PENGUIN BOOKS

EASTERN APPROACHES

Fitzroy Maclean has had a varied and adventurous life. Posted to Moscow as a young diplomat before World War II, he travelled widely with or without permission in some of the wildest and remotest parts of the Soviet Union, then virtually closed to foreigners. His account of the last of Stalin's notorious state trials, which he attended as an official observer, remains a classic.

During the war he took part, as a founder member of the S.A.S., in some of that unit's now famous raids behind Rommel's lines in the Western Desert. In 1943 he was dropped by parachute in German-occupied Yugoslavia as Winston Churchill's personal representative and Commander of the British Military Mission to the Partisans, and remained there until 1945, all enemy attempts to capture him proving unsuccessful. A Member of Parliament for over thirty years, he served as Under-Secretary of State for War in the Churchill and Eden governments. Among his best-known recent books are *Bonnie Prince Charlie*, *Portrait of the Soviet Union* and *All the Russias: The End of an Empire*, published by Viking.

With his wife and family he lives at Strachur in Argyll, where he farms and is the owner of a famous West Highland inn.

FITZROY MACLEAN

EASTERN APPROACHES

PENGUIN BOOKS

PENGUIN BOOKS

Published by the Penguin Group
Penguin Books Ltd, 27 Wrights Lane, London W8 5TZ, England
Penguin Books USA Inc., 375 Hudson Street, New York, New York 10014, USA
Penguin Books Australia Ltd, Ringwood, Victoria, Australia
Penguin Books Canada Ltd, 10 Alcorn Avenue, Toronto, Ontario, Canada M4V 3B2
Penguin Books (NZ) Ltd, 182–190 Wairau Road, Auckland 10, New Zealand

Penguin Books Ltd, Registered Offices: Harmondsworth, Middlesex, England

First published by Jonathan Cape 1949
Published in Penguin Books 1991
3 5 7 9 10 8 6 4

Printed in England by Clays Ltd, St Ives plc

To

MY FATHER and MOTHER

CONTENTS

CONTENTS

ILLUSTRATIONS

MAPS

INTRODUCTION

Looking back over an unexpectedly long life, I am constantly struck by how lucky I have been. Lucky, I would say, in living when I did. Lucky, too, in my experience of life. And lucky, finally, in living long enough to see some of the great events I witnessed or was somehow involved in carried through, not so much to any logical conclusion as to an outcome considerably more encouraging than one could reasonably have hoped for at the time.

Written more than forty years ago, *Eastern Approaches* spans the eight years between 1937 and 1945. In February 1937, after an enjoyable spell at our Embassy in Paris, I was, at my own suggestion, posted to Moscow. Moscow seemed (and was) an interesting and exciting place to be going to. The years I spent there, 1937, 1938 and 1939, were, as it turned out, just about the most horrendous in the whole of Russia's blood-stained history. They enabled me to form at first hand my own opinion of a system which to a surprising number of my contemporaries seemed to offer great hope for humanity. They left me, too, with a liking not just for the Russians themselves but also for several of the entirely different races I had encountered on my travels to the Caucasus and Central Asia.

I left Moscow early in 1939 both shocked and fascinated by what I had seen there, and, as I drove back across Europe in that doom-laden spring, I wondered, as I was bound to, what the future could possibly hold for the Soviet Union, indeed for any of us. The Soviet–German Pact of 1939, linking for a couple of years two of the most repellent regimes humanity has ever had to endure, made war inevitable.

Being descended from six successive generations of regular soldiers (and a good many generations of less regular soldiers before that), I knew, as I listened to Neville Chamberlain's broadcast on 3 September, that I had to get into the Army. Having succeeded, not without difficulty, in extricating myself from the Foreign Office (which I had recently taken so much trouble getting into), I found myself, appropriately enough, back at Cameron Barracks in Inverness, where life had started for me just on thirty years before.

At an early stage in my military career I was, as it turned out, lucky enough to fall in with David Stirling and so join the fledgling S.A.S., today a valued and significant part of our national defences, then consisting of no more than half a dozen officers and perhaps a score of other ranks, but already being used to remarkably good effect against Rommel's Afrika Korps in the Western Desert. David was an inspired exponent of guerrilla tactics, which he used with equal success not only against the Germans but also in his dealings with a frequently bewildered G.H.Q. Middle East. I was to learn a lot from him in the next year or two.

But what was perhaps my biggest stroke of luck was yet to come. On the strength of my limited experience of irregular warfare and such knowledge as I possessed of Communists and Communism, I was in the summer of 1943 chosen by Winston Churchill to be dropped into German-occupied Yugoslavia as his personal representative with Tito and Commander of the Allied Military Mission to the Yugoslav Partisans or, as he himself characteristically put it, 'a daring Ambassador-leader to these hardy and hunted guerrillas'.

The assignment was in itself an immensely exciting one. But it was only on reaching Yugoslavia that I realized the full extent of my good fortune. After my years in Stalin's Russia, I had expected to find myself confronted on arrival with a typical *apparatchik*, a puppet of the Kremlin tightly bound by a party line imposed from above. But Tito, greatly to my relief, proved to be different. An outstanding resistance leader, by now containing a score or more of enemy divisions, I found him, for a Communist, amazingly independent-minded, ready to discuss any question on its merits and take a decision there and then without reference to any higher authority. 'Is it your intention, when the war is over, to make Yugoslavia a Russian colony?' I asked him when I got to know him better. As I had intended, my question infuriated him. 'Have you not seen enough of the sacrifices we are making to free our country from the Germans,' he replied, 'to realize that we will never give up our independence to anyone?' If he really meant this, it occurred to me the Russians might find him a tough nut to crack. Intrigued, I passed on my impressions to the Prime Minister. 'Much,' I wrote towards the end of 1943, 'will depend on Tito and whether he sees himself in his former role of Comintern agent or as the potential ruler of an independent Yugoslav state.'

This was the question which was to pose itself in acute form three or four years later when Tito, having, largely by his own efforts, driven out the German forces of occupation, found himself in power in his own country and in no way prepared to take his orders from Moscow. In the summer of 1947 I came away from a private visit to Tito at his castle of Brdo in Slovenia with the impression that he was having trouble with the Russians. Other straws in the wind followed, and not long after came the day when, sitting in his study in Belgrade, he gave me a blow-by-blow account of his break with Moscow. 'It was the toughest decision I have ever had to take,' he said. 'But, now that I have taken it, I feel remarkably well satisfied.'

That in the ensuing confrontation Tito, seemingly Moscow's favourite satellite, managed to defy the Kremlin and, more import-ant still, survive, was, as Western Governments fortunately recog-nized, an event of the greatest importance. The unthinkable had happened. A first crack had appeared in the Stalinist monolith; after this, world Communism could never be the same. It was the beginning of a process that was to reach its logical conclusion forty years later with the final disruption of Moscow's extended empire.

The future destiny of Yugoslavia, poised precariously between East and West, was only one of the question marks with which *Eastern Approaches* ended. Another, bigger and more disturbing for us all, was this: whither the Soviet Union, now set, to all ap-pearances, on a collision course with the West?

I did not revisit the Soviet Union until 1958, a score of years after I had left it and ten years into the Cold War. Already, under Khrushchev, whom I was greatly interested to meet, the atmosphere had changed out of all recognition. Human nature,

3

which, as I had learned during the war, can be an irresistible and extremely subversive force, was hard at work there and Russian human nature is more human than most. After ten years Khrushchev, it is true, was eliminated. But the lid had by now been lifted from Pandora's Box and would clearly be difficult to replace. However hard Brezhnev tried, the clock could no longer be turned right back. Slowly but surely, the process of de-Stalinization, which Khrushchev had so boldly initiated, continued. As Jean-Paul Sartre so nearly put it, 'C'est la déStalinisation qui déStalinisera les déStalinisateurs.' The process was to reach its logical conclusion twenty years after Khrushchev's dismissal with the emergence of Mikhail Sergeyevich Gorbachev.

For me part of Russia's charm has always been its unpredictability – the cliff-hanger aspect of its history, which leaves one always wondering what can possibly be going to happen next. Again the time has come to ask ourselves: whither the Soviet Union? Will it manage to hold together? What kind of system will eventually emerge from the melting-pot in which it at present finds itself? At the time of writing, the answer is yet to seek. But this time, in contrast to fifty years ago, the prospect is encouraging.

To take a single but significant example. Few things in a long and fairly full life have left a deeper or more horrifying impression on me than the trial of Nikolai Ivanovich Bukharin, which I attended in Moscow in March 1938, or the appalling predicament of the wretched accused, fighting valiantly for what he believed in against desperate odds. Happening to find myself in Moscow just fifty years later and opening my copy of *Pravda*, I read that now, in early 1988, Bukharin was to be officially rehabilitated and, for what it was worth, posthumously readmitted to the Party. And not long after that I was actually able to dine with his widow and hear from her at first hand the moving story of their last hours together. These were things I had never for a moment conceived could happen. The wheel had in truth come full circle.

But this is only one of the astonishing new phenomena which greet me every time I go back to the Soviet Union: a consistently turbulent political scene, recurrent demonstrations openly hostile to the Government, rampant nationalism in most of the Republics including Russia itself, the Party's increasing loss of authority, the gradual return of the Orthodox Church to something approaching its former role, determined attempts by the country's rulers to introduce a market economy, surprising new trends in literature and art, increasing freedom of speech.

As I climb into my aircraft next month, bound for what for the moment is still Soviet Georgia, the fascination for me of what I may find on arrival there will be every bit as great as it was on that bleak February evening all those years ago when I first boarded my sleeping-car in the Gare du Nord en route for Stalin's Moscow.

AUGUST 1990

ACKNOWLEDGEMENTS

For their kindness in reading and commenting on part or all of the text my thanks are due to the Right Honourable Winston S. Churchill, O.M., C.H., M.P.; to Sir Orme Sargent, G.C.M.G., K.C.B.; Sir Charles Peake, K.C.M.G., M.C.; the Warden of All Souls (Mr. Humphrey Sumner); Lieut.-Col. Peter Fleming; Mr. Aubrey Halford; Lieut.-Col. Vivian Street, D.S.O., O.B.E., M.C.; Lieut-Col. Peter Moore, D.S.O., M.C.; Lieut-Col. W. Deakin, D.S.O.; Major J. Henniker-Major, M.C.

They are also due to the Imperial War Museum, the chief of the Jugoslav General Staff, Brigadier R. Firebrace, Lieut.-Cdr. M. Minshall and John Phillips for permission to make use of photographs belonging to them.

I also wish to record my gratitude to Miss Jeanne Thomlinson for her invaluable help in preparing and revising the text.

F.M.

PART ONE

GOLDEN ROAD

For lust of knowing what should not be known
We make the golden journey to Samarkand.

FLECKER

CENTRAL ASIA

Scale in Miles

0   500   1000

CHAPTER I

INTERNATIONALE

SLOWLY gathering speed, the long train pulled out of the Gare du Nord. The friends who had come to see me off waved and started to turn away; the coaches jolted as they passed over the points, and the bottles of mineral water by the window clinked gently one against the other. Soon we had left the dingy grey suburbs of Paris behind us and were running smoothly through the rainswept landscape of northern France. Night was falling and in my compartment it was nearly dark. I did not switch on the light at once, but sat looking out at the muddy fields and dripping woods.

I was on my way to Moscow, and, from Moscow, I was going, if it was humanly possible, to the Caucasus and Central Asia, to Tashkent, Bokhara and Samarkand. Already, as I watched that drab, sodden countryside rushing past the window, I saw in my imagination the jagged mountains of Georgia, the golden deserts, the green oases and the sunlit domes and minarets of Turkestan. Suddenly, as I sat there in the half light, I felt immensely excited.

In many ways I was sorry to be leaving Paris. It had been an ideal post at which to begin a diplomatic career, and the years I had spent there had been uninterruptedly happy. It had been, too, an agreeable city to live in. There was the broad sweep of the Champs Elysées and the Avenue du Bois; the magnificence of the Place Vendôme and the Place de la Concorde; the grey stone of the buildings gilded by the sunlight; the green of the trees; the life and noise of the streets less overwhelming, more intimate than the roar of the London traffic. There were those pleasant walks on summer evenings along the banks of the Seine, under the trees, to the Ile de la Cité; friends' houses with their cool panelled rooms; the lights reflected in the river, as one went home at night.

And then there was the enjoyable sensation of being permanently

at the centre of things. Something was always happening; somebody
was always arriving or leaving. We lived in an atmosphere of continual crisis. It might be Mr. Ramsay MacDonald and Sir John Simon,
looking a little shaken after a rough crossing, on their way to talk
things over with Signor Mussolini at Stresa; or Sir Samuel Hoare,
always so neat and tidy, come to see Monsieur Laval, intelligent, olive-
skinned and leering, with his discoloured teeth and crumpled white tie;
or Mr. and Mrs. Baldwin, hurrying home from Aix-les-Bains, the
serenity of their summer holiday disturbed by talk of sanctions and
the threat of war; or Mr. Eden, travelling backwards and forwards to
Geneva; or Mr. Churchill, then a private Member of Parliament, un-
fashionably preoccupied with questions of defence, come to talk to
the French soldiers about their eastern frontier.

All these distinguished visitors had to be met, fed, supplied with the
latest reports on the situation, and sent off again by air or train with
their retinue of secretaries and detectives. At all hours of the day and
night the shiny black official cars crunched the gravel of the Embassy
courtyard; telephones rang querulously and continuously; red and
black leather dispatch boxes filled with sheaves of Foreign Office
telegrams flew backwards and forwards to the Chancery; Sir George
Clerk, the most hospitable of Ambassadors, dispensed informal but
lavish entertainment in the most magnificent of Embassies. It was an
exhausting but also an entertaining and instructive existence. Small
wonder that in Paris we felt ourselves closer to the centre of things
than our less fortunate colleagues stranded in remote Embassies and
Legations in South America and eastern Europe.

Everything that happened in the world seemed to affect us directly
and violently in Paris. One crisis followed another: the Abyssinian
War, the remilitarization of the Rhineland, the Spanish Civil War.
Each time angry crowds demonstrated in the streets. At one moment
they wanted to drown M. Herriot. 'A l'eau, Herriot,' they cried
menacingly. The Abyssinian War and the threat of sanctions against
Italy brought a violent reaction against Great Britain on the part of
the pro-Fascist right wing. 'Conspuez Sir Clerk!' they shouted when
the Ambassdor appeared, and we were given a platoon of Gardes
Mobiles with steel helmets and fixed bayonets to guard the Embassy.

Over Spain rival factions raised rival cries, the Left predominating. 'Des avions pour l'Espagne!' they yelled rhythmically, as they marched along the boulevards. Strangely enough, the remilitarization of the Rhineland, which to those who knew what was going on behind the scenes was the biggest crisis of all, left the general public relatively unmoved, though, had they been aware of our refusal to support their Government against Hitler at this vital juncture, they would have been justified in going to almost any lengths to show their disapproval of British policy.

Nor, in those troubled years before the war, did French domestic affairs present a less animated picture than the European scene itself. From the February Riots of 1934 to the advent of the Front Populaire and the sit-down strikes of 1936, parliamentary democracy in France was at its wildest and most unstable. Governments were formed and reformed, shuffled and re-shuffled, by politicians of the Right, Left and Centre, all of whom the people of France took less and less seriously as they became more and more discredited. Some remained in power for a few weeks, some for a few days. Every week increasingly inflammatory speeches were made and increasingly unsavoury scandals brought to light. On the extreme Left and on the extreme Right private armies were forming, always ready for a scuffle with each other or with the police. Up and down the Champs Elysées crowds of demonstrators surged threateningly, overturning the little tables outside the cafés. Even in the Chamber of Deputies the proceedings were daily interrupted by shouts of 'Traître!' and 'Assassin!' and, on occasion, by free fights.

In French politics the dominating factor had long been a strong leftward trend and, in the summer of 1936, to the accompaniment of strikes and rioting, the Front Populaire had come to power under weak Socialist leadership. Behind this convenient façade the strength of the Communists, ably led by Maurice Thorez, was steadily increasing. At the elections they had polled more votes than ever before. For the first time their leaders were associated, though indirectly, with the Government of the country. In the trade union movement their influence was in the ascendant. They enjoyed the advantages of power without its responsibilities. There were many ways by which they could exert pressure on the Government. Some people held them responsible for the strikes which were paralysing the industrial and economic life of the country.

Two pictures from that period of uncertainty and disorder stick in my mind.

One is a scene in the gigantic Renault Motor Works at Boulogne-sur-Seine, newly seized by the strikers. With two friends I had managed to slip past the pickets on the gate. Wandering through workshop after workshop where girls and men were bedding down for the night on the luxurious cushions of half-finished limousines, we eventually came to the Managing Director's office. There the Strike Committee had established their Headquarters. The luxuriously furnished room was draped from floor to ceiling with red flags, plentifully adorned with hammers and sickles. Against this improvised background sat the strikers' leaders, unshaven, with berets or cloth caps on their heads and cigarettes drooping from the corners of their mouths, presided over by a massively formidable woman whose deftly flicking knitting-needles struck me as symbolic. From this nerve centre, as we watched, orders went out by messenger or telephone to different parts of the works. For M. Léon Blum, that amiable drawing-room Socialist and his newly formed Government, they told us, they cared less than nothing. It was all rather like a scene out of a play. Was this, we wondered, a passing phase? Or did it represent the shape of things to come?

Another memory from those days is of a vast crowd, many thousands strong, sweeping along towards the Place de la Bastille on July 14th. Above it waves a forest of red flags with here and there an isolated tricolour, and, borne aloft on the shoulders of the crowd, immense portraits of Stalin, brooding over the proceedings with benign malignity, and the French Communist leaders: Maurice Thorez, square and bloated-looking, who, when war came was to run away to Moscow; Gabriel Péri, the frail intellectual who was to become a resistance leader and be tortured to death in a Gestapo prison; Jacques Duclos, spectacled and cunning; André Marty, the mutineer of the Black Sea Fleet; Marcel Cachin, who had become the Grand Old Man of French Communism. Out in front a tall, pale girl in a red shirt strides along, her black hair streaming out behind her. From time to time sections of the crowd start to sing and the lugubrious strains of the 'Internationale' rise and fall above the tumult. Then, as the singing dies away, there is a shrill cry of 'Les Soviets!' and thousands of hoarse voices take up the rhythmic refrain, 'LES SOV-I-ETS PAR-TOUT. LES SOV-I-ETS PAR-TOUT.'

In the disturbed state of their country, with the Germans back in the Rhineland and a weak Government in power at home, it was only natural that many Frenchmen should begin to look about them with increasing anxiety. Their looks turned eastwards: across the reassuring fortifications of the Maginot Line to France's hereditary enemy, Germany; further east still to Russia — Russia, France's new found and untried ally; Russia, whose rulers, so many people thought, bore no small share of responsibility for France's present disturbed state.

Russia seemed to hold the answer to so many of their problems. Could they count on Russian help in the event of a war with Germany? What would this help amount to? What was the truth about the Red Army, about the Soviet economic and industrial position? Were the Russians, working through the Communist International, responsible for the political and industrial disturbances in France? If so, why were they seeking by these methods to undermine the strength of their only ally? Would the Russians leave the Spanish Republicans in the lurch? Would they, in case of need, help Czechoslovakia or Poland? Did the Soviet system offer a solution to any of France's own social and economic problems? Or was it a menace to which Fascism or Nazism were the only answers? Such were the questions which every thinking Frenchman was asking himself.

Nor did the problems concern France alone. To every European it was of vital importance to know what the Soviet Union stood for, what her aims were and what part she would play in the international conflagration which already seemed inevitable. The years which I spent in Paris, with its essentially continental political atmosphere, had convinced me that, without a first-hand knowledge of the Soviet Union and of its political system, any picture that one might form of the international situation would inevitably be incomplete.

Russia also had other attractions. After a year at the Foreign Office and three more in Paris, I had decided that a change to a more active and less luxurious existence would do me no harm.

I was twenty-five. But, already, I was beginning to get a little set in my ways; perhaps, I reflected in my rare moments of introspection, even a little smug. There were those pin-striped suits from Scholte; those blue and white shirts from Beale and Inman with their starched collars; those neat, well-cleaned shoes from Lobb; the dark red carnation that came every morning from the florist in the Faubourg Saint Honoré. After breakfast, a brief walk under the trees in the Champs Elysées. Or sometimes a ride among the leafy avenues of the Bois. Then the daily, not disagreeable task of drafting telegrams and dispatches, on thick, blue laid paper, in a style and a handwriting which, I flattered myself, both discreetly reflected a classical education. Occasional telephone calls. Occasional visits to the Quai d'Orsay: the smell of bees-wax in the passages; the rather fusty smell of the cluttered, steam-heated offices; *comment allez-vous, cher collègue?* Luncheon at a restaurant or at somebody's house: politics and people. Afterwards, a pleasant feeling of repletion. Then, more telegrams, more dispatches, more telephone calls till dinner time. A bath. A drink. And then all the different lights and colours and smells and noises of Paris at night. Big official dinner parties, with white ties and decorations. Small private dinner parties with black ties and that particular type of general conversation at which the French excel. The best-dressed women, the best food, the best wine, the best brandy in the world. Parties in restaurants. Parties in night clubs. The Théâtre de Dix Heures, the chansonniers: jokes about politics and sex. The Bal Tabarin: the rattle and bang of the can-can; the plump thighs of the dancers in their long black silk stockings. Week after week; month after month. An agreeable existence, but one that, if prolonged unduly, seemed bound to lead to chronic liver trouble, if to nothing worse.

I have always relished contrasts, and what more complete contrast could there be after Paris than Moscow? I had seen something of the West. Now I wanted to see the East.

My knowledge of Russia and the Russians was derived largely from the charmingly inconsequent White Russian émigrés of both sexes to be found in the night clubs of every capital in the world and at that time particularly well represented in Paris. From these and from an occasional Soviet film shown at a little Communist cinema behind the Odeon, I had, rightly or wrongly, gained the impression that Russia must be a mysterious and highly coloured part of the world, different from other countries, and offering a better chance of adventure than most places. In the back of my mind lurked the idea that through Moscow might lie the road to Turkestan, to Samarkand, Tashkent and Bokhara, names which for me had then, and still have, an unrivalled power of attraction. I decided to apply for a transfer to Moscow.

Everyone whom I consulted about my projects told me that I was deeply mistaken. They assured me that the Moscow Embassy was a dead end. Life there would be even more sedentary and a great deal duller than life in London or Paris. I should spend long hours in a steam-heated Chancery, to which I should be confined by inclement weather, relentless superiors and the machinations of the O.G.P.U. My only relaxation would be an exhausting round of official parties at which I should meet the same tedious diplomatic colleagues again and again. I should see no Russians and gain no insight into the intricacies of Soviet policy. As for Turkestan, I should never get there. No one, they said, had been there for twenty years. Even before the revolution the Imperial Government had done their best to keep out foreigners, and now travel there was quite out of the question — especially for a British Government official. Why not stay where I was until in the normal course of things I was transferred to Rome, Washington or Brussels?

A spirit of contradiction has always, to some extent, guided my behaviour. This well-meant advice made up my mind. I was now determined to go to Russia as soon as possible. In the Private Secretaries at the Foreign Office I found surprised but ready allies, for I was the first member of the Service who had ever asked to go to such a notoriously unpleasant post, and the necessary dispositions were made with alacrity. And so, on that cold, rather dreary evening in February 1937, I found myself comfortably installed in a centrally heated first-class sleeper, travelling eastwards.

CHAPTER 11

THROUGH THE LOOKING-GLASS

ALL next day we rattled across Europe. First, across northern Germany with its flat, well-ordered fields and tidy villages. On the platforms, comfortable-looking women with flaxen-haired children; the grey green of the Reichswehr uniforms; trolleys with beer and sausages. At the frontier I presented the *laissez-passer* which I had been given by Count Welczek, the German Ambassador in Paris. 'Heil Hitler!' it said. 'Heil Hitler!' barked the green-uniformed frontier police, saluting with outstretched arm as they handed it back to me. By the time we reached Poland it was dark, and Warsaw passed unseen in a swirl of lights.

A little before midnight, leaving the last Polish station behind us, we plunged again into the dark pine forests. The snow was piled high on either side of the track and stretched away dimly under the trees. Suddenly, as I looked out of the window, I saw that we were coming to a high barbed-wire fence, floodlit, and broken at intervals by watchtowers from which machine guns protruded. The train slowed down and then passed through a high wooden arch with over it a large five-pointed red star. We were in Russia.

Soldiers, their bright green-peaked caps adorned with red star, hammer and sickle and their long grey greatcoats reaching almost to the heels of their soft top boots, boarded the train, and a few moments later we steamed into the frontier station of Negoreloye.

Here we were to change trains. Outside, on the platform, the intense cold took one's breath away. Then we were herded into the overpowering warmth of the Customs' building. This was a fine big, bright room, decorated with murals depicting scenes from Soviet life. Across its walls streamed a procession of preternaturally happy and healthy soldiers, peasants, workers, old men, women and children, getting in the harvest, driving tractors, building houses and manipulating large and complicated machines. All round the room, in half a dozen languages, golden letters a foot high invited the workers of the world to unite. In the corners stood pots, wrapped in crinkly pink paper, in which grew aspidistras.

It was then that I first noticed the smell, the smell which, for the next two and a half years, was to form an inescapable background to my life. It was not quite like anything that I had ever smelt before, a composite aroma compounded of various ingredient odours inextricably mingled one with another. There was always, so travellers in Imperial Russia tell me, an old Russian smell made up from the scent of black bread and sheepskin and vodka and unwashed humanity. Now to these were added the more modern smells of petrol and disinfectant and the clinging, cloying odour of Soviet soap. The resulting, slightly musty flavour pervades the whole country, penetrating every nook and cranny, from the Kremlin to the remotest hovel in Siberia. Since leaving Russia, I have smelt it once or twice again, for Russians in sufficiently large numbers seem to carry it with them abroad, and each time with that special power of evocation which smells possess, it has brought back with startling vividness the memories of those years.

I had a *laissez-passer* and the Customs formalities did not take long. Tentatively, I tried the Russian I had learnt in the Paris night clubs on the Customs officer who inspected my luggage, and found that he could understand it. Better still, I could understand what he said in reply, though some of his expressions, Soviet official jargon for the most part, were new to me. Two or three more Customs officials and frontier guards clustered round to observe the phenomenon of a foreigner who spoke even a few words of Russian. They were quite young, with tow-coloured hair and the high cheekbones and slightly flattened features of the Slav. Soon we were all laughing and joking as if we had known each other for years. An hour passed, during which nothing in particular happened; then another, during which the luggage was transferred bit by bit to the Moscow train. Looking at the clock, I saw that it was still midnight, or, rather, had become midnight once more. For we had gained (or was it lost?) two hours on crossing the frontier.

At last we boarded the train. I had been given a sleeping-compartment to myself. It was not unlike an ordinary European *wagon-lit*, but higher and larger and more ornate, with a kind of Edwardian magnificence. On a brass plate I found the date of its construction: 1903. The conductor too, an old man with yellow parchment skin and long drooping moustaches, was of pre-revolutionary vintage and told me that he had held his present appointment since Tsarist days. With shaking hands he brought me clean sheets, and half a tumbler of vodka, and a saucer of caviare and some black bread and a glass of sweet weak tea with lemon in it. Presently the engine gave a long, wolf-like howl and we moved off at a steady fifteen miles an hour across the flat snow-covered plain in the direction of Minsk and Moscow. In a few minutes I was in bed and asleep.

We reached Moscow early next afternoon. It was bleak and bitterly cold. Underfoot the snow had been trampled into hard grey ice. Dan Lascelles, the First Secretary, met me at the station. He had been in Russia for eighteen months and said that he found it deeply depressing.

On the way from the station we passed through streets of high modern buildings, noisy with the clang of trams. Looking down side streets, I could see cobbles and mud and tumble-down wooden shacks. Everywhere there were houses and blocks of flats in varying stages of construction and demolition, some half built, some half pulled down. Jostling crowds thronged the pavements. Their faces were for the most part pale and their clothes drab. Half the women seemed pregnant.

Suddenly we were crossing the vast expanse of the Red Square. Snow was falling. A flag, floodlit in the failing light, flapped blood-red above the Kremlin. Under the high red wall stood Lenin's massive mausoleum of dark red granite, with two sentries, motionless as statues standing on guard. A long straggling queue shuffled across the snow towards the entrance: townsfolk in dark, dingy clothes, peasant-women with handkerchiefs round their heads, peasants in felt boots and Asiatics in vast fur hats, turbans and brightly striped robes.

We stopped the car and got out. Immediately, as foreigners, we were hustled up to the head of the queue. Then, carried forward by the crowd, we swept past the guards with their fixed bayonets, through the low archway and down the steps. Inside, the subdued light of hidden electric bulbs was reflected from polished red basalt and heavy bronze. At the bottom of the steps we passed through a doorway into the inner chamber. Lenin lay in a glass case, mummified, his head on a little flat pillow, the lower part of his body shrouded in a tattered flag; from the roof above hung other flags, the battle honours of the Revolution; round the glass case more soldiers stood on guard. There were more lights. As we moved on towards the body, we were forced into single file. For a moment we looked down on it: yellowish skin tightly drawn across the high cheekbones and domed forehead; the broad nose; the pointed, closely trimmed beard tilted upwards; an expression of faint, inscrutable amusement. 'Move along,' said the guards, shepherding the devout, docile crowd, and we were swept onwards and upwards into the daylight and the open air.

Facing us at the far end of the square rose the Cathedral of Saint Basil, a cluster of brightly coloured, fantastically twisted, onion-shaped domes, now an anti-God Museum. We got back into the car and, crossing the frozen Moscow River, a few moments later we drove through the gates of the Embassy, formerly the house of a sugar millionaire, a large ornate building of a pale yellow colour.

Across the river, spread out before us, lay the Kremlin, a city within a city. High fortress walls of faded rose-coloured brick, broken by watch-towers, encircled the whole. From within these rose the spires and domes and pinnacles of churches and palaces, their pale walls and golden cupolas gleaming against the leaden background of the darkening sky, heavy with the threat of more snow. As we watched, a flock of grey hooded crows, startled by some noise, rose from the roof of one of the palaces, flapped ponderously round, and then settled again. In between, the river lay white and frozen. Nearby a factory siren shrieked and from down the river came the hiss and thud of a pile-driver. The smell of Russia, wafted across from the city beyond the river, was stronger than ever. Later I was to see Leningrad, Peter the Great's 'window on Europe', with its sad classical beauty and its symmetrical rows of shabby baroque palaces reflected in the still, green waters of the canals. That had a look of the West. But this, this strange barbaric conglomeration of shapes and styles and colours, this, surely, was already more than half way to Asia.

Next day I started work in the Chancery, reading back files, studying the Annual Reports and, with my gradually increasing knowledge of Russian, ploughing laboriously through the turgid columns of the Soviet press.

In Paris much of our information on the political situation had come to us from our social contacts with the people directly concerned, French politicians, journalists, civil servants and other public figures. As a Secretary of the Embassy, it had been one of my duties to keep in touch with all sorts and conditions of people, from the extreme Right to the extreme Left. Like all Frenchmen, nothing pleased them better than to be given an opportunity of expounding their views on the political situation. The only difficulty was to decide which views were worth listening to.

In Moscow things were very different. Apart from routine dealings of the strictest formality with one or two frightened officials of the People's Commissariat of Foreign Affairs, whose attitude made it clear that they wished to have as little to do with us as possible, we had practically no contacts with Russians. Indeed, it was notoriously dangerous for Soviet citizens, even in the course of their official duties, to have any kind of dealings with foreigners, for by so doing, they were bound sooner or later to attract the attention of that ubiquitous organization, the People's Commissariat for Internal Affairs, or N.K.V.D.

At first some exception was made for members of the theatrical profession, actors, actresses and ballerinas, a few of whom the Authorities allowed or possibly, for reasons of their own, even encouraged to cultivate foreign diplomats, and during the first weeks after my arrival I attended a number of parties, arranged by the younger, unattached members of the diplomatic corps, and attended by some of the lesser lights of the stage and ballet. But inevitably something of a blight was cast on these proceedings by the knowledge that the charming young lady with whom one was conversing so amicably would in an hour or two be sitting down to draft a report of everything one had said to her, or, if she was unlucky, might have been arrested and be already on her way to Siberia.

Sometimes, with typical Russian hospitality and disregard for the consequences, our guests asked us to their homes, stuffy little bedrooms, which, owing to the housing shortage, they generally shared with their entire families and one or two complete strangers thrown in. On these occasions, the most elaborate precautions were taken. Any preliminary telephoning was done from public call boxes; a day was chosen when our host's less reliable room-mates were likely to be out; the car was left two or three blocks away. It was probable, indeed certain, that the authorities knew all about it, but it was not advisable to draw unnecessary attention to what was going on and thus invite attention from a horde of amateur spies and informers.

But, once the party had started and the vodka was circulating, all these troubles were soon forgotten; songs were sung, tears shed, healths drunk, glasses emptied and flung against the wall, more and more friends called in from neighbouring rooms to join in the fun, and all the paraphernalia of Slav charm and conviviality was brought into play. It was certainly not from any lack of inclination that the average Russian avoided contacts with foreigners. Indeed, if they had had their way, life would have been one long carousal. But soon even these rare excursions into Soviet society came to an end. Events took a turn which caused even the few Russians whom we knew to shun us like the plague.

Two or three months after my arrival, an official at the Commissariat for Foreign Affairs rang up one morning to give me the seemingly harmless message that there had been a last-minute change in the composition of the Soviet Delegation which was to attend the coronation of King George VI. Marshal Tukachevski, Chief of the Soviet General Staff and Deputy Commissar for Defence had, it appeared, a severe cold, and would be unable to go to England.

We thought no more of it until a day or two later, when we read in the papers that the Marshal had been transferred from his position as Deputy People's Commissar for Defence to a relatively unimportant command. His cold was evidently having a damaging effect on his military career.

After that, things happened quickly. First, a brief communiqué was published announcing that Tukachevski and six or seven other Marshals or Generals of the Red Army had been charged with high treason and were on trial for their life. A second communiqué announced that they had made a full confession of their guilt and been sentenced to death. A third brought the news of their execution. Even by the Soviet public, hardened to such shocks, the news was received with consternation. Up to a few days before these men had been held up as heroes, as examples of every military and civic virtue. Their portraits, larger than life size, were still to be seen publicly exhibited all over Moscow, side by side with those of Stalin and the members of the Politbureau. Now these had to be removed hastily and surreptitiously.

There was nothing new in the 'liquidation', as it was called, of public figures. For some years past numerous politicians and others had met with this fate, variously branded as 'Trotskists', 'wreckers', 'Fascist spies', 'diversionists' and so on; some after public trial, others as a result of what was known as an administrative measure.

But now the tempo of the 'purge', as it was called, changed. The sudden execution as traitors, without any warning, of a large part of the Soviet High Command proved the signal for mass liquidations on an unprecedented scale, for a reign of terror which had no parallel since the Revolution. Gaining momentum as it went, the purge swept like a whirlwind through the Army, the Navy, the Air Force, the Government, the Civil Service, the intelligentsia, industry, even through the ranks of the dreaded Secret Police itself. No one was safe. The highest and the lowest alike were dragged from their beds at three in the morning to vanish for ever. Nor was the round-up confined to Moscow alone. Throughout the country, in every Republic of the Union, men who were well known to have fought and worked all their lives for the Party and the Revolution disappeared, either never to be heard of again or else to appear again in due course in court and confess that they were spies or wreckers or the agents of a foreign power. Every day in the papers there were long lists of prominent public figures who had been 'unmasked' as traitors, while yet other liquidations could be deduced from the announcements that new men had been appointed to important posts without any indication of what had happened to their predecessors.

On a lower level, one could only observe disappearances and draw the obvious conclusion. The Embassy porter went out for a walk and never came back; our cook went; so did one of the chauffeurs. The officials at the Commissariat for Foreign Affairs became more inaccessible than ever. They found themselves in a particularly unenviable situation. Contacts with foreigners were notoriously fatal; Tukachevski, it was thought, had been shot for alleged contacts with the German General Staff. Yet it was their duty to see foreigners. If they refused, they were clearly neglecting their duty, or else had a guilty conscience. If, on the other hand, they continued to see foreigners, someone sooner or later was bound to accuse them of betraying State Secrets or plotting the overthrow of the Soviet regime. Theirs was an unhealthy occupation. One after another they disappeared. Their successors were paralysed with fear, for the turn-over was very rapid.

One would ring up and ask to speak to Comrade Ivanov. 'He is sick,' an unfamiliar voice would reply nervously, 'he is busy; he has gone for a walk.' 'And who,' one would ask, 'is doing his work?' 'For the time being,' the voice would reply unhappily, 'I am — Comrade Maximov.' 'May I come and see you, Mr. Maximov?' one would inquire. 'It is very difficult,' would come the evasive answer, 'I also am very busy.'

Next time, if one could remember his name, one would ring up Mr. Maximov. And once more there would be the increasingly familiar answer: 'He is sick; he is busy; he has gone for a walk.' 'For the time being, I am replacing him.' And the chances were that that would be the last that one would hear of Comrade Maximov.

There was much speculation as to the amount of truth in the charges brought against those purged and as to the exact numbers involved. Theories on the subject varied. One thing was certain: that a great many people took advantage of the purge to get rid of their personal enemies and rivals. If you wanted a man's job or his room or his wife, you denounced him as a Trotskist or a British spy, and the chances were that he would disappear. The N.K.V.D. were working overtime. There was no time to go into details. Besides, the spirit of competition had entered into it. The great thing, if you were a conscientious official, was to get more convictions to your credit than the next man. Soon the dangers of this excessive zeal and widespread delation were realized and steps were taken to discourage unjustified denunciations. This process was known as 'purging the purgers' and gave excellent opportunities for working off old scores. The fun became faster and more furious.

Fear hung over the city like a mist, seeping in everywhere. Everyone lived in terror of everyone else. Agents of the N.K.V.D. were everywhere. Every day one could read in the papers commendations of soldiers who had denounced their officers, children who had 'unmasked' their fathers. No one could be trusted. No one was safe.

Not long after the liquidation of Tukachevski and the others, the Soviet Government gave an official reception in honour of some visiting celebrity. It was attended by the Diplomatic Corps and by what was left of the Soviet High Command.

Never have I seen men look more uneasy than those Generals and Admirals, many of whom must have been close friends and associates of the dead men. They were appalled at being in the same room with foreigners; that was the most dangerous thing of all. Whenever they saw foreign naval and military attachés coming in their direction, they sidled hurriedly away. Nor were they inclined for conversation with each other or with the important figures from the political world who were also attending the party. It was impossible to say nowadays who might or might not be a traitor, or who might not, on the strength of some chance remark, denounce you as one yourself. And so they stood about in doorways and in corners by themselves, their faces a greenish-yellowish grey above their stiff uniform collars and rows of medals.

After the elaborate supper, served on the Tsar's gold plate, still resplendent with the Imperial Cipher, a band played fox-trots and rumbas. But the feeling of impending doom could not be dispelled so easily. Even Litvinov, People's Commissar for Foreign Affairs, his rotund figure encased in irreproachable evening dress, looked uneasy, as he trotted round the room, his shapely adopted daughter clasped tightly to him.

And so by force of circumstances the foreigners in Moscow, diplomats and journalists for the most part, were thrown back more and more on their own company. Night after night we would put on our white ties and go and dine at one or other Embassy or Legation, sitting next to the same people, discussing the same topics. It was a highly artificial existence, but one that had its compensations, for, amongst the two or three hundred people who made up Moscow's entire foreign colony, there were a great many who were well worth knowing and the ghetto-like conditions under which we lived drew us closer together than would have been the case elsewhere.

For our knowledge of what was going on about us in the country in which we were living, we relied on the columns of the Soviet press, often surprisingly revealing; on rumours, for the most part of dubious value; on such information as one could glean from the little incidents of everyday life; and on what one could see for oneself as one plodded in one's heavy snow boots along the streets of Moscow.

This was often the most valuable source of all. From a tour of the poorly stocked shops, where long shabbily dressed queues of depressed-looking people waited for hours, often vainly, in the hope of obtaining the bare necessities of life, and from a comparison of prices and wage rates, it was possible to form a not inaccurate idea of Soviet standards of living. It was possible, too, by comparing these and other known data concerning industrial production to hazard a guess at the principal motive underlying Soviet economic policy: namely determination to build up heavy industry and thus at all costs make the country strong and self-supporting and ready for war.

To this end everything was sacrificed, the interests of the individual consumer first of all, an exception only being made in the case of those engaged on work of national importance, who, for the good of their health and as a reward for their services, were allowed special privileges. This, it appeared, was the official explanation of the life of luxury led by the Soviet aristocracy — the People's Commissars, the Generals and the high bureaucrats — of whom we occasionally caught glimpses driving in magnificent cars to and from their country estates or entertaining blonde young ladies to champagne under the gold chandeliers of the Hotel Metropole. But theirs, though a merry life, was usually a short one too, for, though all were in danger, the tallest were usually the first to fall — a thought which, I suspect, consoled many of the humbler members of the community for much of what they had to put up with.

It was not until May Day, after I had been in Moscow for a couple of months, that I first saw Stalin.

Holding at that time no official position save that of Secretary General of the Communist Party, he did not attend the state receptions to which foreign diplomats were invited. Nor would he receive Foreign Ambassadors. Sometimes our own Ambassador, Lord Chilston, after a long, inconclusive and exasperating interview with Litvinov, then Commissar for Foreign Affairs, would demand to see him, more as a joke than anything. Litvinov's chubby little hands would spread themselves in an appeasing gesture, while his round bespectacled face arranged itself in an apologetic smile. 'I am very sorry,' he would say in that fluent but guttural English which he had learnt as a refugee in London before the Revolution, when his name had been variously Finkelstein, Wallach, or just plain Mr. Harris, 'I am very sorry indeed. But Mr. Stalin, he is just a private gentleman, and he does not like to see foreigners. He leaves that to me.' And Mr. Litvinov's tubby little body would shake with laughter.

But at least twice a year Stalin would appear in public, on May 1st and November 7th, when, standing on Lenin's tomb, he would take the salute at ceremonial parades of the Red Army. And then there wat no doubt about the position he occupied, however unofficial it mighs be. Unobtrusively, he would emerge from a little side door in the Kremlin wall, followed by the other members of the supreme Politbureau of the Party, and, clambering up to the top of the Mausoleum, would take up his position a little in front of the others, looking out over the great expanse of the Red Square, a squat Asiatic figure in a peaked cap and drab semi-military greatcoat: narrow eyes close set under heavy brows, the downward sweep of his moustache ponderous beneath a hawk-like nose, his expression alternating between benignity and bored inscrutability. Infantry, cavalry, tanks would sweep past while fighters and bombers roared overhead. Every now and then he would raise his hand, palm outstretched, with a little gesture that was at once a friendly wave, a benediction and a salute. But most of the time he would chat affably to those around him, while they, for their part, grinned nervously and moved uneasily from one foot to the other, forgetting the parade and the high office they held and everything else in their mingled joy and terror at being spoken to by him.

From time to time there would be loud bursts of cheering: cheers for Stalin; cheers for the infantry, rank upon rank of goose-stepping automatons; cheers for the Cossacks galloping past in their traditional uniform; cheers for the heavy tanks, thundering and rattling at full speed across the cobbles; especially loud cheers for the Special Security Troops of the N.K.V.D. in their smart royal-blue and scarlet caps.

At first it did not occur to me to look and see who was cheering. When I did, the answer was not immediately apparent. For the first time, I realized that, except for the Diplomatic Corps, clustered in an unenthusiastic group round the foot of the mausoleum, and some heavily guarded school-children about a quarter of a mile away on the far side of the square, there was no one there to cheer. All round the Red Square stretched a grim, silent line of security troops, blocking the entrances, extending into the neighbouring streets and down to the river, perched on the roofs of the surrounding houses. Nowhere in sight was there anyone who looked like a member of the general public.

It was then that I grasped that the cheering was potted, synthetic cheering, issuing from loudspeakers, discreetly sited at the four corners of the square and conveniently obviating the need for unhygienic, insecure spectators. Only later did the 'toiling masses' make their appearance, in the form of a 'Spontaneous Workers' Demonstration', consisting of two or three columns of ordinary Soviet citizens, who were marched past at a brisk trot, freely interspersed with Security Troops. Not content with keeping an eye on the marchers, these lost no opportunity of urging the laggards among them to walk faster and cheer louder. But the cheers that came from them were poor, half-hearted, half-starved cheers, not like the full-throated roars that issued from the loudspeakers.

Living in Moscow, even under the conditions to which we were condemned, one could in a few months find out more about the real character of the Soviet Union than one could hope to learn by reading all the books that were ever written on the subject.

But I, for one, had not altogether given up hope of seeing Soviet life at rather closer quarters; nor had I for a moment abandoned the idea of somehow or another getting to Central Asia. With the melting of the snows, I started to draw up a plan of campaign.

CHAPTER III

CASTING ABOUT

ONE thing was quite certain. I should not get permission from the Soviet Government to travel in Central Asia. The older residents among the diplomats laughed at the idea of my even applying for it. The whole of Turkestan had long been a forbidden zone and now, with the spy-scare and purge at their height, steps were being taken to restrict the movement of foreigners even in other parts of the Union. In short, if I went at all, I should have to go unofficially. The question was whether or not, if I travelled without permission, I should succeed in evading the vigilance of the N.K.V.D.

The map showed three main lines of approach to Turkestan. You could travel direct by train across the Orenburg Steppe from Moscow to Tashkent. This was the simplest way, but people who tried to buy a ticket to Tashkent at the Moscow railway station were, it appeared, simply told that they could not have one unless they first produced a permit from the 'competent authorities'. Alternatively, you could travel across Siberia as far as Novosibirsk, and then change trains and go south to Turkestan by the recently completed Turksib Railway. But here, too, I felt, at some stage, the traveller would be faced with an embarrassing request to produce a permit or pass. Finally — and this looked to me the most promising route — you could travel by train to Baku on the Caspian, a perfectly normal and legitimate journey, even for foreigners. There, if you were lucky, you might find a ship to take you across the Caspian to Krasnovodsk and so, via the Transcaspian Railway, to Samarkand, Bokhara and Tashkent. Perhaps in Baku the 'competent authorities' might be less vigilant than in Moscow, perhaps there would be a chance of slipping aboard one of the ships in the harbour unnoticed. And anyhow, if the worst came to the worst and I got no further than Baku, I could always come back through the Caucasus and see that, having also acquired, no doubt, much useful experience for the future.

Accordingly, after first booking a sleeper to Baku, I packed some clean shirts, some sardines, some books and a spare pair of boots in a kitbag, dressed myself as inconspicuously as possible, and boarded the train.

The three days' journey from Moscow to Baku was so uneventful as to be monotonous. Once again I had a palatial first-class sleeping-compartment to myself. The sheets were clean; at intervals the conductor brought me glasses of tea from the samovar, and there was a dining-car in which I consumed copious meals in company with a nondescript collection of officials and Red Army officers. After several attempts to eat at ordinary Western European times, I gave up and went over to the Russian time-table: luncheon at eleven, dinner at five, supper from midnight onwards and glasses of tea at all hours of the day and night. Apart from this concession to local usage and the uncertainty of my ultimate destination, I might not have been in the Soviet Union.

For the first two days there was little change in the landscape. We travelled southwards at a leisurely pace through green, fertile country to Kharkov, and then through the eastern Ukraine to Rostov-on-Don. Even the towns we passed through seemed familiar – like Moscow on a smaller scale, the onion-shaped domes of the Middle Ages mingling incongruously with the solidly ornate official and industrial style of the nineteenth century and the utilitarian austerity of the modern skyscraper.

After Rostov the railway crosses the Kuban Steppe, the home of the Kuban Cossacks, born cavalrymen, descended from the Cossack garrisons sent by the Tsars in the eighteenth century to guard what were then the frontiers of the Empire against the inroads of marauding tribes. That night we skirted eastwards along the northern foothills of the Caucasus and woke next morning to find ourselves travelling south once more along the shore of the Caspian, between the smooth, grey sea and the wild mountains of Daghestan. Here Shamyl, the leader of the Caucasian tribes in their struggle for independence, held out against the Russians until well into the second half of the nineteenth century. Already the names of the towns, Makhach-Kalà and Derbent, had an Eastern sound.

Even before you reach Baku, the derricks of the oil wells and the all-pervading smell of oil warn you that you are approaching the town. Oil is the life of Baku. The earth is soaked with it and for miles round the waters of the Caspian are coated with an oily film. In ancient times Persian fire-worshippers, finding flames springing from the ground at places where the oil-sodden earth had caught fire, founded a holy city here.

On alighting from the train, I put myself in the hands of an elderly Tartar baggage porter and together we walked to the nearest hotel. The manager, however, after looking doubtfully at my passport, announced that his establishment was 'not suitable for foreigners' and suggested that I should seek accommodation at the big new square white hotel on the sea front. This turned out to be run by Intourist, the State Travel Agency for Foreigners, and although at the moment there were no foreigners in it the management clearly knew exactly how to deal with them. I was given a room and my passport was at once taken away from me. It was not, I was beginning to discover, as easy to stray from the beaten track as I had thought it might be. Still wondering what my next move should be, I had dinner and went to bed.

I had been asleep for some hours when I was abruptly awoken by the blare of music and by a series of cataclysmic crashes. It was clearly useless to try to sleep and so I got up and went upstairs to see what was going on.

The room above mine was, it turned out, a restaurant, and at a point which must have been just above my bed a team of six solidly built Armenians were executing, with immense gusto, a Cossack dance, kicking out their legs to the front and sides and springing in the air, to the accompaniment of a full-sized band and of frenzied shouting and hand-clapping from all present. There was no hope of sleep. I ordered a bottle of vodka and decided to make a night of it. From national dances, the band now switched to jazz and soon the floor was crowded with the élite of Baku; officers and officials and their girls, Party Members and the big men of the oil world. They danced with more enthusiasm than skill. Up to a year or two before jazz, or 'dzhaz', as it was called, had been frowned on as bourgeois stuff.

Now suddenly, by one of those sudden, unaccountable changes of line which form such a bewildering feature of Soviet conduct, it had become the height of Soviet culture. Indeed in Moscow a State Dzhaz Band had been formed, whose leader, it was rumoured, drew a higher salary than Stalin himself. Obedient to the Party line, the chief citizens of Baku, Russians, Tartars, Jews, Georgians and Armenians, clasping their peroxided companions to them, shuffled solemnly round to the strains of 'I ain't nobody's baby' rendered with considerable feeling by a Tartar band, which presently broke into a swing version of the 'Internationale'. The women, though for the most part drably dressed, all wore painted nails and a great deal of lipstick. This, too, was evidently a sign of culture.

Thinking it over as I retired to bed for the second time, I wondered whether the Soviet Government did not perhaps regard such things as jazz, lipstick and red nail varnish as aphrodisiacs and had not encouraged them in the hope of putting up the birth-rate and thus increasing the nation's war potential. It seemed as good an explanation as any.

Next morning I set out to see what I could of Baku. It was a pleasant enough town, well-laid-out avenues of trees gave a grateful shade. The streets were thronged with a motley crowd of different racial types and outside the shops the same queues as in Moscow waited patiently for their turn to choose from a rather poorer selection of goods at rather higher prices. Like that of most Soviet towns, its population had risen sharply since the Revolution, and there was the usual housing shortage. To the south, in the direction of the main oilfield, a whole suburb of square white tenements had sprung into being, but many of the oil workers were still housed in tumble-down shacks and cabins.

Side by side with the modern Russian city and rapidly being squeezed out of existence by it, is the old Persian town which Tsar Alexander I captured from the Shah of Persia in 1806. Its mosques and minarets and flat-roofed houses of pale, sun-baked, clay bricks reminded me that I was already on the fringes of Asia, as did also a string of camels encountered on its outskirts.

On one of the desolate red hills that overlook the town I found a memorial to the British troops killed in the fighting against the Bolsheviks twenty years before, an episode in our military history which few English people any longer remember. But the Soviet authorities have never ceased to do everything they could to keep alive the memory of Allied intervention, and while I was in Baku elaborate preparations were being made for the celebration of the twentieth anniversary of the death of the Twenty-six Commissars of Baku, said to have been shot after they had been taken prisoner by the British.

I have always heard that the twenty-seventh Commissar (who somehow escaped) was no less a personage than Anastasi Mikoyan, today a prominent member of the Politbureau. Meeting him at official parties, I could not help wondering, as he pressed on us delicious wines 'from my little place in the Caucasus', whether this elegant Asiatic statesman still bore us any ill-will. Looking at his fierce, handsome, inscrutable face above the well-cut, high-necked, silk shirt, smiling so amiably at a visiting British celebrity, I felt that he almost certainly did.

Amongst the local inhabitants, on the other hand, both here and elsewhere in the Caucasus, there were a number who retained pleasant enough memories of the British occupation and of the short-lived independent states of Georgia, Azerbaijan and Armenia. Those, they said, were the days. The Highlanders in particular had won all hearts.

Nowadays, as I was reminded every time I opened a local newspaper or looked at a public notice, Baku is the capital city of the Soviet Socialist Republic of Azerbaijan, one of the federal republics of the Soviet Union, with its own President and its own Government and the right to secede from the Union whenever it likes. In theory the Soviet Constitution grants a considerable measure of autonomy to the sixteen or so Soviet Socialist Republics (the number has been increased by the addition of the Baltic States and other spoils of war) which go to make up the Union. In practice, policy in all save minor administrative matters is dictated from Moscow. It is true to say, however, that in each case the local instruments of Soviet power are for the most part natives of the republic in question rather than Russians. Thus in Azerbaijan the office-holders were mainly Azerbaijanis, a Turko-Tartar race closely akin to the inhabitants of Persian Azerbaijan across the border, while in the neighbouring Republic of Georgia, Stalin's native land, power was in the hands of Georgians. Samarkand, my ultimate destination, was in the Republic of Uzbekistan, the land of the Uzbeks, who are Turkis, akin in language and origin to the Ottoman Turks. And so on; all these different races being no more like European Russians than the people of Birmingham are like Chinese.

As the basis for a policy of imperialism, this system has much to recommend it. Power is vested in the hands of a group of reliable natives, who are responsible for seeing that the wishes of the central authority are carried out. If they prove unreliable, they can be replaced by others, while, if the worst comes to the worst, an emissary of the central authority can be sent to put things right. By this means, no risks are taken and an appearance of autonomy is preserved. Moreover it is a system which is capable of application to any new country which happens to fall under Soviet dominion. Thus, more recently, in Esthonia, Latvia and Lithuania Soviet Socialist Republics have been set up and politically reliable governments formed from members of the local Communist Parties. It is, we are now learning, a stereotyped pattern into which almost any people or country can be made to fit with a little squeezing and pushing.

After two or three days I had seen all I wanted of Baku, and directed my attention to the next stage of my journey. My first move was a blunder. I walked into the local branch of Intourist and informed the seedy little Armenian clerk behind the counter that I wished to book a passage across the Caspian to Central Asia.

I could not have upset him more if I had told him that six Turks were outside waiting to skin him alive. At first he said nothing. Then, when he had recovered sufficiently from the shock, he started, with truly oriental reiteration, to enumerate the reasons which made it impossible for me to go where I wanted. Central Asia was a closed zone; it was dangerous; it was unhygienic; it was of no interest; there were no ships running across the Caspian; if there had been any ships there would have been no room on board; why did I not go back to Moscow where everything was so much more cultured?

I decided that I had better go away and think again. Taking a seat in a restaurant I ordered a late breakfast of vodka and fresh caviare from the Caspian and settled down to read the local newspaper.

The front page, I noticed, was given up to the Twenty-six Commissars, and featured a highly fanciful drawing of their execution by a mixed firing squad composed of Tsarist officers, Turkoman tribesmen and British other ranks, but on the back page an article caught my eye which I was soon reading with the most lively interest. It related the experiences of a scientific expedition of some kind in the neighbourhood of a place called Lenkoran in the extreme south of Soviet Azerbaijan, on the Persian frontier. The expedition, who had travelled by ship from Baku, had found much to interest them in southern Azerbaijan. The climate was subtropical and the flora exotic and luxuriant, while the fauna, it appeared, actually included tigers. The inhabitants, the writer added, were a little backward, but coming on nicely.

Lenkoran might be (and probably was) unhygienic; it might even be dangerous; but no one could tell me that it was not full of interest or that it could not be reached by sea from Baku. Triumphantly waving my copy of the *Bakinski Rabochi* or *Baku Worker*, I burst once more into the Intourist Office. This might not be Central Asia, but it was on the way there and sounded as if it was well worth having a look at.

But the little Armenian knew where his duty lay. No, he said, there were no boats. There had been boats, perhaps, but at present there were none and in any case, when there were boats, they were always full. Nor could you go to Lenkoran by land; there was no railway and no road, nothing but a great howling wilderness. Besides, when you got there it was unhealthy and unsafe, and of no interest whatever.

'But what,' I said, 'about the tigers?'

'Tigers, perhaps,' he replied pityingly, 'but no culture.'

I was clearly barking up the wrong tree. I left the office and strolled aimlessly down to the harbour. There, a mixed crowd of Tartars and Russians were loading ships or standing about and talking. Others queued up for what seemed to be steamer tickets. I attached myself to the nearest queue, which was mainly composed of Tartars, wild, swarthy, unkempt-looking fellows in shaggy fur hats and tight-fitting skull-caps, who jabbered to each other gutturally in their own language.

For an hour or two nothing happened. Then the window of the

ticket office snapped open and we started to move slowly forward. Eventually I reached the front. 'Where to?' said the pudding-faced woman behind the grating. 'Lenkoran,' I said wondering what her reaction would be. 'Three roubles,' she said giving me a ticket. 'What time does the boat sail?' I asked, hoping she would not notice my foreign accent. 'In half an hour,' she said.

There was no time to be lost. Making my way back to the hotel, I extracted my passport from a reluctant management by means of a subterfuge, shouldered my kitbag and, running back to the docks, pushed my way through the crowd and on board the S.S. *Centrosoyus*, a bare minute before the gangway was taken up.

CHAPTER IV

TRIAL TRIP

I N spite of her modern-sounding name the *Centrosoyus* was a survival
of the old regime, having been built on the Volga in the 'eighties.
Every inch of the very limited deck-space was taken up by closely
packed Tartar families who with their bedding and their chickens were
already settling down for the night. A dense cloud of flies accompanied
us as we steamed slowly out of Baku harbour. After a copious but
singularly unappetizing meal the non-Tartar passengers and the crew
settled down for the night on the benches of the saloon. Preferring
the deck, I managed, after much stumbling about in the dark, to find
a vacant corner between two Tartars, where, using my kitbag as a
pillow, I disposed myself to sleep.

We reached our destination an hour or two after sunrise. The scene,
as we neared the shore, contrasted sharply with the barren red hills
round Baku and the even more barren steppe to the south of it.
Orchards and tea plantations grew almost down to the water's edge.
Behind them, in the distance, rose a line of blue mountains. A few
red-tiled roofs jutted out from among the vivid green of the trees.
There were no signs of anything that could be called a town.

High-prowed Tartar boats put out to meet the ship, which lay at
some distance from the shore. Soon, after some preliminary bargaining, they were ferrying backwards and forwards, loaded to the
gunwale with shouting, struggling humanity. To my dismay I found,
that, in addition to my kitbag, I was now carrying a Tartar baby, whose
mother had thrust it into my arms, and which seemed, at first sight, to
be suffering from smallpox.

Lenkoran, when we reached it, proved to be no more than a fishing
village of white-washed houses clustering round a single unpaved
street. Having inquired whether there was an inn, I was told that there
was and that it was a two-storeyed building; on the strength of which
description I had no difficulty in finding it. Here I succeeded in

obtaining a room. On the wall over the bed, I noticed, a previous occupant had amused himself by squashing bed bugs in neat parallel rows, one above the other.

My British passport, which I now displayed, caused considerable excitement and an admiring crowd collected to look at it, most of whom remained my fast friends for the rest of my stay. The information that I was a foreigner clearly conveyed very little to them, and, on ascertaining that I worked in the British Embassy in Moscow they inquired whether that was the same as the Moscow Soviet. I did not seek to enlighten them. In any case they showed no signs of the panic which seized the average inhabitant of Moscow when he found that he had inadvertently come into contact with a foreigner or worse still a foreign diplomat. Indeed for the next three days I spent the greater part of my time walking, talking, eating or playing cards with the local inhabitants or visitors from Baku who were occupying the other rooms in the hotel. Amongst them was a pretty, fair, Russian girl with a small baby, who told me that she was on sick leave from the collective farm where she worked. She was supposed to have gone to a rest home in the Crimea, but had been sent here by mistake. It was, she said, with a flutter of her long eyelashes, nice to meet someone cultured in such an uncultured place.

The principal products of Lenkoran, as far as I could make out, were fish and tea. Apart from the high street where a flyblown and incongruous selection of over-priced Moscow-made goods were exhibited in the window of Aztorg (the Azerbaijan State Co-operative Store), the Westernizing tendency of the Russian colonists was not particularly evident and life centred round the seething Tartar bazaar, where individual enterprise still flourished and whither the peasants from the neighbouring villages ride to sell their wares to the highest bidder. Though the prices of Russian-made goods were exorbitant, local produce was cheap. Bread and dried fish, which form the staple diet of the Turko-Tartar peasant, were plentiful. Meat of sorts was also available at times for those who could afford it. Eggs, always a useful stand-by on such occasions, could, I was told, sometimes be had, but the supply had momentarily failed. There were no vegetables or fruit of any kind except garlic. On the other hand every kind of vodka was to be found, at a price, and weak tea with a judicious admixture of mud and dead flies.

Agriculture in the Lenkoran district and in the rest of Azerbaijan had been almost entirely collectivized, though most of the peasants seemed to take advantage of the rule by which they are allowed to produce and sell on their own account a limited quantity of agricultural produce, while the inhabitants of some of the more remote villages apparently still managed to hold themselves completely aloof from the collective farms.

At first sight the smiling faces of the Tartars and the comparative absence of the outward and visible emblems of the Soviet power gave the impression that this remote corner of the Soviet Union had perhaps not been entirely brought into line. But I was to change my mind before long. Lenkoran possessed no drainage system, or indeed any sanitary arrangements whatever. But it boasted, in addition to a Party Headquarters, a 'School of Marxist-Leninist Propaganda' housed in one of the only decent buildings in the town.

Soon I was to have an even more striking proof of the long arm of the Kremlin. On the second day after my arrival I was awakened by an unaccustomed noise. A succession of lorries were driving headlong through the town on the way to the port, each filled with depressed-looking Turko-Tartar peasants under the escort of N.K.V.D. frontier troops with fixed bayonets. As lorry followed lorry (the procession was to last, intermittently, all day) and it became clear that the operation was taking place on a large scale, the population began to show considerable interest in what was going on. Little groups formed at street corners and, to my surprise, some bold spirits even dared to express their disapproval openly, and ask the guards what they were doing. It seemed that several hundred peasants had been arrested with their families and were being deported to Central Asia. Ships (including the *Centrosoyus*) were waiting to take them across the Caspian.

There was naturally much speculation as to the reason for these mass arrests. The more ideologically correct suggested that the prisoners were kulaks, or rich peasants, a class long since condemned to liquidation, or that their papers were not in order.

A rather more convincing explanation was put forward by an elderly be-whiskered Russian whom I found airing his views in the minute and somewhat ridiculous 'Park of Rest and Culture' with which Lenkoran had recently been endowed. In his opinion, he said, the arrests had been decreed from Moscow and merely formed part of the deliberate policy of the Soviet Government who believed in transplanting portions of the population from place to place as and when it suited them. The place of those now being deported would probably be taken by other peasants from Central Asia. This, he said, had often happened before. It was, he added, somewhat cryptically, 'a measure of precaution'. And he tugged portentously at his white whiskers.

As we watched the lorries rolling down to the shore a youngish nondescript man, with nothing to distinguish him from any other Soviet citizen, came up to me with a copy of *Krokodil*, the official comic weekly. I saw that he was pointing at an elaborate cartoon, depicting the horrors of British rule in India. A khaki-clad officer, with side-whiskers and projecting teeth, smoking a pipe and carrying a whip, was herding some sad-looking Indians behind some barbed wire. 'Not so different here,' the man said, and was gone. It had been a glimpse, if only a brief one, at that unknown quantity: Soviet public opinion.

The deportation of the Turko-Tartars was not without its effect on my own arrangements. On inquiring when the next steamer was due to leave Lenkoran for Baku, Krasnovodsk or any other port, I was told that all available shipping was being used for the transport of the deportees to Krasnovodsk. It was not known when ordinary passengers would be taken again. There were no railways in southern Azer-baijan, but in the bazaar I found some drivers mending a very old motor truck. When enough passengers had collected, they said, the truck would leave for a place called Astrakhan Bazar. Thence buses sometimes ran to another place, Hadjikabul, and from Hadjikabul there was a train to Baku. With luck the journey would not take more than four days. If I did not go by the truck, there was no saying when I should get away.

I had by now seen enough of Lenkoran and this seemed an oppor-tunity not to be missed. One of my new-found friends provided me with a letter to someone who would give me lodging for the night in Astrakhan Bazar where, it appeared, there was no accommodation for travellers, and I returned to the hotel to get my kitbag and my passport. But the latter document was nowhere to be found and by the time I had retrieved it the truck had left. There was nothing for it but to wait.

I consoled myself with the thought that I should now have plenty of time to explore the surrounding country. Looking round, I found in the bazaar a Tartar blacksmith shoeing a horse. He was a large, brawny, jovial man, with high cheekbones, a snub nose and a villainous black moustache that curled downwards round the corners of his mouth. The sweat ran down his brown body in streams as he hammered away. Round him a typical Eastern crowd of Tartars, with here and there a Russian, had gathered to look on and exchange gossip.

The sight of the horse he was shoeing, a sturdy Tartar pony, gave me an idea. I asked him if he or its owner could let me have it for a day or two. 'What will you pay?' he asked immediately. As I had suspected, he did a sideline in horse dealing.

Finally, after a good deal of talk, in which most of the crowd took part, making suggestions and offering advice, I got what I wanted and, accompanied by a friendly Tartar onlooker, set out in the direction of the mountains where, my companion told me, the Moslem villagers lived their own life relatively undisturbed by the doctrines of Marx and Lenin.

It was a fine day, the horses were not bad and I jogged along contentedly enough. Soon we had left the orchards and tea plantations behind us and were riding along a dry river bed, with, on either side, a tangled mass of semi-tropical vegetation. A snake slipped out of the bushes and slid across our path; a brightly coloured bird flew out of a tree, its wings flashing in the sunlight. I had, I felt, left Europe far behind.

After we had been riding some hours, I noticed a troop of cavalry riding across country at full gallop. They were some distance away and I watched them with interest. They were well mounted and were, I noticed, wearing the uniform of the N.K.V.D. Special Troops. They seemed to be heading in our direction. Suddenly, a broad circling movement brought them face to face with us. Then, before I had taken in what was happening, I found myself staring down the barrels of a pistol and half a dozen rifles. 'Hands up,' said the officer, and up went my hands.

I took advantage of the somewhat embarrassing pause which now ensued to explain to my captor, a shifty-looking little Tartar, that I was a diplomat and could therefore not be arrested. Did he know what a diplomat was? To this he replied, his foolish face suddenly crafty, that he knew only too well and that if I went on arguing he would shoot me on the spot instead of waiting till we got home. I said that if he did the consequences would be very unpleasant for him, to which he replied that they would be even more unpleasant for me.

This argument struck me as convincing and I relapsed into a gloomy silence. Then, with my hands above my head, a revolver in the small of my back and two rifles still covering me, we set out on the return journey to Lenkoran.

After we had ridden for two or three miles I thought it time to bring up once more the question of my diplomatic immunity. A first attempt to extract a Soviet diplomatic pass which I was carrying from my note case gave rise to more play with the revolver, but in the end I induced my captor to take it out for me and look at it. It did not, however, produce on him the effect for which I had hoped. Indeed it produced no effect at all and finally after a little hedging he admitted that he could not read Russian, or, as he put it, in his best Soviet official jargon, was 'illiterate as far as Russian is concerned'. I replied that until he could find someone who could read Russian well enough to decipher my card I proposed to answer no questions. (He was anxious to know what I was doing on a horse so near the Persian frontier.) 'Wait and see,' he replied proudly, 'at N.K.V.D. headquarters we shall find any number of people who can read Russian.' Once again we relapsed into silence.

On our arrival the entire force was paraded and each man inspected my card in turn but without success. By this time a certain embarrassment had become evident amongst my captors, and seeing that I had them at a disadvantage, I made some scarcely veiled allusions to the lack of culture prevalent. They began to look more sheepish than ever.

Then someone found amongst my papers a card of admission to the May Day Parade on the Red Square and having succeeded in spelling out the word *propusk* (pass) jumped to the conclusion that it was a special pass to the frontier zone into which I had apparently unwittingly wandered. This increased their dismay. Following up my advantage I said that, as I was apparently the only person present who could read Russian, perhaps the best way out of the difficulty in which we found ourselves would be for me to read them what was written on my pass. Somewhat guilelessly, they consented and I proceeded to read out with considerable expression, and such improvements as occurred to me, what my pass said about the treatment to be accorded to the representatives of friendly Powers and in particular the inadvisability of arresting them. 'Signed,' I concluded, 'Maxim Litvinov, People's Commissar for Foreign Affairs of the Union of Soviet Socialist Republics,' and looked up to see what effect this had had on my captors.

There could be no doubt that it had made a considerable impression. As if by magic, they abandoned the aggressive attitude which they had adopted hitherto and became apologetic and amiable. They begged me to overlook their most regrettable mistake. In particular they hoped that, when I got back to Moscow, I would not mention this unfortunate incident to Comrade Litvinov. I would understand that they had to be careful so near the frontier; some high officers of the Red Army had left hurriedly and illegally by that route a short time ago. I said I quite realized the need for care and after shaking hands with a roomful of Tartar militiamen returned to the inn.

I had not been back long when a messenger arrived from the Chief of Police to say that a steamer had 'arrived unexpectedly' and would leave next evening for Baku. This information caused great rejoicing among all those who like myself had been marooned in Lenkoran and we celebrated the occasion with a card and supper party which lasted late into the night. Next afternoon five or six of us, including the girl from the collective farm and her baby, an N.C.O. in the Chemical Section of the Red Army, and a large, frowsy man who described himself as a Red Economist and whose life seemed to be bound up with the Third Five Year Plan, settled into a four-berthed cabin on a very small paddle steamer bearing the date 1856. Food had run out in the saloon and some tinned Yarmouth bloaters and a bottle of whisky greatly enhanced my prestige. The atmosphere soon became highly convivial and remained so for so long that in the end I was glad once more to find a vacant space amongst the Tartar horde on deck where I spent the remainder of the night.

From Baku, where we arrived next morning, I took the train north-wards to Tiflis, the capital of the Soviet Socialist Republic of Georgia. My plan was to spend a few days there, cross the Caucasus by road, and then return to Moscow. My visit to Lenkoran must, I felt, have attracted so much attention that any attempt I might now make to reach Central Asia would be doomed to failure in advance.

I reached Tiflis after a night in the train spent in the company of a voluble gentleman of oriental appearance who introduced himself as 'a prominent Armenian composer'. Immediately the town took my fancy. It had a graceful quality, a southern charm, an air of leisure, which I had so far found nowhere else in the Soviet Union. In the old city the houses, crazy structures with jutting verandas, hang like swallows' nests from the side of a hill. Beneath them a mountain stream tumbles its rushing waters and more houses cluster on the far side. Where the valley opens out a broad avenue leads to the newer part of the town, built by the Russians after the conquest of Georgia a century ago.

Here I found a room in the Grand Hotel d'Orient, a long low stone building where my grandfather had stayed fifty or sixty years before. The food, by Soviet standards, was good and the cellar contained an excellent local *vin rosé*. The manager, a pale, spare man with a neatly trimmed black moustache, had not learnt his hotel keeping locally. He was a Slovene, a former Austrian subject who had been taken prisoner by the Russians in 1916. Before the war his father had owned the big hotel at Abbazia. When the revolution had broken out the Bolsheviks had set him free, but he had been bitten with the new ideas and preferred to stay where he was. Now, he said, a little sadly, he was a Soviet citizen and could not go back if he wanted to.

Half the charm of Tiflis lies in its people. They are southerners and wine-drinkers, mountaineers and fighters. They combine a truly Mediterranean expansiveness and vivacity with the dash and hardiness of the Highlander. As a race, they are strikingly good-looking: the men dark, wiry and aggressive in their long cloaks and sheepskin hats on the side of their heads; the women high-breasted and dark-eyed, with straight classical features. Racially they are neither Slavs, like the Russians, nor Turks like the Tartars, but belong to a race of their own with its own ancient language and customs.

After the Revolution the Georgians, who had always resented what they regarded as foreign domination, broke away from Russia and set up an independent state, which, despite a certain flavour of comic opera, survived until 1921. Then, on the withdrawal of the British troops who up to then had helped to hold the ring, internal dissensions broke out and the Red Army, swooping across the mountains, completed the task of subjugation which the Tsars had begun a hundred years earlier. In 1924 the Georgians made another bid for independence, but by now the hand of Moscow lay heavy on them and the rising was savagely suppressed.

The Georgians must, I think, regard with mixed feelings the meteoric rise of Stalin, otherwise Joseph Djugaschvili, the local Georgian boy who made good. Stalin was born in a little village up in the mountains, in a region where for centuries warring tribes had swooped down on each others' flocks and burnt each others' villages, where blood-feuds flourished and there was little intercourse between one steep valley and another; and where he learned, as a child, that it did not do to trust your neighbour further than you could see him. As a youth, he was sent to Tiflis by his mother to be educated as a priest at the local seminary and to receive a grounding in dialectics which was also not to be without its uses later. Then, very soon, he became a professional revolutionary, starting strikes, throwing bombs and robbing banks. At different places in the Caucasus one comes on marble plaques commemorating these activities which must have played their part in forming his character. At any rate, looking back on them in later life, he knew the kind of thing that revolutionaries were apt to do, the kind of thing to look out for when you were building up and consolidating a dictatorship which you did not mean to have overturned. For the Georgians, undergoing this iron rule along with the other races of the Union, and watching it extend its authority over the world, it may be some consolation to recognize in the force that directs it some of their own less amiable qualities.

Old Mrs. Djugaschvili, who had sent him to the seminary, was, it seemed, still alive, a determined old lady in her 'nineties. Deeply religious, she was reputed to regard many of her son's activities with distaste, and the relative freedom from persecution of the Georgian branch of the Orthodox Church was generally attributed to her influence on him.

Knowing that somewhere in Tiflis there was a British War Cemetery containing the graves of the British soldiers who had died or been killed during the British occupation at the end of the war, I decided to find it and see what state it was in. As there was a resident Representative of the Commissariat of Foreign Affairs in Tiflis (Georgia, although it had been elevated to the dignity of a Soviet Socialist Republic, was not encouraged to have a foreign policy of its own), I decided that I had better in the first place get in touch with him. I found his office in a side street, in a house with a courtyard. Its occupant turned out to be a large, flabby man called Stark.

This surprised me, for when I had last heard of Stark, he had been Soviet Ambassador in Afghanistan, where for many years he was known to have intrigued actively and conscientiously against our interests and to have organized rebellion in India. He hastened to explain that he had only been transferred to a quieter post because of his health and for no other reason. I replied, perhaps not very tactfully, that there seemed to have been a good many transfers in the Soviet Diplomatic Service recently, and then, to give interest to the conversation, which seemed to be flagging a bit, I mentioned that, while in Baku, I had heard that Podolski, the Representative there of the Commissariat for Foreign Affairs and former Soviet Minister in Vienna, had been replaced only a few days before.

I have never seen a few words, casually spoken, have such an effect. Mr. Stark's large, flabby face turned a dirty white. Clearly he was in the power of a very strong emotion, and from then onwards it became evident that, even if he had wanted to, he could not have kept his attention on the subject under discussion. From time to time he would make an effort to jerk himself back from the terrifying speculations in which he was engrossed; but it was no good. He could not bring his mind to bear on the question of the cemetery, at any rate not of that cemetery. For some reason, he evidently regarded Podolski's fate as linked to his own, and the news of his removal, so short a time after his arrival at Baku, where he occupied the equivalent post to Stark and whither he, too, had been transferred from a more important post abroad, had filled him with terror for himself. After a time I gave up trying and took my leave. As I went down the stairs, I could hear him talking to his wife in low, hurried whispers. I did not see him again. Not long afterwards it was announced that he, too, had been replaced. His forebodings had been justified.

After this unsuccessful attempt to make use of the correct channels, I decided to address myself direct to the local authorities, in this case the Tiflis Municipal Soviet. It was installed in a large building on the main square of the town, opposite the seminary – now the Palace Hotel – where the young Stalin had received his education. I found it to be a hive of mostly misdirected activity. The officials were mostly Georgians, with a sprinkling of Armenians. Every office that I visited was filled with a depressed crowd of citizens in search of somewhere to live; from their remarks, I gathered that most of them were living five to a room. In the end, together with one or two of the more enterprising supplicants, I penetrated to the office of the Vice-President of the Soviet, an indolent-looking Armenian who was treated with exaggerated deference by his subordinates.

But it soon became clear that he was not interested, and I was just going to leave the building in despair when I was stopped by his secretary, a white-skinned, black-haired, Georgian girl of very considerable personal attractions. Her name, she said, was Tamara, and would I like to come to the cinema? This seemed too good an opportunity to miss and so, postponing my inquiries about the cemetery, I repaired with Tamara and some friends of hers to the special cinema run by the Tiflis Soviet for its employees. There we saw a historical film in Georgian depicting a rising of the Georgians against their Russian oppressors. It was received with enthusiasm by the Georgian audience and I could not help wondering if in their applause there was not perhaps a note of wishful thinking. The uniforms of the Tsarist troops, who fell such easy victims to the fusillades of the Georgian patriots, did not somehow look so very different from those of the N.K.V.D. Special Troops who were to be seen walking about the streets of Tiflis.

After the cinema I asked Tamara, who seemed friendly and intelligent, what she thought was the best way of finding out about the cemetery. 'Ask the N.K.V.D.,' she replied without hesitation. 'They are the only efficient people here.' This seemed sound advice and accordingly without further ado I presented myself at N.K.V.D. Headquarters, where I eventually found an official who had heard of the cemetery. He did not, he said, know where it was, but he could give me the address of an Englishwoman who might know.

I could hardly believe my ears. An Englishwoman living in Tiflis was something quite unheard of. I set out for the address I had been given, wondering if the N.K.V.D. really knew what they were talking about.

The house was a large one in the old quarter of the town. In the middle was a courtyard with wooden balconies giving on to it, draped with festoons of washing. A little Georgian boy was playing in the yard. Could this be the right place? I wondered. At that moment a voice issued from the uppermost balcony. 'Come here at once, Tommy,' it said in commanding tones. 'It's time you were in bed.' 'Coming, Miss Fellows,' said the little Georgian in English which bore no trace of an accent, and trailed reluctantly off to bed. It was, I decided, the right house.

Following Tommy up the stairs, I found Miss Fellows at the top, small and white-haired. 'And what do you want?' she asked briskly. I told her about the cemetery. 'Of course I know where it is,' she said. 'I've looked after it for twenty years, ever since our troops left.' Then she told me her story. It was quite simple. She was the daughter of a Colonel in the Indian Army. She had come to Tiflis as a governess in 1912 and had stayed there ever since, through the war, through the Revolution, through the Allied intervention, through the Bolshevik reoccupation. She had never been home. Indeed I was the first Englishman she had seen for many years. She had been with the same family of Georgians ever since she arrived, teaching first one generation and then another. First the whole house had belonged to them. Now they lived in one room of it and she with them. There was another child in bed, a little girl. 'Poor mite,' she said, 'she had a touch of fever, so I put her to bed.' Then she went out and shouted across the court-yard to some neighbours. It was quite clear that hers was the dominant personality in the neighbourhood. I noticed with pleasure that she still spoke Russian with a strong English accent.

I asked her if she had had any trouble with the local authorities. 'None to speak of,' she said. 'They keep trying to make me give up my English nationality. But I tell them not to be silly.'

Later on she took me to see the cemetery, a sad little place, hidden away on the outskirts of the town, which she had cared for and tended for the best part of twenty years, fighting a never-ceasing battle against weeds, stray dogs, hens and marauding Soviet children.

Before leaving, I asked Miss Fellows if there was anything I could do for her. She asked for two things, some English books and help in getting a wall built round the cemetery. I asked her if that was really all she wanted. She said yes, she could manage perfectly well. To anyone who knows the Soviet Union, it will be apparent that Miss Fellows was a very remarkable woman.

There was no longer anything to keep me in Tiflis and my spell of leave was running out. The passes over the Caucasus were now clear of snow and trucks were running across the Georgian Military Road. Without much difficulty I got a seat in one, and, stuffing my belongings into my kitbag, set out on my homeward journey, in company with a miscellaneous collection of Georgians and Russians.

The Georgian Military Road, which runs from Tiflis across the main Caucasus Range to Ordzhonikidze, was built by Russian engineers in the first half of the nineteenth century, primarily as a means of subduing the warlike Caucasian tribes who were still holding out against them in the mountains. By enabling them to move considerable forces rapidly to important strategic points, it made it easier for them to contend with the highly mobile mountaineers and led finally to the defeat of Shamyl and the pacification of the Caucasus.

For some miles after leaving Tiflis we followed the valley of the swiftly flowing Kura. Before long this brought us to Mtzkhet, the former capital of Georgia, now a mere cluster of houses round an ancient cathedral jutting out into the swirling water of the river. Already we were in the hills and soon the road began to climb sharply. The air became sharper and the mountains wilder. From time to time we passed little groups of travellers on foot, on horseback and in carts and sometimes solitary horsemen, fierce shaggy figures. At Pasanaur near the top of the pass we stopped to eat – a surprisingly good meal: freshly caught trout, *shashlik* – mutton grilled over charcoal on a skewer – and a bottle of local red wine. Outside the post house sat a small, rather mangy bear on a chain, a forlorn-looking little animal.

Still we climbed, more and more steeply. Our truck had seen better days and in many places the road had been washed away by the melting snow. At more and more frequent intervals it became necessary for everyone to get out and push, and I began to wonder whether we should ever reach our destination. High above us to the west loomed Mount Kazbek, a massive peak capped with eternal snow. We were passing through the towering Dariel Gap. Sheer rock rose up for thousands of feet on either side of us. Then we started to descend. Soon we found ourselves following the valley of the Terek, flowing down towards the northern slopes of the Caucasus. But our surroundings remained as wild as ever. An expanse of vast boulders lined the river bed and the mountains on either side were barren and craggy. The sun was down and it was bitterly cold. By the time we reached our destination it was dark and we were half frozen.

Vladikavkaz, the Key to the Caucasus, or, as it is now called, after a People's Commissar of that name, Ordzhonikidze, is an agreeably placed little town rather like a decayed French watering place, but otherwise has little to recommend it, and, after spending a night at the inn, I was glad to board the train for Moscow, where I duly arrived forty-eight hours later.

My journey was over. I had not reached Central Asia and I had made a number of major tactical errors. On the other hand I had caught my first glimpse of the East and I had lived on and off in considerably closer proximity to the Soviet population than I would have believed possible. Next time, I decided, I would profit by this experience. Next time. . . .

CHAPTER V

TOUCH AND GO

B Y the end of the summer my turn had come for another spell of leave, and I was free to make a fresh attempt to reach Central Asia.

This time I decided to try a different line of approach: by Siberia. As far as I knew, there was nothing to prevent one from travelling across Siberia by the main Trans-Siberian line. Some friends of mine had recently gone through to China that way. My plan was to take a ticket on the Trans-Siberian Express; leave the train without warning somewhere in the middle of Siberia, and then, stage by stage, make my way southwards as unobtrusively as possible, and without revealing my ultimate destination. I hoped, by this indirect approach, to keep the 'competent authorities' guessing until the final, illicit stage of my journey, by when, with any luck, it would be too late for them to stop me getting where I wanted. I did not expect to remain at large in Central Asia for long, even supposing that I got there, but judging by my last journey, my experiences once I left the beaten track were likely to be unusual and entertaining. The chief danger was that I would be picked up and sent back to Moscow as soon as I left the Trans-Siberian.

I started from Moscow on September 21st with a first-class ticket, bought quite openly, a supply of roubles, some tins of *foie gras*, no more luggage than I could carry on my back, and no definite plans.

For two days I ate and slept and read the excellent novels of Monsieur Simenon. Outside the window, the Russian landscape rolled slowly by, green and monotonous. I decided that I would get off the train at Sverdlovsk, on the far side of the Urals, one of the big new industrial towns which have grown up in Siberia since the Revolution.

We crossed the Urals in the night and reached Sverdlovsk station an hour or two before sunrise. Without saying anything to anyone I shouldered my kitbag and slipped off the train. Snow had fallen in the mountains and it was bitterly cold. Standing on the bleak windy platform, I watched the warm, brightly lighted coach from which I had just alighted sway off into the darkness.

Outside the station a tram was starting. It took me through muddy, unpaved streets of tumble-down wooden shacks to the centre of the town with its groups of vast blocks of recently built but already slightly dilapidated buildings. The largest of these, an immense reddish building, bore in golden letters a yard high the legend 'Grand Ural Hotel'. This looked promising. I pushed my way through the swing doors.

In the hall, even at so early an hour, a seething, shouting crowd was besieging a harassed booking clerk who was trying to make them believe that not one room was vacant. A number of less impatient seekers after accommodation were sleeping peacefully on the benches in the hall, which, like the rest of the hotel, was modernistic in intention, but shabby in effect, and strongly redolent of Soviet humanity. Life-size plaster statues of Lenin and Stalin towered above them. After a struggle, I fought my way through to the booking clerk. 'No rooms,' he said. 'What, no rooms at all?' I asked. 'No rooms unless you have a special permit from the N.K.V.D.,' he said, and started talking to someone else.

This was not at all good news. The last thing I wanted to do was to draw upon myself the attention of the 'competent authorities' at this early stage. On the other hand, unless I applied to them for a permit, I should have nowhere to sleep and probably nothing to eat, and at least in Sverdlovsk I was not in a forbidden zone. I accordingly decided to visit the N.K.V.D., devoutly hoping that they would not ask me too many questions about my future movements.

To my delight, they asked me no questions at all. At N.K.V.D. Headquarters a harmless-looking functionary with pince-nez and a fussy manner, on being told that I was travelling 'on official business', at once issued me with the document I needed. Armed with this, I returned to the Grand Ural Hotel, having achieved something very like official status.

As soon as they saw the document with which I had been issued the attitude of the hotel staff changed completely. After a brief whispered conversation I was provided with a *propusk* (pass) admitting me to the upstair regions and installed in a room of which the furniture consisted of three rather doubtful beds, a wireless loudspeaker which poured out propaganda at me until I succeeded in silencing it, and a large mauve marble inkwell in the shape of a bird. Then, having eaten a greasy but filling meal in the fly-infested hotel dining-room, I set out to inspect the town.

Sverdlovsk, the former Ekaterinburg, where Nicholas II and his family were put to death by the Bolsheviks in 1918, was now one of the chief centres of Soviet heavy industry sited, for strategic reasons, beyond the Urals. Before the Revolution Ekaterinburg with a population of 40,000 must have been a typical Russian provincial town. Now, twenty years later, it could boast a population of close on half a million. Some of the old churches and official buildings still survived but the latter were completely outnumbered and overshadowed by the vast modern constructions which had sprung up of recent years and were still springing up: factories, department stores, Government buildings, cinemas, clubs and blocks of flats.

Seen, or, better still, photographed, from a distance these were impressive both on account of their size and of their up-to-date design. But little attention had been paid to detail. From nearby or from inside the new buildings were considerably less impressive, shoddily constructed and roughly finished. Indeed in many respects they compared unfavourably with the more solidly built and better-finished houses of the old regime. Sverdlovsk had manifestly been modernized in a hurry and the fine asphalted streets of sub-skyscrapers tended to tail off into muddy lanes of wooden shacks. In the outlying parts of the town where the majority of the working population lived there were no paved streets and no stone or brick houses; nothing but mud and hovels.

But in spite of these imperfections, Sverdlovsk gave an impression of energy and progress. The new factories seemed to be working day and night and, although the finest blocks of flats were of course reserved for the new bourgeoisie of Party members, high officials and highly paid skilled workers, a considerable number of more modest buildings were being built to provide accommodation for a considerable proportion of the population and do something to relieve the appalling housing shortage.

Shopping facilities seemed to be confined to one street and indeed to one shop, an enormous Universalmag (State department store). This, by Soviet standards, was well fitted, while the selection of goods for sale was no worse than that to be found in Moscow stores and the prices roughly equivalent to those current in Moscow. As usual, the counters at which the necessities of life were on sale were besieged by a seething crowd of anxious would-be purchasers while there was far less demand for fancy goods and 'luxuries'. In the side-streets the usual queues were waiting outside the kerosene and bread shops. In Sverdlovsk as in every other Soviet town half at least of the shop-windows were filled with Soviet-made scent and soaps.

Considerable attention seemed to have been paid to providing amusements for the population or rather for the portion of it which has the time and money to be amused. One of the most striking modern buildings was the 'Dynamo' sports club, an organization with branches all over the Union, whose members are drawn from the new Soviet *jeunesse dorée*. A fine neo-classical building which was presumably the Governor's residence under the old regime has been converted into a school and Communist Boy Scouts' Club and the garden in front of it into a playground for the children. Near a new basalt-faced block of Government offices and flats for Government officials was a large new cinema and dance hall and there were other cinemas and theatres in other parts of the town. On the outskirts, an attractive 'Park of Rest and Culture' was being laid out on a large scale in a pine wood on the shores of a lake.

But, in spite of all these means of recreation, the crowds which thronged the badly paved streets looked uniformly and profoundly depressed. Almost all were poorly clothed, badly shod industrial workers or rather industrialized peasants. The smartly dressed members of the new bourgeoisie, so conspicuous in Moscow, were few and far between.

On the whole I felt little inclination to linger in Sverdlovsk and it was with feelings of relief that, after rising at three in the morning and waiting for some hours on the station platform, I learned that there was one vacant berth on the incoming train to Novosibirsk. I decided to take it.

Novosibirsk, two days' journey eastwards, had little to distinguish it from Sverdlovsk. Both were centres of heavy industry. There were, in both, the same blocks of pretentious modernistic buildings in the centre of the town and the same fringe of muddy streets and dilapidated shacks on the outskirts; the same factories working day and night and the same crowds of unsmiling workers in the streets. But while Ekaterinburg was already an important provincial town in 1917, Novosibirsk or rather Novonikolaievsk was before the Revolution no more than a medium-sized village, and the present town of 300,000 or more inhabitants with its street-cars and skyscrapers has been entirely constructed under the Soviet regime.

It was at Novosibirsk that I planned to leave the Trans-Siberian line and branch southwards along the Turksib Railway which joins the Trans-Siberian at Novosibirsk and links it up with Turkestan. Accordingly, having seen all I wanted of the town, I took my place in a queue for tickets. For hour after hour I shifted my weight wearily from one foot to the other. Finally, after waiting for no less than ten hours, I was lucky enough to secure the last available ticket for Biisk, two or three hundred miles to the south at the foot of the Altai Mountains. After which the window of the ticket office shut with a snap and the remainder of the queue settled down to wait patiently for another twenty-four hours until the next day's train was due to leave for Biisk and a fresh supply of tickets would be put on sale.

As I turned away from the ticket office, two men who had been standing nearby turned away after me. Their alert expressions, intelligent faces and neat dark suits immediately aroused my suspicions. I took a walk round the block. Glancing over my shoulder, I could see that they were following me. When I stopped, they stopped and pretended to look into a shop window. With a sinking heart, I boarded the southbound train. As I settled into my berth, I found that one was occupying the berth immediately above mine and the other the one below. There could no longer be any doubt about it. I had been provided with an N.K.V.D. escort.

This was a nuisance, but at least it was better than if I had been stopped outright, politely informed that foreigners were not allowed to travel on the Turksib and put on the next train for Moscow, which was what I had half expected. Besides, the carriage in which I found myself was of the 'hard' variety where the cleanliness of one's immediate neighbour is a matter of considerable interest, and my escort, although not so picturesque as the other occupants of the carriage, were less likely to harbour the vermin for which Siberia is famous.

Railway accommodation in the Soviet Union falls into three categories. First there are the 'International' coaches mostly built before the Revolution on the lines of the ordinary European sleeping-cars and divided into compartments for two (or four) passengers. These coaches, in which I had travelled up to now and which are the only form of accommodation ever seen by most foreign tourists, are only included in a very few of the more important luxury expresses and are completely unknown to the average Soviet citizen. Secondly there are the 'soft' coaches, of which there is one on most express trains. These, which are used for the most part by the new bourgeoisie, are divided into compartments with four upholstered berths in each.

Finally there is the 'hard' coach which is the means of transport of 90 per cent of the population, and of which a great many trains are exclusively composed. The 'hard' coach, which is built to hold forty passengers and never holds less though it very often holds more, is not divided into compartments. An open space runs down the middle and on either side there are three layers of planks arranged one above the other on each of which there is just room for a small man to stretch out at full length. In theory an ordinary railway ticket gives the right to travel 'hard'. In reality, however, unless a passenger is ready to spend several days at the railway station on the chance of an empty train coming in, he must buy a supplementary 'place card' of which only a limited number are sold.

'Hard' carriages like everything else in the Soviet Union vary considerably. Some, in spite of the absence of all upholstery, are infested with vermin. Others are perfectly clean. (Much, of course, depends on one's travelling companions.) Sometimes bedding can be hired but often one has to sleep on the bare boards. Sometimes there is electric light, but in the carriage in which I now found myself the forty occupants had to content themselves with the light of a single tallow candle placed in the middle of the central passage.

In several respects, however, all railway carriages in the Soviet Union are alike. The windows are either not made to open or if they are, are kept tightly shut; a general conversation on a variety of subjects is constantly in progress all day and all night, and someone is always eating and drinking.

The town of Biisk, for which I was now bound, had from my point of view two things to recommend it. In the first place it lay at the foot of the Altai Mountains which form the boundary between the Soviet Union and the Republic of Tannu Tuva and stretch far into Mongolia, and I felt that the surrounding country should therefore be worth exploring. Secondly, situated as it is on a branch line some distance along the Turksib, it seemed to me a good starting place for an unobtrusive trip to Central Asia.

Biisk at six in the morning presented an exceptionally depressing spectacle. The weather, which at Novosibirsk had been fine, had broken. It was cold and raining heavily and at the station there was nothing to be had but black bread and greasy soup. Even the vodka had run out. A number of the inhabitants who had collected at the station to witness the arrival of the train hastened to inform me that once it started raining in these parts it went on for weeks.

Before deciding on any course of action the first thing was clearly to inspect the town of Biisk which lay at a distance of several miles from the station. The only available means of conveyance was a strange oval wickerwork coracle on wheels filled with extremely wet hay and drawn by a wet and immensely depressed-looking horse. It was generally used, so the crowd informed me, for redistributing guests after parties. Crouched in this distressing vehicle, I set out in streaming rain along a road which was literally a foot deep in mud.

Biisk did no credit to anyone. The dozen stone-built houses were without exception of pre-revolutionary construction and the wooden houses with their eaves carved in the old Siberian style were unbelievably dilapidated. The row of shops in the high street were a disgrace even by Soviet standards and the unpaved streets a sea of mud. What I saw of the population looked depressed, which indeed they had every right to be. Although Biisk is said to have been originally the centre to which the neighbouring Chinese and Mongols came to sell their corn and wool, the inhabitants are all Russians and I saw practically no Turkis, Tartars or Mongols here or anywhere else in Siberia.

It had by now become quite evident that late September was not the time of year to visit the Altai and having seen the mud in Biisk itself I accepted unquestioningly the assurances of the local inhabitants that the roads up into the mountains were already impassable. Biisk as a pleasure resort had not proved a success. On the other hand it retained its advantages as a jumping-off place for a trip to Central Asia and I felt that in the circumstances the sooner I made a start the better. In the stationmaster's office I found a fairly recent time-table and with the assistance of the acting stationmaster, a friendly though not very intelligent young lady of sixteen, I succeeded in planning out an itinerary which would bring me in the end to Alma Ata, the capital of the Soviet Socialist Republic of Kazakhstan, situated three days' journey to the south at the foot of the Tien Shan range, near the Chinese frontier.

After the usual wait — for in the Soviet Union nothing can be had without waiting — I started off once again on my travels. My immediate destination was Altaisk. Thence I would go to Barnaul, and thence, if I got as far, to Alma Ata.

The 'hard' carriage I was in filled with local peasants who got in and out at the various small stations along the line: gnarled beings whose drab, ragged, sweat-soaked clothes exhaled a sour odour of corruption, and who, in the dim, flickering light of the single candle which illuminated the swaying truck, had a strangely troglodyte appearance.

On learning that I not only came from Moscow but was actually a foreigner — a being of which most of them had only the vaguest conception — they started to describe to me the horrors of life in Siberia, interrupting each other and repeating themselves over and over again, like the chorus in a Greek play. On the collective farms, they said, things were in a poor state. The up-to-date mechanical apparatus was permanently out of order as no one really knew how to work it. They toiled from morning to night and were only just able to keep themselves and their families alive. Altogether the collective-farm system was a failure and whatever I might hear to the contrary I was to understand once and for all that the life of a Siberian *kolkhoznik* was a miserable one. The people to be envied, they said bitterly, were the railway workers who received enormous wages for doing nothing.

Actual figures are always hard to get at, but the agricultural labourer sitting next to me, a man in the prime of life, said that he was quite satisfied when he earned 100 roubles (then roughly equivalent in purchasing power to one pound sterling) a month.

At Altaisk, a few miles from Barnaul where the Biisk branch line joins the Turksib, we stopped for several hours while a number of cattle trucks were hitched on to our train. These were filled with people who, at first sight, seemed to be Chinese. They turned out to be Koreans, who with their families and their belongings were on their way from the Far East to Central Asia where they were being sent to work on the cotton plantations. They had no idea why they were being deported but all grinned incessantly and I gathered from the few words I could exchange with some of their number that they were pleased to have left the Far Eastern territory where conditions were terrible and to be going to Central Asia of which they had evidently been given enthusiastic accounts. Later I heard that the Soviet authorities had quite arbitrarily removed some 200,000 Koreans to Central Asia, as likely to prove untrustworthy in the event of a war with Japan. I was witnessing yet another mass movement of population.

By the side of the track a little Tartar boy was playing with what seemed to be a mouse. On closer inspection it proved to be an enormous spider, several inches across, its body and legs covered with thick black hair. Methodically the little boy pulled off its legs, one after another, until all that was left was a round black hairy body, squirming in the sand.

On reaching Barnaul I went, before trying for a place on the Alma Ata train, out into the town to buy some bread, a commodity not always to be found in the small wayside stations along the line. While I was in the shop I was accosted by a young man with a brisk manner and an alert expression who said he would like a word with me outside in the street.

Recognizing him without difficulty as an agent of the N.K.V.D., I felt little doubt that my travels were about to be brought to an abrupt conclusion. I decided nevertheless to try to brazen things out and replied that before accompanying him outside I must ask him to tell me who he was, as I was not in the habit of discussing my affairs with strangers. At this he seemed somewhat taken aback and embarrassed (I imagine that the average Soviet citizen does not tend to argue on such occasions). Then, after a moment's hesitation, he drew me aside and whispered into my ear that he was an official of the N.K.V.D. and was anxious to avoid a painful scene in public. On being told this I expressed relief which I was far from feeling, explained that at first sight I had taken him for a *khuligan* (hooligan) of whom I understood from the newspapers there were many about and asked him what I could do for him. In reply he told me to hand over my papers and asked me what my business was in Barnaul. I accordingly produced my British passport, a document which completely baffles the average Soviet provincial official and is therefore far more useful than any diplomatic pass, and explained that I was about to leave for Alma Ata. I added that I should not require his services on the journey as — and I pointed to my escort who were hovering rather sheepishly in the background — I had already been provided with two of his colleagues from Novosibirsk, but that I should be very grateful if with his knowledge of local conditions he could help me to get a place on the train.

There followed a pause during which he examined my passport which, with the exception of my expired entry visa into the Soviet Union, he was naturally quite unable to decipher, from all angles and then to my infinite relief touched his cap (all Russians are inclined to be impressed by anything new and unknown) and said that he would see what he could do about reserving me a place on the Alma Ata train.

Under the auspices of my new-found protector I now took my place at the head of the queue amongst the Red Army soldiers, members of the Central Committee of the Communist Party, holders of Soviet orders and decorations, nursing and expectant mothers and other privileged persons, who in the Soviet Union are given preference to all other travellers, and soon secured the necessary place-card entitling me to a place in a soft carriage. All this was done so quickly that I still had an hour to spare before the train left in which to eat a much-needed hot meal.

In the buffet I found myself at a table with two Soviet citizens of the successful and contented type which one occasionally encounters in places like station restaurants which are not frequented by the very poor: bluff, hearty, back-slapping characters. Both were still in their twenties and both, they hastened to inform me, members of the Party. One was foreman in a building organization and earned 900 roubles a month, the other an engineer earning 1000 roubles a month. Both were local men.

The builder was very full of himself. Until recently he had been an ordinary workman. He owed his promotion entirely to his own skill and bodily strength and thanks to his own experience as a workman was able to see that his subordinates did their work properly. On the wages he was earning he could live comfortably and indulge his passion for beer (which we were all three drinking in large quantities at the time).

Did workmen, he asked, live as well as this wherever I came from? I confined myself to saying that I did not think that the British workman was any worse off than his Soviet brother. But even such studied moderation brought the indignant retort that if I believed that, it showed that I had simply been deceived by what I read in the lying capitalist press which was well known to be government controlled. He, on the other hand, knew from reading the Soviet press, the veracity of which no one could doubt, that in all capitalist countries the workers were starved, underpaid and persecuted by the police and by their employers. But soon the world revolution would come and the old system would be swept away in Great Britain as it had been in Russia. Great Britain, he said, had never been the friend of Tsarist Russia and would therefore never really be the friend of the Soviet Union. But, if not a 'genuine democracy', she was at least, he concluded, a 'non-fascist country', and we parted on the best of terms. Indeed both the builder and the engineer announced their intention of coming to see me when they visited Moscow which neither of them had yet seen. Not wishing to cut short two so promising careers, I was careful to give them an imaginary address.

In the train I found myself in a 'soft' compartment with three senior and somewhat supercilious officers of the Red Army, well pleased with themselves in their smartly cut uniforms and top-boots. When I woke up next morning they had gone and their place had been taken by three of the railway employees whose prosperity had been such a source of envy to the peasants I had met the day before. These were friendly and talkative and we shared our supplies of food, while the eldest of the three regaled us with somewhat salacious accounts of night life in Warsaw before the Revolution, which he said compared most favourably with life in Central Siberia at the present time. The three railwaymen got out at Semipalatinsk but were immediately replaced by three more railwaymen. What exact purpose was fulfilled by the hordes of railway officials who filled the 'soft' carriages in Soviet trains, I never discovered. But all had well-filled brief cases and all were travelling, so they said, 'on Government business'.

While my fellow travellers changed at frequent intervals, the country through which we were travelling had so far scarcely varied. From the Urals to Novosibirsk and then down the Turksib as far as Semipalatinsk the landscape remained strictly Siberian: a dead flat plain covered with grey-green moss, occasional clumps of silver birches, and an occasional magpie sitting on a stump. Such villages as I saw consisted of decayed wooden *isbas*, inhabited by miserable-looking Russian peasants.

The change from Siberia to Central Asia came soon after entering the Republic of Kazakhstan near Semipalatinsk which we reached on the second night after leaving Barnaul. From this point onwards the Turksib, after climbing to a higher level, runs through what is apparently a waterless desert, as flat, though far more desolate than the Siberian plain. This we traversed for the whole of one day. The Turksib, which was only completed in 1930, had, unlike the Trans-Siberian, not yet been double-tracked and there were frequent and prolonged halts while we waited for trains coming in the opposite direction.

At the side of the track at intervals were situated clusters of Kazakh *yurts*, or dome-shaped huts, from the inhabitants of which the passengers, in the absence of a dining-car, could buy melons, eggs and other articles of food for the most part rather fly-blown and looking, as indeed was probably the case, as though they had met every train for weeks past. Lovingly a dirty, tattered old woman would produce from the innermost folds of her dress half a roast chicken, black with age, and offer it for sale at an enormous price, which only the very richest passengers could afford to pay. Personally, I stuck to eggs and fruit.

The dwellers along the line and, by now, most of the passengers were native Kazakhs. These vary considerably in type, some having flat, round, moonlike faces with high cheekbones like Mongols and others oval faces with more aquiline features of a more Persian type. All have dark reddish-brown complexions like that of North American Indians. The women wear strange medieval head-dresses; the men long padded coats and, on their heads, skull-caps, round fur hats or helmet-shaped cones of thick white felt with sharply upturned brims. The language they speak is akin to Turkish. Russian for them is a foreign tongue. Though most of the Kazakhs are no longer nomads and have exchanged their tents for villages of mud huts, they are still born horsemen and are never out of the saddle for long.

At sunset we came to a range of small hills, the first I had seen since the Urals. During the day the sun was blazing hot but after dark the desert was bitterly cold and, though I slept fully dressed and wore an overcoat, I shivered all night in my bunk. When I looked out next morning across the sandy waste, I saw something that filled me with pleasurable anticipation.

Far to the south, dimly seen in the remote distance, towering high above the desert, rose a mighty range of mountains, their lower slopes veiled in cloud and vapours, their snow-clad peaks glittering in the sunlight, suspended between earth and sky.

These were the Tien Shan: the Mountains of Heaven. At their foot lay Alma Ata, beyond them Chinese Turkestan.

CHAPTER VI

CITIES OF THE PLAIN

ALL day we trundled across the desert towards those distant peaks. Then, suddenly in the early afternoon, we found ourselves once again amid cultivation: apple orchards, the trees heavily laden with fruit; golden fields of Indian corn ripening in the sun; plantations of melons; rows of tall poplars growing by the side of canals and irrigation ditches. After the desert the foliage seemed lusciously, exuberantly green. We were nearing Alma Ata. Already we could see the white houses of the town. Beyond it the tree-covered foothills of the Tien Shan rose steeply towards the snow-covered peaks behind them.

I was in Central Asia.

Alma Ata lies ten miles from the railway. After an interminable wait, followed by a sharp mêlée, I succeeded in securing myself a place in a lorry that was going there. Next to me was a grubby but cheerful individual, with a snub nose, a mouthful of irregular, broken teeth and a shock of tangled hair, who told me that he had just completed five years in a penal settlement. Life there, he said, had not been so bad, though to this day he did not know why he had been sent there. Perhaps it was because he was a Pole. But now, although he had never applied for them, he had been given Soviet papers, so things would perhaps be easier for him. Before being deported he had been a barber by profession; now he hoped to make a living by picking apples. He seemed a happy-go-lucky sort of fellow, ready to take things as he found them.

After a fierce jolting down long dusty roads lined with poplars, we passed through a colony of dilapidated Kazakh *yurts* on the outskirts and almost immediately found ourselves in the centre of the town.

Alma Ata must be one of the pleasantest provincial towns in the Soviet Union. In character it is purely Russian, being one of the first Russian settlements in Central Asia. From its foundation in 1854 until the Revolution it bore the name of Vierny. In Kazakh its new name means 'Father of Apples', an appellation which it fully merits, for the apples grown there are the finest in size and flavour that I have ever eaten. The central part of the town consists of wide avenues of poplars at right angles to one another. The houses, whether of wood or of stone, are painted white and are for the most part in a good state of preservation. In addition to the ornate pre-revolutionary buildings, a large number of austere ultra-modern constructions have been erected which include a very large block of government buildings, a telegraph, telephone and wireless building, a fine cinema, various scientific and other institutes, shops and several blocks of flats. Other buildings were nearing completion. A tramway system was being installed and many of the streets were asphalted. The shops seemed well stocked, especially the food shops. In the centre of the town there was a large open bazaar to which the Kazakhs from the neighbouring collective farms rode in to sell their wares. The population, which to judge by the crowds in the streets was roughly half Kazakh and half Russian, seemed comparatively contented, and those with whom I spoke showed themselves intensely proud of the town they lived in. I gained an impression of prosperity and progress.

Alma Ata, until a few years ago a smaller town than Semipalatinsk, owes its development almost entirely to the Turksib Railway which has linked it up with the rest of the Soviet Union. Before the Revolution the population was approximately 30,000; in 1929, before the railway reached it, it was 50,000 and now seven years after the construction of the Turksib, it had reached the figure of 230,000.

The population of Kazakhstan of which it is the capital and, which in 1936 became a Union Republic, is only about eight millions, but in area it is approximately equivalent to England, France and Germany put together. Its economic importance is principally agricultural and in the immediate neighbourhood of Alma Ata the country seemed remarkably fertile, producing Indian corn, cotton, wheat and rice and sugar beet besides the apples for which it is famous and other kinds of fruit. It is also the most important cattle-breeding area in the Soviet Union.

On arrival at Alma Ata I immediately set out in search of somewhere to live. I was attracted by what I had seen of the town and its immediate surroundings and I was also determined to see something of the Ala Tau, the portion of the Tien Shan range which lies immediately to the south. From what I knew of Soviet methods it would be several days before I even found out what means existed of getting up into the mountains.

I had ascertained on arriving that there were two hotels, both of recent construction. One was known as the Ogpu Hotel because of its proximity to N.K.V.D. Headquarters and the other, which formed part of the central block of Government buildings, was called the Dom Sovietov or House of the Soviets. At both I was told on applying for accommodation that they were completely full, the management of the Dom Sovietov adding that even if they had had room they would not have given it to me as they only catered for Government and Party officials travelling on official business.

Emboldened by my experience at Sverdlovsk I decided that the time had come to invoke the help of the N.K.V.D. At N.K.V.D. Headquarters I was told that the competent officer was out but would be back in two hours, and on returning two hours later, I found no one except an apparently half-witted Kazakh sentry from whom I gathered that Headquarters had shut down for the night. My own N.K.V.D. escort had no suggestions to offer and seemed in some doubt as to where they were going to spend the night themselves. The immediate outlook was scarcely promising, but before resigning myself to the prospect of a night on the streets, I decided to go back to the Dom Sovietov, which had seemed to me in every way preferable to the ordinary hotel, and see whether I could not by sheer persistence make the management relent. I accordingly deposited my luggage in the front hall and fought my way through the crowd surrounding the booking desk. An hour later, although the management showed no signs of weakening as far as sleeping accommodation was concerned, I had succeeded in securing permission to have supper in the hotel dining-room, a success of which I hastened to take advantage.

I had expected the filthy oilcloth-covered tables, the rude attendants and the greasy, stodgy food with which I had grown familiar at Sverdlovsk and elsewhere. Instead, I found a pleasant room, obsequious waiters and waitresses, and good food. After eating a meal of bortsch, roast duck with apples, and pancakes, which cost me only ten roubles, and drinking several glasses of vodka I felt a great deal happier and more determined than ever not to be turned out of this preserve of the privileged classes.

But the tired, solitary, middle-aged woman who had been left in charge of the booking desk stuck to her guns and an hour or two later, in spite of every kind of threat, taunt and appeal, I had still made no progress and was preparing to spend the night on a bench in the local Park of Rest and Culture, when, suddenly, as is the way in the Soviet Union, her opposition collapsed and she told me that, if I would promise to go away next day, I might have a bed in the Lenin Corner which had been turned into a temporary dormitory. I was issued with the necessary *propusk* or pass and a few minutes later I was installed in a fairly clean bed immediately under the outstretched arm of a life-sized statue of Lenin and opposite an equally imposing bust of Stalin. The fifteen other beds in the room were occupied by snoring Kazakh or Russian minor officials, all of whom woke and protested loudly when I tried to open the window.

Next morning, having been told that the impending arrival of 70 visiting members of the Communist Youth Association made my continued presence in the hotel impossible, I returned to the attack with the N.K.V.D. This time I was received almost immediately by the Commanding Officer, who was clearly unaccustomed to foreigners and seemed at a loss to know what to do with me. In the end he turned for advice to his lady secretary who told him with an air of authority, which under any other system would have been surprising, that he was to have nothing to do with me at all. I was accordingly turned politely away from N.K.V.D. Headquarters and advised to try the Dipagentstvo or Diplomatic Agency.

This, I felt quite convinced, did not really exist. In any case my experience of Mr. Stark in Tiflis made me feel certain that even if there really was a Diplomatic Agent in Alma Ata he would be worse than useless. But I was mistaken.

After a prolonged search I at last found the Diplomatic Agency which, in the absence of the Agent, who I gathered was an official of the

People's Commissariat for Foreign Affairs, was in charge of a most amiable and zealous young Kazakh who assured me that he was delighted to see me as he felt that my arrival justified his existence. In spite of the fact that he was employed in a Diplomatic Agency, I was the first foreigner with whom he personally had ever come into contact. After a brief struggle in which he was completely victorious, he brought the Dom Sovietov into line and a good single room was put at my disposal for as long as I liked. Moreover, on learning of my desire to visit the Tien Shan he provided me with a recommendation to the Society of Proletarian Tourists.

When I applied next day to the offices of that organization I was told that a car and a guide had now been found but that there was no petrol to be had as every drop was required for bringing in the harvest. I accordingly decided to make an excursion on my own. After loitering for some time round the motor-lorry base in the centre of the town I succeeded in obtaining a place on a lorry going to Talgar, a large village in the hills some forty miles to the south-east of Alma Ata.

On reaching Talgar I set out on foot into the hills followed by one of the two local N.K.V.D. men who had relieved their colleagues from Novosibirsk soon after my arrival. After we had gone some distance I allowed my new escort, to whom I had not yet spoken, to catch up with me and remarked on the beauty of the scenery. He agreed and, taking advantage of the opening, inquired whether I proposed to go on walking all day without anything to eat. I suggested that we might pick some apples off the trees. He replied that if I wanted apples and some hot food too we could stop at a peasant's cottage, as he was a Talgar man himself and the peasants were all old friends of his. I agreed and we turned into the next cottage we came to.

The cottage, which was surrounded by three or four acres of ground, including an apple orchard, a plot of Indian corn, a plot of melons and a plot of sunflowers, contained one large room where the occupants slept and ate, a kitchen and a space under the eaves for drying fruit and vegetables. It was built of mud bricks and whitewashed inside and out. Sitting in the sun outside it we found a very old Russian peasant woman and her two grandchildren aged four and five. They seemed delighted to see visitors and the grandmother immediately started to prepare a meal while I played in the garden with the puppy, the children and the N.K.V.D. man. Later we were joined by the children's mother, a fine healthy-looking peasant woman, and their elder sister aged nine who arrived with the bread, and finally by their father who had been into the bazaar with his horse and cart to sell his Indian corn crop.

The meal to which we now sat down after the family had duly crossed themselves in front of the numerous ikons which were hanging in a corner of the extremely clean and quite well-furnished living-room, was a good one. There was no meat; but a large bowl of pancakes with sour milk into which we all dipped, eggs, tea and magnificent apples and melons which the children were sent out to pick. After we had finished, we discussed, as always happens on such occasions in the Soviet Union, our respective modes of life. My hosts told me that they worked on the neighbouring collective farm. In addition to what they earned there, they were able to sell on their own account the produce of their plot of ground which they had bought twelve years before. They also kept pigs and hens. They said that all the peasants in the district had been collectivized but that life there was pleasant and prosperity fairly general. This was certainly borne out by the appearance of most of the peasants I saw near Talgar and Alma Ata.

After refusing an urgent invitation to spend the night, my escort and I set out for Talgar at dusk having failed to induce our hosts to accept any reward in return for their hospitality. Before leaving I was called on to hear the little girl's reading and geography lessons. She seemed to possess a fair knowledge of both subjects and to my relief I found that her reader contained ordinary fairy stories and practically no propaganda. At Talgar we boarded a lorry full of highly Sovietized Kazakh girl students returning to Alma Ata after spending the free day in their villages. They, too, seemed pleased with life and squeaked and giggled shrilly as we jolted along.

Early next morning I again visited the Tourist Base only to find that there was still no petrol. I had by now decided that this was probably a case of deliberate obstruction rather than mere disorganization, but as a last resource I suggested that an attempt should be made to obtain me some official petrol from the Alma Ata Town Soviet, a body with whom I had as yet had no dealings. To my intense surprise the reply came back in a few minutes that the necessary quantity of petrol had been put at my disposal by the Town Soviet and that one of the more active members of that body would himself accompany me on my expedition. An hour or two later I drove out of Alma Ata in an extremely dilapidated open Ford car, accompanied by a decorous young Soviet official in a neat blue suit and a ferocious-looking one-eyed Kazakh guide in a sheepskin. My N.K.V.D. escort were left gaping outside the Dom Sovietov.

First we climbed by a road in a very early stage of construction, south-eastwards through the foothills of the Ala Tau as far as the village of Issik. At frequent intervals gangs working on the road made it necessary for us to make considerable detours through the scrub. At Issik, a mountain village which much resembled Talgar, we turned southwards up a more or less non-existent mountain track, passing on the way a native *aul* with its mud huts clinging insecurely to the almost perpendicular mountain side. The corn cobs were spread out to dry on the roofs as being the only available flat space. The sides of the valley through which we were climbing were thick with wild apple trees and rose bushes. Finally we arrived at the point where the track ceased to exist and, leaving the car in charge of a Kazakh lumberman whose solitary *yurt* happened to be nearby, set out on foot for the lake, climbing up the rocky bed of a mountain stream.

The sun was setting and from where we were at five or six thousand feet above sea level there was a magnificent view over the steppe stretching away for three thousand miles to the Arctic Ocean. By the time we reached our destination night had fallen and we got our first view of the waters of Lake Issik by the brilliant starlight of Central Asia. We slept in a one-roomed wooden hut on the shore of the lake, sharing it with an old man and a young girl of fifteen or sixteen who slept together in the only bed, while the guide and I spent the night on the floor.

In the morning we woke to find ourselves in what might have been a typical Alpine valley, and after a bathe in the icy waters of the lake, I set out to explore the surrounding hills. But the lateness of the season made any further progress out of the question. And so, having extracted from the guide a promise that if I returned next summer he would take me a six-day journey on horseback over the mountains to Frunze and show me lakes full of flamingoes and other even more exotic birds, I made my way back to Alma Ata.

Next morning I left Alma Ata for Samarkand. The critical stage of my journey had begun. If I were not stopped now, nothing could prevent me from achieving my objective.

My departure from Alma Ata was unobtrusive; so unobtrusive that, when I had boarded the train and settled into a densely crowded 'hard' carriage, I found that I had left my escort behind. This, I felt, was just as well. I was doubtful about Alma Ata, but Samarkand I knew was in a forbidden zone and in the circumstances the presence of two representatives of the N.K.V.D. could only have been embarrassing.

My plan was to travel from Alma Ata to Tashkent, to stop there for as short a time as possible and then go straight on to Samarkand.

For most of the 500 miles from Alma Ata to Tashkent the snow-capped mountains of Kirghizia remain in sight to the south. As you travel westwards and southwards, signs of Russian, though not necessarily of Soviet, influence become far less numerous and one has no difficulty in realizing that one is in a part of Asia which, until its conquest by the Tsar's armies some seventy or eighty years ago, had only been visited by half a dozen Europeans. In the villages through which we passed and which I generally had time to explore quite thoroughly before the incredibly slow train started off again, nothing seemed to have changed since the time when the country was ruled over by the Emir of Bokhara. Agricultural methods are primitive and camels and donkeys are still the most common means of transport, while not infrequently one encounters one of the local notables advancing down the poplar-lined village street mounted on a bull. The men wore turbans and brightly coloured striped robes (*khalats*) and most of the women still had heavy black horsehair veils.

On the next bunk to mine lay an Uzbek girl of sixteen or seventeen. A loose-fitting striped *khalat* partly masked her young body and she wore the same soft black riding-boots as the men. On her head was the usual little round black cap embroidered in white, from under which her sleek black hair fell in two long plaits. She wore no veil and from where I lay in the shadows I was free to study her features. They reminded me of a face on a Chinese scroll. She had the high cheek-bones, short upturned nose and almond eyes of the Mongol, but her features were finely formed and the delicate oval of her face showed a trace of some other ancestry, Persian perhaps, or Circassian. Her skin was scarcely darker than my own, its pale, golden hue clear and un-blemished. Most of the day she lay stretched out asleep with her head pillowed on her arm. Once she woke and climbed down from the carriage with the rest of the passengers at a station. When she came back she brought a fine yellow melon and, cutting a slice from it, handed it to me. The firm crisp flesh was snow white and as sweet as honey.

I had decided to stop in Tashkent only on my way back from Samar-kand but a missed connection now gave me several hours there. It was nearly midnight when I started out to explore. In the old town the dimly lighted *chai-khanas* (tea-houses) opening on the street were still filled with squatting Uzbeks and from all sides the flat native drums throbbed rhythmically in the warm Eastern-smelling darkness. Two or three hours before dawn I returned to the station and boarded the Samarkand train without having been asked my business by anyone.

The last stretch was the worst. There was no room anywhere on the train and for hours I squatted, swaying dangerously, on the little iron platform between two coaches. Then, just as I was beginning to wonder whether it was worth it, the train stopped at a little wayside station and I saw the name in black letters on a white ground: 'SAMAR-QAND'. A truck, picked up outside the station, took me at break-neck speed through the long tree-lined avenues of the Russian cantonments and deposited me, without further ado, in the middle of the old town. I had arrived.

Before me, in the early morning sunlight, lay a paved square, the Registan, open on one side to the street and enclosed on the other three by the lofty arched façades of three ancient *madrassehs* or Moslem colleges. At each corner of the square a slim minaret points skywards. The buildings are of crumbling sun-baked bricks, decorated with glazed tiles of deep blue and vivid turquoise that sparkle in the sun. Each *madrasseh* is built round a central courtyard surrounded by cloisters. Into these open the cells once occupied by Moslem scholars and now inhabited by various local inhabitants. On the northern side of the square is the Tillah Kari or Golden Mosque Madrasseh, called after the great mosque which forms part of it. On the western side stands the smaller and more beautiful Madrasseh of Ulug Beg, Tamerlane's grandson, who built it in 1417; opposite it, the Shir Dar. Across the top of the central arch sprawls the form of the great golden lion which gives it its name: Shir Dar — Lion bearing. On either side of the façade rise splendidly proportioned twin domes. After passing through the central arch and exploring the cloisters beyond, I climbed by a narrow twisting stairway to the top of the Shir Dar and from there looked down on the sun-baked Registan and beyond it on the fabled city of Samarkand, on the blue domes and the minarets, the flat-roofed mud houses, and the green tree-tops. It was a moment to which I had long looked forward.

Then, leaving the sunlight of the Registan, I plunged into the semi-darkness of a covered bazaar, where Uzbek merchants offered their goods for sale. From these, as I passed, I received tempting offers for my greatcoat and even for my trousers. Presently, I came to an open air *chai-khana*, or tea-house, where scores of turbaned and bearded worthies squatted on raised wooden platforms strewn with fine carpets, gossiping and sipping bowls of green tea.

Here I sat for a time drinking tea like the rest of them, and then, walking on through the outskirts of the town, came suddenly upon the splendid ruins of the Bibi Khanum mosque, built as the chief ornament of his capital by Tamerlane a year or two before his death in 1405 and named after one of his wives, a Chinese princess. Its great blue dome is shattered, some say by Russian shell fire when the town was captured in 1868, but one immense crumbling arch still remains, poised perilously above the surrounding buildings. From it one can still picture the noble proportions of the original structure.

According to a legend, the Persian architect who built the mosque fell in love with the princess and imprinted on her cheek a kiss so passionate that it left a burn. Tamerlane, seeing this, sent his men to kill his wife's lover. But the Persian fled before them to the top of the highest minaret and then, as his pursuers were about to seize him, sprouted wings and, soaring high above Samarkand, flew back to his native town of Meshed.

Near the Bibi Khanum two or three incongruous modern buildings in the Soviet style have already made their appearance and will no doubt be followed by others. Passing by these and along the main street out in the country I came to a dusty hillside, littered with graves and gravestones all crumbling into decay. Down it ran a walled stairway with, on either side, a row of small mosques of the most exquisite beauty. In these lie buried the friends and contemporaries of Tamerlane. From some, the blue tiles have disappeared completely, leaving a rough crumbling surface of pale sun-baked clay sprouting here and there with tufts of grass. At the top of the stairway stands a larger mosque, the tomb of Kassim Ibn Abbas, a Mohammedan soldier-saint, who, it is said, is only sleeping and will one day rise again sword in hand to perform great exploits. After him the mosque, for centuries a place of pilgrimage, is called Shah Zinda — The Living King. Climbing over the wall, I wandered in and out of the mosques until I was eventually turned away by an angry Uzbek woman ably seconded by an idiot boy. Sightseeing, it seemed, was not encouraged in Samarkand.

Beyond the Shah Zinda stretches the dusty expanse of the Afro Siab, the former site of the ancient city of Maracanda, founded by Alexander the Great. Now it is a desolate undulating plain, sprinkled with crumbling ruins.

At the far end of the old town stands the blue-ribbed dome of the Gur Emir, where the great conqueror Tamerlane himself lies buried. In front of the great entrance arch an old man had set up his bed under a mulberry tree. Rousing him, I induced him to open the gate for me. Inside, the walls are wainscoted with alabaster and adorned with jasper. Tamerlane's tombstone is of polished greenish-black nephrite, carved with Arabic lettering. His body lies in a vault below.

Though the Gur Emir was empty many of the smaller mosques scattered about the old town were in use, and the mullahs seemed still to command the respect of the population. In character the old town had remained practically unchanged by the Russian invasion of 1868. Few Russians were to be seen in the streets. The Uzbeks wore their national dress, long striped quilted coats and turbans or embroidered skull-caps, while many of the women were still enveloped in their traditional thick black horsehair veils, entirely covering and hiding the face and most of the body. The houses were built in the native style of sun-baked mud bricks with flat roofs. There were few windows in the outside walls, though some of the larger houses had balconies. Through open gateways I caught glimpses of courtyards and gardens, and here and there I came on square ponds surrounded by trees. The shops of the merchants were open to the street and their owners sat cross-legged in them manufacturing their goods on the threshold. In the open bazaars great heaps of fruit were offered for sale: melons, apples, apricots and grapes. Life seemed easy and the inhabitants seem to spend most of their time talking and drinking tea out of shallow bowls in the innumerable *chai-khanas*.

But it is only a question of time before all there remains of a bygone civilization is swept away. Chancing to look into the courtyard of a house in the old town, I was not surprised to see some twenty little Uzbek girls of three or four years old being marched briskly up and down in fours and made to sing hymns to the glorious Leader of the People.

Tashkent, the centre of the Soviet cotton industry, is, with its population of half a million or more, a vast city in comparison with Samarkand. It also has a tremendous reputation for wickedness. Returning on the train from Samarkand I was taken aside by the ticket-collector, a comfortable motherly middle-aged female, and solemnly warned against the dangers and temptations to which I was about to be exposed. She could see, she said, that I was young and inexperienced and not accustomed to life in great cities.

After a trying night in a crowded hard carriage, I was glad to find a bench in a garden near the station on which to go to sleep. But I had scarcely closed my eyes when I awoke to find my neighbours on each side shaking me and asking me in agitated tones whether I realized that I had fallen asleep. On my replying that that was what I was trying to do, they seemed profoundly shocked and explained that if you were foolish enough to go to sleep out of doors in a city like Tashkent anything might happen to you. And so, I set out unreposed to explore this latter-day Babylon.

The old town, which is intersected by a network of tortuous narrow streets running between the high walls of the flat-roofed mud-built native houses, has no monuments which can be compared with those of Samarkand. Life, as usual in the East, centres round the teeming bazaar in the centre of which is a vast open space, ankle deep in mud and filled with a seething crowd of Uzbeks packed shoulder to shoulder, each engaged in trying to sell something to his neighbour. The goods offered for sale range from embroidered skull-caps and Bokhara carpets to second-hand trousers and broken-down sewing machines. Once again I received many tempting offers for my overcoat and indeed for everything I had on, although my clothes, which I had slept in for several nights running, were not looking their best. Clearly, wearing apparel had a scarcity value in Tashkent.

The streets leading into this arena are lined with shops, all of which overflow into the street, and are filled with a jostling, shouting crowd, continually being pushed apart to make way for strings of camels or donkeys, or for *arbas*, the high-wheeled native carts.

In Tashkent as in Samarkand the national dress and customs had been largely retained, and many women still went veiled. But while in Samarkand life had seemed a leisurely affair, in Tashkent it was full of noise and strife. A queue had only to form outside a bread-shop for a free fight to begin which generally ended in the shop being taken by storm and in any member of the Militia (a force for the most part recruited locally and treated with scant respect), who was unwise enough to intervene, being left seated in the mud, trying to collect his wits.

This same violence, which, after the stolid patience of Russian crowds, I found rather refreshing, is encountered in acute form on the Tashkent trams, which can be boarded only after a hand-to-hand fight. Fists, teeth and feet are used freely. Once one is on board, however, the trams, which run to every point of the new town and for considerable distances out into the country, provide a most convenient means of seeing Tashkent.

The Russian town, which like Alma Ata and the modern portion of Samarkand, is laid out in broad avenues of poplars, was for the most part built after the capture of the town by the Russians in 1865 but before the Revolution, though there are the usual square white factories, Government offices and blocks of flats in the strictly utilitarian style of modern Soviet architecture. I was not surprised to be told that the best block of flats was reserved for 'specialists', i.e. highly paid technical workers. In the station buffet an extremely 'hot' band with a good sense of rhythm played fairly recent jazz from New York. An institution inherited from the old regime is a formidable turreted and machicolated prison, the crenellated walls of which are continually patrolled by N.K.V.D. troops. On the way from the old town to the new I saw another heavily guarded and apparently fortified enclosure which I took to be the Headquarters of the Central Asian Military district, but not wishing to be arrested as a spy, I kept well away from it. Outside the town, the villages in the surrounding country are purely Uzbek, their inhabitants working for the most part in the cotton fields or in the mills.

I had seen Alma Ata; I had seen Tashkent; best of all I had seen Samarkand. I had done what I had set out to do and, having done it, immediately I conceived new ambitions.

First of all, there was Bokhara, not more than 200 miles southwards and westwards from Samarkand, but harder to get to, and further removed from Western influence, scarcely changed, it seemed, since the downfall of the last Emir. Now that I had come so far, might I not go a little further?

Then, over the mountains from Alma Ata lay Chinese Turkestan or Sinkiang, as it was called, an outlying province of China, which Soviet intrigue and the turbulent nature of its inhabitants had thrown into an uproar, temptingly near and temptingly inaccessible. Might it not be possible to slip across the passes of the Tien Shan to Kashgar, or join a caravan, travelling eastwards along the new road from Alma Ata to Urumchi?

But already I had exceeded my leave, and, if I exceeded it still further, I might well be granted no more. Besides, lucky as I had been so far, I could scarcely hope to reach either Bokhara or Sinkiang without running into trouble with the N.K.V.D. And, with an eye to future enterprises, I wanted to avoid an actual show-down with them for as long as possible. And so, reluctantly, I turned my back, for the time being at any rate, on both these alluring projects, and after spending an entire night from dusk till dawn standing in a queue, I secured a ticket and boarded a train bound for Moscow by the most direct route.

My journey home was uneventful. I made it in a 'soft' carriage on a train with a well-stocked dining-car. The other berths in my compartment were occupied by one of the inevitable railwaymen and two youthful and extremely affected intellectuals from Leningrad with horn-rimmed spectacles and carefully trimmed beards who knew better than to talk to a foreigner and were too class-conscious to talk to a railway man. The result was that the railwayman and myself, thrown together and having exhausted all possible topics of conversation at an early stage in the proceedings, filled up the rest of the four-day journey with ceaseless games of chess. I had not played since I was seven, and so my opponent invariably won, much to his delight.

The first part of the return journey lay through the Kazakh steppe, this time further to the west, the train following the course of the Jaxartes or Syr Daria as far as the Sea of Aral, seen briefly as a glittering expanse of water stretching away into the distance. The second stage, by way of Orenburg, Kuibyshev and Penza to Moscow lay through a typical Russian landscape. All that remained of Asia was the crowd of Uzbeks and Kazakhs in the 'hard' carriages travelling to Moscow on business or for pleasure.

A few miles outside Moscow we passed a long prison train, eastward bound. It was composed of reinforced cattle trucks. At the end of each truck was a guard of N.K.V.D. troops with fixed bayonets. Through cracks in the sides one could see the prisoners' faces, peering out. It served as a reminder that travel in the regions from which I was returning is not always undertaken at the traveller's own wish.

CHAPTER VII

WINTER IN MOSCOW

BACK in Moscow the first snows had fallen and I put aside any further thought of travel until the spring. There was a lot of work to be got through in the Chancery; there was the endless round of official parties. But, with a little ingenuity and enterprise, life could be made agreeable enough.

Chip and Avis Bohlen and Charlie Thayer of the American Embassy had a *dacha*, a country cottage, ten or twelve miles outside the town, and there we kept some horses which we had bought from the Red Army and which, as far as we knew, were the only privately owned saddle-horses in the Soviet Union. On them we ranged far and wide over the green, rolling country round about. When the snow made riding impossible, we took to our skis and plunged inexpertly down the frozen slopes immediately behind the *dacha*. In the evenings, after a hard day's exercise, we would congregate round a roaring open fire in the *dacha* and Avis would dispense frankfurters and peanut butter and corned-beef hash and other unaccustomed delicacies, washed down by plenty of good American coffee and equally good Scotch whisky. Then we would lie about and talk and play the gramophone until it was time to go home. As we drove back to Moscow the air was icy and the stars shone down frostily on the sparkling snow.

Sometimes, at night, we went to the Park of Rest and Culture, an immense amusement park on the outskirts of Moscow. In the winter the whole of it was flooded and on skates one could go skimming along for miles over brilliantly lighted frozen avenues to the strains of Vienna waltzes and Red Army marches, while vast illuminated portraits of Marx and Engels, Lenin and Stalin gazed benignly down on the whirling crowds beneath them. Sometimes, too, we would go to the Hotel Metropole, where the cream of the Red Army and of Soviet officialdom could be seen disporting themselves with their women-folk beneath the same gilded candelabras that had witnessed the antics of their Tsarist predecessors.

But, of the various distractions that Moscow can offer, none surpasses the Theatre and Ballet. The tradition which they represent has endured unbroken from before the Revolution. They would, I think, play an important part in Russian life under any regime. It is in the foyer of the Bolshoi and of the First Arts that the 'new proletarian aristocracy' assemble, immaculate in uniforms and neat blue suits, their wives resplendent in sable and redolent of Soviet scent. In the former Imperial box Stalin and the members of his entourage make their rare public appearances. Round the persons of the leading ballerinas hangs an aura of glamour and romance shared by few save the greatest military and political leaders.

The Soviet authorities do all they can to encourage the Theatre and Ballet. Perhaps they see in them a relatively harmless outlet for a turbulent imagination. By a fortunate dispensation of providence, Russians possess a natural gift of make-believe. Listening to Chaikovski's music and watching the transformation scenes of *Swan Lake* and *The Sleeping Beauty* unfold before them, they have the power to forget their troubles and miseries and transport themselves into a world of plenty, magnificence and romance, with nothing more frightening than an occasional witch or magician to take the place of the more substantial terrors of real life. For them, as for no other race, the real and the imaginary, the actual and the symbolic, the literal and the figurative, tend to overlap and become one. Even the foreigners, diplomats and journalists, sitting isolated in their stalls amid the serried rows of proletarian aristocrats, cannot but share the thrill of excitement that runs through the crowd as the curtain goes up, cannot but feel something of the rapt interest with which they follow every movement and every gesture until it goes down again.

But before the winter was out, the easy routine of our life was to be interrupted by an event which was to leave on me, at any rate, a more profound impression than any other experience during the years I spent in Soviet Russia.

By the beginning of 1938 no important State trial had been held in public for a year. Sentence had been passed on Tukachevski and the Generals behind closed doors; many other high functionaries of Army,

Government and Party had been liquidated, as far as one could ascertain, 'administratively'. People were beginning to think that the unfavourable reaction even of Left-wing circles abroad to the trials of Piatakov and Radek and other Old Bolsheviks, with the fantastic public confessions, orgies of self-abasement of the prisoners and the bloodthirsty ravings of the Public Prosecutor, had at last convinced the Soviet authorities that in the long run displays of this kind did more harm than good, and induced them to abandon the public trial in favour of more discreet methods of liquidation. Every week since the last trial the removal from office of public figures of varying importance had been announced and their names cited in the Press as wreckers and enemies of the people. But after that, in general, no more was heard of them, and their demise was assumed as a matter of course. It seemed likely that there would be no more public trials.

Then, one day at the beginning of March, the news broke.

Outside it was dreary and overcast, and the big shiny black cars of the high Soviet dignitaries spattered the plodding crowds in the streets with half-frozen snow as they rushed past with klaxons blaring on their way to and from the Kremlin. But in the great white-pillared ballroom of the American Embassy it was agreeably warm and the crystal chandeliers shed a cheerful light on the silver trays of highballs and old-fashioneds.

Suddenly a newspaperman hurried in, displaying all the symptoms, the air of suppressed excitement, of scarcely veiled self-importance, of someone who has got a story. News was short in Moscow in those days, and we clustered round him, diplomats and journalists alike. In his hand he held the text of a communiqué which had just been released by the Soviet Government. It was the announcement of a big State trial, the biggest yet. Looking over one another's shoulders, we read the names of the accused.

It was an impressive list: Bukharin, a former Secretary-General of the Communist International, for years the leading theorist of the Party and a close associate of Lenin; Rykov, Lenin's successor and Molotov's predecessor as Premier; Yagoda, who, until eighteen months ago, had been People's Commissar for Internal Affairs, and supreme head of the all-powerful N.K.V.D.; Krestinski, formerly Vice-Commissar for Foreign Affairs, whom most of us remembered meeting at official parties and receptions; Rosengolts, until recently Commissar for Foreign Trade; Faisullah Khojayev, President of Uzbekistan, who ever since the Revolution had been the outstanding figure in Soviet Central Asia; three of the Kremlin doctors, Levin, Pletnev and Kasakov; and a dozen others, all men who had until recently held key positions in the Soviet hierarchy. The charges were equally sensational: espionage, sabotage, murder, high treason.

The trial was to open in a few days' time. Admission would be restricted. A few representatives of the foreign Press and only one member of each Embassy would be allowed to follow the proceedings. On learning this, we dashed off to secure passes and make the necessary arrangements.

The court-room, a day or two later, was full of noise and chattering, like a theatre before the curtain goes up. People were laughing and talking, looking for their seats and waving to friends. The cameramen, setting up their apparatus, shouted to each other across the room. It was a large, high, bright room, rather floridly decorated in characteristic Russian nineteenth-century style: white Corinthian columns against light blue walls. Before the Revolution it had been one of the ballrooms of the Nobles' Club. Now it was fitted with rough wooden benches, like a schoolroom. At the far end there was a raised dais with a long table on it; near it a kind of enclosure or pen. There was no space for a large audience. Admission was by special invitation, and the rows of solid-looking citizens, sitting there like schoolchildren out for a treat, in their neat blue suits and tidy dresses, were all representatives of different organizations, good Party men and women, members of the élite — 'proletarian aristocrats' every one.

These were the successors of the nobles who had danced here in the old days before the Revolution. Now they, too, had come here to enjoy themselves, to meet their friends and to witness proceedings which would be both entertaining and edifying. They were men and women who could be counted on to place the correct interpretation on what they saw and heard, to benefit from the lessons and, for that matter, the warnings which it might contain.

For, like all true drama, the performance on which the curtain was about to go up had the power of affecting the audience personally and directly; the characters in it were familiar to them, were men in whose place they could without any great stretch of imagination imagine themselves. And so they had come not only to be excited and edified, but to be horrified, and perhaps even terrified, by a spectacle which would partake at once both of the medieval morality play and of the modern gangster film.

Suddenly a hush fell on the crowded room. Scores of inquisitive, greedy eyes turned in the direction of a little door in the corner at the far end. Through it filed the accused, twenty-one men, paler and smaller, somehow, than ordinary human beings. With them, herding them along, came a dozen giants in the uniform of the special N.K.V.D. Security Troops, bearing themselves like guardsmen in their well-fitting tunics and scarlet and blue peaked caps, their fixed bayonets gleaming, their sunburnt faces expressionless. One after another the prisoners took their places in the dock, with the guards surrounding them. A ripple of barely audible sound ran through the audience, something between a hiss of detestation and a murmur of horror. For an instant we stared, picking out familiar faces: Bukharin, with his pale complexion and little beard, strangely like Lenin as I had seen him in his glass coffin; Yagoda with his little toothbrush moustache; dark-skinned Faisullah Khojayev; Krestinski, small and nervous-looking.

Then another, larger door was flung open; and in a parade-ground voice an officer called out, 'Silence. The court is coming. Stand up.' We rose to our feet and stood waiting. There was a brief pause and then through the door tripped a fat man in uniform.

His shaven head rose to a point; his neck bulged over the collar of his tunic in rolls of fat; his little pig's eyes darted here and there, from the prisoners to the crowd and back again. This was the notorious Ulrich, the President of the court, the man who had pronounced sentence of death on the prisoners at the previous State trials.

'*Sadityes pojalusta* – pray be seated,' he said, leering amiably at the crowd as he took his seat on the dais. Two other judges took their seats on either side of him; various lawyers, stenographers and technical experts arranged themselves at the foot of the dais.

To the right of the judges, facing the accused, stood Vyshinski, the

Public Prosecutor. His was the leading role. Neatly dressed in a stiff white collar, checked tie and well-cut blue suit, his trim grey moustache and hair set off against his rubicund complexion, he looked for all the world like a prosperous stock-broker accustomed to lunch at Simpsons and play golf at Sunningdale every weekend. 'A rather decent chap. . . .'

In a rapid expressionless voice an officer of the court started to read out the indictment. The trial had begun.

For sheer blood and thunder the indictment left nothing to be desired. The prisoners were charged, collectively and individually, with every conceivable crime: high treason, murder, attempted murder, espionage and all kinds of sabotage. With diabolical ingenuity they had plotted to wreck industry and agriculture; to assassinate Stalin and the other Soviet leaders; to overthrow the Soviet regime with the help of foreign powers; to dismember the Soviet Union for the benefit of their capitalist allies and finally to seize power themselves and restore capitalism in what was left of their country. They had, it seemed, been arrested before they could put this plan into execution, but not before they had organized widespread sabotage and actually made away with several prominent personages, covering the traces of their crimes so that their victims were generally believed to have died a natural death. What is more, despite their distinguished careers and the responsible posts which they had held, they were shown for the most part to have been criminals and traitors to the Soviet cause ever since the Revolution — before it, even. Several were charged with having been Tsarist police spies and *agents provocateurs* posing as revolutionaries under the old regime, while Bukharin was accused of having plotted to murder Lenin and Stalin as early as 1918. They were also shown to have had connections, not only with the German, Polish, Japanese and British Secret Services, but with Trotski, with the accused at the two last big State trials, with Tukachevski and the Generals who had been shot the summer before, and with a number of other prominent citizens whose disappearance had hitherto passed uncommented on. Finally, before coming into court, they had all, it appeared, signed written statements, confessing in detail to the crimes with which they were charged and thoroughly incriminating themselves and each other. The evidence accumulated filled no less than fifty large volumes which could be seen stacked on the judges' desk.

After the reading of the indictment had been completed, the prisoners were asked whether they pleaded guilty. This, too, was pure routine. One after another, using the same words, they admitted their guilt: Bukharin, Rykov, Yagoda.

Then, suddenly, the audience woke up to the realization that things were not going as they should. Krestinski, a pale, seedy, dim little figure, his steel-rimmed spectacles perched on his beaky nose, was saying something different from the others, something appalling. Interest revived; was focused on Krestinski. Even the other prisoners turned to look at him.

'I do not,' he was saying, 'admit my guilt. I am not a Trotskist. I am not a member of the Rightist-Trotskist "Bloc". I did not even know it existed. I am not guilty of any of the crimes with which I am charged. I never had relations with the German Intelligence Service.'

There was an awkward pause. Even Ulrich, gross and self-assured, seemed momentarily taken aback. 'But do you not,' he asked, 'confirm the admissions you made before coming into court?'

But Krestinski only went on repeating what he had said before. 'I was never a Trotskist. I was never a member of the Rightist-Trotskist "Bloc". I never committed a single crime.'

For the moment there was nothing to be done. Ulrich turned to the next prisoner.

'Do you plead guilty to the crimes with which you are charged?'
'Yes, I plead guilty.'

Then, when all the others had returned the prescribed answer, he announced briefly, 'The court is adjourned for twenty minutes,' and, followed by his two colleagues and by Vyshinski, left the room.

When, twenty minutes later, the hearing was resumed, Vyshinski immediately asked leave to begin the cross-examination of the prisoners with Bessonov, formerly the Counsellor of the Soviet Embassy at Berlin, a grim, grey-faced man, with the air of an automaton. The reason for this choice soon became clear. In an orderly, deliberate manner, as became the responsible Government servant he had once been, Bessonov proceeded to describe in detail how, while in Germany, he had acted as the link between Trotski and Krestinski, how, in 1933, he had arranged an interview between Trotski and Krestinski, how Trotski and Krestinski together had plotted to betray the Soviet Union to the Germans.

With heavy sarcasm Vyshinski interrupted him to ask what, in view of all this, he thought of Krestinski's claim that he was not a Trotskist. Bessonov smiled, but did not answer.

'Why,' Vyshinski asked, 'are you smiling?'

'Because,' he replied, 'it was Krestinski who denounced me as his contact with Trotski. If he had not volunteered that information, I should not be here now.'

And, for an instant, those watching had a glimpse of the meshes in which the accused had entangled themselves and each other before ever coming into court.

'And now,' said Vyshinski triumphantly, having piled up the evidence he required, 'I have some questions to ask Krestinski.' But still Krestinski did not weaken. Other prisoners were called and readily added their incriminating statements to those of Bessonov. Still he refused to admit his guilt; refused to admit that he had had a meeting with Trotski; refused to admit that he had sought to betray his country to the Germans.

Again Vyshinski reminded him of the admissions he had made at the preliminary examination. How, he asked him, did he account for these? The answer came back at once, devastating in its directness. 'I was forced to make them. Besides, I knew that if I said then what I say now, my statement would never reach the Heads of the Party and of the Government.' There was a shocked hush in court. Never before had such a thing been said in public.

The court adjourned for two hours. It resumed. Still Krestinski, looking more than ever like a small, bedraggled sparrow, steadfastly maintained his innocence. Vyshinski was beginning to look worried. After all, it was his responsibility to produce the desired results, and who could tell what would happen to him if he failed in his task?

Finally he gave up trying to break down Krestinski's resistance and, leaving him, turned to his companions. Readily, eagerly, they admitted their guilt. Cross-examining them, Vyshinski's self-assurance returned There were no more discordant notes. It was like playing on a well-tuned instrument. Vyshinski looked happier. Late at night the court adjourned. The door at the end of the room was flung open and Ulrich and the other two judges marched out. Then someone opened the little side door and the prisoners filed through it, the guard closing in round them as they went. Back to their cells, back to the nightmare which had become their life.

Next day Vyshinski resumed his cross-examination of Krestinski. At once the change was obvious. After a little preliminary skirmishing and the production of further incriminating evidence, Vyshinski got down to the main point at issue. 'Do you,' he asked, 'still persist in your refusal to confirm your previous declarations?'

'No,' came back the answer. 'I confirm everything.'

'What, then, was the meaning of the statement you made yesterday?'

'Yesterday, influenced by a feeling of false shame, and by the atmosphere of the court, and by my state of health, I could not bring myself to tell the truth and admit my guilt before the world. Mechanically, I declared myself innocent. I now beg the court to take note of the statement which I now make to the effect that I admit my guilt, completely and unreservedly, under all the charges brought against me, and that I accept full responsibility for my criminal and treacherous behaviour.'

The words were reeled off like a well-learnt lesson. The night had not been wasted.

'You may sit down,' said Ulrich, in his soft, oily voice, and Krestinski slid back on to his seat with a look almost of relief. Vyshinski straightened his tie. The situation was saved.

The cross-examination of the prisoners continued. First came several of the smaller fry. The principle followed was clear enough. It was intended that by their admissions they should give a general picture of the activities of the alleged 'bloc' and, incidentally, thoroughly incriminate its leaders. Bessonov had played his part by describing the connection of the 'bloc' with Trotski and with the Germans. Grinko, a Ukrainian, revealed the existence of a terrorist organization in the

Ukraine, working under orders from the 'bloc'. Chernov, a former People's Commissar for Agriculture, confessed that, under instructions from Bukharin and Rykov, he had, in the hope of causing unrest, deliberately persecuted the medium peasants and, in order to diminish the country's resources, arranged for the destruction of tens of thousands of pigs and horses. Several other prisoners followed his example, admitting to agricultural sabotage on a vast scale. One, Zelenski, a former Chairman of the State Planning Board, admitted to having put nails and powdered glass in the butter supplies and on one occasion in 1936 destroyed fifty truck-loads of eggs.

At this startling revelation a grunt of rage and horror rose from the audience. Now they knew what was the matter with the butter, and why there were never any eggs. Deliberate sabotage was somehow a much more satisfactory solution than carelessness or inefficiency. Besides, Zelenski had also admitted that he had been in contact with a sinister foreigner, a politician, a member of the British Labour Party, a certain Mr. A. V. Alexander, who had encouraged him in his fell designs. No wonder that he had put ground glass in the butter. And nails! What a warning, too, to have nothing to do with foreigners, even though they masqueraded as Socialists.

More and more, as the hearing went on, attention became focused on the 'bloc's' connection with foreign governments and intelligence services. Nor were the Germans the only villains. Equally prominent was the role allotted to the British Secret Service. On this subject Rakovski, a venerable-looking old gentleman with a long white beard and a fine record as a revolutionary, who had formerly served as Soviet Representative in London, was a particularly fruitful source of information. In great detail he described how he himself had been 'recruited' over dinner at a little restaurant in Oxford Street. Then he declared that Trotski himself had been a British agent ever since 1926. Two more self-confessed British agents were Ivanov and Rosengolts, who, under instructions from Bukharin, had sold good timber to the British at ridiculously low prices in order to gain British support for their own fell designs. Faisullah Khojayev, for his part, declared that, being well aware of British designs on Central Asia, he had endeavoured to find a British agent in Tajikstan with whom to establish contact, but had not been successful. Looking up at this juncture, I caught Vyshinski's eye and found him regarding me with a significant smile, as though to say: 'You slipped up that time.'

When the court adjourned one of the Secretaries at the German Embassy walked over to where I was sitting. 'Congratulations,' he said. 'They don't seem to like you any more than they do us. Or perhaps it is that we are getting more popular!' and he laughed. The following year this same German was to play a not unimportant part in the negotiations for the Soviet-German Pact.

Bit by bit, as one confession succeeded another, the fantastic structure took shape. Each prisoner incriminated his fellows and was in turn incriminated by them. Readily, glibly, they dwelt on their crimes and on those of their companions, enlarged on them, embroidered them, elaborated them. There was no attempt to evade responsibility. On the contrary, they often argued among themselves as to who had played the more important part, each claiming the honour for himself. Some displayed considerable narrative powers; of some it might almost have been said that they were eloquent. These were men in full possession of their faculties; the statements they made were closely reasoned and delivered, for the most part, with every appearance of spontaneity. It was unthinkable that what they said had simply been learnt by heart beforehand and was now being delivered under the influence of some drug or hypnotic spell.

And yet what they said, the actual contents of their statements, seemed to bear no relation to reality. The fabric that was being built up was fantastic beyond belief. The history of the 'bloc', as a 'bloc', did not, it appeared, go back much beyond 1932 or 1933, when the Right-wing Diversionists under Bukharin and Rykov had joined forces with the Trotskists, with Yagoda, and with the dissident elements in the Red Army, under Marshal Tukachevski, in a kind of counter-revolutionary coalition for the purpose of overthrowing the Soviet regime by force. But the personal history of every one of the accused was taken back to his early youth in an attempt to show that not one of them had been anything but a traitor from the start. Faisullah Khojayev, who was famous for his part in the Soviet Revolution in Central Asia, and who, while still in his twenties, had been President, first of the People's

Republic of Bokhara and then, since its formation in 1925, of the Uzbek Soviet Socialist Republic, announced that he had in fact been a clandestine 'bourgeois nationalist' ever since 1918; that his aim throughout had been to overthrow the local Soviet regime and set up an independent Central Asian State under British influence; that, with this object in view, he had deliberately sabotaged agriculture in order to cause discontent amongst the native population; and that for twenty years his apparent loyalty to Moscow had been no more than a blind. When in 1933 and again in 1936 Bukharin had visited Central Asia and got into touch with him, the Rightists had found a ready recruit.

The counter-revolutionary activities of some of the prisoners were traced back to before the Revolution. With the greatest readiness, they admitted that they had been Tsarist police spies and *agents provocateurs*, masquerading as revolutionaries. One such case afforded an opportunity for a dramatic interlude, which, though in itself unimportant, afforded an interesting illustration of Vyshinski's technique as a stage manager.

In the course of his interrogation Zubarev, a relatively unimportant prisoner, against whom the main charge preferred was one of recent agricultural wrecking in the Urals, admitted incidentally that he had in 1908 been enrolled as a police spy by the Chief of Police of the little town of Kotelnich, a certain Vassiliev. In return for betraying his fellow revolutionaries to the Imperial Police, he had, he said, on two occasions received from Vassiliev payments of thirty silver roubles. ('Twice as much as Judas,' commented Vyshinski in a loud aside, which was greeted with sniggers by the crowd.)

Zubarev's admission gave Vyshinski his cue. He turned to Ulrich. 'Perhaps,' he said casually, 'you will allow me to call Vassiliev as a witness for purposes of verification.'

At once there was a buzz of surprise and excitement in the court. How could Vyshinski call as a witness a man who had been a police officer under the Tsar thirty years ago? Surely he could not still be alive? And even if by a miracle he had survived the Revolution, and the Civil War, and the Famine and the Purge, how had it been possible to find him? It was like bringing back a ghost. It was as though he had offered to produce in court Peter the Great or Ivan the Terrible.

But Ulrich had given his consent and an usher had been dispatched to fetch the witness. Heads turned and necks craned; all eyes were fixed on the entrance.

The doors opened and up the middle of the room tottered step by step a frail little old man, his skin so shrivelled and yellow as to resemble parchment, his sunken features dominated by an enormous pair of moustaches carefully waxed to a point and sticking out on either side. If the powers that be had wanted to symbolize a grotesque and long-dead past, they could have chosen no better means than this faded military ghost. Shakily, he made his way up the whole length of the court-room, between the serried rows of benches; made his way unaccompanied, for this was no prisoner to be guarded, but a free man, enjoying the liberty accorded him by a merciful, forgiving Government.

As he went, the audience followed him with puzzled eyes. How were they to react? Should they register disgust at the sight of this vile old man, this survival from a hated past? Or delight at the victory which the regime had won over such vermin? Or admiration at the ingenuity displayed in producing him? This was something outside their experience.

Anxiously they looked at Ulrich and Vyshinski to see how they were taking it. Both were discreetly grinning. At once all doubts vanished. They might have known. This was a comedy turn. Soon the court-room was echoing with obedient laughter.

Amid guffaws the old man reached the witness box. Silence fell on the crowd. What was coming next? Ulrich asked him his name. In a high, piping squeak he answered: Vassiliev, Dmitri Nikolaievich. The creature could speak. It was too good to be true. The guffaws burst out afresh. Ulrich was at his most genial. His fat frame shaking with half-suppressed mirth, he signalled to the crowd to be quiet and let him get on with his cross-questioning. 'Just leave it to me, boys,' his gestures seemed to say, 'there's plenty more fun to come.'

The old man, his tired, cracked voice barely audible, had launched into an account of how in 1908 (or was it 1909?) he had been Chief of Police at Kotelnich and had paid the prisoner thirty silver roubles to betray his comrades. Sometimes he seemed to lose track of what he was saying and Ulrich, like a showman cracking his whip, had to bring him back to the point. To the accompaniment of delighted titters from the crowd, he completed his statement. Then it was Vyshinski's turn. 'Do you really remember the prisoner after all these years?' he asked. 'Yes,' piped the old man, 'I remember him, but he was younger then.' 'And so were you, I suppose?' said Vyshinski. This sally was altogether too much for the crowd. They roared and bellowed and stamped on the floor, until even the old man woke from his torpor and looked about him in dazed surprise.

And now, having played his part, he was on his way back down the room. The door opened and he shuffled out, back to whatever limbo he had come from.

He had been a success. There was no doubt about it. True, his evidence had added nothing to what the prisoner had already confessed; indeed, it was altogether superfluous. But that only made it the more valuable. If the prosecution could produce a witness to prove in such a spectacular manner something that had happened thirty years ago and that in any case didn't really need proving, then clearly it followed that they must be able to prove with equal ease all the more recent crimes with which the accused were charged. At this thought, a ripple of satisfaction ran through the audience. The nasty taste which the Krestinski episode had left in their mouths had been taken away. Vyshinski preened himself. It had been a master-stroke.

Gradually the trial moved towards its climax. Bit by bit the web was woven more closely round the accused. Sitting there day after day, listening to statement after statement, cross-examination after cross-examination, from early morning until late at night, in the dingy winter daylight and under the stale glare of the electric lamps, in that strange, tense atmosphere, one found oneself unconsciously yielding to the power of suggestion beginning to take what was said at its face value, seeking to follow prosecutor and prisoners step by step through the intricate labyrinths of the structure that they were building up, beginning to assume, as they assumed, that it really existed. Gradually, one came to grasp their mental processes, to understand what was going on in their minds, to see how in time the same ideas and doubts and half-memories might take root in anyone's mind, one's own, for example.

Then, not a minute too soon, the court would adjourn, Ulrich would waddle out to his dinner, the prisoners, dim ghosts, would fade through their little door, and one would emerge, as from an unpleasant dream, to find oneself outside in the fresh air listening to the reassuring chatter of the newspapermen, to the old Moscow hands recalling what had really happened in 1929 or 1932, and how Trotski, or someone else, could not possibly have been where he was said to be.

But the real struggle was still to come. As the trial progressed, it became ever clearer that the underlying purpose of every testimony was to blacken the leaders of the 'bloc', to represent them, not as political offenders, but as common criminals, murderers, poisoners and spies. Again and again came the revelation, following on a long catalogue of improbable misdeeds, that the instigator of this murder, of that piece of sabotage, of those treasonable conversations with the agents of a foreign power, had been Rykov, or Yagoda, or Bukharin.

Particularly Bukharin. To him, it seemed, belonged the role of arch-fiend in this grim pantomime. He had been behind every villainy, had had a hand in every plot. It was he who had planned to murder Lenin in 1918; who had decided on the dismemberment of the Soviet Union; who had plotted with Tukachevski to open the front to the Germans in the event of war and with Yagoda to murder Kirov and Maxim Gorki, Menzhinski and Kuibyshev; who had instructed his myrmidons to establish contact with the agents of Britain, Japan, Poland and Germany, with the White Russians, with Trotski, with the Second International; who had organized agricultural and industrial sabotage in the Ukraine, in Siberia, in the Caucasus, in Central Asia; who had planned, first, a peasant rising and civil war, then a palace revolution and *coup d'état*. Each prisoner, as he blackened himself, was careful at the same time to blacken Bukharin. Methodically, the old picture of the revolutionary fighter, the Marxist theoretician, the friend of Lenin, the member of the Politbureau, the President of the Communist International, was demolished, and a new portrait substituted for it: a demon, complete with horns, hooves and tail, a traitor, a spy and a capitalist mercenary, a sinister figure, skulking in the shadows, poisoning Soviet hogs, slaughtering Soviet stallions, slipping powdered glass into the workers' butter. Lurking memories of a glorious past were obliterated. No one could have any sympathy with such a miserable wretch. Each fresh revelation was greeted by the crowd with murmurs of rage, horror and disgust. Clearly the method chosen was having the desired effect, was working satisfactorily.

Working satisfactorily, that is, so long as Bukharin himself took no part in the proceedings. But, when, as sometimes happened, Vyshinski, leaving the prisoner under examination, turned to Bukharin for confirmation, things did not go so smoothly. Even when he admitted the crimes with which he was charged, he had an awkward way of qualifying his admissions, of qualifying them in such a way as largely to invalidate them, of slipping in little asides which made complete nonsense of them. Besides, he did not answer the Public Prosecutor with at all the same deference as did the other prisoners. He seemed to treat him as an equal, even as an inferior. At times he actually seemed to be making fun of him, and even the good Party men in the audience caught themselves laughing at his sallies.

And his cross-examination was yet to come.

At last, on the evening of March 5th, Ulrich announced that it was Bukharin's turn to be cross-examined. The morning had been devoted to the interrogation of Akmal Ikramov, until a few months before Secretary-General of the Uzbek Communist Party. Prompted by Vyshinski, he had readily revealed that, under personal instructions from Bukharin, he had, with Faisullah Khojayev, for years past, sought to wreck the industry and agriculture of Uzbekistan, with the ultimate object of converting it into a British colony. Bukharin, he said, had visited him more than once at Tashkent and reproached him with not doing enough damage. A suitable frame of mind having thus been induced in the audience, the stage was now set for the appearance of the villain in person.

As Bukharin rose to his feet, there was a stir of interest in the crowd. This was the big moment; this was what they had been waiting for. A stir of anxiety too; for might not the old fox have some trick in store?

But they were soon reassured. Immediately the accused made a full confession of his guilt. Almost too full, for, having declared himself one of the leaders of the Rightest-Trotskist 'bloc', he forthwith announced that he accepted entire responsibility for any and every misdeed which might have been committed by the 'bloc', whether he had had any knowledge of it or not.

This, of course, was satisfactory, but not, it seemed, exactly what was wanted. Vyshinski started in to elicit some more details. But it was not easy to pin down the prisoner to concrete facts. Soon he was launched on an account of the 'bloc's' economic programme. Their first divergence, it appeared, had been on the subject of industrialization. They had considered that it was being carried too far too quickly; that it was putting too great a strain on the budget; that it was defeating its own object and having a harmful effect on production. They had also had doubts about the collectivization of agriculture, had disapproved of the way in which the Government had treated the richer and medium peasants, the *kulaks*, of their mass liquidation, in fact. Gradually, they had moved towards the idea of a system of State capitalism, with smaller collective farms, prosperous individual peasants, foreign concessions and no State monopoly of foreign trade. On the political side, they had evolved in the direction of bourgeois democratic liberty, with more than one party. It was this oppositional tendency, carried to its logical conclusion, that had led them to consider overthrowing the regime by force and to their various other sins of thought and deed, to the project, finally, of a *coup d'état* against the present rulers of the Soviet Union. . . .

Ulrich and Vyshinski began to look annoyed. This was not at all the kind of thing that was wanted. It was essential that Bukharin should appear, not as a theoretician, but as a common criminal, and here he was, quite his old self, evolving a reasoned political and economic theory, and, what was worse, one that for some people might not be without attractions. It was unheard of that a prisoner at a State trial should declare that he had opposed Stalin's policy because he had come to the conclusion that it was wrong, and yet this in effect was what Bukharin was doing.

Hastily Vyshinski raised the question of espionage. Bukharin had been in Austria before the Revolution in 1912 and 1913. Had he not had some contact with the Austrian police? Had they not recruited him as a spy? The answer came back like a flash: 'My only contact with the Austrian police was when they imprisoned me in a fortress as a revolutionary.' And almost immediately he was back in the realm of political theory. When the court adjourned later that night, Vyshinski had made little progress in the desired direction.

Next day, March 6th, was a Rest Day — twenty-four hours in which to prepare Bukharin for the next phase of his cross-examination, and induce in him a more amenable frame of mind. But when, on the seventh, the court reassembled, though showing signs of strain, he was as resilient as ever. His tactics varied. To some charges he replied blandly that he personally had no knowledge of the events referred to, but that he was nevertheless prepared to accept responsibility for them on behalf of the 'bloc'. To others his answer was that he didn't happen to have committed the crimes with which he was charged, but that it would have been a logical consequence of his conduct had he done so and that he was therefore quite ready to admit his guilt, if it would give any pleasure to the Public Prosecutor. Sometimes, displaying all his old dialectical skill, he amused himself by picking holes in the arguments advanced by the prosecution, making free use of such terms as 'nonsense' and 'absurd'. On several points he remained absolutely firm. He refused to admit that he had ever contemplated murdering Lenin; or that he had ever been the agent of a foreign power; or that he had ever agreed to dismember the Soviet Union or to open the front to the Germans in time of war. Nor did he once consent to play the prosecution's game by incriminating his fellow prisoners.

Vyshinski tried arguing; he tried blustering; he used every quibble of a second-rate pettifogging lawyer. Still Bukharin stood firm. Vyshinski re-interrogated several of the other prisoners, eliciting from them the most damning statements. Bukharin flatly contradicted some and dismissed the others as *agents provocateurs*, while others he cross-examined himself, quickly disposing of their allegations.

Then Vyshinski called Rykov, Bucharin's close friend and associate and, allegedly, co-leader of the 'bloc'. 'You will surely not suggest that your good friend Rykov is an *agent provocateur*,' he said triumphantly.

Former President of the Council of Peoples' Commissars, Lenin's successor, Molotov's predecessor, Rykov, as he rose to his feet, was a pathetic figure, tall, with hunched shoulders, swaying slightly, red-nosed and bleary-eyed, his straggling beard wagging unsteadily as he looked round him. Always known for his addiction to strong liquor, he now seemed to have gone to pieces completely. Already, under cross-examination, he had admitted everything that had been required of him, his incoherent utterances punctuated by inane giggles. But still Bukharin held out, and even the poor creature Rykov seemed somehow to rally at his example, refusing after all to betray his friend.

Again and again, on different pretexts, Vyshinski raised the issue of espionage. At all costs the prisoner must be shown to be a criminal, and a criminal hired by the enemies of his country. But Bukharin, unshaken, continued to expound the ideology underlying his alleged conduct and calmly to deny the specific charges brought against him. 'And so you consider yourself an ideologist?' said Vyshinski. 'Yes,' replied Bukharin, quietly. 'You, I suppose, would rather I said I was a spy, but I don't happen to have been one.'

For Vyshinski the most important task of all was to show that Bukharin had planned to murder Lenin in 1918. If he could do that, nothing else would matter. The accused would be finally and irretrievably blackened. The legend of his friendship with the Great Master would be finally disposed of; turned against him, in fact, so that he appeared as an arch-traitor, a Judas. But already the cross-examination had lasted for many hours and still Bukharin showed no signs of weakening.

On the contrary, he was just beginning to get into his stride. 1917, 1918, that was his period, the heroic period of the Revolution. Stalin and Molotov by comparison had been small fry then, and no one had heard of Vyshinski. It was all coming back. Here, he was on ground where few could follow him. With authority he described the intricate relations between Bolsheviks, Mensheviks, Social Revolutionaries, Left-wing Communists; the intrigues; the plots; the counter-plots. Described them as one who had played a leading and a creditable part in it all. Described them as no one else living was qualified to describe them.

No one else living . . . If the situation was to be saved, witnesses must be raised from the dead. Like a conjurer producing a particularly fine rabbit from his hat, Vyshinski raised them. 'Perhaps,' he said, 'I might be allowed to call as witnesses the Left-wing Communists, Jakovleva, Ossinski and Mantsev and the Left-wing Social Revolutionaries Karelin and Kamkov.'

The disappearance from the public scene of the three Left-wing Communists had been comparatively recent; but nothing had been heard of the Social Revolutionaries for twenty years. Their resuscitation was almost as much of a *tour de force* as that of the Tsarist Chief of Police.

One after the other they made their appearance; their bodies clothed in neat blue suits, issued for the occasion, their faces grey and corpse-like. Karelin, in particular, looked as if he had been dead a long time. 'Not quite the man he was,' commented Bukharin, with a suspicion of irony, on being asked whether he recognized him.

Beginning with the woman Jakovleva, a squat figure in her dark blue coat and skirt, they gave the evidence that was required of them in flat toneless voices. There had been a plot in 1918 to murder Lenin, Stalin and Sverdlov. Both the Left-wing Communists and the Left-wing Social Revolutionaries had been associated in it. Bukharin, as the leader of the Left-wing Communists, had been the instigator.

But Bukharin claimed the right to cross-examine the witnesses himself and this, grudgingly, was granted him. Soon he was dominating the scene. His questions were embarrassingly to the point: was it not a fact that he had been in Petrograd and not in Moscow at the time of the alleged conspiracy? That the Social Revolutionaries, with whom he was supposed to have been in league, had sought to assassinate him? Vyshinski did his best to interfere, but Bukharin was irrepressible. If it was really considered necessary to go so carefully into everyone's political history, might it not, he asked, be worth recording that such prominent statesmen as Menzhinski, Kuibyshev and Jaroslavski had all been Mensheviks at that period? And others, too. . . .

And others too. Vyshinski's normally rubicund complexion went several shades paler. He himself had been a Menshevik and did not like being reminded of it. It was not a healthy thing to have been. Was his own position, after all, so very secure? Had not Yagoda taken a leading part in preparing the case against Bukharin and Rykov, only to find himself, when the time came, side by side with them in the dock, an author who suddenly finds himself mixed up in the plot of his own novel? It was a thing that might happen to anyone.

But fortunately it was getting late. Hastily, the proceedings were brought to a close. It had been a bad day for the prosecution. In a final attempt to redress the balance Vyshinski asked Bukharin flatly whether, in view of what the witnesses had said, he still denied having plotted to murder Lenin. Flatly he replied that he did; that what the witnesses had said was a lie. There was no getting away from it, the prisoner, in spite of everything, had scored a moral victory. The court adjourned and one after another the witnesses filed out, shadowy, unsubstantial figures.

But Vyshinski had other fish to fry. Yagoda still remained to be dealt with. Yagoda, who, as People's Commissar for Internal Affairs, as Supreme Head of the O.G.P.U., of the N.K.V.D., had until eighteen months before wielded power second only to that of Stalin himself; whose task it had been to make all arrangements for the personal security of the military and political leaders; who had held their lives in his hand; whose task it was also to keep a check on the activities, public and private, of everyone in the Soviet Union, great or small; in whose power it lay to get rid, by one means or another, of anyone who crossed his path; who for years had, with the approval of the Party and the Government, used these powers to keep up a reign of terror unparalleled in the history of mankind; who had been charged with preparing all the previous State trials; who, in all probability, had made the preliminary arrangements for the present trial.

Having brought his dialectical tussle with Bukharin to a not very satisfactory conclusion, Vyshinski now turned his energies to a task which also seemed likely to present certain difficulties. For Yagoda clearly knew a great deal. Enough of the innermost secrets of the regime to discredit it eternally; enough about everyone's past (Vyshinski's for example) to ruin them irreparably. Besides, might not his technical knowledge of the Soviet judicial machine make him a difficult subject, now that the roles were reversed? The situation was full of interesting possibilities.

Again Vyshinski adopted the technique of methodically blackening his adversary by means of the confessions of his alleged partners in crime. This was the role assigned to the three Kremlin doctors. The story they told was fantastic, more fantastic than anything that had gone before. At Yagoda's instigation they had, it appeared, made away with four of their patients: Maxim Gorki, the writer; his son, Maxim Peshkov; Menzhinski, Yagoda's predecessor as Head of the O.G.P.U.; and Kuibyshev, once the scourge of Turkestan. In a matter-of-fact way, as though they had been addressing a medical congress, they described in detail how they had done it. Menzhinski and Kuibyshev had simply been given the wrong treatment for heart trouble; Maxim Gorki had deliberately been sat in a draught and had caught pneumonia; his son Maxim Peshkov they had got drunk and left in the snow to cool off. In each case the victim had died an apparently natural death. They had not, it seemed, done this of their own accord. Yagoda had terrorized them. They were helpless in his hands. He had both bribed and threatened them. Sometimes, he made them presents of foreign wine, hot-house flowers and even country houses and allowed them to import what they liked duty-free from abroad. But, when the time came, he would remind them that, if they did not comply with his wishes, not only they, but their families would suffer a most unpleasant fate. Coming from the head of the O.G.P.U., such hints were bound to make an impression. They knew that he meant what he said; that he could do anything with them that he liked. And they complied.

Or so they said. But Yagoda himself took a different line. Asked to confirm the testimony of the doctors, he admitted without hesitation, as if it had been quite a normal thing, that he had given instructions for the murder of Kuibyshev and Maxim Gorki, but denied flatly that he had in any way been concerned with the death of Maxim Peshkov or of Menzhinski.

There was a stir among the spectators, a gasp of excitement. Like the filmgoers or readers of penny dreadfuls who in Western countries get a vicarious thrill from the real or imaginary adventures of the titled or criminal classes, they felt that they were seeing life at first hand. The bit about the country houses and the foreign wines and the hot-house flowers had been good. But this was better. It was like a detective story; they could work it all out for themselves. Menzhinski had been Yagoda's boss at the O.G.P.U. He had had him murdered because he wanted his job. It had always been said that Menzhinski, a notoriously vicious character, had died of incurable syphilis, and that it had been a remarkable feat on the part of Dr. Kasakov to keep him alive as long as he did. But now they knew better. And why had Yagoda wanted to get rid of Max Peshkov? Some of the better informed among them knew that too: Max had had an attractive wife, Nadyezhda. Since her husband's death she was rumoured to have become Yagoda's mistress.

And now, while he readily admitted the two 'political' murders with which he was charged (what, after all, did an extra 'liquidation' or two mean to him? He had been responsible for so many thousands in the course of his official duties), Yagoda was steadfastly denying the two crimes for which he might have had personal grounds. From some last remnant of professional pride, perhaps; or from some strange feeling of delicacy, surviving all other emotions. All eyes were on him. Fascinated, the crowd watched the man who up to a few months ago had had power of life and death over every one of them, over every one in court, in fact, judges, prisoners, guards, Public Prosecutor, all of them.

He stood in the dock and contradicted. Contradicted in a tired, an utterly weary voice. A very different figure from the Yagoda we remembered a year or two before. Then he had been youngish and self-satisfied looking. Now he was a broken, white-haired man. His toothbrush moustache, once jaunty, now had a pathetic air. Clearly the Heroic Defenders of the Security of the People had required all their skill in order to subdue their former Commander. Yet something of his former authority still remained. Broken as he was, he still seemed to exercise a strange fascination.

Kasakov had declared that, on instructions given to him personally by Yagoda, he had brought about the death of Menzhinski. Asked by Vyshinski to confirm this, Yagoda rose slowly to his feet. 'The first time I ever saw Kasakov was in this court,' he replied in a low toneless voice. 'I have never dicussed any such matters with him.'

'Then why,' asked Vyshinski, 'did you say that you had done so in the statements which you made before coming into court?'

'Those statements were untrue.'

'And how was it that you came to make statements that were untrue?'

There was a pause. Yagoda put his head a little on one side and looked at Vyshinski. Then he spoke, and his voice, as low as ever, was full of meaning. 'Perhaps,' he said, 'you will allow me not to answer that question.'

Everyone knew what he meant. Hurriedly Vyshinski turned to another prisoner. This time the charge was the murder of Max Peshkov. Again it was alleged that the murder had been committed at Yagoda's instigation. Again Yagoda denied having had any hand in the matter. Again Vyshinski confronted him with his previous statements out of court.

'I was lying,' said Yagoda in a low, level voice.

'And now?'

'I am telling the truth.'

'And why did you lie?'

'Once again,' and this time there was a note of impatience, almost of irritation, in Yagoda's voice. 'Once again, I must ask to be allowed not to reply to that question.'

Earlier in the trial Krestinski had said that his preliminary statements had been obtained from him against his will. This scarcely veiled allusion to the methods of the N.K.V.D., coming from their former Chief, was even more telling.

But, in the long run, even Yagoda could not hold his own. When the court reassembled, it was all too clear that corrective measures had been applied. In a few hours he had aged by ten years. Before, he had looked broken; now, he looked crushed.

Before cross-examining him, Vyshinski called his former private secretary, Bulanov, an individual of sinister but intellectual appearance. There could be no doubt as to the purpose of Bulanov's testimony. It was solely designed to incriminate his master. He began by saying, that during the years he worked for Yagoda, he had fallen completely under his influence, to such an extent that he had lost all contact with the Party. Knowing his devotion, Yagoda had told him all his plans. He had thus at an early stage become aware that Yagoda was a Rightist; that he was in league with the Trotskists and with Tukachevski; and that he was plotting to get rid of the present leaders of the Government and the Party by means of a *coup d'état* and to install himself and his associates in their place. An ardent admirer of Hitler, he had chosen for himself the post of President of the Council of Peoples' Commissars, while Bukharin, as Secretary of the Central Committee of the Party, was to play the part of Dr. Goebbels. Realizing that it would be impossible for them to do this without outside help, the members of the 'bloc' had planned to make their *coup* coincide with a war, and, in anticipation of this, had established contact with the foreign powers most likely to attack their country.

It was the same familiar story over again, with Yagoda's part in it more clearly defined. According to Bulanov, he had used his position at the Commissariat for Internal Affairs and the immense power that went with it to shield his fellow plotters and cover up their treachery and to get rid of anyone who stood in his way. The N.K.V.D. had become a hive of anti-Soviet activity, with Yagoda's men in all the key positions. In detail Bulanov told of the cold-blooded deliberation with which Yagoda had planned the murder of his own chief, Menzhinski, first of all, and then, when he had succeeded him, of Kirov, Kuibyshev, Gorki and Peshkov. When, in spite of his precautions, the activities of some of his associates had been unmasked, he had done everything to prevent their cases from being properly investigated, and had actually visited some of them in prison and 'suggested to them the line they should take when they were brought to trial'.

Finally, towards the end of 1936, he had been relieved of his post as Commissar for Internal Affairs and transferred to the Commissariat of Posts and Telegraphs. Terrified that his successor, Yezhov, would discover his guilty secrets, he had decided to make away with him before it was too late. For some time past he had been interested in poisons. Indeed, he had established a special branch of the N.K.V.D. entirely devoted to their study. It was largely by means of poison that he had planned to carry out his *coup d'état*. Now, with his back to the wall, his thoughts again turned to poison. Summoning the faithful Bulanov, he had produced some bottles of different sizes and a large metal spray. All were of non-Russian, in fact of foreign manufacture.

Taking their cue with both hands, the audience gasped with appreciative horror and disgust: of course such things would be of foreign manufacture. Then they settled down to listen avidly to what was coming next. It did not fall short of their expectations.

Armed with this foreign apparatus, Bulanov continued, he and his master had proceeded to spray with foreign poison the walls and curtains and carpets of the Commissar's office which in a few days would be taken over by Nikolai Ivanovich Yezhov. After his master had left, he had repeated the process hopefully two or three times. But in vain. Yezhov, though his health had been affected by the fumes, had survived this ingenious attempt on his life, had continued conscientiously to hunt down the enemies of the people, and in the following spring both Yagoda and Bulanov had been arrested.

The audience gasped again; this time with relief. There had been a happy ending. All was well. The dog it was that died, or, rather, was going to die.

And now, once again, Yagoda was on his feet. Clearly the treatment which he had received this time, whether physical or mental, had been of the most drastic description. His former pupils had done their work well. Nothing remained of that faint flicker of defiance; all the spirit had been knocked out of him. In a voice that was utterly weary and so faint that it could scarcely be heard in the hushed court, he proceeded to stumble through a written statement, reading it as though for the first time. In it he confirmed what Bulanov and the doctors had said, adding that Bukharin and Rykov must bear their full share of blame for crimes which had been committed in accordance with their orders. But, while no longer denying responsibility for any of the murders, he asked to be allowed to give details of the murder of Max Peshkov in private, and this request was granted. That, even in his present condition, with only a few more hours to live, this poor battered wreck should struggle so tenaciously to keep this one matter from being discussed in public, pointed all too clearly to some internal conflict, to stresses and strains beneath the surface, at the nature of which one could only guess.

To round off this phase of the trial, testimonies were heard from a number of medical experts, designed to bear out what had already been said. They included a statement signed by six leading Soviet scientists to the effect that an analytical examination of Yezhov's urine and of his office furnishings had revealed the presence of appreciable quantities of poison.

The cross-examination of the prisoners was at an end. It was announced that the court would now sit *in camera* to hear statements from a number of the accused regarding their dealings with the official representatives of certain foreign powers.

But Vyshinski wanted the public proceedings to end on a humorous note. With a twinkle in his eye, he asked leave to put a question or two to Rosengolts. When the latter had been arrested, a curious object had been found in his hip pocket and he wanted to ask him about it. He produced a small, rather grubby piece of pink paper with some writing on it. This had been found in a piece of bread, wrapped in newspaper and sewn in a piece of stuff. With the court's permission he would read out what was written on it; and, with a knowing leer at the audience, he started to read.

As I listened, I realized that I had heard what he was reading before. Automatically the Russian sentences translated themselves into English, into the familiar English of the Book of Common Prayer.

Let God arise, and let his enemies be scattered: let them also that hate him, flee before him.

Like as the smoke vanisheth, so shalt thou drive them away: and like as wax melteth at the fire, so let the ungodly perish at the presence of God. . . .

Whoso dwelleth under the defence of the most High: shall abide under the shadow of the Almighty.

I will say unto the Lord, Thou art my hope, and my strong hold: my God, in him will I trust.

For he shall deliver thee from the snare of the hunter: and from the noisome pestilence.

He shall defend thee under his wings, and thou shalt be safe under his feathers: his faithfulness and truth shall be thy shield and buckler.

Thou shalt not be afraid for any terror by night: nor for the arrow that flieth by day;

For the pestilence that walketh in darkness: nor for the sickness that destroyeth in the noon-day.

The sixty-eighth and ninety-first psalms. Odd words to hear in that place and at that time. And yet, perhaps, not so inappropriate.

But Vyshinski was gleefully pursuing his point. 'And how,' he asked, 'did that come to be in your pocket?'

'My wife put it there,' Rosengolts replied sheepishly. 'She said it was a kind of talisman to bring me luck.'

This was what Vyshinski had been working round to. 'To bring you luck!' he said, and he winked knowingly at the crowd. They took their cue. There was a roar of laughter, and the court broke up in an atmosphere of general hilarity.

Next day the Soviet official Rest Day, taking the place of Sunday, came round again and the court did not sit, but in the papers there was a brief communiqué announcing that on the previous evening the court had heard *in camera* statements from the accused regarding their dealings with the official representatives of certain foreign states. Rosengolts, I remembered, had lunched at the Embassy once or twice when he was Commissar for Foreign Trade, bringing his little dark Jewish wife with him. Now, I supposed, their innocent conversation with the Ambassador and Ambassadress about their children, and the Opera and the weather, had, with the help of one or other of the Embassy footmen who possessed a smattering of English, been converted into a sinister plot to murder Stalin or dynamite the Kremlin.

The Court had also heard, it seemed, a statement from Yagoda, who had admitted that he was guilty of the murder of Max Peshkov and had let it be known that he had committed this crime to some extent from personal motives. Once again the shadow of the beautiful Nadyezhda Peshkova fell across the scene.

When, on March 11th, we assembled again, it was to hear Vyshinski make his final speech for the prosecution.

He began with a text. A year ago Comrade Stalin had said: 'Whether these people call themselves Trotskists or Bukharinists, they have long since ceased to be a political movement and have become an unprincipled band of wreckers, spies and assassins, devoid of ideology. They must be mercilessly rooted out.' Therein lay the historical significance of the present trial. It had shown that Comrade Stalin was right. Bukharin and his friends were nothing but common criminals. They were also the agents of foreign countries: Great Britain, Poland, Germany and Japan. More clearly than ever before this trial had shown that the Socialist World and the Capitalist World were deadly enemies, irreconcilably opposed to each other. How right, once again, Comrade Stalin, the Great Master, had been to draw attention to the menace of capitalist encirclement. And so on, for five and a half hours, of which no less than two were devoted to the all-important task of finally and conclusively blackening Bukharin.

What Vyshinski lacked in eloquence, he made up for by the violence of his metaphors, the extravagance of his comparisons. He likened Bukharin to Judas Iscariot and Al Capone; he described him as a 'cross between a fox and a pig'. He had, he said, been the instigating force behind all the crimes of the 'bloc', behind practically all the crimes that had been committed, or planned, in the Soviet Union since the Revolution. At great length he recalled them all, from the attempted murder of Lenin in 1918 to the attempted murder of Yezhov in 1936; launched into a pseudo-scientific disquisition on poisoning and poisoners with references to Pope Clement VI and Philip II of Spain; recalled the espionage, the sabotage; dwelt once again, for the benefit of the audience, on the crimes of Zelenski. 'Powdered glass and nails in the butter!' he exclaimed, 'a monstrous act, in comparison with which all other such crimes fade into insignificance . . . Fifty truckloads of eggs deliberately destroyed. It is clear now why there is famine in the midst of plenty.' And the object of these fell deeds: to strangle the Socialist Revolution with the bony hand of hunger. Such had been from the outset the purpose of Bukharin and his associates.

Gradually he worked himself up. 'Our country,' he declaimed, in a shrill crescendo, foaming slightly at the mouth, 'only asks one thing: that these filthy dogs, these accursed reptiles, be wiped out.' Then, having reached his climax, he ended on a calmer note, his voice oozing adulation. 'The weed and the thistle,' he concluded, 'will grow on the graves of these execrable traitors. But, on us and our happy country, our Glorious Sun will continue to shed His serene light. Guided by our beloved Leader and Master, Great Stalin, we will go forward to Communism along a path that has been cleansed of the sordid remnants of the past.'

The trial was almost at an end. After Vyshinski came the lawyers for the defence, but they spoke only on behalf of the three doctors, the other accused having waived the right to be defended or defend themselves. It now only remained for the accused to make their last statements. These final speeches occupied what was left of that day and all the following day, adding, for the most part, little or nothing to what had gone before. One after the other the accused once more confessed their crimes, declared their repentance and begged for mercy, dwelling, in the most abject terms, on their ingratitude and treachery and on the glories of the Soviet Fatherland which they, miserable wretches, had betrayed. Even Yagoda mumbled with frozen lips a request to be allowed to live and to be sent to the Arctic to work on the White Sea Canal, his own masterpiece, where so many thousands of his victims had met their death toiling amid frost and snow under the most terrible conditions.

But one speech, by its eloquence and dignity, stood out far above the rest. On the evening of March 12th Bukharin rose to speak for the last time. Once more, by sheer force of personality and intellect, he compelled attention. Staring up at him, row upon row, smug, self-satisfied and hostile, sat the new generation of Communists, revolutionaries no longer in the old sense, but worshippers of the established order, deeply suspicious of dangerous thoughts. Watching him standing there, frail and defiant, one had the feeling that here, facing destruction, was the last survivor of a vanished race, of the men who had made the Revolution, who had fought and toiled all their lives for an ideal, and who now, rather than betray it, were letting themselves be crushed by their own creation.

He began by making a formal confession of guilt. He accepted, he said, once more, full 'political and juridical responsibility' for all the crimes which had been committed by the 'bloc'. These crimes, high treason and incitement to revolt amongst them, rendered him liable to the death penalty. There again he was in complete agreement with the Public Prosecutor, who had asked for a death sentence. But, having said this, there were one or two charges which he would like to examine in rather greater detail.

And then, having, in principle, admitted the justice of the case which had been made out against him, he proceeded, uninterrupted this time, to tear it to bits, while Vyshinski, powerless to intervene, sat uneasily in his place, looking embarrassed and yawning ostentatiously.

In the first place, said Bukharin, there was supposed to have been a 'bloc'. It might therefore be assumed that the members of such a 'bloc' would at least have known each other. But, before he came into court, he had never seen or even heard of Charangovich, or Maximov, had never in his life spoken to Pletnev, Kasakov or Bulanov; had never had any counter-revolutionary talk with Rosengolts or Rakovski. In fact, it was impossible legally to maintain that the accused constituted a Rightist-Trotskist 'Bloc'. 'I deny,' said Bukharin, 'belonging to any Rightist-Trotskist "Bloc"; there was no such group.'

Besides there was an obvious lack of connection between the crimes with which the members of the alleged 'bloc' were charged. For example, Yagoda was now known to have murdered Max Peshkov for personal reasons. That had nothing to do with any 'bloc'. Menzhinski was known to have been dying. What could be the object of murdering him? The weakness of the prosecution's arguments was painfully apparent. From the mere fact that he, Bukharin, happened to have been acquainted with Yenukidze, now conveniently out of the way, the story of an elaborate conspiracy had been built up. Because Tomski, also now dead, had once said to him in the course of conversation that the Trotskists were opposed to Maxim Gorki, he, Bukharin, was now accused of having given orders for Gorki to be murdered. In fact what Vyshinski was doing was assuming what he was trying to prove. He would give a concrete example to illustrate his methods of cross-examination.

VYSHINSKI Did you see Khojayev in Tashkent?
BUKHARIN Yes.
VYSHINSKI Did you talk politics?
BUKHARIN Yes.
VYSHINSKI Then I can assume that you instructed him to get into touch with British agents in Tajikstan.

But in fact he had done nothing of the kind. He, for his part, categorically denied having had any connection with any foreign espionage organization. Nor had he ever advocated opening the front to the enemy in case of war, or given instructions for sabotage, which he regarded as useless. As proof of these charges the prosecution produced the testimony of Charangovich, of whose very existence he had been unaware and who now tried to make out that he had been the author of a plan for widespread sabotage.

At this Charangovich, with a fine show of indignation, got up and shook his fist at Bukharin, shouting 'Liar'. But, with vindictive pertinacity, Bukharin continued to pick holes in the case that had been made out against him. He denied, he said, having had anything to do with the murders of Kirov, Menzhinski, Kuibyshev, Gorki and Peshkov. Finally, he denied having ever contemplated the assassination of Lenin. Vyshinski had not been speaking the truth when he said that he had had no answer to the testimonies of the five witnesses who had been called by the prosecution in support of this charge. He had had any number of answers. And he proceeded to recapitulate them at length.

But, said Bukharin, all this did not mean that he was not guilty. The crimes for which he had accepted political and juridical responsibility were sufficient to justify his being shot ten times over. And so, before finishing, he would like to give some account of the political and mental process which had brought him to where he now was.

To some extent his own evolution and that of his friends had been the logical consequence of their opposition to the regime. Having once abandoned Bolshevism, they were inevitably, irresistibly forced into the position of counter-revolutionary bandits. But, despite their disloyalty to their Fatherland, they lacked faith in their own counter-revolutionary cause. Their conscience was uneasy. They had, as it were, a split personality. The compelling spell of Socialist construction was hard to resist. Therein lay the strength of the Soviet State: it had power to sap the will of its adversaries. Ultimately even they were bound to repent and confess.

Western intellectuals who were puzzled by what happened at the Soviet State Trials could not understand this. They did not realize the fascination which the proletarian State exercised even over those who sought to betray it. Such things could not happen in capitalist countries. Only in the Soviet Union.

People had attributed the confessions of the accused to oriental drugs, or hypnotism, or the workings of the Slav soul. But that was all nonsense. Anyone could see, if only by the way he himself argued with the Public Prosecutor, that his mind was perfectly clear, that he was neither drugged nor hypnotized.

Perhaps, he continued, he might dwell on his own case for a few moments more. He would not keep them much longer. He was speaking, probably, for the last time in his life.

Why had he admitted his guilt? In prison he had had time to look back over his past, and he had asked himself this question: If I die, what shall I be dying for? It was then that he had found himself looking into a black abyss, and had realized that, if he died unrepentant, there would be no cause left to him to die for. If, on the other hand, he were by some extraordinary chance to be spared, there would, without repentance, be nothing left for him to live for. He would be an enemy of the people, an outcast, cut off from humanity. It was then that all the positive qualities of the Soviet Fatherland came back to him more forcibly than ever, and it had been this that in the end disarmed him completely and caused him to bow the knee before the Party and the Country. Personal considerations had long since ceased to weigh with him. His repentance and confession represented the moral triumph of the Soviet Union over yet another of its opponents. Left-wing circles abroad would probably seek to defend him. He did not want their defence. They would do better to profit by his example. 'My own fate,' he concluded, 'is of no importance. All that matters is the Soviet Union.'

When all the prisoners had had their say, the court adjourned to consider their verdict. It was half-past nine at night. Sentence would not be pronounced for several hours. Chip Bohlen and I walked through the icy streets to his flat in the American Embassy to get something to eat. We could not take our minds off what we had seen and heard. For ten days we had spent eight or nine hours a day at the trial. We had thought and talked of little else. It had come to be part of our lives. Now, over dinner, in a normal atmosphere once more, we tried to find a theory which would fit the facts as we knew them.

It was not easy.

If what we had heard in court was the literal truth, if, ever since the Revolution, the highest offices of State had been held by a band of traitors, spies, murderers and wreckers, whose sole aim had been to overthrow the Soviet regime, if the whole regime had from the start been riddled with treachery and corruption, how was it that such a galaxy of talent, with such opportunities, had obtained so small a measure of success, how was it that their most important achievements had been to spoil a relatively small quantity of eggs and butter and to hasten the demise of an elderly littérateur, who for forty years had been suffering from an incurable disease? For five years Yagoda, a notoriously ruthless man, had controlled the all-powerful N.K.V.D., had had under his command the Kremlin guards; had had in his power the doctors who attended Stalin and the other leaders of the Party and Government; had had his private laboratory for the preparation of special poisons. Why had he not used these opportunities to eliminate all those who stood in his way?

If, on the other hand, the men now standing their trial had in fact been loyal servants of the regime and the charges brought against them nothing but a tissue of lies, then an answer was no easier to find. What possible purpose could it serve to invent such fairy-tales; to murder, on purely imaginary charges, a large number of key men, and, in the process, to proclaim gratuitously to an already sceptical and hostile world that for years past the Soviet Union had been ruled by a gang of ruffians?

And the accused themselves? If they were innocent, why did they confess? It was hard to believe that torture or drugs alone could produce such ready admissions, such closely reasoned statements, such eloquent speeches. If, on the other hand, they were guilty, if there had really been a large-scale conspiracy against the regime, why did they not seek to justify themselves, why was it that none of their speeches contained a word of criticism of a system of which they had been such bitter opponents?

The answer to some of these questions must lie, it seemed, in Bukharin's last speech. It was, in the first place, a matter of ideological, of psychological atmosphere. Such things, he had said, could only happen in the Soviet Union.

One knew what he meant.

For twenty years past, everyone in court, prisoners, judges, prosecutor, guards and spectators, had lived in the tense atmosphere of unreality, tension, oppression and suspicion which we had come to know so well. Before that, the older ones amongst them had lived in the tense conspiratorial atmosphere of revolutionary circles in Tsarist Russia. On top of this, the accused had endured additional strains and stresses. For years they had known the fear of impending liquidation. Then had come the final shock of arrest, the long-awaited knock on the door at midnight; then the long months of prison, the unceasing interrogations.

All, judges and accused alike, had, for the greater part of their lives, been subjected to propaganda, so constant, so intensive, so insidious, as to leave its mark on the strongest intellect. All had been cut off, as only Soviet citizens are cut off, from any contact with the outside world, from all normal intellectual and political influences, from all valid standards of comparison. In a sense, all their minds must work along the same lines, along different lines, that is, from the Western mind.

Was it altogether surprising that, with this mental background, they should at times have difficulty in distinguishing between the real and the imaginary, the actual and the hypothetical, that their faculties should become blurred, that they should lose their objectivity?

Besides, all were Party Members, deeply impregnated with Communist dogma, their conduct ruled by a Party Line. For them any deviation, however slight, was a crime. To disagree, even mentally, with the leaders of the Party on some minor point of doctrine was as unforgivable as to commit a seemingly much graver crime, as to plan their physical destruction, for instance. 'Having once deviated from Bolshevism,' Bukharin had said, 'we were inevitably, irresistibly forced into the position of counter-revolutionary bandits.' If they had deviated, the rest followed.

Already, the whole problem of guilt and innocence was reduced to a simpler form. In the past, when political discussion had still been admissible, Bukharin and Rykov, Krestinski and Rakovski had all differed openly from Stalin. On the face of it, despite subsequent disavowals, it was improbable that they had since become convinced of his infallibility or that they could be reconciled to the grim new form which the Soviet regime had assumed under his sway. There was much about it that must shock them, much of which, when they remembered the structure that they themselves had planned to build, they must disapprove.

Disapprove. There, already, was something to go on. Enough for Stalin, at any rate. The former seminarist had learnt at an early age the power for evil of 'dangerous thoughts'. The old revolutionary knew from his own experience that, in Russia, every difference of opinion carries in it the germ of a conspiracy. The tribesman, the guerrilla, knew the importance in irregular warfare of thinking quicker than your opponent, of getting your blow in first, before his intentions have had time to take shape.

And if, in fact, there had been a conspiracy, what more natural than that the thinkers, the ideologists, should have made common cause with the men of action, Tukachevski, Yagoda? What more natural, too, than that to the Tukachevskis and the Yagodas, finding themselves in positions of great power, should come the idea of using that power for their own ends. Tukachevski was known to admire Napoleon. As a soldier? Or as a man? An officer of the Imperial Army, he had shifted his allegiance quickly enough, when his interests demanded it. Might he not do so again? And Yagoda. In the service of the State he had shown himself utterly ruthless and utterly unscrupulous. Might he not, with the vast power at his disposal, be tempted to pursue a personal policy? And if he did? Was he not the man who held Stalin's own personal security in his hands? It was an alarming thought.

What more natural, too, than that any potential opponents of the regime should seek, and receive, outside support, among the enemies of the Soviet Union? Some of them had, in the course of their normal duties, had contact with foreigners. Tukachevski, in the old days, had had many dealings with the German General Staff; had been to Paris. Krestinski had been to Berlin, Rakovski to London and Tokio. Rosengolts had lunched and dined at the British Embassy. Had these contacts really been innocent?

And the 'wrecking'? Inefficiency? Or stubbornness? Or malice? Or a combination of all three? In any case a phenomenon which the enemies of the regime, if they knew their job, would be bound to exploit. Something which called for the most ruthless counter-measures.

Looking at it like that, it was possible to see how, in the minds of those concerned, if not in reality, the idea of a conspiracy might have grown up.

Who had thought of it first? The conspired against or the conspirators? Probably the former, at any rate in the concrete form in which it was now presented.

But the conspirators, with their minds working along the same lines as those of their inquisitors, would have had no difficulty in following their line of argument, especially if, in the back of their minds, there lurked a suspicion that if only they had had the chance they might in fact have acted in the way they were supposed to have done.

Once this basis for an understanding between the two parties had been established, the rest would follow naturally. It only remained to prepare the idea for presentation to public opinion, to dress it up in its proper ideological clothes, to paint in the background, to accentuate darkness and light, to link the various scenes so as to present a more or less coherent whole. This, for trained minds, accustomed to such work, was mere child's play.

And if, unexpectedly, any of the puppets did not wish to play the parts allotted to them? Everyone has his weak point. Some would be afraid for themselves, some for their wives and children. We knew that the families of the prisoners had all been arrested at the same time as they had.

The resistance of others could be broken down by more subtle means. All kinds of strange tricks can be played with the human mind, given time and patience.

Time and patience. Most of the prisoners had been in prison for a year or eighteen months. During that time, they would have been cross-examined for days, for weeks, for months on end. They would have been confronted with statements signed by their fellow prisoners, by their closest friends, by their own wives and children, incriminating them hopelessly. They would have felt betrayed, helpless and utterly alone. They would have been reminded of half-remembered episodes, not very creditable to them, perhaps, not very easy to explain, and invited to explain them. They would find that all kinds of seemingly unconnected incidents in their lives had a way of fitting into a pattern, which, taken as a whole, was seen to be utterly damning. They would have been subjected to many different kinds of pressure, sometimes physical, sometimes mental. The N.K.V.D. were reputed to make sparing use of actual torture, as practised by the Gestapo. But there were other ways. Lack of sleep, lack of food, soon sap resistance. In the cells the heating could be left off in winter; left on in summer. A drunkard — Rykov, for example — could be deprived of drink or suddenly given as much as he wanted. Sudden plenty, a carefully timed bribe, could be as demoralizing as the worst privations. There might be some, Tukachevski, for instance, whose resistance was too strong to be overcome, whom nothing would induce to play their allotted parts. For them was reserved liquidation by administrative measure, without a public trial.

And Bukharin himself, a man of a different calibre from the others, for whom personal considerations had long since ceased to exist, whose whole life for years past had been the Party, how was he to be induced to play his part, to declare himself a traitor to all that had been most precious to him?

Once again the answer was to be found in his own words. Faced with death, he had felt the need of a cause to die for, and, for him, a lifelong Communist, there could only be one cause: the Party; the Party which he had made and which was now devouring him; the Party, disfigured and debased beyond all recognition, but still the Party. In other words, he, too, had had a weak point: his loyalty to a cause. Others had confessed for their own sakes or for the sake of their families. His confession had been a last service to the Party.

A last service . . . How could this fantastic nightmare serve the Party, or anybody else?

In a number of ways. Primarily, it seemed, the whole trial was a political manifesto, a carefully worded fable designed to convey a number of carefully selected messages to the hazy minds of the Soviet population. That was why it was necessary for there to be so sharp a contrast between good and evil, between darkness and light, for the characters to be portrayed in such crude colours, to correspond so accurately to the conventional figures of Communist Heaven and Hell.

In the first place Good would be seen to triumph over Evil, and, so that even in the haziest mind, there could be no possible doubt as to the meaning, it would be Absolute Good, with wings and halo, triumphing over Absolute Evil, with horns and tail. That was the *leitmotif*: that it does not pay to rebel against established authority. The trial would serve, too, as a reminder of the dangers besetting both the Soviet State and the individual citizen. It would help to keep up the nervous tension which, extending to every walk of life, had become one of the chief instruments of Soviet internal policy. By making people suspicious of one another, by teaching them to see spies and traitors everywhere, it would increase 'vigilance', render even more improbable the germination of subversive ideas. The stories of foreign spies, of foreign designs on the Soviet Fatherland, would serve to make the population shun foreigners, if possible, more rigorously than before. Much, too, would be explained that had hitherto been obscure. Shortages, famines had been due, not to the shortcomings of the Soviet system, but to deliberate wrecking. The purge, even, would now be seen to be the work, not of the benevolent Father of the People, but of the

Fiend Yagoda, working without his knowledge and against his will. Now the purgers were being purged; the wreckers liquidated and the designs of the foreign spies finally thwarted. Soon peace and plenty would reign.

For months past, to the exclusion of all other intellectual activities, judges, prosecutor, prisoners and N.K.V.D. had been working at high pressure on the production of this legend, as authors, producers and actors might work on the production of a film: piecing together the real and the imaginary, truth and illusion, intention and practice, finding connections where none existed, darkening the shadows, heightening the highlights, embodying it all in the fifty volumes of evidence which littered Ulrich's desk. Inevitably, as work progressed, as their production began to take shape, the distinction between truth and illusion would become in their minds more and more blurred, would be replaced by a kind of pride of authorship, an attachment to accuracy, which, in court, on the day, would cause them to argue with each other, to correct each other on points of detail, which in fact bore no relation to reality, which existed only in their imagination.

In their imagination, in everybody's imagination. In Ulrich's imagination; in Vyshinski's imagination; in the imagination of the N.K.V.D. interrogators; in Yagoda's imagination; in the imagination of the Soviet public.

Perhaps even in Stalin's imagination. That was the most terrifying thought of all. How did the Supreme Puppet Master view the proceedings? With the complete detachment of a *metteur en scène*? Or with the acutely personal interest of a man who finds that his medical attendants are murderers and the arrangements for his personal safety are in the hands of a bitter and unscrupulous enemy? Was the ruler of the Soviet Union a cold and calculating schemer, deliberately eliminating, after first carefully blackening their names, all those who might embarrass him? Or was he a sufferer from persecution mania whose weakness was exploited for their own ends by a gang of unscrupulous police spies?

Of his interest in the proceedings we had direct proof, for at one stage of the trial a clumsily directed arc-light dramatically revealed to attentive members of the audience the familiar features and heavy drooping moustache peering out from behind the black glass of a small window, high up under the ceiling of the court-room.

It was long after midnight. Still talking, we walked back through the dark, frozen, empty streets to the court-house. The judges had still not concluded their deliberations. In the court-room a little group of foreign correspondents were wearily awaiting their return. They were listening to Cholerton of the *Daily Telegraph* who had been in Moscow for twelve years and knew more than any of us. He was talking about the trial.

'What do you make of it, Cholerton?' we asked.

He tugged at his beard, and his eyes twinkled.

'Oh,' he said, 'I believe everything. Everything except the facts.'

It was four in the morning when the judges returned. For the last time the doors were flung open and Ulrich sidled in. Under the ghastly glare of a battery of arc-lights and to the accompaniment of whirring cinema cameras, the prisoners filed into the dock.

In a level voice Ulrich read out the verdict, while all remained standing. The prisoners were found guilty of all the crimes with which they were charged. Once again they were recapitulated: murder, wrecking, espionage, treason. For twenty-five minutes he droned on. At last he reached the last page and, turning it, read out a list of names:

> *Bukharin, Nikolai Ivanovich*, it began,
> *Rykov, Aleksei Ivanovich*,
> *Yagoda, Genrikh Grigoryevich*,
> *Krestinski, Nikolai Nikolayevich . . .*

Fourteen other names followed. Then, amidst complete silence, he read out the sentence: TO BE SHOT.

Then, scarcely noticed, followed the names of the three prisoners who had been sentenced to terms of imprisonment: Bessonov, Rakovski and one of the doctors, Pletnev. When we looked we saw they were no longer there.

The proceedings were at an end. The door in the middle was flung open, and Ulrich marched out. For the last time, the little door at the side was opened and the guards closed in round the eighteen condemned men. They had heard the sentence impassively, and now, impassively, they filed out to their death. The last to go was Yagoda. As he reached the door, he stopped for an instant and looked back. Then he also turned and went out, and the door shut after him.

CHAPTER VIII

CHINESE PUZZLE

THE snows melted. The ice broke and came thundering and crashing down the river past my windows. With the return of warmer weather, my thoughts once again turned to travel. But this time my itinerary, as things turned out, was chosen for me.

After my return from Central Asia in the autumn I had, largely in order to justify my prolonged absence from my desk in the Chancery, tried my hand at writing up my experiences. As it was a long time since any first-hand information had been received from Russian Turkestan, my report attracted more attention in London than it would otherwise have done, and on the strength of it I acquired a largely spurious reputation as a Central Asian expert. Meanwhile, events in another part of Central Asia were causing concern to the Foreign Office and feelings verging on alarm to that more sensitive Department of State, the India Office.

Few inhabited areas of the world are more remote and, to the ordinary traveller, more inaccessible, than Sinkiang, or, as it is also called, Chinese Turkestan. On the maps Sinkiang is simply shown as an ordinary province of China, but, though much can be learnt from maps, they do not always tell the whole story.

Geographically Sinkiang is separated from China by the formidable expanse of the Gobi Desert while its inhabitants are for the most part not Chinese but Turkis, akin in race and language and religion to the inhabitants of Russian Turkestan. Since it first became part of the Chinese Empire half way through the eighteenth century the history of Sinkiang (its name means the New Dominion) has been one of sustained turbulence. Both the Provincial Government and the population have rebelled, sometimes together and sometimes separately, against the hegemony of the Chinese Central Government. Matters were further complicated when, in the nineteenth century, both Great Britain and Russia began to take an interest in this rich, semi-independent province. But Russia had one great advantage. The journey across the Himalayas from British India took six weeks on foot. The natural gate to Sinkiang was from the newly conquered Russian territories in Central Asia. Russian goods gradually squeezed out British competition in the bazaars and the Russian Consul-General's armed escort of Cossacks behaved with increasing arrogance, driving all before them as they galloped through the bazaars.

With the Revolution, Russia temporarily set aside all thought of expansion and withdrew from Sinkiang. Cossacks, Consul-General and traders disappeared from the two main towns, Kashgar and Urumchi. The Chinese Central Government reasserted its authority with that long-suffering perseverance so characteristic of the Chinese, and British Indian trade and traders once again reappeared in the bazaars.

But, in the nineteen-thirties, the Soviet Government once more took up, in Sinkiang as in other parts of the world, the threads of Tsarist policy. Once again Russian Consuls arrived at Kashgar and Urumchi; Russian goods made their appearance once again in the bazaars.

There followed a period of the kind of confusion in which Sinkiang has long specialized. The Tungans or Chinese Mohammedans revolted against the Provincial Government. The Provincial Government appealed for help, not to the Chinese Central Government, who in any case had their hands full elsewhere, but to Moscow. Moscow intervened rapidly and effectively and Soviet troops and aircraft soon accounted for the Tungans. When the Russians returned home, they left behind them considerable numbers of technical and other advisers, who continued to help the Provincial Government. History repeated itself. Russian influence increased, the position of the British community became more and more precarious. The Indian traders in the bazaars found themselves boycotted. Even the British Consul-General at Kashgar was practically a prisoner in his Consulate. He was moreover largely out of touch with the Provincial Governor, or Tupan, who resided at Urumchi, several weeks' journey away, and who in any case was generally believed to be no more than a Soviet puppet.

In 1937 the Tungan revolt had finally collapsed. By the beginning of 1938 Soviet influence seemed firmly established and the position of the few remaining British Indian traders was extremely precarious. Economically they were slowly but surely being squeezed out and, what was worse, were liable to sudden arrest and ill-treatment. The protests of H.M. Consul-General, when he could find anybody to protest to, remained unheeded.

It was at this stage that the scheme was evolved of sending me on a mission to Urumchi to contact the Tupan and plead with him for better treatment for the Indian traders and also for H.M. Consul-General. It was felt, so the telegrams said, that the fact that I came from H.M. Embassy at Moscow would lend weight to what I had to say.

It seemed to me highly improbable that I should meet with any success, but I was delighted at the prospect of another visit to Central Asia, and at once I started looking out my rucksack.

But I soon discovered that this time my travelling arrangements were not to be quite so simple as on previous occasions. The authorities at home insisted (quite properly, I suppose) that I should not set out without having first applied for and obtained through official channels everything that was needed in the way of passes and visas. Furthermore they suggested that the Embassy should inform the Soviet Government of the project and invite them to use their influence with the Sinkiang authorities to facilitate my journey. This, it seemed to me, finally disposed of any chance of success I might ever have had. But I went ahead with my arrangements nevertheless.

First I visited a friend of mine at the Chinese Embassy. He seemed slightly embarrassed when I mentioned Sinkiang, but nevertheless promised to ask his Government by telegram for authority to grant me a visa. I next called at the People's Commissariat for Foreign Affairs to see the head of the Third Western Department, Comrade Weinberg. Having reluctantly agreed to receive me, he listened sardonically while I told him of my plans and expressed, in strict accordance with my instructions, the hope that the Soviet Government would use their influence with the Sinkiang authorities to facilitate my journey. The mention of Soviet influence in Sinkiang gave him his cue. He could not, he said, imagine what made the British Government think that the Soviet Government had any special influence in the province of

China I had mentioned. It was not the practice of the Soviet Government to interfere in the internal affairs of China or of any other country. If I wanted facilities for travel to China I should apply to the Chinese Government. He, for his part, would be delighted to grant a Soviet exit visa if and when I required one. As a special favour he would even give me a letter of introduction to the Soviet Consul-General at Urumchi, who was a friend of his.

Feeling that I had been scored off heavily, but not decisively, I went back to the Chinese Embassy. Permission to grant me a visa had duly arrived from the Central Government and my passport was handed back to me covered with impressive-looking hieroglyphics. Had the Central Government informed the local authorities of my impending arrival? I inquired. They had. What had been the reply? There had not yet been a reply. The local authorities in Sinkiang were sometimes a little slow in answering.

At any rate I had a visa of some sort, which I supposed was better than no visa at all. I asked my Chinese colleague what he advised me to take with me in the way of equipment. 'Visiting cards,' he replied without hesitation, 'plenty of Chinese visiting cards.' Then, seeing my dismay, 'Never mind,' he said, 'I will make you some,' and seizing a quill pen and some Indian ink, proceeded to reproduce again and again the three Chinese characters which represent my name: Ma-Ke-ling, which he explained meant 'The horse that corrupts the morals'. 'I hope,' he added gleefully, 'that they will not think you are anything to do with General Ma, the notorious Mohammedan rebel leader.' I said that I, too, hoped they would not.

I left Moscow on June 6th on the five days' journey by train to Alma Ata, the capital of the Kazakh S.S.R. It was the same route that I had followed on my way back from Tashkent in the autumn. The first two days were taken up with the journey through European Russia. We crossed the Volga near Samara. On the third day we reached Orenburg, the base of the Imperial Russian forces in their campaign against the rulers of Tashkent, Samarkand and Bokhara during the second half of the last century. Soon after Orenburg the barren steppe begins. On the fourth day we reached the Sea of Aral and thereafter roughly followed the course of the Syr Darya. In the appearance of the countryside there was little to show that we were near so great a river. On either side of the railway track the steppe stretched away as far as the eye could reach and cultivated patches were few and far between. It was blazing hot. An enthusiastic Kazakh in the train told me that just out of sight of the railway there roamed vast herds of cattle; and this may well have been so, for Kazakhstan is reputed to be the chief cattle-raising district of the Union.

On the journey I talked to many Kazakhs. Like the Kirghiz, from whom, to anyone but an expert, they are all but indistinguishable, they are — or were until recently — simple, friendly nomads and mountaineers of a far lower standard of culture than the neighbouring Uzbeks, who have behind them the traditions of Samarkand and Bokhara. Although it is admittedly hard to judge from isolated cases, the impression I gained was that they have proved much more malleable material from the point of view of administration and propaganda than the other culturally more developed races of Russian Central Asia. For one thing, they have fewer religious and cultural traditions to break down. Racially, too, they are different, being for the most part of a definitely Mongol type, while the Uzbeks, Tajiks and Turkomans resemble rather Persians or Afghans.

The Kazakhs I met were mostly officials on their way to Party Conferences and the like. All were obviously proud of their Republic (recently promoted to federal status) and filled with a sense of their own personal importance. In conversation they referred quite casually to those of their colleagues who had been 'unmasked'[1] during the recent purge of Kazakhstan which had culminated in the trial and execution of practically all the leading Government and Party officials. The possibility that they themselves might be the next to go did not seem to occur to them, or, if it did, was outweighed by the wireless sets, motor tractors, cheap scent, opportunities for making speeches, and other manifestations of culture which the Soviet regime has brought in its train.

On the fifth day we sighted the snow-clad mountains of Kirghizia which form the western extremity of the Tien Shan range. At the same time there was an abrupt change in the nature of the country

---

[1] That is, arrested and shot as enemies of the people.

through which we were passing. We had left the Hungry Steppe and were in fertile, well-irrigated and cultivated country. Instead of the scattered groups of *yurts* (the round skin tents of the Kazakhs and Kirghiz), which were the only form of human habitation we had seen for the past few days, we now passed through Arys, Chimkent, Mankent and other pleasant country towns standing in groves of poplars. From Chimkent onwards we travelled more or less due east skirting the Tien Shan range which rises like a wall to the south, until we came in sight of the snow-clad Ala Tau, the spur of the Tien Shan which rises behind Alma Ata. The first stage of my journey was completed.

My next object was to get myself to Ayaguz, the station on the Turksib Railway which is the starting-point of the main road linking Urumchi with the Soviet Union. At Alma Ata, however, the higher station officials were nowhere to be found and the subordinates unwilling to take any responsibility, so that there seemed to be little hope of getting a place, whether 'hard' or 'soft', on one of the crowded northward-bound trains passing through Alma Ata on their way from Tashkent to Novosibirsk.

Finally in the early hours of the morning I came upon the assistant stationmaster sitting in somebody else's office with her uniform in considerable disarray, suckling her new-born baby. The station-master was lying unconscious face downwards on the floor, where he remained throughout the interview. Asleep? Drunk? Dead? It was impossible to say. But the assistant stationmaster, like so many Russian women, proved helpful and moderately efficient and in the end I was duly provided with a reserved seat as far as Ayaguz on a train leaving early next morning.

The journey of four hundred miles northwards through the eastern fringe of the Hungry Steppe from Alma Ata to Ayaguz took no less than twenty-four hours, the train never going at more than thirty miles an hour and stopping frequently while the passengers got out and picked flowers. The stops were further enlivened by an enthusiastic sailor of the Red Navy who at every stop insisted upon trying to ride the camels which were grazing near the line and at every stop was kicked off. The Hungry Steppe fully justifies its sinister name but the ice-blue peaks of the Tien Shan, which remained in sight for most of the way, served as a comforting reminder that the whole of Central Asia is not a flat waste of scorching sand.

Ayaguz, where we arrived shortly before sunrise, has sprung into existence since the building of the Turksib Railway eight years ago. It is laid out in American fashion, the streets of square white plaster or wooden houses all running at right angles to each other. It boasts a school, a club and a municipal building, as well as the inevitable statue of Lenin and Park of Rest and Culture, consisting of a few bushes with a paling round them. The population, as far as I could make out, was composed entirely of employees of the Turksib Railway and of the State Trading Organization of Sovsintorg, with a detachment of Frontier Guards and the usual quota of police spies, two of whom devoted their attention to me throughout my stay, padding along the dusty village street twenty yards behind me. At one end of Ayaguz was a small native bazaar to which the Kazakhs from the neighbouring *auls* ride in to sell their produce. Beyond, the desert stretched away bleakly.

The only definite information which I had been able to obtain in Moscow regarding travelling facilities between Ayaguz and Urumchi was derived from an official publication several years old. From this it appeared that the two towns were connected by a road, along which there was at certain times 'regular motor traffic'. Knowing Soviet methods, I was glad that I had the whole day before me in which to explore the possibilities of pursuing my journey to Urumchi.

But I met with fewer difficulties than I had expected. At N.K.V.D. Headquarters, I was told politely and promptly by the officer on duty that I should address myself to the local base of Sovsintorg, the State Organization in Charge of Trade with Sinkiang. From the attitude of the N.K.V.D. I gained the impression that they had already received instructions about me from Moscow. This impression was confirmed when, a few hours later, I was informed by the Director of the Sovsintorg Base that, although normally no bus would be running on that day to the frontier town of Bakhti, he would put one on especially for my benefit. It would leave at two in the afternoon and we should reach Bakhti by eight in the evening. At Bakhti I should be able to pick up a lorry which would take me on to Urumchi. This unexpected, and, in my experience, unprecedented helpfulness, left no doubt in my mind that the authorities at Ayaguz had received explicit instructions to speed me on my way.

Before leaving Ayaguz I witnessed one of those spectacles without which no picture of any part of the Soviet Union would be complete. While I was talking to the stationmaster at Alma Ata, an order had come through by telephone for a detachment of N.K.V.D. troops to be dispatched to Ayaguz and these had travelled with me on the train. Now, as I was waiting for the bus to appear, the detachment paraded on the platform, where they proceeded to take charge of a contingent of prisoners who were then herded into a heavily barred truck. The prisoners, largely Kazakhs, seemed for the most part indifferent to their fate, but one of their number, a burly, red-bearded European Russian, seized this opportunity to harangue the crowd which had collected to witness their departure and had to be driven hastily into the truck at the point of a bayonet. This scene supplied the inevitable undertone of violence and repression.

The bus made its appearance at 4 o'clock – barely two hours late. Although it had been produced especially for my benefit, it was already filled to bursting point with a crowd of Kazakhs, including no less than six small babies. Room was found, or rather made, for me, and we set off as fast as the bus, a four-year-old product of the Stalin Factory, could be induced to go. The heat was stifling and the bus hermetically sealed.

After the first few miles the road emerged from the desert and ran through rolling prairies of fragrant grasses and flowering scrub, from which covey after covey of partridges got up as we passed. To the north the steppe was bounded by the blue craggy foothills of the Tarbagatai Range and to the south it stretched away as far as the eye could see. The road, though rough, was a first-class one by Soviet standards and obviously every effort was being made to keep it in a state of good repair. At frequent intervals we found gangs working on it with every modern road-building appliance. Altogether it bore the mark of a road which had been made, and was being kept up, for a very definite purpose. We passed a number of lorries filled with merchandise going in both directions.

Towards midnight, in spite of furious driving, made all the more noticeable by the absence of springs and the uneven surface of a road not designed for passenger traffic, we were still a hundred miles from the frontier. Most of the other passengers had by now faded away and we decided to spend the night at the village of Urdjar, a group of mud farmhouses clustered on the banks of a stream. Here I was given a kettle of tea and the choice of six not very promising-looking beds.

At four next morning, in the bleak half light that precedes the dawn, we started on the final stage of the journey to the frontier. For the remaining hundred miles the road runs between two ranges of mountains, to the north the Tarbagatai Hills with beyond them the Altai Mountains, and to the south the Dzungarian Range. At ten we reached the Soviet frontier town of Bakhti and drove straight to the headquarters of the N.K.V.D. Frontier Guards.

There I was received in the most friendly manner by the officer in charge, a tall good-looking Russian in the khaki-drill tunic and smart apple-green cap of his Corps. He had clearly been warned of my arrival and, in less than an hour, had commandeered a Sovsintorg lorry and installed me in it next to the driver, a merry fellow in a red and white striped football jersey. In forty-eight hours, he said, I should be in Urumchi. The journey was not a difficult one and I should be able to find food and accommodation for the night at rest houses provided by Sovsintorg for their drivers. Then he shook hands and saluted and we started on our way. Everything seemed to be going surprisingly well.

Leaving behind us the Soviet frontier post where Soviet frontier guards in smartly cut uniforms were exercising their well-groomed horses, we passed through a triumphal arch and entered Chinese territory. The road immediately became narrower and rougher than on the Soviet side of the frontier. Soon we reached the Chinese frontier post where a very old wrinkled Chinaman, with long white drooping moustaches and a very shabby black suit, came out to inspect our passports. In the background a number of Chinese and Turki soldiers in jodhpurs and bedroom slippers lounged about and searched each other for lice. The old man, after looking at my pass-port in a dejected way for some time, finally disappeared into a dilapidated two-storeyed house and I was left sitting outside in the sun.

While I was waiting I was engaged in conversation by an onlooker, who introduced himself as an inhabitant of Chuguchak. His father, he said, had moved there from Tashkent. He himself was a Soviet citizen but his brother had Chinese nationality. By race they were Uzbeks. He then went on to say that what was really wanted in Chuguchak was a good English school. Could I not arrange for one to be founded there? The whole population knew Russian but were longing to learn English and he hinted at promising opportunities for propaganda. He himself already knew a few words of English which he then proceeded to air. On the whole he gave the impression of being an *agent provocateur*. But perhaps prolonged residence in the Soviet Union had made me unduly suspicious.

After half an hour had elapsed I went up to the house to see if I could expedite matters. I was received in the most friendly way by a number of soldiers who ushered me into a small room containing a rack of eight rifles, an incredible number of flies and the largest bed I have ever seen. They then produced a teapot and two bowls, one of which they handed to me while the other was passed round from mouth to mouth. After this ceremony they invited me by means of gestures (to my surprise I found that none of them could or would speak Russian) to lie down and go to sleep. In reply I made it clear to them, also by means of gestures, that at the moment I was not anxious to go to sleep, but wished rather to continue my journey to Urumchi with as little delay as possible. At this they left me, locking the door rather ostentatiously as they went.

Time passed. My prospects, I began to feel, were not so bright as they had at first seemed. Upstairs I could hear Russian being spoken and the sounds of scuffling and female laughter.

Finally the key turned in the lock and the decayed old man in the black suit reappeared and told me that, as soon as my lorry, which had apparently broken down, had been repaired, my documents would be returned to me and I should be allowed to proceed on my way. This was good news. I cheered up and settled down to wait with better grace.

Another hour elapsed. The lorry was now in working order. Again I returned to the attack; but this time the old man announced that my passport had been sent off by special messenger some two hours before to the Governor of the neighbouring town of Chuguchak. We must wait for it to be returned.

We now sat down to watch the road to Chuguchak, which could be seen from where we were winding across the plain towards the blue mountains of Dzungaria. At last in the remote distance, a column of dust appeared moving rapidly along the road. We watched it coming nearer. Out of it there eventually emerged a small black car of Soviet manufacture, rattling along at full speed over the uneven surface. It drew up in front of the guard-house and from it descended a frail-looking young man with spectacles and a small black moustache neatly dressed in a suit of plus-fours and a mackintosh, an officer in a smart black uniform and top-boots with an enormous Mauser automatic strapped to his side and the air of a stage executioner, and a dejected-looking individual in a stiff collar. All three were Chinese.

The young man in plus-fours and the officer disappeared upstairs without a word, and I was ushered into an office where I found the third member of the party looking more embarrassed and dejected than ever. After inquiring in bad but fairly fluent Russian at some length about the state of my health, he very gradually turned the con-versation to the question of my journey. The Governor of Chuguchak, he said, seemed to have received no instructions about me from the Chinese Central Government, or from the Provincial Government at Urumchi. This placed him in a dilemma. He would have liked to help me but it was impossible for him to do so. Indeed he could not even allow me to remain any longer on Chinese territory. The law prevented him. And so, taking everything into consideration, he would advise me to return to Moscow.

In reply, I explained with some vigour that I was proceeding to Urumchi on instructions from the British Government, that I was doing so with the approval of the Chinese Central Government, as was shown by the Chinese diplomatic visa and *laissez-passer* which had been issued to me, and, finally, that the Sinkiang Provincial Government had been notified of my arrival both by the Chinese Central Government and by His Majesty's Consul-General at Kashgar, and that if the authorities at Chuguchak had received no instructions regarding my journey it could only be due to a most regrettable omission on the part of the Provincial Government.

To this he answered that this was as it might be; but without explicit instructions from Urumchi he could not allow me to remain on Chinese territory, diplomatic visa or no diplomatic visa. All he could do was to telegraph to Urumchi for instructions, pending the receipt of which I must wait on the other side of the frontier. Threats and attempts at persuasion proved of no avail and the outcome of a long argument was that my baggage was transferred to a Chinese lorry and that I started off in the direction of the Soviet frontier with the assurance, for what it was worth, that as soon as the necessary instructions arrived, all possible facilities would be accorded to me.

The officer in command of the frontier guards at Bakhti expressed great concern on seeing me back so soon. He had thought, he said, with the suspicion of a smile, that I was going to China. At any rate, he went on with perhaps rather suspicious emphasis, I would agree that the Soviet authorities had done everything in their power to help me on my way. With uncultivated people like the Chinese of course one never could tell. He only wished that he could have allowed me to await the answer of the Urumchi Government at Bakhti. But unfortunately it happened to be in a forbidden area. He would advise me to return to Alma Ata where I could get into touch with Urumchi through the Chinese Consul. It so happened that the bus which had brought me to Bakhti was still there. I could leave immediately.

Feeling that I was being made a fool of, I climbed back on to the bus. It was fuller than ever, and this time there were eight children. On the way we stopped at the village of Makanchi for a much-needed evening meal which we were given in the eating-house of the local collective farm: tea, vodka, fried eggs and beef-stew. The eating-house which was a converted mud hut, seemed to be monopolized by the higher *kolkhoz* officials whom I found engaged in preparations for the forthcoming elections to the Supreme Council of the Kazakh S.S.R.

These consisted in plastering the walls of every building inside and out with the not very prepossessing portrait of the local candidate, a typical officer of the N.K.V.D. troops. He was, needless to say, unopposed.

After driving all through the night I reached Ayaguz in time to throw myself on board a hard carriage bound for Alma Ata, where I arrived, tired, cross and dejected, twenty-four hours later.

On reaching Alma Ata, my first care was to call on the Plenipotentiary Representative of the People's Commissariat for Foreign Affairs, the same pleasant young Kazakh with whom I had had dealings the previous autumn. I explained to him what had happened and asked him to find me accommodation for two or three days while I endeavoured to communicate with Urumchi through the intermediary of the Chinese Consul. He was as usual extremely amiable and, after providing me with a letter to the director of the Dom Sovietov, the hotel where I had stayed on my first visit, proceeded to try to ring up the Chinese Consul on my behalf.

This proved to be no easy matter, and when, after the sixth attempt he had still not got through, I told him that I would walk round to the Chinese Consulate and see what I could do myself. He seemed a little embarrassed at the idea of my paying a personal call on the Chinese Consul and assured me that if I would leave it to him he would arrange everything for me himself. I thought it nevertheless better not to take advantage of his kind offer and set out to find the Chinese Consulate on my own.

It was a revealing experience. The consular offices were installed in a tumble-down native house in a side street. As I was about to enter the front door I was challenged very abruptly by the N.K.V.D. militiaman on duty outside, who asked me where I thought I was going. I replied that, although the matter scarcely concerned him, my intention was to call on the Chinese Consul. At this the militiaman, who had by now, I think, realized that I was not a native of Alma Ata filled with a sudden desire to move in consular society, entered the courtyard of the Consulate, closely followed by myself, and emitted a tremendous bellow. A seedy-looking Chinese appeared in answer to this somewhat unorthodox summons and was told in the most peremptory fashion to 'come and talk to this man'. The Chinese, who introduced himself as the Secretary of the Consulate, was evasive as to the whereabouts of the Consul but assured me that he himself would be glad to deal with any points I might wish to raise. I accordingly explained to him my business and asked him to send a wireless message to Urumchi requesting that instructions for my admission to Sinkiang should be sent to Chuguchak with as little delay as possible. At this he seemed slightly embarrassed and asked me whether I had been to see the Plenipotentiary Representative of the People's Commissariat for Foreign Affairs. He was afraid that the Soviet authorities might be opposed to my visiting Sinkiang. I pointed out that the Soviet authorities had done everything to facilitate my journey and added that I had already in the ordinary course of events been to see the Representative of the People's Commissariat for Foreign Affairs, although I did not see how this affected the matter. After extracting from him a promise to send an immediate wireless message to Urumchi I returned to the Representative of the People's Commissariat for Foreign Affairs to report progress.

The two offices were only a few hundred yards apart and I had hardly arrived there when the telephone rang. It was impossible for me not to hear that this was the Chinese Consulate asking the Government of the country in which it was stationed for instructions with regard to a matter which, in theory at any rate, exclusively concerned China and a third Power. The Plenipotentiary Representative, whom I suspected of being a little simple, made no attempt to disguise this fact from me and proceeded in my presence to authorize the Chinese Consulate to refer the matter to Urumchi without further delay. After putting down the receiver he said, not, I think, without a desire to show off, that he would see to it that an answer was obtained from Urumchi without delay. In the meanwhile, he said, I could rest after my journey and once again enjoy the amenities of Alma Ata. I accordingly went to the hotel and, after a good meal, lay down to rest with the feeling that if I had achieved nothing else my visits had at any rate thrown an interesting light on the position occupied by the Chinese Consulate at Alma Ata.

I was aroused from deep sleep by a loud knock at the door and, sitting up in bed, found myself in the presence of an imposing-looking officer of the N.K.V.D. Militia who opened the conversation somewhat abruptly by announcing that, as the laws of the Soviet Republics of Central Asia did not allow foreigners to reside there without special permission from the N.K.V.D., and as in my case the N.K.V.D. had no intention of giving such permission, I was to leave Alma Ata at once.

At this I got out of bed as quickly as I could and, asking the officer to sit down, proceeded to explain why I was in Alma Ata and pointed out that if the N.K.V.D. refused me permission to remain in Alma Ata until an answer had been received from Urumchi they would in fact be hindering me in the performance of my official duties after the Soviet Government had been requested to afford me all possible assistance on my journey. I further pointed out that I had spent a week in Alma Ata in the previous autumn when the N.K.V.D. had not only made no mention of the regulation which he was now quoting but had shown themselves most helpful in every way, and finally observed that, as there was a Plenipotentiary Representative of the People's Commissariat for Foreign Affairs in residence in Alma Ata, the N.K.V.D. should communicate with me through him and not direct.

The officer replied that he quite saw my point of view but that nevertheless I must leave by the first train. As to the Representative of the People's Commissariat for Foreign Affairs, he had made a mistake in obtaining accommodation for me, and this mistake, I could rest assured, would duly be brought to his notice. In any case he could assure me that the views of the People's Commissariat for Foreign Affairs carried very little weight with the N.K.V.D. He then cut short the discussion by leaving the room.

There was nothing for it but to return to my friend the Plenipotentiary Representative and ask his advice. Before I had had time to explain to him what had happened, he greeted me with the news that the Chinese Consulate had now received a reply from Urumchi and would like me to call in order that they might communicate it to me. In the circumstances I proceeded without delay to the Chinese Consulate where I was once again received by the dejected-looking Consular Secretary. Other Chinese drifted in and out of the room whilst we were talking, interrupting the conversation with vague but polite inquiries about the state of my health. I said I heard that the answer had come from Urumchi. Yes, they said, it had. The necessary instructions had now been sent to Chuguchak. They were to the effect that I was on no account to be allowed to cross the frontier. I said that I regarded the decision of the Provincial Government as most surprising and added that His Majesty's Government would in due course be informed of it. There ensued a further prolonged exchange of courtesies and I then took my leave.

There was no longer anything to keep me in Alma Ata, even if I had not been under an order of expulsion. But I was determined that if the N.K.V.D. wished me to leave Alma Ata, they should enable me to do so in style.

On being told that there were no first-class seats available on the Moscow train, I replied that while I could not prevent them from expelling me from Alma Ata I could at least insist that I should travel in comfort. At once the influence of the N.K.V.D. was brought to bear on the railway authorities, the necessary number of minor officials were arbitrarily evicted from the sleeping-car and I and my escort of police spies left for Moscow in luxury. Anything to get rid of me.

I had been scored off heavily and all the way back to Moscow I turned over in my mind ways of getting even with the N.K.V.D. Long before I arrived, I had decided that I would come back to Central Asia before the end of the year, whether they wanted me there or not. And next time I would not make them a present of my itinerary in advance.

CHAPTER IX

A LITTLE FURTHER

B Y the early autumn it had become clear that, for reasons outside my control, any further attempt on my part to reach Urumchi would have to be postponed at any rate until the spring of 1939. In the circumstances I decided instead to attempt a journey through Soviet Central Asia to the Oxus and thence through Afghan Turkestan to Kabul.

The possibility of the journey from India into Soviet Central Asia being undertaken by a British official had been considered from time to time in the past, but special permission would have been required, and the well-known unwillingness of the Soviet authorities to allow foreigners access to the Central Asian Republics made it extremely unlikely that they would have agreed to grant the necessary entrance visa.

My own case was different. Being in the Soviet Union already, all that I required, in theory at any rate, was a Soviet exit visa, and at that time the exit visas issued to members of the Diplomatic Corps were, strangely enough, technically valid for any frontier point. Having furnished myself, then, with an exit visa no different from those with which we regularly left the Soviet Union when bound for Paris or London, and an entry visa into Afghanistan, obtained discreetly and without difficulty from the Afghan Embassy, I set out again for Central Asia, for once at any rate theoretically well within my rights.

On my first visit to Soviet Turkestan I had left Moscow without informing the Soviet authorities of my intentions and consequently without visas or permits of any kind, and had banked simply on the assumption that, if they could be taken by surprise, their reactions would be too slow for them to put an effective stop to my activities before I had seen what I wanted to see. This had worked once, but was not likely to work again. The best proof was my expulsion from Alma Ata in June. Moreover, since my first trip the N.K.V.D. had taken to following me about everywhere, even in Moscow, where a car, containing sometimes as many as five men, waited outside any house that I visited and two plain-clothes agents sat behind me whenever I went to the theatre.

Careful thought was required. If, I reasoned, I were to travel to the Oxus direct without stopping or turning aside, the authorities were likely to make the best of a bad job and do everything in their power to get me out of Soviet Central Asia across the frontier into Afghanistan as quickly as possible. The prospect of travelling direct to the frontier did not, however, appeal to me particularly. The journey to the Oxus, like almost any journey through outlying parts of the Soviet Union, was likely to be in itself instructive and amusing. But in my eyes its principal interest lay in the fact that it would take me through the station of Kagan which is the nearest point to Bokhara on the main Central Asian line.

On my previous visit to Uzbekistan I had failed to reach Bokhara, and this had rankled, until in my mind it had come to outshine even Samarkand and the other legendary cities of Turkestan. It should, I now decided, be possible to pay an unobtrusive visit to the former capital of the Emirs, either on my way to Afghanistan or on my way back. At any rate, if I were to have trouble with the authorities my position would, I hoped, be pleasanter than that of the Hungarian, Vambery, who visited Bokhara in 1863, disguised as a dervish, and passed some months there knowing that capture meant a singularly disagreeable death in the pit, full of specially bred vermin and reptiles, which the Emir reserved for unwelcome visitors to his domains.

I left Moscow on October 7th by a more or less comfortable express train bound for Askhabad, the capital of Turkmenistan. Not only did it boast a restaurant-car which is apt to be a somewhat problematical feature of Soviet trains, but the crew of the latter turned out to be old friends, already encountered on a previous journey. I was greeted effusively and before I had had time to order anything was confronted with half a tumbler of vodka and a plate of cabbage soup, which had evidently stuck in my friends' memory as staple articles of my diet. My fellow passengers were for the most part officers of the N.K.V.D. Frontier Troops, travelling back to the outposts of empire on the Oxus and in the Pamirs, fully conscious of belonging to a *corps d'élite*.

For two whole days after leaving Moscow we travelled through European Russia: pine woods, birch woods; villages of decayed wooden *isbas* clustering round decayed white churches and inhabited by decayed-looking peasants; magpies on stumps, in flight and on telegraph wires; the Volga, a mighty stream.

On the third evening we reached Orenburg, which for more than one hundred years marked the furthest point of Russia's advance against the Kirghiz and Turkomans and the Khans of Bokhara and Khiva. On a previous occasion when I had passed through Orenburg, presumably merely on account of my doubtful appearance, I had been arrested on the platform outside my railway carriage and had almost been left behind. This time I was more careful and nothing untoward occurred.

By next morning we were well into Asia and for two days travelled through the Kara Kum or Black Desert, a howling wilderness of (paradoxically) pale red sand and parched and distorted shrubs and grass, its monotony broken half way through by the dreary storm-swept expanse of the Sea of Aral and its bleak mud flats. At the stopping-places the Kirghiz and Kazakh women in their high medieval head-dresses and long coats of dirty velvet came out of their round skin tents to sell us *kumiss*, fermented mare's or camel's milk, flat unleavened loaves, melons, skeins of camel-hair, dried fish from the Sea of Aral, necklaces of cockle-shells, and, occasionally, eggs. Remembering journeys when I had been entirely dependent on their products, I was glad of the restaurant-car with its cabbage soup.

In the middle of the fifth night we reached Tashkent and next morning awoke to find ourselves nearing the oasis of Samarkand. To the south, the mountains of Kirghizia, the westernmost extremity of the Tien Shan Range, were in sight and, instead of the Hungry Steppe, the vineyards and cotton fields of Uzbekistan. At the wayside stations, Uzbeks with oval faces and regular features in brightly striped *khalats*, sashes and turbans or embroidered skull-caps had taken the place of the Kazakhs and Kirghiz in their sheepskins. In the villages flat-roofed houses of sun-baked mud bricks had replaced the skin tents of the nomads.

During the long train journey I had had plenty of time to consider my plans and had decided not to postpone my attempt to reach Bok-

hara until my return journey. I would go there at once. Samarkand
would have to be left this time, unless I were to prejudice my chances
of reaching Bokhara; and so I resisted the temptation to revisit the
glittering domes of Shakh Zinda and the Gur Emir, and reluctantly
contented myself with buying some grapes for my breakfast on the
platform of Samarkand railway station. Westwards from Samarkand
I was travelling through a part of Uzbekistan which was new to me,
but which had little to distinguish it from the country further east,
except that it was perhaps rather more fertile, for we were now following the course of the Zaravshan, the river which waters the oases of
both Samarkand and Bokhara.

At Kagan, which we reached in the afternoon, and which looked
very much like any other small Soviet railway station, I shouldered my
luggage and slipped unobtrusively from the train. Two alert-looking
young men, whom I had already noticed in the dining-car, did so too.
I deposited my luggage in the luggage office. They followed my
example. I strolled into the station buffet. They came too, developing
a sudden interest in a bun whenever I stopped. There was no doubt
who they were. So long, however, as they did not interfere with me,
I had no objection to being followed by them. If, as I suspected, their
purpose was to see what I did, rather than to stop me from doing it, I
had no reason to anticipate trouble from them. What I needed to
avoid at all costs was unduly attracting the attention of the local
authorities who were far more likely to interfere.

My first object was to ascertain as discreetly as possible how to get to
Bokhara. I believed that an occasional train still ran along what used
once to be the Emir's State Railway. This idea, however, had to be
abandoned almost immediately, for the first person I met on emerging
from the luggage office was a portly local Jewess lamenting loudly that
the only train of the day had already gone and that there was no bus
service. While I was condoling with her and wondering what to do
next, I caught sight of a lorry laden with bales of cotton moving off
down the only road in sight which, I felt, probably led to Bokhara. A
short sprint and a flying jump landed me head first in a rather loosely
packed bale of cotton, from which I emerged to see one of my N.K.V.D.
men running after the lorry, which he obviously had not a hope of

catching, while the other disappeared into the door of the Militia guard-room presumably in order to get help. Meanwhile, the lorry, with me on board, was heading for the open country and showing a pretty turn of speed. The situation, I felt, was fraught with amusing possibilities.

At this point the lorry suddenly stopped for no apparent reason, and a few seconds later a breathless N.K.V.D. man landed in the next cotton bale to mine. I felt reassured and hoped that his colleague would not now persist in his intention of turning out the guard and that I should be able to complete my journey to Bokhara undisturbed in this providential vehicle.

But this was not to be. The sight of two people jumping on to a lorry had put the same idea into a number of other heads. There was a rush and we were trampled over and rolled on as the lorry filled with a variegated crowd of Uzbeks, kicking and biting, as only Uzbeks can, in their efforts to get themselves on and their friends off.

All might yet have been well, had not the driver, who had let in the clutch and was moving off again, at this point put his head round the corner and caught sight of this multitude of uninvited passengers. It was, he said, overdoing it. One or two might pass, but not a whole crowd. We must all get off at once. There ensued a general argument which ended in the driver letting down the sides of the lorry and pushing off as many of his passengers as he could reach, while others climbed in again on the other side.

This might have lasted indefinitely, when I saw something which caused me to get off the lorry hurriedly and disappear into some trees at the side of the road where I was joined by my N.K.V.D. man.

A car was coming down the road from the station, containing my other N.K.V.D. man and a uniformed officer of State Security. Meanwhile the lorry, having got rid of most of its passengers, had started once again on its way. It was quickly overtaken by the police car and stopped a hundred yards further on. The driver was made to get out and was cross-questioned and finally every bale of cotton was gone through. Meanwhile the first N.K.V.D. man, crouching beside me in the bushes, remained, inexplicably, where he was without giving any sign of life. As I watched the progress of the search from my hiding-place, I decided that the interest which the local authorities were showing in my movements was far from reassuring. I consoled myself, however, with the thought that the zeal which they were now displaying might peter out, as so many things do peter out in Central Asia.

Having completed his search of the lorry and allowed the somewhat bewildered driver to proceed on his way, the officer of State Security now climbed back into his car and drove off, leaving his plain-clothes colleague from the capital standing in the middle of the road. From the bushes, I watched his departure with feelings of unmixed relief. I had by this time decided that my only hope of reaching Bokhara was to walk there and wondered why I had not thought of this before. My ideas about distance were vague, but I had an idea that the Emir's little train was supposed to take about an hour, so that it could not be very far. The road taken by the lorry was the only one in sight, so I came out of the bushes and started off along it, while my escort fell in behind at a discreet distance, wondering, I imagine, what was coming next.

Apart from the railway station, N.K.V.D. Headquarters, one or two cotton mills and a distressing structure of uncertain use combining all the worst features of both European and Oriental architecture, Kagan has little claim to be called a town, and we were soon in the open country. On either side of the road flowering fields of cotton stretched as far as the eye could reach, intersected by irrigation ditches. From time to time I passed clusters of two or three native farmsteads amid poplars and other trees. Through an occasional open gate, set in high mud walls, I caught sight of a courtyard, with, in the living-quarters on the far side, an open door and a fire burning in the living-room. Uzbek houses have changed very little since the days of Tamerlane.

From time to time the road branched and I was left in some doubt whether to go to the left or the right. The sun was setting and the prospect of spending the night wandering about Uzbekistan looking for Bokhara in an entirely wrong direction did not appeal to me. On the whole I allowed myself to be guided by the endless caravans of two-humped Bactrian dromedaries, which, I imagined, were, like myself, making for the city of Bokhara. The peculiarly sweet tone of their bells sounded reassuring in the gathering darkness. Behind me my followers in their neat Moscow-made blue suits and bright yellow shoes padded along disconsolately in the acrid-smelling, ankle-deep dust.

I walked for what seemed a very long time. It was by now quite dark and there was still no sign of Bokhara. I had come to feel less well-disposed towards the dromedaries. With their vast bales of merchandise they took up the whole road entangling me in their head ropes, breathing menacingly down my neck and occasionally lumbering up against me and pushing me into the ditch.

I was beginning to wonder if I had not after all taken the wrong road, and, if so, where it would lead me, when I noticed that the sky in the direction in which I was walking seemed slightly more luminous than elsewhere. It might, or it might not, be the reflected lights of a city. Soon the farmsteads along the road and in the fields became more numerous and the road took me between high mud walls enclosing orchards of apricot trees. It was very unlike the Soviet Union.

Then all at once the road took a turn, and topping a slight rise I found myself looking down on the broad white walls and watch towers of Bokhara spread out before me in the light of the rising moon.

CHAPTER X

BOKHARA THE NOBLE

IMMEDIATELY in front of me stood one of the city gates, its great arch set in a massive fortified tower which rose high above the lofty crenellated walls. Following a string of dromedaries I passed through it into the city.

I possessed a fair knowledge of the writings of most of the European travellers who visited Bokhara during the past century and this made easier the task of identifying the principal buildings. Entering the city from the south east, I followed the fairly straight street leading to the bazaars and centre of the town which has for centuries been followed by travellers and caravans from India, Persia and Afghanistan.

It was along this street that there passed in 1845, to the consternation of the population who had assembled in their thousands to witness his arrival, the Reverend Joseph Wolff, D.D., 'garbed', by his own account, in 'full canonicals', clergyman's gown, doctor's hood and shovel hat, and carrying a bible under his arm. By origin a Bavarian Jew, the son of a Rabbi, by vocation (after a brief but spirited passage with the Pope) a Church of England clergyman, the Eccentric Missionary, as he was known to his contemporaries, had set out at an advanced age to ascertain the fate of Colonel Stoddart and Captain Conolly, two British officers who had been sent sometime previously by Her Majesty's Government on a mission to the Court of the Emir Nasrullah, with the ultimate aim of making Bokhara a British dominion before it became a Russian one.

Dr. Wolff ascertained the fate of the envoys soon enough. After months of what was in fact imprisonment they had been consigned to the well, twenty-one feet deep, where the Emir kept his specially bred vermin and reptiles. When, two months later, 'masses of their flesh having been gnawed off their bones', they had finally refused to turn Mussulman, they had been beheaded outside the Citadel. This had happened many months before Wolff's arrival. He himself attributed the failure of the mission to the action of the Prime Minister, 'that bloodhound Abdul Samut Khan, in whose character, it seems to me, the Foreign Office has been deceived'.

Soon the question of his own religious proclivities was raised. The Chief Executioner was sent, a little pointedly, by Abdul Samut Khan to ask him whether he was prepared to embrace Islam. To this inquiry he replied 'Decidedly not!' and sat down to write a farewell letter to his wife, the Lady Georgiana,[1] with whom he had kept up an animated correspondence throughout his journey.

But his life, as it turned out, was saved by the strangeness of his appearance and behaviour. On his being brought before the Emir, still clad in full canonicals and with his bible still under his arm, that potentate, of whom he writes vividly, 'His Majesty has the whole appearance of a *bon vivant*', was seized with a fit of uncontrollable laughter, which redoubled when the Eccentric Missionary prostrated himself thirty times, stroked his beard thirty times and cried 'Allah Akbar' thirty times, instead of the usual three. For, though not prepared to become a Mohammedan, Dr. Wolff was ready to go to considerable lengths in order to keep out of the vermin pit. The interview was thus a distinct success and culminated with the appearance of a 'musical band of Hindoos from Lahore' who gave a spirited rendering of 'God Save the Queen'. After further adventures, which included his temptation by means of an unveiled woman specially sent for this purpose by the Prime Minister, Dr. Wolff was eventually suffered to leave Bokhara, greatly to the surprise of the population, who were not accustomed to such clemency and hailed the Emir's astonishing decision as a sign from heaven.

Following in the steps of the Eccentric Missionary, I reached the centre of the town. Seen thus, Bokhara seemed an enchanted city, with its pinnacles and domes and crumbling ramparts white and dazzling in the pale light of the moon. High above them all rose the Tower of Death, the oldest and most magnificent of the minarets. Built seven hundred years ago by the Karakhanides, who ruled in Bokhara before the Mongol invasion and the advent of Genghis Khan, it vies in purity of line and beauty of ornament with the finest architec-

[1] Daughter of Lord Orford.

ture of the Italian Renaissance. For centuries before 1870, and again in the troubled years between 1917 and 1920, men were cast down to their death from the delicately ornamented gallery which crowns it. Today a great Red Flag flaps from its summit.

Before me gaped one of the cavernous tunnels of the covered bazaar. There I bought from a plump Uzbek merchant sitting cross-legged at the entrance of his dimly lighted shop a flat round loaf of sour-tasting black bread, some fruit and a bottle of sweet red wine, and, repairing to the garden of a nearby mosque, sat down under a bush to rest and eat. Under the central arch of the old mosque the present rulers of Bokhara had erected a gleaming new white marble monument to Lenin and Stalin, lavishly draped with red bunting.

As I took a pull at my bottle of wine, I became aware of someone hovering uncertainly near me, and a quavering voice said, 'Please leave some for me.' Then a very frail, very tattered old Russian, with long white drooping moustaches emerged ghostlike from the shadows and stood waiting expectantly. I gave him the wine. Tilting back his head, he raised the bottle to his mouth. There was a sound of gurgling, and he put it down empty. Then, with a mumbled word of thanks, he shuffled off into the darkness, leaving me with an odd sense of satisfaction at having thus by chance supplied a much felt need.

Cheered by this encounter and by my share of the wine, I took another stroll through the empty streets, and then returned to the garden, which I had decided to make my home for as long as I remained in Bokhara.

An attempt to secure a bed in one of the *chai-khanas* would have necessitated the production of documents and probably have led to trouble with the local authorities. So long as I did not formally announce my presence, they were not formally obliged to take steps to get rid of me, and my chief concern was accordingly to avoid any kind of incident which would have made it necessary for me to declare my identity. I therefore made myself as comfortable as I could under some shrubs, while my escort reluctantly followed my example a few yards away. They were not, I think, particularly pleased. They had taken a good deal more exercise than they liked; they had been made to look at a great many ancient monuments in which they were not particularly interested and, worst of all, their evening's work had added nothing to their knowledge of British intrigues in Soviet Central Asia.

Wrapped in my greatcoat I passed the remainder of the night undisturbed. After midnight few of the inhabitants venture out, and there was no noise save in the distance the snarling and barking of the thousands of dogs which stray about the streets, the melancholy whistling of the night-watchmen and the flapping of the great Red Flag on the Tower of Death.

Next day I resumed my wanderings through the town. My escort had now been reinforced by an Uzbek colleague, an amiable native of Bokhara, with whom I soon made friends and who showed me my way about, told me in broken Russian where I could buy the local products and even helped me to identify some of the buildings. He was a simple soul, clearly delighted at coming into contact with a genuine foreigner, especially one so full of admiration for his native city.

In many ways Bokhara resembles Samarkand or the old city of Tashkent. There are the same intricate labyrinth of narrow lanes between high windowless mud walls, the same jostling, brightly clad crowds in the streets, pushed aside here and there to make way for strings of donkeys or camels, the same *chai-khanas* crowded with clients sitting on piles of carpets, drinking tea, talking, telling each other stories, or selling each other whatever comes to hand.

But, while in Tashkent and Samarkand East and West lie side by side and often intermingle in the most disconcerting way, Bokhara has remained, and, I think, cannot but remain, so long as it survives at all, wholly Eastern.

With the capture in 1868 of Samarkand and the upper reaches of the Zaravshan by the Russians, who thus gained control of his water supply, the Emir of Bokhara was obliged to accept the suzerainty of the Tsar and Russian control of his relations with the outside world; but inside his own dominions he maintained his own army and enjoyed absolute power of life and death over his unfortunate subjects. The Russian population was limited to a few officials and merchants, while the Emir excluded other Europeans from his domains with a jealousy which has been emulated by his Bolshevik successors. Bokhara thus remained a centre of Mohammedan civilization, a holy city with a hundred mosques, three hundred places of learning, and the richest bazaar in Central Asia. It was not until 1920, three years after the downfall of his imperial suzerain, that the last Emir, after vainly invoking the help of both the Turks and the British, fled headlong across the Oxus to Afghanistan, dropping favourite dancing boy after favourite dancing boy in his flight, in the hope of thus retarding the advance of the pursuing Red Army, who, however, were not to be distracted from their purpose by such stratagems. A leading part was played in these events by the same Faisullah Khojayev, whom I had seen condemned to death in Moscow six months earlier.

In Bokhara the process of Sovietization can have been neither rapid nor easy. The population were accustomed to being oppressed and tortured by the Emirs, but they were not accustomed to interference with their age-old customs and their religion. There were the mullahs to be reckoned with, who possessed great influence over the population, and there were the capitalist class, the Begs, the merchants, both large and small, and the landowners.

The problem which faced the Bolsheviks in the domains of the former Emir, and particularly in such a stronghold of Moslem culture as the city of Bokhara itself, was as hard as any with which they were confronted in Central Asia. The solution adopted was perhaps the only one possible. The capital of the Emirs could not be converted into a Soviet town unless it was to be razed to the ground and built up afresh. And so it was left to decay. In contrast to that of most provincial towns in the Soviet Union, which in many cases has increased tenfold, the population of Bokhara has fallen steadily until now it is less than half what it was thirty years ago. With the exception of a highly incongruous Pedagogic Institute which has made a somewhat half-hearted appearance within its walls, the dying city of Bokhara has remained purely Eastern. The only changes are those which have been wrought by neglect, decay and demolition.

The city is still surrounded by its high crenellated walls with their eleven gates and one hundred and eighty-one watch towers, believed by some to be a thousand years old. Immediately inside the walls on the outskirts of the city lie what must once have been the gardens and houses of the rich. Outwardly little has changed, and the high walls, pierced by no windows, make it impossible to tell by whom they are now occupied.

In the centre of the town, clustering round the Tower of Death stand the principal mosques: the Kalyan, or Kok Gumbaz (Blue Dome), formerly the place of worship of the Emir, and the vast Mir Arab which lies beyond the Tower of Death and formerly possessed the largest *madresseh* in Central Asia. Neither is of great architectural beauty, though the dome from which the Kok Gumbaz gains its name, with its tiles of the brilliant blue only found in Turkestan, provides pleasant relief from the dust-coloured buildings which surround it. Both were built in the sixteenth or seventeenth century.

Like those in Tashkent and Samarkand, the mosques and *madressehs* of Bokhara are constructed of mud bricks of different shades of pale red and brown. The design is nearly always the same: in the centre of the façade, the central arch or *pishtak*, reaching the whole height of the building, with, on either side, a double row of smaller arches. In the *madressehs* the central arch forms the entrance to one or more court-yards surrounded by cloisters and rows of cells. Most of the mosques in Bokhara have lost the coloured tiles which formerly adorned their façades and which to a large extent still survive in Samarkand; but the *madressehs* of Ulug Beg and Abdul Azis, which stand facing each other not far away from the Tower of Death have retained that much of their former splendour, their façades being still decorated with their original intricate arabesques. The Ulug Beg *madresseh*, like the *madresseh* of the same name in Samarkand, was built by Ulug Beg, the grandson of Tamerlane and famous astronomer, at the beginning of the fifteenth century. Bokhara abounds with smaller mosques and *madressehs*. Of the former a very few are still in use, but for the most part they stand abandoned or have been turned to other uses. Everywhere heaps of masonry and rubble testify to the process of demolition, which is robbing the city of its splendours.

Round the Tower of Death and the principal mosques lies the bazaar quarter. Formerly the covered bazaars stretched for miles throughout the centre of the town. Now little is left of what was once the richest bazaar in Central Asia save the Char-su or clusters of domes at the points where two or more bazaar streets intersect. A few shops and stalls still survive, but individual enterprise, though possibly it survives in Central Asia to a greater extent than elsewhere in the Soviet Union, has been all but stamped out, and even the brightly striped *khalats* are now produced by collectivized seamstresses working under the auspices of some State combine or trust. Only the fruit and vegetable bazaars have retained something of their former magnificence with their splendid heaps of grapes and melons.

Not far from the Kalyan and Mir Arab mosques, on the north-west side of the town, rises the grim thousand-year-old Ark or Citadel of the Emirs, where Stoddart and Conolly and innumerable other prisoners met such singularly unpleasant ends. Constructed on an artificial mound, its lofty walls and crumbling fortifications cover an enormous amount of ground. The entrance gate, with its twin turrets, now bears, in Russian and Uzbek, the inscription, 'Town Soviet'. In front of it stretches a large open space, formerly the Registan, or main square of the city, but now bereft of any signs of life. Shakh Rud, a canal linked with the Zaravshan and constituting the city's only water supply, still flows through Bokhara, but many of the *khaus*, or tanks, which were formerly filled by it, seem to have been abolished, no doubt in an attempt to check the ravages of the Sartian Sickness or Bokhara Boil so prevalent in Uzbekistan and largely due to the particular foulness of the water.

I could have spent months in Bokhara, seeking out fresh memories of its prodigious past, mingling with the bright crowds in the bazaar, or simply idling away my time under the apricot trees in the clear warm sunlight of Central Asia. But my position was precarious and my time limited. Reluctantly I decided that it was time for me to continue my journey to the Oxus.

My decision was greeted with enthusiasm by my two followers. They had never taken to Bokhara, finding the alfresco existence we led there particularly trying. Now that we were leaving, they were too tired even to walk to the station, and their Uzbek colleague had to make room for all three of us in a very small bus, already completely filled by rank-smelling local inhabitants in their padded chintz *khalats*. This took us to the point outside the walls where the Emir's little train was waiting with an antiquated engine and two or three open coaches. Up and down the train, wandered a very old blind man with a straggling white beard and an elaborate and very dirty turban, chanting prayers in a high nasal wail and gathering a large crop of kopeks from his fellow passengers.

Eventually the train started and eventually we arrived at Kagan. The next thing was to take the first train bound for Stalinabad, the capital of Tajikstan. This was not so easy. To have left a through train at a point which was not a terminus was a risky step in the, at times, rather painful game of railway travel in the Soviet Union. The trains which pass through such wayside stations generally come in completely full. If there are any vacant places, they are given to travelling officials or Red Army soldiers. The general public simply waits in the station, sometimes for days, until something turns up. This had happened to me in the past and I was determined that it should not happen to me now. I accordingly explained to my escort, with whom I was by now on quite intimate terms, though we kept up the polite fiction that we were simply travellers whose ways happened to coincide, where I wanted to go, adding casually that, if by any chance I should fail to obtain accommodation on the train, I should simply walk back to Bokhara, with which, I said, I had been most favourably impressed. This hint of more walking exercise did the trick. The stationmaster, that most elusive of Soviet officials, was found almost immediately. A word was whispered in his ear, and, when the next south-bound train came in, room was somehow made for us in a hard coach. It was, we were told, the best that could be done.

My intention had been to get some sleep on the way in order to be fresh for my impending struggle with the frontier authorities in the early hours of next morning and so I stretched myself on one of the hard wooden shelves, from which the 'hard' carriage gets its name. But this was not to be. 'Hard' carriages are always lively places. This was the liveliest I had ever experienced. My immediate neighbours were two dark-skinned, almond-eyed characters in *khalats* and skull-caps. I had no sooner got to sleep than they dug me in the ribs and introduced themselves as Tajiks. They had been in Kirghizstan, they said, and were going back to their native Tajikistan, which was a much better place and they were sorry they had left it. Where had I come from and where was I going to? I explained that I had come from Frengistan (roughly: Europe) and was going to Afghanistan and possibly Hindustan. This did not seem to convey much to them, though they must have spent most of their lives within a hundred miles of the North-West Frontier of India, and though, as recently as ten years ago, the Tajiks were known to have been collecting sterling by devious means and smuggling it across the frontier to the Aga Khan, whom they still regard as their spiritual leader. But now, all possible contact with the outer world had been cut off and interest in outside affairs had waned correspondingly, at any rate amongst the uneducated classes, though a Russian I once met told me that Tajikstan was full of people who spoke English fluently.

Having found out all they wanted to know about me, and having observed that 'anyone with so many belongings' (I had a kitbag and a rather disreputable bundle) must be a rich man, the two Tajiks now proceeded to regale me with an account of their own affairs. They were, they said, laughing heartily, poor men, and badly treated at that. They had been sent to Kirghizia to build a road in some horrible mountains. (They were far from explicit, but must I think have meant the new road from Frunze to Osh.) They had been badly housed and only given eighty roubles (rather less than sixteen shillings) a month, which was not enough to live on. They were glad to have seen the last of Kirghizia.

They next proceeded, still laughing loudly (for they were irrepressibly cheerful), to pass round a bottle of bright pink vodka and then to take off the elaborate system of wrappings swathed round their feet in the place of socks. This, they explained to me, somewhat superfluously, was a thing they only very rarely did, but they thought it might interest me as a Frengi. I could not help wishing that they had postponed the operation a little longer.

Then we all went to sleep for a time, one of the Tajiks occasionally waking me, in order to tell me of some amusing thought which had occurred to him. This happy state of affairs did not last long. Soon, a Russian with a basket of vodka bottles and another basket of pink Soviet sausages appeared and announced that the shelves on which we were lying were reserved for refreshments. We said that we had never heard of such a thing, but the consensus of opinion in the carriage seemed to be definitely on the side of the sausage seller, who had all the demagogic attributes of his classical prototype, and we eventually suffered ourselves to be moved, protesting, to some other shelves further up.

I now gave up all hope of sleep and spent the rest of the daylight looking out of the window. We were travelling through typical Central Asian country, occasional oases and stretches of pale, yellowish desert, broken by ranges of low red hills, across which the pilgrims used to make their Golden Journey. At intervals there were strange-looking tumuli. To pass the time I discussed their origin in a desultory manner with my neighbours. These now included an elderly and benevolent Russian couple, who seemed perpetually concerned at the discomfort in which they imagined me to be, and a rather weedy young man, travelling to Central Asia for the first time to take up an appointment in Stalinabad, who kept on comparing 'all this sand' most unfavourably with the forests and villages of European Russia. We did not come to any particular conclusion about the tumuli.

Meanwhile, the sausages and vodka had begun to have their effect. A little further up the carriage a group of travellers had formed themselves into what is known in the Soviet Union as an *ansambl* or concert party, and were giving spirited renderings of various folk-songs and dances. Vodka flowed more and more freely and soon pandemonium was let loose. Even the elderly couple's benevolent smile broadened into a bleary grin. Several members of the party were entirely overcome by their exertions and we had to hoist them like sacks on to the top shelves, from which at intervals they crashed ten feet to the floor, without any apparent ill effects. When we reached my destination, Termez, an hour or two before dawn, the party was at its height.

For the last part of the journey the railway had followed the course of the Oxus (Amu Darya) passing through eastern Turkmenistan. The far bank of the river was Afghan territory. It only remained to get across the river. I foresaw that it would take a lot of doing.

I was right.

ACROSS THE OXUS

M Y first care, on alighting from the train at Termez, was to establish contact with the local authorities, who, I imagined would, as soon as they became aware of my presence, lose no time in getting me over the frontier and out of the way.

The Militia officer at the station was most accommodating. He put me on a lorry with a mixed escort of a dozen Militia and N.K.V.D. troops, somehow reminiscent, in the bleak half light that precedes the dawn, of a firing squad, and dispatched me to the centre of the town. If, he said, I would present myself at Militia Headquarters at eight, the necessary arrangements would immediately be made for me to cross the river.

At eight I was duly received by the local Chief of Militia, a corpulent Uzbek of great complacency, who explained amiably that he could do nothing until twelve o'clock because the frontier guards did not get up till then. I said that in the meanwhile I would do some shopping and have some food. I was provided with an official escort of one uniformed militiaman, who was told, in a loud aside, that there were to be 'no personal conversations', and, thus accompanied, I started out to explore Termez.

Like almost every other town between Tashkent and Kabul, Termez was founded by Alexander the Great, sacked by Genghis Khan in about 1220 and later visited by the Spanish traveller, Clavijo, in whose day it was so considerable a city that the noise made by its inhabitants could be heard at Balkh, sixty miles away across the Oxus. Now, nothing remains of its former splendour save a few ruins in the country to the north of the town, and it is like any other Russian settlement in Central Asia, the new town having been entirely built since 1894, when the Tsar took over the fortress of Termez from the Emir of Bokhara and made it the principal Russian military post on the Afghan frontier.

Accompanied by my militiaman, who carried my purchases and

whose presence greatly increased my prestige with the shopkeepers, I wandered up and down the broad dusty avenues of low white shops and houses and eventually succeeded in accumulating an enormous round loaf, some melons and some eggs. From this comparatively successful expedition, I returned to Militia Headquarters and, after further attempts at prevarication by the Commanding Officer, was eventually put into a car and sent down to the frontier post on the river bank, where, I was assured, all arrangements had been made for my passage across the river.

The frontier post is situated at Patta Hissar. Along the river, stretch for a mile or so in a narrow strip, the barracks of the frontier troops, the officers' bungalows and piles of merchandise awaiting transshipment; then, as far as the eye can reach, a jungle of reeds ten or eleven feet high, reputed to harbour tigers as well as a great deal of smaller game. The Oxus must at this point be almost a mile wide, a vast muddy river full of mud flats and sandbanks, flowing between low mud banks. I have seen more exciting rivers, but its name and the knowledge that very few Europeans except Soviet frontier guards have ever seen it at this, or any other point of its course, made up for its rather drab appearance. In the distance there were some blue mountains.

The captain of the frontier guards, a smart-looking young Russian officer, received me most politely, but on hearing that I wished to cross the river, looked surprised and distressed. Previous experience of Soviet methods prevented me from feeling much astonishment on now realizing that the Town Militia had made no attempt whatever to communicate with the frontier post. I said that it was admittedly unfortunate that he had not been warned of my arrival, but that I imagined that this need not delay matters. At this he looked more embarrassed than ever, and I was filled with gloomy forebodings.

They were fully justified. The frontier, he said, was not working. I said: Did he mean it was closed? He said: No, he would not go so far as to say that; it just wasn't working. Nobody knew when it would start working again and in the circumstances he would advise me to return to Moscow and see if I could not take an aeroplane to Kabul. It would be much more comfortable. I saw that it was not going to be an easy matter to get across the river that day.

After an hour or two I had extracted from my interlocutor the admission that, while the frontier would in effect have been closed to anyone else, he would, in view of my official position, in principle have been prepared to let me cross it, if there had been any means of getting me across. Unfortunately there were no boats. I asked him whether he meant to tell me that there was not so much as a rowing boat on the whole of the Oxus? He replied that there were three paddle boats, but two were completely out of action and the third was undergoing a *kapitalny remont* or complete overhaul. If I waited a day or two, it might be possible to put her into commission.

This, I felt, was a distinct advance. At any rate I should get across the Oxus sooner or later. It now only remained to accelerate the *remont* of the third paddle boat. I observed that on a recent visit to the Chinese border I had gathered that foreigners were not allowed to linger in the frontier zones of the Soviet Union. Moreover, I had reasons of my own for wishing to be in Afghanistan that same day. From what I had heard of Soviet 'shock' methods a group of Stakhanovites or shock-workers should be able to put any paddle boat in order in an hour or two. He said: Possibly, but he must first get authority from his Commanding Officer.

This was a blow, as nobody knew where the Commanding Officer was. By about four in the afternoon, however, his authority having either been obtained or dispensed with, to my considerable surprise, a 'brigade' of somewhat half-hearted-looking 'shock-workers' appeared, and we went down to look at the craft at my disposal. Two paddle boats were obviously incapable of keeping afloat. The third, which rejoiced in the name of *Seventeenth Party Congress*, though, to judge by her antiquated appearance, she must have been built long before the Communist Party was ever thought of, was handicapped by the absence of an engine or motor of any kind. Eventually it was decided to take the motor out of one of the first two and transfer it to the third. It turned out to be an ordinary unadapted tractor motor from the Stalin Factory, and as it was heaved on the shoulders of the shock brigade I felt glad that I was not embarking on a more considerable voyage.

While the finishing touches were being put to the *Seventeenth Party*

Congress, I stood talking to the Captain of the frontier guards and his wife and children, all well dressed and good-looking in a stolid Soviet kind of way. Proudly displaying his dog, an amiable animal of uncertain parentage, which he explained was a cross between a pointer and a setter, the Captain told me that he was something of a shot and frequently went out, not only after the Trotskists and Diversionists, with which the frontiers of the Soviet Union were known to swarm, but also after pheasant and sometimes even wild pig and tigers. He told me, too, that he was learning English from a work entitled *London from the top of an Omnibus* which made him feel as if he had known Westminster Abbey and Buckingham Palace all his life. For purposes of conversation, however, his knowledge of the English language seemed to be limited to the one cryptic expression: 'Very well by us!' of which he was inordinately proud, and it was to repeated shouts of 'Very well by us!', heartily reciprocated by myself, that some time later I embarked on the *Seventeenth Party Congress*.

Once I was on board, the Red Flag was hoisted; the crew of seven counted and recounted in case any should try to escape; the tractor engine (an anxious moment) started up; and we set out on our somewhat unsteady course across the Oxus. On the river bank my plain-clothes escort stood and waved their handkerchiefs — somewhat ironically, I thought, but then our relations had been tinged with irony from the start.

The crossing took half an hour or more, the sandbanks making navigation rather complicated. From the upper floor of the two-storeyed cottage which combined the functions of bridge, engine-room and sleeping-quarters for the crew, I commanded an extensive view of the river and of the jungle on both shores, with, on the Soviet side, watch towers at intervals and a patrol of frontier troops setting out to look for Diversionists. On the Afghan side there was, as far as I could see, nothing except jungle.

Such knowledge as I possessed of the point for which we were making was derived from the narrative of Colonel Grodekov of the Imperial Army who in 1878 earned himself the name of 'The Russian Burnaby' by riding (in full uniform) from Samarkand to Mazar-i-Sharif and Herat, an exploit which appears to have caused considerable amusement to the natives and no little alarm to Her Majesty's Government, who were at that time perturbed by the situation in Afghanistan and suspicious, as indeed they had reason to be, of Russian policy in Central Asia. Colonel Grodekov, who had ridden from Bokhara to Patta Hissar, where he too crossed the Oxus, had not a good word to say for the point at which he landed on the Afghan side, which, as far as I could make out, is also called Patta Hissar. Any village which had ever been there had long since slid into the river and been washed away. All he found was three reed huts and a small group of rather hostile Afghans. It had been his intention to push on to Mazar-i-Sharif and thus avoid spending a night in a place where 'it was clear to him that he would catch ague'. He was, however, forced by the Afghans to spend a night in one of the reed huts and almost lost his life next morning by explaining to an audience of devout Moslems, in his anxiety to impart knowledge, that the brush with which he was cleaning his teeth was made of the best hog's bristles.

When we had approached close enough to the Afghan bank, I saw that there were perhaps a dozen Afghans standing on it, watching us come in. Two were soldiers in uniform; the remainder wore *khalats* and turbans. In the background there were three circular reed huts exactly like the *kibitkas* of Russian Central Asia. There were also two or three horses. Apart from these there was nothing except the jungle.

The *Seventeenth Party Congress* grounded with a bump, a plank was put down, my luggage was hastily tossed to me, the engines were reversed, and that remarkable craft started off stern first for the Soviet Union as if the whole capitalist world was infected with the plague. At this point it occurred to me rather forcibly that I knew not a word of Persian or Urdu and that my knowledge of Turki was limited to about a dozen not very useful phrases.

As a first step, the twelve Afghans, to whom I was later to become quite attached, picked my baggage out of the mud and deposited it in a neat heap near the huts. The sun now set. My luggage was abandoned; carpets were produced; a mullah appeared, and the whole twelve turned in what I imagine to have been the direction of Mecca and prostrated themselves. By the time they had completed their devotions it was quite dark. They next inspected my passport and *laissez-passer*, which did not seem to convey anything to them at all. As I spoke neither Persian nor Urdu, and they spoke no European language, while neither party spoke any Turki worth mentioning, we were, until I had acquired three or four useful words of Persian, entirely reduced to signs. I accordingly said 'Mazar-i-Sharif' very loud and clear and made as if to get on to one of the horses. In reply my audience gave me to understand that I had better have something to eat (gesture) and then go to sleep (gesture) and we would see about Mazar-i-Sharif tomorrow (series of gestures of extreme complication accompanied by shouts of Mazar-i-Sharif from all present).

From Colonel Grodekov's narrative I had gathered that Mazar was about one hundred versts (roughly, 60 miles) away, through jungle and desert, so that this advice seemed on the whole sound. Some food was produced and tea made, one of the reed huts cleared out, carpets spread and a charpoy installed and, after an adequate meal, I retired to rest, while one of the soldiers took up his position on guard outside. I have seldom slept better.

Next morning at dawn a delegation came to watch me pack my few belongings. Everything pleased them enormously, but nothing so much as a copy of the *New Yorker*, thoughtfully provided by my American colleagues before my departure from Moscow, and which I now left behind, a morsel of American culture on the shores of the Oxus. Two horses were then led forward with high Turkoman saddles adorned with inconveniently situated brass bosses and enormous stirrups permanently and irremediably the wrong length. I mounted one and one of the Afghans mounted the other. My bundles were packed into saddle-bags and distributed between us and after cordial farewells we set off at a rapid, uncomfortable amble into the jungle.

After a few miles riding we emerged from the reeds of the jungle into the desert. It was very much like any other desert in Central Asia, with its dunes of drifting sand and shrivelled tamarisk bushes. Marmots with their short forelegs, long hindlegs and bushy tails whistled petulantly and scuttled in and out of their holes. From time to time we came on the bleached skeletons of horses and camels. Then, after some miles of crawling up sand dunes and slithering down the other side, we came out on to a flat, completely barren plain with absolutely nothing in sight. Underfoot was hard white clay. There was no road, but something approaching a track had been worn by the caravans making their way down to the Oxus.

Finally, after riding for a good many miles we sighted a large *sarai*, or mud fort, standing on a slight rise. My companion signed to me to keep away from it, but I was anxious to see it from nearer and was riding towards it, when a horseman, a splendid figure, armed to the teeth, and riding a very much better horse than either of us could boast, emerged from the gate at full gallop and rounded us up. We were taken inside the crenellated walls of the *sarai* and made to dismount. A score of Afghans in turbans and *khalats* clustered round me, jabbering excitedly. Then I was led into a small room in which there were a great many flies and a rack of German service rifles.

The inhabitants of the *sarai*, who I hoped were soldiers or frontier guards, but who from their lack of uniform and ferocious appearance, might equally well have been brigands, seemed distressed to find that I spoke no known language and took little interest in my passport. We seemed to have reached a deadlock. After a suitable interval had elapsed I accordingly said 'Mazar-i-Sharif' and made as if to remount my horse. But this I was gently but firmly prevented from doing.

A further interval elapsed at the end of which, feeling hungry and thirsty and finding an orange in one of my bundles, I began to suck it, spitting out the pips on the floor. For some reason this made more impression on my captors than anything else I had hitherto said or done. At once the horses were brought round, our temporary captors waved goodbye and we started off again, I, at any rate, none the wiser. As an afterthought an escort was sent galloping after us. For miles he rode abreast of me with a loaded rifle held loosely across his saddle bow and pointing exactly at my stomach. I was glad when he tired of our company and eventually faded away.

An hour or two later we sighted a small earth-coloured hump on the horizon. The drab, khaki-coloured desert was absolutely flat and it was a very long time before we came near enough to see that it was the immense dome of a ruined mosque, apparently of very great age. From now onwards the plain was scattered with ruins, sometimes a few crumbling stones, at others, whole cities with mosques and watchtowers and city walls stretching for miles. Away to the west lay what is left of Balkh, the ancient Bactria, the Mother of Cities. These were the remains of a civilization which had been founded by Alexander of Macedon, had been destroyed by Genghis, had recovered, and had then gradually crumbled into decay. There are no signs of vegetation near any of these ruins and any water supply there may have been must have dried up or been diverted.

Towards sunset we came to the cultivated fields and plantations of the oasis of Seyagird, the first we had seen since the Oxus. Here a large military fort, with crenellated mud wall, towers over a cluster of houses and gardens surrounded by high walls and a small mosque, all built of the mud bricks used throughout Turkestan. In a large open space before the fort the camels of a number of caravans were resting, before setting out once more. We dismounted at the house of the Headman of the village, with whom I made, by means of signs, place names and a lavish use of the three or four Persian words which I had by now acquired, polite conversation over a cup of tea until it was time to go on. One of the horses was by now beginning to show signs of distress, so the luggage was transferred to a cart and we continued on our way in the dark over the flat clay plain. After what seemed a long time we saw the lights of Mazar reflected in the sky and just before ten clattered down the main street past the great mosque from which the town derives its name and dismounted in front of the inn. My horse, in spite of its unprepossessing appearance, had done sixty miles over bad country under a scorching sun without turning a hair.

The inn turned out to be clean and well-appointed. Unfortunately, no one spoke a word of any European language, and all that I was able to discover from the inn-keeper with regard to my onward journey was that the only motor vehicle in the place was 'out of order', a Persian phrase which was to impress itself forcibly on my memory in the course of my travels.

The conversation had taken place outside the inn. Turning away, somewhat depressed by what I had learned, I walked into the first door I came to where a light was showing. A couple were lying in bed under a mosquito net. As far as I could judge they were Europeans. I addressed them in English. They replied in Russian that they did not speak German. A few minutes later they were making me some tea on a spirit lamp and I was giving them the latest news from the Soviet Union.

My host, a large, jovial man, came from Tashkent and was employed as a technical adviser at the local cotton mill. Since the removal of the Soviet Consulate earlier in the year he and his wife had been the only European residents in Mazar. My arrival, it seemed, had not been entirely unexpected to him, for he produced from his pocket a torn and crumpled letter which I found was from the British Minister in Kabul and intended for me. The somewhat excessive interest which he showed in my affairs was however amply made up for by his helpful and amiable attitude. With his help I succeeded in arranging that the car which was to take me to Kabul should be repaired without delay and that we should start for the mountains next morning.

Like so many Soviet citizens, once they get outside their own country, the cotton expert and his wife showed no signs of the agonized reserve to which foreigners grow so accustomed in Moscow, but talked away gaily about all manner of things: night-life in Tashkent, the uncultured-ness of the Afghans and the fate of Czechoslovakia. They seemed particularly astonished to hear that I had been allowed to cross the Oxus. I explained, not without pride, how I had argued my way across. They said that they could not understand why the frontier authorities had let me across in view of the cholera. On my inquiring innocently what cholera, they proceeded to explain, with evident gusto and great wealth of detail, clearly delighted at such an opportunity of making anyone's flesh creep, how northern Afghanistan, and in particular the town of Mazar, was being swept by a devastating epidemic of cholera, and added that, now that I had entered the stricken area, I should not be allowed to continue my journey until I had spent a week in an Afghan quarantine station. There I was certain to catch cholera if I had not got it already.

This prospect did not please me at all and, having politely got out of a pressing invitation to make up a party for the local circus, I retired to bed, determined to leave for Kabul next day as I had originally arranged.

By an early hour next morning I had succeeded in collecting in my bedroom the head doctor of the hospital, a Turk who could speak one or two words of each of a number of languages, and the local Director of Sanitation, an elegant young Afghan in a European suit and karakul hat. Having, with considerable difficulty, first convinced them that I was not myself suffering from cholera, which was what they had been led to suppose by whoever had fetched them, I explained the situation and asked them for their advice. After a good deal of desultory talk during which I lost no opportunity of assuring my audience of my admiration for Afghanistan and for all Afghan institutions, including the local sanitary authorities, and also hinted darkly at the vital and urgent character of my mission, we came to the conclusions that the best way of smuggling me through the sanitary cordon would be to furnish me with a document certifying that I had already had cholera and recovered. An impressive-looking medical certificate to this effect was accordingly drawn up and signed and a similar document made out in favour of the driver of the truck. I was left with some hours in which to look round before setting out.

Mazar-i-Sharif, now the chief town of Afghan Turkestan with a population of 50,000, has supplanted Balkh and the other cities of which the ruins are strewn over the desolate and malarious plain in which it is situated. In the midst of it stands the fifteenth-century mosque from which it derives its name, the Noble Shrine. The walled gardens, the windowless fronts of the houses and the *chai-khanas* open on the dusty street, recalled Bokhara and the cities of Soviet Turkestan, but there was a striking difference in atmosphere and in the demeanour of the population. In the bazaar, a noisy, brightly clad crowd pushed its way through narrow streets of stalls containing, in addition to local products, a rich selection of goods from Birmingham, Yokohama and Berlin. Here and there one or two European-built buildings testified to the modernizing tendencies of the Government. It was the King's birthday and a stream of somewhat superficially Europeanized troops in khaki and steel helmets were marching to the music of brass bands along recently laid out avenues under flag-bedecked triumphal arches to a review.

Towards midday the truck, which, I gathered, had been repaired, made its appearance and I settled into the front seat with the feeling that there was nothing more for me to do but sit still until we got to Doaba, the village approximately half way to Kabul, where it had been arranged that I should meet the British Minister, Colonel Fraser-Tytler.

Once we had left the outskirts of the town I found myself once again in a typical Central Asian desert, complete with sand, tamarisks, marmots and skeletons, but travelling this time at forty miles an hour along a very fair road. This took us eastwards for some fifty miles to the foot of the mountains and the village of Tashkurgan, the namesake of the fort which dominates the road from Kashgar to the Indian border. Here we stopped to show our medical certificates and noticed that the petrol tank had sprung a leak. We collected from some amused villagers a handful of raw cotton and a handful of raisins, ground them together between two stones, spat on them, and effected the necessary repair, only to find that the steering gear was also out of order. A summary inspection revealed that at least one important part was missing. This was replaced by a metal collar-stud and, well pleased with our resourcefulness, we then proceeded contentedly on our way up into the mountains.

The pass through the mountains which I was to follow as far as Doaba and thence on to Kabul corresponds roughly to the branch of the Silk Road leading from Turkestan over the Oxus into India. This was the way followed by the pilgrims from China searching for the Buddha, by the caravans and by Genghis on his way to the plains of India.

The present road, which twists beside rushing mountain streams between towering crags and cliffs of light red volcanic rock, has only been in existence since 1937 and represents one of the most important achievements of the reign of Nadir Khan. Besides being no mean feat of engineering this road, some three hundred miles long, possesses considerable economic and political significance. It is only natural that Afghan Turkestan, cut off as it is by geographical and, to a certain extent, by ethnological barriers from Kabul and southern Afghanistan, should be drawn towards the rest of Turkestan and, in particular, to Soviet Turkestan, from which it is separated by no natural barriers save the Oxus for a part of the length of the frontier. Until the construction of the present road northern Afghanistan was only connected with Kabul by a few mountain passes only negotiable by pack animals, while to the north a number of roads, or at any rate potential roads, across flat country, connected Mazar-i-Sharif and Herat with the Soviet frontier and, what is more, with the Central Asian Railway which now runs for a considerable distance along the Soviet frontier and of which a branch line joins up with Kushk. The chances were that northern Afghanistan, besides being exposed to a military attack, would, even without this, fall completely under Soviet economic domination, which is apt to be followed by Soviet political and even military domination. This would almost certainly have meant the end of Afghanistan which would scarcely have been able to exist without its richest province. By this road, however, along which a steady stream of lorries runs from Kabul to Mazar-i-Sharif, Nadir Khan enabled the northern province to turn southwards for its supplies and markets.

After leaving Tashkurgan, we climbed through rocky gorges until, towards nightfall, we reached Hai-Bak, with its long street of bazaar-stalls and *chai-khanas*, in front of which the male population were sitting smoking and drinking tea in the soft evening light. The bazaar was overflowing with saddle-bags, skull-caps, Afghan national flags and melons. We laid in a large store of the latter and drove on in the dark over a dusty plain, cultivated in places, until again we reached another craggy range of mountains and started to climb once more. As we negotiated hairpin bends in the dark at a steady fifty miles per hour with a wall of rock rising above us on one side and a rushing torrent at the bottom of a precipice on the other, I wondered sleepily how the collar-stud, which occupied so important a position in the steering gear, was standing up to the strain.

We reached Doaba at three in the morning and here found, very much to my surprise, a rest house built by the Afghan Government on Anglo-Indian lines and reserved apparently for travelling Europeans and high Government officials. The caretaker was roused and I was soon asleep in a bed with blankets and clean sheets. I afterwards learned that it was generally considered a poor sort of place by the Diplomatic Corps in Kabul, but to me it seemed at the time the height of luxury.

I devoted most of next day to preparations for my meeting with His Majesty's Minister. The rest house boasted a bathroom with fittings by Messrs. Doulton, but these were very definitely 'out of order' and had long since been turned to other, by local standards no doubt more practical, uses. In the end a number of buckets of tepid water were brought and poured over me and by the time the Legation car arrived I was, if not very elegant, at any rate moderately clean.

The next two days, spent in camp on the banks of a rushing stream beneath a great natural wall of rock in the valley of the Andarrab, a tributary of the Oxus, were amongst the pleasantest of the whole journey. In Mrs. Fraser-Tytler I found a fellow clanswoman with whom my friendship dated back to the days of my childhood in Inverness, while from her husband I learned more about Afghanistan in forty-eight hours than I should otherwise have learnt in as many days. Finally, large quantities of excellent food, partaken of in magnificent natural surroundings and in circumstances of extreme luxury, contributed still further to my contentment.

From the Andarrab valley I did not travel direct to Kabul, but turned aside westwards along the river valley to Bamyan. Here two immense Buddhas are cut in the side of a red sandstone cliff, honeycombed with the cells and passages of a monastery which the Chinese pilgrim Hsijan-Tsang visited at the height of its splendour in 630 A.D., six centuries before the Mongol invasion. On the summits of the crags on either side of the valley stand the forts and watch towers which guarded the approaches of the great city of Bamyan, of which the ruins are scattered over the plain into which the valley broadens out. High above these rises the castle of the King, which, so the story goes, was betrayed to Genghis Khan by the King's lovesick daughter. After which Genghis sacked the city and defaced the great Buddhas and, incidentally, put the King's daughter to death.

Not many miles south of Bamyan the road crosses the watershed of the Oxus and the Indus at a height of some 12,000 feet above sea level. Thence it descends again until it emerges from the rocky gorges of the Hindu Kush into a flat plain. Crossing this, we came in the evening to Kabul, a rambling, featureless town with its miles of covered and uncovered bazaars.

HOMEWARD BOUND

IT was time to consider how to get back to Moscow. My original plan had been to make my way back to the Soviet frontier by way of Herat, to cross it at Kushk and to rejoin the main line of the Transcaspian Railway at Merv in Turkmenistan, the capture of which by the Russians in 1884 had caused us such acute 'Mervousness', as the Duke of Argyll facetiously put it at the time, and which is thought to be the oldest city in the world, though little now remains to be seen save a few crumbling ruins. Thence I intended to travel westwards across the Caspian to Baku and Moscow.

But when I called at the Soviet Embassy it was gently but firmly explained to me that the reports of the cholera epidemic in northern Afghanistan were now more alarming than ever and that, although the frontier guards might have been misguided enough to let me cross the frontier into Afghanistan, there could be no question of my returning to the Soviet Union via the infected area.

It was not clear to me how far the cholera in northern Afghanistan was being used as a pretext to prevent me from paying another visit to Soviet Central Asia, but it was quite evident that in the circumstances there was nothing for it but to return by an alternative route. I accordingly decided to leave next morning by the Legation lorry for Peshawar, travel thence to Delhi, fly from Delhi to Baghdad and make my way as best I could from Baghdad to Moscow by way of Persia and the Caucasus.

Leaving Kabul at dawn, we crossed the highest point of the pass towards the middle of the day, sharing the road with long caravans of wild-looking nomad tribesmen from the hills who were making their way down to the plains at the approach of winter with their families, their flocks and herds and all their worldly goods. In the early afternoon we reached Nimla, where the great cypresses still stand in the garden of Shah Jahan. A few miles further on was Jalalabad, a typical

Central Asian town approached through long dusty avenues of poplars. Here we spent the night as guests of His Majesty's Consul, an Indian Moslem of charm and distinction, with a beard like an ancient Assyrian, who had made the pilgrimage to Mecca and thus earned the title of Haji.

Next morning we left Jalalabad while it was still dark and by dawn were climbing up into the mountains towards the Khyber. By half-past ten we had come in sight of the first British fort, with the Union Jack fluttering from the summit, and a few minutes later were on British territory and travelling along a perfect asphalt road. The Oxus, though only four days' journey by road and as many hours by aeroplane, seemed very remote.

From the Khyber the road twisted down into the plain of India and by midday we were in Peshawar. There I spent a happy day, wandering first through Peshawar city, completely Central Asian in character, with its citadel and bazaar, and then through Peshawar Cantonment with its shops, its Club, its rows of neat bungalows. Sitting at tea with a friend in the garden of the Peshawar Club I could hear the pipes and drums of the Highland Light Infantry beating Retreat. It was all refreshingly unlike anything in the Soviet Union. That evening I took the train to Delhi. I have always enjoyed contrasts and certainly the splendours of the Viceroy's House, the abundance of delicious food and drink, the amiability of everyone with whom I came in contact made a welcome change after the austerities of Central Asia.

From Delhi I flew to Baghdad in an Imperial Airways mail-carrying aeroplane. Beneath us the country unrolled itself, panorama fashion: the plains of India; the howling wilderness of Baluchistan; the Indian Ocean; the Peninsula of Oman; the Persian Gulf; Bahrein, with its palm trees and oil-wells; Basra, where we were allowed to sleep for an hour or two in an unbelievably large and up-to-date hotel; and, next morning, the gigantic ruins of Ktesiphon, the Tigris and finally, Baghdad, a disappointing city.

After a pleasant day and a comfortable night at the Embassy, I left for Teheran at four next morning with two German spies, thinly disguised as commercial travellers, in a very old American car driven by an Armenian of Egyptian nationality. At dawn we crossed the frontier at Khanikin where we waited for hours, while one of the Germans cleared his calculating machine at the Customs House. This was an imposing building in a mixture of the late baroque and Moorish styles, lavishly decorated with Iranian lions, agonizingly entwined with cupids and acanthus leaves. Outside three or four dozen vultures hovered over a dying camel.

Khanikin lies at the foot of the mountains and we drove all day through craggy light red hills along a road built for the most part by our troops during and after the First World War. At nightfall we came to Kermanshah, which lies pleasantly enough amongst groves of poplars in a valley. Leaving again at sunrise we drove all next day through the same kind of country as the day before. The dusty roads, the poplars, the reddish hills in the foreground, the bluish hills in the background and the strings of camels and donkeys, all reminded me of Turkestan. But the inhabitants trudging along the roads and lounging in the villages in the shabby European suits forced on them by Reza Shah were disappointing after the Uzbeks of Samarkand and Bokhara in their striped *khalats*, and the Afghans in their flowing robes and turbans.

We stopped for a meal at a *chai-khana* by the roadside and in the early afternoon reached Hamadan, the Ecbatana of the ancients, and reputedly the burial-place of Esther and Mordecai. The car had by now broken two springs and something had to be done. It took a long time to do it, and in the meantime I was able to look round Hamadan. Everywhere there were signs that the old order of things, had been swept away and very little put in its place. The mosque and bazaar were decayed and uninteresting and the central square, with its public garden, a feeble caricature of a European town. Soon after nightfall we emerged from the mountains into the plain and at midnight arrived at Teheran.

There had been rumours that the Soviet-Iranian frontier was closed and, after endless inconclusive telephone conversations with the Soviet Embassy which left me still in doubt whether the Soviet-Iranian frontier at Djulfa was open or shut, I finally set out in a very small car with four extremely bulky Iranians to find out for myself what the position was. We stopped at Kazvin to eat and at Zenjan to sleep and, after passing rapidly through Mianeh, where according to legend the bite of the bed-bugs is apt to be fatal to the victim, arrived next afternoon at Tabriz, the capital of Persian Azerbaijan, where I was most hospitably welcomed at the British Consulate.

Tabriz is a pleasant town. From the towers of the ancient Ark or Citadel, which commands a view of the surrounding mountains, the flat-roofed houses seem more spacious than one would ever suspect by looking at them from the street, and the high mud walls enclose pleasant gardens. The covered bazaars stretched for miles and, besides foreign wares, were full of local carpets and other local products. The inhabitants, mostly Turko-Tartars and Armenians, were indistinguishable in appearance from the Soviet Azerbaijanis I had met at Lenkoran. The famous Blue Mosque is a ruin and the other mosques were for the most part shut. In the main square of the town I saw a policeman tear the veil from a woman's face and throw it in the mud. The Persians were being modernized, whether they liked it or not.

After forty-eight hours, spent for the most part in arguing with the local Civil Governor, who at first denied the validity of the exit visa which I had obtained in Delhi and refused to accept the responsibility of issuing me with one himself, and then finally admitted that the visa which I already had was all that I required, I started on the last stage of my journey to the Soviet frontier.

The road to Djulfa follows for the most part the railway line from Tabriz to Djulfa built by the Russians in 1916. After some two or three hours we emerged from the light red mountains of Iran into the valley of the Araxes. This marks the frontier between Iran and the Soviet Union and also, in theory at any rate, between Europe and Asia. Far away beyond the Araxes rose the black wall of the Caucasus.

The Customs formalities on the Iranian side did not take long and I soon found myself standing with my two bundles half way across the bridge which crosses the Araxes at this point. I shouted to the sentry at the Soviet end, explaining that I was anxious to enter the Soviet Union. He did not reply, but looked rather pointedly down the barrel of his rifle. After half an hour of more or less continuous shouting neither he nor the frontier guards on the far bank had shown any signs of departing from their hostile attitude. One of the Iranian sentries, who for some reason spoke Italian, said that the frontier seemed to be shut, and advised me to keep away from the Soviet end of the bridge as they did not want a frontier incident. He only wished he could let me return to Persia, but that was unfortunately impossible. It was cold and wet and I had had enough of hovering in uncertainty between Europe and Asia and was trying to devise some safe means of shaking the Soviet's sentry's composure, when a car drove up on the Soviet bank of the river and an officer got out who, after a certain amount of parleying said reluctantly that I might come across, though it would have been better if I could have waited till next day.

I was back in the Soviet Union.

Soviet Djulfa, like its Iranian counterpart, is of little interest, consisting almost entirely of one dusty street of low white houses. It was the day after the anniversary of the November Revolution and at the post office, where I went to draw some money, an uproarious party was in progress. Vodka was flowing freely and the post office staff were far too busy singing and dancing to attend to customers. It was not till midnight that I got what I wanted.

The relatively large sum I had drawn attracted universal attention and there was much whispering as I left to go back to the inn. After I had been asleep for an hour or two I was wakened by the door opening stealthily. When my visitor had reached my bedside, I asked him what he wanted. He replied that he was the landlord and had come to see that I had everything I needed. Outside in the yard a crowd of Persians were encamped, who had been expelled from the Soviet Union and were on their way back to Persia. Ceaselessly they talked and murmured amongst themselves. I did not sleep much that night.

Next morning I took the train to Erivan, the capital of Soviet Armenia. As we were starting, two Armenians, dark, furtive men, got into the carriage and sat on either side of me. When an officer of the frontier troops came to ask them for their passes to the frontier zone they winked at him significantly. The officer, however, clearly not realizing the significance of the wink, insisted on seeing their papers and, when these were at last reluctantly handed over, held them rather clumsily under my nose while he inspected them. They showed their holders to be agents of the N.K.V.D., and I could not resist the temptation of winking in my turn at my neighbours over the unfortunate slip which their uniformed colleague had made. They were to be my constant companions for the rest of my journey.

The railway follows the red stream of the Araxes, which marks the Iranian frontier, almost all the way to Erivan, a distance of about a hundred miles, with, to the north, the range of the southern Caucasus and to the south the pale red mountains of Iran culminating in Mount Ararat, which stands near the point where the frontiers of Turkey, Iran and the Soviet Union intersect. The only important town between Djulfa and Erivan is Nakhichevan, the capital of the tiny autonomous Soviet Socialist Republic of that name, in which Djulfa is situated. Its white buildings are dominated by a large straggling fort on a hill, dating back to the days when the whole region was a bone of contention between Russia and Persia. The inhabitants were Turko-Tartar rather than Armenian in type and the women who came down to the station to look at the train were almost all heavily veiled. Along the valley of the Araxes the ruins of mosques alternated with those of Armenian churches.

Erivan is a pleasant enough town. Armenia had once occupied a privileged position in the Soviet scheme of things. The Katholikos, or Head of the Armenian Church, had been allowed to remain in the Monastery of Etchmiadzin a few miles from Erivan, and religious persecution was, it seemed, considerably less savage than in most other parts of the Soviet Union. The population were not entirely cut off from all contact with Armenians abroad, many of whom sent considerable sums of money to their relations and friends in Soviet Armenia. At one time even immigration was encouraged and a number of Armenians from America and elsewhere returned to the land of their fathers, a step which some of them may since have regretted. National pride was fostered and individual prosperity not discouraged. These advantages, combined with the fruitfulness of the land and the natural business instincts of the inhabitants, made the Armenian Soviet Socialist Republic and its capital an oasis of prosperity of which it was no doubt hoped that rumours might even filter across the frontiers into Turkey and Persia and thus add to the prestige of the Soviet Union.

Of this prosperity many indications still survived. Erivan had, to a very great extent, been built since 1921 when Armenia came under Soviet rule, and was still being built. The new buildings, built of the local reddish stone in the neo-classical style or in an adaptation of the Armenian national style, compared favourably, both as regards appearance and solidity of construction, with new buildings elsewhere in the Soviet Union. As usual the tendency had been to concentrate on immense public buildings: a new University, a new cinema, a new Institute of Marxist Propaganda, a State Opera House, and an enormous hotel for travelling officials, not to mention great blocks of offices which house the various Government and Party organizations. But, in addition to the usual blocks of luxury flats built to accommodate highly paid officials and specialized workers, streets of humbler dwellings were being erected where room might perhaps be found for members of the less privileged classes. Of the old Persian town practically nothing remained save a gaudy eighteenth-century mosque and a few hovels on the slopes of the surrounding hills.

The shops of Erivan, including the food shops, seemed, by provincial standards, well stocked. They were not overcrowded and I saw no queues. The food at the hotel was good and the clothes of the members of the privileged classes eating it, up to the highest Moscow standards. In the surrounding country the little stone houses and walled orchards and vineyards recalled Tuscany and gave me the feeling of having indeed crossed from Asia into Europe.

From Erivan I travelled by train to Tiflis and thence direct to Batum on the Black Sea, where I hoped to find a ship which would take me to Sochi, the principal seaside resort of the Soviet privileged classes, which I felt should be of considerable sociological interest. On the second morning of the train journey from Erivan I awoke to find that we had left the barren mountains of the central Caucasus and were travelling through the green hills, the orange-groves, the tea and tobacco plantations and the steaming sub-tropical swamps of Adjaristan. In the villages through which we passed the men, lean, swarthy figures, wore strange black headgear, half way between hoods and turbans.

Batum struck me as being different from other Soviet towns. Of Turkish rule before 1878 no signs remained save a solitary mosque. Most of the town had been built between 1878 and 1914 and this fact was proclaimed by every brick of it. During the years which succeeded the British evacuation and the final occupation by the Reds, Batum seemed to have been left out of the general scheme of demolition and reconstruction. It lacked the rows of half-built and half-demolished houses and the vast incongruous modernistic buildings which gave most towns in the Soviet Union so desolate an appearance. Its streets were made up of rows of solidly built, typically bourgeois houses and shops. Along the main boulevards the well-grown rows of trees had not been rooted up to make way for imaginary traffic.

Nor had Batum been allowed to decay. According to a local inhabitant whom I met in the train, Batum, after a long period of eclipse, had during the past four or five years returned to favour. Certainly a large new hotel was being built on the sea front; the houses and shops had been freshly painted; the streets seemed in excellent repair, and, most important of all, a large number of the villas in the neighbourhood had been converted into rest-homes reserved for the members of various important State organizations, and were fulfilling their original function of a playground for the upper classes. Thus Batum had by chance retained the appearance of a fairly prosperous seaside town in a capitalist country.

Batum, I knew, produced mandarines, tea and tobacco. Having read in the local papers that a crop of several million mandarines had just been gathered, I was disappointed to find that none were for sale locally. They had all been sent off to Moscow. The population, I was told by a rather cynical young man who sold me three clandestinely, were being punished for the failure of the mandarine trees to fulfil the plan.

There seemed to be little shipping in the harbour. The only foreign vessel I could see was flying a Turkish flag. Along the sea front, to the west of the town, stood the refineries which receive the oil which comes from Baku by pipe-line.

On the wall of a factory near by, I found a large and ornamental marble plaque to the greater glory of Joseph Stalin who, in 1903, 'provoked in the former factory of Rothschild a strike which ended in the victory of the workers'. Looking through the window of the factory, where clearly nothing had been changed since 1903, I could not help considering what would be the consequences if one of the ragged, badly paid, underfed workers were now to try to emulate the youthful exploits of the Leader of the People.

The hotel at Batum was not very clean and manifestly a survival of the old regime. So, I think, was the cook, for the *bœuf Stroganov* and the cooking generally were the best I had tasted in the Soviet Union. The dining-room was filled with a noisy delegation of collectivized peasants from Armenia and the Ukraine, who seemed for no particular reason to be making a triumphal progress through the Caucasus. Later they visited Gori, Stalin's birthplace, whence, I read in the paper, they sent him an ecstatic telegram.

Meanwhile, I had learnt (rather to my relief, for the Black Sea looked far from inviting) that there would be no sailings from Batum for an indefinite period on account of the storms; and so there was nothing for it but to return to Tiflis.

In Tiflis a number of brand new buildings had made their appearance since my previous visit eighteen months earlier: a new Government Building; a new Stalin University, and a vast new triumphal pavilion which had sprouted on the very top of St. David's Mountain overlooking the town. From beneath its towering cement colonnades loudspeakers blared forth continuously Georgian translations of Soviet patriotic songs. Behind it lay an ornamental garden centring round a colossal statue of Stalin.

Things had tightened up, too, since my last visit. The first time I ventured outside the town I stumbled into what was apparently a forbidden zone. Before I knew where I was I was staring down the muzzle of a rifle with my hands above my head. My N.K.V.D. escort, needless to say, chose this moment to fade discreetly away. After a great deal of talk I finally persuaded my captor, a stolid character who seemed quite content to stay where he was all day, to summon help by firing his rifle off in the air. Reinforcements arrived at the double and

I was eventually marched off in the middle of a platoon of N.K.V.D. troops to their Headquarters. There I spent the rest of the day arguing about Marxism and the international situation with half a dozen N.K.V.D. officers, while the duty-officer tried vainly to get into touch with someone sufficiently senior to authorize my release. It was not until late at night that the local Commandant, a florid-looking Georgian with fiercely curling moustachios, made his appearance and, having looked at my papers, sent me back to the hotel.

I was beginning to feel that I had had enough of Tiflis and next day I was glad to find room in a lorry that was leaving for Ordzhonikidze by the Georgian Military Road. It was fine but bitterly cold and the snow already lay thick on the passes. The truck was open and everyone in it had wrapped themselves in everything they possessed. Tugged down over my ears I wore an enormous fur hat bought from a villainous old Georgian in a side-street, while disposed about my body were the entire contents of my kitbag, shirts, sweaters and socks pulled on, one on top of the other. Above us Kazbek glistened and sparkled in the sunlight against the pale blue of the sky. Constant stops to dig the truck out of the snow restored our circulation and at Pasanaur we ate a filling meal and drank as much vodka as we could hold. Then came the descent in the gathering darkness, with the high crags looming above us and below us the icy rushing waters of the Terek River. By the time we reached Ordzhonikidze I was half frozen and glad to take refuge in the comforting stuffiness of the Moscow train.

I reached Moscow late at night a couple of days later. My cook had gone off duty. The memory of those lavish meals in Delhi and Teheran had long since faded; I was tired and once again very hungry. Amongst the letters in my flats was an invitation to a supper-party that night at the Belgian Legation. The Belgian chargé d'affaires and his wife were a charming couple. They also had the best food in Moscow. There was just time to get there.

I shaved a week's growth of beard; soaked myself briefly but luxuriously in a badly needed bath; struggled into a stiff shirt and white tie, and set out. Ten minutes later I was sitting down to a large slice of fresh *pâté de foie gras*, specially flown from Strasbourg, a plate of endive salad and a glass of Burgundy. Soon, I felt much better.

It was a young party and I was on Christian-name terms with most of the people there, Counsellors and Military and Naval Attachés, Secretaries of Embassy and their wives and daughters. French, Americans, Germans, Italians, Persians, Roumanians, Swedes, Finns, Norwegians, Chinese and Japanese, we had all ski-ed together, ridden together, bathed together, played bridge and tennis and danced together, day after day, night after night, in the artificial isolation of Moscow diplomatic life, until international barriers had largely disappeared amid individual friendships and quarrels, jealousies and romances.

Now, I noticed, the talk was of war: Was it inevitable? Or could it still be avoided? Much had happened in Europe in that autumn of 1938, while I had been away on my travels. The professional diplomats, drinking their brandy, regarded the international scene with cold detachment, in terms of underlying motives, of objectives to be achieved and relative military potentials. And, having so regarded it, they did not share the real or affected optimism of the professional politicians.

I sat with Johnny Herwarth von Bittenfeld, my opposite number at the German Embassy and an old friend. A patriotic German, he was, I believe, strongly and genuinely anti-Nazi. Now, the news of Munich had filled him with despair. 'After this,' he said, 'the Führer will think that he can get away with anything. He will be wrong, for he does not understand your mentality. He does not realize that, whatever line your Government may take, there is a limit beyond which you, as a nation, will not be prepared to let him go. This last fatal surrender of yours will embolden him to overstep this limit; it will weaken the hand of such restraining elements as still remain in Germany; it will make war inevitable, war which in the long run will bring about the destruction of Germany.' He paused and then went on again in a lower voice: 'If there is to be war, then there can be only one hope for Germany: an agreement with these people here. Then, at least, we should not have a war on two fronts.'

Not long after our conversation I was transferred to London and left

Moscow for good. Some months later Johnny, mobilized as a Reserve Cavalry Officer, marched into Poland; then into France; then into Russia. Later he fought on other fronts. I did not see him during the years that followed, though sometimes, as chance would have it, we were only a few miles apart. Sometimes I was on the run; sometimes he was. When, finally, after the war we met again, everything that he had foretold that evening in Moscow had come true.

PART TWO

ORIENT SAND

> Death has no repose
> Warmer and deeper than that Orient sand
> Which hides the beauty and bright faith of those
> Who made the Golden Journey to Samarkand.
>
> FLECKER

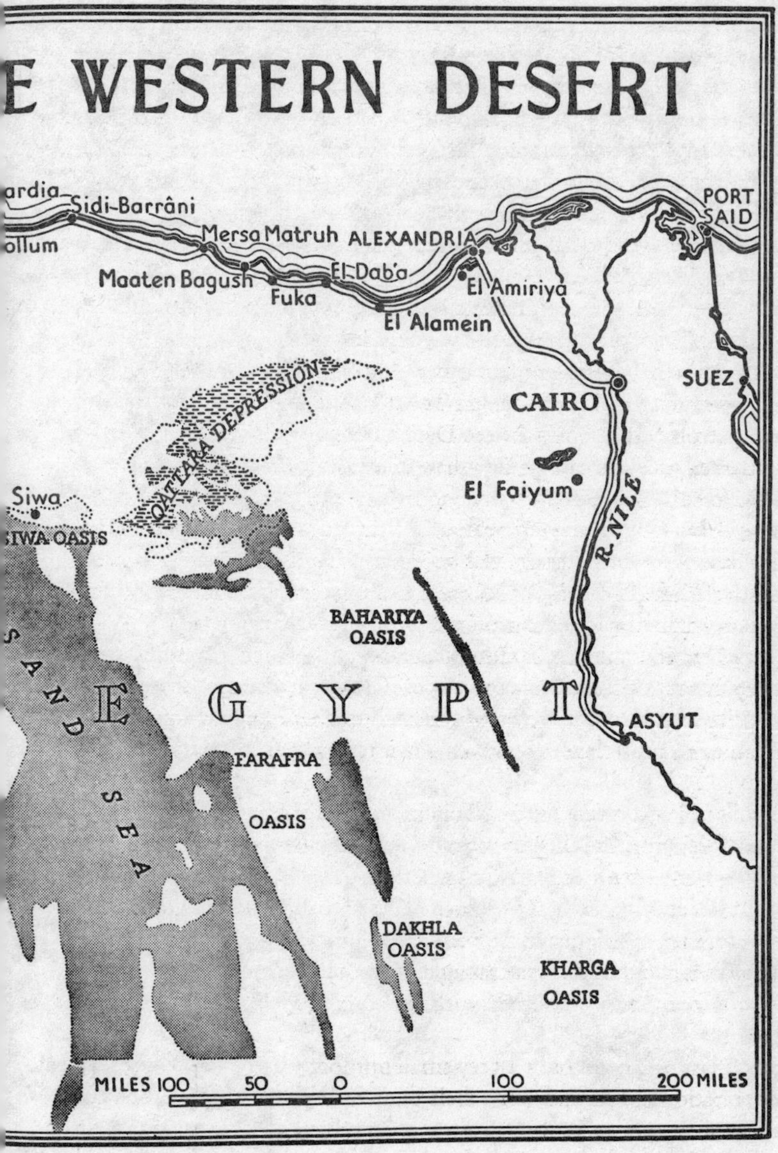

E WESTERN DESERT

ardia
Sidi-Barrâni
ollum
Mersa Matruh ALEXANDRIA
PORT SAID
Maaten Bagush   El-Dab'a
Fuka
El Amiriya
El 'Alamein

QATTARA DEPRESSION

CAIRO

SUEZ

Siwa
SIWA OASIS

El Faiyum

R. NILE

BAHARIYA
OASIS

SAND

E G Y P T

ASYUT

FARAFRA

OASIS

SEA

DAKHLA
OASIS

KHARGA

OASIS

MILES 100   50   0   100   200 MILES

CHAPTER I

FEET ON THE GRAVEL

WAR, it has been said, is diplomacy continued by other means. Certainly, to me, as I sat at my desk in the Foreign Office, my own occupation, once hostilities had begun, seemed suddenly to have lost its point. I decided to resign my commission in the Diplomatic Service and to enlist.

But this was easier said than done. No sooner had I mentioned my intention of resigning than it was pointed out to me, in no uncertain terms, that my behaviour was extremely unpatriotic. For six years, they said, I had been learning my job. Now, just as I was beginning to be of some slight use, I wanted, in order to satisfy my personal vanity, to go off and play at soldiers; I must lack all sense of responsibility. But, in any case, my resignation would not be accepted. The new Defence Regulations gave the Secretary of State full powers in this respect.

'And what if I simply go off and enlist?' I asked.

'If you do that,' they said, 'the War Office will be asked to send you back at once. In irons, if necessary.'

They had me there. I decided to go away and think again.

I allowed some time to elapse before making my next approach. Then I asked for an interview with the Permanent Under-Secretary for Foreign Affairs, Sir Alexander Cadogan. In the meanwhile I had made a careful study of the Foreign Office Regulations. Paragraph 22 gave me what I needed.

'And what do you want?' said Sir Alexander, who was a busy man, looking up from his desk.

'I want to go into politics,' I said.

'In that case,' he replied, without enthusiasm, for the idea of Party politics is repugnant to the permanent official, 'In that case, you will have to leave the Service.'

I replied that I was prepared for that. In fact, if he liked I could let him have my resignation at once. And, laying a neatly written letter of resignation on his desk, I escaped from the room. A few minutes later I was in a taxi and on my way to the nearest Recruiting Office. It had been simpler than I had expected.

The processes of medical examination and enlistment took their usual somewhat lengthy course. What to me was the beginning of a new phase in my life was, to the clerks and doctors who took my particulars, so much dreary routine. After swearing the Oath and filling in a number of forms, I was given the King's Shilling and a railway warrant to Inverness. I was a Private in the Cameron Highlanders, my father's old regiment.

I arrived at Inverness with a batch of several hundred other new recruits, for the most part nineteen-year-old youths from Glasgow. It was cold and grey and drizzling. In moist, undecided groups, we hung about the barrack square, our hands in the pockets of our civilian suits.

Then, suddenly, we were pounced on by half a dozen N.C.O.s And given numbers. And divided up into squads. And herded into bleak-looking barrack-rooms named after battles in the Peninsular War: Salamanca, Corunna and Ciudad Rodriguez. And issued with things: boot brushes, tooth brushes, knife, fork, spoon, blankets, boots, overalls (denim), bonnets (Balmoral). And told not to —ing lose them. And told to look out and look sharp and hurry up, and use our —ing initiative. And given mops and pails and scrubbing brushes and told to —ing scrub the —ing floor.

My military career had begun.

After we had scrubbed the floor, we were turned on to heaving coal and tipping rubbish and cleaning the latrines and polishing the brass and peeling potatoes for dinner. It was not for some days that our Sergeant Instructors attempted to initiate us in the arts of war in the narrower sense of the word.

When they did, it was not a success. There was the difficulty, the ever-recurring difficulty, of remembering at short notice which was your left foot and which was your right; of saying, off hand, what you did with your bren gun after it had jammed for the second time; of putting a name, when suddenly confronted with it, to this or that apparently insignificant, but doubtless vital part of the same gun; of explaining the presence of that unaccountable but altogether shameful speck of dirt on your rifle; of finding things that had got lost; of being constantly in the right place at the right time with the right equipment. We were sadly afflicted by what has been called the total depravity of inanimate things.

Our instructors watched us gloomily. We were, they said, just terrible. In twenty years they had never seen recruits like us. All we could do was eat and sleep.

And, indeed, eating and sleeping bulked large in our scheme of things. From the moment when the first piercing notes of the pipes dragged us forcibly from our slumbers, as from a well of treacle, until the last post sounded and the lights were put out in a barrack-room half of whose occupants were already asleep and snoring, we were perpetually hungry and sleepy. At meal-times we threw ourselves upon our food like a pack of wolves; and whenever we were given a chance we slept, indoors, out of doors, in broad daylight, in the middle of a room full of men, shouting, singing and swearing.

Then bit by bit life became less bewildering and took on a new interest. We made friends amongst our fellow recruits. Even the N.C.O.s assumed the proportions of ordinary mortals. On occasion some of them would even try to explain to us what it was all about. 'You and me,' our own Sergeant Instructor would observe philosophically from time to time, 'You and me are nothing but —ing cogs in this gigantic — organization.'

Slowly the purpose of many of the seemingly incomprehensible things that we were required to do became apparent. The mere task of existing became less formidable. The bren gun ceased to be a meaningless conglomeration of oddly shaped bits of steel and became a weapon which some day one might conceivably use in action. Yelling hoarsely, we plunged our bayonets with ever greater conviction into the straw-stuffed entrails of the defenceless targets. One by one our fellow recruits assumed particular characteristics, developed particular aptitudes, stood out from the mass. As inmates of one hut or barrack-room we acquired a corporate existence. We helped each other out of difficulties; we lent each other missing bits of equipment;

we did each other's fatigues; we told lies on each other's behalf to those in authority; we showed each other snapshots of our families, and went together to the pictures.

My own closest associate was Eddie McIntosh, a compact, smiling, sensible young man from Edinburgh, whose father, like mine, had been a Cameron. We were first thrown together because our names came next to each other on the list, but I soon came to like him for his natural friendliness, his abundant good nature and his quiet enthusiasm for whatever he happened to be doing. Poor Eddie, he was to be killed a couple of years later in Burma with the 1st Battalion.

Physically, as well as mentally, we were undergoing a change. On the barrack square we stamped and wheeled and turned about with ever greater precision under the supervision of a Regimental Sergeant Major with the gift of projecting his voice from one side of the square to the other and bringing it down on an offender with the deadly accuracy of a stock whip. Week by week the training became more arduous and the distances greater, until, plodding along the road behind the pipes, or ranging over the moors in sleet and snow and rain, we seemed to have covered most of the north of Scotland. We felt fitter than ever before. The pale, spotty, narrow-chested corner boys changed as though by magic into robust men who before the war was over would give a good account of themselves on many different fronts. However senseless much of it might seem, nobody could deny that recruits' training served its purpose.

By now, too, our initial bewilderment and exhaustion had worn off. We discovered that there were ways out of every difficulty. It was simply, as we had been told on our arrival, a question of using your —ing initiative. We began to find our way round. We discovered the value of contacts in the cookhouse, in the armoury, in the Company Office, in the Quartermaster's store. We found that there were other ways out of the barracks than past the guard at the main gate. We discovered a hundred and one more or less ingenious methods of avoiding unnecessary exertion, of avoiding detection, of acquiring merit, of escaping punishment. We ceased to be recruits and became trained soldiers. Effortlessly, we fell into the linguistic habits of the army; every other word in our conversation was the same meaningless and monotonous, yet somehow satisfying expletive.

For me, this new existence had not come a moment too early. Very soon I found that it possessed unsuspected tonic qualities. Despite, perhaps because of, its limitations, it had a stimulating, a humanizing, a rejuvenating effect. All of a sudden, I felt very much younger, both physically and mentally. For years, I had led my own life, seeing my own circle of friends and following my own tastes and inclinations; doing on the whole what I felt like doing. In detached fashion, I had dealt with ideas and ideologies, tendencies and trends, situations and relationships. Now, plunged suddenly into this new life, among companions assembled by the hazards of conscription, I was dealing at close quarters with people and things. And I was thoroughly enjoying it.

Months passed and the time came when some of us were given a Lance Corporal's stripe, Eddie McIntosh and myself included. The position of Lance Corporal was one of considerable influence. We doled out the food at meal-times; we directed the peeling of potatoes; we put people on charges. As Orderly Corporal we walked round the messes behind the Officer of the Day, hissing 'That'll do from you,' at any hint of a complaint about the food. Occasionally, when the Sergeant could not be bothered to do it himself, we gave instruction in the use of the rifle, the bren gun and the two-inch mortar. Followed obediently, though uncomprehendingly, by our Sections, we led midnight attacks on waterworks and sewage farms and became hopelessly and irretrievably lost in the all-enveloping confusion of Company and Battalion exercises. There was an improvement, too, in our social standing. Instead of being hailed as 'Jock' by all and sundry, we were now addressed as 'Corporal' by the young ladies in the shops and behind the bars. We were even admitted to the company of some of the more easy-going Sergeants. It was an agreeable, relatively carefree existence.

Then one day, I was summoned to the Orderly Room and given unexpected news that I had been given an immediate commission and posted as a subaltern to the 1st Battalion.

This sudden advancement was not regarded by my companions as a matter for congratulation. 'Poor old Corporal,' they said pityingly.

'he's away to the 1st Battalion to be a ——ing officer.' 'But cheer up, Corporal,' they said consolingly, 'all you'll be needing is bags and bags of ——ing patter.'

And indeed, it did not take me long to adapt myself to the life and duties of a Platoon Commander. There was no very great difference between it and the life I had just left. My chief preoccupation was still with bren, rifle and two-inch mortar; with boots, webbing equipment, cap badges and greatcoat buttons; seeing they were not lost, seeing they were properly cleaned, seeing that they and their owners were in the right place at the right time performing their proper functions. The burden of responsibility was heavier, but still not overwhelming.

From time to time came rumours that the Battalion was going overseas. But the prospect of going into action, of really using those carefully preserved weapons, that carefully checked ammunition, still seemed oddly remote.

There were other rumours too, disquieting hints from friends in London that my failure to enter politics had not passed unobserved; that steps were being taken to secure my return to the Foreign Office, at that time painfully under-staffed. It began to look very much as though, after a promising start, my military career might be brought to a premature end.

Only one thing could save me; early election to Parliament. I had already been in touch with Conservative Central Office. I returned to the attack with renewed vigour. I was told that there was to be a by-election at Lancaster; a Conservative candidate had not yet been adopted. If I liked, I could go up there and see what the local Association thought of me. I applied to the Colonel for a few days' leave and went.

Diffidently I presented myself at the local Party Headquarters. It was my first experience of politics. I did not know the answer to half the questions I was asked; it was no good pretending I did. With a sinking heart I admitted my ignorance. The Executive Committee adjourned to discuss the rival merits of the various potential candidates. Surprisingly, when they came back, I was told that I had been adopted. All the more surprisingly, since I had made it clear that, if I was elected, my military duties would have to come first and my political duties second.

There was about a month before the poll. I applied for a month's leave and started electioneering. I had hardly ever attended a political meeting. I had never made a speech in my life. By the end of a week, I was making three a night. By the end of a fortnight I was almost enjoying it. Not only my supporters, but everyone I met, took me in hand. They fed me; they stood me drinks; they gave me advice; they told me what to do and what not to do; they told me, with characteristic North Country frankness, what they thought of my speeches. Dazed but happy, I drank gallons of beer and shook thousands of hands. Perpetually late for my next appointment, I walked or drove from house to house and street to street and village to village.

Wherever I went, among supporters or opponents, I met with the same forthrightness, the same friendliness. I had hardly ever set foot inside the House of Commons and I had no means of telling whether the life of a parliamentarian would suit me or not. But of one thing I was quite sure: that, if I was to be a politician, these were the sort of people I should like to represent.

Then came the eve of the poll: packed, noisy meetings; polling day; a tour of the constituency decked with rosettes and favours like a prize bull; the count; hushed suspense in the Town Hall; the result: I was in: M.P. for Lancaster.

Member of Parliament, or Platoon Commander?

As things turned out, I was not called upon to try to play this dual role for long. One night after a long day's training on the moors, I was roused from my sleep by a dispatch rider and told to report at once to Battalion Headquarters. There I was shown a signal from the War Office. I was to proceed forthwith on embarkation leave. I had told my constituents repeatedly that, if ordered abroad, I should go. And so, leaving them in the able and experienced hands of Jim Thomas, an old friend from Foreign Office days, I went.

A week later I was in a seaplane on my way to Cairo. I had no idea what awaited me at the other end. But at least I was bound for what, in that bleak autumn of 1941, was the only active theatre of operations: the Middle East.

CHAPTER II

SPECIAL AIR SERVICE

WHEN I got to Cairo, I took a taxi to the address at which I had been told to report. 'Ah,' said the villainous-looking Egyptian who drove me, when he heard the address. 'You want Secret Service.'

Hopefully I sent up my name and was shown into a comfortably furnished office. There I was given some idea of what lay in store for me. It sounded exciting but improbable.

Then I was introduced to some of my companions in the proposed venture. What they told me made me even more sceptical. For months already they had been standing-by to leave at twelve hours' notice for a special operation. They had been trained in map-reading and demolitions and mountain warfare, and the workings of the internal combustion engine. They had been sent on ski-ing courses and language courses, and courses in leadership and administration. They had been promoted to the rank of Major and then demoted to the rank of Captain. They had drawn special equipment and special weapons, and special pay and allowances. Everything they had done had been treated as if it was of the utmost urgency and importance. But nothing ever happened. They longed to get back to their regiments.

It was accordingly with little surprise or regret that I learned quite soon after my arrival that whatever I had been wanted for was not going to happen after all and that I was free to return to regimental duty. The 2nd Camerons were in the desert and there was nothing to prevent my being posted to them immediately. But things turned out otherwise.

On my way to the Adjutant-General's branch of G.H.Q. I ran into David Stirling, a subaltern in the Scots Guards, whose brother Peter, then Secretary at the Embassy in Cairo, was an old friend of mine. David was a tall, dark, strongly built young man with a manner that was usually vague, but sometimes extremely alert. He asked me what my plans were. I told him. 'Why not join the Special Air Service Brigade?' he said. I asked what it was. He explained that it was not really a Brigade; it was more like a Platoon. It was only called a Brigade to confuse the enemy. But it was a good thing to be in. He had raised it himself a month or two before with some friends of his after the Commando with which they had come out to the Middle East had been disbanded. Now there were about half a dozen officers and twenty or thirty other ranks. He had been made a captain and commanded it. He was also directly responsible to the Commander-in-Chief. I asked what Special Air Service meant. He said it meant that everyone had to be parachute trained. I asked him if he liked parachuting. He said that he found it most disagreeable, but thought that it might be a useful way of getting to places – behind the enemy lines, for instance. Once you were there you could blow things up and find your way home by other means. I asked what they had managed to do so far. He said their first operation had been a disaster. But since then they had had several successes; all in the desert. They had taken the enemy by surprise and done a good deal of damage. He went on to elaborate his ideas on small-scale raiding. They were most illuminating. We could operate in the desert first of all; then in southern and eastern Europe. Small parties could be dropped there by parachute and then picked up on the coast by submarine. There were endless possibilities.

It sounded promising. I said I should be delighted to join.

Special Air Service Headquarters were in the Suez Canal Zone. I travelled down with two Sergeants coming back from leave in a truck that was full of tommy-guns and parachutes and packets of high-explosive. It was a long bleak drive. A bitter wind filled one's eyes with sand and chilled one to the bone. On either side of the narrow tarmac road, with its never-ending stream of cars and trucks, the desert stretched away dismally. From time to time we passed camps and dumps: huts and tents and barbed wire and sign posts and clouds of flies, an uninviting smell of food rising from the cookhouses; the sickly smell of disinfectant rising from the latrines.

Now and then, as we jolted along, I caught snatches of the Sergeants' conversation. They were talking about the last operation. 'Dropped in the wrong place . . . rations all gone . . . ammunition all gone . . . water all gone . . . couldn't make out if their parachutes hadn't opened or what . . . dead when we found him . . . enemy patrol . . . gave them a burst for luck . . . couldn't see in the dark . . . must have stepped on a mine.'

It was dark when we arrived. The wind was still blowing the sand about. I was told that Guardsman Duncan would look after me. He was a large, imperturbable man from Aberdeen. Before the war he had been a male nurse. There was, it seemed, a shortage of tents. Together we set out to look for one, plodding through the soft sand. In the end we found one that looked empty. But it had someone else's kit in it. I asked if it mattered taking someone else's tent. 'Ah,' said Duncan gloomily, 'the poor gentleman will not be requiring it any more; or his kit.' Then he brought me a hurricane lamp and a petrol-can full of water, spread my sleeping-bag on the previous occupant's camp bed and went away.

By the light of day things looked a good deal more cheerful. Our camp was pitched on the shores of the Great Salt Bitter Lake. The wind had fallen in the night and the sun was shining on the blue water. There was good bathing only a few hundred yards away. There was an R.A.F. station on one side of us and a Naval camp on the other. Some landing-craft were riding at anchor off the shore. A lot seemed to be going on.

As I was unpacking my kit, the flap of the tent was pulled back and a wild-looking figure with a beard looked in. 'My tent,' he said. It was the owner, Bill Fraser. He was not dead at all. Finding himself cut off, he had walked back across two hundred odd miles of desert to our own lines, keeping himself alive by drinking rusty water from the radiators of derelict trucks. It showed what could be done.

Resignedly Guardsman Duncan set out to find me a new tent. This time he erected outside it a small board, labelled, quite firmly: THE CLACHAN. I had settled in.

More operations were being planned. David Stirling had said that, as soon as I was trained, I could go on one. The next thing was to get trained.

Parachuting was only part of the training. So far the S.A.S. had attempted only one parachute operation, and it had not been a success. They had been dropped in the wrong place; they had had difficulty in reaching their target; they had run into every kind of trouble; they had lost several of their men; their stock had gone down at G.H.Q. After this setback, David had come to the conclusion that, in the desert, parachuting was not necessarily the best way of reaching one's target.

The survivors of the first operations had been picked up by Long-Range Desert Group. This was a specially equipped, specially trained unit, which had been formed the year before primarily for reconnaissance purposes. In patrols of half a dozen trucks, carrying their own water and petrol, they pushed far into the vast expanse of waterless desert which stretched away for hundreds of miles to the south of the relatively narrow coastal strip where the Desert War was being waged. They thus circumnavigated the flank of the two armies, and re-emerged miles behind the enemy lines. There they stayed for weeks on end, hiding in the desert with their trucks camouflaged, watching enemy troop movements and returning with much vital information. The desert, particularly that part of it which was nominally enemy territory, became a second home to them.

We had to have the L.R.D.G. to bring us back (for the idea that we were 'expendable' or a 'suicide squad' was strongly discouraged by all concerned). Why, David argued, should we not make use of their trucks to take us to the scene of the intended operation or at any rate to a point from which the target to be attacked could be reached on foot? It would be a safer, more comfortable and, above all, more practical way of reaching our destination than parachuting. And it would involve no great loss of time, for, when necessary, the L.R.D.G. could cover great distances very quickly.

Henceforward the Long-Range Desert Group provided expert knowledge of the desert, skilled navigation and first-rate administration — vital necessities where one's life and the success of the operation depended on getting to the right place at the right time and on carrying with one a sufficient load of food, petrol and water to last the trip. David, for his part, brought to these ventures the striking power and, to their planning and execution, what Lawrence has called 'the irrational tenth ... like the kingfisher flashing across the pool': a never-failing audacity, a gift of daring improvisation, which invariably took the enemy by surprise. The resulting partnership was a most fruitful one.

The best targets were aerodromes. From these the Luftwaffe and their Italian allies regularly attacked our convoys, fighting their way through the Mediterranean to Malta, and Eighth Army, now driven back to the Egyptian frontier. Situated hundreds of miles behind the front, these desert airfields were not heavily defended: some wire, some machine-gun posts and an occasional patrol were considered sufficient protection. After carefully studying the lie of the land, it was possible to slip through the wire under cover of darkness, and surreptitiously deposit charges of high explosive in the aircraft where they stood dotted about the airfield. The high explosive, mixed for better results with an incendiary substance, was made up into handy packages and provided with a device known as a time-pencil which could be set to detonate the charge after an interval of a quarter or half an hour.[1] This gave the attackers time to put a mile or two of desert between themselves and the airfield before their bombs exploded and the alarm was given. After that it only remained for them to make their way back to wherever the L.R.D.G. trucks were waiting to pick them up.

Working on these lines, David achieved, in the months that followed, a series of successes which surpassed the wildest expectations of those who had originally supported his venture. No sooner was one operation completed than he was off on another. No sooner had the enemy become aware of his presence in one part of the desert and set about taking counter-measures than he was attacking them somewhere else, always where they least expected it. Never has the element of surprise, the key to success in all irregular warfare, been more brilliantly exploited. Soon the number of aircraft destroyed on the ground was well into three figures. In order to protect their rear the enemy were obliged to bring back more and more front-line troops. And all this was done with a handful of men, a few pounds of high explosive and a few hundred rounds of ammunition. One thing, perhaps, con-

[1] They were known as Lewis Bombs after their inventor, Jock Lewis, who had helped raise the S.A.S. and was killed in one of the first operations.

tributed more than anything else to the success of these operations: that David both planned them and carried them out himself, and that, in the early days at any rate, every man in the unit had been picked by him personally.

Second only to David Stirling's own part in the history of the S.A.S. was that played by Paddy Mayne, a large and formidable Ulsterman, who combined immense physical strength with great agility both of mind and body and at the same time possessed a total disregard of danger and a genuine love of fighting for fighting's sake which can rarely have been equalled. In twelve months he destroyed over a hundred enemy aircraft on the ground with his own hands, a record which puts into the shade the performance of the most successful fighter pilots. A tremendous figure of a man, with a deceptively quiet manner, he inspired absolute devotion and confidence in those he led and utter terror in the hearts of those who were unfortunate enough to encounter him in battle.

Training was based on this practical experience. Physical fitness was clearly of the utmost importance. For days and nights on end we trudged interminably over the alternating soft sand and jagged rocks of the desert, weighed down by heavy loads of explosive, eating and drinking only what we could carry with us. In the intervals we did weapon training, physical training and training in demolitions and navigation.

Two Free French officers, Captain Berger and Lieutenant Jordan, had joined the S.A.S. at about the same time as I had, bringing with them a dozen or so French other ranks, and it was with them that I did most of my preparatory training. Berger came from southern France; Jordan from the north. The one was excitable; the other calm and phlegmatic. Both had one idea in life: to get at the enemy. They took their training very seriously, marching twice as far as anyone else and prolonging the periods of physical training almost beyond human endurance. I went with them. It was a stimulating, but exhausting experience.

Someone had to teach the French about explosives. We put in to G.H.Q. for a sapper. They sent us Bill Cumper. After twenty years in the Army, Bill had recently been given a commission. He had spent the last few weeks hastily blowing up Eighth Army stores and installations to prevent them falling into the hands of the advancing Germans. He knew all there was to be known about demolitions. He arrived straight from the desert in a fifteen-hundredweight truck full of high explosive. As he got out, I noticed that he was wearing a detonator behind his ear as if it were a cigarette. He had sandy-coloured hair and a jaunty appearance. His hat was worn well over one eye. He had a loud and penetrating voice. His pockets were bulging with explosive devices of one kind or another.

Soon it became clear that we had made a remarkable acquisition. In addition to his knowledge of explosives, Bill had a gift for repartee which pricked anything approaching pomposity as though with a pin. He was never bad-tempered and never at a loss. He also had an unrivalled command of cockney rhyming slang and a most revealing stock of anecdotes. After an initial period of total bewilderment, the French, who only understood one word in three of what he said, took to him whole-heartedly, and he to them. Soon the whole camp echoed with the crash and thud of exploding charges. When at the end of a fortnight he left us, our knowledge of the theory and practice of demolitions had increased out of all recognition and Bill had become an important part of our lives.

So important a part that we decided that we must get him back at all costs. David and I went up to Cairo to look for him. We found him sitting in an office in the Chief Engineer's Branch, dispensing sanitary fittings and looking, for once, profoundly unhappy. Some strings were pulled (an art in which David specialized), and a few days later Bill was with us once more, this time on a permanent basis.

I still had my six parachute jumps to do. Despite the failure of the one operation in which parachutes had been used, David insisted that everyone joining the S.A.S. should be parachute trained. Already he was looking forward to the time when we should be operating, not only in the desert, but on the continent of Europe, and then the parachute would be essential. He also thought, rightly or wrongly, that parachute training had a good effect on morale. So we all jumped.

In the light of later experience I now realize that our parachute course was not on strictly orthodox lines. Our preliminary training consisted in jumping from a fifteen-hundredweight truck while it was being driven across the desert at a brisk thirty miles per hour, or alternatively in stepping from the top of a fifteen-foot tower. Several students broke arms and legs doing this, thereby bringing their career as parachutists to a close.

Then came the real thing. The aircraft from which we jumped were Wellington bombers, borrowed from the R.A.F. station across the road on days when they were not needed for bombing operations. On these occasions they were temporarily fitted up for parachute jumping by our instructor, Peter Warr, a resourceful young man with curly hair and an excitable manner, who had recently arrived out from England and who was the only man in the Middle East who knew anything about parachuting at all. The method of attaching the static lines to the plane was, he said, one that he had invented himself. He hoped that it would work. So did we.

In common with every other parachute instructor Peter had a considerable natural gift for dramatization. Somehow he contrived to make the unpleasant but relatively simple act of stepping out of an aeroplane appear as the climax of a great drama. While we were still on the ground he would dash round yelling instructions on a noisy and entirely unnecessary motor bicycle, followed by an equally noisy and even more unnecessary Alsatian dog. We fitted our parachutes and climbed into the aircraft amid pandemonium. Once we had taken off he would continue to shout above the noise of the engines, occasionally breaking off to whisper vaguely disturbing and only half-comprehensible technicalities into one's ear. As the moment to jump approached, he would work himself up into such a frenzy of excitement that he almost fell out of the plane, jumping up and down, waving his arms and screaming the order in which we were to jump at the top of his voice: ONE, TWO, THREE, FOUR . . .

One good thing about all this was that, when we had done our six jumps and could wear our wings, we felt delighted with ourselves, as if we had really done something. The more so as we were the first Allied parachute unit in the Middle East and there was therefore no competition. Few of us, I think, enjoyed jumping, at any rate not after the first jump; but it was agreeable to think about afterwards.

Indeed, looking back, I am not sure that Peter Warr's dramatic approach was not perhaps as good as any. At any rate it lent excitement to what might have otherwise been a dreary and unpleasant routine. He himself soon got tired of teaching and joined a parachute battalion, with which he greatly distinguished himself three years later at Arnhem.

Now that I had done my jumps my training was completed. I was due to go on the next operation. I had pictured it as an attack on a desert aerodrome. But, as things turned out, it was on different lines.

CHAPTER III

OUTWARD BOUND

I N the spring of 1942 Benghazi was a place of considerable importance.

Despite the demolitions carried out before our withdrawal the previous autumn, the enemy had soon put the harbour back into commission, and it was now serving as the principal supply port for Field-Marshal Rommel's Afrika Korps, who were standing opposite Eighth Army in the neighbourhood of Gazala, two or three hundred miles further east. At the same time, enemy aircraft based on the complex of airfields situated in the Benghazi area, Regima, Benina and Berka, were affording the enemy valuable support and decimating our convoys on their way through the Mediterranean to Malta.

Something had to be done to stop this.

Night after night the bomber pilots from the R.A.F. station across the road dropped ton upon ton of high explosive on the docks and aerodromes of Benghazi. Once Peter Warr managed to smuggle himself on board a Wellington as rear gunner and came back with a highly coloured story of bombs whistling down and *flak* streaming up.

But air bombardment was only one way of dealing with the problem, and not necessarily the most effective. The S.A.S. had already made a number of extremely successful attacks on the aerodromes round Benghazi. G.H.Q. were now toying with the idea of a raid on the docks and installations in the town itself.

The plan was that, as a first step, a small party should enter the town surreptitiously and make a stealthy tour of the harbour. If they found suitable targets – shipping in particular – they were to attack them. They were in any case to spy out the land for an eventual large-scale operation.

David had said that I could go on the first operation after my training was completed. This was it.

For an operation of this kind it was necessary to wait for a moonless period. The next one was in the second half of May. This gave us plenty of time to make our preparations.

The first question to decide was how to get into Benghazi. There was clearly no advantage to be gained by parachuting. For a time we considered the possibility of landing from the sea. But in the end we fell back as usual on the good offices of the L.R.D.G. They would escort us to within reach of Benghazi, after which we would go on into the town by ourselves, taking with us a supply of explosives and some kind of light boat to use in the harbour. We would travel in the 'battle-waggon'.

This was a new, cut-down Ford station waggon, with room in it for six people and a certain amount of kit. It was well sprung and had a powerful engine, and the removal of the roof and sides had considerably increased its speed. It was fitted with mountings for two machine guns in front and two behind. The guns themselves could be removed at will and placed out of sight on the floor, thereby giving it a more innocent appearance. For our present purpose we had it painted dark grey to resemble a German staff car with the enemy air-recognition mark, a broad white stripe across the bonnet.

The question of the boat was left to me. We wanted something that would fold into a small space and was easily portable. First, I borrowed a selection of R.A.F. rubber-dinghies from a thoroughly mystified administrative officer at the R.A.F. station next door. But these were oddly shaped and hard to manage in the water. They were also for the most part orange or lemon-yellow in colour, being designed so as to be visible from as far away as possible; which was not what we wanted. They were inflated, too, by means of a small cylinder of compressed air, which, when we tried to use it, went off with a noise like the last trump, setting all the dogs barking for miles round.

Then I remembered an article of army equipment known as a Boat, reconnaissance, (Royal Engineers), and with the help of Bill Cumper procured two of them. They were small and black and handy and you inflated them by means of a small pair of bellows, which emitted a wheezing sound. Each held two men with their equipment.

The party for the operation was made up of three officers, David Stirling, Gordon Alston and myself, and three N.C.O.s, Corporal

Rose, Corporal Cooper and Corporal Seekings. Gordon Alston, a recent arrival, knew Benghazi well, having spent some time there while it was under British occupation the year before. He would act as guide. The three Corporals had been with the S.A.S. since it was first raised and had taken part in most of David's operations.

We now started on an intensive course of boating. Every night, after dark, we carried our little black boats down to the Great Salt Bitter Lake, inflated them, and paddled about, while one of the party played sentry and shouted out as soon as he heard or saw us. This was generally very soon. The bellows made a noise; our paddles made a noise; the smooth luminous surface of the lake made a background against which we showed up all too clearly. But we consoled ourselves with the thought that, on the night, there would be no moon and the sentries in Benghazi would not be expecting us.

We were also encouraged by the success of our dress rehearsal. One night after dinner we all piled into the battle-waggon, with our rubber boats in the back, and motored over to Suez. Despite the enemy recognition mark on the car and the fact that none of us were wearing proper uniform, the guard at the entrance to the docks made no difficulty about admitting us. Once inside, we drove down to the water's edge, unpacked the boats and started to inflate them.

A gunner from a nearby Anti-Aircraft site strolled across and stood watching us. 'What are you blokes on?' he inquired in a friendly way. 'Never you —ing mind,' we replied offensively. 'You — off'. 'All right; all right,' he said in an aggrieved tone 'I didn't mean no harm,' and walked sadly away. Would a German, we wondered, have been as easy to get rid of?

As soon as he was out of sight, we embarked: David and Corporal Cooper in one boat, and Seekings and myself in the other. The rest of the party stayed by the car. Taking a bearing on a convenient light, we paddled off in the direction of two tankers that we had seen from the quayside. It was further than we thought; a long row in choppy water; and hard to keep direction amid the many flickering lights of a big port. But we got there in the end. When we were within a dozen yards of our tanker, Seekings and I shipped our paddles and let our little boat drift up against her side. Then, holding ourselves in position by the tanker's hawser, we fixed a couple of 'limpets' to her stern. These were half-spheres of metal, made to contain a pound or so of high explosive and fitted with a magnetic device to hold them to the side of the ship. They could be detonated by a time-pencil and were guaranteed to blow a sizable hole in a hull of ordinary thickness. This time we used empty ones.

For a moment, we hung listening to snatches of the crew's conversation which floated through the lighted porthole. Then we let go and paddled back again. On the jetty we found David and Corporal Cooper who had been equally successful; we deflated the boats, packed them into the car and drove out of the harbour area and out of Suez without further incident. It was too easy.

Next morning we rang up the Port Authorities and asked them to return our limpets. They were not amused.

The next few days were taken up with drawing stores, with tommy-gun and pistol practice, and with other last-minute preparations. It was not easy to stave off the well-meaning curiosity of our friends, most of whom had guessed that something was afoot, though none except those of us who were actually taking part in the operation knew our destination.

Meanwhile the S.A.S. had gained a new recruit: Randolph Churchill, who had left a Staff job in Cairo to join us. Randolph had too good a nose for news not to find out in a very short time that we were going on an operation. And, as soon as he had discovered this, he wanted to come too.

David objected that he had not done his training and that in any case there was only room for six in the car. But Randolph continued to plead, and in the end a compromise was reached. Randolph would come as an observer on the first part of the trip, but would stay behind with the L.R.D.G. patrol who accompanied us, while we went into Benghazi. Randolph grudgingly accepted this arrangement, but it was clear from the start that he would not be happy until he got his own way.

Eventually the appointed day arrived and we set out for Alexandria where we were to receive a final briefing from the Intelligence Authorities.

Alexandria looked inviting in the early morning sunshine: white houses glistening in the sun round the wide sweep of the blue bay. At the Naval Intelligence Office at Raz-el-Tin everything was ready for us; maps, air-photographs, the latest intelligence reports, and, finally, a large wooden model of Benghazi, with its Cathedral, its government buildings, its docks, streets and houses all accurately constructed to scale. In a little white-washed inner room, barred to all save the initiated, we settled down to impress its features on our memories, working out on the model our best way into the city and the best route down to the docks.

At the base of one of the jetties in the harbour was what seemed to be a narrow strip of shingle. On the model it was marked by a tiny dab of yellow paint, between the grey of the jetty and the green of the harbour. This, if we could reach it, would be a good place to launch our boats. But first we would have to get through a barbed-wire entanglement and past the sentries who were known to patrol the docks.

Always assuming that we managed to get into the town. This would largely depend on the sort of check which the enemy kept on the main roads leading into Benghazi. Anxiously we asked what we might expect in the way of check posts or road blocks. The latest photographs and reports were studied, and we were told that if we approached it by the Benina road, it should be possible to get into the city without being challenged. There had been a check post, but it seemed to have been abolished. We heaved a sigh of relief. In any case an isolated night-watchman or sentry should be easy enough to deal with.

Before we left we arranged to be kept supplied by wireless with any fresh information that might come in. We also arranged with the R.A.F. to leave Benghazi alone the night we were there, but to give it a good bombing the night before we went in. This, we hoped, would help to cause confusion and lower the powers of resistance of any members of the garrison that we might encounter during our visit.

Then, after an excellent luncheon, we piled into the battle-waggon and started off westwards along the coastal road. As we were leaving the outskirts of Alexandria, I noticed a sign-post put up before the war by the Royal Egyptian Automobile Club. 'BENGHAZI', it said hopefully, 'KM.1000'.

We spent the night at Mersa Matruh, a cluster of white buildings and green palm trees nestling among the sand dunes on the edge of the Mediterranean.

It was from Matruh that my father had set out in 1916 across the desert, first to reconnoitre and later to capture Siwa Oasis. At that time the Senussi Arabs, whose stronghold Siwa was, had risen against the Italians, then our allies, and, with the help of Turkish and German officers landed by submarine, were causing us great embarrassment and tying up in Egypt considerable forces which could otherwise have been diverted elsewhere. Against them we employed Light Car Patrols, the first units to use motor vehicles for long-range work in the desert. Armed with machine guns and equipped with T. model Fords they finally captured Siwa in 1917.

After the fall of Siwa the Senussi gave us no more trouble on the Egyptian side of the frontier, though, in spite of the most brutal repression, they kept up for twenty years a spasmodic resistance to the Italians across the border in Libya. Now, with the Italians fighting against us, the Senussi, throughout the desert, both in Egypt and Libya, had become our allies, and Siwa was the Headquarters of the L.R.D.G. and the jumping-off place for our raids. Sometimes L.R.D.G. patrols, far out in the desert, came on the tracks made in the gravel by their predecessors, the Light Car Patrols, and found rusty bully-beef tins marking their camp sites.

Next day we too set out for Siwa, branching inland and travelling in a south-westerly direction across the desert by what was now a well-marked track. On the following morning, after a night in the open, we came in sight of the oasis; first an escarpment of red and yellow sandstone and then, lying in a trough, surrounded by salt marshes and palm groves, Siwa itself.

Ever since I was a child I had been brought up on stories of Siwa. In the years before 1914 a cousin of mine had been one of the relatively few Europeans to enter the oasis, and he and my father had played their part in the operations which led to its capture. Now, it did not fall short of my expectations. Under the palm trees were pools of clear fresh water bubbling up from a great depth. Round one of them was an ancient stone parapet. I remembered my father telling me what a joy it was to plunge into these pools after long weeks in the desert, and now, at an interval of a quarter of a century, I followed his example. The water was deliciously refreshing and gushed up with such force that it was like bathing in soda water.

In the middle of the oasis rose what was left of the fortress-town of the Senussi, built of mud and shaped like a beehive. The shells of 1917 had torn great breaches in its walls, revealing inside it the columns of the ancient Greek temple of Jupiter Ammon, whose oracle was famous in the time of Herodotus. Nearby, among the palm groves, were some older ruins, dating back to the ancient Egyptians. In the market place the Arabs clustered round us, friendly and curious, and soon I found myself being entertained to tea and mutton by several of the leading citizens. As in Central Asia, the food was placed in a large central dish, from which we all helped ourselves with our fingers. An elaborate pipe was also passed round for each of us to take a pull at in turn as we squatted on the ground. Meanwhile the L.R.D.G. Medical Officer, who had accompanied me on this expedition, was fascinated by the disease from which my immediate neighbour was suffering. 'Very interesting,' he kept saying, 'and no doubt highly contagious.'

The L.R.D.G. had their mess in some modern buildings built by the Egyptian Government, and there they made us welcome. The unit was made up of a number of patrols recruited from volunteers from different regiments or formations. There was a Guards Patrol, a New Zealand Patrol, a Rhodesian Patrol and so on. We were to be escorted on our present venture by the Guards Patrol, and we were now taken charge of by Robin Gurdon, who commanded it.

We could not have had a better host. Robin had come to the L.R.D.G. after a long spell in the desert with the Coldstream Guards. Though no longer, by our standards at any rate, so very young, he had spent all his war as a junior regimental officer and most of it fighting. He performed the arduous duties which he had chosen superlatively well and obstinately refused the many Staff appointments which would have been open to him. He was to be killed on his next patrol, continuing to direct operations to the end after he had been mortally wounded.

Now, a tall elegant figure with a heavy fair moustache, his face burnt black by the sun, he made us welcome in the two-roomed, doorless and windowless mud hut in which he lived, as hospitably as though it had been a country house at home: showing us where to spread our bedding rolls, arranging for us to be called with tea and shaving water, and arranging for trucks to take us down to bathe.

At the Headquarters Mess we met the Commanding Officer, Colonel Prendergast, and Bill Shaw, the Intelligence Officer. Both had known the Western Desert well before the war, when they had spent their leave exploring it on their own account in company with Colonel R. A. Bagnold. Now that the desert, from being a geographical curiosity, had become an area of first-rate strategical importance, their knowledge was of inestimable value. Fortunately General Wavell, with characteristic insight, had been quick to grasp this and in 1940 had entrusted Bagnold and his companions with the task of raising the L.R.D.G.

The more I saw of the L.R.D.G., the more impressed I was. There seemed to be nothing they did not know about the desert. In the two years since the unit had first been formed, their patrols had covered immense areas of country which the two conflicting armies, as they fought their way up and down the narrow coastal strip in the north, had left completely untouched. With the help of the sun-compass and the theodolite they had perfected the art of desert navigation and could bring you unerringly to a given hillock or heap of stones hundreds of miles away in the middle of a vast expanse of featureless sand and gravel. They had mapped and charted great stretches of unknown desert and could tell you with unfailing accuracy what to expect in the way of going, where you could hope to get through with a light truck and where with a three-tonner, where to look for cover and how to find the occasional well, half choked up with sand, upon which your survival might easily depend. They had worked out to the last ounce and the last gallon the amount of food, water and petrol needed to take so many men and so many vehicles so far. They had made dumps of food and petrol in safe places which patrols could fall back on if necessary and which meant that they could stay away from their base far longer than would otherwise have been possible. Finally they had a first-class system of wireless-communications which enabled the patrols to keep in constant touch with Headquarters and flash back immediately the vital information which they collected from hundreds of miles behind the enemy lines.

Officers and other ranks alike were volunteers. They needed to be, for staying in the desert for weeks on end, short of food and short of water, is not everyone's idea of fun. But these men had deliberately chosen this life, and few units could compare with them for morale.

When our preparations were completed, we left Siwa. The L.R.D.G. had provided us with the Arab head-dresses which they wore themselves. We were delighted with them. Apart from their romantic appearance, they were extremely practical articles of equipment. They were cool to wear and gave good protection against the sun, and, when you were not wearing them, you could use them as a towel or a dish-cloth or spread them over your face and go to sleep, oblivious to sun, sand and flies.

At first the going was good — a surface of hard smooth gravel over which we bowled along at forty miles an hour. Then, a little further on, we struck our first patch of soft sand and were soon out pushing and pulling in the midday sun, while our vehicles plunged and floundered helplessly. Desert travel is a succession of such contrasts, but, under the expert guidance of the L.R.D.G., we fared on the whole remarkably well, encountering a minimum of difficulties.

First we drove almost due north for 80 miles or so in the direction of Sollum, which brought us to the Wire. This was a barbed-wire entanglement, six feet high and thirty feet wide, running southwards for two hundred miles from the coast along the Libyan-Egyptian frontier, which had been erected ten years earlier by Marshal Graziani at a cost of a quarter of a million pounds, in the hope of better controlling the permanently disaffected native population of the province of which he was governor. But by now there were a number of gaps in it, and through one of these we slipped, like rabbits into a bed of lettuces.

During the first days we moved from dawn till dusk. Taking off our shirts, we drove in nothing but drill shorts and sandals. The Libyan sun was blazing hot, but at the speed at which we were moving there was always a breeze and we did not feel its heat. At midday we stopped briefly for lunch — tinned salmon or sardines and tinned fruit, unwonted luxuries included in the L.R.D.G.'s special scale of rations. Then, when the wireless operator had made contact with Siwa and the navigator checked our position, we climbed back into our trucks and drove on till sundown.

After driving for twelve hours or more, the evening halt would be something to look forward to. Night falls quickly in the desert and the air grows suddenly cold. All at once you would feel the need of every scrap of clothing you possessed. Supper did not take long to prepare: hot bully stew; tea, and sometimes a tot of rum. It was cooked over a desert fire, made by pouring some petrol into a tin filled with sand, which then burned with a steady flame for a surprisingly long time. After we had eaten, and filled our water bottles from the water tank in preparation for the following day, we would sit round the fire muffled in our greatcoats. Robin had a white Hebron sheepskin coat. Sometimes when the day's signals had been sent and received, the wireless would be turned to more frivolous uses and we would listen to jazz music, or to Tommy Handley, or to the eight o'clock news from London. Or to Lili Marlene, the new German *chanteuse*, singing her special song for the Afrika Corps from Radio Belgrade, now in enemy hands:

> Unter der Laterne,
> Vor dem grossen Tor . . .

Husky, sensuous, nostalgic, sugar-sweet, her voice seemed to reach out to you, as she lingered over the catchy tune, the sickly sentimental words. Belgrade . . . The continent of Europe seemed a long way away. I wondered when I would see it again and what it would be like by the time we got there.

Soon the fire would die down and we would seek out a soft patch of sand on which to spread our sleeping-bags. We slept soundly under the stars with a cool breeze playing on our faces.

The noise of the cook getting breakfast woke you before dawn. From your sleeping-bag you watched the desert fire flare up against

208

the lightening sky. There were five short minutes more before you need get up. Then 'Come and get it' shouted the cook, rattling his can, and you crawled out of your sleeping-bag, pulled on your boots, collected mug and mess-tin and stumbled sleepily over to the fire.

It was a good breakfast: porridge, sausage, sometimes tinned bacon, biscuit and hot sweet tea. Afterwards you cleaned your mug and mess-tin in the sand, for water was too precious to waste on washing up; rolled up your bedding roll; helped load the trucks; and drove on. Soon the sun was high in the sky and you could shed, first your great-coat, then your sweater, and then your shirt.

Our course, now that we were through the wire, lay roughly north-west. The desert was sometimes flat, sometimes broken and undulating; sometimes sandy, sometimes hard and stony; in colour a mixture of greys and browns and yellows and reds, all bleached by the sun and merging one into the other. We came upon nothing resembling an oasis; but in some places the rains had produced an ephemeral crop of coarse grass and scrub. Once or twice we saw gazelle, tiny creatures hardly larger than hares, bounding away in front of the trucks. One night I killed a snake as it was crawling into my sleeping-bag. One day a Beaufighter flew over us and we felt uncomfortably conspicuous with our enemy recognition mark exposed to view.

Soon we were parallel with Gazala where, further north on the coast, the two armies were facing each other. In our own very small way, we were turning the enemy's flank. From now onwards we would be behind his lines, and must look out for trouble.

For the last part of the journey we travelled by night and lay up by day. Our routine was reversed. We moved off after supper and stopped to bivouack at first light. Breakfast would be more welcome than ever. After a long chilly night's drive, straining our eyes in the darkness for unseen obstacles and pitfalls, we found that there was a lot to be said for a dram of whisky stirred into our porridge. It made a sustaining and stimulating mixture which I can warmly recommend as a breakfast dish to all engaged on similar enterprises.

Our first care when we halted was to camouflage our trucks against observation from the air. We usually chose as a stopping-place a dip in the ground, or some rocks, or a patch of scrub. Carefully disposing our vehicles so as to make the best use of such cover as there was, we would then set about blending them into the background, with bits of scrub and camouflage nets stretched right over them. The L.R.D.G. trucks were painted with a bold design of rose-pink and olive-green, which, oddly enough, made them practically invisible against the desert. Later the S.A.S. adopted the same camouflage, and several times I was caught with a vehicle in the open by low-flying enemy aircraft without the pilot seeming to notice us.

Our camouflage completed, we would settle down to try and get some sleep. But it was hard to escape the glare of the sun which beat down mercilessly, pursuing us, as it rose higher, from one dwindling patch of shade to another. Then there were the flies, which appeared by myriads in a place where, an hour before, there had been no sign of life, and buzzed and crawled over your face as you lay. It was hard, too, lying there sweating, with nothing else to think of, to forget how thirsty you were. But in the end exhaustion would get the best of it and you would drowse off and wake to find the cook warming up the bully stew in readiness for a start at dusk.

On one such day, as we were dozing fitfully beside the trucks, we were brought back to our senses half-way through the morning by a shout from the look-out man, who came running up to say that he could see something moving on the skyline. In turn, we took the glasses and peered at it, distinctly recognizable as a motor vehicle of some kind and now disappearing rapidly over the horizon.

Where we were, we had to assume that any vehicle we encountered was an enemy one. And we could not afford to let an enemy vehicle get back to its base with the news that it had seen us. Snatching up our tommy-guns, David and I jumped into the battle-waggon and set out after it at top speed.

We soon began to gain on it. From nearer by it looked like a British truck, but there were too many of our trucks in enemy hands to go by this alone. When the driver saw us he accelerated sharply, and went careering wildly off across the desert, ignoring our signals to stop. But our Ford was the faster car and we had soon headed him off and brought him to a standstill.

The truck stopped and two figures in grubby khaki shirts and shorts got out of it. We asked them who they were. 'S.A.S.,' they said resentfully with a strong foreign accent.

We thought we had them there.

But then they explained in guttural English that they were members of a South African Survey Unit, now engaged in surveying this part of the desert. When we pointed out to them that they were miles behind the enemy lines, they seemed mildly surprised. They didn't, they said, bother about anything much except their work, and it hadn't occurred to them that anything might be wrong until we had started to chase them. We advised them to be more careful in future and left them. They made off as fast as they could go.

Afterwards we wondered if we should not have perhaps examined their credentials rather more closely.

Between us and our destination, running from Agedabia north-eastwards to the sea, lay the Trigh-el-Abd, an ancient caravan route between the coast and the interior. It consisted of innumerable trails, spreading over a wide stretch of country, and was strewn along its whole length with the whitened bones of camels, and no doubt of men, who in the course of centuries had fallen by the way and been left to die.

Of more immediate interest to us was the fact that it was also strewn with 'thermos' bombs. These handy little devices, the size and shape of a thermos flask, were broadcast by the enemy over areas where they thought that our patrols might pass. Half covered by loose sand, they were hard to see and, exploding, did considerable damage to any vehicle that drove over them. We accordingly timed our departure from our previous stopping-place so as to perform this part of our journey in daylight, and, keeping a sharp look-out for bombs, emerged unscathed on the other side.

After crossing the Trigh-el-Abd, we skirted round to the east of Msus, where there was an enemy garrison, and turned in a north-westerly direction towards the coast. Now, more and more frequently, we came upon little groups of burnt-out tanks and trucks, some bearing enemy markings and some British, some with the mangled bodies of their crews still in them, reminders of the bitter fighting of the previous winter. Sometimes, too, the wrecks of aircraft, fighters and bombers, lying where they had crashed far out in the desert, would loom up like ghosts in the moonlight.

Then, one morning, after we had driven all night, first light showed us a completely new landscape. Instead of the Libyan Desert, we might have been in the Highlands of Scotland. We were driving across brownish-green hills and moorland thickly covered with scrub, with here and there stunted trees. The spring flowers had faded, but the wind was heavy with the scent of wild thyme. We passed a Moslem shrine with its tattered banners, such as I had seen in Central Asia. We passed a heap of stones, marking a well, the earth round it trampled by sheep, goats and donkeys.

We had reached the Gebel Akhdar — the Green Mountain — the hilly country which lies south from the coastal plain and which was to serve us as a temporary base. We were within a few hours' drive of Benghazi.

Well watered, by comparison with the desert, the Gebel was fertile enough to support the flocks and herds of the Beduin who dwelt in it. These were nomads for the most part and, like the people of Siwa, belonged to the Senussi sect. Their bitter hatred of the Italians made them the loyal allies of anyone who, like ourselves, was fighting against them. We were thus, in a sense, in friendly country. There was water, too, and, by desert standards, reasonably good cover. Apart from occasional punitive expeditions or search parties, the enemy were inclined to keep out of the whole area.

To the north and east the Gebel fell away abruptly in a steep escarpment at the foot of which lay the coastal plain. Coaxing our trucks across country, along goat tracks and dried-up water-courses, we made our way to a point near the top of the escarpment from which, twenty miles away across the plain, we could see the white walls of Benghazi and beyond them the blue Mediterranean shimmering in the sunlight. Then, camouflaging our trucks among the plentiful natural cover, we camped near them on the sandy bed of one of the dried-up water-courses or *wadis* with which the Gebel abounds.

We did not remain alone for long. We had not seen any Arabs on the way, but they had seen us and now several of them came to visit us. We gave them cups of tea and they gave us eggs. Then we showed them a photograph of Sayed Idris es Senussi, head of their sect and grandson of its founder, who at that time was living under British protection in Egypt. They fingered it admiringly, looking first at it and then at us and grinning.

It was May 20th. We were to go into Benghazi on the twenty-first. We had another twenty-four hours. That night, as we lay in our sleeping-bags, we could see the flashes of the bombs bursting over the town. The R.A.F. were doing their stuff. The moist sea breeze was relaxing after the dry air of the desert and we were soon asleep.

Next morning we made our final preparations. Weapons were cleaned and ammunition counted out and distributed. The rubber boats were taken out; inflated; deflated; and packed up again.

Our friends the Beduin came back and watched us. This time they were accompanied by an Arab we had not seen before, a more sophisticated figure wearing a trilby hat and carrying a neatly rolled umbrella. The newcomer, whom we named the City Slicker, spoke fluent Italian and showed more interest in our affairs than we liked. Reports had reached us of Italian agents sent into the Gebel to watch for British patrols and report on their movement. Could this be one? It looked as though he might be. We were debating as to the wisdom of taking him into protective custody, when, looking round, we found that he had gone.

Meanwhile, in their corner of the *wadi*, Cooper, Seekings and Rose were getting the explosives ready: unpacking the bombs and limpets and fitting the time-pencils and detonators to them. Suddenly there was a sharp report and an oath. We hurried across to see what had happened. A detonator had exploded in Corporal Seekings's hand. He was not badly hurt, but his hand was out of action and there could be no question of his going with us. We were one man short.

It is an ill wind . . . The crack of the detonator had hardly died away, when Randolph appeared, jubilant. His exclusion from our expedition had been a sore point, but this, it seemed to him, made everything easy. Already he was oiling his tommy-gun and polishing his pistol in preparation for the night's work.

Such keenness, David felt, could not be left unrewarded. A spare

N.C.O. who had come with us as a possible replacement in an emergency, was told, much to his disgust, that he would not be needed, and Randolph took Corporal Seekings's place.

We set out in the late afternoon. Two of the L.R.D.G. trucks came with us. It was getting dark as we reached the escarpment. We followed the bed of one of the smaller *wadis* down into the plain, easing the battle-waggon as carefully as we could over the rough ground and boulders. Here and there we passed little groups of Arabs working in the fields. They waved to us and we threw them cigarettes. The going was difficult and it was not till ten that we reached the main Barce-Benghazi road, where the L.R.D.G. trucks were to leave us. It had taken us five hours to do fourteen miles.

Round about us on the plain we could see the camp fires of the Arabs twinkling in the dark. We lit a fire too and brewed up. It was cold and the hot strong sweet tea was welcome. Then we said goodbye to the L.R.D.G., told them to expect us for breakfast in the morning, switched on our headlights and drove off. David and I sat in front with Gordon Alston between us. Randolph and the two N.C.O.s sat in the back. David was driving.

Once we had left the desert and were on the smooth tarmac road, we noticed that the car was making an odd noise. It was more than a squeak. It was a high-pitched screech with two notes in it. Evidently one of the many jolts which they had received had damaged the track-rods. Now the wheels were out of alignment and this was the result.

We lay back on our backs in the road and tinkered. It was no use. When we got back into the car and drove off again, the screech was louder than ever. We could hardly have made more noise if we had been in a fire engine with its bell clanging. It was awkward, but there was nothing we could do about it now. Fortunately it did not seem to affect the speed of the car.

Soon we were passing the high wire fence round Regima aerodrome. We were not far from Benghazi now. We were going at a good speed and should be there in five or ten minutes. I hoped that the Intelligence Branch were right in thinking there was no road block. It was cold in the open car. Feeling in my greatcoat pocket I found a bar of milk chocolate that had been forgotten there. I unwrapped it and ate it. It tasted good.

Then, suddenly, we turned a corner and I saw something that made me sit up and concentrate. A hundred yards away, straight ahead of us, a red light was showing right in the middle of the road.

CHAPTER IV

SHORT WEEKEND

DAVID jammed on the brakes and we slithered to a standstill. There was a heavy bar of wood across the road with a red lantern hanging from the middle of it. On my side of the road stood a sentry who had me covered with his tommy-gun. He was an Italian. I bent down and picked up a heavy spanner from the floor of the car. Then I beckoned to the sentry to come nearer, waving some papers at him with my free hand as if I wanted to show them to him. If only he would come near enough I could knock him on the head and we could drive on.

He did not move, but kept me covered with his tommy-gun. Then I saw that beyond him in the shadows were two or three more Italians with tommy-guns and what looked like a guardroom or a machine-gun post. Unless we could bluff our way through there would be nothing for it but to shoot it out, which was the last thing we wanted at this stage of the expedition.

There was a pause and then the sentry asked who we were. 'Staff Officers,' I told him, and added peremptorily, 'in a hurry.' I had not spoken a word of Italian for three years and I hoped devoutly that my accent sounded convincing. Also that he would not notice in the dark that we were all wearing British uniform.

He did not reply immediately. It looked as though his suspicions were aroused. In the car behind me I heard a click, as the safety catch of a tommy-gun slid back. Someone had decided not to take any chances.

Then, just as I had made my mind up that there was going to be trouble, the sentry pointed at our headlights. 'You ought to get those dimmed,' he said, and, saluting sloppily, opened the gate and stood aside to let us pass. Screeching loudly, we drove on towards Benghazi.

Soon we were on the outskirts of the town.

Coming towards us were the headlights of another car. It passed us

Then looking back over our shoulders, we saw that it had stopped and turned back after us. This looked suspicious. David slowed down to let it pass. The car slowed down too. He accelerated; the car accelerated. He stopped altogether; the car did the same. Then he decided to shake it off. He put his foot down on the accelerator, and, screeching louder than ever, we drove into Benghazi at a good eighty miles an hour with the other car after us.

Once in the town, we turned the first corner we came to and, switching off our headlights, stopped to listen. The other car shot past and went roaring off in the darkness. For the moment our immediate troubles were over.

But only for the moment. As we sat listening a rocket sailed up into the sky, then another, and then another. Then all the air-raid sirens in Benghazi started to wail. We had arranged with the R.A.F. before we started that they should leave Benghazi alone that night; so this could not be an air-raid warning. It looked very much as though the alert was being given in our honour. We remembered the two South Africans, and the City Slicker with his homburg hat, and the suspiciously casual behaviour of the sentry, and last, but not least, our pursuers in the car. It all added up to the same unpleasant conclusion: they were on to us.

Clearly the battle-waggon, with its distinctive screech, was no longer an asset now that the alarm had been given. We decided to get rid of it at once and take a chance of escaping on foot. Planting a detonator timed to go off in thirty minutes, amongst the explosives in the back, we started off in single file through the darkness.

We were in the Arab quarter of the town, which had suffered most heavily from the R.A.F. raids. Every other house was in ruins and, threading our way over the rubble through one bombed-out building after another, we had soon put several blocks between ourselves and the place where we had left the car to explode. Once or twice we stopped to listen. We would hear people walking along the adjacent streets, but no one seemed to be following us.

Then passing through a breach in a wall, we emerged unexpectedly in a narrow side-street, to find ourselves face to face with an Italian Carabiniere.

There was no avoiding him and it seemed better to take the initiative and accost him before he accosted us. The rockets and sirens provided a ready-made subject for conversation. 'What,' I asked, 'is all this noise about?' 'Oh, just another of those damned English air-raids,' he said gloomily. 'Might it be,' I inquired anxiously, 'that enemy ground forces are raiding the town and that they are the cause of the alert?' Even in his depressed state, he thought this a good joke and gave a chuckle. 'No,' he said, 'there's no need to be nervous about that, not with the British almost back on the Egyptian frontier.'

I thanked him for his reassuring remarks and wished him good night. Although we had been standing under a street light, he did not seem to have noticed that I was in British uniform.

This encounter put a different complexion on the situation. We seemed to have been unduly pessimistic. We might have a go at the harbour yet. And save ourselves a long walk back to the Gebel.

We hurried back to the car. Our watches showed that about twenty-five minutes had elapsed since we had set off the time-pencil. If it was an accurate one, there should still be five minutes to go before it detonated and blew up the car. If it was an accurate one. Nervously, we extricated it from the back of the car and threw it over the nearest wall. A minute or two later we heard it go off with a sharp crack. We had not been a moment too soon.

The next thing was to make our way to the harbour, which was about a mile off. The screech made it inadvisable to take the car. Accordingly we left Randolph and Corporal Rose to find somewhere to hide it, while David, Corporal Cooper and myself, with Alston as guide, started off for the harbour, armed with tommy-guns and carrying one of the boats and a selection of explosives in a kitbag. Soon we had left the dark alleyways of the Arab quarter behind us and were in the European part of the town. High white buildings loomed up round us, and our footsteps echoed noisily in the broad paved streets. Then, just as we were coming to the barbed-wire fence which surrounded the harbour, I caught sight of a sentry.

Laden as we were, we made a suspicious-looking party, and once again I thought it better to try to set his suspicions at rest by accosting him, rather than attempting to slink on unnoticed. 'We have,' I said, thinking quickly, 'just met with a motor accident. All this is our luggage. Can you direct us to a hotel where we can spend the night?'

The sentry listened politely. Then he said he was afraid that all the hotels had been put out of action by the accursed English bombing, but perhaps, if we went on trying, we would find somewhere to sleep. He seemed well disposed and had apparently noticed nothing wrong either with my Italian accent or with our uniforms. An unobservant man. We wished him good night and trudged off.

As soon as we were out of sight, we started to look for a place to get through the wire. Eventually we found one and dragged the boat and the explosives through it. Then dodging between cranes and railway trucks we made our way down to the water's edge. Looking round at the dim outlines of the jetties and buildings, I realized with a momentary feeling of satisfaction, that we were on the identical strip of shingle which we had picked on as a likely starting-point on the wooden model at Alexandria. So far, so good.

David, who possesses the gift of moving silently and invisibly by night, now set off on a tour of the harbour with Alston, leaving Cooper and myself to inflate the boat. Crouching under a low sea wall, we unpacked the kitbag and set to work with the bellows. There was no moon, but brilliant starlight. The smooth, shining surface of the harbour was like a sheet of quicksilver, and the black hulls of the ships seemed no more than a stone's throw away. They would make good targets if only we could reach them unobserved. At any rate, we should not have far to paddle, though I could have wished for a better background than this smooth expanse of water. Diligently we plugged away at the bellows, which squeaked louder than I liked, and seemed to be making little or no impression on the boat. Several minutes passed. The boat was still as flat as a pancake. We verified the connection and went on pumping.

Then suddenly we were hailed from one of the ships. It was a sentry. 'Chi va la?' he challenged. 'Militari!' I shouted back. There was a pause and we resumed pumping. But still the sentry was suspicious. 'What are you up to over there?' he inquired. 'Nothing to do with you,' I answered, with a show of assurance which I was far from feeling. After that there was silence.

Meanwhile the boat remained flat. There could only be one explanation. Somehow, since we had inspected it in the *wadi* that morning, it had got punctured. There was nothing for it but to go and fetch another. It was fortunate we had two. Hiding the first boat as best we could under the shadow of the wall, we crossed the docks, slipping unseen through the hole in the wire, and walked back through the silent streets to where we had left the car. There we found Randolph and Rose in fine fettle, trying with the utmost unconcern to manœuvre the car through a hole in the wall of a bombed-out house. Occasionally passers-by, Arabs for the most part, gaped at them with undisguised interest and admiration.

Wishing them luck, we pulled the second boat out of the car and started back to the harbour. Once again we got safely through the wire and down to the water's edge, but only to find that the second boat, like the first, was uninflatable. It was heart-rending. Meanwhile there was no sign of David. We decided to go and look for him.

As we reached the hole in the wire we saw, to our disgust, someone standing on the other side of it. I was just thinking what to say in Italian, when the unknown figure spoke to me in English. It was David, who had been down to the water to look for us and had been as alarmed at not finding us as we had been at not finding him.

There followed a hurried council of war. All this tramping backwards and forwards had taken time and our watches showed that we had only another half-hour's darkness. Already the sky was beginning to lighten. We debated whether or not to plant our explosives haphazard in the railway trucks with which the quays were crowded, but decided that, as targets, they were not important enough to justify us in betraying our presence in the harbour and thus prejudicing the success of an eventual large-scale raid. If we were to blow them up, the alarm would be given. We should probably be able to get away in the confusion, but another time we should stand a much poorer chance of raiding the harbour unnoticed. Our present expedition must thus be regarded as a reconnaissance. It was a hard decision to take, now that we had got so far.

If we were not to excite suspicion, it was essential to take away anything that would betray the fact that intruders had been in the harbour area. This meant going back to the water's edge to retrieve the boats, a nerve-racking trip of which we were beginning to get rather tired. This time, as I started to crawl through the hole in the wire, I suddenly found myself staring into a coal-black face, with round goggling eyes and a set of dazzling white teeth, like a nigger minstrel. It was an Ascari from Italian Somaliland. I did not like the look of him at all. Standing over me, he grunted menacingly and pointed his bayonet at the pit of my stomach. I felt at a distinct disadvantage. David and Corporal Cooper looked on with evident interest. It seemed a more intractable problem than we had hitherto encountered.

Infusing as much irritation into my voice as I could muster, I asked this formidable blackamoor what he wanted; but he only answered, 'Non parlare Italiano,' and went on prodding at me with his bayonet.

This gave me an opening. I have always found that in dealing with foreigners whose language one does not speak, it is best to shout. I did so now. 'Non parlare Italiano?' I yelled, working myself into a fury. 'Non parlare Italiano!! And you a Caporale!!' And I pointed to the stripe on his sleeve.

This seemed to shake him. He lowered his bayonet and looked at me dubiously. My confidence returned. Trying to give as good a representation as I could of an angry Italian officer, I continued to shout and gesticulate.

It was too much for the black man. With an expression of injured dignity, he turned and walked slowly away, leaving us to continue our progress down to the water's edge. There we stuffed the boats and explosives back into the kitbags and started on our return journey, a weary and despondent little party.

It was at this stage that, looking round, I noticed that there were more of us than there should be. Two sentries with rifles and fixed bayonets had appeared from somewhere and fallen in behind.

These were a most unwelcome addition to the party. There was clearly no hope of shaking them off in the harbour area, and, with such companions, it would be fatal to try and negotiate the hole in the wire. Alternatively to try and shoot it out with them would bring the whole place about our ears. There was only one hope, and that was to try somehow to brazen it out.

Assuming as pompous a manner as my ten days' beard and shabby appearance permitted, I headed for the main gate of the docks, followed by David and Corporal Cooper and the two Italian sentries. At the gate a sentry was on duty outside the guard tent. Walking straight up to him, I told him that I wished to speak to the Guard Commander. To my relief he disappeared obediently into the tent and came out a minute or two later followed by a sleepy-looking Sergeant, hastily pulling on his trousers. For the second time that night I introduced myself as an officer of the General Staff, thereby eliciting a slovenly salute. Next, I reminded him that he was responsible for the security of this part of the harbour. This he admitted sheepishly. How was it, I asked him, that I and my party had been able to wander freely about the whole area for the best part of the night without once being properly challenged or asked to produce our identity cards? He had, I added, warming to my task, been guilty of a gross dereliction of duty. Why, for all he knew, we might have been British saboteurs carrying loads of high explosive (at this he tittered incredulously, obviously thinking that I was laying it on a bit thick). Well, I said, I would let him off this time, but he had better not let me catch him napping again. What was more, I added, with a nasty look at the sentry, who winced, he had better do something about smartening up his men's appearance.

Then I set off at a brisk pace through the gate followed by David and Corporal Cooper, but not by the two Italians who had shuffled off into the shadows as soon as they saw there was trouble brewing. My words had not been without effect. As we passed him, the sentry on the gate made a stupendous effort and presented arms, almost falling over backwards in the process.

By the time we got back to the car it was nearly light, and we were relieved to find that Randolph and Corporal Rose had disposed of it in the lower part of a half-demolished house. Hurriedly we set about camouflaging it as best we could with any old bits of planks and sacking that came to hand, and then looked round for somewhere to hide ourselves. For there could be no question of getting back to the Gebel in daylight, and the only alternative was to lie up in Benghazi itself.

On further investigation, the upper storey of the house where we had hidden the car proved to be empty. It consisted of two rooms reached by an outside staircase in a courtyard. The shutters were down and the whole place looked reassuringly derelict. We went inside and closed the door after us.

We might have been very much worse off. There were some tins of bully in the car and someone had a flask of rum. Our quarters were not luxurious, but at any rate there was plenty of floor space on which to lie down and go to sleep.

As we were settling in, we heard a roaring, and, looking out of the window we saw the early morning sky filled with flight after flight of German and Italian bombers coming over the city at roof-top level, doing victory rolls. They had, I suppose, just come back from the front or from a raid on Alexandria.

Gradually the town began to wake up all round us. Many of the Arabs spent the night in the palm groves outside, in order to avoid the bombing, and we could not be sure that suddenly someone would not burst in on us. Through a hole in the wall we watched a wizened old Arab woman next door cooking her breakfast in the courtyard. On the other side of the road, as we looked through the closed shutters, we could see a German Sub-Area Headquarters starting its day's work, with dispatch riders dashing in and out on motor bicycles, and busy-looking officers arriving and leaving. Further down the street an Arab shop was opening its shutters. From where we were we could hear the passers-by in the street below talking in German, Italian and Arabic.

It grew hotter. After we had eaten we each took it in turn to watch whilst the others slept. We still had an uneasy feeling that our presence in the town might somehow have become known and that there might be search parties out after us.

The hours passed. Then, suddenly, as we lay dozing, we heard the sound that we had been half expecting all day: heavy footsteps ascending the stairs.

Randolph, who was keeping watch, was outside first. There was an exclamation and a stampede. Snatching our tommy-guns we reached the door to see a frightened-looking Italian sailor disappearing into the street, whilst Randolph, his beard bristling, stood majestically at the top of the stairs.

Had the intruder been sent to spy on us, or was he simply on the look out for loot? Had he noticed that we were in British uniform? If so, would he do anything about it? We had no means of telling. For the next couple of hours we sat clasping hand-grenades and tommy-guns ready to give any visitors a warm reception. But no one came.

As soon as it was dark, we left our temporary home and set out for a walk round Benghazi, past the Cathedral and along the sea front, keeping a sharp look out for anything that might be of interest on our next visit. For we were determined to return under, we hoped, more auspicious conditions. We walked down the middle of the street arm in arm, whistling and doing our best to give the impression that we had every right to be there. Nobody paid the slightest attention to us. On such occasions it's one's manner that counts. If only you can behave naturally, and avoid any appearance of furtiveness, it is worth any number of elaborate disguises and faked documents.

Our most interesting discovery was a couple of motor torpedo boats tied up to the quayside opposite a large square building, which, from the lights blazing in all the windows and the sentries on duty at the gate, seemed to be some kind of Headquarters. So interesting that we decided that it would be worth trying to blow them up on our way out of town. We accordingly went back to our temporary quarters, extricated the battle-waggon and returned with a supply of bombs.

But our luck was out. As we drew up by the side of the road opposite to where the boats were moored, we saw that in our absence a sentry had been posted there. He looked at us suspiciously. I got out of the car, and, while Corporal Rose tried to get near enough to slip a bomb on one of the boats, I engaged the sentry in conversation.

But it was no use. The sentry was far more interested in what Corporal Rose was doing than in what I was saying, and two more sentries were now watching the scene with increasing interest from the building on the other side of the road. We had missed our opportunity. Reluctantly David called off Corporal Rose and we got back into the car and drove off, screeching disconsolately. Our attempts at sabotage seemed doomed to failure, but we had thoroughly spied out the land and felt by now like old inhabitants of Benghazi. We must hope for better luck another time.

Meanwhile, time was passing and we wanted to be in the Gebel

before first light. We made for the Benina road. On the way out of
the town we drove for a short time in a convoy of enemy trucks. Then
came the road block. Once again the sentry accepted my statement
that we were Staff officers, and in a few minutes we were bowling
along the road towards the Gebel.

We reached our rendezvous with the Long-Range Desert Group at
six on Sunday morning, exactly twenty-four hours late. They had
long since given us up and were having breakfast, preparatory to
moving off. Hungrily we threw ourselves upon mugs of tea and
steaming mess tins of porridge.

CHAPTER V

BACK TO BENGHAZI

OUR journey back across the desert to Siwa was on the whole uneventful. But once in the night we heard a rumble of big guns away to the north and David, who made a detour to visit Eighth Army Headquarters, had his car shot up by marauding enemy fighters at a place called Bir Hakim, soon to become famous for the stand made there by the Free French under General Koenig.

Back at Siwa, the thing that I remember most clearly was the long-awaited plunge into the clear bubbling waters of Cleopatra's pool, a luxury to which we had looked forward all through the parching days in the desert, when there had been very little water for drinking and none at all for washing. But we were in a hurry to get back to Cairo to report and make plans for the future.

In such a hurry that, half-way between Alexandria and Cairo, the battle-waggon left the road and turned over, and it was not until two or three days later that I regained consciousness, through a haze of morphia, to find that I was in hospital in Alexandria with a fractured collar bone, a broken arm and what seemed to be a fractured skull. The rest of the party were all more or less out of action, except for David, who was hardly hurt at all.

At the beginning of July I left hospital to convalesce, and spent the weeks that followed in enforced, but not disagreeable, idleness, waiting for the plaster to be taken off my limbs. Various people came to see me on their way through Alexandria, where I was staying in great luxury with the Teddy Peels. George Jellicoe, who had just joined the S.A.S., came with Georges Berger of the Free French Squadron. They were just starting by submarine for an operation in Crete, and their visit was a reminder that our ultimate goal lay beyond the Mediterranean, in Europe. While in Crete they were betrayed to the enemy and, though Jellicoe got away, Berger spent the rest of the war in a German prison camp.

Meanwhile, to pass the time, as I lay idle on the beach at Sidi Bish, I started to learn modern Greek from the many fair Greek ladies who adorned it. It might, I felt, come in useful.

Then one day David appeared. He had just come back from the desert and was full of plans for a further large-scale raid on Benghazi. He wanted me to come back to Cairo with him at once and start making preparations. A doctor was found to certify that I was once again medically A.1, and we set out.

One night, while we were in Cairo, we dined at the Embassy. The party was a distinguished one: Mr. Churchill, the Chief of the Imperial General Staff, General Smuts and General Alexander, the latter newly arrived from England. Wondering what they had come out to Egypt to do and little realizing that their visit betokened a complete change in the high command, we took the opportunity to put in a word for the S.A.S. We told the distinguished visitors what we planned to do and asked for some equipment to do it with.

I had not seen the Prime Minister since I had become a Member of the House of Commons. Someone had told him of the stratagem which I had employed to extricate myself from the Foreign Office, and this had amused him. 'Here,' he said, dragging me up to General Smuts, 'is the young man who has used the Mother of Parliaments as a public convenience.'

Meanwhile, the plans for a raid on Benghazi had been greeted with enthusiasm at G.H.Q. With such enthusiasm that, by the time they came back to us they were practically unrecognizable. The latest scheme envisaged a major operation against Benghazi, to be carried out in conjunction with similar large-scale operations elsewhere.

The military situation in the Middle East had deteriorated very sharply since May. The gunfire which we had heard on our way back from Benghazi had heralded Rommel's attack on the Gazala line, which was followed by a general offensive. This had begun at the end of May. Bitter fighting had followed: Knightsbridge, Bir Hakim, the fall of Tobruk. Finally, Rommel's advance to El Alamein had brought the Afrika Korps to within eighty or ninety miles of Alexandria. In Cairo the staff at G.H.Q. Middle East were burning their files and the Italian colony were getting out their black shirts and Fascist badges in preparation for Mussolini's triumphant entry. The Long-Range Desert Group had been forced to leave Siwa in a hurry, and that pleasant oasis was now occupied by a detachment of Fascist Youth, who had been specially sent over from Italy for the forthcoming victory parade. Now, Rommel, having consolidated his position at Alamein, was pouring in supplies through Benghazi and the recently captured port of Tobruk, and at the same time centring all available resources before a knock-out blow against Eighth Army.

Our task was to cause a diversion, thereby interfering with this process. Altogether four operations were planned. We were to attack Benghazi, but this time with a force numbering some two hundred men. At the same time a similar raid was to be made on Tobruk with naval and air support. Two patrols of the Long-Range Desert Group were to raid the airfield at Barce, 50 miles east of Benghazi along the coast. Finally the Sudan Defence Force were to take and hold the oasis of Jalo, which was situated in the desert 300 miles due south of Benghazi. Now that Siwa was in enemy hands, the base for these operations would have to be Kufra, an oasis 800 miles south of Benghazi, which had been captured from the Italians in 1941.

Very considerable preparations and much detailed planning were needed for an operation on this scale. Clearly it was no easy task to transport several dozen vehicles and a couple of hundred men across 800 miles of waterless desert without attracting the attention of the enemy.

While David was busy attending conferences, collecting new recruits, begging, buying or stealing additional transport and equipment, I went down to Faiyum, where the L.R.D.G. had made their home after leaving Siwa, to look at maps with Bill Shaw. I also went down to Alexandria to see the Naval Intelligence Division and have a look at the model of Benghazi which had now been brought up to date and was kept in a closely guarded room, together with an equally handsome model of Tobruk.

For obvious reasons, secrecy was vital, and only a very small number of those taking part in the operations were told what their destination was to be. But long before we were ready to start there were signs that too many people knew too much. At Alexandria a drunken marine was heard boasting in a canteen that he was off to Tobruk; a Free French officer picked up some startling information at Beirut; one of the barmen at the hotel, who was generally thought to be an enemy agent, seemed much too well informed. Worse still, there were indications that the enemy was expecting the raids and was taking counter-measures.

Eventually the plan was completed and David and I left for Kufra in a Hudson bomber. We first flew due south down the Nile to Wadi Halfa; then westwards across the desert. It was an unpleasant flight. The hot air rising from the scorching surface of the desert made air pockets through which the aircraft fell like a stone. Looking down, we could see beneath us strange red sandstone conformations. We were glad when we finally jolted to a standstill on the airfield at Kufra.

Up to 1931 Kufra, like Siwa, a stronghold of the Senussi, had been visited by only half a dozen Europeans, the first being the German explorer Rohlfs who reached it by camel in 1879 and narrowly escaped with his life. His exploit was repeated by explorers once or twice in the intervening years, while an occasional unwilling European visitor was taken there as a prisoner of the Arabs. Then in 1931 the Italians, determined to consolidate their North African Empire, launched a motorized expedition against Kufra from the north, and once there, easily reduced it with the help of aircraft and artillery, thus mopping up the last pocket of active resistance in Libya.

Ten years later, almost to a day, a Free French column under General Leclerc arrived unexpectedly from Lake Chad, disposed of the Italian garrison without difficulty, and established an Allied base, which was to serve as a jumping-off place for the L.R.D.G. until the end of the Libyan campaign.

The Italians had erected a fort on a hill dominating the oasis. In the middle of the courtyard a Fascist emblem, made of cement and bearing a pompous Latin inscription which no one had bothered to deface, still celebrated the establishment of this outpost of an empire which even then was already beginning to crumble. From the fort one had a good view of the oasis and the surrounding desert. In many ways Kufra resembled Siwa; the same bright green date palms, the same clusters of Arab huts, built of wattles or mud, the same patches of cultivation.

Amongst the palms there were two lakes of brilliant turquoise-blue, so salt that you could float sitting upright in the water as though in an armchair with half your body above the surface. The fort was occupied by a garrison of French and British troops. Our own forces, together with the L.R.D.G., Sudan Defence Force and the party which was to attack Tobruk, were already encamped under the palms, and there we joined them. All the original members of the unit were there and with them a hundred or more new recruits, thrown in to swell our numbers for the largest operation undertaken hitherto.

There was a lot to be done in a short time. The fitters were hard at work on the trucks, some of which had suffered considerably on the long journey down. Some trucks had got lost in the desert between Wadi Halfa and Kufra, and an aircraft was out looking for them. Bill Cumper's sappers were making bombs, and navigators were busy with their maps. All were cleaning up their weapons. Finally, now that we had the party isolated from outside contacts, all those going on the operation had to be briefed.

Everyone was collected and we unfolded the full plan; we were to rush Benghazi, taking the garrison by surprise, and, once inside, to destroy everything we could lay hands on. If the situation developed favourably, we might even manage to hold out until relief arrived. In any case, we could make it useless to the enemy for quite a time. This news was enthusiastically received by the assembled troops. Now they knew what the little party of sailors was for: they were to take any available ships to the mouth of the harbour and sink them there. They also knew that the purpose of the two light tanks, borrowed from the Tenth Hussars, was to blast their way into Benghazi at the head of our column. (In the event, they stuck in the sand a short distance from Kufra and had to be abandoned.) Altogether, they thought, it sounded a promising plan.

Everywhere little scattered groups sat round the camp fires under the palm trees until late at night talking. Some were coming with us. Others were taking part in the simultaneous and equally ambitious attack on Tobruk, in which a leading part was to be played by a party of German Jews in enemy uniform, who were to bluff their way past the sentries, as the spearhead of a larger force. Nearby, the black troops of the Sudan Defence Force were preparing for their attack on Jalo, the success of which was vital to us, for we would pass within a few miles of Jalo on our way back from Benghazi, and if it was not by then in Allied hands, our retreat would be cut off. On all sides there was a buzz of anticipation.

Next day our advance party, under Paddy Mayne, started for the Gebel and I went with it. We had a formidable array of vehicles. Of these the greater part were our own, for, although we had a patrol of the L.R.D.G. with us and relied on them to a great extent for navigation, we now owned our own transport. This consisted chiefly of Ford three-tonners, carrying petrol, water and supplies, and a fleet of jeeps, mounted with Vickers-K machine guns, which had been found were invaluable for desert raiding. David came to see us off. He himself would follow with the rest of the party in three or four days' time. Everyone was in high spirits, and we gave him a cheer as we drove by.

For the first part of the journey we travelled by day and slept at night. North of Kufra the desert was pinkish in colour and full of fantastic rock formations.

On the second day out, I was awakened before dawn by screams of pain. One of the cooks getting breakfast had carelessly thrown petrol on the fire from a bottle. The flame had shot back up the stream of petrol into the bottle which had burst in his face. He was terribly burnt and in agony. We dressed his burns as best we could and, giving him some morphia, sent him back to Kufra in one of the jeeps. It was lucky for him that we were not further out.

For a convoy as big as ours there was only one practicable route from Kufra to the Gebel. Between us and our destination lay the Sand Sea. This was an expanse of deep, soft, fine sand the size of Ireland, ribbed with long parallel dunes several hundred feet high, following each other in monotonous succession like the waves of the sea. The L.R.D.G. had long ago proved that it was not impassable if you knew how to tackle it, but it was bad going for heavy trucks. Accordingly we aimed for Zighen, a point where the Sand Sea narrows down to a bottleneck not more than twenty miles wide. Here we would cross it and then drive northwards, skirting along its western fringe, and passing through the narrow gap which separates it from the oasis of Jalo, then in enemy hands.

Our crossing of the Sand Sea was something of an ordeal. With increasing frequency the leading truck would suddenly plunge and flounder and then come to an ominous standstill, sinking up to its axles in the soft white sand. Once you were stuck it was no good racing the engine. The wheels only spun round aimlessly and buried themselves deeper than ever. There was nothing for it but to dig yourself out with a spade and then, with the help of sand mats — long strips of canvas with wooden stiffening — back precariously on to the firm ground you had so unwisely left. Then the whole convoy would wait while someone went cautiously on ahead to prospect for a safe way out of our difficulties.

Or else we would find our way barred by a sand dune, or succession of sand dunes. These were best negotiated by rush tactics. If you could only keep moving you were less likely to stick. The jeeps, making full use of their extra range of gears, would lead the way, with the three-tonners thundering along after them like stampeding elephants. Very rarely we all got through safely. Generally someone hesitated half way up and immediately went in up to the running boards in sand. Then out came the spades, sand mats and towing ropes, and the whole dreary business of 'un-sticking' would start again.

But too much dash had its penalties. Many of the sand dunes fell away sharply on the far side and if you arrived at the top at full speed, you were likely to plunge headlong over the precipice on the far side before you could stop yourself, and end up with your truck upside down on top of you forty or fifty feet below.

The tracks we left gave a vivid picture of our progress. Sometimes, when the going was good, they ran straight and even like railway lines; at others when things were going less well, they wavered and branched off; where disaster had overtaken us, they ended in a confused tangle of footprints, tyre marks and holes in the sand.

But ours were not the only tracks which scarred the face of the desert and, fortunately, from the air fresh tracks are not easily distinguishable from old ones. Otherwise it would not have been difficult for enemy aircraft to track us down from the air. Even so, a party as large as ours, trundling across the open desert in broad daylight and throwing up a great cloud of dust, could not hope to be as unobtrusive as a single patrol, and we knew that, once spotted, we should offer a splendid target. Above all, it was important that we should not attract the attention of the Italian garrison, while passing Jalo, for they were known to be in wireless touch with Benghazi, and a message from them at this stage of the proceedings announcing our approach would have deprived us of any hope of success.

Accordingly we timed our journey so as to pass the Jalo gap at midday, when the heat haze made visibility poor. When the navigators reckoned we were abreast of the oasis, we halted and I climbed to the top of a little conical hill to have a look round. There was nothing to be seen except a few depressed-looking camels chewing at the almost non-existent scrub, and westwards on the horizon, some black specks, jumping up and down in the haze, which, by a stretch of imagination might have been the palm trees of Jalo. On the top of my hill I found a chianti flask. I wished that it had been full. Then we had a hurried meal of tinned salmon and biscuits, washed down with half a mug of tepid water, and hurried on.

Now that we were nearing the coast, where we were more likely to encounter patrolling aircraft, we only moved by night, lying up by day and camouflaging the trucks. Once again we picked our way cautiously across the Trigh-el-Abd, keeping a sharp look out for thermos bombs.

But not sharp enough. As we were half way across, I heard an explosion immediately behind me, and looking round, saw that the three-tonner which had been following in my tracks had had a wheel blown off by a thermos bomb, which my own jeep had gone over but had been too light to explode. Fortunately the height of the three-tonner from the ground had protected the occupants and no one was hurt. The three-tonner's load was distributed among the other trucks and we continued on our way.

Two or three days later we reached the welcome cover of the Gebel. So far as we could tell, our convoy had completed its journey across 800 miles of open desert, to a destination 600 miles behind the enemy's front line, without being spotted either from the air or from the ground. This was encouraging.

Our first care on reaching the Gebel was to get into touch with Bob Melot. Melot was a middle-aged Belgian cotton merchant who lived in Alexandria. Before the war he and his wife had for their own amusement taken some trips into the desert in their Ford car; he also spoke some Arabic. When the desert campaign started he offered his services to the British Army, and was commissioned as a subaltern. Thereafter he only paid occasional visits to his home in Alexandria. The rest of his time was spent in the desert, hundreds of miles behind the enemy lines. He lived on his own or with the Beduins for months on end, picking up information which he sent back by wireless. For food, he depended on dumps of rations left for him by the Long-Range Desert Group and on what he could get from the Arabs. He was obliged to keep moving from hiding-place to hiding-place, in order to avoid the search parties which the enemy sent out after him. It would have been an arduous life even for a much younger man.

After asking at a number of Beduin tents, we were directed to the *wadi* where Melot was lying up. He was cheerful, but tired and extremely hungry, for Rommel's advance to Alamein had interfered with his supplies. I cooked him some rather stodgy bully beef rissoles fried in oatmeal, which he ate avidly. At last I had found someone who appreciated my cooking.

Then we got out our maps and discussed the forthcoming operation. It appeared that there had been a number of rather suspicious enemy troop movements in the neighbourhood during the past week or ten days. In particular, various outposts on the edge of the Gebel had been strengthened. It looked rather as though we were expected. I remembered what I had been told in Alexandria before we started.

We decided to make further investigations. First of all we had a talk to two of the local Sheikhs, dignified old gentlemen with grey beards, who were friends of Melot's. We squatted on the ground on a hilltop, brewed up some tea, and talked inconclusively in a mixture of Arabic and Italian. The gist of their information was that the enemy seemed to be uneasy about something.

In view of this further confirmation of our suspicions, Melot suggested that he should send one of his Arabs, a deserter from the Italian army who was a native of Benghazi, to the town itself to see what he could pick up. That afternoon we took the Arab as far as the edge of the escarpment and started him off on his twenty miles' walk to Benghazi, with instructions to spend the next day there and come back to us the following night. He set off down the escarpment, grumbling as he went. We shouted after him to buy us some cigarettes and matches in Benghazi. He looked, I thought, singularly unreliable.

Melot and I settled down to wait for him in a nearby *wadi*. The rest of the party were camping five or six miles back. I cooked some more rissoles.

All next day we lay low and waited, lying in the scrub. Melot told me about the First World War, in which he had taken part as a pilot in the Belgian Air Force and about his life in the Gebel.

That night we sat up waiting for our spy. There was no sign of him. Then, after breakfast, just as we were beginning to give up hope, he limped in complaining that his feet hurt him and looking more unreliable than ever. But he had brought us some cigarettes, decorated with a large Fascist badge on the box and some little Italian wax matches — *cerini*. I had not seen any since before the war. We gave him something to eat and started to question him; Melot in Arabic and I in Italian.

He had a lot to tell us. He had stayed the night with relatives. He had also been round the bazaar. The bazaar, he said, was full of the news of our impending attack, which had upset local opinion quite considerably. The civilian population was being temporarily evacuated; a strong German machine-gun detachment had arrived as well as Italian infantry reinforcements, minefields had been laid at different points round the city perimeter, including the place where we hoped to force our way in. Finally, the actual date of our attack — September 14th — was being freely mentioned.

In fact his report was far from reassuring.

Taking our Arab with us, we made our way back to the *wadi* where the rest of the party had camped. When we got there, we found that David and the main force had just arrived. They had been delayed by a number of breakdowns on the way, and in order to make up time had travelled day and night. They did not think they had been spotted from the air. A jeep had been blown up by thermos bombs crossing the Trigh-el-Abd and the occupants killed. One was an elderly lieutenant in the R.N.R., who had been harbour master at Benghazi during the British occupation of the town the year before and was coming to show us round when we reached the harbour. It seemed hard that he should have been killed in this way at such an early stage in the proceedings.

We told David our news, and after some discussion he decided to send a signal to G.H.Q. asking whether they wished to make any change in the original plan in view of the extensive publicity which it seemed to have received. Clearly, now that we had got so far, there could be no question of coming away again without making our raid, but a change of time-table might help to put the enemy off his guard.

The answer came back in a few hours: we were to disregard bazaar gossip and carry out the operation according to the original time-table.

Evidently there was nothing in the rumours we had picked up. It looked as though Melot's Arab had simply been trying to make our flesh creep, and put us off an operation in which he had no wish to take part. We continued our preparations, feeling reassured.

Our plan was simple. The main body, relying on the element of surprise, so essential in operations of this kind, would make its way down the escarpment at nightfall, cross the intervening plain, rush the road block and drive at full speed down to the harbour, where various targets had been allotted to different parties. After that we would see how things went.

A problem was caused by the existence of an Italian wireless post in a small fort on the edge of the escarpment, so situated that we were bound to pass close to it on our way down. It was decided that a party should set out, slightly in advance of the main expedition, for the purpose of silencing the occupants before they could give the alarm.

In order to lower the morale of the enemy, and also to make them keep their heads down until the last possible moment, the R.A.F. had been asked to bomb the town and harbour as hard as they could for the two hours preceding our arrival, which was timed for half an hour before midnight.

By the early afternoon of September 13th, our preparations were complete. The guns, which even their close-fitting quilted covers could not entirely protect against the all-pervading sand, had been cleaned once again. The explosives, under Bill Cumper's care, were ready. The doctor, we noticed, was busy preparing bandages, splints and blood plasma against our return. Each of us was issued with our 'escape set' in case we got left behind or captured; a map of the Western Desert printed on fine silk, to be hidden in the lining of our battle-dress; a small compass masquerading as a button; some benzedrine tablets; a collapsible water-bottle; and various other ingenious devices to be distributed about one's person.

The party that was to attack the fort started first. Bob Melot insisted on leading it. With him went Chris Bailey, a new recruit to the S.A.S. whom we all liked and who, before the war, had run a hotel in Cyprus.

Then our own turn came. The branches and camouflage nets were stripped from the vehicles and the covers taken off the guns; we ate rather hurriedly a bar of chocolate and a tin of sardines; the convoy assembled, and we jolted off in the failing light, following a winding valley down towards the plain.

For the first hour or two the country was familiar. We were following the route that Melot and I had taken to the edge of the escarpment. The maps were inaccurate and we found our way through a maze of *wadis* largely by the help of landmarks; a burnt-out German truck; a Mohammedan shrine; the unusual outline of a hilltop.

Clearly it was going to be no easy matter for a convoy the size of ours to negotiate the precipitous escarpment, especially as our choice of routes was limited by the latest enemy troop dispositions. Melot's Arab, who claimed to know a good way down, was brought up to the front of the column and used as a guide.

He turned out to be a very poor one. It was now quite dark. The track soon became increasingly precipitous and showed signs of petering out altogether. It was strewn, too, with immense boulders which grated ominously on the sumps of the trucks. After a good deal of whispered barracking from me in Italian, our guide finally agreed that we must be in the wrong *wadi*. The process of extracting the column from it, and searching for a new way down was long and painful.

Meanwhile the R.A.F. had been bombing Benghazi for some time. We could see the bombs bursting. By the time we reached the foot of the escarpment and started out across the coastal plain, the bombardment had stopped. The searchlights flicked round the sky once or twice more and then went out. The moon was down. We should not now reach Benghazi until well after the appointed hour. We seemed to have been on the way a long time. It was cold and the effects of the rum we had drunk before starting had long since worn off. We cursed the Arab roundly.

At last we reached the tarmac road and a few minutes later were nearing the outskirts of the town. It would not be long now before things began to happen. So far there had been no sign of the enemy.

We were almost on top of the road block before we saw it. This time there was no red light and no sentry. Only a bar across the road. Beyond it, in the shadows, something was flapping in the wind. The leading vehicles stopped and word was passed back for the rest of the column to halt, while we investigated matters further. On either side of the road there was wire and in places the soil seemed to have been dug up. This looked unpleasantly like the minefield we had heard about. If so, it meant that our only line of approach lay along the road and through the road blocks. David summoned Bill Cumper, as the expert on mines, and invited him to give his opinion of this somewhat disquieting discovery.

Bill made one of his inevitable jokes and then we watched him while he went forward and poked about in the darkness. Evidently our suspicions were well founded, for after a quick look round, he turned his attention to the road block. He fiddled with the catch for a second or so, and then the bar flew up, leaving the way open for us to advance.

The situation, Bill felt, called for a facetious remark, and, as usual, he rose to the occasion. 'Let battle commence,' he said in his best Stanley Holloway manner, stepping politely aside to let the leading jeep through.

The words were hardly out of his mouth when pandemonium broke loose. From the other side of the road block a dozen machine-guns opened up at us at point-blank range; then a couple of 20-mm. Bredas joined in, and then some heavy mortars, while sniper's bullets pinged viciously through the trees on either side of the road.

From the front of the column we opened up with everything we had. The leading jeep, driven by Sergeant Almonds of the Coldstream Guards, drove straight at the enemy with all its guns firing and was already well past the road block when an incendiary bullet hit it in the petrol tank and set it ablaze. Another followed and met the same fate. The Bredas in particular, gave our opponents a considerable advantage, while the blazing jeeps furnished a light to aim by. Then, after a time the combined fire of our leading vehicles, now dispersed on both sides of the road, began to tell and there was a marked falling off in the violence of the enemy's opposition.

But it was abundantly clear that we had been expected and it could only be a question of time before fresh reinforcements were brought up. There was no longer any hope of rushing the defences. The element of surprise had gone, and with it all chance of success. Meanwhile time was passing. Hopelessly outnumbered as we were, we could not afford to be caught in the open in daylight. Reluctantly, David gave the order to withdraw. Still returning the enemy's fire while they could, our vehicles dispersed on the open ground on either side of the road and headed singly and in groups for the Gebel, in a race to reach cover before the sun rose.

First light caught us just short of the foot of the escarpment. Looking back we saw a most unwelcome sight. From Regima, Benina, and the other airfields round Benghazi, aircraft were rising like angry wasps. We barely had time to run our trucks into the scanty cover afforded by the rocky ravines, with which the face of the escarpment was scarred, before the first aircraft were upon us, bombing and machine-gunning. There were about a dozen of them in the air at a time. They flew round in a circle, one after another peeling off and swooping down to drop its bombs or fire a long burst from its guns. Now and then one would fly off back to its airfield to collect a fresh supply of ammunition and another would take its place.

But they seemed uncertain of our exact position, and a good deal of their bombing and machine-gunning was going wide of the target. From where we lay we could see a little party of Arabs making their way across the plain, taking their produce to the bazaar; first two greybeards on donkeys and then some women following on foot. At last the Italians had a target they could see. Once again they swooped and dipped; there was a burst from their guns, and the Arabs were left crumpled and struggling on the ground.

Then a lucky shot found the truck containing the bulk of our explosives and ammunition, and set it alight. A column of smoke rose from it, followed by a series of flashes and explosions. Seeing that they were at last on to something, the enemy started methodically to comb the neighbouring *wadis*. Another truck full of explosives went up, taking with it all my personal kit. That was another two trucks gone. My equipment was now reduced to an automatic pistol, a prismatic compass and one plated teaspoon. From now onwards I should be travelling light.

The day wore on, but the enthusiasm of our tormentors showed no signs of waning. Sometimes they would fly off, bombing and strafing empty *wadis*, and we would hope that our troubles were at an end. Then suddenly they would come circling back, flying low over our heads, and we would dive for cover again. Meanwhile there was nothing that we could do. To open up at them would have drawn their fire and betrayed the exact position of our remaining vehicles. For the same reason any attempt to move would have been disastrous. There was nothing for it but to lie low and hope for the best.

From where we were, half way up the escarpment, we looked across the plain to the white walls of Benghazi, with beyond them the blue waters of the Mediterranean. But we gave little thought to what in happier circumstances would have been a delightful view. To us it seemed inevitable that the enemy, having pinned us down from the air, would now send out a mechanized force to mop us up. We scanned the wide expanse of plain anxiously and heaved a sigh of relief as each successive scurry of sand in the distance resolved itself into a harmless dust devil, and not, as we feared, into the forerunner of a squadron of armoured cars.

The morning passed slowly. A speckled chameleon, hardly noticeable against the stones, crawled out of a hole and looked at us, a miniature gargoyle. Someone put it on his bandana handkerchief. It put its tongue out and turned a rich shade of red.

Soon after midday the circling aircraft flew off one after the other and we were left in peace. As we sucked at our tepid water-bottles, we imagined our tormentors giving a colourful account of their exploits over iced drinks in a cool mess. After a brief respite they reappeared, and, working in relays, kept it up until sunset. Meanwhile, to our great relief, there was still no sign of enemy land forces.

As night fell and the last aircraft flew off, we set to taking stock of our position.

It left much to be desired.

CHAPTER VI

LONG TRAIL

We were separated from our base by 800 miles of waterless desert, dotted with enemy outposts and patrols, now all on the look out for us. We had lost several of our trucks, some of our food and a good deal of our ammunition. The enemy knew, within a few hundred yards, where we were. Twenty miles away in Benghazi there was an enemy garrison, presumably at that very moment preparing a sortie against us. We had already had a taste of what the Luftwaffe and the Regia Aeronautica could do, and might expect that the experience would be repeated at frequent intervals all the way back to Kufra.

After dark we were joined by the little party that had attacked the fort. They had succeeded in their task. They had stormed and taken the fort, killing or capturing the bewildered Italians who manned it. But the cost had been heavy. Bob Melot had been badly wounded about the legs and body by a hand-grenade; Chris Bailey had been shot through the lung; one of the N.C.O.s, Corporal Laird, had had his arm shattered. All were in considerable pain. The first thing was to get the wounded back to the doctor. We made them as comfortable as we could in the backs of our trucks and set out up the escarpment.

It was a nasty drive. Our way led across precipitous country. If we went fast the pain caused to the wounded by the jolting became unbearable. If we went slow we were in danger of being caught by the daylight in the open at the mercy of enemy planes. When I was not driving I sat with Chris, who was lying on a bedding roll perched up on the top of the petrol cans and paraphernalia with which the truck was filled. Though every jolt and lurch of the truck hurt him, he was as cheerful and gay as ever.

We reached the *wadi* where we had left the doctor just before dawn. He was there and took charge of the wounded. Everything seemed much the same as when we had left it thirty-six hours earlier. We divided ourselves up between the different *wadis*, camouflaged the trucks, driving them into patches of scrub or up against rocks and pulling camouflage nets over them. Guardsman Duncan arrived as though by magic with mugs of strong sweet thick tea, which he could always be counted upon to produce under any circumstances. Then, as dawn was breaking, we lay down to get some sleep while we could.

The first part of the day passed quietly enough. In the intervals of inspecting our camouflage and discussing our future movements, I interrogated the Italian prisoners who had been captured in the fort. Like everyone else in the neighbourhood, they seemed to have had warning of our impending arrival, but failed to connect it with themselves in their own cosy little fort, so that in the event it had come as a very severe shock to them. Now that they had had time to sum up the position, they were frankly terrified, for they had no doubt in their minds whatever that, when they had been interrogated, they would be killed. To them it seemed inconceivable that anyone in our position would burden themselves with useless mouths or alternatively release prisoners who could betray their position. And so they drew touching pictures of aged parents and chubby children awaiting them at home and begged us to be merciful. No sooner had I reassured them on this point, than their attention was once again distracted, this time by the activities of their own side.

Soon after it got light, the air sentries, from their look-outs on the hilltops, had signalled the first enemy 'recce' plane searching for us. Now others followed. But evidently our camouflage was too good for them. We lay quiet behind our respective bushes and stones and felt a little more optimistic about the future. If the enemy failed to discover us before dark, we should have the whole of the following night in which to increase the distance which separated us from him and would thus gain a valuable start. We were careful not to move or to do anything else which might betray our position.

It was then that we saw the jeep. It was one of ours and it was driving towards us from a neighbouring *wadi* at a good brisk pace. As it came it sent up a column of dust. I never discovered who was driving it or what had induced him to set out on his early morning round of visits. We were not the only people who saw it. For some time an enemy plane had been circling overhead looking for us in a desultory manner. On the appearance of the jeep it came lower in order to investigate. The jeep continued its headlong progress in our direction, the dust billowing out behind it. The plane circled and then turned and flew off in the direction of Benghazi.

Could it be that it had not seen us after all? I was sharing the cover afforded by a good large boulder with a Royal Australian Air Force pilot who had come with us to arrange for air-supplies, should we need them. Cautiously we put our heads out from behind it. As we did so, the earth all round was kicked up by a burst from the plane's tail-gunner. Hurriedly we dived back. 'This,' said the Australian, 'is going to be a shaky do.'

He was right.

The enemy had not wasted the intervening night. The neighbouring airfields had been heavily reinforced — at the expense, we learned later, of his troops in the front line at Alamein. Before long the pilot who had discovered us came back accompanied by a swarm of fighters and bombers, which settled down to circle monotonously over our *wadi*, diving down, heedless of the small-arms fire coming up at them, to discharge bombs and cannon into what was left of our transport, and into anything they could see moving. Lying on that bare hillside under a blazing sun, I have seldom felt more disagreeably exposed.

This time there was no pause for lunch and a midday siesta, or if there was, the pilots were working in shifts and we did not notice it. My watch had stopped, and the sun seemed to move incredibly slowly across the sky. There were always twenty or thirty aircraft in the air over our heads. As the day wore on, first one truck and then another was hit and caught fire.

Watching the plane circling overhead and wondering where the next bomb or the burst from their cannon would strike, any distraction was welcome and I found myself calculating the minimum number of trucks required to get us home. As truck after truck disintegrated before our eyes, it became clear that it would be a tight fit. And then there was the water and the petrol, can after can of which was being spilt out into the sand. 'Shaky do', it seemed to me, summed up the position very neatly.

Eventually, with sickening deliberation, the sun went down; the last aircraft cleared its guns and flew off home to supper; and we turned once again to computing our losses and our assets. Considering the strength and the duration of the air attack, comparatively few of us had been killed or wounded. But we were short of transport, short of food, short of water and our only remaining wireless set had been blown up.

Several trucks were still blazing and by their light we inspected the others. Some of those which had been hit seemed capable of repair. In the end we came to the conclusion that if we jettisoned everything except the barest necessities and if every jeep and truck was loaded to its maximum capacity, there would be just enough transport for everyone.

The situation as far as food, water and petrol were concerned was less promising. Food and water were shortest. If we ate and drank barely enough to keep us alive, with luck there should be enough to last us the 400 miles to Jalo, which, if all had gone well, we should find in the hands of the Sudan Defence Force. If all had not gone well, we should have to think again when we reached Jalo. Sufficient, we felt, unto the day. . . .

Our calculations were interrupted by a sudden torrent of excited Italian. Following up the noise, I found our three prisoners in tears with spades in their hands. A perplexed Sergeant was standing over them with a tommy-gun. Seeing no reason why they should not be usefully employed, he had decided to make them dig graves for our men who had been killed. But the Italians, on being handed spades and seeing that he was carrying a tommy-gun, jumped to the conclusion that, in true Fascist style, they were being made to dig their own graves. Once again they took a great deal of reassuring.

Before we moved off there was a hard question to be decided; what we were to do with the wounded. A long and necessarily arduous journey, under a blinding sun, in open trucks, over rough country lay before us. We were likely to run into all kinds of trouble before we reached our destination. Already the wounded had spent one whole day under constant air attack. Were we justified in exposing them to further danger and exhaustion? In the end the doctor decided to risk it in the case of Bob Melot and Corporal Laird. Chris Bailey and some of the other wounded he decided were too ill to move any further; even the journey of the night before had tried them severely. We accordingly made them as comfortable as we could where they were and left behind a medical orderly and one of the Italian prisoners with instructions to drive into Benghazi next day under a Red Cross flag and ask them to send out an ambulance for them. It was a hard decision and we left them reluctantly.

It was a long time before we received news of them, though we knew from our own rearguard, who had stayed behind to watch, that the Italians had come to fetch them. Then, many months later, we heard that they had died in hospital in Benghazi.

Now, in the light of the burning trucks, we divided ourselves up into two main parties, and a third smaller party under David Stirling, who was going to try to collect various stragglers who had not yet been accounted for, and catch us up later.

Then, having filled our water-bottles and destroyed everything worth taking out of the derelict trucks, we piled into our vehicles and started off into the darkness. My own jeep had a crew of eight, all fortunately travelling as light as I was myself. We drove as best we could by starlight, for it was rough going and we were still too near the enemy to show a light. There was some confusion at first. 'Les camions français par ici!' shouted the French. Then we got going.

We did not make much progress that night. The going was bad; there was no moon. Clearly our best course would be to move only as far as the southern edge of the Gebel and take advantage of the comparatively good cover to lie up there for another whole day, in the hope of throwing the enemy off the scent, before we set out on our long trek across the open desert. Just before dawn we halted in what seemed a likely *wadi*, camouflaged the trucks and then settled ourselves into the scrub and rocks near them to await developments.

The transition from darkness to light is a rapid one in the desert. Soon the sun was beating down on us fiercely. With it the flies returned to the attack. Time passed slowly.

Before starting the night before, we had worked out a scale of rations designed to eke out our meagre supplies as far as Jalo. This allowed each of us about a cup of water and a tablespoonful of bully beef a day. To simplify matters, we decided to eat our rations in the evening. There would be supper, but no breakfast, lunch or tea. Our diet for the last forty-eight hours had been scrappy in the extreme, and now we found ourselves looking forward to the evening meal with painful fixity. The time was about six a.m.

Gordon Alston and I climbed to the top of a nearby hill, from which we had a view of the surrounding country, and made ourselves as comfortable and as invisible as we could inside a rough circle of stones used as a shelter by the Beduin. A ground-sheet spread across it gave us some shade. As the sun moved across the sky we moved our ground-sheet to keep pace with it. The flies buzzed. I could feel the sweat trickling in a steady stream down my spine. I thought about food. And drink — long drinks in tall tumblers with the ice clinking against the sides.

Suddenly our day-dreams were interrupted by the sound of bomb-bursts and machine-gun fire. From our look-out, we could see, some miles away, a swarm of enemy aircraft circling and swooping like wasps round a jam pot. Soon, first one column of smoke and then another showed that they had found what they were looking for. Someone, either Paddy Mayne or David, was catching it again. A fighter, on its way to join in the fun flew right over us, without seeing us. Eventually the aircraft went away and did not come back. In the distance we could still see the smoke from the burning trucks curling up into the sky. Once more we settled down to wait for darkness.

From high in the sky the sun blazed down on us. The flies were worse than ever. Whenever one of us hit out at them, the ground-sheet fell down on us. Time passed very slowly. We watched the sun reach its meridian, stay there for what seemed an unconscionable time, and then, almost imperceptibly begin to sink lower. The aircraft did not come back. In another few hours it would be dark. We gave up thinking of imaginary meals and began to visualize our actual rations; the bully, the biscuit and the cup of water. Time passed slower than ever.

Later we made an exciting discovery; two small and very dirty bits of half-melted barley sugar, forgotten in the pocket of my great coat. We ate them greedily. They seemed as stimulating as a stiff whisky. I suppose because we had not had much to eat for some time.

At last the sun set, sinking below the horizon as quickly as it had risen. In the sudden dusk, we walked down from our hilltop towards the ration truck, where a little group was already gathering. The big moment of the day had arrived.

But it was soon past. A spoonful of bully beef is quickly eaten. The camouflage nets were pulled off the trucks and stowed away, and, feeling refreshed, though by no means sated, we started on the next stage of our journey.

After much floundering about in the dark, one or two abortive excursions up *wadis* that turned out to have no outlet and various other misadventures, we finally emerged from the Gebel into the open desert. The going, by comparison, was now quite good, and in the early hours of the morning by the light of a waning moon, we considerably increased the distance between ourselves and the enemy.

The dawn found us in the middle of a perfectly flat expanse of gravel, stretching as far as the eye could see and dotted here and there with a solitary, scrubby, leafless bush, some eighteen inches high. There can be few places in the world with less natural cover. Hurriedly, before it was quite light, we dispersed the trucks as widely as we could. Then, pulling over them their camouflage nets, enlivened with an occasional twig, we proceeded to convert them into what we hoped optimistically would look from the air like a series of natural mounds or knolls. Having done this, we lay down and composed ourselves hopefully to sleep.

Fortunately on this occasion our powers of camouflage were not put to the test. Inexplicably, no aircraft came our way. Our slumbers were interrupted only by the usual flies, which appeared from nowhere, buzzing gaily in the sun. I spent an hour or so talking to Bob Melot. He had suffered a good deal from the heat and the jolting and he was too weak to hold his own against the flies. But he was as cheerful as ever and talked confidently of getting back home to Alexandria. His cheerfulness made one forget one's own minor discomforts.

It was September 17th. At nightfall we ate our rations and started off again. We kept going all that night and all the following day. It was a risk driving by day, but, with our supplies of food and water as low as they were, it was one that had to be taken. It was very hot and the soft sand swirled up at us, as though a sand storm were threatening. With seven or eight of us to a jeep, it was not easy to relax, even when one was not actually driving. The sun blazed down relentlessly from a brazen sky. Occasionally someone would go to sleep and fall off, and we had to stop, waiting irritably, while he picked himself up and climbed back on again. The tyres, too, were beginning to feel the strain after so many hundreds of miles of rough going under a hot sun, and punctures came with increasing frequency. Changing a wheel, or digging the jeep out of soft sand began to seem more and more arduous as we grew weaker. Our throats were dry and it required an effort to speak. We counted the hours and minutes which separated us from the blissful moment when we could next allow ourselves to take a pull at the rapidly dwindling supply of warm, dirty, brackish water in our water-bottles.

When we halted at dusk on September 18th, after driving more or less continuously for twenty-four hours, we had covered a considerable distance, and were now not more than twenty or thirty miles from Jalo. Tracks in the sand, made apparently by heavy Italian trucks, led in the direction of the oasis. Once again we took stock of our position.

We had very little petrol left and enough food and water for one more meal. Another four or five hundred miles separated us from Kufra. Everything depended on what we found at Jalo. If it was still in enemy hands, the outlook would be poor.

Our meal that night was on a more luxurious scale than anything that we had tasted for some time. In addition to the usual spoonful of bully beef, we used up some of the remaining water in making some hot porridge and brewed up some tea. We also scraped up enough rum for a small tot all round. This we drank after supper, lying on a little sandbank and watching the sun sinking behind the dunes.

We had all been beginning to feel a bit low, and this unexpected treat restored our spirits. I, for one, will always recall it with pleasure. Indeed, looking back over a varied gastronomic experience, ranging from strawberry messes at Eton and sheep's entrails in Central Asia to the more sophisticated fare of Larue and La Pérouse, I cannot remember a meal that I enjoyed more or that seemed more wildly and agreeably extravagant. Extravagant it certainly was, for, when we had finished eating, there was no food left at all, and only enough water to half fill one water-bottle for each man.

The next thing was to ascertain unobtrusively how matters stood at Jalo. Sandy Scratchley and I decided to take two jeeps and go and look.

Sandy had come to the S.A.S. from the Fourth County of London Yeomanry. After a brief career as a regular soldier before the war he had left the army to become a steeplechase jockey, a profession in which he very soon made his mark. It was his boast that he had broken every bone in his body and that he was the best-dressed man on the turf. There seemed no reason to doubt the veracity of either claim. One of the Stirling family's more spectacular motor accidents had accounted for most of the limbs which had escaped fracture in a long series of racing accidents, while, even at this stage of our adventures, Sandy, in a shirt and an old pair of corduroy trousers, with a straggling reddish beard and with sand clogging his shock of curly reddish hair, managed to achieve an appearance that was somehow reminiscent of Newmarket.

We cleaned our Vickers-K guns, drew our ration of water, filled up with petrol and started off, leaving the rest of the party to await our return. In my jeep came Sergeant Seekings, the Cambridgeshire farmer and old S.A.S. operative, the mishap to whose hand had caused him to be left behind when we paid our first visit to Benghazi in the spring. In my pocket I carried my teaspoon. I sincerely hoped that I should before long find a use for it.

It was midnight when we started. Our object was to get as near to the oasis as we could under cover of darkness and then try to find out who was in possession of it. If we ran into an Italian patrol we proposed to make a hasty withdrawal without further ado. If, on the other hand, we were challenged by Sudanese, we should have to try and make them understand who we were, which in the dark and in the absence of any common language was likely to be a no less ticklish operation.

There was no moon and we kept direction as best we could by the stars, one man looking out and one man driving. Mike Sadler, our navigator, who had started us off, had told us that if we kept on a westerly course, we should not have much difficulty in finding the oasis, which covered a comparatively large area.

After we had been jolting along in the dark for some hours, Sergeant Seekings, who was looking out, drew my attention to a flash of greenish light across the sky in front of us. It was, he said, a green Very light, which was our usual recognition signal. The other jeep had seen it too. They had taken it for a shooting-star, but, on second thoughts, they were not sure.

Should we assume that it was a signal and reply with the appropriate signal of a red, followed by a green light — an unwise proceeding if there happened to be any enemy in the immediate vicinity? Or should we, on the other hand, dismiss the whole thing as an astronomical phenomenon? In the end Seekings won the day. Our Very pistol was produced and fired off twice. First a red, then a green star soared up into the sky, blossomed out, illuminating the surrounding desert as it did so, and faded away. Then we settled down to await some reaction. None came. The shooting-star school of thought made no attempt to disguise their triumph, and elaborated on the folly of advertising our position to everyone in Central Libya by totally uncalled-for firework displays.

Before going any further, we checked up on our position as best we could, and came to the conclusion that we must now be very near the edge of the oasis. There seemed very little to be gained by pushing on any further in the few hours that remained before dawn. Indeed it seemed quite likely that, if we did so, we might blunder into unnecessary trouble. We accordingly revised our plans and decided to stay where we were for the time being and move on just before first light. Each of us took turns at keeping watch, while the rest slept. We were by now all very tired and were glad of the rest.

Before going to sleep, I finished what was left of my water. It was a comfort to take a good long pull at it after so many days of sipping, and as I drained the last tepid drops, I reflected that the next day was in any case likely to solve the water problem radically one way or the other.

The brief grey twilight that precedes the dawn showed, as we had expected, the palm trees of Jalo a few miles away on the western horizon. Nothing else was in sight. There were no signs of any human activity. We got back into our jeeps and drove cautiously towards Jalo.

Half an hour's driving brought us to the outer fringe of the oasis. A little wind was stirring the palms; the sky was limpid. Still we saw nothing. We were wondering what to do next when the familiar sound of aircraft engines fell on our ears. Looking to the horizon, we saw three bombers flying straight towards us in formation. We had barely had time to get the jeeps under cover of the palms, when they were over us. Looking up we could see that they bore German markings.

Simultaneously it occurred to us that here was a simple means of finding out by whom the oasis was held. If the Germans bombed it, we could safely assume that it was in the hands of our own troops. If, on the other hand, they landed, or dropped supplies, or did nothing, we should know that it was still held by the enemy.

The bombers took a run over the oasis, flying so low over the palm trees that from our hiding-place we could see the faces of the pilot and rear-gunner. We watched them intently. Nothing happened. From where we were we could see through the palm trees the flat sand of the landing-strip, empty save for the wreck of a fighter. If they landed now we should have ringside seats; in fact, we should have to do some very quick thinking.

As we watched, they circled out over the desert and came back a second time. Once again they flew over us at a low altitude and disappeared over the palm trees. Then, just as we were beginning to give up hope, came the crash and roar of three sticks of bombs. I had never thought that I should derive such pleasure from the sound of German bombs bursting in my immediate vicinity.

The attack was short and sharp and soon the three aircraft, having dropped their bombs, turned and flew off again towards the north, leaving the coast clear for us to make contact with our friends of the Sudan Defence Force, for we felt now certain that they must be in possession of the oasis. Rising above the palm trees, about half a mile away, we could see the little Italian fort which forms the centre of Jalo, and thither we prepared to go, licking our lips at the thought of the abundance of food and drink which awaited us there. The Sudan Defence Force always lived well, and there would be captured Italian rations too.

We had already scrambled back into the jeeps and were starting up the engines when a new and, at this juncture, unexpected sound fell on our ears: the screeching of a salvo of shells. As we watched, they burst fair and square on the fort. At this, the comfortable certainty which we had derived from the hostile behaviour of the German aircraft that had just flown off gave way to fresh doubts. If the Sudan Defence Force had, as we assumed, captured the fort, how was it that there was any enemy left to shell them? We decided that we should be wise to investigate the situation further before driving up to the fort for breakfast.

All this had happened so quickly that we had hardly had time to look round. A closer inspection of our surroundings now revealed a solitary Arab half-heartedly tilling an unpromising-looking vegetable patch some distance away under the palm trees. I walked over and engaged him in conversation. I was, I told him in a mixture of Italian, troops' Arabic and dumb-crambo, anxious to know who was in the fort. 'Taliani,' he replied succinctly, with evident contempt for one so ill-informed about local events. 'And what,' I asked, 'about the English.' 'The English,' he said, 'tried to get in several days ago.' 'And now,' he added, turning back to his digging, as a shrill whistling announced the arrival of another salvo of shells, 'they are trying again.'

This made things much clearer. We were, it appeared, occupying part of the Italian advanced positions and under heavy fire from our own side. The Italians themselves had wisely evacuated these positions at some earlier stage of the encounter. The sooner we followed their example the better it would be for us.

But this was easier said than done. A fair number of shorts and overs were coming our way, making the shallow, rather smelly little trenches in which we found ourselves no place for a rest cure. But, on the other hand, the sudden appearance of two stray jeeps silhouetted on the skyline would have provided a heaven-sent target to all concerned. We decided that we would have to stay where we were for the time being and wait for a lull in the proceedings.

Time passed slower than ever in our new surroundings and we became painfully aware of hunger and thirst. My friend the Arab seemed the only possible source of refreshment. Once again I made my way over to him, this time rather more cautiously than before, for things were beginning to warm up round us, and opened negotiations. The first thing was to find out where he kept his water supply. It turned out that there was a well in the sand by the side of his allotment. Lying on the sand, with the help of an old leather bucket and a long bit of string, I managed in a short time to pull up enough water to fill two large water-bottles. The slimy, brackish liquid thus produced seemed more delicious than vintage champagne. At any rate the water problem was solved for the time being.

I next asked him whether he could sell us anything to eat. Always a man of few words, he pointed to a bright green vegetable marrow growing at his feet. 'Any eggs?' I said. 'No,' he said. It was only too clear that the vegetable marrow was all that we were going to get; and eventually it changed hands for a thousand lire note. It was not cheap, but it was the smallest note I had and one could hardly expect change in the circumstances. Carrying it as proudly as if it had won a prize at the Crystal Palace, I started back to the jeeps by a suitably circuitous route. On the way I filled my pockets with unripe dates off the date palms. We had all the makings of a feast.

We had scarcely sat down to breakfast when a fierce controversy broke out over our *plat de résistance*. My own claim that it was a vegetable marrow was brushed scornfully aside by Sandy, who said that he knew that it was a cucumber. On being told that cucumbers did not grow to that size, he said that anyone who knew anything about vegetables could see that it was a tropical cucumber. Nettled by this I retorted rather unjustly that anyone who knew anything at all could see that he was nothing but a city slicker whose knowledge of the country was derived solely from the low suburban race courses which he frequented.

Prolonged lack of food and drink is apt to fray the nerves. Our tempers were not at their best, and we both felt by now that we could have cheerfully used up our remaining strength in fighting each other over the identity of the rather sad-looking vegetable which lay between us, cut up into unappetizing green slices already covered with sand and flies. Fortunately a breach of the peace was avoided thanks to Sergeant Seekings, the only real agricultural expert of the party, who drew the fire of both parties by suggesting that the object of our controversy must be a kind of pumpkin, a diagnosis so manifestly outrageous that Sandy and I sank our differences in a united but entirely unsuccessful attempt to persuade Seekings that he was talking nonsense. Not long after eating it, whatever it was, we were all attacked by the most violent stomach ache. Altogether it was an unsatisfactory vegetable.

While awaiting our chance to make a dash for it, we took turns at reading a volume of admirable short stories by the late Damon Runyon, which Sandy had brought with him. The sufferings of Good-time Charley, Harry the Horse and the rest of them at the hands of less peaceable characters helped to distract our thoughts from our own predicament. But two stories made painful reading. One contained an account of an eating competition; the other concerned a character whose favourite drink was 'Rock candy and rye whisky, without the rock candy.' What, we reflected sadly, could we not have done at that moment with some rye whisky, or, for that matter (for we were not fussy) with some rock candy, whatever that might be.

It was some time before a suitable opportunity to leave our hide-out presented itself. When it did, we lost no time in decamouflaging the jeeps and getting under way. Once we were clear of the trees we drove as hard as we could and managed to get away unpursued.

From where we were we had been able to form a pretty good idea of the approximate position of the attacking force, and thither we now made our way after taking a fairly wide sweep out into the desert before approaching. The first thing we saw was a number of blazing trucks, set on fire by bombing or gun-fire. Vainly trying to fight the flames, we found one of the S.D.F. officers who told us the whole story.

Just as we had done at Benghazi, the S.D.F. had approached their objective to find the entire garrison of Jalo sitting waiting for them at their machine guns behind a new and well-placed minefield, clearly expecting to be raided. In spite of this, they had managed to fight their way inside the fort, but had been thrown out again with heavy losses. They had subsequently withdrawn and reassembled their force, and now, after shelling the Italians all day, and being shelled back in return, were preparing to make a fresh assault on the fort, as soon as it got dark. In this they invited us to join them. We said that there was nothing we should like better and, if they would give us some food and water we would go and collect the rest of our party in time for the evening's proceedings. They accordingly provided us with a supply of bully beef and biscuits, and we drove off in triumph, Seekings and I with an open tin of bully between us, at which we took alternate stabs with my teaspoon.

But, by the time that we had found the main party and joined up once again with the Sudan Defence Force, there had been a fresh development, necessitating a further change of plans. The S.D.F. had received over their wireless a signal from G.H.Q., M.E., of which the first paragraph ordered them to abandon the idea of making a further assault on Jalo and to return to base forthwith. This in itself was disappointing.

The reason for the decision, however, which was contained in a second paragraph, delighted no less than it surprised us. Strategically, we were told, our respective operations, which to us had seemed from a tactical point of view such dismal failures, had already achieved their main object. For they had caused the enemy to divert from the front disproportionately large numbers of aircraft and troops, which would otherwise have been used to counter certain operations now being undertaken by Eighth Army. These, as we learned later, were the preliminary moves which were to culminate soon after in the grand attack on Rommel's lines at El Alamein.

Thus, seen as part of a larger canvas, the decision of G.H.Q. to stick to the original time-table, come what might, at last became comprehensible. I was reminded of my Sergeant Instructor's admonition in the early days at Inverness. As he had said, we were nothing but ——ing cogs in a gigantic ——ing organization. On our eventual return to civilization we were gratified to find ourselves and our operation described in the popular press in such glowing terms as to be scarcely recognizable.

Meanwhile a third paragraph of the signal contained some other news which was of immediate interest to us. We had, it appeared, been successful in diverting, not only enemy aircraft and infantry, but a column of armoured cars, which were even now scouring the desert for us. In the light of this information, the order which we had received to withdraw seemed a good deal more sensible and we pressed on with our preparations for departure. These were simple. With several trucks still blazing in the dusk and a machine gun rattling half-heartedly from the fort, we collected some dates from the surrounding palm trees; drew from the nearest well as much water as we could carry; borrowed from the S.D.F. all the petrol and rations they could spare, and then, piling back into our jeeps and trucks, formed ourselves into column and drove off again southwards into the gathering dusk.

Our encounter with the S.D.F. had made it possible for us to go on; but only just. After we had pooled all the available petrol and rations between us, it still seemed uncertain whether there would be enough to carry both units safely back to Kufra. There would certainly be no marked improvement in our standard of living, and bully beef would still have to be doled out by the spoonful. Water, on the other hand, was more plentiful than it had been for a long time, and there was every prospect of finding more en route.

With aircraft and armoured cars about, it was advisable to put as many miles as possible between ourselves and Jalo before dawn. There was no moon, and, to save time, we decided to take the risk of being spotted and using our headlights, to drive as fast as we could.

My recollections of that night's journey are dim but wholly unpleasant. A few yards ahead, illuminated by the red glare of the tail lamp, and, as it were, suspended in mid-air, the bearded, sand-blanched faces of the men huddled on the back of the jeep in front of us jerked and jolted before our eyes, like puppets in a peep-show. The soft sand billowed up, and, in the glare of the headlights formed itself into fantastic shapes. Hunger and exhaustion helping, we seemed to be travelling through a constantly shifting landscape. Suddenly you could fancy that your headlights were lighting up, not a strip of desert, but a narrow lane bounded by high walls or hedges, with overhanging trees and, here and there, houses. Sooner or later you found that your eyes were focusing themselves irresistibly on some one point in this non-existent countryside and that you yourself were drifting further and further from reality, until a sudden jolt brought you back to consciousness. Then, if you were driving, it was high time to hand over the wheel to someone else, and climb on to the back, there to doze uneasily, every now and then clutching wildly at the guns to save yourself from being pitched off.

First light found us amongst surroundings no less fantastic than the imaginary landscape of the night. We were in the middle of a kind of desert archipelago. The desert was flat and sandy, like the sea floor. From it rose abruptly a group, as it were, of islands, with cliffs towering above our heads, the summits crowned with startlingly unfamiliar greenery, shrubs and even small trees. Against the dazzling blue of the sky and the white expanse of sand, the scene recalled early representations of the Thebaid; at any moment you expected to see hermits and demons start from the caves which here and there dotted the sides of these strange little hills. Insects of all kinds abounded. Yet nowhere was there any sign of water. The place must have been all that remained of a dying oasis, somehow deprived of the water supplies to which it owed its origin. The maps showed no trace of it.

Here we spent the day, undisturbed by the enemy, the shade of the high overhanging cliffs providing ideal hiding-places for the trucks. Sleep was a less easy matter. Immediately on our arrival the insects, their appetites sharpened by a lifetime of privation, and now roused at the prospect of an undreamed-of feast, came hopping, crawling and flying out to greet us. The rest of our stay was spent in unavailing attempts to fight them off.

At dusk we ate our food; shared our once again dwindling supply of water with the thirsty radiators of our trucks, and set off. That night's drive was a repetition of our journey of the night before; the same struggle to keep awake at the wheel, the same, sharply illuminated clouds of dust playing tricks with the imagination, the same halts while your own or someone else's puncture was repaired. Just before dawn we halted for an hour's sleep, and then, deciding that we were far enough south to risk travelling by day, set off again once more, following this time the line of beacons set up before the war by the Italian authorities to mark the route from newly captured Kufra to Jalo and the coast. Here and there little heaps of bleaching bones were proof that for many generations caravans to and from the interior of the continent had passed the same way.

Towards evening we reached Zighen and the oasis of Bir Harash, to find the S.D.F. already installed there. To us this fly-infested patch of scrub in the middle of a howling wilderness seemed a veritable outpost of civilization. Not only were there unlimited supplies of brackish water to drink, but in the remote past some visiting patrol of the L.R.D.G. had amused themselves by opening up one of the wells, and, with the aid of some flattened petrol cans, converted it into a tin-lined bathing pool. Here, sharing our ablutions with a crowd of splashing Sudanese, our feet slipping in the slime on the bottom, we indulged in the nearest approach to a wash that we had had for some time.

The remainder of our homeward journey was relatively plain sailing. There was no longer any doubt that our supplies of food, water and petrol would see us through, and, as the distance from the coast grew greater, the danger of interference from the enemy grew less, although we kept a sharp look out for aircraft and in fact a few days later a sharp bombing attack caused considerable damage and a number of casualties at Kufra.

From Zighen we plunged once more into the dunes and valleys of the Sand Sea. 'Unsticking' had been a wearisome-enough business when we were fresh; now that we were tired, it was a nightmare. We were glad to see the last of the Sand Sea.

Next day we found ourselves among black cliffs and towering red sandstone pinnacles. With luck we should reach Kufra next morning. That night, we lay down to sleep on a soft patch of sand with a new and not altogether agreeable feeling of security and of certainty as to how it would all end. Some of the more musically inclined members of the party celebrated our last night out with a sing-song, and the last sound that drifted across to me as I fell asleep was the rich tenor of Sergeant Phillips, a hardened offender on such occasions, giving a particularly soulful rendering of 'The green eye of the little yellow god'.

In the event, we did not reach Kufra until the following evening. So far both our tyres and the vehicles themselves had stood up well enough to the bashing which they had been given. Now both began to fail and the short journey took us all day. Every few minutes the despairing hooting of a horn apprised us that a truck or a jeep had broken down, either with a puncture or a mechanical defect. Then the whole convoy would grind to a halt, while the necessary repairs were carried out. With increasing frequency the shout of 'Fitter's Jeep!' would ring out, and the chief fitter, Sergeant Lilley, dark, thin and efficient, would come dashing up with his team of experts to carry out what seemed miraculous repairs on the battered and sand-crusted engines. Even a puncture was a serious matter. Spare wheels and jacks were things of the past. Each time, the truck or jeep had to be lifted by bodily force, the wheel taken off, the old tattered tube patched and re-patched and put back again. When we had set out, it had been an easy matter for four of us to lift a jeep. Now, it was all that eight of us could do to get it off the ground, and the more often the punctures occurred the more exhausted we became. Tempers grew frayed, only Guardsman Duncan remaining completely imperturbable, as again and again our jeep came to a shaky halt with its klaxon sounding, and all eight of us climbed down to heave, pull and wrench at the offending wheel.

It was late when we finally reached Kufra, and after we had completed the necessary administrative processes, we were glad enough to lie down wherever we happened to be under the palm trees and go to sleep.

Next day was a memorable one. After a long lie and a bathe in the lake we lined up for breakfast at an improvised cookhouse under the palms. Porridge, with whisky in it, was followed by eggs from the Arab village, bacon and sausages. Next came bread, Australian butter and marmalade and finally tinned pineapple, produced from somewhere by a benevolent Quartermaster. The whole, piled high in borrowed mess tins, was washed down with copious draughts of strong tea, thick with condensed milk and sugar, drunk from elegant enamelled mugs. This last refinement provided a welcome contrast to the empty bully-beef tins to which we had been reduced of late.

When we had finished, we strolled over to where the other parties were encamped to hear in detail how they had fared. All had reached Kufra within a few hours of ourselves, and like us were enjoying to the full the new-found luxury of a life of leisure. Paddy Mayne's party had got back without special misadventure. David Stirling had waited as long as he could in the Gebel, had ascertained that the wounded we had left behind had duly been picked up by the enemy, and then, collecting all the stragglers he could find had brought up the rear.

The other raiding parties who had started out from Kufra had fared no better than we had. A patrol of the L.R.D.G., under David Lloyd Owen, had been given the task of escorting as far as their destination the party who were to try to bluff their way into Tobruk in German uniform, while a larger force was landed simultaneously from the sea. Lloyd Owen had duly navigated his charges across the desert to Tobruk, and had then waited for them to return. This they had not done, and, after waiting as long as he could, he had been obliged to return without them. From the pandemonium which, he said, had broken loose in Tobruk as soon as they entered it, we drew the conclusion that their operation, like our own had been anticipated by the enemy and had not gone according to plan. We were right. As at Benghazi, the Germans at Tobruk were expecting the attack. Matters were made worse by unfavourable weather which interfered with the naval side of the operation. Two of the destroyers and four M.T.B.s taking part in the landing were lost, and such troops as were landed were taken prisoner. Of the party which entered Tobruk from the desert, John Haselden, who commanded it, was killed. Tommy Lambton of the Irish Guards and David Russell of the Scots Guards managed to get away and, after an epic walk, made their way safely to the British lines at Alamein.

To balance this there was one piece of good news. Two L.R.D.G. patrols from Faiyum under Jake Easonsmith had crossed the full extent of the Sand Sea and, emerging from its northern end, had made a devastating surprise attack on the airfield at Barce, fifty miles east of Benghazi, where they had put the fear of God into the garrison and destroyed thirty aircraft on the ground.

Meanwhile David Stirling was already, characteristically, full of fresh ideas for the future, turning over in his mind plans for more operations in the desert, operations in Europe, operations (should the Germans get as far) in Persia. Later that day he left by air for Cairo and Bill Cumper, Guardsman Duncan and I went too. With us, on their stretchers, travelled Bob Melot and Corporal Laird, both of whom had borne the journey back with immense fortitude, and were now on their way to the comparative comfort of a general hospital.

We reached Cairo next day, having still not had time to remove our beards, change our shirts, or indeed indulge in more than the most perfunctory washing operations. The only means of transport we could find at the airport was a fifteen-hundredweight truck, and into the back of this we piled, a thoroughly disreputable-looking crowd. Someone wanted to be dropped at Shepheard's Hotel, and there we drove, to find the terrace packed with a well-dressed throng. How little our own garb did us justice was forcibly brought home to us when we overheard someone asking indignantly 'why there was no proper guard on that grubby-looking batch of German prisoners'?

Clearly it was high time we got ourselves a wash and brush up.

CHAPTER VII

A PASSAGE TO PERSIA

IN September 1942 one arm of the vast German pincer-movement which was threatening the whole Allied position in the Middle East had arrived at a point less than one hundred miles from Cairo and Alexandria. The other was reaching down through the Caucasus towards Persia. In Egypt the newly arrived Commander of Eighth Army, General Montgomery, was marshalling his forces for an assault on the enemy positions at El Alamein. In south Russia the Germans had attacked the town of Stalingrad and bitter fighting was in progress there.

If Eighth Army's offensive failed and the Germans broke through to the Nile delta, there was a danger that they would continue their progress through Egypt and Palestine into Iraq and Persia. Likewise, it seemed probable that the fall of Stalingrad would shortly remove the last obstacle to a German advance into these same countries from the north.

Persia was the gate to India. It was the source of immensely important oil supplies. Through it ran the main Anglo-American supply line to the Soviet Union. It was occupied at this time by a small force of British and Soviet troops, whose timely arrival had forestalled Reza Shah's plan of turning Persia into a Nazi base. But it seemed unlikely that they would be able to hold up the progress of a victorious German army, advancing either from the north or from the west.

It was against this general background that, on my return from Kufra, I was ordered to proceed to G.H.Q. Persia and Iraq Command at Baghdad to discuss with the Commander-in-Chief, General Maitland Wilson, the possibility of raising a small force on S.A.S. lines to operate on enemy-occupied territory in Persia in the event of a German break through.

There was no time to be lost. I hurried down to the Canal Zone, collected a new jeep, some maps and a week's rations, some warm clothes and Guardsman Duncan, and set out post haste for Baghdad and points east.

We had an uneventful journey across the Suez Canal and through the Sinai Desert to Gaza and Beersheba; through Palestine to the Lebanon and Syria and from Damascus across the desert to Baghdad. On the way we cooked our meals by the roadside and slept where night overtook us. In one way it seemed like a continuation of the drive back from Benghazi. But now we had plenty to eat and drink, we could sleep in peace at night, and we did not need to be perpetually scanning the skies for enemy aircraft.

On reaching Baghdad, I had a talk with General Wilson, who gave me authority to raise from the troops under his command a force of about 150 volunteers with a high proportion of officers and N.C.O.s, and told me to lose no time in making a reconnaissance of the areas in which we should be operating, if Persia fell into enemy hands.

A map was produced and together we studied it with a view to finding suitable bases from which irregulars might operate. The Commander-in-Chief was a massive man physically and it was not until we came to look at the map together that I realized that he combined a somewhat weighty manner with great alertness of intellect and an altogether remarkable eye for country.

The 'A' and 'Q' branches of G.H.Q. provided me with an agreeably elastic establishment and a lavish scale of arms and equipment. For operational purposes my private army, which was to be known as M Detachment S.A.S. Regiment, was to be directly responsible to G.H.Q. Persia and Iraq Command. The training programme was to include parachuting and any other methods of infiltration that might be called for.

Guardsman Duncan and I refilled the jeep with petrol and food and set out for Persia.

At the frontier at Khanikin, the baroque Customs House was still there, but this time Indian sentries had replaced the soldiers of the Shah. Thereafter we followed the same route that I had taken in 1938: Kermanshah, Hamadan, Kazvin, Teheran. I was glad to be back in Central Asia, with its clear light and pure dry air, its distant ranges of blue mountains, its arid plains and its little villages of flat-roofed mud

1. THE KREMLIN

2. THE SILK ROAD

3. THE MIDDLE EAST: SAS PATROL

4. LEAVING SIVA

5. LONG-RANGE DESERT GROUP

6. TITO

7. BOSNIA: IN THE WOODS

8. BOSNIA: ALL ROUND, THE SNOW LAY DEEP

9. DALMATIA

10. SIR FITZROY WITH TITO (*on left*)

11. BOKHARA — FIRST LIGHT

houses clustering amid a grove of green poplars on the bare hillside.

I spent the next two or three weeks pleasantly enough touring British units in Persia, calling for volunteers and at the same time making a reconnaissance of those parts of the country which seemed most likely to furnish bases for irregular operations. Prolonged inactivity made our troops in Persia long for a change and there was an abundance of volunteers from which to make a choice. All were ready to give up rank and pay in return for the prospect of early action.

The results of my reconnaissance were no less encouraging. Everywhere the mountains provided ideal conditions for irregular operations. From Teheran I went north over the Elburz Range into the Soviet-occupied provinces of Gilan and Mazanderan on the shores of the Caspian where the semi-tropical jungle offered excellent cover for guerrillas. Then westwards into Luristan, a traditional hide-out for bandits. Then south into the Dasht-i-Kavir, the vast and largely unexplored Salt Desert stretching right across Central Persia, traversed only by occasional camel tracks and dotted with salt marshes and quicksands. Here there were clearly possibilities of reproducing the conditions under which we had operated in the Western Desert. Aircraft could land, supplies could be dropped. There were excellent facilities for camouflage and lying up. Most important of all, the railway line, the main roads and Teheran itself were all within striking distance. Indeed the possibilities of making things hot for an occupying force were everywhere so good that it seemed to me incredible that the Germans had not tried something of the sort.

Then, just as I was thinking of pitching my camp and starting to train the nucleus of my force, I received a signal instructing me to report at once to General Wilson's Chief of Staff, General Baillon, who, the signal informed me, had just arrived in Teheran from Baghdad.

At Teheran, I found General Baillon at the British Legation in conference with the Minister, Sir Reader Bullard. They told me that they had a job for me. For some time past, they said, there had been signs that some kind of trouble was brewing in south Persia. The tribes, the Qashgai and the Bakhtiari, had German agents living amongst them and seemed likely to rise at any moment, just as they had in 1916 when their rebellion had caused us a disproportionate amount of trouble. Were this to happen, our supply route to the Persian Gulf might be cut. There was also discontent in Isfahan and other towns, largely caused by the hoarding of grain by speculators, which we were unable to prevent. This discontent, might at any moment flare up into open rebellion. Worse still if there were trouble, the Persian troops in south Persia were likely to take the side of the rioters.

A sinister part was being played in all this by a certain General Zahidi, who was in command of the Persian forces in the Isfahan area. Zahidi was known to be one of the worst grain-hoarders in the country. But there was also good reason to believe that he was acting in co-operation with the tribal leaders and, finally, that he was in touch with the German agents who were living in the hills and, through them, with the German High Command in the Caucasus. Indeed, reports from secret sources showed that he was planning a general rising against the Allied occupation force, in which his troops and those of the Persian general in the Soviet-occupied northern zone would take part and which would coincide with a German airborne attack on Tenth Army, followed by a general German offensive on the Caucasus front. In short, General Zahidi appeared to be behind most of the trouble in south Persia.

The situation was a delicate one. The Allied forces of occupation in northern Persia had been reduced to a minimum, in order to meet demands from the fighting fronts; there were practically no Allied troops in south Persia at all. The nearest British troops to the seat of the trouble were at Qum, two hundred miles north of Isfahan. There was very real danger that any sudden movement of British troops in a southward direction might provoke a general rising which we should have serious difficulty in containing with the small forces at our disposal. On the other hand, if we allowed events to take their course, the results would be equally disastrous.

In short it was essential to nip the trouble in the bud, while avoiding a full-scale showdown. General Baillon and Sir Reader Bullard had decided that this could best be achieved by the removal of General Zahidi and it was this task that they had decided to entrust to me. How it was to be done they left me to work out for myself. Only two conditions were made: I was to take him alive and I was to do so without creating a disturbance.

My first step was to go to Isfahan and see for myself how the land lay. That city's mosques and palaces, unrivalled in the whole of Asia, provided an excellent pretext for visiting it. I let it be known in Teheran that I was going to spend a few days' leave sight-seeing in the south, and set out.

I reached Isfahan the same night after driving all day across a bleak plateau fringed with distant snow-capped mountains. Finally the flickering lights of an isolated *chai-khana* shone out of the darkness, showing two or three dim figures squatting in the doorway, drinking their tea and smoking their long pipes; then a group of houses; then some shops; and then we were in the main street of Isfahan in a seething stream of carts, donkeys and camels, whose owners turned round to stare at the first jeep and the first British uniforms to make their appearance in Isfahan.

I drove to the British Consulate, where I was welcomed by the Consul, John Gault, with the same lavish hospitality that I have always met with at the hands of His Majesty's Consular Representatives in Persia. Soon Duncan and I, in the time-honoured phrase of the British soldier, had 'our knees under the table', and were making good progress with a brace of the local brand of partridge, washed down by delicious wine from the town of Shiraz, which, according to some, disputes with Xeres the honour of being the birthplace of sherry.

Over dinner I disclosed to my host, a robust-looking young man who gave the impression of being equally alert both mentally and physically, the true purpose of my visit. He was delighted. General Zahidi, though pleasant to meet, was, he said, a really bad lot: a bitter enemy of the Allies, a man of unpleasant personal habits, and, by virtue of his grain-hoarding activities, a source of popular discontent and an obstacle to the efficient administration of south Persia. He, too, had heard that he was plotting with the Germans and with the tribal leaders. Indeed, according to information which had reached him, one of the opening moves in General Zahidi's plot was to be the liquidation of the British Consul in Isfahan, a piece of news which completely outweighed all the General's personal charm, as far as he was concerned.

I asked Gault where Zahidi lived. He said he would show me, and after dinner we strolled out of the Consulate, across a narrow many-arched bridge, and along a broad avenue of plane trees, until we came to a massive pair of gates, set in a high stone wall and flanked by a sentry box and guardroom. Outside, a Persian infantryman was marching up and down while others, all well armed, slouched at the door of the guardroom. We took a turn round the back premises, where the surrounding wall was pierced by another gate, guarded by another sentry. This was the General's residence. Then we continued our stroll along the avenue under the trees. A few hundred yards further along we came to a large modern barracks, which according to Gault contained the greater part of the garrison of Isfahan, ready to rush to the assistance of their commander in case of trouble. It did not look as though a frontal attack by a small raiding party would have much chance of succeeding.

If Zahidi could not conveniently be winkled out of his place of residence, the obvious alternative was to ambush him when he was away from home, travelling from one point to another. I ascertained from Gault that at the same time every morning he crossed the bridge on his way to his headquarters. Would it not be possible to take advantage of the narrow bottleneck formed by this ancient monument to hold up his car, drag him out of it, and make off with him?

I gave this plan careful consideration, but there were two serious objections to it. In the first place Zahidi was reputed to go nowhere without a heavily armed bodyguard, whom it would be necessary to overcome by force. Secondly, even assuming that we managed to avoid a pitched battle with the bodyguard, we were unlikely to succeed in kidnapping a General in broad daylight in the middle of so populous a town as Isfahan without attracting a good deal of attention. The two of us driving peaceably along in the jeep had been a sufficiently novel spectacle to hold up the traffic in the main street of Isfahan; the same party with the addition of a struggling general and his bereaved bodyguard could scarcely fail to introduce into the proceedings that very element of uproar which my superiors were so anxious to avoid. I went to sleep that night with the feeling that the problem before me was not as simple as it had at first sight appeared.

Next day, after further thought and another talk with Gault, I came to the conclusion that, unless I was prepared to risk a serious incident which might have unforseeable repercussions, I should have to rely primarily on some kind of a ruse in order to get my man. In short, what was needed was a Trojan horse.

Once I had started thinking on these lines, it was not long before a plan began to shape itself in my mind, which seemed to offer a better chance of neatly and successfully eliminating the source of the trouble without setting light to the powder-magazine of South Persia. That afternoon I sent off a cipher telegram to Teheran giving my proposals for 'Operation PONGO', which was the code-name I had chosen for the abduction of the General.

The first thing was to find a pretext for introducing myself into Zahidi's house. I suggested that I should be given authority to assume for the occasion a Brigadier's badges of rank; that I should then ring up the house and announce myself as a senior staff officer from Baghdad who wished to pay his respects to the General. If the latter agreed, I would drive up in a staff car, accompanied by Duncan and one or two other resourceful characters, hold him up at the point of the pistol, hustle him into the car, and drive away with him out of Isfahan before the alarm could be given. I also asked for a platoon of British infantry to lend a hand in case anything went wrong. I undertook to work out some means of introducing these into Isfahan, in such a way as to attract as little attention as possible.

Having sent off my telegram, I spent two agreeable days in Isfahan, making a detailed reconnaissance of the city, with special attention to the best line of withdrawal in case of an emergency, and at the same time enjoying its peerless beauty.

Isfahan is, with Peking and Bokhara, one of the few places in the world which does not belie its reputation. Gault had installed himself in a charming old Persian house, with in front a lofty veranda looking out on to a walled garden. Thence, a short walk along a poplar-lined avenue brought you to the Maidan-i-Shah, the vast main square of the city, once the royal polo ground. On one side stands the Ala Kapu, or Great Gate. This is the entrance to the royal palace, known on account of its forty pillars as the Chehel Situn. Above it there is a splendid veranda, from which, when Isfahan was the capital, the monarch could watch polo, or wild beast shows or the arrival of foreign envoys, coming in state to pay homage to the King of Kings. At the southern end of the Maidan, near the palace, is the great royal mosque, the Masjed-i-Shah, while opposite it, on the eastern side, stands the smaller, more exquisite mosque of Sheikh Lutfullah. Within and without the dome is encrusted with glazed tiles: dazzling under the direct rays of the hot Persian sun beating down on the square; blue, cool and mysterious in the filtered light which penetrates the intricate arabesques of the narrow windows.

At the northern side of the square stands the entrance to the labyrinthine passages of the Great Bazaar. Along these, if you feel so inclined, you can wander for hours amongst piles of pomegranates, heaps of saddle-bags, prayer-mats and lamb-skins, in and out among the stalls of cobblers, rope-makers, confectioners and goldsmiths, all crying their wares at the top of their voices and at the same time bargaining noisily with each other and with their customers. Despite the hideous modern statue of the late Shah still standing there and despite his misguided attempts, fortunately abandoned by his successor, to bludgeon Persia into giving a half-hearted and entirely superficial imitation of a modern Western industrial state, Isfahan recalls the great capital city of the Middle Ages.

The arrival of an urgent message from G.H.Q. in reply to my telegram, submitting my proposals and requesting instructions, brought me back to the realities of the Second World War. My plan was approved in principle and I was instructed to go ahead with my preparations. Only one item of my highly unorthodox programme stuck in the throats of the well-trained staff officers at the other end. It was not (repeat: not) possible, they said, to authorize an officer of my age and seniority (I was a Captain) to masquerade, even for a day, as a Brigadier. Rather than allow this, they would place at my disposal, for a limited period of time, a genuine Brigadier, for use as bait, or for any other purpose within reason. Moreover this officer, for the purposes of the operation, would receive his instructions from me. For administrative purposes I was directed to report to General Anderson, the Corps Commander, at Qum, some two hundred miles from Isfahan, who had been asked to furnish the Brigadier and also such troops, equipment and transport as I might require.

I lost no time in reporting to Corps Headquarters, where I was provided with a platoon of Seaforth Highlanders, who were told that they had been specially selected for training in commando tactics. As surprise was clearly essential to the success of our enterprise, secrecy was of the utmost importance, and at this stage practically no one except the Corps Commander and myself was aware of our real objective. The Seaforths were equipped with tommy-guns and hand-grenades and we repaired to a secluded part of the desert near Qum to rehearse our act.

I had decided that the Seaforths should only be used in case of an emergency. My plan was that on the appointed day they should arrive in Isfahan in two covered trucks, disguised as far as possible to look like civilian vehicles, shortly before I set out for the General's house. One would draw up under the plane trees on the far side of the avenue, opposite the main entrance to the house and stay there. The other would take up a position covering the back entrance. The men, clutching their tommy-guns and hand-grenades would remain in the back of the trucks, out of sight. Only if they heard firing or a pre-arranged signal of three blasts on the whistle would they emerge from their hiding-place, overpower the guard and force an entrance, after which their task would be to cover the withdrawal of the party in the staff car, which it was hoped would include Zahidi whatever happened. If, on the other hand, all went well, the two trucks would simply wait until the staff car drove out with Zahidi in it, and then fall in behind and escort us out of Isfahan to a point in the desert where an aircraft would be waiting, ready to fly our prisoner out of the country.

For our rehearsals I chose a ruined fort in the desert. Again and again the two trucks took up their positions outside; the staff car drove in; the whistle sounded; the Seaforths poured out of the trucks and into the fort; an imaginary victim was bundled unceremoniously into the car, and all three vehicles drove off in triumph, the occupants tossing dummy hand-grenades out of the back at imaginary pursuers, as they went. The Seaforths gave a splendidly realistic performance. Indeed their enthusiasm was such that my only anxiety was lest on the day itself they would emerge from their place of concealment, whether things went well or badly, and massacre a number of harmless Persians out of sheer ebullience.

It now only remained to fix the day. This was done after a further exchange of signals with G.H.Q. Baghdad and with the Foreign Office via Teheran. I also extracted from the authorities, not without difficulty, permission to shoot General Zahidi, should he be armed and resist capture.

Our D-Day was fixed, and, on D minus one, we set out from Qum. I had decided that the Seaforths should spend the night well out of sight in the desert about ten miles from Isfahan. Next day, while the main party entered the town in the two trucks, smaller parties were detailed to cut the telegraph wires connecting Isfahan with the neighbouring Persian garrisons. Meanwhile I collected the Brigadier, a distinguished officer whose well-developed sense of humour caused him to enter completely into the spirit of the somewhat equivocal role that had been allotted to him, and set out for the British Consulate.

On our arrival there a telephone call was put through to the General's house and an appointment duly made for the same afternoon. After a copious lunch we took our places in the staff car which was flying a large Union Jack. A reliable N.C.O., armed to the teeth, occupied the seat next the driver, while Guardsman Duncan and a Seaforth Highlander, both carrying tommy-guns, crouched in the luggage compartment at the back, under a tarpaulin. Gault followed in his own car. As we approached Zahidi's house, I was relieved to see our two trucks, their tarpaulin covers concealing the battle-hungry Seaforths, drawn up in their appointed places. At the gate the Persian sentry was deep in conversation with Laurence Lockhart, a Persian linguist from the R.A.F. Intelligence, whose services I had enlisted for the occasion. So far everything had gone according to plan.

On our appearance, the sentry at the gate reluctantly put out the cigarette which Lockhart had given him, broke off his conversation, and presented arms. We drove on up the drive and drew up in front of the house immediately outside a large pair of open French windows. A servant ushered us in through these and went off to fetch the General.

When, a couple of minutes later, General Zahidi, a dapper figure in a tight-fitting grey uniform and highly polished boots, entered the room, he found himself looking down the barrel of my Colt automatic. There was no advantage in prolonging a scene which might easily become embarrassing. Without further ado, I invited the General to put his hands up and informed him that I had instructions to arrest him and that, if he made any noise or attempt at resistance, he would be shot. Then I took away his pistol and hustled him through the window into the car which was waiting outside with the engine running. To my relief there was no sign of the much-advertised bodyguard. As we passed the guardroom, the sentry once again interrupted his conversation to present arms, and the General, sitting bolt upright, with my pistol pressed against his ribs and Duncan breathing menacingly down his neck, duly returned the salute. The two 'plain vans', with their occupants now bitterly disappointed, fell in behind; and the whole convoy swept at a brisk pace over the bridge and into the main avenue leading out of Isfahan.

Some miles outside the town we passed a large barracks, full of General Zahidi's troops, but the telephone wire from the town had duly been cut by the wire-cutting party, and there was no sign of the alarm having been given. Meanwhile Zahidi continued to sit bolt upright and to assure me that there was a very good explanation of any aspects of his conduct which might at first sight have seemed at all suspicious. Soon we reached the point in the desert where we had spent the night and here I handed over my captive to an officer and six men who were standing by to take him by car to the nearest landing-ground where an aeroplane was waiting to fly him to Palestine. This was the last I saw of General Zahidi, but, reading my newspaper recently, nearly five years after his 'liquidation', I was amused to see an announcement that he had returned to Persia and once again been placed in command of the south Persian military district.

Having said goodbye to the Brigadier, whose duties were now at an end, and sent a signal to General Wilson announcing the completion of Operation PONGO, I went back into the town to clear up any outstanding points, taking a few Seaforths with me. My first objective was Zahidi's Headquarters, which I entered at the head of six Seaforths carrying tommy-guns. Gault had told me that Zahidi's Chief of

Staff was also very hostile to the Allies, and, in addition to this, extremely truculent in manner. The exaggerated amiability with which this dignitary now greeted me accordingly left me in no doubt that news of what had occurred had already got out. Taking him with me, I next returned to Zahidi's house which I proceeded to search methodically. In the General's bedroom I found a collection of automatic weapons of German manufacture, a good deal of silk underwear, some opium, an illustrated register of the prostitutes of Isfahan and a large number of letters and papers which I took back with me to the Consulate.

That night the Seaforths camped in the Consulate garden in case there was trouble, and Gault and I sat down to examine Zahidi's correspondence. One of the first letters that caught our eye was a recent communication from a gentleman styling himself 'German Consul-General for south Persia', and apparently resident in the hills somewhere to the south. He spoke of Zahidi's activities in terms of general approval and asked for more supplies. His letter left no doubt that the General's arrest had not come a moment too soon.

CHAPTER VIII

NEW HORIZONS

AFTER the kidnapping of General Zahidi, I settled down to the more orthodox task of assembling my new detachment and training them in S.A.S. methods. As a training area we were allotted Isfahan and the surrounding country, in the hope, I was told, that, by showing the flag there, we might act as a deterrent to any other Persians who might be contemplating rebellion or co-operation with the Germans. As there were only about one hundred and fifty of us all told with no other British troops for several hundred miles, it seems doubtful whether we counted for very much in the calculations of any potential fifth-columnists, but we nevertheless did our best with the material at our disposal to convey the impression that we were a large and well-equipped force.

Sandy Scratchley and Bill Cumper brought over a load of high explosives and a convoy of fully fitted jeeps as a present from David Stirling. The unaccustomed sight of these nimble little vehicles, bristling with machine guns fore and aft, would we hoped, strike terror into the hearts of General Zahidi's late accomplices. In addition to my original volunteers 'Operation PONGO' had brought me in a number of Seaforths, including a piper, whose spirited performances were no doubt equally disconcerting to such Persians as heard them. Another valuable acquisition was Sergeant Charlie Button from Sandy Scratchley's regiment the Fourth County of London Yeomanry, a rubicund and uniformly cheerful character, who after serving in the First World War and winning a very good Military Medal in the Western Desert in the Second, had now decided, on reaching the late forties, that it was time he learned to parachute. He was soon installed as Quartermaster Sergeant, and, by the time we started our training programme, had accumulated by methods which, if not strictly orthodox, were remarkably effective, a magnificent collection of weapons, equipment, vehicles, clothing, tentage and rations. We laid out an impressive camp some twenty miles from Isfahan and the next two months were spent training arduously amidst the ice and snow of the hill country of southern Persia.

Meanwhile, further west, the battles of El Alamein and Stalingrad had checked the German advance, and by the end of 1942 it had become clear that the threat to Persia had been removed. I accordingly flew to Baghdad to try to find out what plans were being made for our future. When I got there, I found General Wilson on the point of leaving for Cairo to take up the appointment of Commander-in-Chief, Middle East. This meant that the eastern Mediterranean, an area with unrivalled opportunities for small-scale raiding, would come under his operational control. It was too good a chance to miss. Before he left, I extracted from him a promise that we should be transferred to Middle East Command forthwith. With any luck, the training in mountain warfare which we had acquired on the Iranian plateau would be put into practice amongst the hills and valleys of southern and eastern Europe. I took the first aeroplane back to Persia, and a week or two later we had struck our camp and were moving as fast as our vehicles would take us back across Persia and Iraq to our new scene of activities.

In Middle East Command there had been many changes since Duncan and I had set out for Persia in the autumn. Eighth Army was now at the other end of North Africa, preparing for the landings in Sicily. The Middle East, for so long almost the only active theatre of war, was being converted into a gigantic jumping-off place and supply base for the invasion of southern Europe.

In the S.A.S. there had also been changes. David Stirling, after so many miraculous escapes, had at last been taken prisoner in Tunisia while operating hundreds of miles ahead of Eighth Army. With the end of the war in the desert, too, the S.A.S. had lost a medium ideally suited to their type of warfare. The desert had played a vital part in their operations. Now they would have to adapt themselves to completely new conditions, to use completely new methods, if they were to achieve the same successes on the continent of Europe. I wished that David, so quick to grasp the potentialities of the desert for irregular warfare, had been there to help evolve a new 'continental' technique.

After David Stirling's capture the S.A.S. had split up into a number of parts. On our arrival from Persia my party joined up with George Jellicoe who was training with canoes and rubber dinghies on the coast of Palestine at Athlit, romantically situated at the foot of Mount Carmel, where the ruins of a vast Crusader's castle, complete with dungeons and banqueting hall, tower above the blue waters and sandy beach of a little Mediterranean bay. After some weeks of this I moved my detachment northwards up the coast to the Lebanon to complete our training in mountain warfare. For this purpose we were based on the village of Zahle high up in the mountains behind Beirut.

Situated in a typical Alpine valley, with rushing past its half-French-provincial, half-Arab houses, a mountain stream, which the inhabitants used for cooling bottles of delicious wine from the neighbouring vineyards, Zahle sticks in my memory as one of the most agreeable places to which my travels have taken me. We had, however, by now all had enough of training, however agreeable the surroundings might be. We had also had enough of the Middle East. Our objective now was Europe, to which prolonged inaccessibility had lent an entirely new glamour. Eighth Army were preparing to land in Sicily. We did not see why we should be left behind.

A few weeks after our arrival from Persia, I was summoned to Cairo and told to select a small party of officers and N.C.O.s with which to attack a German fighter base on Crete. We were to be landed by night on a secluded part of the coast; make our way across the island to our target; blow up any aircraft there might be on it and then find our way back to the coast to be taken off again. Large-scale maps and air photographs were procured, and we settled down to the detailed planning. We soon felt as if we had known that aerodrome and the rocky gullies by which we should have to approach it since our earliest childhood. We drew our operational rations from Sergeant Button, discussing the relative merits on a long march of dates or raisins, biscuits or oatmeal, bully or bacon. We made up and packed our explosives and oiled and cleaned our weapons.

As we were preparing to leave for Beirut to go on board the motor launch which was to drop us, I was once again summoned to Cairo, to receive, I assumed, some last-minute instructions. But on arriving there, I was told that the latest air photographs showed that the

Germans were no longer using the aerodrome for which we were bound and that our operation had therefore been cancelled.

I left G.H.Q. feeling quite unwarrantably aggrieved. Things, it seemed to me, were going from bad to worse. Twelve months earlier the Germans would never have behaved like this. In the desert, if you stuck around long enough, something always turned up; you didn't have to fabricate operations.

It was in this frame of mind that I went to see Rex Leeper, an old friend from Foreign Office days, and now His Majesty's Ambassador to the Greek Government then in exile in Cairo. Looking back to our first attempt at parachute training I had a dim recollection of mysterious figures who had passed through our hands and who were, as far as we knew, preparing to be dropped into enemy-occupied Greece, not to perform a single operation, but to stay there indefinitely, just as Bob Melot had lived for months at a time behind the enemy lines in the desert. It seemed to me that a job of this kind might meet my requirements. Presumably, if one lived permanently in enemy-occupied territory, there would be no need to go out of one's way to find excitement.

I found the Ambassador in a pleasant flat in Zamalek, overlooking the grounds of the Gezira Sporting Club, with a long drink waiting for me that was most welcome after a frustrating morning in the sweltering offices of G.H.Q. Better still, there was, it appeared, every prospect of a job on the lines I had in mind. He would make inquiries and let me know the result. Being blessed with a fairly lively imagination, I started on my return journey in a much better frame of mind, already picturing myself in any number of fascinating and agreeably spectacular situations amongst the thyme-scented mountains of Greece. When I got back, I asked Duncan and Sergeant Button whether they would like to come to Greece with me. They replied that they didn't mind if they did.

The response to Rex Leeper's inquiries came sooner than I had expected. I had hardly got back to Zahle when I received a message from him, asking me to return to Cairo without delay. On my arrival he showed me a telegram from London, saying that I was needed; but not in Greece. I was to be dropped in Jugoslavia. I was to fly to

London forthwith and report to the Prime Minister himself, who would tell me what was required of me.

I did not have long to think out the implications of this telegram. An aircraft was leaving for England the same night. There was barely time to notify G.H.Q. and get the necessary movement order. I had not been home for nearly two years and to be going back was, in itself, exciting enough.

I knew little of the situation in Jugoslavia. I had never been there before the war and, since the German occupation, the only news of Jugoslavia which I remembered reading in the occasional copies of the *Egyptian Mail* which had happened to come my way, concerned the activities of General Mihajlović, who, by all accounts, was conducting a spirited resistance movement in the mountains. In so far as I speculated at all about the future, my guess was that I should in some way be associated with this legendary figure.

Once I reached London, I was soon put in the picture. Information reaching the British Government from a variety of sources had caused them to doubt whether the resistance of General Mihajlović and his Četniks to the enemy was all that it was made out to be. There were indications that at least as much was being done by armed bands bearing the name of Partisans and led by a shadowy figure known as Tito. Hitherto such support as we had been able to give had gone exclusively to Mihajlović. Now doubts as to the wisdom of this policy were beginning to creep in, and the task which I had been allotted was to form an estimate on the spot of the relative value of the Partisans' contribution to the Allied cause and the best means of helping them to increase it. For this purpose I was to be dropped into Jugoslavia by parachute as head of a Military Mission accredited to Tito, or whoever I found to be in command of the Partisans.

My inquiries revealed that in fact little or nothing was known of the Partisans in Whitehall. Three or four British officers had been dropped in to them by parachute a few weeks before, but there had been fierce fighting in Jugoslavia since their arrival and no comprehensive report of the situation from them had reached London. It was, however, believed that the Partisans were under Communist leadership and that they were causing the Germans considerable inconvenience (an impression that was principally derived from German sources). Their principal sphere of activity was thought to be in Bosnia and it was there that I was to be dropped.

As to Tito, there were various theories concerning his identity. One school of thought refused to believe that he existed at all. The name, they said, stood for *Tajna Internacionalna Teroristička Organizacija*, or Secret International Terrorist Organization, and not for any individual leader. Another theory was that it was simply an appointment, and that a new Tito was nominated at frequent intervals. Finally, the more romantically inclined claimed that Tito was not a man, but a young woman of startling beauty and great force of character.

A day or two after I arrived in England I was rung up from No. 10 Downing Street and told that Mr. Churchill wanted me to come down to Chequers for a weekend so that he could himself explain to me what he had in mind.

When I reached Chequers, I wondered if the Prime Minister would ever find time to talk to me about Jugoslavia. The Chief of the Imperial General Staff was there, and Air-Marshal Harris, of Bomber Command, and an American General, and an expert on landing-craft, and any number of other people, all of whom clearly had matters of the utmost importance to discuss with Mr. Churchill. Red leather dispatch boxes, full of telegrams and signals from every theatre of war, kept arriving by dispatch rider from London.

Then there were the films; long films, short films, comic films and serious films, sandwiched in at all hours of the day and night. The great men stood by, waiting their turn, hoping that it would not come in the early hours of the morning, a time when the ordinary mortal does not feel at his brightest, especially if he has seen three or four films in succession, but when the Prime Minister, on the contrary, seemed filled with renewed vigour of mind and body.

Towards midnight, in the middle of a Mickey Mouse cartoon, a memorable interruption took place. A message was brought in to Mr. Churchill, who gave an exclamation of surprise. Then there was a scuffle and the film was stopped. As the squawking of Donald Duck and the baying of Pluto died away, the Prime Minister rose to his feet. 'I have just,' he said, 'received some very important news. Signor

Mussolini has resigned.' Then the film was switched on again.

As we went downstairs, I reflected that in view of this startling new development it was now more unlikely than ever that the Prime Minister would find time to attend to my affairs. But I was mistaken. 'This,' he said, turning to me, 'makes your job more important than ever. The German position in Italy is crumbling. We must now put all the pressure we can on them on the other side of the Adriatic. You must go in without delay.' Mr. Churchill then went on to give me a splendidly lucid and at the same time vivid account of the strategic situation and of what he wanted me to try and do in Jugoslavia. I was amazed, as so often afterwards I was to be amazed, by his extraordinary grasp of detail in regard to what was, after all, only one of the innumerable problems confronting him.

After he had finished, there was only one point which, it seemed to me, still required clearing up. The years that I had spent in the Soviet Union had made me deeply and lastingly conscious of the expansionist tendencies of international Communism and of its intimate connection with Soviet foreign policy; after all, in my day, the Communist International had sported a brass plate in one of Moscow's main thoroughfares and had numbered Stalin and several other leading Soviet public figures amongst the members of its Executive Committee. If, as I had been told, the Partisans were under Communist leadership, they might easily be fighting very well for the Allied cause, but their ultimate aim would undoubtedly be to establish in Jugoslavia a Communist regime closely linked to Moscow. How did His Majesty's Government view such an eventuality? Was it at this stage their policy to obstruct Soviet expansion in the Balkans? If so, my task looked like being a ticklish one.

Mr. Churchill's reply left me in no doubt as to the answer to my problem. So long, he said, as the whole of Western civilization was threatened by the Nazi menace, we could not afford to let our attention be diverted from the immediate issue by considerations of long-term policy. We were as loyal to our Soviet Allies as we hoped they were to us. My task was simply to find out who was killing the most Germans and suggest means by which we could help them to kill more. Politics must be a secondary consideration.

I was relieved at this. Although, as a Conservative, I had no liking for Communists or Communism, I had not fancied the idea of having to intrigue politically against men with whom I was co-operating militarily. Now, in the light of what the Prime Minister had told me, my position was clear.

Meanwhile the first thing was to refresh my knowledge of the country for which I was bound. While I was in England, I read every book about Jugoslavia that I could lay hands on. Seen from the angle of someone about to plunge headlong into it, the turbulent stream of Balkan history had a new fascination. The details were as confusing as ever, but certain basic characteristics, certain constantly recurring themes, seemed to run right through the bewildering succession of war and rebellion, heroism, treachery and intrigue. In these might lie the key to much that was now happening.

I should be among Slavs once more. Some fifteen centuries ago, the forbears of the principal races which now inhabit Jugoslavia, the Serbs, Croats, Slovenes, Montenegrins and others had migrated there from the north to become a southern outpost of the Slav world. They were Jugo-Slavs, South Slavs. Even now their language, Serbo-Croat, which I had set myself to learn, had so much in common with Russian that soon I found that I could understand it and make myself understood in it.

From the first their history had been eventful, a story of bloodshed and violence: of feudal lords contending amongst themselves for supremacy in their own country; of overlords, their supremacy once established, seeking to impose their rule on neighbouring races and countries; striving to weld these into an Empire strong enough to hold its own in the rapidly diminishing power-vacuum between East and West. To overthrow each other, to rid themselves of dangerous rivals and settle their own internal quarrels, these Balkan chieftains would enlist the aid of outside powers, Byzantium, the Turks, the Emperor or the Pope. Then they would unite once more amongst themselves to cast off the foreign allegiance which a short time before they had seemed so ready to accept. They understood above all the art of playing off the Great Powers against each other: East against West, Rome against Byzantium, Pope against Emperor, Teuton against Turk.

But the purpose of these manœuvres remained the same: the preservation of their own national independence. This end they pursued with a violence, a devotion, a turbulence and a resilience all of their own.

But for small national States the struggle for survival was then, as it is now, a hard one. The advance westwards of the Osmanli Turks grew ever harder to check. In 1389, at Kossovo, the famous Field of the Blackbirds, the Serbian Prince Lazar was killed and his people passed under Turkish sway. The neighbouring principalities succumbed one after another. Soon the whole peninsula was under alien domination, the Turks occupying the south and east, while the Austrians and the Hungarians advanced to meet them from the west and north, and the Venetians established themselves along the coast. It was destined to remain so for over three centuries.

In this way the South Slavs were divided up, the southern and eastern area of their territory, now Serbia, falling under Turkish rule and the northern and western, now Croatia and Slovenia, under Austro-Hungarian. The Dalmatian coastal strip passed into the hands of the Doges of Venice, until eventually, with the decline of the latter, it too was absorbed by Austria-Hungary.

Thus, although their language and racial origin were identical, the two groups of Slavs found themselves separated by the national frontiers of the Great Powers and gradually grew apart culturally, politically and traditionally. In the matter of religion also, for by now the division between the Eastern and Western Churches, Orthodox and Catholic, had finally crystallized into a fixed pattern. The results of this cleavage still make themselves felt today.

Under the loose, though often savage rule of the Sultans, the Serbs, while enjoying a certain degree of liberty and even autonomy, inevitably looked towards Constantinople as the political, religious and cultural centre of their world. For them the Church was the Eastern Orthodox Church, with the Patriarch of Constantinople at its head, while some, particularly in Bosnia, even went over to the faith of their conquerors and embraced Islam.

The Croats and Slovenes, on the other hand, looked westwards towards Vienna, the upper classes basking at a respectful distance in the reflected glory of the Imperial Court. In religion they were, like their

Austrian masters, Roman Catholics, Christianity having in general first come to them with the Teutonic invaders from the north. Altogether, they became in their outlook generally, in their standard of civilization and in their attitude towards life, a Western rather than an Eastern people.

The Serbs, for their part, made, under Turkish rule, but little progress towards civilization as it existed in Western Europe. As administrators, the Turks were not greatly concerned with culture. In the outlying provinces of their Empire their main preoccupations were financial and military in nature: the levying of tribute and the defence of their frontiers. While Zagreb came to resemble a European town, Belgrade remained an oriental fortress.

But if the Serbs in some ways lagged behind their Slav brothers beyond the frontier, in one important respect they did not. They never lost their love of freedom, their sense of nationhood. All through the centuries of Turkish rule the spirit of independence was kept alive in the hill-country of Serbia by little bands of guerrilla fighters who harried the Turks, partly for the fun of it, and partly to keep in existence a nucleus, however small, of national independence. Most successful of all in this were the Montenegrins, who, in their mountains, held out unsubdued against all-comers for century after century. This tradition of resistance was to endure both in Serbia and in Montenegro.

At the start of the nineteenth century there came a change in the situation. The Ottoman Empire began to crumble. The new spirit of liberty and national independence which was sweeping through Europe like wildfire made itself felt in the Balkans with redoubled force. For the first time progressive elements in Europe, following the fashionable example of Lord Byron, began to interest themselves in the fate of the Balkan Christians. With the Russians the ties of race, language and religion carried particular weight; Panslavism, the all-Slav movement, was born. All of a sudden the patriots of the Balkans found that they had powerful friends.

In Serbia they also had effective leaders. The revolt which flared up in 1804 was led by Kara Djordje, or Black George, peasant, turned mercenary, turned brigand, turned guerrilla. Kara Djordje, who was to be the founder of the Karadjordjević dynasty, was a black-a-vised man, owing his name equally to his swarthy appearance and savage, morose nature. With his own hands he is said to have killed over a hundred men, including his own father and brother. A man of great determination and an effective commander in the field, he showed himself a forceful rather than a skilful statesman. By 1807 he had driven the Turks from Serbia. In 1809 they returned. With Russian help he drove them out again. In 1813 they returned again, this time in overwhelming force, and Kara Djordje was driven out and obliged to take refuge, first in Austria, then in Russia. The Turks appointed Miloš Obrenović, a former herdsman, to rule the conquered province for them.

But in 1815 there was a fresh rising against the Turks. This time it was led by Miloš Obrenović, the man the Turks had made their Viceroy. He, too, showed himself a man of determination. In a single campaign he expelled the Turks and proclaimed himself Prince of Serbia. After this he obtained Turkish recognition and in return accepted Turkish suzerainty. When Kara Djordje came back in 1817 he was assassinated and his head sent to the Turks. Miloš Obrenović, it was thought, had not been entirely unconnected with his assassination.

For the next hundred years Serbia presents an extraordinary picture of intrigue and unrest. Rival dynasties, founded by the two peasant-liberators, Kara Djordje and Miloš Obrenović, served as rallying points for opposing factions. Princes and Kings, Prime Ministers and Commanders-in-Chief followed one another in a bewildering succession, regulated by mob-violence, political assassination and the intrigues of the Great Powers. In her external relations, Serbia sided first with one Great Power and then with another, as her interests or the personal inclinations of her rulers demanded, while the Great Powers, for their part, lent their support first to one Serbian faction and then to another.

Seen from close by, these proceedings are far from edifying; but, regarded in the light of later events, they fall into their proper place as incidents in the struggle of a proud and naturally turbulent people for unity and nationhood. For that was the ultimate aim: the reunion with Serbia of the Croat, Slovene, Dalmatian, Bosnian and other provinces, still under Austro-Hungarian or Turkish rule, and the maintenance, by judicious manœuvring, of Serbia's independence in relation to the Great Powers.

With Kara Djordje out of the way and Russia supporting him, Miloš Obrenović reigned as Prince of a semi-autonomous Serbia under Turkish suzerainty until 1839. The ferocity of his despotism equalled that of the Turks. In 1839 he was ousted by his own son, Milan. But Milan died the same year and was succeeded by his brother, Michael, and Michael was in turn dethroned two years later by Alexander Karadjordjević, the son of Kara Djordje, who enjoyed the support of Austria-Hungary and Turkey. The Obrenovićs went into exile.

But Serbia had not seen the last of the Obrenović dynasty, or indeed of its founder, Miloš. Alexander's policy of friendship with Austria was not popular, least of all with the Tsar, who was inclined to regard himself as the Protector of Serbia. In 1859 Alexander was driven out and, after twenty years of not entirely misspent exile, that aged but persistent herdsman, Miloš Obrenović, returned to the throne from which he had been driven by his son twenty years earlier. He, for one, knew the value of friendship with Russia.

In less than two years Miloš Obrenović was dead, succeeded by his son Michael, who had also returned from exile, and who now reigned wisely and well until 1868, when he was assassinated. The Karadjordje faction were, it was thought, not entirely unconnected with his demise.

This time, however, there was no change of dynasty. The Karadjordje plot misfired and Michael Obrenović was succeeded as Prince by his cousin Milan. Under Milan Obrenović, Serbia embarked on a more adventurous policy, undertaking or joining in no less than three wars. In 1876, having attacked the Turks, she was defeated by them and her autonomy seemed in danger. But she was rescued by the Russians, whom she then joined in their war of 1877-78 against Turkey. As a reward she was granted complete independence from Turkey and Milan was proclaimed King. But even so he felt that the Russians had not done enough for him and, abandoning the traditional pro-Russian policy of his dynasty, turned towards Austria. When in 1885 the Serbs were defeated by their neighbours the Bulgars, who now, in their turn, enjoyed the favour of the Russians, it was the Austrians who came to their rescue. Leaning heavily towards Austria, Milan continued to reign until 1889, when, following his divorce from his Russian wife, Natalie, he abdicated unexpectedly in favour of his young son Alexander. With his departure, Serbia swung back once more towards Russia.

But the young Alexander, finding himself in difficulties, soon recalled his father, the ex-King, from exile to advise him, making him Commander-in-Chief of the Serbian Army. With Milan's return, Serbia inclined once more towards Austria-Hungary. Inclined, that is, until Alexander fell in love with and married Draga, one of his Russian mother's ladies-in-waiting. Then he exiled his father once more and threw Serbia back into the arms of Russia.

But by now Alexander Obrenović was popular neither with the Great Powers nor with his own subjects. Plots, disturbances and conspiracies became the order of the day. He played with the idea of changing his foreign policy or, alternatively, divorcing his wife. But he was not quick enough. On June 15th, 1903, he and Queen Draga were assassinated and their horribly mutilated bodies thrown from the window of their ornate little palace. It was generally supposed that the supporters of the rival dynasty had not been unconnected with the assassination.

At any rate it was Peter Karadjordjević, the grandson of Kara Djordje, who now ascended the throne, while the Ministry of Public Works (a lucrative appointment) went to a certain Colonel Mašin, who was known to have played an important part in the assassination. He was also, as it happened, the brother-in-law of the murdered Queen, but had clearly not allowed family ties to interfere with his political convictions. The first act of the new Parliament was to pass a vote of thanks to the regicides and the Russian Ambassador was among the first to congratulate King Peter on his accession to the throne. Russian influence was on the increase.

From now onwards Serbia's relations with Austria-Hungary became increasingly strained. For she was clearly destined to be the rallying point for South Slav irredentism, and most of the South Slavs outside Serbia dwelt in Croatia, Slovenia and Dalmatia, and were subjects of the Austrian Emperor. Thus Vienna viewed the rise of

Serb nationalism with ever-growing concern. In 1908 the Austrians, who believed in leaving nothing to chance, formally annexed Bosnia and Herzegovina, Slav provinces which were nominally still part of Turkey, although since 1878 they had, to the disgust of the Serbs, been administered by Austria-Hungary.

The Serbs were indignant, but powerless to intervene. They too started to reinsure. In 1912, in company with the Greeks, Bulgars and Montenegrins, they fought a victorious war against the Turks, forcing them to cede most of what remained of Turkey in Europe. Then in 1913 they fought the Bulgars, their allies of the year before, for the fruits of their common victory, the Turks joining in on their side. Serbia emerged from these struggles with her territories enlarged and her national consciousness now thoroughly awakened.

The concern felt by Austria increased still further. She decided to settle the South Slav problem once and for all. An opportunity offered itself in June of the following year, 1914, when the Archduke Franz Ferdinand of Austria was assassinated, while on a visit to the newly annexed provinces of Bosnia and Herzegovina, by a young Bosnian Serb named Gavrilo Princip. The Serbian Government, so the Austrians maintained, had not been entirely unconnected with the assassination. The Austrian Government delivered in Belgrade an ultimatum which the Serbs could not possibly be expected to accept.

The issue did not long remain a purely Austro-Serb one. Russia came to the help of Serbia, while Germany supported Austria. France and Great Britain were soon involved, and within a month Europe was at war. The effects of the shot fired by Gavrilo Princip were to be far-reaching.

During the four years of war the Serbs fought well against overwhelming odds. With Prince Alexander Karadjordjević, the great-grandson of the Liberator, at their head, both the Army and the civilian population performed remarkable feats of valour and endurance. They knew they were fighting for their existence as a people. They believed that victory would bring them unity with the Slav minorities in Austria-Hungary. Already during the war deserters had come over to them from the Croat and Slovene troops in the Austrian Army and in 1918 a Committee was set up to discuss the eventual establishment of a unified kingdom of Serbs, Croats and Slovenes under the rule of the Karadjordjević dynasty. When the war was over, this was duly sanctioned at Versailles, the name being later changed to Jugoslavia, the Land of the South Slavs. In one respect, it is true, the peace settlement left Jugoslav aspirations unsatisfied. Under the peace treaty Trieste was awarded to Italy, while a band of Italian nationalists, led by the poet, d'Annunzio, seized the town of Fiume by main force.

Prince Alexander Karadjordjević, King Peter's second son, who had led the Serbian forces to ultimate victory in the war, was proclaimed Regent of the new State. King Peter was old and his eldest son Prince George had been persuaded to give up his rights to the throne. His valet had died in suspicious circumstances some time before and Prince George, or so his younger brother maintained, had not been unconnected with his death. It was thought better for him to take a back seat.

The dreams of the early Serb patriots had come true. After bitter struggles and great tribulation the hereditary enemies, first the Turks and then the Austrians, had been overcome and driven out and now at last a true South Slav kingdom set up, ruled over by a descendant of Black George and uniting within its frontiers all their long-lost Slav brothers. All, or so it seemed, was for the best in the best of all possible worlds. But the South Slavs were not destined to live for long in peace.

The Serbs, on the whole, had little to complain of. A Serb King was on the throne. Serb officers commanded the Army. The capital remained in Belgrade, a Serbian city. This, they felt, was as it should be. Victory, after all, had been won by a Serb Army and not by their long-lost, new-found Slav brothers from across the border. Many Croats and Slovenes, they recalled, had not come over to them, but had continued to fight for the Austrians as long as there were any Austrians left to fight for. They were also, as it now appeared, different from the Serbs in many ways: in their outlook, in their habits and finally in their religion. Thus, although in the new State the newcomers amounted to about forty per cent of the total population, the feeling among the Serb ruling class was that the Croats and Slovenes must work their passage before they were admitted to full and equal partnership.

This 'Pan-Serb' attitude was from the outset bitterly resented by the

Croats who were in any case inclined to regard the Serbs as barbarian parvenus, and now clung jealously to what they regarded as their national rights, which, some said, had been better safeguarded under the old and reactionary, but at least civilized, Austrian Empire. Thus, scarcely had the longed-for union of all the South Slavs been effected, than Serbs and Croats were at each others' throats in the best Balkan style.

During the years that followed the setting up of the new kingdom, Jugoslav internal affairs were dominated by the Croat problem, which loomed even larger than the Irish question in British politics before 1914. Like the Irish question, it tinged the political life of the country with violence, with religious rivalry and with a spirit of fanaticism. The proceedings of the Skupština or parliament were constantly disturbed by the increasingly violent clashes of the Croat nationalists and their Pan-Serb opponents.

Finally matters reached a crisis when in 1928 Stepan Radić, the leader of the Croat Peasant Party, was shot dead by a political opponent during a debate of the Skupština. Reckoning that things had gone too far for parliamentary government to be any longer a practical possibility, King Alexander, who had succeeded his father as King in 1921, abolished the constitution, dissolved the Skupština and set up what was in effect a personal dictatorship with the power concentrated in the hands of the monarch and authority ruthlessly enforced by a large and ubiquitous police force backed up by the Army. Little pretence at parliamentary democracy remained.

The new regime was repressive and finally confirmed Serb domination. On the other hand it stood for the preservation of order and increased administrative efficiency. Alexander, too, enjoyed a certain personal popularity. A grim, determined, conscientious man, he commanded the respect of his people by the way in which he had shared their dangers and hardships during the war, by his capacity for work, and by his undoubted devotion to what he conceived to be his duty.

But, like so many of his predecessors, Alexander was to meet with a violent end. The end of parliamentary government had driven the more extreme Croat nationalists underground or into exile. In Italy and also in Hungary the most violent, calling themselves Ustaše, formed themselves into a terrorist organization vowed to liberate Croatia from Serb domination, and enjoying the protection of Mussolini, who saw in it a useful means of furthering his own aims in the Balkans. Their leader was a certain Ante Pavelić, a lawyer from Zagreb. From Italy and Hungary the Ustaše sent clandestine emissaries back into Jugoslavia, but Alexander's police state was so firmly established that there was little that they could do against it. He himself lived in a closely guarded palace on a hilltop outside Belgrade, surrounded by massive blocks of barracks, housing the Royal Guards. The Ustaše waited. Their opportunity came in 1934, when Alexander paid a State visit to France. Then, as the King was driving through the streets of Marseilles with Monsieur Barthou, the French Foreign Minister, an Ustaša shot them both before he was himself cut down by the police. Looking back, I remembered the consternation which this assassination had caused in Paris. Subsequent investigations, I recalled, had shown that Ante Pavelić had not been unconnected with the murder. Indeed his connection with it was so close that in his absence he was condemned to death.

In his absence. For he continued to live in Italy under Mussolini's protection, awaiting the opportunity to carry his plans a stage further.

Meanwhile, in Jugoslavia King Alexander's assassination did not lead to any change in the character of the regime which he had established. If anything it became more oppressive under the rule of his cousin, Prince Paul, who assumed the regency during the minority of Alexander's son, Peter.

In 1939, however, the outbreak of war in Europe, of war which might at any time spread to the Balkans, brought home to the rulers of Jugoslavia the need for some kind of effort on their part to conciliate the Croats and thus unite the people of Jugoslavia in the face of the danger which now threatened them. An approach was accordingly made to Dr. Maček, the leader of the Croat Peasant Party and a man of very great influence in Croatia. As a result of this, Maček agreed to enter the Government as Vice-Premier, his Party exchanged their attitude of abstention and obstruction for one of limited co-operation, while the structure of the Jugoslav State was remodelled on a federal basis, involving a marked improvement in the position of Croatia.

Hardly had these changes been finally agreed upon, when the blow fell. In March 1941 the Jugoslav Government were presented with what amounted to an ultimatum demanding the incorporation of Jugoslavia in the Nazi New Order. For Jugoslavia to comply with such a demand would have been to sacrifice her independence. On the other hand, to refuse it meant almost certain annihilation. The men in whose hands the decision lay, the Regent Prince Paul and the Prime Minister Cvetković, decided to capitulate. Leaving hastily for Vienna at Hitler's bidding, Cvetković returned a few days later having signed a comprehensive agreement with Germany.

But they had reckoned without the Jugoslav people. As soon as the news of their deal with Hitler became known, a spontaneous popular rising swept Cvetković's Government out of office and Prince Paul out of the elegant white palace which he had built himself on a hill outside Belgrade. A new Government was formed under General Simović; the eighteen-year-old King Peter was declared to have attained his majority, and the pact with Germany was formally denounced.

The popular rejoicing provoked by these events was not to be of long duration. On April 6th German bombers made devastating attacks on Belgrade and on a number of other Jugoslav towns. They were followed by the German Army in force, with the Italians yapping at its heels.

Against an enemy so overwhelmingly superior in training, numbers and equipment the Royal Jugoslav Army, poorly armed and supplied, badly led and with no hope of Allied support, could do little. It was moreover still further weakened by corruption and treachery. Cases of ammunition were found, when they reached the front, to be empty or filled with sand, and, particularly among the Croat troops, there was large-scale desertion to the enemy. After a few days the capitulation was signed; King Peter and General Simović's Government fled abroad, and the Jugoslav Army laid down their arms. Resistance, or so it appeared, was at an end, and the Germans were now free to proceed with the occupation and dismemberment of Jugoslavia.

In Croatia a new independent State was set up on strictly Fascist lines. Ante Pavelić, arriving in the train of the conquering Axis armies, was given the title of Poglavnik or Leader. The Ustaše flocked over to become his Praetorian Guard. Their patience had at length been rewarded.

In Serbia, now separated from Croatia and reduced to her former frontiers, the role of Quisling — or perhaps it would be fairer to say of Pétain — was played by General Nedić, the former Chief of Staff.

Such Jugoslav territory as was not included within the boundaries of the new Serbia and the new Croatia was distributed amongst her neighbours. Most of Dalmatia and part of Slovenia went to Italy. Hungary received the Bačka; Bulgaria part of Macedonia, while Germany herself took part of northern Slovenia. Axis forces remained in occupation of the whole country.

Thus, once again, the South Slavs had fallen under foreign domination. But once again their love of independence was finding expression in widespread guerrilla resistance to the invader. Inevitably the issue was clouded and confused by racial rivalry and internecine feuds and factions. This time, moreover, there was a new complication, the ideological factor.

Judging by their history, the Jugoslavs might be expected to take to Fascism and Communism with the same violent enthusiasm that in the past they had devoted to religious controversy. Indeed they might even seek to improve on the originals.

We were going to Bosnia. And had not the Bosnians almost immediately after their conversion to Christianity, embraced Bogomilism, a particularly lively heresy which had caused endless irritation to the Pope? Had not these same Bosnians, having later been converted to Mohammedanism by the Turks, denounced the Sultan as false to Islam and embarked on a holy war, a jehad, to reconquer the Ottoman Empire for the true faith? There was no telling what might not happen to ideas in the Balkans.

But I found two things in all this to encourage me. First, the war-like qualities of the Jugoslav peoples and the tradition of resistance to the foreign invader, running like a golden thread, all through their national history; and, secondly, their love of independence, which again and again in their history had served to extricate them from every sort of entanglement. Mine was primarily a military mission, and for me military virtue must therefore be the first consideration. This we seemed certain to find. What else we should find remained to be seen. But we could be sure of one thing; we should not be bored.

Before I left, the Prime Minister gave me a copy of a directive he had issued concerning my appointment. 'What we want,' he had written, 'is a daring Ambassador-leader to these hardy and hunted guerrillas.' It would not, I felt, be an easy role to fill. But I could have a try.

On reaching Cairo, I immediately found my hands full with half a dozen urgent tasks. General Wilson, now Commander-in-Chief Middle East, who was very much alive to the importance of Jugoslavia as a subsidiary theatre of war, and who had also taken a friendly interest in my activities since our first meeting in Baghdad, did everything he could to help with the preparations for our departure.

My first care was to pick up a strong side. Being only a very amateur soldier myself, I realized that it was essential for me to have a really first-class regular soldier as my second in command. The name that immediately occurred to me was Vivian Street. Vivian had given up a Grade I staff appointment at G.H.Q. to come to the S.A.S. as a Major and had had the bad luck to be taken prisoner on his first operation. Then the submarine in which the Italians were taking him to Italy was depth-charged and he was picked up by one of our own destroyers, in time to take an active part in the remainder of the North African campaign. At the age of 29 he had the well-deserved reputation of being one of the best regimental officers and also one of the best of the younger staff officers in the Middle East. He also had three qualities, which were no less important for my purposes, namely great personal courage and determination, a flexible and original mind and the gift of getting on well with all kinds of people.

But I was not the only person who was aware of Vivian's value. When I told General Wilson that I had chosen him as my second in command, he said that he would rather have let me have anyone else, as he had earmarked him to command a battalion of his own regiment, the Rifle Brigade. However, he eventually agreed to let him go, feeling, I suspect, that Jugoslavia would be all the better for a judicious sprinkling of 'Black Buttons'.

Following up this train of thought, Vivian and I next proceeded to select another Rifleman, John Henniker-Major, who had passed into the Diplomatic Service a year or two before the war, but, like myself, had managed to get out of it again and join the Army. He had been shot through the chest while serving with the Rifle Brigade in the desert, but had now fully recovered and was ready for anything. We felt that this combination of military and diplomatic training should be very useful for our kind of job.

In all irregular warfare success depends to a great extent on the skilful use of high explosive, and one of our most important requirements was therefore a really good Sapper as C.R.E. One walked straight into our arms in the shape of Peter Moore, another regular soldier, who, after distinguishing himself during a long spell in the desert where he had won a good D.S.O. and M.C., had been sent to the Staff College and was now spending a few days' leave in Cairo, looking out for something more active to do. His quest was brought to an end over a drink in the bar of Shepheard's Hotel, and he was soon scouring the R.E. dumps and depots round Cairo in search of the latest infernal machines for us to take in with us. With him Peter brought Donald Knight, a promising young Sapper subaltern, who had served with him in the desert.

One of our most important tasks seemed likely to be equipping and supplying the Partisans by air. This meant that the post of D.A.Q.M.G., for which we had made room in our Establishment, would need to be particularly well filled. A careful search produced another Sapper, Mike Parker, in civilian life an electrical engineer, who had divided his time in the desert between taking up the latest and trickiest types of German mines and serving as D.A.Q.M.G., Seventh Armoured Division. This sounded the right type of man for the job. We also felt that anyone who had been good enough for Seventh Armoured Division and General John Harding would be good enough for us. We were quite right.

Then there was the question of Intelligence. As soon as it became known amongst the Intelligence experts of G.H.Q. and the War Office that we were going to Jugoslavia, we were swamped with requests that we should keep various branches supplied with information about enemy order of battle. As we should be living right in amongst the enemy, they said, they reckoned that we should know everything there was to be known about them. To this, we replied, rather doubtfully that we supposed we should, and set about looking for an order of battle expert. This conjured up visions of spectacled intellectuals, admirably suited, no doubt, to poring over captured documents in G.H.Q., but a good deal less well equipped for the life of Balkan brigands which we were looking forward to. It was then that I thought of David Stirling's Intelligence Officer, Gordon Alston, who has already appeared in these pages as a fairly regular visitor to Benghazi during its occupation by the enemy.

By the time he reached the age of twenty-five Gordon had managed to have a remarkably full life. Having got off to a flying start when he left Eton at seventeen to become a racing motorist in Italy, he had later tried his hand at journalism in France and brewing beer in Germany. Since early in the war he had served in Commandos or Commando-type units. This varied experience had left him with a taste for adventure, a knowledge of foreign languages, and, most conveniently for us, an altogether remarkable flair for military intelligence. In particular, he possessed the gift of being able to piece together a coherent picture of the enemy's order of battle from half a dozen captured pay books, two or three hat badges, some buttons and a newspaper cutting. We signed him on without further ado, and sent him off on a tour of G.H.Q. collecting maps and other useful information.

Another of my original companions was Robin Whetherly, who had a first-class record as a fighting soldier in the K.D.G.s in the desert and whom, as our only cavalry officer, we promised to put in charge of the first horses, or alternatively armoured vehicles, that we captured.

These, with Duncan (promoted from Corporal to Sergeant for the occasion), Corporal Dickson of the Scots Guards, Corporal Kelly of the Seaforth Highlanders and two specially trained wireless operators, made up our party. At thirty-two, I was, I think, the oldest of them all.

We left behind David Satow, an extremely efficient young staff officer, and Sergeant Charlie Button to follow on later. Satow was to act as our rear link with G.H.Q., while Button collected chocolate, bacon, marmalade and other delicacies, which we fondly hoped might eventually be dropped in after us.

A few days before we left, we were greeted one morning with the news that we were not a British Military Mission, after all, but had been converted overnight into an Allied one by the addition of an American officer, Major Linn Farish. I was glad of this, as, ever since I had shared a stable with my American colleagues in Moscow, I had had invariably agreeable experience of Anglo-American co-operation, and I also felt that, working as we were in a theatre of war commanded by a Supreme Allied Commander with an integrated Anglo-American staff, there was every advantage in securing American co-operation in the present venture.

We were even more pleased when we met Farish, a large rugged man like a bear, with an amiable grin. He was wearing, we noticed to our surprise, the uniform of a Major in the Royal Engineers. We asked him how this had happened. 'Why,' he said, as if it had been the most natural thing in the world, 'Why, when the war started over in Europe, I felt I just had to get into it, so I joined the British Army; and I've never got around to quitting it since the States got into the war.' 'Now I'm coming on this job,' he added, 'I guess I'll need to join the United States Army,' and the next day appeared resplendent in the uniform of a Major in the United States Engineer Corps, but with British parachute wings still on his shoulder. 'Call me Slim,' he said, and we did, although the name was singularly inappropriate for one so robust.

We asked him what he could do. He said that he could build aerodromes, an answer that was greeted with loud acclamations. It was, we told him, the one thing that we needed most. The sooner he put an end to the present uncomfortable mode of entry into Jugoslavia the better, especially as it was confined to one-way traffic. He promised to see what he could do, and we told him to be sure that there was a comfortable waiting-room with a well-equipped bar.

From then on Slim Farish was one of us, and Anglo-American co-operation was of the closest. It continued so when, a year later, after

Slim himself had been killed, the Americans decided to send in a full-scale American Mission, and we reverted to our original status.

Our last days in Cairo were spent in feverishly collecting information, weapons, equipment, sleeping-bags, explosives, special portable wireless transmitting and receiving sets, batteries and charging engines; in marking maps and in making signal plans. Absolute secrecy was a most important consideration, as Cairo was known to be full of enemy agents and we had no wish to find the Germans waiting for us when we landed. Very few people, even at G.H.Q., knew our destination, and, for the most part we had to keep up an elaborate pretence of having nothing particular in view. I remembered the reception we had had from a forewarned and forearmed enemy on the occasion of our last visit to Benghazi, and hoped devoutly that this time our security was better.

At last we were ready. There had been a lull in the fighting in Jugoslavia, and a signal arrived to say that the situation was now sufficiently stable for the Partisans to be able to give a definite map reference to which we could be dropped without undue likelihood of finding the Germans there. The place suggested was a secluded valley in the mountains of Bosnia. We were glad to leave the sweltering heat of Cairo for the airfield in Tunisia from which we were to make our entry into Europe.

We went down to the airfield a little before midnight. Our aircraft was still being loaded and a beam of light shone out across the field from its open door. It was a Halifax bomber, and, as we came nearer, we could see the huge dark outline of its wings, four engines and elongated body looming above us against the starlit sky. An R.A.F. Sergeant with an agreeably reassuring manner fitted our parachutes, jerking and easing the webbing straps into position over our shoulders and between our legs. The Station Commander, who had come down to see us off, shook hands with us, his last words lost in the roar of the engines. We climbed in. The doors were shut. We could feel the wheels jolting over the uneven runway. The roaring of the engines grew louder and steadier. We felt the ground slip away from under us. We were airborne.

Inside the aircraft it was cold and dark and stuffy and there was hardly room to move. A gleam of light came from the crew's cabin, forward. Every spare inch of space was filled with the long cylindrical containers which were to be dropped with us. As best we could, we disposed ourselves to sleep.

I was wakened by a hand on my shoulder. It was the 'dispatcher', a Flight-Sergeant with a flowing moustache. For a moment I could not think where I was. Then I remembered. I looked at my watch. It was half-past three. 'Getting near now,' the dispatcher shouted in my ear above the roar. 'Ran into some flak as we were crossing the coast.' Then he crawled on past us, picking his way through the containers, and we saw him stoop down and pull open the two halves of the trap-door which covered the circular hole in the floor through which we were to make our exit. The aircraft was losing height rapidly. We readjusted our parachute harness. But it was not our turn yet. The containers had to go first. As they were rolled out, their static lines slapped against the sides of the hole with a noise like gunfire. It was nearly four by the time the last one had gone out. As it disappeared, the dispatcher beckoned to us and Vivian and I scrambled along to him, and made fast the static lines to the special hooks on the inside of the fuselage. I was to go first and Vivian was to follow. Slim Farish and Duncan were to go after that.

I sat on the edge of the hole waiting, with my legs dangling in space. A glance downwards showed some points of light twinkling a long way below — fire signals. Looking up again, I saw that the warning red light was showing. The dispatcher's hand was raised. Slowly, deliberately, he started to lower it. Then, suddenly, the light turned to green and I jumped out and down, into the breath-taking tumult of the slipstream.

PART THREE

BALKAN WAR

We shall go
Always a little further: it may be
Beyond that last blue mountain barred with snow,
Across that angry or that glimmering sea.

FLECKER

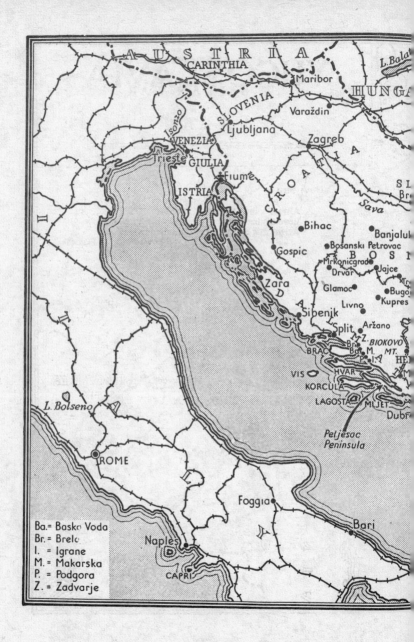

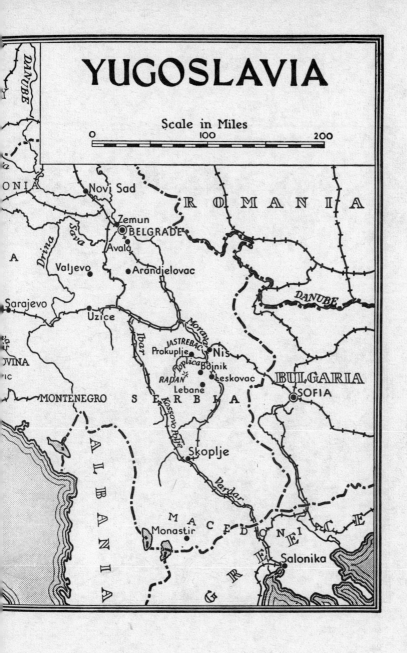

YUGOSLAVIA

Scale in Miles

0   100   200

CHAPTER I

INSIDE EUROPE

WITH a jerk my parachute opened and I found myself dangling, as it were at the end of a string, high above a silent mountain valley, greenish-grey and misty in the light of the moon. It looked, I thought, invitingly cool and refreshing after the sand and glare of North Africa. Somewhere above me the aircraft, having completed its mission, was headed for home. The noise of its engines grew gradually fainter in the distance. A long way below me and some distance away I could see a number of fires burning. I hoped they were the right ones, for the Germans also lit fires at night at different points in the Balkans in the hope of diverting supplies and parachutists from their proper destinations. As I swung lower, I could hear a faint noise of shouting coming from the direction of the fires. I could still not see the ground immediately beneath me. We must, I reflected, have been dropped from a considerable height to take so long in coming down. Then, without further warning, there was a jolt and I was lying in a field of wet grass. There was no one in sight. I released myself from the harness, rolled my parachute into a bundle, and set out to look for the Partisans.

In the first field I crossed there was still no one. Then, scrambling through a hedge, I came face to face with a young man in German uniform carrying a sub-machine gun. I hoped the German uniform was second-hand. '*Zdravo!*' I said hopefully, '*Ja sam engleski oficir!*' At this the young man dropped the sub-machine gun and embraced me, shouting over his shoulder as he did so: '*Našao sam generala!*' – 'I have found the general.' Other Partisans came running up to look at me. They were mostly very young, with high Slav cheek-bones and red stars stitched to their caps and wearing a strange assortment of civilian clothes and captured enemy uniform and equipment. The red star, sometimes embellished with a hammer and sickle, was the only thing common to all of them. Together we walked over towards the fires, which I could now see flickering through the trees. The Partisans chattered excitedly as we went.

It was cold and I was glad to get near to the blaze. I found Vivian Street, Slim Farish and Sergeant Duncan there already, none the worse for their jump. Together we piled on more sticks and straw, for there was as yet no sign of the second aircraft in which the rest of the party had started from Bizerta a few minutes after us, and it was important to keep the fires up to guide them in.

Someone gave me an apple. As I was eating it a tall dark young Partisan, whose badges, well-cut uniform and equipment proclaimed him a person of some importance, came up and introduced himself as Major Velebit of Tito's personal staff. He had, he said, been sent to welcome me and to escort me to Tito's Headquarters. Having thus greeted me, Velebit lost no time in getting down to business. The Partisans, he said, were glad I had come. They hoped my arrival meant that they would get some supplies. Did the Allies realize that for two years they had been fighting desperately against overwhelming odds with no arms or equipment save what they had been able to capture from the enemy?

It was some time before I could get a word in. Then I told him that it was precisely because the British Government wanted to know more about the situation in Jugoslavia that I had been sent there. Their policy was a simple one. It was to give all possible help to those who were fighting the enemy. This seemed to reassure him, and soon we dropped into the tones of ordinary conversation.

Presently, as we talked, sitting round the fire, it began to get light. It was no longer any use waiting for the other aircraft. It would not come now. We could only hope that the others had not been dropped in the wrong place and were not now in German hands.

The Partisans had collected the supplies which had been dropped from our aircraft and, having loaded them on to peasant carts, were carrying them off to a place of safety. There were German troops in the nearby hills and German aircraft, too, in the neighbourhood, so that the open valley was no place to stay in by daylight. The fires were extinguished; horses were brought, and we set out, accompanied by several dozen Partisans, as escort.

Our way took us along the banks of a rushing mountain stream between high green hills. The sun was shining. From time to time we met peasants who greeted us cheerfully. Vlatko Velebit proved an agreeable companion. Before the war he had been a lawyer and a young man about town. By descent a Serb, he came of a distinguished military family. His father had been a general. He had read and travelled widely. In the early days of the resistance, before coming out to join them in the mountains, he had worked underground for the Partisans in Zagreb and other German-occupied towns — a singularly perilous occupation. In addition to his other qualities he possessed a quick brain and a well-developed sense of humour, both valuable assets in time of war. I was to see a lot of him during the next eighteen months.

After an hour or two's ride we came to a tiny sunlit village, set high in the Bosnian hills. Its wooden houses clustered round a tree-shaded square. Above them rose the minaret of a mosque. Its name was Mrkonićgrad, or, as Sergeant Duncan called it, Maconachie-grad. In it were the Headquarters of the local Partisan commander, Slavko Rodic, with whom we were to breakfast.

Rodic, a dashing young man of about twenty-five, came out to meet us, riding an officer's charger captured from the Germans. With him were his Chief of Staff and his Political Commissar, a big jovial Serb with a long flowing moustache. Together we repaired to a peasant's house where breakfast was ready. At the door a robust sentry armed with a sub-machine gun saluted with his clenched fist. A pretty girl with a pistol and a cluster of murderous-looking hand-grenades at her belt, poured some water over my hands from a jug and dried them with a towel. Then we sat down to breakfast, some dry black bread washed down by round after round of pink vanilla brandy. We discussed all manner of topics, horses, parachuting and politics, but the conversation had, I found, a way of drifting back to the one subject which was uppermost in everyone's mind: when were the Allies going to send the Partisans some arms?

While we sat there, messengers kept bringing in situation reports from nearby areas where operations were in progress. As they delivered their messages, they too gave the clenched-fist salute.

Somehow it all seemed strangely familiar: the peasant's hut, the alert young Commander, the benign figure of the Political Commissar with his walrus moustache and the hammer and sickle badge on his cap, the girl with her pistol and hand-grenades, the general atmosphere of activity and expectation. At first I could not think where I had seen all this before. Then it came back to me. The whole scene might have been taken, as it stood, from one of the old Soviet films of the Civil War which I had seen in Paris seven or eight years earlier. In Russia I had only seen the Revolution twenty years after the event, when it was as rigid and pompous and firmly established as any regime in Europe. Now I was seeing the struggle in its initial stages, with the revolutionaries fighting for life and liberty against tremendous odds.

With enemy aircraft and troops patrolling the neighbourhood it was not, it appeared, advisable to continue our journey to the Headquarters until evening, and we for our part were glad of some rest. In a nearby orchard we lay down in the shadow of some plum trees. The sunlight, filtering through the leaves, made a shifting pattern on the grass. The last thing that I remember before going to sleep is the noise of a German aeroplane droning high overhead in blessed ignorance of our presence.

When I woke, the sun was down and it was time to start. The Partisans had a surprise in store for us. Drawn up in the village square was a captured German truck, riddled with bullet holes, but apparently still working. Two or three Partisans were pouring petrol and water into it and another was cranking energetically. A crowd of small children were climbing all over it. An immense red flag waved from the bonnet, though whether to denote danger or to indicate the political views of the driver was not clear. It was a great occasion. Feeling unpleasantly conspicuous, we piled in and drove off.

The track took us along the shores of a lake, with hills running steeply down to it on all sides. We followed it for some miles. Then all at once the valley narrowed and we found ourselves looking up at the dark shape of a ruined castle rising high above the road. Round it clustered some houses, while the lights of others showed from the other side of a mountain stream. From somewhere nearby came the roar of a waterfall. Still at top speed our driver swerved across a shaky wooden bridge and jammed on his brakes. We had reached our destination: Jajce.

We had hardly stacked our kit in the house which had been allotted to us when Velebit, who had temporarily disappeared, came back to say that the Commander would be glad if I and my Chief of Staff would join him at supper. Clearly a Chief of Staff was a necessity; in fact, while I was about it, I might as well have two, one British and one American. Accordingly both Vivian and Slim Farish were raised to that position. Sergeant Duncan became my Personal Bodyguard, and we set out.

With Velebit leading the way, we re-crossed the river and climbed up to the ruined castle on the hill which we had noticed earlier. As we picked our way through the trees, a Partisan sentry, stepping from the shadows, challenged us, and then, on being given the password, guided us through the crumbling walls to an open space where a man was sitting under a tree studying a map by the light of a flickering lamp.

ARMS AND THE MAN

As we entered, Tito came forward to meet us. I looked at him carefully, for, here, it seemed to me, was one of the keys to our problem. 'In war,' Napoleon had said, 'it is not men, but the man who counts.'

He was of medium height, clean-shaven, with tanned regular features and iron-grey hair. He had a very firm mouth and alert blue eyes. He was wearing a dark semi-military tunic and breeches, without any badges; a neat spotted tie added the only touch of colour. We shook hands and sat down.

How, I wondered, would he compare with the Communists I had encountered in Russia? From the members of the Politburo to the N.K.V.D. spies who followed me about, all had had one thing in common, their terror of responsibility, their reluctance to think for themselves, their blind unquestioning obedience to a Party line dictated by higher authority, the terrible atmosphere of fear and suspicion which pervaded their lives. Was Tito going to be that sort of Communist?

A sentry with a Schmeisser sub-machine gun slung across his back brought a bottle of plum brandy and poured it out. We emptied our glasses. There was a pause.

The first thing, clearly, was to find a common language. This, I found, presented no difficulty. Tito spoke fluent German and Russian, and was also very ready to help me out in my first attempts at Serbo-Croat. After a couple of rounds of plum brandy we were deep in conversation.

One thing struck me immediately: Tito's readiness to discuss any question on its merits and, if necessary, to take a decision there and then. He seemed perfectly sure of himself; a principal, not a subordinate. To find such assurance, such independence, in a Communist was for me a new experience.

I began by telling him the purpose of my mission. The British Government, I said, had received reports of Partisan resistance and were anxious to help. But they were still without accurate information as to the extent and nature of the Partisan movement. I had now been sent in with a team of military experts to make a full report and advise the Commander-in-Chief how help could best be given.

Tito replied that he was glad to hear this. The Partisans had now been fighting alone and unaided for two years against overwhelming odds. For supplies they had depended on what they captured from the enemy. The Italian capitulation had helped them enormously. But outside help was what they needed most of all. It was true that, from time to time during the past few weeks, an occasional parachute load had been dropped at random, but the small quantity of supplies that had reached them in this way, though gratefully received, was of little practical use when distributed among over 100,000 Partisans.

I explained our difficulties; lack of aircraft; lack of bases nearer than North Africa; the needs of our own forces. Later we hoped to move our bases to Italy. That would be a help. Meanwhile, as a first step towards improving our organization, I suggested that I should have an officer with a wireless set dropped to each of the main Partisan Head-quarters throughout the country. These would be in touch with me and in touch with our supply base and could arrange for supplies to be dropped in accordance with a central scheme which he and I could draw up together.

Tito at once agreed to this suggestion. It would, he said, help him and enable us to see for ourselves how the Partisans were fighting in different parts of the country. Then he asked whether we had thought of sending in supplies by sea. Following on the Italian capitulation a week earlier the situation in the coastal areas, which had been occupied by the Italians, was extremely fluid. Indeed, the Partisans were at the moment actually holding the town and harbour of Split, though it was unlikely that they would do so for long. If some shiploads of arms could be run across the Adriatic from Italy and landed at specified points on the Dalmatian coast, it should be possible to transport them back into the interior by one means or another, before the Germans had had time finally to consolidate their position in the areas vacated by the Italians. In this way, the equivalent of several hundred aeroplane loads of supplies could be brought into the country in a few days.

This possibility seemed worth exploring and I said that I would ask G.H.Q. urgently for their views by signal. We also agreed that our Chiefs of Staff should start work next day on a joint scheme, providing for British or American liaison officers under my command to be attached to all the main Partisan formations and for a system of priorities as between different parts of the country and different types of supplies.

As the night wore on, our talk drifted away from the immediate military problems which we had been discussing, and Tito, whose initial shyness had long since worn off, told me something of his past. The gaps in his narrative I filled in later.

The son of a Croat peasant, he had fought in the First World War in the ranks of the Imperial Austro-Hungarian Army. He had been sent to the Russian front, where he was wounded and taken prisoner by the armies of the Tsar. Thus in 1917 at the time of the Bolshevik Revolution he had found himself in Russia. All prisoners of war were set free and he himself volunteered for the newly formed Red Army. He served in it throughout the Civil War. It was his first taste of the new ideas. He returned to his own country a convinced Communist.

The life which now began for Tito, or Josip Broz, to give him his true name, was that of a professional revolutionary, of a loyal servant of the Communist International. Of that he made no secret. In the new kingdom of Jugoslavia, of which he was now a citizen, the Communist Party was declared illegal almost as soon as it was formed, and severely repressive measures taken against its members. And so he spent the next twenty years in and out of prison; in hiding; in exile. Proudly, he showed me a photograph of himself which the Partisans had found in an old police register and which he kept as a memento of this period of his existence.

Then in 1937 a new phase opened in his career. The Communist International were purging the foreign Communist Parties. In Jugoslavia they found that the Party had become badly disorganized and had fallen into grave heresies. A key point in south-eastern Europe was endangered. A reliable, determined man was needed to put matters right. Gorkić, the Secretary-General of the Jugoslav

Communist Party, was liquidated and Josip Broz appointed in his place.

He was a good organizer. In his underground army he made new appointments, allotted new tasks and established a new discipline. He would send for people and tell them what to do. 'You,' he said to them, 'will do this; and you, that,' in Serbo-Croat, 'Ti, to; ti, to.' He did this so often that his friends began to call him Tito. The name stuck. It grew to be more than a nickname. It became a call to action, a rallying point.

The German invasion of Jugoslavia in 1941 was bound to cause some uneasiness in Moscow, despite the Soviet-German Pact. The pundits of the Kremlin still refused to believe in the stories of an impending German attack on the Soviet Union, but they could nevertheless scarcely regard with pleasure the extension of Hitler's rule to the Slav countries of the Balkans, historically a Russian preserve. Elsewhere Communists all over the world continued to denounce the struggle of Great Britain and her allies against Nazi Germany as the 'Second Imperialist War'. In occupied Jugoslavia the Communist Party, still underground, appear to have received different instructions from those sent to their comrades in other countries, instructions which were not altogether in accordance with the spirit of the Soviet-German Pact. Even before June 1941, when the German invasion of the Soviet Union turned the 'Second Imperialist War' into the 'Heroic Struggle of Democracy against Fascism', Tito and the Jugoslav Communists had begun to prepare for resistance to the invader. By the summer of 1941 the first Partisan detachments were operating in Serbia and elsewhere under Tito's command. At first they consisted of small groups of determined men and women, who had taken to the hills and forests, armed with cudgels and axes, old sporting guns, and anything else they could lay hands on. For all further supplies they depended on what they could capture from the enemy and what the country people would give them.

When the Partisans first entered the field in the summer of 1941, they found another resistance movement in existence: the Četniks, formed round a nucleus of officers and men of the Royal Jugoslav Army, under the leadership of Colonel Draža Mihajlović. They were in the early days more numerous and better equipped than the Partisans. At no time, however, was their discipline so ruthless or their organization so good.

At first, Jugoslavia had been dazed by the suddenness of the German attack. Now, when the first shock had passed, there returned to the people of Jugoslavia the fierce spirit of resistance for which they have been famous throughout history. The rising which took place in Serbia in the summer of 1941 was essentially a national rising. In it Partisan and Četnik bands fought side by side. It was astonishingly successful. The Germans were taken by surprise. Large areas of country were liberated, the peasants flocking to join the resistance. A unified command and a united effort against the invader seemed possible, indeed probable.

It was in these circumstances that a meeting took place between Tito and Mihajlović in the neighbourhood of Užice. At it some kind of provisional *modus operandi* seems to have been arrived at, although it was not possible to reach full agreement for a unified command. In the operations that followed, however, each side accused the other of treachery, the Partisans, in particular claiming that the Četniks had betrayed their positions to the Germans and had joined in the German attack on them. A further meeting between the two leaders led to no better results. Thereafter clash after clash ensued between them.

Meanwhile, the Germans had had time to collect themselves. The necessary forces were assembled, the liberated areas re-occupied, the guerrillas driven off with heavy losses, and savage reprisals undertaken against the civil population. While surviving Partisans and Četniks licked their wounds in the woods and mountains, the towns and villages of the plain were burned and devastated and thousands of hostages, men, women and children, taken out and shot.

To this and to subsequent disasters Partisans and Četniks reacted differently. In this difference of attitude lies the explanation of much that followed later.

In the eyes of the Četniks the results achieved by their operations could not justify the damage and suffering caused to the civilian population. Their aim was to preserve rather than to destroy. Henceforward they inclined more and more to avoid active operations; soon some even arrived at mutually advantageous accommodations with the enemy.

The Partisans, on the other hand, with true Communist ruthlessness, refused to let themselves be deterred by any setbacks or any reprisals from accomplishing the tasks which they had set themselves. Their own lives were of no account. As for the civilians, they too were in the firing-line, with the same chance of a hero's death as they themselves. The more civilians the Germans shot, the more villages they burned, the more enemy convoys the Partisans ambushed, the more bridges they destroyed. It was a hard policy, especially for men operating in their own part of the country, but in the end it was justified by events and justified notably by the unwilling respect which it imposed on the Germans, a respect which no amount of appeasement could ever have inspired.

As we sat talking under the stars, I asked Tito whether now, two years after his original negotiations with Mihajlović, there was any hope of reaching agreement with the Četniks and thus forming a united front against the enemy. He replied immediately that there might be some hope if the Četniks would stop fighting the Partisans and start fighting the Germans and if those of them who had come to terms with the enemy could either be brought to heel or finally disowned. He did not, however, regard such a change of heart as any longer within the bounds of possibility. Two years ago, when he met Mihajlović, he had even been prepared to place himself under the latter's command, but Mihajlović had sought to impose conditions which he could not accept.

He recalled the scene in the peasant's cottage near Užice: both parties very much on their guard; he himself, for so many years wanted by the Royal Police, feeling it strange that he should be dealing on equal terms with the Royal Minister of Defence; Mihajlović, very much the professional staff officer, not knowing what to make of this Communist agitator turned soldier, and half believing him to be a Russian; both feeling that the other perhaps had something to offer that was worth having.

In those days, he said, the Četniks had the advantage. Now the Partisans were the stronger and it would be for them to impose their terms.

But in any case he thought the Četniks had become too undisciplined and demoralized from long inaction and had gone too far in their collaboration with the enemy for any real change of heart. Much, too, had happened in the last two years that could not be lightly forgotten.

I asked him whether any Četniks had come over to the Partisans of their own accord. 'Many,' he said. 'Father Vlado will tell you about them.' And he beckoned to a man with a striking red beard and an unrivalled collection of pistols, bandoliers and hand-grenades strung round him, who seemed to be the life and soul of a little group of officers at the other end of the table. When he had joined us I saw that, in addition to the usual red star, this walking armoury was wearing a gold cross as a cap badge. He was a Serbian Orthodox priest who at the time of the German occupation had collected all the able-bodied parishioners he could find and taken to the woods. He had first joined Mihajlović and had been given command of a Četnik formation. At an early stage, however, he left the Četniks for the Partisans. This, he explained, he had done because he did not get enough fighting with Mihajlović. With the Partisans, on the other hand, he got all the fighting he wanted, while at the same time he ministered to the spiritual needs of the Serbs among Tito's forces. Many other Četniks, he said, had done the same thing as he had for the same reasons.

Father Vlado soon showed that his prowess was not solely confined to the pulpit and the battlefield, for he more than held his own both as a raconteur and a trencherman. Altogether he was a remarkable figure.

After Mihajlović we talked of King Peter. Tito said that the question of whether or not the dynasty should be restored could not finally be settled until after the Germans had been driven out. The King had done himself good by his conduct at the time of the *coup d'état*. But his people's enthusiasm for him waned when they reflected that he was living in comfort in London while they were fighting for their lives in the mountains and forests. Moreover some of his pronouncements, broadcast over the wireless, had caused bitter resentment. For example, some months earlier he had awarded the Karadjordje Star for 'gallantry in the face of the enemy' to one of Mihajlović's Commanders who at the time was actually living at Italian Headquarters, while his award of the Karadjordje Star to another Četnik leader had coincided with the award of the Iron Cross to the same man by Hitler. Recently, too, they had been listening to the Serbo-Croat broadcasts from London, when it was announced that the King had outlawed Tito's own Chief of Staff as a traitor.[1] The announcement had reached them after an extremely bloody battle with the Germans, and Tito said that the Chief of Staff, a tall, gloomy-looking man sitting at the other end of the table, had taken it very much to heart.

To this I retorted that I thought they were being rather hard on the King, who was no doubt misinformed on certain aspects of the situation, and, who, I felt sure, as a young man of spirit, asked for nothing better than to be allowed to fight if given the chance. If it came to that, would he be allowed to join the Partisans, if a way could be found of getting him there?

Turning the idea over in his mind, Tito was clearly rather tickled at the thought that he a Communist outlaw should have a King under his command. It might, he said, add to the prestige of the Movement in Serbia, though not in Croatia, where the dynasty was unpopular. It would lead to all kinds of complications, but he did not entirely exclude the possibility. Only, if he were to come, the King must come as a soldier and not as a reigning sovereign; for, once again, the question of the future form of government of the country was one which could only be settled once the war was over.

We talked of politics in general. I said that I was a Conservative; he, that he was a Communist. We discussed the theory and practice of modern Communism. His theme in its broad lines was that the end justified the means. He developed it with great frankness. I asked him whether it was his ultimate aim to establish a Communist State in Jugoslavia. He said that it was, but that it might have to be a gradual process. For the moment, for instance, the Movement was based politically on a 'popular front' and not on a strictly one-party system. At the same time, the occupation and the war were rapidly undermining the foundations of the old political and economic institutions, so that, when the dust cleared away very little would be left, and the

[1] Arso Jovanović – shot in 1948 by Tito's frontier guards on similar grounds.

way would be clear for a new system. In a sense the revolution **was** already in progress.

'And will your new Jugoslavia be an independent State or part of the Soviet Union?' I asked. He did not answer immediately. Then: 'You must remember,' he said, 'the sacrifices which we are making in this struggle for our independence. Hundreds of thousands of Jugloslavs have suffered torture and death, men, women and children. Vast areas of our countryside have been laid waste. You need not suppose that we shall lightly cast aside a prize which has been won at such cost.'

It might mean something. On the other hand, I reflected, it might not.

These were interesting thoughts to go to bed on. As we made our way down the hill and across the river, I tried to sum up my impressions of the man with whom I had been talking, and reached the conclusion that it should not be impossible to get on with him. Militarily, it was too early to form any opinion of the Partisans or of Tito as a leader. First I must see all I could for myself. But he clearly possessed energy, determination and intelligence. Also, he seemed to my relief to have a sense of humour. Though strangely shy socially (a rather engaging weakness) he was perfectly sure of himself when it came to fundamentals. He relied, too, on his own judgment and was ready to give his views on any subject that happened to crop up.

In short, here at last was a Communist who did not need to refer everything to the 'competent authorities', to look up the Party line at every step. He himself was the competent authority and, as for the Party line, he knew it instinctively, or perhaps even evolved it as he went along. At the same time, there was no pretence at liberalism or 'social democracy' or any question of his being anything but a Communist. In this respect, at any rate, I knew exactly where I stood.

Might he, as time went on, evolve — become more of a nationalist, less of a Communist? Might his allegiance to Moscow weaken? Would he ever be able to throw off a mental habit, painfully and rigorously built up over twenty years? It seemed unlikely.

And yet there was that unexpected independence of mind, that odd lack of servility. . . .

CHAPTER III

ORIENTATION

Late next night the remainder of my party arrived looking a good deal the worse for wear. We were relieved to see them, for, as time passed and there was still no sign of them, we had grown more and more certain that they had been dropped to the enemy.

Their journey had gone a great deal less smoothly than ours. They had left Bizerta, as had been arranged, a few minutes after us, but their pilot had lost his way and, finding himself shortly before dawn over what appeared to be Bulgaria, had wisely decided to go home without dropping his passengers. And so the latter had arrived back at Bizerta in time for breakfast, having spent a frustrating and rather worrying night over Hitler's Europe, alternatively putting their parachutes on and taking them off again.

The following night, feeling sleepy and faintly irritable, they had set out again. This time the pilot found his way and they were successfully dropped in the right place. They were given a warm welcome by the Partisans and, after finishing off the remains of the pink vanilla brandy, had set off from Mrkonićgrad in the captured truck, still gaily flying the red flag. They had not expected such luxury. Things, they felt (quite mistakenly), were beginning to look up.

Then, when they had gone some distance, a German reconnaissance aeroplane, which had no doubt got wind of the previous night's doings, had appeared, hovering inquiringly over the tree-tops. After one look at the red flag, it settled down to machine gun them with characteristic thoroughness, the observer from time to time light-heartedly tossing a hand-grenade over the side. Having emptied their automatics at their tormentor without apparent effect, the occupants of the truck had wisely left it for the extremely damp ditch by the side of the road. There they remained until the aeroplane, having exhausted its ammunition, left for home.

When at length they emerged from their hiding-place, moist but fortunately unscathed, it was to find that the engine of the truck, never very sound mechanically, was now completely unserviceable, having received a number of machine-gun bullets in the radiator. Its wheels, on the other hand, were still on, and the driver was reluctant to abandon it. Besides, it was loaded to the brim with the various supplies which had been dropped in with them, including our rum ration, and these, apart from a few bullet holes, were still intact. Accordingly, they decided that the right course was to tow it with its contents to a place of safety, and set out in search of a means of propulsion.

After scouring the countryside for several hours, they returned, towards dusk, with a team of oxen borrowed from a neighbouring peasant. By the time the oxen had been made fast to the truck, it was quite dark and raining steadily. With the truck's headlights illuminating the rumps of the oxen, they set off for Jajce. Their troubles, they reflected, were over at last.

Once again they were mistaken. They had not gone very far when a fusillade broke out from the bushes at the side of the road. With a merry cry of 'Četniks!' their escort returned the fire and a confused skirmish ensued in the course of which the headlights were put out and the oxen stampeded. The remainder of their journey, undertaken in pitch darkness and drenching rain, they preferred not to discuss. Now that they had reached their destination, a double rum all round comforted them and they went to sleep on the floor where they lay.

Now that we were all there, we could get down to work. Next morning we started on full-dress 'staff conversations' with the Partisans, with the object of obtaining from them, as a first step, their picture of the military situation in Jugoslavia, which we could then check against information available from the other sources at our disposal.

Vivian Street, as my 'Chief of Staff', spent his days poring over large-scale maps with the Partisan Chief of Staff, Arso Jovanović. Peter Moore discussed demolitions and explosives with Tito's Chief Engineer, who, strangely enough turned out to be a White Russian émigré. Parker's opposite number was known as the Intendant and together they worked out an elaborate draft scheme of requirements and priorities on the best staff college lines. Gordon Alston, his confidential manner more accentuated than ever, repaired daily to a house at some distance from the others to confabulate with the chief of the Partisan Intelligence, piecing together from agent's reports and captured German pay books and badges a patchwork of information about the enemy's order of battle, which we then signalled diligently to Cairo and London, to be compared with the information on the same subject collected from elsewhere.

Every two or three days, when we had had time to sift and digest the material we had collected, I would climb up to the fortress for a general survey of the situation with Tito, in the course of which we would talk over the latest developments, discuss the various courses open to the enemy and to the Partisans, and clear up any outstanding questions.

These preliminary discussions showed us one thing: that the Partisan Movement in Jugoslavia possessed an efficient central organization with which it was possible to make plans and exchange information, and which, in turn, was in more or less close touch, by courier, and in some cases by wireless, with Partisan forces throughout the country.

The information which the Partisans gave us about their strength in the country as a whole, about the number of German divisions they were containing, and, above all, about the quantities of supplies they required, we were inclined to take with a grain of salt, at any rate until we had had an opportunity of checking it for ourselves.

Meanwhile there was no doubt as to the shape which my mission must assume and the functions which it must seek to perform. As we had thought, my own Headquarters must remain with Partisan Head-quarters, while suitably trained officers, linked to us by wireless, must be attached to all of the principal Partisan formations. On the basis of the information thus obtained, it should be possible to form a fairly accurate idea, both of the extent and effectiveness of Partisan resistance and of the degree of material assistance which we should be justified in giving them. Once sufficiently good liaison had thus been established, it should further be possible for us to concert and co-ordinate Partisan operations with Allied operations in the Mediterranean theatre of war as a whole.

The first step was to establish direct contact with the three or four British officers who had been dropped to the Partisans earlier in the summer and were now with Partisan formations in different parts of Jugoslavia. Their views, which for one reason or another did not seem to have reached the outside world, would clearly be of the greatest value to us in attempting to assess the situation.

In our own area there was Bill Deakin. He had been away at the time of our arrival and was now on his way back. A history don from Oxford, he had been with Tito's Headquarters during the bitter fighting of the past two or three months, and I felt that he should be able to give us a better idea than anyone of what the Partisans were worth.

The others were harder to reach, being separated from us by much wild country and many enemy garrisons. In Croatia there was a regular soldier, Anthony Hunter, a Scots Fusilier, who had commanded a patrol of L.R.D.G. Further north, in Slovenia, was Major Jones, a picturesque figure, whose personal courage was only equalled by the violence of his enthusiasms. Having won the D.C.M. and bar as an N.C.O. with the Canadians in the First World War, and subsequently risen to command a company, he had, when well over fifty, somehow contrived to have himself dropped into Jugoslavia, where his powers of endurance and his spirited, though at times somewhat unorthodox behaviour astonished all who met him.

Meanwhile Peter Moore had concluded his technical talks with the Partisan demolition experts and was now anxious to see something of their practical work. His journey to the north, which, according to the Partisans, could be accomplished in about six weeks, would serve several purposes. He could visit first Hunter and then Jones, obtain their views and arrange for them in future to report direct to me by wireless or courier. He would also, in the course of a journey of two or three hundred miles on foot through German-occupied Jugoslavia, inevitably collect a good deal of valuable information on his own account. Finally he was instructed to discuss with the Partisan commanders in Slovenia the possibility of intensified operations against the Ljubljana-Trieste railway, a strategic line of first-rate importance

Italian front and which offered a number of tempting targets in the shape of bridges and aqueducts.

The Partisans provided a guide and late one evening Peter set out on his travels, his kit reduced to what he could carry on his back. To read on the journey, he carried one formidable-looking technical work on engineering. We all went out to watch him start. Someone shouted to him to put the charges in the right place. He replied over his shoulder that he certainly would. We were not to see him again for several months.

Soon after Moore had left, Deakin arrived. We had expected a forbidding academic figure, and were relieved to find that he looked like a very young and rather untidy undergraduate and managed to combine an outstanding intellect with a gift for getting on with everyone. When he had had something to eat and got rid of the lice, which were an almost unavoidable accompaniment to Partisan warfare, we settled down to cross-question him about his experiences. They had been remarkable.

He had arrived, straight from an office desk in Cairo, to find the German Fifth Offensive in full swing and the Partisans on the move. He had moved with them, on short rations, on foot and at a great rate. He had been moving ever since. In Montenegro the main body of the Partisans had been surrounded, forced on to the defensive, and very nearly wiped out by an overwhelmingly strong enemy force, including seven German and four Italian divisions, supported by armour, artillery and aircraft. He and Tito had been wounded by the same bomb. Only their superior mobility and knowledge of the country had enabled the Partisans to escape complete annihilation.

Deakin's conduct during these trying times had, I soon found, earned him the respect and admiration of the Partisans and built a solid foundation for our relations with them.

We asked Deakin what he thought of the fighting qualities of the Partisans. He was loud in their praises. He spoke of their almost unlimited powers of endurance. As to their military effectiveness, the unceasing efforts of the enemy to wipe them out were the best proof of that.

We went on to talk of the Četniks and of their alleged collaboration with the enemy, and found that, after his experiences in Montenegro and Bosnia, Deakin had few doubts on this score. There the Četniks had fought side by side with the Germans and Italians against the Partisans, while captured documents provided evidence of the contacts which existed between the commands. Still a historian at heart, Deakin had already gone into this question at some length and I accordingly now gave him the task of sifting the undigested mass of evidence at our disposal and producing a considered report on the subject.

Soon after Moore had left for the north, I dispatched Slim Farish with Knight, our other Royal Engineer, to Glamoć, a village lying in a mountain valley some forty miles to the south-west of Jajce. The problem of our communications with the outside world was all-important, and at Glamoć, nestling among the surrounding hills, we had found a flat bit of land on which, if a few trees were cut down and some hummocks flattened, it should be possible to land an aircraft.

Thus Farish, the expert airfield designer, found himself back at his peace-time occupation sooner than he had expected, helped in his work by the men, women and children of Glamoć, who, under his direction, toiled away with pick and shovel, making the way smooth for the Dakotas which we fondly imagined would land there when all was ready. Once we had a landing-strip, we told ourselves optimistically, we should be able to start a regular courier service with Cairo and most of our difficulties would disappear. Meanwhile, we signalled endless measurements and details to R.A.F. Headquarters in the hope of overcoming the scepticism and distrust which in those early days they still displayed towards amateur-run, improvised landing-strips. When not actually at work, Farish and his party carefully replaced the bushes that they had uprooted, so as to cover up their traces and thus avoid exciting the curiosity of passing enemy aircraft.

The frequency with which these visited our area, sometimes bombing and machine-gunning, sometimes merely hovering, left no doubt as to the interest which they took in us and our activities. For purposes of propaganda, however, the Germans continued to deny my existence and to maintain that the Partisans had no contact with the Allies. The story of our arrival, which had spread like wildfire through

Bosnia, they disposed of with some ingenuity by announcing in the local quisling newspaper that the whole thing was a hoax. The Communists, they said, had got hold of a Moslem sausage-seller and dressed him up as a British Brigadier. It was not until some months later that the enemy propaganda authorities decided to face up to the ugly fact of our existence in their midst. When they did, the result was almost equally fanciful.[1]

Sometimes at night, before going to sleep, we would turn on our receiving set and listen to Radio Belgrade. For months now, the flower of the Afrika Korps had been languishing behind the barbed wire of Allied prison camps. But still, punctually at ten o'clock, came Lili

---

[1] 'So this', wrote the *Donauzeitung* of February 4th, 1944, with heavy Teutonic irony, 'is Tito's Grey Eminence.'

'It was in May 1943. Somewhere in the Bosnian Mountains, in the neighbourhood of Tito's H.Q. there was great excitement. The liaison officer of His Majesty the King of England was expected. He was to land by parachute.

An Anglophile Swiss review describes the surprise of the bandits to see the landing of the following human being: 'A young man, in a grey overcoat, armed to the teeth, with a Kodak and a bush-knife, having as luggage a pipe and an Anglo-Croatian dictionary . . .' Apparently it took the bandits some time to get used to this 'extravagant Englishman', to this 'curious man with high military and social ranks', to this 'adventurer' and to respect him as Tito's 'Grey Eminence'.

Who is this romantic parachutist, who landed with a Kodak and a bush-knife among the savages of the Bosnian jungle? Some time ago, Anthony Eden lifted the veil of the mystery: Fitzroy Maclean, member of the House of Commons and deputy of the town of Lancaster, newly appointed brigadier, thirty-year-old chief of the British mission at Tito's H.Q. is depicted to us, as a robust red-haired adventurer of a Scottish officer family.

His career developed according to the schemes of the British plutocratic tradition: Eton and Cambridge, Embassy Attaché in Paris and Moscow, Eastern European Department of the Foreign Office, Lieutenant of the Highlanders. Bribed elections in his native town of Lancaster gave him the possibility of imposing a by-election, in which he was elected. When the war broke out this smart young man felt himself as a hero.

Apparently he cannot keep quiet, he is dreaming of adventures in foreign countries and of military glory, he remembers that he is an officer who renounced the exemption from military service to which he is entitled as a member of the House of Commons, and joins the Highlanders, fighting in North Africa against Rommel.

In short he is: an adventurer, who in the middle of the war remembers he is an officer. But, he does not stay a long time with his Highlanders. He joins the Parachute troops, and is awarded the rank of colonel, for a landing behind the lines of the Italians, who were already demoralized at that time. He named his parachute company 'Mystery column'. This energetic youth was chosen by England, when the need was felt by His Britannic Majesty to send a mission to Tito's bands. An adventurer, who dreams of glory and heroical deeds, in remote countries and who intends teaching Tito's bandits with a Kodak and a bush-knife the meaning of English culture. . . .'

Marlene singing their special song, with the same unvarying, heart-rending sweetness that we knew so well from the desert.

> Unter der Laterne,
> Vor dem grossen Tor . . .

Belgrade was still remote. But, now that we ourselves were in Jugoslavia, it had acquired a new significance for us. It had become our ultimate goal, which Lili Marlene and her nostalgic little tune seemed somehow to symbolize. 'When we get to Belgrade . . .' we would say. And then we would switch off the wireless a little guiltily, for the Partisans, we knew, were shocked at the strange pleasure we got from listening to the singing of the German woman who was queening it in their capital.

It grew colder: sharp, crackling autumn weather. The leaves fell and a bitter wind swept up the valley, ruffling the waters of the lake. Winter was not far off; a hard time for guerrillas. For the Partisans it would be the third spent in the woods, '*u šume*'. Already food was scarcer and the lack of proper boots and clothing was making itself felt.

Once again the Germans were attacking. Split had fallen, and, with the enemy in strength at Banjaluka and Travnik, just up the road, our position was none too secure. Daily their patrols pushed closer. Between us and the coast the Germans were forcing their way back into the areas which the Italians had evacuated.

War breaks down the barriers which divide us in peace time. Living as we did amongst the Partisans, we came to know them well, from Tito and the other leaders to the dozen or so rank and file who acted as our bodyguard and provided for our daily needs.

All had one thing in common: an intense pride in their Movement and in its achievements. For them the outside world did not seem of immediate interest or importance. What mattered was *their* War of National Liberation, *their* struggle against the invader, *their* victories, *their* sacrifices. Of this they were proudest of all, that they owed nothing to anyone; that they had got so far without outside help. In their eyes we acquired merit from the mere fact of our presence among them. We were living proof of the interest which the outside world was at last beginning to take in them. We were with them 'in the woods'. This, in itself, was a bond.

With this pride went a spirit of dedication, hard not to admire. The life of every one of them was ruled by rigid self-discipline, complete austerity; no drinking, no looting, no love-making. It was as though each one of them were bound by a vow, a vow part ideological and part military, for, in the conditions under which they were fighting, any relaxation of discipline would have been disastrous; nor could private desires and feelings be allowed to count for anything.

But, for all that, the Partisans were not dull people to live among. They would not have been Jugoslavs if they had been. Their innate turbulence, their natural independence, their deep-seated sense of the dramatic kept bubbling up in a number of unexpected ways.

Tito stood head and shoulders above the rest. When there were decisions to be taken, he took them; whether they were political or military, took them calmly and collectedly, after hearing the arguments on both sides. My own dealings were with him exclusively. From him I could be certain of getting a prompt and straightforward answer, one way or the other, on any subject, however important or however trivial it might be. Often enough we disagreed, but Tito was always ready to argue out any question on its merits, showing himself open to conviction, if a strong enough case could be made out. Often, where a deadlock had been reached owing to the stubbornness of his subordinates, he, on being approached, would intervene and reverse their decision.

One line of approach, I soon found, carried great weight with him: the suggestion, advanced at the psychological moment, that this or that line of conduct did or did not befit an honourable and civilized nation. By a discreet use of this argument I was able to dissuade him more than once from a course of action which would have had a calamitous effect on our relations. At the same time he reacted equally strongly to anything that, by the widest stretch of the imagination, might be regarded as a slight on the national dignity of Jugoslavia. This national pride, it struck me, was an unexpected characteristic in one whose first loyalty, as a Communist, must needs be to a foreign power, the Soviet Union.

There were many unexpected things about Tito: his surprisingly broad outlook; his never-failing sense of humour; his unashamed delight in the minor pleasures of life; a natural diffidence in human relationships, giving way to a natural friendliness; a violent temper, flaring up in sudden rages; a considerateness and a generosity constantly manifesting themselves in a dozen small ways; a surprising readiness to see two sides of a question. These were human qualities, hard to reconcile with the usual conception of a Communist puppet, and making possible better personal relations between us than I had dared hope for. And yet I did not for a moment forget that I was dealing with a man whose tenets would justify him in going to any lengths of deception or violence to attain his ends, and that these, outside our immediate military objectives, were in all probability, diametrically opposed to my own.

Of the men round Tito, we saw most during those early days of his gaunt Montenegrin Chief of Staff, Arso Jovanović, who as a regular officer of the old Jugoslav Army had studied at the Belgrade Staff College under General Mihajlović. A stiff, angular, unbending, unlovable man, he kept strictly to the business in hand, unimaginative, but coldly competent, supporting his arguments with facts and figures and frequent references to a captured German map. During Tito's outbursts of anger or merriment he would remain silent. Then, when he had finished, he would resume his accurate and conscientious appreciation of the situation.

But Arso was not one of Tito's real intimates. These, we soon found, were men with the same background as himself; professional revolutionaries, who had shared his exiles and imprisonments, helped him to organize workers' cells and promote strikes, run with him the gauntlet of police persecution. Gradually we got to know them.

Perhaps the most important of all was Edo Kardelj,[1] a small, stocky, pale-skinned, black-haired Slovene in the early thirties, with steel-rimmed spectacles and a neat little dark moustache, looking like a provincial schoolmaster, which, as it happened, was what he was. He, I found, was the theoretician of the Party, the expert Marxist dialectician.

There were a lot of questions about the theory and practice of

---

[1] Now Vice-Premier and Minister for Foreign Affairs.

Communism that I had always wanted an answer to. Now was my opportunity. Kardelj knew all the answers. He was a fascinating man to talk to. You could never catch him out or make him angry. He was perfectly frank, perfectly logical, perfectly calm and unruffled. Muddle; murder; distortion; deception. It was quite true. Such things happened under Communism, might even be an intentional part of Communist policy. But it would be worth it in the long run. The end would justify the means. Some day they would get their way; some day their difficulties would disappear; their enemies would be eliminated; the people educated; and a Communist millennium make the world a happier and a better place. Then the need for strong measures would disappear. He might not live to see this happen. But he was quite ready, as they all were, not only to die himself, but to sacrifice everybody and everything that was near and dear to him to the cause which he had chosen, to liquidate anybody who stood in his way. Such sacrifices, such liquidations, would be for the greater good of humanity. What worthier cause could there be? And he looked at me steadily and amiably through his spectacles.

Then there was Marko, a Serb whose real name was Aleksander Rankovic.[1] 'Marko', it seemed, was his conspiratorial code-name. And indeed, everything about him was conspiratorial. He had a way of keeping in the background, and it was not for some time that I realized what an important part he played in the Movement. Chiefly as an organizer. He it was who, under Tito's supervision, operated the Party machine; got rid of unreliable characters, promoted good men in their place; planted underground workers in the big towns; penetrated the quisling forces; penetrated the Gestapo. Still, like Kardelj, in his early thirties, he had been in prison before the war; had been with Tito from the start, taking an active part in the first uprising in Serbia in the summer of 1941. The son of a peasant, he had the stubborn, rather sly look which peasants often have. Not, you felt, a man who would come off worst in a bargain. And yet, somehow, a rather engaging character. 'Konspiracia!' he would say gleefully, winking and laying his finger at the side of his nose, 'Konspiracia!'

There was Džilas, too, Montenegrin, young, intolerant and good-

[1] Now Minister of the Interior.

looking, with a shock of hair like a golliwog; and Moše Pijade, an elderly intellectual from Belgrade, who, as almost the only Jew amongst the Partisans, became a favourite target for Nazi propaganda; both high up in the Party hierarchy. And the girls, Ždenka and Olga, who took turns at working for Tito, keeping his maps and lists and bundles of signals. Ždenka, a strange, pale, fanatical little creature. Olga, tall and well-built, in her black breeches and boots, with a pistol hanging at her belt, speaking perfect English, for before the war she had been sent to a smart finishing school in London by her father, a Minister in the Royal Jugoslav Government, in the hope of keeping her out of trouble. A hope which was doomed to disappointment, for no sooner was she back in her own country than, despite her background and upbringing, she joined the Communist Party, pledged to overthrow the Government of which her father was a member, and for her part in Communist disturbances was promptly thrown into prison by that same Government's police. Now, for two years, she had hidden in the woods and tramped the hills, had been bombed and machine-gunned, an outlaw, a rebel, a revolutionary, a Partisan. But when she spoke English, it was like talking to a young girl at home before the war; the same words and expressions, the same way of talking, the same youthful tastes and enthusiasms – all pleasantly refreshing in these grim surroundings. Somehow one never thought of her as being married, but she had a husband who was a Bosnian Moslem and a baby that she had left behind when she joined the Partisans. Now the baby – a little girl – was in Mostar, a German garrison town down towards the coast, at the mercy of the Gestapo and of frequent R.A.F. bombings. She wondered if she would ever see her again. Once a photograph was smuggled out by an agent who had been working underground in Mostar for the Partisans, a tiny, blurred snapshot, which, as Vlatko Velebit said, made the child look like a tadpole. But Olga was delighted. At least her baby had been alive a week ago.

Finally, to complete Tito's entourage, there were Boško and Prlja, his bodyguards, a formidable pair of toughs who never left his side, and his dog, Tigger, an enormous wolfhound, originally captured from the Germans and now his constant companion.

Two things struck me about this strange group over which Tito presided with a kind of amused benevolence; first their complete devotion to the Old Man, as they called him, and secondly the fact that all of them, young and old, men and women, intellectuals and artisans, Serbs and Croats, had been with him in the woods from the early days of the resistance, sharing with him hardships and dangers, setbacks and successes. This common experience had overcome all differences of class or race or temperament and forged between them lasting bonds of loyalty and affection.

The Partisans who formed our own escort were old stagers too, in battle-experience, that is, for some were boys in their teens. Not much to look at in tattered German and Italian tunics and heavily patched trousers tucked into leaky boots, they were alert and determined, and handled their weapons, gleaming and well cared for against the drab shabbiness of their clothes, like men who have borne arms all their lives.

Their leader had the rank of *ekonom*, or quartermaster sergeant, for his tasks included drawing our ration of black bread and stew from the cookhouse, supervising our baggage train of two or three weedy little Bosnian ponies and various other functions of an administrative rather than a combatant nature. To us he was known as the Economist. At first we did not altogether take to him. He looked, we thought, too clever by half with his sallow skin and crooked features. But, as time went on, and we had more opportunity of judging of his qualities, we conceived a certain affection for him, finding him willing, friendly, resourceful and dependable in an emergency. Later, he confided to me his greatest ambition: to become a 'real soldier'. As a first step to this end, he hoped to qualify for special training of some kind, after which, with luck, he might even become a warrant officer. But for the present he remained our guard commander and general factotum.

Gradually, from our own observation, and from the reports which I was now receiving from my officers in different parts of the country, we began to form some idea of the extent and nature of the Partisan Movement in Jugoslavia. Here, it seemed, was something far more important both militarily and politically than anyone outside Jugoslavia suspected.

At first, the tiny Communist-led guerrilla bands had, when opportunity offered, used the few weapons they possessed to attack isolated enemy outposts, to ambush convoys on lonely roads, killing the enemy soldiers and taking their arms and equipment. Then, better armed and better equipped at the expense of an unwary enemy, they had been able to undertake more ambitious operations; had come into possession of ever-larger quantities of weapons and supplies. Their numbers increased with their successes. As their victories became known, their ranks were joined by Jugoslavs from all over the country, men and women of all ages and from every walk of life. Of widely differing views and creeds, they were united by the belief that the Partisan Movement under Tito's leadership offered the best chance of striking a blow for the liberation of their country, and all were filled with unquenchable enthusiasm for the fierce struggle in which they were engaged and for the new and better Jugoslavia which they saw as their ultimate aim and reward. Thus the Movement grew in strength.

Strategically the situation was well-suited to irregular operations. Everything in Jugoslavia favoured the guerrilla: the enemy's long drawn-out lines of communication, his isolated garrisons and installations. The terrain, too, was well suited to the purpose. In the hills and woods the Partisans had a background for their operations which could be made to serve at will as a base, as a jumping-off point, as space in which to manœuvre, as a place in which to hide. It was an element as essential to their kind of warfare as the sea to naval warfare. By emerging unexpectedly from it they were able to achieve the surprise which is the essence of irregular operations. By fading back into it, once their immediate task was completed, they could deny the enemy any solid target at which to strike back. They enjoyed, too, the support of a civilian population deeply imbued with the tradition of resistance to the foreign invader, Teuton or Latin, Magyar or Turk.

But it was perhaps in the character of their leaders that resided the ultimate reason for the Partisans' success. These leaders were Communists. In guerrilla war, ideas matter more than material resources. Few ideas equal Communism in strength, in persistence, in insidiousness, in its power over the individual. Their Communist leaders furnished the Partisans with the singleness of purpose, the ruthless determination, the merciless discipline, without which they could not have survived, still less succeeded, in their object. They possessed themselves and inspired in those about them a spirit of absolute devotion which led them to count as nothing either their own lives or the lives of others; they neither gave nor expected quarter. They endowed the Movement with an oracle: the Party line. They brought it a ready-made intelligence system, a well-tried, widespread, old-established underground network. To what had started as a war they gave the character of a revolution. Finally — and this was perhaps their most notable achievement — they succeeded in inducing their followers to forget the old internecine feuds and hatreds and, by throwing together Serbs, Croats, Slovenes, Montenegrins and the rest in the fight against the common enemy, produced within their own ranks a new sense of national unity.

By 1943, the Partisans numbered, so far as it was possible to ascertain, about 150,000, perhaps more. This force, composed of formations of varying strength, was distributed over the whole of Jugoslavia, being based for the most part in the mountains and forests. Each Partisan formation had its own Headquarters, and these subordinate headquarters were directly or indirectly responsible to Tito's General Headquarters, which thus exercised effective operational control over the whole force. Communications were by wireless, use being made of captured enemy sets, or by couriers who travelled precariously from one part of the country to another across the intervening enemy lines.

The war waged by the Partisans was a strange one. There was no fixed front. Fighting for the most part with small arms only and limited stocks of ammunition, against a well-trained, well-armed, well-equipped, well-supplied and motorized enemy, supported by armour, artillery and aircraft, it was necessary for them to avoid pitched battles in which they would inevitably have come off worst. If they were to succeed, it was essential that they should retain the initiative themselves, and not allow it to pass into the hands of their opponents. Their aim must be to attack the enemy where he presented the richest target, where he was weakest, and, above all, where he least expected it. It was equally important that, having attained their purpose, they should not linger but should fade once again into the background of hills and woods, where pursuit could not reach them. This necessitated a high degree of mobility. Their human resources, like their material resources, were precious. Any engagement in which enemy losses did not outnumber their own losses by at least five to one the Partisans reckoned a defeat.

If guerrillas are to survive in conditions comparable to those in which the Partisans were fighting, they must at all costs deny the enemy a target at which he can strike back. As their numbers and the scale of their activities increased, this became harder. They had to resist the temptation to follow up and consolidate their successes. All gains had to be regarded as temporary. Villages and small towns captured by sudden attacks had to be abandoned again when the enemy counter-attacked in force. For the Partisans to allow themselves to be forced into the role of a beleaguered garrison would have been a fatal mistake, as individual Commanders were to learn on occasion by bitter experience. And so towns and villages changed hands time after time with their inhabitants, and each time became more battered and lost more inhabitants in the process.

For the support which they gave the Partisans the population suffered atrociously. In addition to famine and want, which swept the ravaged country, the Germans, the Italians, the Bulgars and the various local Quislings inflicted savage reprisals on the people of the country in revenge for the damage done by the Partisans. But neither the Partisans nor their civilian supporters allowed anything to deter them from resistance to the enemy. And, in fact, the enemy, by their barbarity, defeated their own object, for such were the hatred and bitterness that it engendered, that the violence and intensity of the national resistance were redoubled.

Long before the Allies, the Germans and Italians came to realize that the Partisans constituted a military factor of first-rate importance against which a modern army was in many respects powerless. In the course of three years they launched against them no less than seven full-scale offensives, each employing upwards of ten divisions with supporting arms. Once or twice large forces of Partisans came near to being surrounded and wiped out. Enemy aircraft, against which they had no protection whatever, played an important part, seeking out their positions and pinning them down while additional land forces were brought up to deal with them. But, each time they succeeded in extricating themselves, fading away, reappearing elsewhere and attacking the enemy where he least expected it. During each of these offensives, the extensive troop movements involved exposed the enemy more than ever to the attacks and ambushes of the Partisans. Thus these offensives failed in their object, and the Partisans, though tired, hungry and poorly equipped, continued their resistance undismayed. Meanwhile, the Germans, with an elusive enemy, with unreliable allies and without enough troops of their own to occupy the country effectively, could do little more than garrison the large towns and try to guard the lines of communication between them. And, merely to do this, they were using a dozen or more precious divisions which they could with advantage have employed on other fronts.

In the areas temporarily held by them the Partisans set up a provisional administration. This was based on a People's Anti-Fascist Front or Coalition under Communist leadership, the political and administrative unit being the Odbor or Council which corresponded roughly to the Russian Soviet. Liaison between the Partisan civil and military authorities was maintained by Political Commissars who also cared for the ideological welfare of the troops. In order not to alienate non-Communists in the Movement and amongst the civilian population, a relatively moderate line was followed, the Communists being careful not to dwell more than necessary on their ultimate aims and to avoid controversial topics. But everywhere the key posts were held by Party Members, and policy was in practice dictated by them. Everywhere, too, I found Communist propagandists hard at work preaching the gospel, bringing waverers into line.

Of actual Soviet Russian intervention and control there was no sign. No official Soviet representative had as yet reached the Partisans, though wireless contact of a sort seemed to have been established with the Soviet Union. But with a Moscow-trained Communist of Tito's calibre at the head of the Movement, there was clearly no need for day to day instructions to be issued from Moscow. Indeed, with the familiar Communist jargon on everyone's lips, the same old Party slogans scrawled on every wall and red star, hammer and sickle on the cap badges of the Partisans, 'an observer familiar with the Soviet Union might', I wrote in one of my earliest reports, 'imagine himself in one of the Republics of the Union'.

Gradually, too, we learned something of the situation in the rest of the country. Where large areas were constantly changing hands, this was not difficult.

Bosnia, where we now found ourselves, was part of the independent State of Croatia. Nominally this was a kingdom, but its King, the Italian Duke of Spoleto, had wisely omitted to take up his appointment and power was in the hands of Ante Pavelić and his Ustaše, supported by the Wehrmacht. The form of government was a dictatorship on Fascist or Nazi lines, with Pavelić in the role of Poglavnik or Führer and the Ustaše as his Praetorian guards. In addition to the Ustaše, who formed units of their own corresponding to Hitler's S.S., the new Croat State boasted its own army and air force, both under German operational control. These were more lukewarm in their loyalty to Pavelić and deserters from them came over to the Partisans in large numbers.

Pavelić's accession to power had been followed by a reign of terror unprecedented even in the Balkans. He had a lot of old scores to settle. There were widespread massacres and atrocities; Serbs, first of all, especially in Bosnia, where there was a large Serb population; then, to please his Nazi masters, Jews; and, finally, where he could catch them, Communists and Communist sympathizers. Racial and political persecution was accompanied by equally ferocious religious persecution. The Ustaše were fervent Roman Catholics. Now that they were at last in a position to do so, they set about liquidating the Greek Orthodox Church in their domains. Orthodox villages were sacked and pillaged and their inhabitants massacred; old and young, men, women and children alike. Orthodox clergy were tortured and killed, Orthodox churches were desecrated and destroyed, or burned down with the screaming congregation inside them (an Ustaše speciality, this). The Bosnian Moslems, equally fanatical and organized in special units by Pavelić and the Germans, helped by the Mufti of Jerusalem, joined in with gusto and a refined cruelty all of their own, delighted at the opportunity of massacring Christians of whatever denomination. At last the Croats were getting their own back for twenty years of Serb domination.

In Serbia the Germans kept most of the power in their own hands. The German puppet government was headed by General Nedić, formerly Chief of Staff of the Royal Jugoslav Army, a considerably milder character than Pavelić, who took the line that in accepting office and collaborating with the Germans, he was acting in the best interests of the Serbian people. This did not, however, prevent him and his Government from acquiescing in the confinement of large numbers of Serbs in concentration camps, the massacre of Serbian hostages and in all the other usual accompaniments of a Nazi occupation. A more actively pro-Nazi part was played by Ljotić, the Serb Fascist leader, and by the Serb Volunteer Corps, which largely consisted of his supporters and whose principal task was the suppression of the Partisans.

Of most interest to us were the Četniks. Theirs was essentially a Serb movement. From the start the main strength of the Četnik Movement was in Serbia, though Četniks were also active in Bosnia, Dalmatia and Montenegro. They derived their name from the Serb *četas* or companies which had fought the Turks in the Middle Ages. Their leader, Draža Mihajlović, was a Serb, a regular officer of the Royal Jugoslav Army who after its capitulation had taken to the woods with such of his men as he could gather round him with the intention of organizing resistance to the invader.

So much we knew. What followed during the summer of 1941 was less clear. Četniks and Partisans had, it seemed, fought side by side against the Germans in Serbia. Then there were mutual accusations of treachery (I had heard Tito's version) and by the end of 1941 they were fighting against each other. The combined onslaught of Germans and Četniks proved too much for the Partisans, and early in 1942 they were driven out of Serbia with heavy losses, to lick their wounds in the mountains of Bosnia and Montenegro.

The way in which the situation now developed was truly Balkan in its complexity. Mihajlović by all accounts continued to hate the

Germans and to hope for an Allied victory and the eventual liberation of his country. But the Četniks could not fight the Partisans and Germans simultaneously. From now onwards their attitude towards the Germans became increasingly passive, while they redoubled their efforts to crush the Partisans.

The motives underlying this policy were not far to seek. In their early encounters with the Germans, the Četniks, like the Partisans, had suffered heavy casualties; their operations had also led to savage enemy reprisals against the civilian population. They lacked the ruthless determination of the Communist-led Partisans, and this had discouraged them. They had also received over the wireless messages from the Royal Jugoslav Government in exile and from the Allied High Command telling them to hold their hand. Henceforward their aim became to preserve rather than to destroy; to keep alive the flame of Serb patriotism, as their ancestors had done under the Turkish occupation, in order that at some future period, after the Allied victory to which they looked forward, they might restore the old Serb-dominated Jugoslavia, which had meant so much to them.

But to be able to do this, they must first eliminate the Communist-led Partisans whose revolutionary tendencies clearly constituted a dangerous obstacle to the restoration of the old order, while their presumed allegiance to Moscow represented a threat to Jugoslav independence. What had started as a war of resistance became in a very short time a civil war, in which, needless to say, the Partisans gave as good as they got.

The Germans were well pleased. Nothing could suit them better than for the Četniks to stop fighting them and turn all their energies against the Partisans, whose stubborn, savage resistance was already beginning to cause them serious embarrassment. A tacit agreement grew up by which Germans and Četniks left each other alone and concentrated on putting down the Partisans.

It was the start of the slippery slope which leads to collaboration; collaboration from motives which were understandable, patriotic even, but nevertheless collaboration. What was more natural than that units fighting against a common enemy should co-ordinate their operations? Some Četnik Commanders went further still and attached liaison officers to German and Italian Headquarters, accepting German and Italian liaison officers in return. Some placed themselves and their troops under German and Italian command, allowed themselves to be supplied and equipped by them.

Who was being fooled and who was getting the best of it? The Germans, who had succeeded in neutralizing what had started as a resistance movement? Or the Četniks, who were actually being armed by an enemy, against whom they hoped one day to rise? It was all in the best Balkan tradition. Had not Miloš Obrenović alternately fought the Turks and acted as their Viceroy? Had he not sent to Constantinople the severed head of his fellow-liberator, Kara Djordje?

Mihajlović himself seems to have disapproved of actual collaboration with the enemy though he himself had originated the policy of abandoning active resistance and concentrating on the elimination of the Partisans. But the control which he exercised over his commanders was remote and spasmodic. Soon, while some Četnik commanders were still rather half-heartedly fighting the Axis forces, and others doing nothing, a number made no secret of their collaboration, and were living openly at German and Italian Headquarters.

Already this kaleidoscope of heroism and treachery, rivalry and intrigue had become the background to our daily life. Bosnia, where we had our first sight of enemy-occupied Jugoslavia, was in a sense a microcosm of the country as a whole. In the past it had been fought over repeatedly by Turks, Austrians and Serbs, and most of the national trends and tendencies were represented there, all at their most violent. The population was made up of violently Catholic Croats and no less violently Orthodox Serbs, with a strong admixture of equally fanatical local Moslems. The mountainous, heavily wooded country was admirably suited to guerrilla warfare, and it had long been one of the principal Partisan strongholds, while there was also a considerable sprinkling of Četnik bands. It had been the scene of the worst of the atrocities committed by the Ustaše, of the not unnaturally drastic reprisals of the Četniks and Partisans.

For anyone who was not himself in German-occupied Europe during the war it is hard to imagine the savage intensity of the passions which were aroused or the extremes of bitterness which they engendered. In Jugoslavia the old racial, religious and political feuds were, as it were, magnified and revitalized by the war, the occupation and the resistance, the latent tradition of violence revived. The lesson which we were having was an object-lesson, illustrated by burnt villages, desecrated churches, massacred hostages and mutilated corpses.

Once, after a battle which had raged all day amid the green hills and valleys, I came on the terribly shattered corpse of an Ustaša. Seeing that capture was inevitable, he had taken the pin from a hand-grenade and, holding it against him, blown himself to bits. Somehow his face had escaped disfigurement, and his dead eyes stared horribly from the pale, drawn, disordered features. From under his blood-stained shirt protruded a crucifix, and a black and white medal ribbon, probably the Iron Cross, still hung to the shreds of his German-type tunic. Fighting for an alien power against his own countrymen, he had destroyed himself rather than fall into the hands of men of the same race as himself, but of different beliefs, beliefs to which they held as savagely as he held to his, for which they would kill and be killed as readily as he for his. There could have been no better symbol of the violence and fanaticism of this Balkan war.

From this confused, this typically Balkan situation, one or two facts stood out clearly.

Mine was a military mission; I had been told that politics were a secondary consideration; what mattered was who was fighting the Germans. And of that there could be no doubt. The Partisans, whatever their politics, were fighting them, and fighting them most effectively, while the Četniks, however admirable their motives, were largely either not fighting at all or fighting with the Germans against their own countrymen. Moreover, regarded as a military force, the Partisans were more numerous, better organized, better disciplined and better led than the Četniks.

I had been told to consider how we could best help the Partisans. This, too, was clear. The Partisans were already containing a dozen or more enemy divisions. By increasing our at present practically non-existent supplies to them, and giving them air support, we could ensure that they continued to contain this force. Moreover their operations, if co-ordinated with our own, could be of direct assistance to the Allied armies in Italy. They would not need to change their strategy. Indeed it was most important that they should not depart from their guerrilla methods. If, by supplying them with arms and equipment and the air support for which they asked, we could ensure that they maintained and if possible intensified their present effort, we should be getting good value for what we gave them.

There was another aspect of the supply situation. We were getting, it seemed, little or no return militarily from the arms we dropped to the Četniks, which had hitherto exceeded in quantity those sent to the Partisans. Indeed, in so far as they were used against the Partisans, who were fighting the Germans, they were impeding rather than furthering the war effort. Logically, therefore, and on purely military grounds, we should stop supplies to the Četniks and henceforth send all available arms and equipment to the Partisans.

Politically, too, certain facts were clear. In the first place, the Partisans, whether we helped them or not, were going to be a decisive factor in the new Jugoslavia. Indeed there seemed no reason to doubt that, with their widespread and efficient organization, they would, when the Germans were driven out, become its effective rulers. Secondly, they were Communists, and must therefore be expected, when they came to power, to set up a totalitarian form of government on Soviet lines, in all probability strongly orientated towards Moscow.

These, too, were facts of first-rate importance, likely to affect the future political orientation of the Balkans and ultimately the balance of power in Europe. Should they affect the British Government's decision to give military support to the Partisans?

The question was one which would have to be decided by the Government. I had, before ever leaving England, raised the then hypothetical question of whether or not we were concerned to check the spread of Soviet influence in the Balkans, and had been told that our policy was not influenced by such considerations. Would the Government change their mind when confronted with the more definite information which would now be laid before them? I could not tell. But, instinctively, I carried the argument a stage further.

Clearly, whatever anyone might say, we could not regard with enthusiasm the establishment in Jugoslavia of a Communist regime under Soviet influence. But did the future political orientation of Jugoslavia depend on us? As far as I could see, it did not. If I had read the situation aright, nothing short of armed intervention on a larger and more effective scale than that undertaken by the Germans would dispose of the Partisans. And that, in the middle of a war in which they and their Soviet sponsors were our allies and at a time when we were in any case desperately short of troops, did not seem a practical proposition. Two years earlier, before the situation had crystallized, we might have been able to influence the course of events one way or the other. But not now.

This being so, we might as well extract such benefit as we could from the situation militarily. To refuse to help the Partisans on the ground that they were Communists at a time when we were doing everything in our power to strengthen the Soviet Union would indeed be to strain at a gnat and swallow a camel. Besides, if, as seemed probable, the Partisans were going to be the future masters of Jugoslavia, the sooner we established satisfactory relations with them, the better; although, if I knew anything about Communists, this would not be easy to do.

There was one other factor to be considered. Human experience shapes human character. The impact of events on the individual cannot altogether be left out of account. Tito had been through a lot since 1937, when, as a reward for his orthodoxy, Moscow had appointed him Secretary-General of the Jugoslav Communist Party. Since then he had undergone the innumerable hazards and hardships of a bitter war fought for the independence of his own country; he had experienced the satisfaction of building up from nothing a powerful military and political organization, of which he himself was the absolute master. Would he emerge from these strenuous and stirring years completely unchanged? Would he accept Soviet dictation and interference as unquestioningly as before? Already I had been struck by his independence of mind. And independence of any kind was, I knew, incompatible with orthodox Communism.

That Tito and those round him might in the course of time evolve into something more than mere Soviet puppets seemed too remote a possibility to serve as a basis for our calculations. But it was nevertheless an eventuality which seemed worth bearing in mind. 'Much,' I wrote in the report which I now started to draft against the day when I should find means of sending it out, 'will depend on Tito, and whether he sees himself in his former role of Comintern agent or as the potential ruler of an independent Jugoslav State.'

CHAPTER IV

ALARMS AND EXCURSIONS

THE weeks passed, and meanwhile the supply problem was no nearer solution. We still relied on what could be dropped by an occasional aeroplane, flying haphazard from North Africa, while for communications we still depended on a rather shaky wireless link with Cairo. Our improvised landing-strip at Glamoć was now ready but, from the messages we received, the R.A.F. seemed disinclined to risk one of their aircraft on it and it was unlikely that the Partisans would be able to hold for much longer the area in which it was situated.

Then one day came the news that the Navy were considering my suggestion that supplies could be run across the Adriatic by fast naval craft and landed by night on the Dalmatian Coast. They did not like the idea of running right in-shore, but they thought that they might take their cargoes as far as the outlying islands, now in Partisan hands, if we could find shipping to carry them from the islands to the coast and some means of carrying them inland from there.

This was something. I climbed up the hill to talk things over with Tito in his castle.

He greeted the news with enthusiasm. The Partisans, he said, had captured a certain number of light craft at the time of the Italian collapse. These they had manned with crews from their Dalmatian Brigade, the Dalmatians being born sailors, and had mounted with captured machine guns and twenty-millimetre Bredas. In fact, he said, they were already well on the way to having their own navy and could easily undertake the task of trans-shipping any quantity of supplies and ferrying them across the E-Boat infested coastal waters to a point in Dalmatia where they could be landed. But, if such operations were to do any good, they must begin at once, for already the Germans were pushing down towards the coast with tanks, artillery and air support, determined to re-occupy the territory which the Italian collapse had left unoccupied and which the Partisans were now holding as best they could against overwhelming odds. The port of Split had been recaptured by the enemy. Soon the Partisans would be cut off from the coast altogether, and then there would be no means of distributing supplies inland, even if they could be landed on the coast.

When I got back to my Headquarters, a fresh signal had arrived, asking for details of suitable landing-places on the islands; evidently the Navy meant business. I answered at once, stressing the need for immediate action and suggesting the island of Korčula as the best place for landing supplies. I added that I would go to Korčula myself as soon as I could, taking a wireless set with me. This would enable me to give further particulars of landing facilities from the island itself when I reached it, and also to form an idea of the problems of onward trans-mission of any supplies that were landed. On the way to the coast, too, I should see new country and the Partisans operating under new conditions.

I decided to take Street, Henniker-Major and Sergeant Duncan with me. Preparations for the journey did not take long. The greater part of it would be on foot and our kit accordingly had to be reduced to what we could carry on our backs. A Partisan officer and two men were allotted us as escort. We would be passed from one Partisan band to another and would rely on them for rations. Our exact route was still uncertain and would depend on the future movements of two enemy columns which at the moment were converging to cut the route down through Dalmatia to the coast. Parker and Alston were left in charge at Jajce and we set out.

The first stage of our journey was accomplished, rather surprisingly, by train. In the course of the counter-offensive, during which Jajce had fallen into their hands, the Partisans had managed to capture intact a railway engine and a number of trucks. Boasting amongst their number a professional engine-driver and guard as well as several ex-stationmasters, they lost no time in putting together a train which operated clandestinely and somewhat spasmodically up and down the short stretch of line between Jajce and the neighbouring village of Bugojno, which it had been decided would be a good jumping-off point for our journey to the coast. After years of weary tramping over the hills, the Partisans were inordinately proud of their train, and Tito had placed his private coach, an imposing structure of planks with a stove in the middle, at my disposal, so that there could clearly be no question of our covering the first short lap of our journey by any other means without causing serious offence.

Our departure from Jajce was scheduled for the middle of the night, which would allow us time to reach our destination before dawn and the appearance of the first enemy reconnaissance planes. After we had eaten and got our packs and the wireless set ready for the road, we made our way across the river to the ruins of Jajce railway station.

The station was a depressing, evil-smelling place. It had been shelled and fought over repeatedly and before the Germans had left the last time, a few weeks before, they had put several score of hostages into what was left of it and burnt it down with them inside. Now the bustle of our departure lent its ruined buildings a certain rather misleading air of animation under the sickly glare and flicker of home-made carbide lamps.

Our packs and the wireless set were put into one truck and then, after an interval, taken out and put into another. Some horses made an unexpected but welcome appearance; were entrained; detrained; and finally, with a good deal of cursing and shouting, entrained again. From time to time the engine, which had had steam up from the outset, and was belching flames, smoke and sparks from furnace and funnel, emitted a cloud of steam and a piercing blast on the whistle. Then, after another long interval, three of the retired stationmasters appeared complete with magnificent peaked caps liberally adorned with gold braid, flags, whistles, and all the paraphernalia of office. We shook hands with Velebit who had come to see us off, and jumped into our private coach; a large number of people who happened to be going our way followed our example; the engine gave a final blast on the whistle, which was echoed by the chorus of stationmasters on the platform; and, with a great deal of puffing and blowing, we rattled and creaked out into the dingy grey dawn which was coming up over the tree-tops. From the door of our truck I kept a look-out for aircraft in the lightening sky, but there were none to be seen. The next time we were in Jajce we heard that a few days later the train, after an even less punctual start, had had an encounter with a particularly active Henschel, after which there had been a badly needed tightening up of the time-table.

After all these elaborate preparations our train journey lasted for little more than half an hour. Under a cold, penetrating drizzle Bugojno station was bleak and cheerless. A score of prisoners were assembled there shivering, their faces yellowish-white above their tattered grey-green uniforms. At first I took them for Germans and reflected uneasily that they were probably on their way to be shot, the fate meted out by the Partisans to all Germans captured by them, in retaliation for the execution and often torture of all Partisan prisoners and of thousands of civilian hostages.

On closer inspection, however, they proved to be Domobranci, conscripts in the militia of the independent State of Croatia. These the Partisans regarded with good-natured toleration. They were for the most part miserable troops — very different from the Ustaše formations which formed the *élite* of Pavelić's army — and generally took the first opportunity of deserting or letting themselves be taken prisoner. When they fell into their hands the Partisans either enrolled them in their own forces or else disarmed them and let them go back to their homes. A favourite Partisan story is told of a Partisan who, having disarmed a Domobran, instructed him to go back to his unit and draw another rifle so that he might again be taken prisoner and thus once more contribute to the Partisans' supply of arms.

At Bugojno we found that we were having breakfast with Koča Popović,[1] then in command of Partisan First Corps. We walked down the battered main street of Bugojno. Like every other town and village in Bosnia it had been fought over a score of times in the past two years and was largely in ruins. On its poor bullet-scarred white-washed walls the inscriptions of the previous occupants: MUSSOLINI HA SEMPRE RAGIÓNE; EIN VOLK, EIN REICH, EIN FÜHRER, had been crossed out and replaced in flaming red paint by the slogans of the Partisans; ŽIVIO TITO; SMRT FAŠISMU, SLOBODA NARODU.[2] If you looked carefully you could see that the still earlier Partisan inscriptions of a previous occupation had been painted out by the Germans when the village had changed hands before.

We found Popović living in a peasant's cottage on the outskirts of

---

[1] Now Chief of Staff of the Yugoslav Army.
[2] Long live Tito. Death to Fascism. Liberty to the People.

the village. It was my first meeting with a man of whom in future I was to see a good deal and who was one of the outstanding figures of the Partisan Movement. I have seldom met anyone who gave a more vivid impression of mental and physical activity. He was of less than average height and sparely built, with a brown skin, twinkling eyes and fine-drawn, hawk-like features. A fierce black moustache gave him a faintly piratical air. Though barely thirty, he had the same tense, strained look as all the Partisan leaders, a look which comes from long months of physical and mental stress. But in his case the life he had led seemed to have fined him down rather than worn him out. Vitality radiated from his leathery, drawn features.

We sat down round a table in the fusty little room with an elaborately framed photograph of the owner's parents in their Sunday best on the white-washed wall and a sad-looking plant in a pot. Sour milk was brought and black bread with a lump of bacon and the usual flask of *rakija*. After the first few mouthfuls my temper, tried by the vicissitudes of our grotesque railway journey, mellowed and gave way to a comfortable feeling of drowsiness and well-being.

Popović, I soon found, was excellent company. He had been educated in Switzerland and France, spoke French like a Frenchman (and a very witty Frenchman at that) and had a startlingly wide range of interests. The son of a well-known Serbian millionaire he had at an early age become a convinced Communist. His interests had, however, in the first place been literary and intellectual rather than political. He had made a study of modern philosophy and had also won a considerable reputation as a surrealist poet, and, in Belgrade society, as something of an eccentric, which, considering the limitations of Belgrade society, was perhaps hardly to be wondered at. He had served his time in the pre-war Jugoslav Army, but the science of warfare had first become a reality to him in Spain, where he had fought for the Republicans, an experience which had left a profound impression on him. After the Germans invaded his own country, he had been one of the first to raise a Partisan band in Serbia and had soon shown himself to possess outstanding qualities as a military leader.

Now, while innumerable flies buzzed on the dirty window panes, our conversation skipped lightly from one topic to another: infantry tactics, Karl Marx, the Atlantic Charter and the latest French play-wrights. I was sorry when an orderly came in to announce that it was time for us to start. I went away with rather clearer ideas on a number of subjects and the impression of having met a man who would have been bound to make his mark in life under almost any circumstances.

Outside, we found our escort and two pack-ponies laden with the wireless set and some of our kit. We said goodbye to Koča and started out. The drizzle of the early morning had cleared off and it was now a sparkling autumn day. The track ran flat and straight before us across a little green plain, dotted with farmsteads and orchards, to the foot of the wooded range of hills which lay between us and Livno, a small town some fifty miles away in the direction of the coast. Beyond the hills fighting was in progress. Livno, which lay astride the road to the coast, had until recently at any rate been held by the enemy, as were most of the intervening villages. We should not know what route to follow until we had reached the other side of the hills and spied out the ground for ourselves.

As we tramped beside the horses I talked to Mitja, the officer in charge of our escort, a tall, smart-looking lad of about twenty-one, wearing on his new suit of British battle-dress the badges of a second lieutenant. He told me that when the Germans had invaded Jugoslavia he had been a cadet at the Royal Military College. He had at once taken to the woods and joined Draža Mihajlović. Then, finding that the Četniks were no longer seriously fighting the enemy, he had left them and gone over to the Partisans. With them he had had all the fighting he wanted. It was a story that we had heard often enough from former Četniks. No doubt my present escort had been specially chosen in order to drum it into me once again.

When we reached the foot of the hills, we left the track and followed more circuitous paths through the forests, climbing steeply most of the way. Once or twice we saw German aircraft flying above us and once from the direction of the main road came the roar of several heavy internal combustion engines. This, rightly or wrongly, was greeted by the Partisans with shouts of '*Tenkovi! Tenkovi!*' — 'Tanks! Tanks!' — a point which we did not stop to investigate. Once we encountered a Partisan patrol making their way in the opposite direction to ourselves,.

but with little idea of what was happening beyond the hills. One of them was a woman, a sturdy-looking girl who carried rifle, pack and a cluster of German stick-grenades like the men.

At midday we rested for a few minutes and ate our rations. The Partisans produced large crusts of black bread from their pockets and we got out our water-bottles. Farish had provided us before we left with pocket-size hermetically sealed packets of the new American K-ration, which none of us had ever seen before, and I was anxious to open one and find out what there was inside. Each mysterious-looking brown packet, though only a few inches long, was labelled 'Breakfast', 'Lunch' or 'Supper', and to our imaginations, whetted by plenty of fresh air and exercise on not very much food, conjured up visions of three-course meals. Indeed Vivian objected that it would be in the worst of bad taste to produce such luxurious fare in front of our less fortunate companions who had nothing to eat but dry bread. However, our natural curiosity overcame these scruples and we opened first one and then another of our packets.

They were certainly very ingenious productions. They contained tiny cellophane packets of lemonade powder, specially primed with Vitamin C and tiny tinfoil packets of soup powder, specially primed with Vitamin B and a lump of special sugar, neatly wrapped in paper and containing, according to the label, a surprisingly high proportion of Vitamin D. They also contained (all wrapped in cellophane) a piece of chewing gum and two cigarettes, two small water biscuits, one small bit of chocolate and finally one very small tin containing a mouthful of Spam or, as the case might be, cheese.

The Partisans, gnawing their bread, watched us pityingly as we fumbled with the cellophane and tried to mix the soup powder in our mugs. Before we had got anywhere at all, the cry of '*Napred*' rang out, and we were off again. We were as hungry as ever, and we had also lost face. We regained it, however, at the next halt, when, during a general showing-off of weapons, I produced my Colt automatic — another product of lease-lend — which was fingered lovingly by the whole party and greeted with gasps of admiration.

Finally, after several more hours of steady climbing and marching through thick woods, we emerged to find ourselves looking out over a wide sunny plain, with the road winding away in the distance. There were no signs of the enemy or indeed of the Partisans. Then, as we were debating what to do next, we noticed a small German staff car climbing up the hill towards us. As it came closer we saw that in it was a Partisan officer, whom we all knew, Lola Ribar, the son of Dr. Ivan Ribar, who had been President of the Jugoslav Constituent Assembly of 1920 and now was a leading figure on the political side of the Partisan movement. Young Ribar, who was still in his early twenties, had a distinguished fighting record and was regarded as possessing considerable all-round ability.

Now he was full of news of the battle. The Partisans had succeeded in recapturing Livno and were fighting in Kupres, a smaller village, lying between Livno and the point at which we now found ourselves. By the time we reached it it would be in their hands.

We piled into the car and drove off down the road at full speed leaving our escort and the baggage train to follow at their leisure. After a few miles we came to the smoking ruins of Kupres. Scattered corpses and burnt-out trucks testified to the defeat of the enemy. Partisan Brigade Headquarters was established in one of the few surviving houses, overlooking the market place. Here we found the Brigade Commander discussing the disposal of the wounded with his Medical Officer, a formidable-looking woman Partisan, who emphasized her points by thumping his table with her fist. As soon as this question had been settled, wine was brought in (we were approaching the vineyards of Dalmatia) and scrambled eggs and bread, and we were told, at length, the story of the battle, in which the Partisans had achieved a notable tactical success by the use of some captured enemy armoured cars. The enemy, not realizing that the Partisans possessed anything of the kind, had assumed that they were their own reinforcements arriving, and had greeted them, literally, with open arms, a mistake for which they paid dearly. When we had finished our meal we were taken to admire the armoured cars, now safely camouflaged behind some haystacks.

We waited at Kupres whilst our wireless operator, who had erected his aerial in the market place, tried in vain to make contact with Cairo. As so often happened, weather conditions or the neighbouring hills intervened and he tapped and twiddled unavailingly in the midst of a large and admiring crowd of Partisans and villagers.

It was late when we started for Livno, this time in a captured motorbus driven by a handsome young Italian dressed in a splendid white sheepskin coat. He was, it seemed, the pilot of an Italian aeroplane which had come over and bombed the Partisans every day until one day someone had succeeded in shooting it down with a rifle. As he did not seem a very convinced Fascist and as they were very short of drivers, they had turned him on to driving a truck. This he did with tremendous gusto, manœuvring his clumsy vehicle as if it had been a dive-bomber, and accompanying each flick of the wrist with a burst of grand opera delivered in a rich tenor. But by now we were too tired to mind anything and nodded in our seats as we jolted over the uneven surface of the road and shot round hairpin bends.

At midnight a single lantern, only half illuminating the market place and masking the squalid debris of battle, gave Livno a romantic air. We were billeted above a shop in a room where holy pictures alternated with portraits of Hitler and Pavelić, which there had presumably been no time to remove. We were tired and, having failed to obtain any food from a sour-looking landlady, fell asleep almost immediately.

Next morning we called on Milić, the local Partisan Commander, to make arrangements for our onward journey. The situation between Livno and the coast was obscure. Milić produced maps to illustrate the progress of the German pincer movement. The two claws seemed almost to have met. He hoped to have more detailed information the following day. Until this had been obtained it would be foolish to try to get through. In any case the journey to the coast and across to Korčula was not likely to be an easy one. Clearly we should be lucky if we got away in twenty-four hours.

Resignedly we settled down to explore the town. Livno lay in the sunshine, a little cluster of white houses at the foot of a great rock cliff. From amongst them rose the dome and minarets of a mosque. Beyond the town, Livansko Polje, the great rolling plain to which it has given its name, spread away into the distance. On the outskirts of the town earthworks had been thrown up and the houses, used as strong-points, had been battered and scarred in the recent fighting and in previous battles, for Livno had changed hands many times.

Now, on the day after the battle, the shops were open again, displaying a rather fly-blown collection of German-made fancy goods for sale in exchange for hundreds of *kunars*, Pavelić's heavily inflated currency. We went into a watchmaker's to try and buy a strap for my wrist watch. The watchmaker greeted us with a brisk 'Heil Hitler' and a Nazi salute, redeemed, on second thoughts by a sudden convulsive clenching of the fist. Clearly he found the military situation rather hard to follow, but this did not worry him for long and he was soon doing his best to sell us a monumental marble clock for which we could have no possible use.

Next we visited the waterworks and power-station, stumbling upon them by mistake at the foot of the cliff behind the town where a spring of water gushed suddenly from the face of the rock. The plant and the shed that housed it were undamaged and working away merrily, dispensing water and light indiscriminately to Fascist and anti-Fascist alike. As the engineer in charge, who had worked for both sides, explained to us, the Germans had not bothered to demolish the installation when they were driven out, because they knew they would be back soon and wanted to find it in working order when they returned. In this they were disappointed, for some weeks later the retreating Partisans blew it sky high.

Livno was a notorious Ustaša stronghold and we found the population surly and ill-disposed to both Allies and Partisans. Even the cajolery of Sergeant Duncan, generally infallible, and backed with the offer of a golden sovereign, could not prevail on our landlady to provide us with food from her well-stocked larder. She remained aloof amongst the pictures of the Führer, the lace antimacassars and the religious oleographs in her prim little parlour, preparing for herself and eating enormous meals and twanging provocatively on a large shiny yellow mandolin, decorated with a bunch of ribbons in the colours of the independent State of Croatia. Clearly appeasement formed no part of her nature.

Looking back, I suppose that her conduct was in fact heroic and dignified. At the time and on an empty stomach, I must confess that I found it extremely irritating, which is doubtless just what it was intended to be. Later we discovered that, as soon as I left, she had sent a messenger to the nearest German Commander informing him of my movements. She was, at any rate, nothing if not consistent. We christened her The Little Ray of Sunshine.

Having failed to get anything to eat at home, we turned to the Partisans who, after a whispered discussion, at once made us members of their Town Major's mess. This functionary turned out, somewhat surprisingly, to be an elderly general of immense distinction of manner. His career had been consistent in one respect only. Throughout his life he had remained a regular officer, though not always in the same army. He had held his first commission in the forces of the Austro-Hungarian Empire, in which he had fought against the Serbs and the Italians in the First World War. After the defeat of Austria in 1918 he had joined the Royal Jugoslav Army in which he had, during the twenty years between the wars, risen to be a general. On the dismemberment of Jugoslavia in 1941 he had thrown his lot in with Pavelić who had made him a general in the Domobran. Then on second thoughts, prompted perhaps once again by the course of events, he had gone over to the Partisans, who, with commendable caution, while leaving him his rank of general, by which, I suspect, they were not unimpressed, had given him an appointment where his actions were unlikely materially to affect the course of hostilities.

The general (he and I invariably addressed each other as Excellency) made a charming host. He was, he said, only sorry that he could not entertain us in a manner more worthy of such distinguished guests. His present establishment was a very squalid affair compared with the old days in Vienna before 1914. In his regiment they had had silver plate and champagne every night. Even in Belgrade, between the wars, things had not been too bad. Now, he missed all that. Indeed there was much about Partisan life that he actively disliked; sleeping out, or in bug-infested hovels, being constantly on the move, and the table-manners of his brother officers.

At the moment he had another cross to bear. After his long and varied military career he had retained strong feelings on at any rate one subject: he very much disliked the Italians. He had fought them on the

Isonzo in 1917. He would like to have fought them over Fiume in 1921. They had come yapping and snapping into Jugoslavia at the heels of the Germans in 1941. They had, even from the point of view of the Domobran, been unsatisfactory to collaborate with. For an all too short period, after he first joined the Partisans, he had once again had the pleasure of fighting them. Now they had capitulated, and some Italian units had actually joined the Partisans. To his disgust they were once again his allies. On top of everything else, an Italian Colonel had now been quartered on him and was actually going to sit down to lunch with us. 'Here he is — the swine,' he added as the smartest Italian officer imaginable, complete with varnished boots and rows of medals for *valore*, bowed his way into the room and introduced himself all round as Colonel V . . . commanding the Garibaldi Brigade.

The meal that followed was highly diverting. The General and the Colonel had no language in common; but this did not prevent them from wishing to communicate, or rather argue, with each other, and my services were soon enlisted as an interpreter. Battle by battle, we re-fought, in Serb, Italian and sometimes German, the Isonzo campaign of 1917, in which, it now appeared, the Colonel had also taken part on what he called the Allied side, pointing proudly to the ribbon of the Military Cross which nestled snugly next to that of the Iron Cross on his much decorated chest.

Soon mutual accusations of cowardice, treachery and barbarity were flying freely back and forth, only partially mitigated in the process of translation. When we reached the present war, the fun became faster and more furious, for now the mess waiter, a gigantic, bewhiskered Serb who had been a Partisan ever since 1941, plunged into the dispute, feeling, no doubt, that he was able to put the Partisan case rather better than his General. 'Here, hold this!' he would say, handing the dish of stew to his assistant, a fair-haired, well-built Partisan girl, her shapely body straining the buttons of a very tight dark green captured German tunic, and the usual couple of hand-grenades dangling from her belt. 'Hold this, while I explain to the Comrade General what really happened.' Soon the discussion became general, more Partisans came in and sat down, the stew went out of circulation altogether and in the ensuing confusion we managed to slip away.

Dinner that night was a repetition of the midday meal and by next morning I had come to the conclusion that if I stayed in that mess for very much longer I should have a nervous breakdown. Besides, it was imperative that I should reach the coast before it was too late. We went round to see Milić, only to be told that he was away on a reconnaissance. There was nothing for it but to wait another day.

We walked out into the Livansko Polje and looked at some ancient white Turkish tombs, topped with stone turbans. We made a tour of the defences and looked at the turf-covered 'bunkers' in which the Germans and Ustaše had made their last stand. We were shown the place where a twelve-year-old girl had dropped a hand-grenade into the turret of a German tank, killing the crew to a man. We talked to innumerable citizens of Livno, some of whom liked the Partisans, while some clearly preferred the Germans and others frankly didn't care, but wished that both sides would go away and leave them to earn their living in peace.

I talked, too, at length, with the Italian Colonel. He was delighted at finding someone who could speak his own language, and to whom he could at last unburden himself freely and I was also glad to have an opportunity of talking Italian again after so many years. His chief concern, I soon found, was to get himself and his men back to Italy, whither their General, who evidently believed in leaving nothing to chance, had already preceded them in the first aeroplane he could find. The Colonel made no attempt to disguise his horror of the Partisans, or *bolscevicchi* as he called them. They had, he said, been terrible enemies, and now he had no wish to fight for them, or indeed for anyone else; he simply wanted to go home. I asked him if he had come across the Četniks of General Mihajlović. At this he brightened. He said that, although the rank and file were sometimes undisciplined and gave trouble, he had always found the Četnik leaders very civilized and easy to deal with. Indeed one of the best parties he remembered since the beginning of the war had been given at his General's Headquarters to celebrate the award of the Karadjordje Star by King Peter to Pop Djuić, one of Mihajlović's principal Commanders in Dalmatia. What had made it all the more enjoyable, he added, was that this high decoration had been bestowed upon Djuić for gallantry in the face of the enemy, and there he was in person carousing at enemy Head-quarters. That, the Colonel commented contemptuously, bursting with national pride, was the sort of thing that could only happen in the Balkans.

When we got back to our billet, we found that a signal had come in over the wireless from Cairo. I had arranged that only urgent and important messages should be passed to me while I was on my way down to the coast, and so we looked at it with some interest. As we read it, our interest turned to amazement. The message was largely corrupt, but one sentence was quite clear. 'King now in Cairo,' it read, 'Will be dropped in to you at first opportunity.'

It could only mean one thing. For some time London had been concerned to effect a gradual rapprochement between King Peter and the Partisans. As a first step, I knew, the King was to move to Cairo, where it was felt, for some reason, that he would be better placed than in London to know what was going on in his own country. I had been kept informed, step by step, of the progress of these deliberations. But now, clearly, someone on a high level, Mr. Churchill perhaps, or possibly King Peter himself, had lost patience and decided to take the bull by the horns, and without more ado to precipitate the King head-long into the seething centre of the Jugoslav cauldron.

We were dumbfounded. The way had not been prepared at all. We had no means of telling how the Partisans would receive the King. In my conversations with Tito I had so far hardly touched on the extremely ticklish subject of the monarchy. My own guess was that if King Peter dropped without warning from a British aeroplane, the Partisans would simply hand him back to me and ask me to get rid of him again, which under existing circumstances would be easier said than done. Our minds boggled at the thought of the embarrassing situations which might arise.

My first thought was to get into touch with Cairo and find out what they really had in mind, but our wireless, temperamental as ever when most badly needed, now suddenly refused to emit a flicker. There was nothing for it but to wait and see.

Meanwhile Milić had returned from his reconnaissance and we went round to see him. He looked tired and worried. Once again the maps were brought out and we traced the progress of the German pincer movement. It had been all too rapid. The two claws had now joined up and the way to the coast was blocked. He himself had had a hard time getting back to his Headquarters. It would, he said, be out of the question for us to attempt the journey. The last courier from the coast had only just managed to get through.

I prepared for an argument. His last remark gave me the opening I wanted. If a courier could get through, I said, I could get through. He replied, with some justice, that it was not at all the same thing. The Germans were firmly established across our route and the only way of reaching the coast was to get through their lines at night. If we were taken prisoner or killed, he would get into trouble. At this I reminded him that my journey to the coast had been planned with Tito personally and that future supplies for the Partisans depended largely on my getting there. This seemed to shake him and I followed up my advantage. In the end he agreed that I should press on as far as Aržano which the Partisans were known to be still holding, and see for myself what arrangements I could make for my onward journey from there.

I was convinced that we should get through somehow and it seemed to me most important to maintain at all costs the principle of our freedom of movement. At the same time, even supposing that Milić had exaggerated the difficulties of the onward journey for our benefit, there was clearly a good chance of our running into an enemy patrol, in which case we should look very foolish if both Vivian and myself were taken prisoner. I accordingly decided to send Vivian back to Jajce with the bulk of the kit, and to go on to the coast myself, taking with me John Henniker-Major and Duncan. We left Livno in the early afternoon. With us came the Professor, a schoolmaster from Split with a remarkable talent for languages, whom I recruited at Livno and who was to be attached to one or other part of my Mission for the remainder of the war, covering immense distances on foot and enduring hazards and hardships most unusual in the career of a peace-loving man of letters.

356

CHAPTER V

ROAD TO THE ISLES

WE were to travel by truck as far as Aržano. After we had gone a very short distance it became evident that our driver did not know the way. This was disturbing, for the situation was still extremely fluid and no one seemed very certain of the exact extent of the enemy's advance.

The next village which we entered at full speed turned out to be still occupied by Italians. With the exception of the Colonel at Livno they were the first I had seen since the capitulation and for a moment the sight of their grey-green uniforms, so long the mark of an enemy, took me by surprise. Then they flocked forward, clenching their fists in the Communist salute and I remembered that we were amongst friends or at any rate co-belligerents.

I talked to several of them while the driver once again asked the way. They were the usual friendly peasants whose chief concern was to get out of Jugoslavia, with its unpleasant memories, and back to 'la Mamma' in Italy. I felt somehow that, despite the heroic echoes of their name, the Garibaldi Brigade which the Partisans were trying to form would not be an unqualified success from a military point of view. They had clearly not much enjoyed fighting for the Germans and the prospect of now fighting against them filled them with alarm and despondency.

Meanwhile the nature of the country through which we were passing had begun to change. The grey rocks and crags of Dalmatia were gradually taking the place of the wooded hills and green valleys of Bosnia. Everywhere there were traces of the recent fighting. The bridges were down and, scattered along the road and in the stony fields were burnt-out tanks and armoured cars with German, Italian and Croat markings. Towards evening, after a good deal of casting about, we came to Aržano, a few tiny white-washed houses, clinging to the side of a hill. Across the valley, dark against the setting sun, rose the first of the ranges of hills, which lay between us and the coast.

We were made welcome by the local Brigade Commander and his Political Commissar, two hilarious characters with heavy moustaches, almost indistinguishable the one from the other. Brigade Headquarters were sitting down to their evening meal. We pulled out our mess tins; they were filled with stew and black bread and a bottle of *rakija* was opened.

While we were eating, we explained who we were and what we were doing and broached the subject of our onward journey. To my relief the Brigade Commander seemed to take it as a matter of course that people with urgent business to transact should slip through the German lines at night. For the greater part of the way, he said, it was simply a question of knowing the lie of the land and dodging German patrols. There was only one place where we were likely to run into trouble. That was a road which we should have to cross and which was strongly held by the enemy.

We produced our map. He gave us in some detail an account of the latest fighting, and a plan was made without further ado. We were to be given two dozen men who would act as guides and escort during the first part of the march. When we reached the road, they would cause a diversion while we slipped across. Thereafter we would make our way by ourselves to a house in a certain village, where we would find reliable men who would put us on the right road to the coast.

This seemed a good plan in the best Fenimore Cooper tradition and before we set out a good many healths were drunk to the success of our venture. Then some songs were sung; plaintive Dalmatian folk songs, rousing Partisan marching songs, bitter Communist political songs, and, in our special honour, 'Tipperary' in Serbo-Croat by an old gentleman who remembered (rather dimly) hearing it sung on the Salonika front in 1917.

The last chorus was still ringing out as our little party wound down the hillside in the gathering dusk. From the west, where the daylight was dying away behind the hills for which we were making, came the flash and boom of some fairly large guns. The fighting was flaring up again.

At first our way lay through the cultivated land of the valley. Then we started climbing, still through muddy fields, up the long slope opposite. At the top we had our first halt. We had been going for about three hours and from now onwards we would have to march as silently as possible. Hitherto a couple of pack-ponies had carried our kit and the wireless set. Now, to avoid making more noise than was essential, we sent these back and divided the load amongst the members of our own party. After we had started on our way, we could still hear for some time the gradually fading sound of hoof-beats in the distance.

Soon we were over the crest and picking our way down a precipitous track towards the next valley. Somewhere beneath us lay the road with its German patrols. Under foot the loose jagged stones clattered noisily against each other. There was no moon and in the dark there could have been no worse surface to walk on for heavily laden men trying not to be heard. In single file the long procession wound its way painfully downwards in the pitch darkness, stopping from time to time to listen.

After several false alarms of enemy to the front, to the rear and on both sides, and many whispered confabulations, we reached the bottom, and there parted with our escort who filed off to create their diversion.

How they fared, we never knew. After some time had elapsed, there were 'noises off' from which those of us who remained concluded that the attention of the enemy was fully engaged elsewhere, and, taking advantage of the opportunity thus offered us, slipped down to the road and across its broad white dusty surface.

Once we were all safely on the other side, we mustered our diminished force and continued on our way, this time through dense bushes and scrub. All of a sudden a new obstacle blocked the way; a fast flowing river, too wide and too deep to be fordable. By now we had been marching for six or seven hours over rough country in the dark, and we were glad to sit down while someone was sent to look for a means of getting across. But waiting was a cold business, and we were not sorry when, half an hour later, our scout returned to say that further down-stream there was an old man who would put us across on a raft.

The raft, when we got to it, was a minute, flimsy affair, not much larger than a big soap box, on which there was barely room for one passenger besides the aged ferryman, who, grumbling to himself as he went, propelled it across the rapid current with vigorous but erratic strokes of his pole. Eventually, after a series of individual journeys, each of which landed the passenger, soaked to the skin, at a different point on the opposite bank, we were all across. We bid farewell to the boatman, still grumbling to himself in the darkness, and set out to look for our next target, the village where we were to find reliable guides.

The need for guides was already beginning to make itself felt. We had not gone far when there was the usual hoarse whisper of 'enemy'. As usual we all stopped dead in our tracks and held our breath, but this time, instead of silence, we heard the unmistakable sound of men making off at full speed through the scrub. This was too much for the Partisans. On all sides of me I could hear the rattle and click of machine pistols and sub-machine guns being cocked and I reflected with alarm that, in our present formation, at that moment a rough semi-circle, an attempt to shoot it out in the darkness with an unseen and possibly imaginary enemy, besides rousing the entire neighbourhood, would almost certainly inflict heavy casualties on our own party. But fortunately more prudent councils prevailed and, while we inflicted, it is true, no damage on the intruders, we at least succeeded in preserving our anonymity.

The incident had convinced me of the advisability of finding our guides as quickly as possible and then continuing our journey to the coast by the most direct route. Somebody, probably, to judge by his behaviour, the enemy, now knew where we were, and, if we continued to wander aimlessly about in the dark, would almost certainly come back in force to deal with us. Mitja, who was in charge of navigation, was accordingly summoned, maps and an electric torch were produced, and a more direct route plotted. Then, hoisting our packs back into position, we started once again to pick our way upwards over the ever-shifting scree of the hillside, our feet sliding back half a yard for every yard that we advanced.

The village for which we were bound lay on some flat ground at the top of the next range of hills. There were, it appeared, Germans quartered in it. The house we were looking for was a farm on the outskirts of the village. The rest of us lay behind a hedge while one of the Partisans went and knocked at the door. For a time nothing happened. Then the door opened a few inches and a whispered conversation took place. Clearly nocturnal visitors were regarded with suspicion.

Finally, after much whispering, a tall, gaunt, elderly man in a cloth cap emerged, with long, drooping moustaches, and a rifle slung over his bent shoulders. He was, it seemed, the Partisans' chief contact-man in the village, where, under the nose of the Germans, he conducted his own miniature underground movement. Should the Germans be driven out, he would come into his own and probably become mayor. Meanwhile, he led a clandestine, surreptitious existence, full of nerveracking episodes such as this. He took the lead and we moved silently off. The going — loose, sharp-edged stones — was as bad as ever.

After another hour or two of marching it began to get light. By now we were out of the danger zone and our guide turned back to his village; we had only to follow a clearly marked track which plunged downwards into the valley. There was not much further to go and the knowledge that we were nearing our destination suddenly made us feel tired and sleepy. We plodded along in silence. Dawn, coming up over the hills we had just crossed, was beginning to light the topmost pinnacles of the great range which rose like a jagged wall on the far side of the valley, the last barrier between us and the sea. As the rays of the rising sun touched them, the mountain tops turned to gold. The mist still lay thick in the valley beneath. We wondered, with an increasing sense of urgency, what, if anything, there would be for breakfast.

The country which we were now traversing was almost incredibly rugged and desolate. In some places, amid the great whitish-grey boulders, the stones had been cleared away to form tiny patches of cultivated ground, not large enough to merit the name of fields, where the vivid green of the vines contrasted vividly with the drab background of the rocks. Here and there stood the remains of a peasant's cottage, its blackened stones an eloquent reminder of the results of Italian military government. Then, rounding a corner, we came upon a church, with three or four houses round it, and a group of Partisans with tommy-guns standing in the roadway. We had reached Zadvarje — our immediate destination.

We asked for Brigade Headquarters and were taken to an upper room in the priest's house, the largest in the village, where we found the Brigade Commander, a young man in his early twenties, sitting down to a breakfast of black bread and captured ersatz coffee made from roasted grain. He asked us to join him and eagerly we did so. It was not the breakfast I should have ordered from choice, but it was very welcome all the same, and was rendered doubly so by a bottle of *rakija* which was produced to wash it down. By now it seemed to us the most natural thing in the world to gulp raw spirits at breakfast.

By the time breakfast was over we felt as if we had known the Brigade Commander (and the dozen or so other people who had flocked in to watch us eat) all our lives. Each of them had told us his or her life-story and we, in response to a volley of questions, had reciprocated with a great many personal details of an intimate and revealing nature. The Brigadier, who in civil life was an electrician's mate and who had been one of the first Partisans in Dalmatia, could not take his eyes off us. To him we seemed, as indeed in a sense we were, beings from another world. How, he wanted to know, had we got here? We explained. What did it feel like to be dropped out of an aeroplane? Had we been sent or had we come because we wanted to? What were we going to do, now that we were here? Might our Government send in arms, and ammunition, and boots, and greatcoats, and food? And would some be sent to Dalmatia?

It was all that we could do to stem the flood of questions and bring the conversation round to our onward journey. This, according to the Brigade Commander, presented no great difficulty. Standing outside the door, he showed us our route. As far as the river at the bottom of the valley, we could travel in a truck which they had captured a few days before. From there onwards — over the last great ridge of Biokovo, and down to the sea — we should have to walk, for the next bridge was down and there was no means of getting the truck across. If we left at midday, we should reach the pass over Biokovo at dusk, which would enable us to complete our journey to the sea under cover of darkness. This was advisable as practically the whole coast was now in German hands, save for the tiny harbour of Podgora, for which we were bound and where we hoped to find some kind of craft to take us across that night to the island of Korčula.

Having thus planned our route, the Brigadier next turned his attention to the truck and was soon hard at work at the head of a gang of amateur mechanics. I asked him what was the matter with it and he answered that it had been shot up by a Henschel the day before. 'The driver was killed,' he added, 'but the engine was not badly damaged, and we will soon get it right again.' He asked us if there was anything we would like to do in the meantime. We said there was: we would like to lie down and go to sleep.

When we woke the sun was high, the truck was ready and it was time to start. We said goodbye to the electrician turned Brigadier. We had only been his guests for a few hours, but I still remember his efficiency, his friendly straightforwardness and his obvious gift of leadership. He was, it seemed to me, a good man by any standards. I tried afterwards to get news of him, but there was bitter fighting in the coastal area in the months that followed and it seems likely that he and most of his men were killed.

Before we started, someone took a group with a camera taken from a German officer, a copy of which was, much to my surprise, to reach me by a courier months afterwards. Then we climbed into the truck; everybody pushed, and we rattled off down the hill in fine style.

The length of the ride hardly justified all the trouble which had been taken to put a vehicle on the road. We had scarcely started when we reached the demolished bridge and it was time for us to get out again and walk. But at least our friend the Brigadier had been able to assert the claim of his Brigade to be regarded as partially mechanized, a great source of prestige amongst the Partisans.

Just before we reached the summit of the ridge, we were overtaken by a thunderstorm and torrents of drenching rain, and for a few minutes we sheltered in a peasant's hut by the roadside, full of smoke and smelling of garlic, like a mountaineer's hut in the Alps.

Then the rain stopped as suddenly as it had started, and a few minutes later we reached the top and were looking down on the Adriatic, with the islands in the distance, the jagged outline of their mountains grey-blue against the fading red of the sunset. Neither Mitja nor my bodyguard had ever seen the sea before, and so we waited while they accustomed themselves to the idea of so much water. Then the sun sank behind the islands, and we started on our way down.

Below us on the right we could see the lights of Brela, where there was an Ustaše garrison. Further to the north, out of sight, lay Split, where the Germans were now firmly established. Immediately to the south, on our left as we descended, was Makarska also held by the enemy, and, beyond it stretched the peninsula of Pelješac, along which German troops from the garrisons at Mostar and Metković were beginning to advance, in preparation, no doubt, for an invasion of the islands. Somewhere in the darkness at our feet lay Baška Voda, still, for the moment, in Partisan hands.

Once or twice on the way down we were challenged by Partisan patrols, gave the password, and went on. Then, at last, we heard the dogs barking in Baška Voda, were challenged once more, and, passing between high white-washed walls, found ourselves on a narrow jetty, looking out over a tiny harbour.

There was no time to lose if we were to reach Korčula before daylight. While we made a frugal meal off a bottle of Dalmatian wine and a couple of packets of German ship's biscuits, two Partisans in bell-bottomed trousers and fishermen's jerseys started work on a fishing smack, fitted with an auxiliary engine, which was to take us across.

Soon everything was ready. The storm had cleared the air and it was a fine night. The wireless set and our kit were put on board; we followed them; I made myself comfortable in the bows with my pack under my head for a pillow, and, with the engine spluttering away merrily in the stern, we set out across the smooth star-lit waters of the Adriatic.

I have seldom slept better. When I woke, we were some way out and, looking back, we could see the lights of Makarska and of the other villages along the coast twinkling across the water. All around us, an unexpected and rather startling sight for one waking from a deep sleep, the dazzling white acetylene lights which the Dalmatians use for fishing flared and flickered from dozens of little boats. In war as in peace, black-out or no black-out, they continued to make their living in their own way, unmolested by Germans or Partisans. I asked our crew whether the Germans made no attempt to keep a check on what was going on. 'Yes,' one of them said, 'they patrol these waters regularly,' and as he spoke, as if in answer to my question, there came the louder, more regular chugging of a more powerful engine, and a strong searchlight went sweeping over the surface of the sea a mile or two away.

The course which we followed was perforce a roundabout one, in and out amongst the islands. Once we stopped to drop a message at Sučuraj on the eastern extremity of the island of Hvar, half of which was held by the Partisans while the other half was occupied by a force of Ustaše, who had landed on it and were digging themselves in. As we approached Sučuraj, one of the crew, muttering '*Signal!*' started fumbling in the locker and eventually produced a small lantern, which he lit, and then, standing up, waved a couple of times in the direction of the shore.

The response was immediate; a shower of machine-gun bullets ploughed up the water all round us. 'Wrong signal,' said our Partisan gloomily and waved his lantern three times instead of two. Once again the machine gun opened up, this time with rather better aim, and I began to wonder whether we had not perhaps struck the wrong part of the island and were not signalling to Ustaše. Meanwhile we had kept on our course and were by now within hailing distance of the shore. '*Partizani!*' we shouted hopefully.

To my relief the sentry did not give us another burst. 'Is that you, Comrade?' he shouted. 'I thought it must be, but why did you give the wrong signal?' And an argument started which was still in progress when, after delivering our message, we once again put out to sea. Soon I was asleep again and when I next woke the sun was coming up behind the mountains on the mainland and we were nearing our destination.

CHAPTER VI

ISLAND INTERLUDE

THE wooded hills of Korčula stood out black against the pale sky. As we rounded the point and entered the harbour, the first rays of the rising sun were beginning to fall on the old houses of the port. Picking our way through a motley assortment of fishing vessels, we tied up by some stone steps which ran down to the water at the base of an ancient circular tower, emblazoned with the Lion of St. Mark, the symbol of former Venetian domination.

We had arrived.

Although by my watch (Cairo time? Greenwich Mean Time? Central European Time? Double British Summer Time?) it was only five in the morning, a small crowd had soon collected to look at us. It included, I noticed with pleasure, one extremely pretty girl. After the tired, ragged villagers of the mainland, the islanders seemed prosperous and well, almost smartly, dressed. The houses, too, with their white, yellow, or pink walls and their green shutters, were undamaged and looked bright and inviting in the early sunlight. The sea was blue and clear as glass. The whole place had a holiday air that was most agreeable after our exertions and the austerity of Partisan life. Sleepily we tumbled out of our boat and up the steps and asked for Partisan Headquarters.

Everybody knew where it was and everybody came with us to show us the way, chattering merrily to us as we went, for the Dalmatians have something of the cheerful volubility of the Italians they dislike so much. As usual we were plied with innumerable questions. What was happening on the mainland? Were the Germans going to invade the islands? How were they to defend themselves if they did? Had we met Tito? What was he like? Were we English or American? Had we been to California, where their aunt lived? (The Dalmatians are great settlers.) Or Australia, where they had cousins? Would we take a letter to their father's brother in New Zealand? Did we realize

366

what devils incarnate the Italians were, and how the island had suffered under the occupation? What had we come for? How long were we staying? Were we married? Did we like dancing?

Answering some questions and avoiding others, we made our way, followed by an excited, gesticulating crowd which increased in size as we went along, through the winding streets of the town to the old Venetian palace which housed its new rulers. Over the doorway the Lion of St. Mark stood headless, decapitated by some over-zealous Partisan, anxious evidently to celebrate the end of Mussolini's rule by destroying the symbol of an earlier period of Italian domination. We went in, through a magnificent colonnade and up a fine Renaissance staircase, at the top of which was a door. We knocked, someone answered, and we entered to find ourselves face to face with a Franciscan friar, who rose to greet us with the clenched fist salute. He was, he said, the Chairman of the Odbor, the local Soviet. We, for our part, explained who we were and what we had come for. He replied that he was delighted to see us and that all the resources of the island would be placed at our disposal. Meanwhile, while we were waiting for a house to be got ready, perhaps we would like to have something to drink.

We said we wouldn't mind if we did. He rang and a bottle was brought in, closely followed by a curly headed youth of about twenty, who was introduced as the commander of the garrison, a tall, elegant, Edwardian-looking character with a drooping moustache, who turned out to be his political commissar and a brisk little man in a white silk shirt and sun-glasses who had been skipper of a merchant vessel. Glasses were taken out of a cupboard and filled. The wine, a sunny Dalmatian vintage from the islands, called, with admirable succinctness, *grk*, was heady and delicious, and soon we were all engaged in animated conversation.

By the time a Partisan arrived to announce that our house was ready we felt that there was hardly anything we did not know about the war-time history of Korčula. We were told of the brutality and licentiousness of the Italians, of the girls who had been seduced and the hostages who had been taken out and shot. Of how the Padre, as our Franciscan was known, had from his monastery kept in touch with the Partisans in the hills. Of how these, under the leadership of the curly headed youth, had been a thorn in the flesh of the Italians, way-laying them on lonely roads and blowing up their lorries and cutting their throats when they least expected it. Of the reprisals. And the counter-reprisals. Of the capitulation and what they had said and done to the Italians before they left for Italy; and the magnificent stores and equipment which they had forced them to leave behind.

When we left, they all came with us and the crowd, who had waited outside, followed along in our wake. We were taken to a little white-washed house perched on a rocky point overlooking the harbour. From it rough steps ran down to the sea and you could plunge straight into two or three fathoms of clear blue water. The rooms were light and airy and the sun was streaming in through the open windows. In the kitchen a cook was busy preparing a succulent meal. We felt slightly bewildered. It was as though we had rubbed a magic ring and suddenly found ourselves miraculously provided with all the things we had been dreaming of for weeks past. Then the Padre asked us anxiously whether it would do and, having been assured that it would, went off back to his office, promising to come back and see us later.

After he had gone, we stripped off our dusty sweat-soaked clothes and, running down the steps, jumped into the sea. It was late enough in the year for the water to be cold and its chill refreshed us. Soon we were swimming far out into the narrow straits, scarcely a mile wide, which divide Korčula from the Pelješac peninsula. In front of us, as we swam, the high, dark hills of Pelješac ran steeply down to the sea, the fishermen's cottages clustering by the water's edge. As we watched some fishing boats put out from the shore. A few miles to the south, where the peninsula joins the mainland, we knew that the Germans were beginning their advance along it. Looking back, we could see the whole town of Korčula spread out round the harbour, the old churches, houses and palaces golden in the morning sunlight.

We swam till we were tired. Then we came in and dried ourselves and put on the clean shirts which each of us had kept rolled up in his pack against just such an occasion as this. An enormous and delicious meal, half breakfast and half luncheon, was waiting for us: fish, eggs, meat, cheese, coffee, fruit, Dalmatian wine, Maraschino from Zara as well as all kinds of luxuries left behind by the Italians in their flight. The cook, it seemed, had worked in one of the royal palaces. He might well have done. We certainly did justice to his cooking.

When we had finished eating, we lay down on our beds and fell deeply and dreamlessly asleep.

I was awakened, sooner than I would have liked, by the rustle of the Padre's robe and by the slapping of his sandals on the stone floor. Grudgingly, I struggled back to consciousness. Outside a little Italian staff car was waiting, its exhaust puffing impatiently. The skipper was there too, and the garrison commander. We were off on a tour of the island.

My recollections of that afternoon are confused. It began at I suppose two with a *vin d'honneur* and a snack with the oldest inhabitant of the next village (a process, which, as we found to our cost, was to be repeated at every other village and township in the island). It ended with a municipal dinner and a dance in the early hours of the following morning. It had the same nightmarish and exhausting quality as the last frantic days of an election campaign, with, in addition, a fantastic comic-opera character all of its own.

At each village, after we had swallowed the inevitable *vin d'honneur* and snack, we inspected the local Partisan detachment. At our first stopping-place we had greatly admired the detachment Commander, a magnificent figure of a man with fierce black moustaches, mounted on a fine black horse.

We were no less impressed by the handsome appearance and military bearing of the detachment Commander at the next village, also a typical Dalmatian and equally well mounted, though his horse, perhaps, did not seem quite so fresh or so full of spirit as the first we had seen. When, after we had visited the oldest inhabitant, we looked round for him to say goodbye, he was strangely enough, no longer there.

At our next halt, once again, the local detachment and with it its Commander was there to greet us. This time we looked closely at the Commander. His horse's flanks, we noticed with some surprise, were heaving and flecked with foam as if it had just had a hard gallop.

And then, that curving neck, that flowing mane and tail, those magnificent moustaches — surely it was more than a resemblance? But in his eye there was no flicker of recognition as he saluted and shook hands, and so, once again we congratulated him on the smartness of his detachment and then turned tactfully away, leaving him to gallop on ahead on his charger — the only one on the island — and place himself at the head of his troops in readiness for our arrival at the next village along the line.

His must have been, I think, an engaging character, a mixture of southern *panache*, rustic guile, and a childlike desire to please. I was never able to find out what became of him in the fierce fighting that was soon to sweep over Korčula.

Other isolated incidents remain ineradicably impressed on my memory. I remember being pelted with flowers by some nuns. I remember noticing that, in contrast to the Roman Catholic clergy on the mainland, here the priests in most of the villages on Korčula seemed to be leading lights in the Partisan Movement. I remember visiting a hand-grenade factory; and a hospital where a man was having his leg cut off by a German-Jewish doctor; and a printing press where nothing in particular was happening. I have a vivid recollection of making several speeches in Serbo-Croat, one from a balcony. I shall also always remember meeting Sergeant Duncan, from whom we had somehow got separated, coming round the island in the opposite direction on a triumphal tour of his own, standing up in a lorry, swaying slightly and loudly acclaimed by the crowd. Finally I have hazy memories of the dance at a village called Blato which rounded off our day's entertainment and which was dramatically interrupted by the explosion of a small red Italian hand-grenade which became detached from one of the girls' belts as she whirled round the barn in which it was being held.

That night we slept very soundly.

During the days that followed our chief concern was with our wireless. We had had no contact since Livno. Mechanically the set seemed in order, but clearly something was radically wrong. Try as we would, Cairo remained deaf to our tappings, and we seemed to be able to pick up nothing of theirs.

This was a serious matter. I had undertaken to send the Navy detailed landing instructions for their motor launch. They had agreed in principle to come to Korčula, and were due to make the attempt any day now, but would they in fact risk one of their light craft so near the enemy coast without an explicit assurance that all was well? Worse still, the absence of any message from us would probably be taken to mean that I had never reached Korčula, or that it was now in enemy hands. Anxiously we tried heightening the aerial, fiddling with the crystal, taking the whole set up to the top of a nearby hill. Nothing did any good. There was also the question of the King still weighing heavily on my mind.

The only hope was to try to send a Partisan courier through to Jajce with instructions that my message should be relayed from there. But that might take weeks. Resignedly we copied out the signal on a sheet of paper, leaving it in cipher in case it should fall into the hands of the enemy. I addressed it to Vivian Street, and that night we watched the courier start off by boat for the mainland. Until I had had an answer one way or the other I myself was bound to stay where I was, for otherwise the M.L. might arrive and find no one there to meet it. I accordingly settled down to wait.

The days went by, fine and bright. Our wireless remained obstinately silent. There was no news of the courier. The fighting on Pelješac seemed to have bogged down. From time to time excited Partisans came running in to tell us that our ship had been sighted or had arrived at one of the other islands, or had been sunk and was now floating off the island bottom upwards. On investigation none of these stories were found to have the slightest foundation, but they relieved the tedium of waiting.

For some time it had almost seemed as if the Germans had wind of our intentions or at any rate of my presence on the island.

Once I had occasion to visit a neighbouring islet. It was so near that it had seemed unnecessary to take the usual precaution of waiting for darkness. The Partisans placed at my dispsoal a magnificent speedboat, resplendent with glistening white paint and shining brass, the relic of some pre-war millionaire holiday-maker. From the stern a large Partisan flag fluttered gaily in the breeze. Behind us, as we roared out of Korčula harbour, an immense foaming wake surged up and sped in ripples towards the shore. For a moment I wondered if all this was wise. Only for a moment. Then I knew it was not. Above the roar of our own engines another, only too familiar sound had reached my ears. As I looked round to see where it came from, a large three-engined German flying boat, flying very slowly and so low that I could see the rear-gunner's face, came suddenly over the brow of the nearest hill. Our steersman took immediate and spectacular evasive action, thereby rendering us even more embarrassingly conspicuous than we were already. Turning over in my mind the possibility of a quick dive over the side, I watched the rear-gunner anxiously to see how he was reacting. Apparently he was not interested, thinking perhaps that only Ustaše or other Axis sympathizers would circulate by day in such a showy craft. Or else he had left his ammunition at home. In any case he did not attack us, but continued peaceably on his way towards the main harbour, where, we heard afterwards, he scared the life out of our cook by skimming past our house at what is known by the R.A.F. as 'nought feet' and peering in at the windows. It was hard to avoid the conclusion that the enemy was looking for somebody or something.

A few days later we had further confirmation of this. I had climbed to the top of the hill that overlooked the harbour and was looking across towards the mainland when suddenly out of the sun there came with a roar a dozen Stukas. There was no mistaking those disagreeably tilted wings, that wasp-like undercarriage. In other theatres, perhaps, the Stuka had had its day, but for us, in our kind of warfare, without fighter support or anti-aircraft defences, it had kept all its old terror.

They took their preliminary run high over the harbour and out to sea again. But immediately they turned and came back and, as I watched, their leader peeled off from the formation, and, with the sunlight flashing on his wings, came screaming downwards past where I was standing, to send his bomb crashing amidst the shipping in the harbour. Almost at sea level, he pulled out of his dive and turned back out to sea, as the next and then a third and a fourth Stuka after him followed him down. Soon high columns of water were twisting up into the air from all over the harbour, matched by clouds of dust and rubble from the shore. Then, as quickly as they had come, the raiders were gone and silence followed, broken only by shouts for help and the wailing of frightened children which rose from the town at my feet. Korčula had had its first experience of aerial warfare.

The days passed. And still there were no signs of the Navy. The wireless was dead and no message had come from the mainland, where the military situation seemed to be deteriorating. I was out of touch both with G.H.Q. Middle East and with Tito.

I decided to give them another twenty-four hours and then, if nothing happened, to start back for Jajce.

That night I was wakened at about two by a confused shouting outside the house. My first thought was that the Germans had landed from the mainland. Then, as I was reaching for my pack and my automatic in preparation for a quick move, our Partisan guard burst excitedly into the house, followed by three naval officers and David Satow, the latest addition to my staff. One of the sailors I recognized as Sandy Glenn, an old friend with a number of adventurous exploits to his credit in the less orthodox branches of naval warfare. The Navy had arrived.

I was delighted to see Sandy, the more so as I had reason to know that he was not supposed to be there at all. But that was not likely to deter him. Nothing could have been more deceptive than his mild, even slightly owlish appearance, as he peered at you benignly from behind a large pair of round spectacles. In fact he possessed gifts of determination and ingenuity which enabled him to get the best of almost any staff officer — enemy or Allied — however obstructive. From now onwards he was never to be far away from us. His next assignment was in enemy-occupied Albania where he lived mysteriously in a cave looking out over the Adriatic and waited upon by a retinue of Italian prisoners. Thence he emerged to rescue an aircraft load of American hospital nurses whose pilot had lost his way and crash landed in the interior, after which they were smuggled down to the coast by the Partisans under the noses of the Germans, marching for days in high-heeled shoes and silk stockings. Finally, towards the end of the war, he was to be dropped by parachute on the banks of the

Danube, with the task of blowing up barges, or something of the kind, for which he was awarded a much-deserved bar to his D.S.C.

Sandy and his friends had, it appeared, taken a chance that Korčula was still in Partisan hands. Having brought their M.L. into a cove on the other side of the island they had then made their way across country to where I was living. I gave them some *rakija* and we discussed what to do next. They had brought several tons of arms and supplies for the Partisans and these needed to be unloaded. It was also essential to ensure that the M.L. was properly camouflaged against air reconnaissance before daylight.

Fortunately, the cove which they had picked was admirably suited for both purposes, with high, wooded sides and a path running down to the water's edge, by which the supplies could be got away, so that a move was not necessary. The Partisans were wildly excited at this impromptu naval visit. We collected as many of them as possible and started work unloading the M.L. and camouflaging her up. By dawn the last case of ammunition had been carried on shore and camouflage nets, all stuck about with leaves and branches, had been ingeniously stretched over the M.L. and from her side to the shore, so as to break up her outline. From the top of the nearest hill, whither we retired to survey our handiwork, she might have been part of the island.

We were not a moment too soon.

As I stood on the deck of the M.L., looking out from under the bowers and trellises of the camouflage, the beat of aircraft engines fell once again on our ears and two little black 'hedge-hoppers' — Fieseler Storchs — came poking inquisitively over the hill. But the M.L.'s camouflage was too good for them and they flew away without noticing us and did not come back. It was tempting to think what a shock we could have given them, had we chosen, by suddenly opening up at close range with the M.L.'s Oerlikon.

They had scarcely gone when the Partisan brigade commander arrived from Pelješac. Things, it seemed, were going very badly indeed in his sector. German reinforcements were pouring in and according to his latest information the enemy were collecting a regular invasion fleet of small craft at the mouth of the Neretva for purposes which were all too clear. Unless we could do something to help, the Partisans would be swept off Pelješac and the way would lie open for a German invasion of the islands. Thus, our new-found supply channel was likely to be shut before we had had time to use it.

Bogdan, the Brigade Commander, was generally a merry little man, but that morning he had a worried look and his long moustaches drooped dismally. I took him on board the M.L. and his eyes, accustomed to the bare hillside, opened wide at the shaded lights and polished brass and mahogany of the chart-house. Then, as maps were produced, the strangeness of it all was forgotten and he was soon completely absorbed in his task of explaining the position and showing us how he thought we could best help.

By now I was accustomed to Partisan demands for air support, which in general showed little comprehension of what could and could not be done from the air and bore but little relation to reality. But this time it looked as though, if the R.A.F. could only spare the aircraft, we might really be able to give decisive tactical support. There was also a chance that the Navy might be able to help, though not, as Bogdan seemed to expect, then and there by means of our one and only M.L.

Sitting down at the cabin table, I wrote out two signals to which I gave the highest priority I could. The first was to Air Vice-Marshal Coningham, who was commanding the old Desert Air Force in Italy, explaining the position and asking him if he could spare some aircraft from the battle in Italy to attack the German troop concentrations at Mostar and Metković, their advanced positions on Pelješac and their invasion barges at the mouth of the Neretva. I added that, to be of any use, the help would have to come at once.

The second signal was to the Flag Officer Taranto, or F.O.T.A., as he was called, suggesting that, if he could spare some M.T.B.s, they would be well employed patrolling off the mouth of the Neretva, in case the enemy should decide to try a landing.

The M.L. had instructions to keep the strictest wireless silence as long as she was in enemy waters, but we had decided that she should leave again at nightfall, and her captain promised to send off my signals as soon as he got out to sea. Bogdan seemed impressed by so much activity. The galley was out of commission, but we gave him some bully and biscuits and he went off back to his hard-pressed men, much more cheerful than he had come and clearly hoping for great things. I only hoped that my signals would have some effect.

The M.L. left that night and next day we, too, having established contact with the Navy, started to prepare for our return journey. It took some time to plan our journey and make the necessary arrangements for it, and, before we finally left, we had the satisfaction of seeing a number of Spitfires flash overhead in the direction of Pelješac and the mainland and of hearing a little later that they had played havoc with the enemy's preparations for a big attack. The Navy, too, came up to scratch and patrolled so successfully that, for the time being, nothing more was heard of the enemy's invasion fleet. By the time I left, the German advance on Pelješac had been temporarily checked and the Partisans were holding their own.

But this temporary tactical success had not solved the much bigger, strategical problem. Everything showed that the intention of the enemy was, first to consolidate their hold on Dalmatia and the coast, and then to push across to the islands. They would use whatever forces they considered necessary to achieve this purpose, and, in an encounter of this kind they were clearly in a position to bear down the Partisans by sheer weight of numbers and armament. For the Partisans to make a stand, either on the coast or on the islands, for them to attempt, in other words, to hold fixed positions would be to flout the first principle of guerrilla warfare, and, to my mind, could only end in disaster.

On the other hand, if we lost the islands, we should be losing a very valuable asset. The secure possession of even one of them would provide a link with the outside world, a kind of advanced supply base, from which, even without a firm foothold on the coast, it should be possible, by judicious gun-running, to send a steady trickle of supplies over to the mainland and up into the interior. It might well be possible, if we could somehow manage to hold an island, to use it as a base from which M.T.B.s could raid enemy coastal traffic and shipping up and down the Adriatic. The first M.L. had after all shown the way and the success of her venture would, I felt, serve to reassure the Navy and encourage them to experiment further. Perhaps, though at that early stage the thought seemed almost fantastic, we might be able to find, somewhere among the crags and woods and olive groves, a flat strip from which fighter aircraft from Italy might operate, thereby greatly extending their range.

These were ideas which, if they were to come to anything, must be followed up at once. First I must see Tito. Then I must come out of Jugoslavia to report. My signals, it is true, had produced results. But before we could go any further there was still much that needed saying, many points that needed clearing up, the question of the islands among them. And the sooner they were cleared up the better.

That night we left for the mainland.

CHAPTER VII

BACK AND FORTH

THE Padre and his friends from the Odbor came down to the harbour to see us off. The news that the German advance was being held had cheered them up, but they were still worried about the future, knowing full well what a German occupation would mean for a civilian population which had sided so whole-heartedly with the Partisans.

I felt mean to be leaving them at such a time and tried to reassure them by saying that I would do what I could to help. They wished us God speed. It was beginning to get dark. We fitted ourselves into our little boat. The engine spluttered and chugged. We were off.

Baška Voda, the point from which we had crossed to Korčula, was now in German hands, and this time our destination was Podgora, another little port further to the north. At first we hugged the coast of the island. Then, when it was quite dark, changed our course and made straight for the mainland. Clearly the visit of the M.L. and the events which followed it had put the enemy on their guard, for now their patrol-boats were more active than ever. One of the Partisans had brought a concertina, which he played in a disjointed sort of way, the tune tailing off uneasily as the roving eye of a searchlight came swinging across the water in our direction. We were all suffering, I suppose, from the sensation which it is so difficult to escape on such occasions, and which leads so many fugitives from justice to betray themselves unnecessarily; the unpleasant feeling that you have no business where you are, that everyone is looking for you and that you are immensely conspicuous.

What, I remember wondering, would happen if they spotted us? Would they hail us and come and investigate? Or would they simply open fire down the beam of the searchlight? It would depend, I supposed, on how much they could see from where they were. Neither prospect was at all agreeable. But fortunately we seemed to be getting out of the stretch of water where the patrol-boats were most active.

Then, all at once I became aware of the chugging of a powerful engine unpleasantly close on our port bow. Simultaneously the accordion player, who had been in the middle of a spirited rendering of 'Alexander's Ragtime Band', broke off abruptly. With startling suddenness, the searchlight was switched on and, from quite close to us, a broad white beam started methodically to explore the surface of the sea. In a matter of seconds it caught us, and then, instead of continuing its search, stopped dead and held us dazzlingly illuminated while our little boat bobbed pathetically up and down in the choppy water.

Never have I had the feeling of being so utterly, so hideously conspicuous. Everyone, I felt, for miles round could see me, and I could see no one, except my immediate companions, also brilliantly illuminated: the accordion player, clutching his instrument as if his life depended on it, John Henniker-Major, looking faintly sheepish, and David Satow, looking, as he always looked, however unpromising the circumstances, every inch a professional soldier.

There was clearly nothing that we could usefully do except sit still, and so we sat still, counting the seconds and enduring the leisurely scrutiny of the anonymous German sailors at the other end of the beam. Would they, I wondered, notice my Balmoral, and David's very English and very military-looking hat and the Partisan flag fluttering so unnecessarily at the stern. Seen from close to, we did not look at all like fishermen.

But I suppose that a guilty conscience made us feel more noticeable than we really were, for, after examining us for what seemed an eternity, the patrol boat switched off its searchlight and chugged off busily to look for evildoers elsewhere. Once again darkness enveloped us; the accordionist struck up a new tune, and we continued on our way, shaken but thankful. The outcome had been an anticlimax, but it was an extremely welcome one.

We took as a matter of course the usual burst of machine-gun fire which greeted us as we entered the harbour of Podgora and flashed our little lantern what our steersman insisted was the prescribed number of times. Amid a string of oaths, followed by an animated discussion as to the merits and validity of different types of 'signals' we scrambled out of our boat and announced that we wished to continue our journey inland that night. We were told that this was inadvisable. At the moment a battle was in progress with a mixed force of Germans and Ustaše from Makarska, a village about a mile up the coast; the situation was confused; the exact position of the enemy was uncertain, and we should do much better to wait until morning before trying to move. As he spoke, the rattle of machine guns and the crash of mortar bombs from further up the road lent force to his words.

We still had some chocolate brought over by the M.L. and with this we decided to make some hot cocoa, before going on. Having repaired for this purpose to a nearby house, we were about to open the door of the living-room when we were stopped by a worried-looking peasant. There were some very important foreign officers inside, he said. They must on no account be disturbed. Clearly the situation had all kinds of fascinating possibilities and, ignoring the owner's panic-stricken protests, we pushed past him into the room.

Two prostrate figures, muffled in German-type sleeping-bags and snoring loudly, were stretched on the floor. We prodded the nearest one gently. It grunted resentfully and, on receiving a further prod, sat up, revealing the tousled head and unshaven chin of Gordon Alston. The other bag contained his wireless operator.

Gordon had, it appeared, just arrived from Jajce on his way to the islands, bringing me another wireless set and the latest news. He had completed the greater part of this journey in a one-horse shay, driven by a Bosnian Moslem, wearing a tarboosh and looking for all the world like a Cairo *gharri*-driver. He had had the greatest difficulty in communicating with this strange character and to this day is not sure whether the route they followed led them through country occupied by Partisans or not. As they drove along the inhabitants could be seen peering at them through the cracks of their doors. Nothing he could say or do would make the driver stop in a village for the night. To all Gordon's entreaties his only reply was to wink broadly, point at the village, and draw his hand meaningly across his throat, at the same time emitting an unpleasant guttural sound. Then he would whip up the horse and they would jolt relentlessly onwards. By the time they reached Podgora both Gordon and the horse were completely exhausted. It had, he said, been a very Balkan journey.

With them they had brought some mail from home which had been dropped in by parachute. They were the first letters to reach us and soon we were sitting round the stove drinking cocoa and reading them, while outside the sounds of the fighting up the road alternately receded and drew near again. The scenes and memories they evoked seemed somehow very remote.

Meanwhile there was one problem which needed clearing up immediately. 'What,' I asked, 'about the King?' 'What King?' said Gordon. 'King Peter,' I said. 'Have they dropped him in yet?' Gordon looked at me as if I had gone mad. Then I told him about the telegram. 'Oh,' he said, 'that wasn't about King Peter. That was about your new signal officer. His name is King.' I felt foolish, but relieved.

When we set out next morning, the fighting had died down and the enemy had withdrawn to Makarska, which we could see from the road, lying below us in the pale morning sunshine. A little further along we found some Partisans, lobbing shells into it with a captured 105-mm. gun, while from time to time the enemy rather half-heartedly returned the compliment from somewhere below. The remainder of our journey was by Partisan standards uneventful, though enlivened by the usual doubts as to where exactly the enemy was, whether we were on the right road and whether or not we should be able to get through.

As soon as we arrived at Jajce I went to see Tito to give him the latest news from the coast and to find out how the Partisans were faring elsewhere. He was fully alive to the threat to the islands and we discussed at length how it could best be countered. The conclusions we reached were not particularly encouraging. Clearly it would be a mistake for the Partisans to attempt more than a series of delaying actions, and this meant that sooner or later first the coastal strip and then the islands would fall into the hands of the enemy. Thus the only hope lay in direct and immediate Allied intervention, which, from all I knew, it would be no easy matter to secure.

I told Tito of my plan to return to Cairo to report, explaining that this would give me an opportunity of finding out for myself what prospect there was of securing effective Allied support in Dalmatia. I added that I would return as soon as possible. He agreed that this was a good idea and asked whether I would like to take two Partisan officers with me as emissaries of good will. I replied that I should be glad to, provided my twin masters, the Commander-in-Chief and the Foreign Office, agreed. After some discussion, two delegates were chosen, Lola Ribar and Miloje Milojević, and that night Tito brought them round himself to share our evening meal. When they had gone, we agreed that Tito's choice of delegates had been a good one.

Miloje Milojević was a fighting soldier. A regular officer in the old Jugoslav Army, he had joined the Partisans at the outset. In the years that followed he had lost an eye and been wounded in almost every part of his body. In recognition of repeated acts of gallantry, he had been made, in an army of brave men, the first and (at that time) only People's Hero, an award equivalent to our own Victoria Cross. A fierce little man, with a black patch over his eye and a scar on his face, he lived, as far as I could judge, only for fighting. No one who met him could doubt for long that the Partisans meant business.

Lola Ribar, whom I had met on my way down to the coast, was a different type. He, too, had had his full share of fighting. But his role in the Partisan movement had been primarily political, and, still in his twenties, he was one of the handful of men round Tito who seemed clearly marked out for fame in the new Jugoslavia. His father, Dr. Ivan Ribar, a venerable-looking elder statesman with a fine head of white hair, was one of the Movement's few links with the old regime. But Lola was an out and out Communist, and now, in a tattered German tunic, with his burning intensity of manner, his bronzed features and his characteristically Slav cast of countenance, he might have served as model for the portrait of a soldier of the Revolution. Once again I welcomed the choice. Young Ribar enjoyed Tito's confidence and was near enough to the centre of things to know the Party line on any given subject instinctively. He would be able to speak for the Partisans with assurance and authority. At the same time, his personal charm, which was great, and his knowledge of affairs would help to fit him for the task of emissary to the outside world which was totally strange and unfamiliar to most other Partisans, who were only at home in their own forests and villages.

Next morning I dispatched a signal asking for permission to come out to report, bringing two Partisan representatives with me. I added that it seemed likely that before long we should be completely cut off from the coast and that I hoped that it would be possible to send me a very early reply.

This, I realized from the start, was a pious hope. Politically, the decision which I had asked the Government to take was not an easy one. For the British authorities to receive Partisan representatives, although in a sense it was the logical sequel of the dispatch of my own Mission, was a step which would arouse the fiercest opposition on the part of the Royal Jugoslav Government, who were our allies and with whom we were in official relations. I pictured to myself the embarrassment which my signal would cause at home, did my best to explain it to Tito and settled down resignedly to a long wait.

As the days went by, the news from Dalmatia became more and more depressing. The Germans were steadily consolidating their position in the coastal strip and pushing along Pelješac in preparation for an invasion of the islands. Even our carefully prepared but never used landing-strip at Glamoć seemed unlikely to remain in Partisan hands much longer. Soon we should be completely cut off from the outside world. And still there was no reply to my signal.

In the end I decided to go back to the islands and await developments. Once there, I could easily make my way across the Adriatic by light naval craft or by Partisan schooner to Italy, and, in the meantime, while I was waiting for an answer, I could at any rate watch the military situation from close to. Ribar and Milojević stayed behind, ready to follow as soon as they knew they were wanted.

I started back to the coast in the first light of a chilly autumn morning. Of the journey I have no special recollection and therefore assume it to have been uneventful. In this I was lucky, for by now the German occupation in strength of this whole area was far advanced and we were fortunate to slip through with so little trouble.

This time our ultimate destination was the island of Hvar. We reached it after the usual midnight crossing in a fishing boat, landing just before dawn at the town of the same name at the western end of the island. The eastern end was occupied by a small force of the enemy, who had landed there from the mainland and whom it had so far proved impossible to dislodge.

Hvar was a pleasant enough place. On a hill overlooking the harbour the Spanish fort, a romantic looking castle built by Charles V, stood guard over the town. At its foot clustered crumbling palaces and churches, an arsenal and an ancient theatre – small, but of a magnificence recalling the splendours of Venice and surprising in what is now only a fishing village. Across the bay stretched a chain of small islands and black jagged rocks, sheltering the harbour from the westerly gales and squalls of the Adriatic. It was warm and sunny, a Mediterranean day, typical of Dalmatia and very different from the bleak, wintry weather which we had left inland.

Just as I had waited on Korčula for news of the Navy, now I waited on Hvar to know whether or not I was to come out and bring the Partisans with me. This time, at least, my wireless was working. We hitched our aerial to a convenient tree and soon a series of plaintive reminders were winging their way to Cairo and London. Would the answer come in time for Ribar and Milojević to reach the coast before it was too late?

The people of Hvar did their best to make my stay agreeable. Speeches were made, healths drunk and bouquets presented by small, squeaky anti-Fascist children, and there was much talk of victory and liberation. But the military situation scarcely justified much rejoicing, and through all the celebrations there ran an undercurrent of anxiety.

The last courier from the mainland, though travelling light and by himself, had narrowly escaped capture on his way down to the coast. According to his report, the large-scale German troop movements already in progress would soon make further communications between the coast and the interior practically impossible. The fighting on Pelješac, too, had flared up again, and the improvised hospital on Hvar was filling with fresh wounded, many of them boys and girls of twelve or thirteen, some with their arms and legs crudely amputated, a result of heavy and accurate German mortar-fire. Meanwhile, the enemy force which had landed at the other end of our own island, only a few miles away, though quiescent, were a constant reminder of what was to be expected. In fact, we now heard, it had already happened on the neighbouring island of Mljet, which for some days had been in German hands. The policy of the Germans was clear enough; to consolidate their position on the mainland and then pick off the islands at their leisure one by one. Nor could the Partisans muster locally a sufficient weight of men or equipment to resist this piecemeal encroachment.

The outlook was far from cheerful.

Finally the answer to my signal arrived. I was to come out to report forthwith. There was, it appeared, a special reason why I should come to Cairo immediately. Nothing had been decided about the Partisan delegation, who, the signal added nonchalantly, could follow later if required.

Reading it, I could not help wondering whether the official who, no doubt after leisurely reflection, had drafted it and placed it in his 'out' tray for dispatch, quite realized the difficulties of travel in German-occupied Europe. Already the journey down to the coast was extremely risky and in a matter of days it was likely to become quite impossible. The chances of Milojević and Ribar being able to follow when required seemed poor. I sent off a message to Tito, explaining as tactfully as possible that his delegation would have to mark time for a bit, and then set about making arrangements for my own journey.

The Navy, I had ascertained, were not prepared to come to Hvar to fetch me; the nearest that they would now venture to the coast being Vis, the most outlying of the whole group of islands. The journey from Hvar to Vis would accordingly have to be made by fishing boat.

A boat was produced, and at dawn on the following morning, after a night of buffeting on a rather choppy sea, I reached Vis. The M.L. that was to fetch me was not due until the following night, and I had the whole day in which to inspect the island.

The little town of Vis is built round a fine natural harbour at the northern end of the island. Commanding the entrance to the harbour, perched on rocks, one on each side of its mouth, stand two old forts. Climbing up to one, I found it decorated, surprisingly, with the crown and royal cipher of King George III of England. Its name, they told me, was Fort Wellington, while its companion, across the bay, was called Fort St. George. Both dated from the island's occupation by the British, who, I now learnt for the first time, had held it for several years during the Napoleonic wars, as had also, strangely enough, the Russians.

Not far away, as I strolled idly back to the town, I came upon an old walled garden, long since overgrown and fallen into decay. In the middle stood a marble obelisk, with on it an inscription in English celebrating a British naval victory won in 1811 over the French off Vis. Then, looking more closely, I found, hidden in the high grass and amongst the shrubs and undergrowth a dozen or so tombstones, commemorating British naval officers and seamen who had lost their lives in the battle, their names, good English names, almost obliterated by moss and weather.

Nearby, another monument, more flamboyant in style, proclaimed a later naval victory, that won here by the Austrians over the Italians in 1866, and somewhere in the back of my mind I seemed to remember, too, learning that Vis — the Issa of the ancients — had been the scene of a great battle in classical times.

But even without the reminders of history, a glance at the map shows clearly enough the strategical importance of Vis in any war fought round the Adriatic and in its waters. Lying, as it does, within striking distance of the coast and the other islands, yet far enough out to sea for it to be reasonably easy to hold and at the same time, easy of access from Italy, it makes an ideal base for an enemy wanting a foothold in the eastern Adriatic, particularly if he has a taste for piracy, a pursuit for which those waters have always been famous. Here, it seemed to me, was the base for which we were looking — if only help could be obtained in time.

The M.L. arrived that night and I went on board, as excited as a schoolboy going home for his first holidays. I felt as though I was going from one world to another. The wardroom of the M.L., with its framed photographs of wives and girl-friends, paper-backed novels, illustrated papers and cups of tea, seemed the height of civilization. The officers and crew treated us as though we were visitors from another planet and we were well on our way across the Adriatic before we turned in.

CHAPTER VIII

OUTSIDE WORLD

THE sun was up when I woke, and the coast of Italy was in sight. We had come straight across the Adriatic and were now sailing southwards along the Italian coast. I had spread my sleeping-bag on deck by one of the guns, and, propped on my elbow, I could see the church towers and white-washed houses of the little towns which stretch almost continuously along the east coast of southern Italy. In another hour we would reach our destination, Bari, which had been captured by Eighth Army not long before. I got up, rolled up my sleeping-bag, and went below to shave in preparation for my return to the outside world.

I had not been in Italy since 1939. Before the war, I had known it well. Since my last visit the Italians had become first our enemies and now, by another swing of the pendulum, our co-belligerents. It seemed strange to be going back. Vaguely I wondered what it would be like.

It was, needless to say, much the same.

The sun was shining and the Italians were busy basking in it. At every street corner good-looking young men, some in uniform, loafed with their hands in their pockets and cigarettes hanging out of the corner of their mouths. On the walls of the harbour, in letters a yard high, the Duce's inscriptions still proclaimed; VINCEREMO — VICTORY WILL BE OURS. Clearly it would have been a waste of energy to rub them out. They were the kind of inscriptions which did equally well whichever side you happened to be on.

In the Hotel Imperiale, which the Army, I was glad to find, had not yet had time to take over, there were hot baths and plenty of food and wine and officers on leave from the front dancing with nursing sisters to the animated strains of an Italian jazz band. 'Lili Marlene!' they shouted, and 'Lili Marlene' the Italians played, just as they must have played it for the Luftwaffe and Wehrmacht officers a few weeks before.

But, I had hardly had time to take it all in before I had been swept on board an aeroplane and was far out over the Mediterranean on my way to Cairo. At Malta we came down, circling low over the stony little fields and the bomb-scarred houses of Valetta. Lord Gort, the Governor, wanted to see us and we went to have a drink with him, a reassuringly solid figure amidst the Italianate magnificence of Government House.

Then we took off again and, falling asleep, I woke to find myself high above Libya, flying eastwards along the coast towards Egypt. Looking down, I could make out Benghazi, then Derna, then Tobruk and Sollum and the Qattara Depression. Here and there clusters of burnt-out tanks, planes, trucks and guns together with a myriad tracks, still scarring the desert, showed where one, two or three years before the fighting had been heaviest.

We reached Cairo in time for dinner. I accepted gratefully an invitation to stay with Kit Steel, in whose comfortable house in Zamalek I had spent the last week before leaving for Jugoslavia, in the days when we were still debating whether Tito existed at all, and, if so, whether he was a woman or a committee. I had left all my kit there, and so, when I went up to my room I found clean linen and a spotless tunic laid out for me, with highly polished buttons. My filthy battle-dress was discarded and I emerged a perfect 'Gaberdine Swine', as the leaders of military fashion in Cairo were known.

From Steel I heard why I had been so urgently summoned to Cairo. Mr. Eden, Sir Alexander Cadogan, William Strang, Oliver Harvey and half a dozen other Foreign Office officials were there on their way back from Moscow where they had been conferring with Molotov. Moreover it appeared that an even higher-powered conference was going to take place somewhere in the Middle East, which the Big Three themselves would attend, and Cairo, in those days of roundabout communications, lay on the road to almost everywhere. If I was ever to get a decision on our policy in Jugoslavia, now was the time and here was the place.

We were to have dinner that night with Cadogan. As I lay in my bath, I reflected that the last time I had seen him had been in his room in the Foreign Office when I had handed him my resignation from the

Diplomatic Service. It seemed a long time ago. Looking back on the few but crowded years between, it occurred to me forcibly how fortunate I had been in my decision and how lucky not to miss the experiences which had fallen to my lot in the intervening space of time. To me, it was not disagreeable to look forward to a future full of uncertainty and insecurity, with none of the slow inevitability of a career in the Government service; to feel myself, in however small a way, the master of my destiny. With my left foot I turned the hot-water tap full on and wallowed contentedly.

We dined under the stars on the roof of the Mohammed Ali Club, eating and drinking, under the supervision of Costi, that truly great *maître d'hôtel*, all the things that I had dreamt about in my hungrier and thirstier moments for months past, perfectly cooked and perfectly served. Round us at the other tables sat the collection of Egyptian pashas, Greek millionaires, exiled Princes, high-ranking British officers and cosmopolitan beauties that constituted Cairene society during the war. They gave an impression of great wealth and considerable elegance. It all seemed faintly improbable, but none the less agreeable. Contrasts, as I have said before, have always appealed to me and this after the life we had been leading was one with a vengeance.

Next day I saw Mr. Eden and gave him a written report on the situation in Jugoslavia which he undertook to pass on to the Prime Minister in time for his forthcoming meeting with Stalin and with the President of the United States, at the same time sending a copy to the Chief of the Imperial General Staff. Verbally, I repeated my main conclusions: that the Partisan Movement was of infinitely greater importance than was generally realized outside Jugoslavia; that it was very definitely under Communist leadership and firmly orientated towards Moscow; that as a resistance movement it was highly effective and that its effectiveness could be considerably increased by Allied help; but that, whether we gave such assistance or not, Tito and his followers would exercise decisive influence in Jugoslavia after the liberation.

When I flew back to Italy, nothing had been decided, but my report had caused something of a stir, and I was under instructions to return to Cairo in a few weeks, when, I gathered, Mr. Churchill himself would be there. In the meanwhile I was to go and fetch the Partisan delegation and bring them back with me.

This was easier said than done.

At Bari the news that greeted me was bad. The German offensive was in full swing in Bosnia and Dalmatia and the way to the coast definitely blocked. Not even single couriers were getting through. If Ribar and Milojević were to come out, an aeroplane would have to be landed to pick them up.

I sent a signal to Jajce, asking whether our carefully prepared landing-strip at Glamoč was still in Partisan hands. The answer came back that it was, but was unlikely to remain so very much longer. There was no time to be lost. The reluctance of the R.A.F. to let us have one of their aircraft for a fancy job of this kind must be overcome and an attempt made before it was too late.

The high-powered instructions which I had brought back with me from Cairo were a help. I went down to the H.Q. Tactical Air Force to see Air Vice-Marshal Broadhurst and came back with the promise, in principle, of an aircraft. The question now was, what sort of an aircraft? If the operation was to be carried out at night, it would have to be something that did not require too elaborate landing arrange-ments, for at Glamoč there would be no lights except a few bonfires, and the runway, to the best of my recollection, was distinctly undulat-ing. If, on the other hand, we were to go in by day, we should need something that could hold its own against enemy fighters, which at that stage of the war were fairly thick over Jugoslavia.

I explained this, diffidently and, I felt, rather amateurishly to T.A.F.

They were not impressed. They had, they said, plenty of far better uses for their aircraft than smashing them up in futile attempts to bring futile foreigners out of the Balkans. Nothing they had could land at night under the conditions described except a Lysander, and that was too small and would probably never get there. As to a landing by day, any aircraft that could carry passengers would almost certainly be shot down by the first enemy fighter it met.

It was at this stage of the proceedings that an entirely new character appeared on the scene. Realizing the importance to us of air operations,

I had asked the Air Officer Commander-in-Chief, Middle East, Air-Marshal Sholto Douglas, for a good air liaison officer, someone, I specified, with plenty of ordinary operational experience, and at the same time with a taste for irregular activities of the kind in which we were engaged. The result was Wing-Commander John Selby, D.S.O., D.F.C. It had taken some time to find him, but, when in the end he arrived, we agreed that he had been well worth waiting for.

John Selby's principal characteristic was his overwhelming enthusiasm. A large, plump, jolly man, he threw himself into whatever he was doing with an exuberance that at times was positively alarming. Before the war he had been an announcer on the B.B.C. Now, within a comparatively short time of joining the R.A.F., he had become a spectacularly successful pilot of night fighters and Mosquitoes. It appeared that he needed a rest from serious operations and was coming to us for a change. As a first step he had taken a course in parachuting and demolitions and bought himself a grammar of the German language, which he spoke with vividness rather than accuracy of expression. He arrived at T.A.F. H.Q. in a small and dangerous-looking aeroplane which he landed with unnerving suddenness. Vivian Street, who had accompanied him, got out of it looking rather green. I sympathized and decided to keep out of it at all costs.

I told Selby of my plans and of the difficulties which we were encountering. 'Leave that to me!' he said reassuringly, and went off to see a friend of his (every R.A.F. Headquarters abounded with long-lost friends of John Selby).

From these consultations he returned shortly after with the promise of a Baltimore, a fast light bomber, which, he assured me, was 'just the kite for the job'. All we now needed, he said, was a fighter escort, and I could then go in by day.

A fighter escort, however, was not so easy to come by. Glamoč was out of range of all but long-range fighters and nobody had any of these except the Americans. After some preliminary telephoning I accordingly set out, complete with Baltimore, for American 82nd Fighter Group, then situated at Lecce, to see what I could pick up from our American allies.

82nd Fighter Group had Lightnings. With their twin tails and bristling cannon, they were formidable-looking aircraft, like something out of H. G. Wells. They possessed sufficient range to do the round trip easily. It only remained to borrow half a dozen for an afternoon.

The Commanding Officer, on being approached said, Sure, I could have them. He was a tall, dark, rather saturnine young man in his twenties, with a full colonel's eagle badges and fine crop of decorations. His name was MacNichol and he had a great many German aircraft to his credit.

We fixed a date for the operation a couple of days later, and I at once sent a signal to Robin Whetherly and Bill Deakin, whom I had left in charge at Jajce, telling them to move the party down to Glamoć at once and stand by there for our arrival. In addition to Ribar and Milojević, the party for evacuation included Robin Whetherly himself, who, as an experienced regular soldier, would, I had decided, be a good man to watch developments on the islands, and Bill Deakin, who was going back to Cairo to act as my rear link with G.H.Q. With them to Glamoć went our liaison officer, Vlatko Velebit, and Donald Knight, the Sapper, whose job it was to get a landing-strip ready for us.

Next day a signal arrived from Robin to say that they had all arrived at Glamoć and would be ready to receive us there the day after. They would set fire to piles of damp straw, when they heard our engines, so as to guide us in by the smoke. 'Very cold here,' he added, 'please bring rum ration.'

While we were waiting to start I lived in the American mess, sharing a room with MacNichol and his second in command, Major Litten, another ace fighter-pilot. We had our meals in a vast mess room, all ranks eating together. The food was delicious once you got over the shock of finding a sly dab of jam amongst your sausages, or a cube of pineapple with the meat. It included such delicacies as tinned grapefruit and Frankfurter sausages and seemed unendingly varied after the monotony of our own rations. But the Americans grumbled about it. What they liked, they said, was that wonderful bully beef and meat and vegetable stew the British had.

At supper, while we were eating our corned-beef hash, MacNichol would walk round the tables picking pilots for the next day's missions.

Then next morning after breakfast there would be briefing; one would hear the roaring of the engines, as they warmed up, and then the Lightnings would take off. In the evening at supper they would be back, talking of their experiences, escorting the heavy bombers over Austria or northern Italy. Once or twice there were gaps at the tables, where someone had not come back. After supper there was usually a film. In bed at night, as I dropped off to sleep inside a vast American Army sleeping-bag, I could hear MacNichol and Litten talking over the day's operations and the prospects for the morrow. Some weeks later I heard that MacNichol had been shot down and killed.

The day appointed for my own venture dawned fine and bright. After breakfast there was briefing. At the request of MacNichol, who was flying one of the Lightnings himself, I gave a short account of the situation in Jugoslavia for the benefit of any of our escort who might be forced to crash-land or bale out, at the same time extending a cordial invitation to anyone who might find himself in such a predicament to come and stay at my Headquarters in the hills for as long as he liked. Then we went down to the airfield. My pilot and I (the rest of the crew had been eliminated to make room for the passengers we were to pick up), clambered up through the belly of the Baltimore; he showed me how the rear cannon fired, and how the intercom. worked; I fitted myself in as best I could; the engine roared, and we took off. Soon we were flying eastwards across the Adriatic, with the Lightnings wheeling and plunging round us till the sunlit sky seemed full of them. All was well that ended well. By the evening, I calculated, Ribar and Milojević would be safely out of Jugoslavia and we should all be on our way to Egypt.

But I had reckoned without the Jugoslav climate. Beneath us the Adriatic was a brilliant blue; the islands and the Dalmatian coast, when we reached them, were bathed in sunshine. Then, crossing the coast, we came to the Dinaric Alps and, climbing to fly over their jagged crests, suddenly found ourselves enveloped in a blinding snowstorm. Turning back, we skirted along the mountain range, looking for a gap. But it was no good. Along the whole length of the range there stretched a forbidding, impenetrable wall of black storm clouds, marking, as it were, the frontier between one climatic system and another. There was nothing for it but to turn back and try again another day. Over the wireless we consulted the Lightnings. They thought so too. Soon we were all heading back for Italy.

Next day we repeated the attempt, with the same result. The sea and the Dalmatian coast were bathed in sunshine, but once again over the mountains we ran into the same insuperable barrier of cloud. When we got back I found a rather plaintive signal from Robin Whetherly asking when we were coming and reminding me about the rum. The outlook was poor, for I knew that the Americans needed all their fighters for some days to come to escort the heavy bombers on a series of all-out attacks on targets in northern Italy.

The day after, I asked my pilot, a cheerful young New Zealander, if he thought we really needed an escort. He said that, unless we had bad luck, he could probably get away from anything except a very up-to-date fighter. I asked him if he would get into trouble if we went without an escort. He replied cheerfully that, if we came back safely, no one would say anything, and, if we didn't, it wouldn't matter anyway. This seemed sound enough logic, and so we sent off a signal to Robin, announcing our arrival, and set off on our own.

The weather was fine when we started, and we skimmed across the Adriatic, just above the crests of the waves, keeping well out of the way of marauding enemy fighters. As we approached the coast, we began to climb, leaving Vis, Korčula, Hvar and the other islands far below us. There was cloud over the coast, but this time it was not so thick, and through the gaps we could see the town and harbour of Split, with its dockyards and shipping spread out beneath us. Evidently we, too, could be seen from the ground, for almost immediately shells from the city's anti-aircraft batteries began to burst round us in white puffs of smoke.

Soon we had left the coast behind us and were in the hills, flying over the same barren, rocky country through which I had tramped on my way down to the coast in the autumn. From the air the mountain tracks were discernible as thin lines winding across the grey rock face. But as we flew inland, the cloud grew thicker and patches of snow began to show on the hillsides. Caught in sudden air currents, the little bomber lurched and jolted sickeningly. For several minutes at a time we would be flying through dense white cloud, then, with unnerving suddenness, a dark hill-top would plunge into view alarmingly near, and the pilot would swing the aircraft upwards or sideways to avoid it. I held on tight.

Peering first out of the side window and then, rather gingerly, through the gaping hole in the floor, I tried to make out where we were. I could see nothing but a blanket of mist, with, projecting from it, half a dozen nondescript mountain spurs. I was contemplating these gloomily, when a buzzing from the intercom. indicated that the pilot wanted to talk to me. I put on the headphones.

'We're over the place now,' he shouted. 'Hold on tight, I am going to try to get under the cloud.'

I held on tighter than ever. There followed some minutes of plunging and swerving through white obscurity. Then the intercom. buzzed again.

'It's no good,' the pilot said. 'I can't make it. We may as well go home.'

It was maddening to think of the Partisans with Robin Whetherly and Bill Deakin standing in the snow a few hundred feet beneath us, listening to the sound of our engines as we circled round and peering upwards through the mist. I was wearing a parachute and for a moment I considered an impromptu jump. But, apart from the pleasure which it would have given me to see my friends again, this would clearly have served no useful purpose, for the Partisan Mission would have been as far from Cairo as ever. So, reluctantly, I signified my agreement to the pilot, and once again we turned for home.

Even now our troubles were not at an end. Crossing the Adriatic we found the whole of southern Italy enveloped in a vast thunderstorm. The rain streamed down in torrents and great mountains of dark cloud, shot with lightning, towered over the coast. At Lecce we found we could not land because of low cloud. From the ground they suggested that we might try Foggia, a hundred and fifty miles to the north. There, we found visibility no better than at Lecce. Meanwhile it was getting dark and our petrol was running out. There was nothing for it but to make the best landing we could and trust to luck. As we finally skidded to rest on a waterlogged airfield, after prolonged circling through successive layers of cloud and rain, I felt that I had had enough flying for one day.

The next forty-eight hours we spent grounded at Foggia in a downpour of rain, vainly trying to communicate with the outside world over a singularly shaky field telephone. When, two days later, we finally reached Bari, events had taken a new and surprising turn. A signal had been received from Robin Whetherly to say that the Partisans had succeeded in capturing a small German aeroplane intact and were proposing to fly the party out in it at once. There was barely time to warn the R.A.F. and the anti-aircraft batteries not to shoot down a small aircraft with German markings, coming from the direction of Jugoslavia. Then we settled down to wait for news of the party's arrival in Italy.

The signal, when it came, was from Bill Deakin, still in Jugoslavia. The news it brought was bad.

The captured aircraft had duly been brought to the landing-strip outside Glamoč at dusk on the evening before the day fixed for the flight. There, it had been filled with enough petrol, it was hoped, to carry it across the Adriatic. Everything had been done to keep the move secret and to avoid attracting attention.

At first light on the appointed day the party had assembled on the bleak windswept plain. It was bitterly cold and the engine took some time to start. As the pilot, a deserter from the Croat Air Force, was warming it up, the passengers and those who had come to see them off had gathered round the aircraft, for there was no time to be lost.

It was at this moment that, looking up, the little group round the aircraft saw, coming over the crest of the nearest hill, a small German observation plane. Before they could move, it was over them, only a few dozen feet above their heads, and, as they watched, fascinated, two small bombs came tumbling out. One fell near where Robin Whetherly and Bill Deakin were standing and without exploding, came trundling over the ground towards them like a football. Robin, who saw it first, clutched at Bill's arm to warn him and they both threw themselves to the ground. As they did so, the bomb exploded, killing Robin who had not been quick enough. The other bomb burst full on the aircraft, destroying it completely and killing Donald

Knight and Lola Ribar, and wounding Miloje Milojević. Then, having dropped his bombs, the German flew off, machine-gunning the survivors as he went. Afterwards we learned that a traitor had warned the enemy, whose nearest outposts were only a few miles away, of what was afoot.

It was sad news indeed. In Robin Whetherly and Donald Knight I had lost two good friends and two of my best officers. In Lola Ribar the Partisans had lost yet another of their outstanding younger leaders and one who had seemed destined to play a great part in building the new Jugoslavia. For his old father, too, whose other son had been killed in action a few weeks before, it would, I knew, be a crushing blow. We had paid heavily for the two or three weeks which it had taken to reach a decision as to the movements of the delegation. Now one of them was dead and the other wounded and Cairo as far away as ever.

But the Jugoslavs had not given up the idea of dispatching representatives to Cairo. Velebit, our liaison officer, who had been standing by the aircraft at the time of the bombing, but had somehow escaped injury, was appointed to take Ribar's place, while Milojević was to go to Cairo, too, wounds or no wounds. Once again I set about trying to find an aeroplane and an escort. Meanwhile, fierce fighting was in progress in Bosnia and the landing-strip at Glamoć seemed unlikely to remain in Partisan hands for much longer.

This time the operation was given a higher priority, and on the first fine day I set out for Glamoć in a troop-carrying Dakota, lumbering along massively, while half a squadron of Lightnings circled and twisted round us, suiting their pace to ours. John Selby, on his way in to join my Headquarters, was amusing himself by flying the aircraft, while the pilot, who had no doubt heard of his exploits in night fighters and Mosquitoes, looked on in awe.

The flight, under John Selby's expert guidance, was uneventful, and presently, having circled the plain of Glamoć and located the signal fires, our Dakota was jolting to a standstill on the uneven turf of the landing-strip, as if it was the simplest thing in the world to land in the middle of an enemy-occupied country in broad daylight.

The doors were opened and we scrambled out. Snow lay on the surrounding hills and a cold, blustering wind was blowing across the plain. Bill Deakin and Vlatko Velebit came running towards us. Above us the Lightnings circled, on the look out for the enemy. There was no time to be lost. Miloje Milojević, wrapped in a blanket and lying on a roughly made stretcher was hoisted gently into the aircraft and after him Vlado Dedjer, another leading Partisan, who had been dangerously wounded in the head and whose life, it was thought, might be saved by an operation. Next followed Anthony Hunter, who had been with the Croatian Partisans and was coming out to report.

Finally, at the point of Sergeant Duncan's tommy-gun, came Captain Meyer of the German Abwehr, who had had the ill chance to be captured by the Partisans while on his way to visit a neighbouring Četnik commander, and was now being sent to Italy for expert interrogation.

On his face was a look of blank amazement, which was perhaps scarcely to be wondered at if you considered his recent experiences. First, the ambush as he was driving peaceably along the road in his car; next his few hours of captivity with the Partisans, with, in the back of his mind, the certainty that death was imminent; then the journey with his hands tied and under escort, to this lonely spot, so well suited for an execution; and finally, when he was convinced that his last moment had come, the sudden appearance in broad daylight of an Allied aeroplane, by which he was evidently going to be removed to an unknown destination. To complete his bewilderment came a cordial handshake from one of the new arrivals who was anxious to make a favourable impression on everyone and had in the confusion taken him for a Partisan.

As soon as all those who were remaining behind were out and all those who were leaving were inside, the doors were shut, the engines, which had been kept running all the time, roared and we jolted off again in a successful, but somewhat unorthodox take-off. As we rose abruptly into the air, we could see John Henniker-Major, who had come to take charge of the newcomers, striding off at the head of his little party. The first landing operation to be carried out in enemy-occupied Jugoslavia had been successfully completed.

At Bari, where we landed, feeling rather pleased with ourselves, there was no one to meet us and one or two explosive telephone calls elicited the information that no one had heard of us, that no arrangements had been made for our onward journey and that no aircraft was available to take us to Egypt, where we were due next day.

This was deplorable. Clearly someone had blundered. I was particularly anxious that the Partisans should be impressed by the smoothness and efficiency of the arrangements which had been made for their reception and it was only too clear that this result was not being achieved. Velebit, restored to civilization for the first time for three years, was looking about him without enthusiasm. Milojević was evidently suffering great pain from his wounds. Dedjer, lying unconscious on his stretcher, his head wrapped in bloodstained bandages, his face a greyish green, his breathing stertorous, seemed on the point of death. The Abwehr man, with Sergeant Duncan's tommy-gun still in the small of his back and with no one to take him away was still looking bewildered. The pilot and crew of the aeroplane, having done what was required of them, had packed up and were preparing to go off duty.

Clearly, if we were going to get anywhere, something would have to be done quickly. I put our problem to the captain of the Dakota. He explained that his orders had been to bring us back to Bari and no further. 'But,' he added with a broad grin, 'if you were to give me a direct order to fly you on to Alexandria, it would be impossible for me to refuse. There will probably be a row afterwards, but that will be your look out.'

This was good enough. The direct order was given with alacrity, and the crew, who clearly fancied the idea of a trip to Egypt, immediately set about filling up with petrol and finding out whether Malta, where we would have to come down, was equipped for night landings. There only remained our German prisoner to dispose of. Eventually, after much searching, two military policemen, resplendent in their red caps, pipe-clayed belts and shining brass, were found to take charge of him, and with these he went off, glad to see the last of Sergeant Duncan and finally convinced, I think, that he was not going to be shot. Then the rest of us, wounded and all, bundled back into the plane; the engines started up; soon we were far out over the Mediterranean.

CHAPTER IX

TURNING POINT

A T Alexandria, where we landed at dawn next morning, everything was ready for us. An agreeable villa had been set aside for the Partisans and, as we drove up to the gate, a guard of Riflemen turned out and presented arms with a rattle and crash. An ambulance swept off the two wounded men to hospital. I recognized the work of my old friends Mark Chapman Walker and Hermione Ranfurly, the Commander-in-Chief's highly efficient Military Assistant and Private Secretary.

An operation was needed to extract the fragments of the bomb from Miloje's much scarred body and it would be some days before he would be able to do any work. Vlatko, too, clearly required time to recover from the stress and strain of the last few days and the sudden plunge back into civilization after the long months and years of guerrilla life. Leaving them to settle into their new surroundings, I went up to Cairo to report, taking Bill Deakin with me.

Cairo was buzzing. In spite of the most elaborate security arrangements, everyone knew that Mr. Churchill and the President of the United States were there. They had arrived a few days before from Teheran, where according to the latest Press releases, there had been a conference with Marshal Stalin. Now, it appeared, a further conference was in progress at which Generalissimo Chiang-Kai-shek would also be present. The whole place was swarming with high officials, admirals, generals and air-marshals. All Whitehall seemed to be there. If we did not get our particular problem cleared up now, we never should.

The first thing was to see the Prime Minister. We found him installed in a villa out by the Pyramids. He was in bed when we arrived, smoking a cigar and wearing an embroidered dressing-gown. He started by telling us some anecdotes about the Teheran Conference and his meeting with Stalin. This, it appeared, had been a success.

Then he asked me whether I wore a kilt when I was dropped out of an aeroplane, and from this promising point of departure, we slid into a general discussion of the situation in Jugoslavia. He had read my report, and in its light and in the light of all other available information, had talked over the Jugoslav problem with Stalin and Roosevelt at Teheran. As a result of these talks, it had been decided to give all-out support to the Partisans.

There remained the question of the Četniks of General Mihajlović, to whom up to then we had been giving rather more help than to the Partisans and to whom a British Military Mission was still accredited. It appeared that evidence from a number of sources, and notably the reports of British officers attached to Četnik formations, confirmed the impression which I myself had gained, namely, that General Mihajlović had for some time past been anything but whole-hearted in his resistance to the Germans; that discipline amongst his forces was poor, and that many of his commanders were collaborating more or less openly with the enemy. In short, his contribution to the Allied cause was by now little or nothing, such operations as were performed being largely the work of the small number of British officers who were attached to the Četnik forces. In the circumstances, it was proposed to give Mihajlović a last chance. He was to be requested through the British Mission attached to his Headquarters, to blow up a certain railway bridge of considerable strategic importance on the Belgrade-Salonika railway. If he failed to carry out this operation by a certain date, the Mission would be withdrawn and supplies to the Četniks would cease. This seemed fair enough.

I now emphasized to Mr. Churchill the other points which I had already made in my report, namely, that in my view the Partisans, whether we helped them or not, would be the decisive political factor in Jugoslavia after the war and, secondly, that Tito and the other leaders of the Movement were openly and avowedly Communist and that the system which they would establish would inevitably be on Soviet lines and, in all probability, strongly orientated towards the Soviet Union.

The Prime Minister's reply resolved my doubts.

'Do you intend,' he asked, 'to make Jugoslavia your home after the war?'

'No, Sir,' I replied.

'Neither do I,' he said. 'And, that being so, the less you and I worry about the form of Government they set up, the better. That is for them to decide. What interests us is, which of them is doing most harm to the Germans?'

Thinking our conversation over afterwards, I felt convinced that this was the right decision. In 1943, the turning-point of the war had been reached, but this was by no means as clear then as it is now. In Italy our armies were still south of Rome and making but slow progress. The Normandy landings were only a remote project. On the Eastern Front, the Germans still stood at the gates of Leningrad and Moscow. The American war effort was as yet only beginning to get into its stride. In the Far East the Japanese were still undefeated. If we were to make certain of achieving ultimate victory and of achieving it without unnecessarily prolonging the bloodshed and destruction, we could not afford to neglect any potential ally. In 1941, when we stood alone, we had thankfully accepted Russia as an ally, without examining too closely her political system or the circumstances which had brought her into the war on our side. Ever since, we had done everything in our power to bolster up her war effort. Having once taken this major decision of principle, to refuse help to the Jugoslav Partisans on ideological grounds would have been scarcely logical. Nor would it have been an easy decision to defend on any grounds, for we should have been abandoning to their fate, on the basis of a long-term political calculation, brave men, who, whatever their motives, were fighting well and effectively on our side in a desperate struggle against a common enemy. Besides, taking a long view, it seemed just conceivable that in the end nationalism might triumph over Communism. Stranger things had happened in the Balkans.

But there was one aspect of the situation which was still disturbing Mr. Churchill. In 1941, after Prince Paul had come to terms with the Germans, King Peter of Jugoslavia, still in his teens, had headed the revolt which threw out the Regent and his Government and brought the country into the war on the side of Great Britain, at that time fighting alone against the Axis. Then, when the German invasion and occupation had forced him to fly, he had taken refuge in Great Britain where he had formed a Government in Exile. This Government had from the outset backed Mihajlović and shown a corresponding hostility towards Tito, whom they regarded as a dangerous revolutionary upstart.

The British Government now found themselves in an awkward situation. Morally, they were under a definite obligation to King Peter, who had thrown in his lot with Great Britain in her hour of need, and politically they were committed to his Government, with whom they were in diplomatic relations. But they were now about to commit themselves militarily to the Partisans, whom both King and Government regarded with repugnance and distrust — sentiments which the Partisans were inclined to reciprocate.

King Peter had recently moved to Cairo, theoretically in order to be nearer Jugoslavia, and it was felt that it might be useful if, while I was in Cairo, I saw the King and gave him a first-hand account of the situation in Jugoslavia. It was accordingly arranged that we should dine t›gether with Ralph Stevenson, who at that time held the post of British Ambassador to the Jugoslav Government in Exile.

King Peter, I found, was a friendly young man, happiest when he was talking about motor cars and aeroplanes, but also, I feel certain, genuinely interested in the fate of his unfortunate country and people. He asked me what the Partisans and the other Jugoslavs I had met thought of him. I told him that they resented some of the proclamations which had been made in his name over the wireless, condemning their leaders to death as traitors. Apart from that, they did not take much interest in him. Their day to day life gave them too much to think about. Next he asked me what prospect I thought he had of recovering his throne after the war. I replied, None, unless he could somehow go back and take part in the war of liberation, side by side with his people, as his father had done in the last war. Otherwise the gap between him and them would be too wide. They had undergone too much, and were too obsessed with their experiences, ever to be ruled over by a King who, through no fault of his own, had spent most of the war years in London or Cairo.

King Peter listened attentively. 'I wish,' he replied as he said goodbye, 'that it only depended on me.'

The decision to give all the help in our power to the Partisans provided a new and firm basis for the military discussions which now opened at Alexandria. These covered a wide range of subjects. Air-Marshal Sholto Douglas, the Air Officer Commander-in-Chief, promised to train and equip a Jugoslav fighter squadron, and General Wilson a tank regiment, while the Naval Commander-in-Chief, Admiral Willis, undertook to find some light naval craft to form the nucleus of a Partisan navy, in addition to the British naval forces, which, it was agreed, should operate off the Dalmatian coast.

But these were long-term projects, affecting a much later phase of the war, for clearly, under existing conditions, there could be no question of sending either tanks or aircraft to operate from bases in Jugoslavia, and it would take a considerable time to find men suitable for the purpose, get them out of Jugoslavia and train them in Italy or North Africa. In reality, the most important subjects discussed at Alexandria were the burning questions of air supply and air support, both of which directly affected the immediate conduct of operations in what was coming to be regarded as the Jugoslav theatre of war.

Here the decisions taken were of immediate and far-reaching importance. In the first place it was decided to increase substantially the allotment of supplies to the Partisans, and, equally important, the number of aircraft set aside for supply dropping. These would operate from airfields in southern Italy and a supply base would be established at Bari. It was also confirmed that the scope of my Mission should be extended and that a number of British officers serving under my command should be dropped to the principal Partisan formations throughout Jugoslavia. Their main task would be to organize supplies, but they would also include a certain number of technical advisers and instructors.

With the expansion of my Mission, I needed more officers, and, before leaving Egypt, I set about recruiting some. The first cover to draw, I decided, was Peter Stirling's flat in Cairo. Now that David Stirling was a prisoner and Bill in Algiers with the 2nd S.A.S. Regiment, it no longer had quite the same air of an operations room or an armed camp as previously, but there were nevertheless generally still quite a number of enterprising characters to be found there. Moreover, now that Cairo had become more or less of a backwater, you could be certain that any likely recruits would jump at the chance of a fairly active job.

Peter's food and drink, I found, was as good and plentiful as ever and was still served by Peter's Arab servant, Mohammed or Mo, to the same accompaniment of grumbling and backchat. The party was a cheerful one. Though not, it appeared, quite so animated as another party which had taken place there some weeks earlier, after which the host had woken next morning to find an entirely unexplained donkey tethered to the foot of his bed and quietly nibbling a basketful of Gloire de Dijon roses.

A few days before, the Foreign Secretary had announced for the first time in a speech in the House of Commons that I had been dropped by parachute into Jugoslavia, thereby causing, I believe, a mild sensation, for I had never attended the House and none of my fellow members had the faintest idea who 'the honourable Member for Lancaster' was. Now someone produced a copy of the *Daily Express*, which had made headline news of the announcement. Down the middle of the front page stretched an immensely elongated photograph of myself in uniform, with, beneath it, the caption: KILTED PIMPERNEL, and, beneath that, a good deal more colour stuff in the same vein.

This took a lot of living down. In the end it was Mo, who came to my rescue. 'Bugadier very fine fellow,' he remarked soothingly. 'One day he catchit scissors,' — a prophetic reference to the crossed swords of a Major General, which was only to be temporarily fulfilled at a very much later date. After that we mixed a delicious drink in the bath tub, and a good time, as the saying goes, was had by all.

This made a pleasant change from the round of staff talks and conferences. Nor did I leave Cairo empty handed. Before flying back to Italy, I made several additions to my officer strength. One was Andrew Maxwell, of the Scots Guards, a cousin of the Stirlings, who, while on leave from his Battalion, had accompanied the S.A.S. on their last expedition to Benghazi. Another was John Clarke, a former Adjutant of the 2nd Scots Guards and a regular soldier, who, having just emerged from a course at the staff college, was desperately afraid of being put into a sedentary staff job. Then there was Geoffrey Kup, a gunnery expert, who I intended should instruct the Partisans in the use of a battery of 75-mm. Pack Howitzers which we had promised them, complete with mules. Finally there was Randolph Churchill. After taking part in the Salerno landings with Bob Laycock's Commandos, he had accompanied his father to Teheran and Cairo and was now at a loose end. Randolph, it occurred to me, would make a useful addition to my Mission. There were some jobs — work, for instance, of a sedentary description at a large Headquarters, full of touchy or sensitive staff officers — for which I would not have chosen him. But for my present purposes he seemed just the man. On operations I knew him to be thoroughly dependable, possessing both endurance and determination. He was also gifted with an acute intelligence and a very considerable background of general politics, neither of which would come amiss in Jugoslavia. I felt, too — rightly, as it turned out — that he would get on well with the Jugoslavs, for his enthusiastic and at times explosive approach to life was not unlike their own. Lastly I knew him to be a stimulating companion, an important consideration in the circumstances under which we lived.

On my return to Italy I found the news from Jugoslavia was increasingly disquieting. The enemy's drive to the coast had developed into a general offensive and Livno and Glamoć had fallen. In the islands the situation was more serious than ever; island after island had been recaptured by the enemy, and it seemed likely to be only a matter of weeks, if not days, before we lost our last foothold there.

This brought my mind back from the general problem to the particular one, and to my old project of establishing a firm base on Vis or one of the other islands before it was too late. I decided that before rejoining Tito in Bosnia I would go across and have a look for myself.

We made the journey this time in a motor-torpedo boat, roaring across the Adriatic in what must have been record time. As we reached the open sea, we met two Hunt Class destroyers, returning from a patrol in enemy waters. They were a fine sight, travelling at full speed, with the sea boiling and seething in their wake. Evidently the Navy were already beginning to devote more attention to these parts.

Our first port of call was Velaluka on the island of Korčula, where we landed the arms and ammunition we had brought with us. The Pelješac peninsula had been evacuated under heavy pressure from the enemy and the whole island was now filled with Partisans from the mainland preparing as best they could to beat off the German landing in force which was bound to follow soon.

From Velaluka we made our way across the island to the town of Korčula, where the brunt of the attack seemed likely to fall. Here the bulk of the defending forces was concentrated, and little remained of the peaceful scene which I remembered from the autumn. Gun positions and strong-points were established everywhere and many of the buildings had already been damaged by enemy shell-fire. From the garden of the little house in which I had lived during my previous visit, we could see the Germans moving about on Pelješac across the water. At the same time they saw us and a salvo of shells came whistling across the straits and landed in the rocks behind the house; the Partisans, with the guns they had taken from the Italians, replied, and we ate our lunch to the accompaniment of an artillery duel.

But it was only too clear that the Partisans had but little prospect of holding out. In the first place the defence of fixed positions was manifestly the wrong role for guerrilla forces, and, in any case, the enemy forces opposing them possessed a crushing superiority both in numbers and armament. And indeed, a few days later, Korčula fell to the Germans.

This applied with equal force to the other islands. Once one had fallen, the others would be likely to follow. Nor would it be sound strategy for the Partisans to devote more than limited resources to opposing the German landings. Indeed, in the long run, it might actually prove to our advantage to allow the Germans to establish garrisons on the islands, for these, from the German point of view, would be useless and costly to maintain, while to us they would offer easy targets for raids, sabotage and harassing operations of all kinds. But, to put this policy into effect, we must have a base and if such a base was to be held, the necessary measures would need to be taken quickly, and outside help would be required.

The more we talked the problem over and the more we studied the map, the clearer it became that, our base, if there were to be one, would have to be Vis. I decided to go there at once and study the problem on the spot, taking Velebit with me.

Vivian Street, who had remained on the islands while I had gone to Egypt, was there to meet us. It was after midnight when we arrived and, turning off the road at the first gate we came to, I spread out my sleeping-bag on a flat stone and went to sleep. When I woke, the sun was up and, looking round me, I found that I had been sleeping in a graveyard. The priest's house was nearby, and there we washed and ate our rations. After breakfast we set out to make a thorough reconnaissance of the island.

Vis, like its neighbours, is a craggy, rock-strewn island, with every square yard of arable land under cultivation. Two parallel ranges of hills run the whole length of the island from east to west. Between them lies a long fertile valley, planted at that time with vines and olives. Most of the population is concentrated in the two small towns of Vis and Komiša, of which the first lies at the eastern end and the latter at the western end of the island. Both cluster round the two principal harbours of the island and are little more than fishing villages, though deriving a certain dignity from the crumbling forts and mansions bequeathed to them by the Venetians and those who followed them.

We stopped to eat our midday meal at a farm-house, perched on a hill overlooking the smiling vineyards and olive groves of the central valley. The R.A.F. officer whom we had brought with us was in a state of some excitement. He had examined the valley from every angle and had come to the conclusion that it could be converted into a first-class airfield. To the uninitiated this was not so immediately obvious and one's mind dwelt involuntarily on the destruction which this transformation would involve. But he was the expert and the conclusion which he had reached was clearly of very considerable importance, as Velebit and the other Partisans present were the first to recognize. If Allied fighters could be based here or could even land here to refuel, their range, for operations over Jugoslavia, would immediately be increased by the whole width of the Adriatic.

This discovery constituted another, very cogent argument for the establishment of a firm base on Vis. The Royal Navy, whose light craft were already operating most successfully against enemy shipping from temporary bases in the islands, though without any real security of tenure, were, we knew, strongly in favour of the idea and would clearly welcome the prospect of occasional fighter support.

But before we could go any further, a garrison had to be found. It was calculated that a force of at least two Brigades would be required to hold the island. The Partisans offered to provide one Brigade, if we would furnish the other. Clearly it was most desirable that we should find one. I left the island wondering where it was to come from.

I had made tentative soundings as to the possibility of British troops taking part in the defence of the islands before leaving Cairo, but without success. Our fighting troops in the Middle East had long since been reduced to a bare minimum and every man who could be spared sent to Italy. Our troops in Italy came under a separate command, 15 Army Group, with whom I had as yet had no direct contact. From what I knew of the military situation in Italy, however, I did not imagine that General Alexander, then commanding 15 Army Group, would have even a Brigade to spare for a side-show like ours.

A first approach to 15 Army Group met with the reply which I had expected, namely, that they wished they could help, but were themselves short of men. Then, by chance, I stumbled on what seemed a possible solution.

Randolph, essentially gregarious by nature, happened to meet in Bari a friend and also a namesake of his, Jack Churchill, then commanding No. 2 Commando, whom he had known at Salerno. Jack Churchill and his brother Tom, who was commanding the Commando Brigade, of which No. 2 Commando formed a part, then asked Randolph and myself to come to a party which they were giving on New Year's Eve in their mess at Molfetta, up the coast from Bari.

Once there, I soon realized that the Churchill brothers were an outstanding pair. Both were regular soldiers. Jack, the elder, had the dashing and formidable appearance which one generally associates with a Barbary corsair or a condottiere of the Renaissance, an impression which was enhanced by a highly polished and extremely deadly looking dagger which he was wearing in his Sam Browne belt, while the medal ribbons on his tunic showed that it was not only their dashing appearance that he shared, but their soldierly qualities as well. Tom, the younger brother, who commanded the Brigade, was also an experienced fighting soldier. Half an hour's conversation with him showed me that he possessed a penetrating intelligence.

Inevitably we talked shop. I asked him what plans he had for his Commandos. He asked me whether I had ever thought of the possibility of harassing operations on the Dalmatian coast and islands. I replied that for some weeks past I had been thinking of little else.

While the party continued to run its somewhat noisy course next door, Tom Churchill and I repaired to his room, where we could look at the maps and talk in peace. I explained to him the situation in the islands, and we discussed its possibilities from an operational point of view. It seemed to me that, if only one Commando or even a smaller detachment could be sent to Vis immediately, we could find plenty for it to do, and the mere fact of its presence would show that we meant business. Tom, who had long felt that the Dalmatian Islands offered great possibilities for his type of troops, was keen on the idea, and, by the time that 1944 had been seen in, it had been agreed that I should go and see General Alexander and put the idea to him personally.

This I did a day or two later. I found the Commander-in-Chief and his Chief of Staff, General John Harding, much more interested in the Jugoslav situation than I had expected. They felt it had a direct bearing on the problems with which they themselves were faced in Italy. This in itself was hopeful. When I broached the subject of the Commandos, they repeated what I had already heard about their shortage of men, but added that the future of the Italian campaign and of the whole war in the Mediterranean was to be discussed at a high-level conference in the immediate future and that, once future plans had been decided, it might after all prove possible to make one or more Commandos available for garrisoning Vis. The conference was to take place at Marrakech in Morocco, where the Prime Minister was convalescing after the severe attack of pneumonia which had struck him down immediately after the Cairo Conference, and General Alexander said that, if I liked, he would give me a lift there in his own aeroplane. The point could then be put to Mr. Churchill and a decision obtained. Randolph, who welcomed this opportunity of seeing his father, came too.

The flight to Morocco in the Commander-in-Chief's aeroplane was a comfortable one. We landed briefly at Algiers, and then set out across the Sahara. General Alexander, I noticed, was reading a German grammar. General Harding had gone to sleep. I followed his example. When I woke, we were over what I took to be the Atlas Mountains, and already starting to come down.

The air over Marrakech aerodrome seemed full of Flying Fortresses and Liberators landing or taking off, for it was a staging-point on the supply route from America to the Mediterranean. Lined up on the ground were numerous aircraft of varying degrees of magnificence, belonging to the various British and American generals, admirals and air-marshals who were attending the conference. General Wilson was among them and Mark Chapman Walker, his Military Assistant, came to meet us. As we were getting into one of the immense American staff cars, which were to take us to our destination, Mark told me that General Wilson had been appointed Supreme Allied Commander, Mediterranean theatre, in succession to General Eisenhower. He added that I was to remain directly responsible to him, as I had been when he was Commander-in-Chief Middle East. I was glad to hear that this association, always a happy one as far as I was concerned, was to continue.

The Prime Minister was installed in an agreeable villa in the Moorish style on the outskirts of Marrakech. He was wearing a bright blue boiler-suit, and, considering how ill he had been a week or two before, appeared remarkably well. It soon became abundantly clear that he had lost none of his old energy or resilience.

I took no part in the formal meetings of the conference. Indeed I made a special point of not being told more about the proceedings than was absolutely necessary, for in a few days' time I was due to be dropped back into an enemy-occupied country, where the possibility of being taken prisoner could never be excluded, and, with the Gestapo's methods of interrogation as good as they were known to be, it was inadvisable for anyone who ran any risk of falling into their hands to know more about the future conduct of the war than was absolutely necessary. The project under discussion was, I gathered, an 'aquatic hook' which was to be carried out on the west coast of Italy, not far from Rome, with the object of breaking the deadlock which had set in in the Italian campaign. The operation in question was to become famous not long after as the Anzio landing, but, at that time, my chief concern was to discover how it would affect the employment of Tom Churchill's Commando Brigade.

On this point I eventually succeeded in obtaining the assurance I needed. Even if the whole Brigade could not be made available immediately, a token force would be sent to Vis at once and other troops would follow later.

Soon the conference, having made their plans for an aquatic hook, dispersed, leaving Mr. Churchill to convalesce in peace, though it was a peace that was continually interrupted by the arrival of dispatches and telegrams requiring immediate decisions. He now turned his attention once again to Jugoslav affairs.

We had just heard that Jajce had fallen to the Germans and that Tito was again on the move. The Partisans, Mr. Churchill felt, needed some encouragement in their time of trouble, and he accordingly sat down and wrote a personal letter to Tito, congratulating him on his past achievements and holding out the hope of future help. This he entrusted to me, with instructions to deliver it personally without delay. In order to expedite my return, he lent me his own aircraft for the first part of the journey, and Randolph and I were soon soaring above the Atlas Mountains on our way to Bari.

At Bari we found that, although the enemy offensive was still in progress, the military situation was sufficiently stable for it to be possible to fix a map-reference to which we could be dropped. The point chosen was near Bosanski Petrovac, in Bosnia. At this time of year the weather over Jugoslavia was so bad that weeks might pass without there being an opportunity for a night drop, and by then the military situation might again have deteriorated. I was in a hurry to get back and it was accordingly decided that we should go in at once by day with a fighter escort. For this purpose we were allotted a Dakota troop-carrying aircraft and an escort of a dozen Thunderbolts. With me came Randolph, Sergeant Duncan, my new wireless operator, Sergeant Campbell, another signaller, Corporal Iles, and Slim Farish, who had just returned from a lightning visit to the United States.

This time our drop lacked the feeling of plunging into the unknown which had lent such zest to my original venture. It was a fine morning and we ate a large breakfast of bacon and eggs before taking off from Bari airfield. Soon we had crossed the by now familiar Adriatic and were over the Jugoslav mainland, but there were no signs of life from the anti-aircraft batteries and no enemy fighters ventured to try conclusions with the Thunderbolts. Then came the mountains, and some cloud. By now we were not far from our destination and it was time to adjust our parachutes. I felt for the Prime Minister's letter. It was there, securely buttoned inside my tunic. Then the doors were opened and the dispatcher signed to us to get into position.

I had decided to jump first with the others following in a 'stick', and I now took my place at the open door with Randolph next to me. Looking down, I could see the houses of a village, with, near them, an open expanse of green grass. A number of figures were running about, and, as I watched, the signal fires were lit and smoke billowed up from them. It all looked very close and I could not help wondering whether we were high enough for our parachutes to open before we reached the ground. Then the light turned from red to green; the dispatcher touched me on the shoulder, and I fell forwards and downwards into space.

CHAPTER X

BACK TO BOSNIA

I WAS right: we had been dropped from very low indeed; no sooner had my parachute opened, than I hit the ground with considerably more force than was comfortable. Looking up, I saw Randolph coming down almost on top of me. The expression of satisfaction which dawned on his face as he realized that his parachute had opened rapidly gave way to one of disgust as he glanced down to see the ground rushing up to meet him. Then, narrowly missing a telegraph pole, he came to rest with a sudden bump in a patch of melting snow and mud. A little further away Slim Farish and the rest of the 'stick' were landing at intervals of a few yards from one another — a neat bit of grouping on the part of the pilot, though personally I should not have minded if we had had a little more height to spare.

But we were not left long to reflect on such technicalities. Already John Selby, in the role of master of ceremonies, was upon us. Six weeks with the Partisans, which had included several forced marches, had, I noticed, made him a good deal less portly, and changed him in appearance from an immaculate Wing-Commander to something between a brigand and a dispatch rider. But his salute was as spectacular and his manner as urbane and soothing as ever. With him came Slavko Rodić, tall, pale and elegant with a neat dark moustache. His troops had provided the reception party for my first drop at Mrkonicgrad and were now performing the same service again.

They had not greatly changed. Weather-beaten and battle-stained, they wore the usual medley of captured enemy equipment and uniforms, only now there was here and there a suit of British battle-dress, a pair of boots, a Mills grenade or a Sten gun as a token of our aid. No sooner had my feet touched the ground, than a guard of honour was formed, ready for me to inspect. From the violence of their ceremonial drill it was clear that they more than made up in keenness for anything they might lack in orthodoxy of appearance.

Then horses were brought and Rodić and I, having played our part in the ceremony, sprang into the saddle and set off at a gallop up the road to the village, followed by the rest of the party, while the guard of honour turned to the task of collecting the containers of supplies which had been dropped at the same time as we had.

Bosanski Petrovac lies on the verge of one of the rare stretches of flat grassland in the highlands of Bosnia. On the far side, perhaps two or three miles away, was a range of dark hills, and in front of us, as we rode, the ground rose again, sloping gently up towards the village, which itself was built on the side of a hill, a typical Bosnian hamlet with its wood and plaster cottages.

In the upper room of one of these a meal had been prepared. It was a good meal, though not so good, our hosts explained with engaging frankness, as the one they had prepared the day before and then eaten themselves when they found we were not coming. At any rate we were hungry and did justice both to the stew which they gave us and to the local *slivovica*.

As we ate, I discussed plans with Slavko Rodić. The military situation was still fluid, and Tito and his staff were living in the woods until they could find somewhere to re-establish their H.Q. I wanted to see Tito as soon as possible, and Rodić said that he would take me to him himself. After Slim Farish, Randolph and the others had been installed in a peasant's house with instructions to stay where they were until further notice, we set out. It was getting dark as we rode down the village street and lights were beginning to twinkle in some of the windows.

Slavko had always prided himself on having good horses, and the two which we rode were admirable. The escort, which accompanied us, were also well mounted and we pushed along at a brisk pace. It was getting dark when we left, and, as we reached higher ground it grew colder and the snow lay deep on the track we were following through the forest. The snow deadened the sound of our horses' hooves, and, in the darkness, you could only dimly discern the form of the horse and rider in front of you. As I rode, muffled in the warm privacy of my greatcoat, I turned over in my mind the various points which I had to discuss with Tito. Then Slavko, who had been riding with the rearguard, caught up with me, and we fell to talking of our lives before the war and of what we hoped to make of them when the war was over. In peace time he had been some kind of engineer or surveyor; now, still in his twenties, he was a Partisan leader; when the war was over, if he survived, there would be work of some kind for him to do in the new Jugoslavia. That this new Jugoslavia would emerge triumphant, whatever the obstacles to be overcome, was for him, as for them all, a certainty, and had so been from the first.

We had a long way to go, and, even though we rode fast, it was after midnight when, in the thickest part of the forest, we were suddenly challenged by an unseen sentry. We gave the password and our names and, having done so, were allowed to proceed. It was still snowing and, as we rode on, we could make out lights dimmed by the falling snow, shining among the trees, and, going towards these, came on a group of wooden huts. A Partisan took our horses, and another, recognizing me, came forward and said that Tito was waiting up and wanted to see me as soon as I arrived. If I would come he would take me to him.

Picking our way through the trees, we came to a small, roughly built hut of freshly sawn planks. Inside, a light was burning. A sentry, on guard at the door, made way for me, and I went in.

As he came forward to meet me, I saw that Tito no longer had on the plain dark tunic and breeches which he used to favour, but was wearing instead a kind of uniform with, on his sleeve, a roughly embroidered laurel leaf encircling a star. Since our last meeting, the Anti-Fascist Council, meeting at Jajce, had bestowed on him the specially created rank of Marshal of Jugoslavia, at the same time setting up a 'provisional Government' in which he occupied the dominant position. When I congratulated him on this honour he seemed slightly embarrassed. 'They would do it,' he said, and smiled deprecatingly. For a moment it occurred to me that, while characteristically enjoying the magnificence of his new title, he perhaps at the same time rather regretted the days when, holding no other office save that of Military Commander of the Partisan forces, he had been known to all by an unadorned nickname. Then we sat down; food and drink were brought, and we started to talk.

417

We had much to tell each other. As a start, I handed Tito the letter which I had brought him from the Prime Minister. He had had no warning of it, and I watched his face closely to see how he liked it, as one watches a child with a new toy.

There could be no doubt of the effect. As he broke open the seal, and, unfolding the crisp sheet of heavy paper within, saw the address of 10 Downing Street at the top and the Prime Minister's signature at the foot, a broad smile of unaffected delight spread slowly over his face, which became broader still when he found a large signed photograph of Mr. Churchill in a separate envelope. I offered to translate the letter for him, but he insisted on trying to make it out on his own, turning to me for help over the more complicated passages, and giving way to fresh demonstrations of pleasure as he came to complimentary references to the prowess of the Partisans and promises of Allied assistance. He was clearly very much pleased.

He had reason to be. Tito's career up to now had taken him underground, behind the scenes. He had been perpetually in conflict with the established order. Despite this, perhaps because of this, he attached great importance to outward appearances. Already the revolutionary process which he had set in motion was carrying him, the revolutionary, upwards and onwards towards a new established order which, ultimately, would take the place of that which was being overthrown. The high-sounding title of Marshal of Jugoslavia which had been bestowed on him by his own people was an outward and visible sign of this, even though its recipient might still be hiding in the mountains and forests. But, hitherto, he had received but little recognition from the outside world. The Germans, it is true, had put a price, and a very high one, on his head, but the Great Powers, whose ally he was, had been slow to discern in him and his Movement a force to be taken into account; even the Russians showed little active interest in him. Now, at last, with the arrival of Mr. Churchill's letter, he was beginning to come into his own internationally. He was in direct and formal communication with one of the Big Three, with the Prime Minister of a Great Power. Mr. Churchill made it clear that he regarded him as an ally and as such promised him all possible help. Moreover he invited him to correspond with him through me on all matters of importance. This was no longer so very far removed from official recognition. It was at any rate a very big step forward.

Next I gave Tito some account of the greatly increased assistance which he was now to receive. I told him in detail of the steps which were being taken to improve the existing system of air supplies and air support; of the scheme for training his men as pilots and tank-crews. He was delighted and said that he would immediately set about collecting good men from all over the country to be trained. These he would then have smuggled down to the coast and shipped across the Adriatic by schooner.

Then I asked what progress the German offensive was making. He replied that the first fury of the German attack had spent itself without the enemy being able to win a decisive success. Now the Partisans, having once again successfully denied the enemy a target, were beginning to hit back all over the country, and the Germans were getting as good as they gave. The trouble was that his men lacked everything: food, clothing, boots, ammunition. He could only hope that the promised supplies would come before it was too late. Meanwhile the situation had to some extent been stabilized locally, and he expected to be able to move his Headquarters before long to the neighbourhood of Drvar, a part of Bosnia which had long been outstandingly faithful to the Partisan cause.

Finally we talked of the islands and of the prospect of converting Vis into a firm base from which we could harass the enemy and smuggle across supplies to the mainland. The other islands had by now all been occupied by the Germans, and we agreed that we should need to act quickly if we were to be in time to save Vis from their fate.

We talked till the early hours of the morning. Then, bidding Tito good night, I followed one of the guards through the snow to the hut which had been allotted me. Gordon Alston and Hilary King, my new signals officer, were lying asleep in some straw which was spread on a kind of shelf stretching the whole length of the hut. Waking, they told me of their adventures since their hurried departure from Jajce. A Partisan with immense moustaches was sitting by an improvised stove, stoking it from time to time, and in the intervals inspecting by its light the recesses of his shirt, which he had taken off and was

419

examining with meticulous care. 'Uši', he said resignedly. 'Lice.' I took the canvas Foreign Office bag in which I had brought the Prime Minister's letter, filled it with straw to make a pillow, wrapped myself in my greatcoat and was soon asleep.

Next morning we were wakened with a mug of captured ersatz coffee and a mess tin of yellow maize porridge by the bewhiskered Partisan, who, in addition to being my bodyguard also fulfilled the roles of cook and batman. Having eaten my breakfast, I cleaned out my mess tin and used it for boiling some snow-water on the stove, to shave in. It was an agreeably compact mode of life, with no time, space or energy wasted on unnecessary frills.

The days that followed were uneventful. We led a patriarchal existence in our huts in the forest. All round, the snow lay deep. I ate with Tito and his staff, several of whom had now blossomed out as Cabinet Ministers. Kardelj was Vice-Premier; Father Vlado, Minister of the Interior; and so on. After much drafting and re-drafting, a reply to Mr. Churchill's letter was composed and sent off over my wireless.

Then, one evening, with the suddenness which always characterized such moves, it was announced that we were leaving the same night for the new Headquarters. The message added that the Marshal would be glad if I would travel in his special coach — an invitation which I was at a loss to understand until, on making inquiries, I discovered that my old friend the Partisan Express had somehow survived the offensive and been brought to a nearby siding and that it was in this that we were going to travel.

Sure enough, when the time came, there it was, the same as ever, whistling gaily and puffing out clouds of sparks, but with the addition of a large specially built wooden box-wagon, which looked exactly like one of our huts on wheels. Into this we all bundled: Tito, the dog Tigger, several members of the Cabinet, Olga, Alston and King, Tito's bodyguard and myself.

Our short train journey had an improbable, dreamlike quality, which even while it was actually in progress, made it hard to believe that it was really happening. From the inside, Tito's special coach was even more like a hut than from the outside, with an open stove in the middle and benches round the wall. The stifling heat of the stove induced sleep. The benches on the other hand were just too narrow to sleep on with any security. On the floor lay Tigger, in a bad temper and snapping at everyone's ankles. At last, after a great deal of fussing and settling down, he went to sleep, only to be woken again almost immediately by a Cabinet Minister falling off one of the benches on top of him, whereupon pandemonium broke loose. It was not a restful journey, but, as Tito pointed out, it was the only train in Jugoslavia in which you could travel with reasonable certainty of not being blown up.

Eventually, some hours before dawn, we arrived, and, detraining, set out with a guide to look for our new quarters. After what seemed a long walk in the dark through muddy half-frozen fields, we found them; a little cluster of wooden houses on the side of a hill. In one of these had been installed a system of double-decked wooden sleeping-shelves, sufficient to accommodate the whole Mission. The owner of the house, an elderly peasant, announced with considerable pride that the whole contraption was 'specially reserved for President Churchill himself', who was shortly expected on a State visit to Marshal Tito — presumably a garbled reference to Randolph's impending arrival. But we were too tired to argue with him and, undeterred by his warnings, we stretched ourselves out in a row on the bottom shelf and were soon heavily asleep.

When we woke, it was broad daylight and we could get a better idea of our surroundings. From where we were, we looked out over a wide green valley, with, on the far side, a range of hills, rising abruptly in cliffs from a river which flowed at their foot. Between us and the hills lay what was left of the village of Drvar, a few gutted houses clustered round the gaunt ruins of what had once been a factory. Behind us open fields, dotted here and there with farmsteads and copses, rose more gradually into another range of hills, on which the snow was still lying.

Our own house stood amid plum orchards, sloping down to a little brook. From their huts round about, the peasants eyed us curiously, staring at our wireless sets and the rest of our gear and listening in surprise to the strange language we spoke. The Partisans they knew; and the Četniks; and the Germans. But we were something different. At first they hung back. Then their curiosity got the best of their shyness. The girls were the boldest. Laughing, and pushing each other forward, first one and then another invented a pretext for engaging us in conversation. The discovery that we could speak their language emboldened them still further, and soon we were the centre of an amused crowd of neighbours, who fired every kind of question at us, and responded to our answers with confidences of their own, generally of an extremely intimate kind. Meanwhile, our whiskered bodyguard, who was supposed to be helping us unpack and stow away what was left of the Mission kit and supplies stood beaming in the middle of a group of small children, to whom he was displaying with a proprietor's pride all the more interesting articles of our equipment, personal or otherwise, each of which was greeted with cheers by his youthful audience. Amongst the latter was a little girl of two or three with a singularly dirty face and flaming red hair, who had toddled up to see what was going on. To her we gave the name of Ginger, by which she was known thereafter by the whole neighbourhood, including her own parents.

The arrival, a couple of days later, of the rest of the party including Randolph, Sergeant Duncan and Slim Farish, who had brought with him a large supply of genuine American 'candy', set the seal on our success. From now onwards our position in the community was assured. Before many days were past, we were sleeping in one house, eating in another, and doing our cooking in a third, an operation which was conducted over an open fire by Ginger's mother under the general supervision of Sergeant Duncan.

Once we had established ourselves, I went to see Tito. I found him living in a cave half way up the rock face on the far side of the valley. It was a stiff climb and I arrived out of breath at the mouth of the cave where I was greeted by Tito, Olga, Tigger and Tito's personal bodyguards, Prlja and Boško, who all seemed delighted with their new abode. At the back of the cave a waterfall roared and chattered and ferns grew in the crevices of the rock. From where we stood we commanded a fine view of the valley and its approaches. Altogether, it was a pleasant enough place. On and off, I was to spend much time in that cave during the months that followed, talking, eating and, above all, arguing.

The life to which we now settled down, while it also partook of the atmosphere of the 'Robbers' Cave' in Act II of a pantomime, had, strangely enough, a good deal in common with that of an important Headquarters in a normal theatre of war, even though the nearest German outposts were never more than a few miles away. In the past six months and particularly since the Italian capitulation, the Partisan Movement had greatly increased both in numbers and in scope, and there had inevitably been a corresponding increase in the size of Tito's staff. But what the latter gained in executive and administrative efficiency, through this increase in staff, it inevitably lost in mobility, and mobility is an essential condition of successful guerrilla warfare. Tito accordingly now found himself confronted with the problem of how best to secure his base. For the time being, it is true, his H.Q. did not seem to be in any immediate danger. The force of the German sixth offensive, which had culminated in the capture of Jajce some weeks earlier, was now largely spent, and the initiative was rapidly passing to the Partisans. Locally, the approaches to Drvar were well defended. To the north, Slavko Rodić and Fifth Corps were based on Bosanski Petrovac. Koča Popović, commanding First Corps, had established his Headquarters at Mokri Nogi, a few hours' walk up the valley. These troops, it was hoped, would be sufficient to protect Drvar against any sudden attack by such German forces as were known to be in the neighbourhood at the time.

But this situation could not be expected to last indefinitely. On the contrary, it was not long before evidence reached us from several different sources that the enemy knew where we were and had no intention of leaving us to vegetate. The most cogent proof of this interest came in the form of enemy air activity. First single aircraft and then groups of three or four would circle overhead, sometimes bombing and machine-gunning, and sometimes just looking or possibly photographing. More disturbing still were reports, received from the R.A.F. and passed on by me to Tito, of concentrations of gliders and troop-carrying aircraft at Zagreb and elsewhere. Then, from captured enemy documents and intercepted messages, came evidence of various German plans to kidnap or assassinate Tito, his staff and my Mission. For this purpose, it appeared, Serbo-Croat speaking members of the notorious S.S. Brandenburg were to be used, dressed as Partisans. Another time, a lightning raid by ski-troops of the First Mountain Division seems to have been contemplated. Going through these documents, I was interested to read the instructions for my own disposal. They gave, in their order, the various formations to which I was to be sent after capture: from Division, to Corps, to Army Headquarters, after which I was to be flown by special aircraft to Germany for further investigation and ultimate disposal by means not specified.

Apart from this, we knew that the Germans, if they took their time, could in the end always concentrate against any given point held by the Partisans an overwhelming weight of troops and particularly of armaments, and, if at any time they decided to take such action against Drvar, Tito and his staff would once again be obliged to take to the woods, with a consequent interruption of the central conduct of the campaign.

This, Tito was naturally anxious to avoid. The question was whether it was feasible to render the base at Drvar secure against attack, if the Germans were really determined to wipe it out. Certain of Tito's advisers were in favour of attempting to convert Drvar and its immediate surroundings into an impregnable fortress and concentrate a considerable garrison within its shelter. They felt, he explained, that it would be good for morale and strengthen the Movement as a whole, if there could be at any rate one permanent strip of 'liberated territory'.

In telling me of the project, Tito asked me what I thought of it and whether, if it were adopted, we would be able to supply the armaments, and in particular the mines, guns and tanks which would be needed to put it into execution.

I replied that, as he knew, we were already supplying the Partisans with mines and that we were hoping to supply them shortly with pack artillery. But I did not think that he would be putting either of these to their proper use if they were employed in an attempt to establish a permanent base in any one given area. For one thing, we could not bring by air a sufficient weight of armaments to give them the security at which they were aiming. For another, to assume a primarily defensive role, even locally, would, in my view, be to fly in the face of a fundamental principle of guerrilla warfare. It seemed to me that the Partisans must at all costs retain their mobility. I saw their need for some kind of base from which operations could be directed, but to my mind they could best achieve the security which they desired by keeping the enemy engaged elsewhere.

This, in fact, they were doing to an ever-increasing extent, and, what is more, it was now possible, owing to the presence of my officers with Partisan formations throughout the country, to co-ordinate their operations with those of the Allied Armies in Italy.

From our point of view special importance attached to Partisan activities in Slovenia and in particular to the possibility of interrupting traffic on the Trieste-Ljubljana railway, which was one of the principal supply lines for the German forces in Italy and also constituted a vital link between the eastern and western fronts. Peter Moore had now returned to Bosnia after a further visit to Slovenia, and, in Vivian Street's absence, was acting as my second in command. I thus had the advantage of his local knowledge and first-hand experience in planning any operations that A.F.H.Q. or 15th Army Group might ask for in the north.

Peter's knowledge and experience were to stand us in good stead, when, sometime later, I was instructed by General Wilson to ask Tito whether his men could attack the Stampetov bridge, one of the main viaducts on the Trieste-Ljubljana railway, the operation to be so timed as to coincide with certain moves by General Alexander in Italy. Tito agreed immediately and undertook to send the necessary instructions to his local commander in Slovenia at once. After talking the proposed operation over with Moore I decided to send him back to Slovenia, in order to provide direct liaison with the troops carrying out the operation and also to help them with technical advice, which he, as a Sapper, was well qualified to give when it came to blowing things up.

Moore was delighted, and, having provided himself with a photograph of the viaduct and all available information about it, set to work calculating the quantities of explosive which would be needed to put it out of commission for an appreciable time. It soon became clear that the undertaking was likely to prove a formidable one. The viaduct was known to be heavily guarded. Moreover it was so constructed that very considerable quantities of high-explosive would be required to make any impression on it. Arrangements were made for the necessary supplies to be dropped in to Slovenia, and Moore left for the north with his professional enthusiasm thoroughly aroused.

For a week we heard nothing. Then a signal came from Moore to say that they had arrived, that they had discussed plans with the local Commander, that the supplies had duly been dropped and that everything was now ready for the operation, which had been given the code name 'Bearskin', to be carried out on the prescribed date. I passed this information on to General Wilson and General Alexander. Then we waited anxiously for news.

The news, when it came, was wholly good, and I hastened to pass it on to Tito. After a long and skilfully executed approach march, the Partisans had rushed the viaduct in the face of heavy opposition and had held the enemy off long enough for the charges to be laid and detonated. When they finally withdrew, the bridge was down, and likely to remain so for some time. Moore was full of praise for the Partisans, who, he said, were ably commanded and had fought with great dash and determination.

Later Tito received an account of the action from H.Q. Slovenia. It only differed from Moore's version in that it contained an enthusiastic account of the part which the latter had himself played in the planning and execution of the operation.

We heard later from Italy that the destruction of the viaduct had achieved its purpose. As a result of it, the railway had been put out of action for some considerable time, and thus denied to the enemy at a critical stage of the campaign. From General Alexander there came a message of thanks which we duly passed on to those concerned. For his part in the operation Moore received a well-deserved bar to his D.S.O.

CHAPTER XI

NEW DEAL

WITH the approach of spring and the improvement in weather conditions, air supply and air support became easier, and we in Jugoslavia now began to feel in the country the results of the new policy of all-out assistance which had been decided on at Cairo.

Supplies were dropped to Partisan formations all over the country in accordance with a system of priorities which Tito and I had worked out together on the basis of estimated operational requirements and which we reviewed periodically. He and I generally reached agreement without much difficulty, but it was often hard to persuade the local Partisan Commanders and the British officers attached to them that they were getting their fair share.

In the neighbourhood of Drvar our principal dropping ground remained Bosanski Petrovac, the Headquarters of 5th Corps, whence the supplies received were distributed by pack-horse and peasant's cart. For a time this was done by day, but soon the enemy discovered what was happening and, on receiving news of a drop, sent out aircraft to patrol all the tracks leading away from Bosanski Petrovac. After one or two of our supply caravans had been caught in the open and badly shot up, it was decided only to move by night.

Sometimes supplies were dropped direct to Drvar or to Koča Popović's Headquarters at Mokri Nogi further up the valley. This was no easy matter for the pilots carrying out the dropping operation even under the most favourable weather conditions. The valley was narrow, surrounded by high hills and often filled with cloud. But somehow the R.A.F. and American Army Air Force brought it off again and again in all weathers, there and all over Jugoslavia.

Often the message to stand by for a drop would reach us on the day itself. For us often much depended on supplies arriving in time and a drop was a big event. The first thing to be done was to prepare the signal fires. After that we would settle down to wait on the bleak hillside for

427

the sound of the aircraft. Sometimes it never came and we would wait all night in vain. This meant that weather had stopped them from getting through. At other times they would be punctual to the minute. Then, as soon as we heard them, we would run out and set light to the fires. Some pilots would let go their loads from a considerable height, and the parachutes, caught by the wind, would drift a mile or more from their proper destination, often ending up with the enemy. Others, with more experience of the job, would edge their aircraft right into the valley and make the drop from a couple of hundred feet above the fires, banking steeply immediately afterwards so as to avoid the hillside. Sometimes they came so low that, looking up in the darkness, we could see for an instant the figure of the dispatcher, outlined against the dim light of the open door, as he rolled out the containers. As the shortage of parachutes became more acute, the R.A.F. took to making 'free drops' of supplies which could be safely dropped without them. These called for considerable agility on the part of those on the ground: a hundred pairs of ammunition boots whistling through the air at a hundred miles an hour, their fall unbroken by a parachute, were a serious menace to life and limb.

At times bad weather would stop all supplies for weeks on end and there would be long, anxious periods of waiting, with reports coming in from all sides of troops hard-pressed for want of arms and our own food supplies getting so low that our few remaining tins of bully and bars of chocolate began to assume an inflated importance and it was hard to prevent oneself from starting to think about the next meal as soon as one had swallowed the one before. Nor were these lean phases easy to explain to the Partisans, to whom meteorological conditions, often brilliantly fine locally when they were altogether impossible in Italy, meant nothing, and who were only too ready to put the whole thing down to Capitalist Intrigue.

But, despite occasional stoppages, air-supplies were now arriving on a far larger scale. Air-support, too, was increasing by leaps and bounds. More and more often we would hear the roar of hundreds of aeroplane engines and looking up at the sky, see the serried squadrons of Fortresses and Liberators glittering high above us in the sunshine, on their way to bomb strategical targets. Sometimes we could count a hundred or more. Until then it had been safe to assume that any aircraft seen in the sky over Jugoslavia was an enemy one and meant mischief, and it was only gradually that the Partisans and the local inhabitants accustomed themselves to the idea of a friendly aircraft. Eventually, however, they did, and then, after the look-out man had taken careful stock of them, the warning cry of '*Avioni!*' — 'Aircraft!', would be followed by joyful shouts of '*Naši!*' — 'Ours!' whenever the R.A.F. or the American Army Air Force made their appearance.

I recall one very satisfactory demonstration of Allied air superiority, when, in the middle of a particularly irritating low-level bombing and machine-gunning attack by two or three medium-sized German planes, a louder, deeper roar suddenly made itself heard above the buzz of the Germans' engines and the rattle of their machine guns, and, looking up, we saw, so high as to be scarcely distinguishable, a vast, silvery armada, set on its relentless course northwards, the escorting fighters diving and weaving on its fringes. Evidently our tormentor saw it at the same moment as we did, and, although it was most unlikely that the Allied pilots had even seen them or would have bothered about them if they had, decided that discretion was the better part of valour and made a hasty exit over the nearest hill-top, followed by derisive shouts from the assembled population.

Tactical air support on a much larger scale also became possible now that we had officers attached to Partisan formations throughout the country. We had arranged that they should have direct wireless communication with the R.A.F. in Italy, and it became relatively common for Beaufighters, Spitfires or rocket-firing Hurricanes to be rushed in the nick of time to the support of some hard-pressed Partisan outpost. or prepare the way for a Partisan attack on a German strong-point.

John Selby, in the meantime, had gone to North Africa to train the Partisan fighter squadron formed under the Alexandria Agreement. Tito, delighted at the prospect of having his own air force, had sent out some of his best officers to be trained and John found himself confronted with the ticklish problem of converting these hardy guerrilla warriors into fighter-pilots. This transformation he effected in a remarkably short time, and, before the end of the war, Partisan pilots, flying Hurricanes bearing a red Partisan star superimposed on the red, white and blue roundel of the R.A.F., were taking an active part in air operations over Jugoslavia.

By now our party included several technicians. Perhaps the most useful work of all was done by a stocky little Major in the New Zealand R.A.M.C. Doc. Rogers, as he was called, had seen a lot of fighting in the Western Desert, where he had commanded a field ambulance. Now, rather than work at a base hospital, he had volunteered for special service in Jugoslavia, not, I think, because he took any particular interest in that country, but simply so as to be in the thick of things.

His wish was granted. At the time when he arrived, it was winter and the sixth German offensive was in progress. Casualties from wounds, disease and frost-bite were heavy. For the Partisans, to whom mobility was a prime consideration, the question of what to do with their wounded was a major problem. If they carried them with them, they hampered their movements. If they abandoned them, they met a terrible death at the hands of the Germans. Apart from this, they were short of doctors and lacked medical supplies almost completely. As a result, men were dying like flies.

This was the kind of assignment that Rogers had been looking for. Accompanied by a R.A.M.C. Corporal of similar character, he set himself to solve it. He organized hospitals wherever he could, in peasants' houses or in the woods. In them he insisted on standards of hygiene and medical discipline unheard of before his arrival. He sent over my wireless link unorthodox but effective signals to the high-ranking officers of the medical world, demanding that they send him at once by parachute large quantities of medicaments and other supplies. He started to make preliminary arrangements for the evacuation of the worst cases to Allied hospitals in Italy as soon as we gained control of a landing-strip. Having got all this going, he and his Corporal moved rapidly from one part of the country to another, descending on his improvised hospitals like a tornado, organizing, reorganizing, interfering, operating by candlelight in stables and cowsheds, arranging for the removal of a group of wounded threatened by a German attack or the isolation and treatment of typhus cases, of which, as usual, there were many. All this was done in a country occupied by the enemy, under conditions of considerable rigour, on short rations, in the middle of constant skirmishing and air attack.

In the military or political situation, as such, he took little interest, and of the language he spoke not a word, working entirely by gesture or through interpreters. On the other hand, he had seen too much of their courage, of their capacity for enduring pain, and of their numerous very human qualities, not to feel a kind of admiration mingled with affection for the 'Pattersons', as he called them. And they, too, liked and admired him, wondering at such devotion and unquestioningly accepting his authority and his knowledge. Indeed such was his popularity that on occasion rival Partisan Commanders quarrelled over him and Tito had to be called in to settle the dispute.

Two other new recruits at this time were John Clarke and Andrew Maxwell, both from the 2nd Scots Guards. The arrival of a newcomer from the outside world was a big occasion, and their drop was eagerly awaited by us all and preceded by a number of signals, reminding them to bring in various odds and ends of which we were short. On the day on which they were due to arrive I rode over to Koča Popović's Headquarters, near which it had been arranged that they should be dropped, taking with me Hilary King who was hoping for some wireless stores. Allied aircraft were short at the time and they were accordingly to be dropped by aircraft of the co-belligerent Italian Air Force, now operating under Allied Command. The experiment was also to be tried of making a mass daylight supply drop. Altogether it seemed likely to be an interesting occasion.

There was deep snow in the valley through which our route lay and we made slower progress than we had expected, our horses plunging and floundering up to their bellies in the snow as soon as we left the beaten track. We were still a long way away when suddenly we heard the noise of aircraft, and, looking up, saw, at a distance of some miles from where we were, several Savoia-Marchetti transport planes flying slowly along at a considerable height.

As we watched them, still a couple of thousand feet up, expecting to see them circle down towards the dropping area, a dozen or so parachutes suddenly burst from them one after another, opened out like Japanese paper flowers immersed in water, and floated slowly down, swaying gently, over a wide area of the countryside; from where we were, we could not see whether their burdens were human or not. While the parachutes were still in the air, the Savoia-Marchettis turned round and departed in the direction from which they had come. Worried by what we had seen, we pressed on anxiously, wondering what we should find.

Some distance further along the track, we met an old peasant coming in the opposite direction. We asked him if the British officers had landed safely. 'Dead,' he replied unhesitatingly, 'all dead. They were dropped on the mountain-tops, and their bones were shattered by the fall. They are bringing their bodies down at this very moment.' Then, evidently feeling that he had adequately summed up the situation, he passed on down the valley, muttering irritably to himself as he went.

This was a blow. John Clarke and Andrew Maxwell were both old friends of mine and it was sickening to think of their lives being thrown away like this. We kicked our horses into a gallop and plunged on through the snow.

The first person that we saw when we arrived was Andrew. He was standing outside a peasant's hut, talking politely to Koča Popović in rather bad French and from time to time inquiring anxiously about his personal kit. He had, it appeared, been dropped from a great height, followed by a free drop of several hundred pairs of boots, which had passed him at high speed, missing him by inches, and had finally landed on an extremely steep mountain-side, covered with sharp stones. The containers dropped at the same time were scattered for miles around. There was no sign of John Clarke, who had been due to jump after Andrew, but search parties were out looking for him.

Koča produced some black bread and cheese and some *slivovica* and we went inside to wait. One after another, Partisans arrived bringing in containers and parachutes that had been found scattered all over the countryside. The Italians, no doubt anxious to be home, had let them go from far too high and they had drifted miles out of their course. Some must undoubtedly have fallen to the Germans. Of John Clarke there was still no sign, but it was something to learn that, in spite of the gloomy prognostications of our original informant, no shattered corpses had yet been brought in.

Our minds were not finally set at rest until a day or two later, when I received a signal from John from Italy, reporting with suitable expressions of regret that Major Maxwell, owing to an unfortunate error on the part of the Italian pilot, was thought to have been dropped to the enemy. The pilot, it appeared, had announced his supposed mistake as soon as Maxwell had jumped and Clarke had therefore naturally not followed him, but had returned to Italy with the plane, having first thrown Maxwell's kit after him, so that he should not be unnecessarily uncomfortable in his prison camp.

To this startling communication we returned a reassuring and mildly facetious reply. When John Clarke was eventually dropped in a week or two late, it was from a British aircraft.

An even more sensational entry on the Jugoslav scene was made at about this time by a full-blown Soviet Military Mission, headed by a General of the Red Army, whose appointment had been announced some months before. It may be imagined with what frantic excitement the news of the impending arrival of some real Russians, the first they had ever seen, was received by the devoutly Communist Partisans.

As the Russians still had no air bases of their own within range of Jugoslavia, the vital task of safely introducing the Mission into the country had to be entrusted to the R.A.F. We were without landing-strips, the enemy were in control of the coast, and it was therefore only possible to enter Jugoslavia by parachute.

A first difficulty was encountered when the Russians announced that they were not prepared to be dropped by parachute. Feverish attempts were made to clear a flat piece of ground of snow, so that at any rate the General might be brought in by light aircraft; but the harder the Partisans worked, the harder it snowed. As time passed and there were still no Russians there began to be whispers of 'capitalist sabotage', when fortunately someone had the brilliant idea of bringing them in by glider. Two Horsa gliders were borrowed from Airborne Forces, and one fine day we were told to stand by to receive them.

We collected on a neighbouring hill-top to watch their arrival. They made an imposing spectacle; the gliders, swimming along behind two Dakotas, with a fighter escort circling round them. Despite the latter, they would have made a fine target for enemy fighters, but fortunately none made their appearance, and the landing was safely accomplished, the gliders cutting adrift as we watched and circling down to the ground under the expert guidance of two glider-pilots, who now joined the strength of my Mission until a means could be found of evacuating them.

Naturally we were much interested to see what the Russians would be like. To our relief they turned out to be charming. In addition to a natural conviviality it was evident that they had been instructed to make themselves particularly agreeable to me and my staff. Furthermore they had filled the gliders with vodka and caviare, which, coming as they did after a long period of relative austerity, were exceptionally welcome. After one or two encounters we decided unanimously that they were a great social asset.

What other purpose they served was less clear. They had no bases within range from which they could bring in supplies, though later half a dozen American Dakotas, bearing Soviet markings, but under British operational control, made occasional appearances from Bari. Nor did they take any part in the direction of military operations or the technical training of the Partisans. Finally, it seemed most unlikely that they were there to interpret the Communist Party line for Tito, who, in my experience, usually knew instinctively what was in the Kremlin's mind without being told and certainly did not need a Red Army General to direct his conscience.

General Korneyev, the Commander of the Mission, was a soldier of some distinction, who had served as Chief of Staff to an Army Commander on the Stalingrad front before taking up his present appointment. Like so many senior officers of the Red Army, he was not of proletarian origin and had held a commission in the Imperial Russian Army before the Revolution. I did not get the impression that he particularly enjoyed being in Jugoslavia or that he thought much of the Partisans. His second in command was a much younger man and an expert on guerrilla warfare, having commanded a Partisan band behind the German lines in Russia. But he, too, seemed to find time hanging heavy on his hands. Of the other officers, I have no very clear recollection, save only of one who bore all the familiar marks of being the local representative of the People's Commissariat for Internal Affairs.

The arrival of the Russians solved a problem which had been exercising me for some time, namely, how to get my old friend Sergeant (now Sergeant-Major) Charlie Button into Jugoslavia. With Sergeant Duncan, he had volunteered to come with me in the first place, but had, like General Korneyev, been forbidden to parachute on account of an old wound in the foot. Now the gliders provided an opportunity and, sure enough, on the day there was Button bringing up the rear of the Soviet party and looking as solid and as rubicund as ever. From now onwards he took charge of the Mission's administrative arrangements, and Gospodin Charlie, as he was known, could be seen planning moves, negotiating for pack-horses, bartering strips of parachute silk for honey or eggs with buxom peasant girls, or instilling into our wireless operators a standard of smartness which would uphold the prestige of the British Army.

In all this his constant companion was the child Ginger, whose blazing red hair had at once won his heart and who had conceived for him in return a passion perhaps not entirely unconnected with the fact that he controlled the chocolate ration.

The task of imparting technical knowledge to the Partisans, which was one of my Mission's functions, was not always an easy one. When introduced to completely new weapons and explosive devices, they were inclined to brush their instructors aside, exclaiming gaily that they knew all about that already, and give a spirited and often alarming demonstration of their alleged technical skill.

Provided, however, that sufficient tact was exercised, they made excellent pupils, grasping with remarkable rapidity the mechanism of a new weapon and showing the greatest ingenuity in applying it to the peculiar conditions of guerrilla warfare. They made, for instance, good use of the Fiat mortars, which had begun to reach us. These ingeniously constructed little weapons, which fired a rocket-like projectile of great penetrating power and high explosive content, and were intended for use by infantry against tanks, were ideally suited for our present purposes and were used by the Partisans with devastating effect against houses, vehicles, railway engines, enemy strong-points and any other targets that presented themselves, to the dismay of the other side who at first could not make out what they were being bombarded with or where it was coming from. To Peter Moore, also, with his immense experience of tank warfare in the Western Desert and his great technical knowledge of explosives, the Partisans were prepared to listen on the subject of mines and anti-tank devices of one kind and another.

But, even so, with the greatest tact, accidents sometimes crept in through the excessive anxiety to assert their own independence. There was the sad case of some dehydrated food, which was dropped to us at a stage of the winter when we had run very short indeed of ordinary food. It was the first time that any of us had seen dehydrated food, and the pleasure with which we regarded the first sacks of strange dried-up looking flakes, variously labelled 'milk', 'mutton', 'eggs', 'carrots', 'onions' and 'potatoes', but all looking strangely alike, was mingled with curiosity and, to some extent, with misgiving. At any rate, before trying them, we read, and carried out meticulously the written directions which accompanied them, of which the principal was to soak them in water for twenty-four hours before cooking and eating them. The result was astonishing. On being soaked, the uninteresting looking flakes swelled up to several times their original size and became lumps of meat or slices of vegetable, as the case might be, and we soon found that a judicious mixture of dehydrated mutton, onions and potatoes properly soaked and then baked in Ginger's mother's oven made a very creditable shepherd's pie, an undreamed-of luxury in our rather straitened circumstances. Clearly, dehydrated food was just the thing for us, especially as its light weight made it far more easily transportable than tinned food.

Delighted, we immediately signalled for further supplies in order that we might share with the Partisans the benefit of our new discovery. On their arrival, we handed them over to the Quartermaster's department, being careful to add full instructions for their use. But these they brushed aside light-heartedly. 'We know all about that,' they said, and started to distribute the sacks to various neighbouring units. We had our doubts, but thought it better not to voice them.

It was only afterwards that we heard what had happened. The dehydrated food had not been soaked, but gulped down as it was. This was dry work, or so the Partisans thought, and so they washed it down with copious draughts of water from the neighbouring brook. Then, with disconcerting suddenness, the stuff began to swell inside them until it had reached several times its original dimensions. Their ensuing discomfort was considerable, though not so acute as that of another Partisan, who at about this time ate a stick of plastic high-explosive, mashing it up with milk, under the impression that it was some kind of maize porridge.

The snow melted in the valleys. Food grew more plentiful. Movement became easier. The fighting flared up again. Meanwhile the Allied High Command had begun to direct their attention increasingly to Serbia.

The strategic significance of Serbia is obvious. It lies right across the Belgrade-Salonika railway, a vital enemy line of communication, of which the importance would have increased still further in the event of an Allied landing anywhere in the Balkans, which at that time was still a possibility.

Hitherto, Serbia had been regarded by us as being primarily a Četnik preserve. Such supplies as had gone there had been dropped to Mihajlović. But the results had in the view of G.H.Q. Middle East been disappointing. In particular there had been little or no interruption of traffic on the Belgrade-Salonika railway. It will be recalled that Mihajlović had been given a limited period in which to carry out a certain specific operation. This had now elapsed without his having complied with this request, and the important decision was accordingly taken to withdraw the Allied Mission from his Headquarters and send him no further supplies. Supplies ceased at once; the extrication of the British liaison officers took longer, and it was not until the end of May that Brigadier Armstrong, my opposite number in the other camp, took leave of a reproachful but still courteous Mihajlović. In the House of Commons Mr. Churchill explained the Government's action. 'The reason,' he said, 'why we have ceased to supply Mihajlović with arms and support is a simple one. He has not been fighting the enemy, and, moreover, some of his subordinates have been making accommodations with the enemy.'

Thus ended a connection which from the first had been based on a misapprehension. With the help of our own propaganda we had in our imagination built up Mihajlović into something that he never seriously claimed to be. Now we were dropping him because he had failed to fulfil our own expectations.

The decision to drop the Četniks having once been taken, it became our policy to build up Partisan strength in Serbia as quickly as possible. The Partisan Movement had had its origin in Serbia, but, after the first bloody set-backs of 1941, the main body of Tito's forces had withdrawn northwards and westwards into Bosnia and Montenegro, and such Partisans as remained had largely gone underground, whence they waged a bitter and uphill struggle against both Germans and Četniks, making raids and ambushes and attacking communications in true guerrilla fashion, but for the most part not operating as formed units, as they did elsewhere in Jugoslavia.

The Serbian Partisans were now given a high degree of priority in allotting supplies, while Tito, for his part, sent no less a person than Koča Popović, himself a Serb, to take command of them. In order that we should also have a good man to represent us there, I now recalled John Henniker-Major from 8th Corps and dispatched him to Serbia, where he arrived by parachute at the end of March or beginning of April. His knowledge of Serbo-Croat was by now extremely fluent and, as well as being a good fighting soldier, he was a trained political observer. Meanwhile I decided that I would take the first opportunity of visiting Serbia myself.

Apart from its military importance the situation in Serbia possessed considerable political interest. The peasants were believed to be in the main loyal to the monarchy and were certainly not communistically inclined; the rather half-hearted collaborationist regime of General Nedić was by no means as unpopular as it might have been; finally, the influence of the Četnik Movement was considerable. Partisan strength on the other hand was to all intents and purposes an unknown quantity. For us it was important to be able to form some estimate of the degree of popular support which the Partisans, in these by no means favourable circumstances, might be able to command there — important both for the purpose of our military planning and in order that we might be able to forecast with reasonable accuracy the course of events in Jugoslavia after the end of the war.

The latter subject was by now beginning to engage the attention of all concerned to an increasing extent. Hitherto the British Government had tended to regard the group of Jugoslav politicians who had come to England with King Peter in 1941 as adequately representing the Jugoslav people. It now became clear that during the years which they had spent in exile these gentlemen had, not unnaturally, lost touch with what was going on in their own country. The Serbs among them had, it is true, managed to establish wireless contact with General Mihajlović, who in his absence had been given the position of Minister of Defence in the Royal Jugoslav Government. The Partisan Movement, on the other hand, they appear to have regarded as a disagreeable and unimportant phenomenon which was on the whole better ignored.

Automatically the decision, taken on military grounds, to drop Mihajlović and support Tito posed a political problem. In the first place, it provoked the strongest opposition from the Royal Jugoslav Government and from King Peter's entourage, although the King himself eventually acquiesced in it. Secondly, it raised the question whether or not our military recognition of Tito as an ally was to be accompanied or followed by any measure of political recognition.

The problem which faced the British Government was an awkward one. The assumption that the London Jugoslavs really represented the people of Jugoslavia and would be able to return upon the cessation of hostilities and start again where they had left off had now worn very thin. By breaking off relations with Mihajlović, we had undermined it still further. Tito, on the other hand, was, for his part, becoming more and more inclined to expect some measure of political recognition in return for the services which, as we had repeatedly recognized, he was rendering to the Allied cause. In support of this claim he could also point to the impressive administrative and political organization which he possessed throughout the country, and to the popular support which his Movement at that time undoubtedly possessed, facts which it was no longer possible to ignore. On the other hand, the Royal Jugoslav Government in exile, however little relation it might possess to the realities of the situation in Jugoslavia, was recognized by us and by the remainder of the United Nations as an Allied Government, and, as such, could not simply be left out of account. Nor could we forget that we were under a very real obligation towards King Peter personally for the part he had played in entering the war on our side at a time when we were fighting entirely alone against tremendous odds. Each side clung with equal intransigeance to its point of view, and showed equally little inclination to compromise or come to terms.

Such was the gap to be bridged. True, the end of the war and the liberation of Jugoslavia still seemed relatively remote contingencies, and, under the terms of the Atlantic Charter, the issue would in the ultimate analysis have to be decided by the people of Jugoslavia, but events, both inside the country and out, were by now moving so rapidly that a continued refusal on our part to face up to the problem could only have made matters worse.

Accordingly, very discreetly at first and without any noticeable measure of success, both parties were sounded out as to the possibility of a compromise. Of the proceedings in London, whither King Peter and his Government had now returned after six months in Cairo, I had no direct knowledge. But Tito, I found, had, as usual, a very clear appreciation of the situation. He knew that when the Germans were finally driven out of Jugoslavia, he would find himself a popular hero, at the head of a *de facto* administration and of a very considerable armed force, which, as a convinced Communist, he would, if necessary, be ready to use for the purpose of achieving his political ends. This put him in a very strong position when it came to bargaining, for in the ultimate analysis nothing short of superior force could turn him out. On the other hand, it was clear that he attached importance to keeping up appearances and to securing, if possible, the recognition of the Allies for his administration; first of all because such a policy would facilitate his task internally and secondly because he had no wish at this stage to cut off his principal source of supplies. His response to our soundings was accordingly not entirely negative, and in return some hope was held out to him that he might ultimately obtain an increased measure of political recognition.

By the spring these mutual soundings, for it would be too much to call them negotiations, had been carried as far as they could be by the somewhat precarious medium of my mobile wireless set in its suitcase container. Simultaneously, a number of other questions had arisen, which, it seemed, could best be settled by my visiting London, possibly in company with a representative of Tito. As usual, the question of supply loomed large. Supplies to the Partisans were by now on such a scale that a change in the administrative arrangements at base was being considered and it was clearly desirable that I should take part in the discussions.

I was accordingly not altogether surprised to receive early in April instructions to stand by to be evacuated and authority to bring with me Vlatko Velebit, whom Tito had once again wisely chosen as his delegate.

CHAPTER XII

CHANGE OF SCENE

IT was a fine, gusty, spring day when Duncan and I set out for Bosanski Petrovac. The snow was still lying on the hills, but in the valley the sun was quite hot. Marching was thirsty work and from time to time we stopped to drink from a mountain stream. The track took us up the cliff face, across a stretch of open moorland, and then, climbing again, into thick pine forests, ankle-deep in snow. German aircraft were in the habit of patrolling the track, and we kept a sharp look out for them while we were crossing the open moorland, where several bomb-craters and the shattered carcasses of two pack-ponies, showed what happened to you if you were caught in the open. But we were lucky, and it was not until we had reached the cover of the woods and had stopped to eat our rations, that the first enemy plane made its appearance, circling harmlessly high above the trees.

Late in the afternoon we emerged from the woods and found ourselves overlooking the flat country round Petrovac, where I had dropped some months before. More recently we had contrived a landing-strip two or three miles from the village and it was from this that we were to be picked up that night by an aircraft from Italy. As we were making our way down to the plain, we fell in with Vlatko Velebit, who had come by a different route. Together we walked on into the village, where we were to rest until it was time to go out and wait for the arrival of the aircraft.

We had a long wait that night in the cold, mist-laden darkness out on the landing-strip, and we had almost given up hope, when we heard the noise of an aeroplane, first faint in the distance, and then louder as it came nearer. Was it a friend or an enemy? That was the first thing to find out. Corporal Price, my wireless operator, came running up to say he had made contact with it and that it was one of ours. A week or two later Price was badly wounded by a bomb from a German plane within a few hundred yards of the same spot.

But this time all was well and by now our aircraft was circling overhead. We hurried to light flares along the improvised runway to guide it in. At the same time, we started to get ready for evacuation a group of badly wounded Partisans who were to be taken out in the same aircraft, bringing them as near the landing-strip as possible, for the pilot would not want to spend more than a few minutes on the ground and there would be no time to be lost.

It made a strange scene, in the flickering light of the flares with the darkness surrounding us like a curtain: the muffled shapes of the wounded, stretched out on the ground or sagging limply in the arms of their comrades, here and there a greyish-white face and a blood-stained bandage, momentarily illumined. Then, suddenly, the pilot, circling ever lower, switched on his searchlight as he touched down and, for a few moments, everything was bathed in dazzling radiance. We saw the wheels bump over the uneven surface of the grass until they finally came to a stop. Then, while the engines were kept running, the doors opened and we started hauling and hoisting the wounded up into the body of the plane. When they were all inside, we followed them; the doors were shut; the engines roared and we jolted off again over the turf to the take-off. Another few seconds and we were airborne. Finding a vacant space among the wounded Partisans on the Dakota's crowded floor, I lay down and, using my pack as a pillow, was soon asleep.

As we came in from the sea, Algiers lay bright and inviting in the sunshine, its red-roofed white-washed houses and green trees spread over a natural amphitheatre of hills rising steeply from the sparkling waters of the bay. We were met at the aerodrome by Mark Chapman Walker, with an invitation to stay from the Supreme Allied Commander and a programme of staff talks which were to begin at once. Soon, in a magnificently tiled bathroom in General Wilson's villa overlooking the harbour, I was wallowing in the first bath I had had for months and Sergeant Duncan was negotiating for some clean khaki drill with his friend the mess Sergeant. Shortly afterwards we sat down to a copious and deliciously cooked meal.

The next few days were full enough. Velebit was by now an old hand at negotiating with the Allied High Command and the staff talks went more smoothly than those at Alexandria. Moreover the decisions of principle had already been taken, as far as material help was concerned. It was our established policy to give the Partisans all the material help in our power and aircraft and supplies were becoming every month more plentiful. It now only remained to perfect the administrative machinery and the proposed changes designed to meet this need were already far advanced, including the establishment at Bari of a Rear Headquarters to my Mission under one of my own officers, and the creation of a new air formation to be known as the Balkan Air Force, which would be responsible for the planning, co-ordination and, to a large extent, execution of air operations in the Balkans.

Meanwhile, the political problem, arising inevitably out of our military policy, remained in the background, unsolved, a constant source of uncertainty and embarrassment. And this, if a solution was to be attempted, would have to be solved in London.

But any doubts as to the next step were shortly to be resolved. Hardly had I reached Algiers when I received a message to stand by for a long-distance wireless telephone conversation with Mr. Churchill, who was going to ring me up from 10 Downing Street at a specified time.

I have never liked the telephone as a means of communication, and this particular conversation seemed likely to prove an exceptionally alarming ordeal. In a state of some apprehension, I repaired to the brightly lighted and heavily guarded underground room containing the Algiers end of the apparatus. First of all, the technicalities involved were explained to me by an officer of the United States Army Signal Corps, while a pretty W.A.C. Sergeant prepared to take a recording of what was said. The best link with London was, it appeared, for some obscure reason via New York and Washington and what we said would somehow be rendered incomprehensible to enemy listeners-in by a 'scrambling' process, thus obviating the necessity of using code. All this struck me as far from reassuring and I continued to view the whole proceeding with the innate alarm and despondency of one who hates telephones.

Finally the appointed time arrived and, after a series of infinitely disturbing clicks and buzzes, Mr. Churchill's well-known voice came booming and rasping over the ether. Closely following the instructions at the beginning of the London telephone book, I began by announcing my own identity. At this, the Prime Minister seemed unaccountably annoyed and told me to shut up. A bad start, I felt. Then he inquired hurriedly and surprisingly, whether I had talked to the Pumpkin. On my asking politely what he meant, he replied in a loud whisper, after hesitating a moment, 'Why that great big General of mine, of course, but look it up, look it up,' and then went on to inquire what I had done with the Pippin.

I was in despair. It was clear to me that one of us was off his head. I hoped that it was not me; on the other hand it was most disturbing to think that at this vital juncture of the war Mr. Churchill should have been overcome by insanity. Clearly there was nothing for it but to admit that I had no idea what he was talking about or how all these vegetables came into it. I did so in some trepidation.

There was a pause, during which nothing could be heard save the inhuman wailing and crackling of the ether. Then, projected over the air, first of all across the Atlantic from Downing Street to Washington, then back again from New York to the north coast of Africa, came, quite distinctly, an exclamation of horror and disgust. 'Good God,' I heard him say, 'they haven't got the code.'

Not a moment too soon, the technicians came to our rescue, breaking in hurriedly on the conversation from either end and arguing it out amongst themselves as to whether it was necessary for us to use a code or not.

Evidently my American won the day, for, when we resumed our conversation, the Prime Minister was off on a new tack. 'Shall we scramble?' he said gaily. I replied that I thought I was scrambled. There was a rumbling noise, followed by a silence, and Mr. Churchill's voice came on the air once more. 'So am I,' he announced.

Then, in ordinary unadorned English, though continuing to refer to the Supreme Allied Commander-in-Chief as Pumpkin, and to his son Randolph as Pippin, two pseudonyms which seemed to delight him, he gave me my instructions. I was to come to London at once and bring Velebit with me.

Having laid down the receiver with relief, I started off to find Velebit and tell him to get ready to leave. On the way I remembered that I had left something downstairs and went back to get it. As I opened the door, I was startled to hear my own voice coming out of it. 'Pumpkin, Sir?' I was saying, 'I'm afraid I don't quite understand what you mean.'

I looked in. The pretty W.A.C. Sergeant was playing a record of the conversation back to herself. I have seldom seen anyone more genuinely amused. 'And an English accent too,' I heard her say delightedly. I decided not to disturb her.

Next day Velebit and I flew to London.

In England, in that spring of 1944, the feeling of suspense dominated everything. Arriving, we found the whole of the southern counties one immense armed camp. Every country lane was crowded with trucks, armoured vehicles and guns; everywhere there were aerodromes and all day long the sky was black with bombers, fighters and transport planes. The restaurants and night clubs were full of young men in uniform having a last fling before plunging into Armageddon. In the streets, American and Allied troops seemed to outnumber our own. London was full of rumours. Everyone knew for certain when the invasion was going to be, and everyone knew different.

I did not expect people to take much interest in Jugoslavia. But they did. They were, I suppose, glad of an excuse to turn their minds to something else, to escape temporarily from the subject of the invasion. The Press descended on us as only the Press can, telegraphing, ringing up and hovering on the doorstep with batteries of cameras. All kinds of people in all kinds of departments wanted to see me and hear about Tito. We were taken to see the Chief of the Imperial General Staff and officers of almost equally exalted rank at the Admiralty and Air Ministry. We were sent for by General Eisenhower, at that time engaged in putting the finishing touches to the preparations for D-Day. Finally we were summoned to No. 10 Downing Street and there received by Mr. Churchill, a formidable figure sitting smoking his cigar at the long table in the Cabinet Room.

Velebit was, I think, well pleased with the results of his visit. He had been able to put his point of view to Mr. Churchill personally; he had been received officially by various other important people and he had also made a number of useful unofficial contacts with the Press, who could henceforward be counted on to keep Tito and the Partisan Movement before the mind of the public. He now returned to report to Tito on the results of his visit. Vivian Street had flown back some days earlier to take charge of the Mission in my absence. I stayed on, as Mr. Churchill needed me for further discussions and there were a number of other people who wanted to see me.

The people to be seen and the matters to be discussed were numerous and varied. First of all there were the Joint Planners. In an electrically lit, air-conditioned subterranean vault, reached by a network of underground passages far below Whitehall, I found a soldier, a sailor and an airman, planning the future course of the war. With them I discussed at length Yugoslavia's relation to the other theatres of operations and the best way to help the Partisans and increase their contribution to the war effort as a whole.

On the political side, it was harder than ever to see a way out. I was sent for by King Peter, now back in London, and had with him a friendly enough conversation, which ended in a discussion of the relative merits of various brands of motor cars. In the course of it I told the King how things were shaping in his country and mentioned that Tito had agreed that he should be a pilot in the new Jugoslav squadron which was now being trained in North Africa and would eventually operate over Jugoslavia. It was a one in a thousand chance, but, for King Peter, it seemed to offer the only hope, however remote, of recovering the position which he had gained by his conduct in 1941 and since lost by his absence from his country during the past three years. To Peter himself, who was a trained pilot, the idea clearly appealed, but, from the reception which it received in other quarters it was obvious to me that nothing was likely to come of it.

Meanwhile, the Foreign Office was doing what it could to bridge the gap between Tito and the Royal Jugoslav Government in London. It was no easy task. The gap was one not only of space, but of time, a difference not only of outlook, but of experience. King Peter, it is true, had, as a gesture, publicly broken with Mihajlović and called

447

upon his people to support Tito. But, coming when it did, this *volte-face* only served to antagonize one faction without impressing the other. Moreover his Government, on the whole, were strongly opposed to such a course of action.

The next thing was to find one that wasn't. And now, in the strangely unreal limbo of exiled politicians which existed in London during the war, there started once again the gropings and shufflings which heralded the formation of a new Allied Government in Exile.

This time the object of the manœuvre was to find a Cabinet which could somehow or other come to terms with Tito before it was too late. At a luncheon party in London I met one of the promoters of the new idea, Dr. Ivan Šubašić, a former Governor of Croatia. He asked me what I thought of their prospects of success. I told him that in my opinion any bargain with Tito at this stage was likely to be a very one-sided one. Dr. Šubašić did not seem unduly disturbed by this. He was a rather flabby-looking man of medium size with his hair *en brosse* and small uneasy eyes. His yellowish skin hung loosely, as though it were too big for him. He looked every inch a politician. He would, I reflected, need to be one, if he were to save anything from this particular wreck.

While I was in England I also met some of the British officers who had been attached to General Mihajlović's Headquarters and had recently, after various adventures, been evacuated and returned to England. Mr. Churchill himself presided over one of these meetings, which was held at Chequers. We found there was little or no disagreement between us as to the facts. It was common ground that the Četniks, though in the main well disposed towards Great Britain, were militarily less effective than the Partisans and that some of Mihajlović's subordinates had undoubtedly reached accommodations with the enemy. I was interested to find that some of those who knew him best, while liking and respecting him as a man, had little opinion of Mihajlović as a leader. They felt that, under new and more determined leadership and with better discipline, the relatively weak Četnik detachments could, in Serbia at any rate, be built up into a force which could play an important part in the liberation of their country.

But at this stage such a reorganization was no longer a practical proposition. Two years earlier something of the kind might have been possible. Indeed, had action on the right lines been taken soon enough, it might have been possible to weld Partisans and Četniks into one unified resistance movement. Now Tito was in a position to dictate his terms and the only condition of co-operation which he was prepared to offer the Četniks was absorption in the Partisan ranks, an offer of which many were to avail themselves.

A few days after my visit to Chequers I received a telephone message from Buckingham Palace to say that the King wished to see me. He wanted, it appeared, a first-hand account of the Jugoslav situation. I was surprised at this, for it seemed to me remarkable that His Majesty should have time to interest himself in what was after all only a relatively minor question of policy, by comparison with the great issues that confronted him at that time. I was even more astonished to find, as soon as he started talking, that the King knew as much or more about the Jugoslav problem as anyone I had met since I had been back in England. He also took an entirely realistic view of it. But what seemed to interest him most was the purely military side of my activities. In fact I gained the impression that there was nothing he would have liked better than to try his own hand at irregular warfare.

I soon became so absorbed in our conversation that I almost forgot where I was and to whom I was speaking. Then I remembered with a start that the young, alert-looking man in R.A.F. uniform sitting facing me in an armchair on the other side of the fireplace was the King of England. I went away very much impressed.

A day or two later I had completed my business and was preparing to start back, when a signal arrived from Vivian Street, now back in Bosnia. It was very short, only a couple of sentences. It had every possible indication of priority, and it was the kind of communication that took your breath away. It announced that the enemy had made a large-scale airborne attack on Partisan Headquarters with glider and parachute troops; that the Partisans had suffered heavy casualties, although Tito himself was believed to be safe; that the Mission had so

far managed to escape capture, although whether they would do so for
much longer was uncertain, for they were in the woods with strong
enemy forces closing in on them from all sides.

We waited anxiously for more news. When it came it was only
slightly more reassuring. Vivian and his party had joined up again
with Tito and with the surviving Partisan Headquarter troops. But
they were still on the run, the enemy having followed up their airborne
attack with an all-out offensive.

On the receipt of this news, urgent instructions were sent to the
R.A.F. in Italy to give the Partisans all possible help from the air. A
few days later the situation was sufficiently stable for it to be possible
to land aircraft on an improvised landing-strip and evacuate Tito and
his staff and the British, American and Soviet Missions.

Having in the meantime reached Italy, I now heard for the first time
a full account of what had happened.

A few days after Vivian reached Partisan Headquarters an incident
had occurred which aroused his suspicion. One morning a single
German aircraft made its appearance over the valley, and, instead of
dropping bombs or machine-gunning, as these aerial visitors usually
did, had spent half an hour or more flying slowly up and down at a
height of about two thousand feet. Each time it passed directly over
the little house on the rising ground outside the village where he and
the others were living. Standing outside in the orchard, in the warm
spring sunshine, looking up at it, they discussed what it could be doing,
and came to the conclusion that it was making a photographic
reconnaissance.

Now the Germans would not do this without a reason, and Vivian's
guess was that the visit of the little aeroplane would be the forerunner
of a heavy air attack that would put anything else we had experienced
into the shade. Accordingly he sought out Tito in his cave and told him
what he thought was going to happen, adding that in the circumstances
he proposed to move a little further out. That afternoon he and the
others transferred themselves with wireless sets and escort to a little
house in the hills a mile or two away from the village.

Two days passed; and nothing happened. Then a third day. Vivian began to wonder if he had not perhaps been rather over-cautious. That night he dined with Tito and after a good meal walked home to bed through the orchards.

Next morning he was wakened, just as it was getting light by the familiar shout of '*Avioni!*' from the Partisans on guard outside. The shout was repeated, so he went out to see what was happening.

A number of small aircraft, considerably more than usual, were bombing the village, circling round and then, when they had dropped their bombs, pulling away to make room for others that were coming in from every direction. Then, just as those who were watching were reflecting what short work a couple of Spitfires would make of the intruders, a deeper note fell on the ears of the watchers, and out of the sun came six great JU 52s, flying in formation down the valley. The Germans were doing things in style.

They waited for the whistle and crash of the bombs. The planes reached the village and circled it. Then, as they watched, something fell from the leading plane, and, falling, billowed out into a great canopy with a man dangling from it. Then more and more, from one plane after another. The air seemed full of them. More planes followed, and gliders, bringing guns and reinforcements to the parachutists, who by now were shooting their way into the village. A glider seemed to be landing almost on top of the little house which the Mission had left three days before.

For a few moments Vivian and the others stood and looked. Then, taking the wireless sets and anything else they could carry, they moved off along the hillside to establish contact with the Partisan Corps Headquarters situated further up the valley.

Meanwhile, in Drvar itself, the Partisans had driven back the Germans from the village. But they were still firmly established on the slopes outside it. A glider which had come down on the flat ground immediately below Tito's cave had crashed and the crew had been killed. But now some other Germans had succeeded in gaining a position from which they commanded the mouth of the cave and this was now under heavy fire. Tito's position was precarious, for to use the ordinary way down would have meant almost certain death. But, with the help of a rope he hoisted himself up a cleft in the rock to the high ground above his cave. From there he was able to join the main body of Partisans.

Now came the news that, on top of the airborne attack, strong forces of the enemy were converging on Drvar from all sides. The Partisans had already suffered heavy losses. They could not hope to hold Drvar in the face of such overwhelming odds. The order was given to withdraw into the hills.

After a ten hours' march Vivian and the others reached the little group of huts buried deep in the forest which we had left some months before, to find Tito and his staff already there. Soon the wireless was working and a message on its way to Bari saying what had happened and asking urgently for air support.

Meanwhile, the enemy had taken Drvar. They had inflicted severe casualties on the Partisans, but at heavy cost to themselves, and they had failed to capture Tito or the Allied Missions. For this failure, they revenged themselves on the defenceless civilian population, known to be loyal to the Partisans. When the village was recaptured some months later it was found that most of the inhabitants had been massacred. One of our officers who went back with the Partisans tried to find some of the peasants who had lived near us. At last he found one who had somehow survived. He said that during the fighting the Germans had forced the civilians to carry ammunition for them at the point of the rifle, making them go on even after they had been wounded and could barely crawl: old men, women and even children. After the fighting was over and they no longer had any use for them, they had shot them. And the child Ginger? Ginger had been shot too.

Having missed Tito at Drvar, the enemy began to close in on him in the woods. Soon they reached the edge of the forest. Firing could be heard coming nearer. Tito decided to break out.

The break out took place at night. Fierce fighting was in progress. Flashes could be seen on the ridge above them. The sound of firing came ever closer. From time to time a Very star shot up into the sky.

Then Vivian saw something that amazed him. There, on a siding in the woods, was drawn up the Partisan Express, with steam up and smoke and sparks belching from the funnel. Solemnly, Tito, his entourage and the dog Tigger entrained; the whistle blew; and, with much puffing and creaking, they started off down the five miles of track through the woods, with the enemy's bullets whining through the trees all round them.

During the days that followed, Tito and his staff, with the Allied Missions and a force of a few hundred Partisans, were almost constantly on the move: dodging through the woods, lying up in the daytime, moving at night. Again and again they had narrow escapes from the enemy. German patrols, aircraft and light tanks seemed to be everywhere. Food and ammunition were getting desperately short, but once they managed to stop long enough to receive a supply drop from British planes, based in Italy. At the same time other British aircraft were giving much needed air support, wherever they could. During the week that followed the attack on Drvar, our planes flew over a thousand sorties in support of the Partisans, thereby doing much to relieve the pressure on them.

All this time Vivian kept in close touch with Tito. He was, he told me afterwards, impressed throughout by the way in which Tito dominated the situation, remaining calm and collected under the severest strain, personally directing the operations of the small body of troops which accompanied him as well as those of the other Partisan formations in the neighbourhood, quietly giving orders to the Partisans round him. This from Vivian, an experienced soldier and a severe judge in such matters, was high praise.

Then one day, as they were resting after a long march, Tito sent for him. Vivian found the Marshal looking tired and depressed. He had, he said, reluctantly reached the conclusion that it was impossible for him to direct the operations of his forces throughout Jugoslavia while being chased through the woods and kept constantly on the move. The complexity of this task now made it essential for him to have a relatively firm base for his Headquarters. Already he had lost touch with nearly all the formations under his command. He must ask Vivian to arrange for the evacuation of himself and his staff by air to Italy until such time as the situation permitted his return to Jugoslavia.

At first Vivian was surprised. Tito was connected in his mind with the hills and forests and it was hard to imagine him leaving them. But he soon realized that the decision which he had taken was the right one.

A signal was dispatched to Bari and the answer came back almost immediately. The R.A.F. would do everything in their power to pick them up from a nearby stretch of flat ground, now held by the Partisans. That afternoon they set out for the landing-strip.

They reached it after dark. It was raining and there was low cloud. Not much hope, it seemed, of getting out. Then the moon came through the clouds and they cheered up a little. Anxiously they waited. At last, came the sound they were waiting for: the faint hum of an aircraft engine in the distance. Bonfires were lighted and soon the Dakota was circling the field, ready to land. It touched down; they climbed in. Tito, his dog Tigger, half a dozen of his staff, Vivian and the Russian Mission. Almost immediately they were airborne.

As Vivian got into the plane, he saw that it was manned by Russians. It was a Dakota, supplied under lease-lend, which the Russians were operating from Bari under British operational control. The Soviet officer concerned had shown considerable astuteness in securing this particular assignment for his plane. Afterwards the Russians were to make great capital out of the claim that it was they who had rescued Tito in this emergency.

An hour or two later they reached Bari.

The next thing to be decided was where Tito and his Headquarters Staff were to establish themselves. I went and called on him at the suburban villa on the outskirts of Bari in which he had been temporarily installed and found him in favour of moving over to the island of Vis until such time as the military situation made it feasible to return to the interior. This, indeed, seemed the obvious solution. Vis was Jugoslav territory; at the same time, thanks to its now substantial garrison and ever-present British naval and air support, it offered a degree of security and stability which was not to be found on the mainland of Jugoslavia.

The task of conveying the Marshal to his new abode was entrusted to the Royal Navy and H.M.S. *Blackmore*, a Hunt Class destroyer, under the command of Lieutenant Carson, R.N., was allotted to us for the purpose, with another destroyer for the rest of the party.

Carson and the officers and crew of the *Blackmore* immediately entered into the spirit of the thing as only the Navy can. In order to avoid any risk of enemy interference, the crossing was made at night. At about six in the evening Tito, followed by Tigger, was piped on board in fine style, and at once taken below and plied with gin. His original Marshal's uniform had fallen into the hands of the Germans during the attack on Drvar and been taken away to grace a museum somewhere in Germany, but a substitute had been found, and he once more looked and, I think, felt the part.

By the time we weighed anchor any initial shyness had completely worn off and I could see that we were in for a convivial evening. We sat down to dinner in the wardroom to find ourselves confronted with a menu magnificently illuminated by one of the crew and written in Serb as well as English. I noticed at once that the wine list was a formidable one: sherry followed the gin, then red wine, then white, then port, then liqueurs. The Marshal drank some of everything, only hesitating momentarily when a large bottle was produced mysteriously draped in a napkin. For an instant he wavered.

'Cheri-beri?' he inquired, cryptically.

'No, Champagne,' said the Captain proudly.

'Ah, Champagne!' said Tito and drained a tumbler of it.

It was not till later that we discovered that by Cheri-beri he meant Cherry Brandy, though when, in due course, that stimulating beverage made its appearance, any distrust which he might have felt for it earlier in the evening had evidently completely vanished.

By this stage of dinner the Marshal, to my surprise, was speaking quite fluent English and rounded off the proceedings by giving a spirited recital of 'The Owl and the Pussy-Cat'.

> The Owl and the Pussy-Cat went to sea
>   In a beautiful pea-green boat.
> They dined on mince and slices of quince,
>   Which they ate with a runcible spoon;
> And hand in hand, on the edge of the sand,
>   They danced by the light of the moon. . . .

After that, we went up on deck.

By now the sky was starting to get lighter, and, outlined against it, we could already see the jagged outline of the Dalmatian mountains. Tito sat in an armchair on deck, contemplatively smoking a cigar. Soon we could make out the dark shape of Vis, rising from the sea, and twenty minutes later Carson, on the bridge, was bringing us skilfully alongside in the little harbour of Komiša.

CHAPTER XIII

ISLAND BASE AND BRIEF ENCOUNTER

DESPITE his experience at Drvar, Tito had not lost his liking for caves. On Vis he discovered one three-quarters of the way up Mount Hum, which rose stark and barren at one end of the island, and there installed himself. I, for my part, chose a little house by the water's edge, which, though strategically less well placed in the event of an enemy attack, was a good deal more commodious and boasted the best bathing in the island. Swimming out a little way, you could see, as you lay floating on your back in the clear blue water, the whole panorama of the Dalmatian coast, stretching hazily away into the distance, with the sunlit island of Korčula, now in German hands, standing out in sharper relief in the foreground. Sometimes Tito would come down from his mountain to visit me and we would swim out together, with Olga, Tigger and the bodyguard cleaving the water in perfect formation behind us.

Vis itself had undergone a startling change since I had last been there. In the place of the peaceful little Dalmatian island, with nothing more warlike to show than the crumbling battlements of Fort St. George, a veritable military, naval and air base had sprung into being in the space of a few months. In the central valley the olive trees had disappeared and the red earth had been flattened out to form a full-sized landing-strip, from which fighters and fighter-bombers were constantly taking off on their way to attack shipping up and down the coast or objectives inland. On one side were drawn up sometimes as many as a dozen four-engined American bombers, Fortresses and Liberators, which had run into trouble while on operations over the mainland, and, unable to get back to their bases in Italy, had limped as far as this and crash-landed on Vis. The narrow roads were crammed with Army trucks and jeeps, stirring up clouds of red dust as they rushed along. Every few hundred yards dumps of stores and ammunition, surrounded by barbed wire and by brightly painted direction

457

posts, advertised the presence of R.E.M.E., of N.A.A.F.I., of D.A.D.O.S., and of the hundred and one other services and organizations whose very existence we had forgotten in our year away from the Army. From the surviving olive groves the old familiar bugle calls rang out and through the branches we could see the green berets and khaki drill of Tom Churchill's Commandos as they moved about making ready for some raid on the mainland or on a neighbouring island. Down by the harbour at Komiša was the Naval Headquarters, presided over by Commander Morgan Giles, R.N., who had what was practically an independent command over a considerable force of M.T.B.s and other light naval craft, with which he engaged in piratical activities against enemy shipping up and down the whole length of the Jugoslav coast from Istria to Montenegro.

Though Morgan Giles possessed the high-sounding title of Senior Naval Officer, Vis, or, in its abbreviated form, S.N.O.V.I.S. (his assistants, for reasons which will be obvious, were known as the Seven Dwarfs), the island boasted another even more distinguished sailor (not to mention, for the moment, the Partisan Major-General who commanded Tito's fleet of schooners). No account of events on Vis would be complete without some mention of him.

Admiral Sir Walter Cowan had, after a long and distinguished career, retired from the Navy in 1931, at the age of sixty. In 1939, on the outbreak of war, he had managed to get himself re-employed, and, not wishing to stay at home, he had himself sent out to the Middle East which, he felt, offered more scope to a man of his tastes. He had always enjoyed fighting on shore, preferably hand to hand, as much or more than fighting at sea, and had won his D.S.O. in the Sudan serving under Lord Kitchener in the 'nineties.

Accordingly, at the age of seventy, he attached himself to an Indian Cavalry Regiment serving in the Western Desert, with the rank of Commander R.N. and in the somewhat ill-defined position of Naval Liaison Officer. In this capacity he took part in a number of Commando raids, startling all concerned by his complete disregard of danger. But in those days things were not going as well as they might in the desert and one day the party he was with had the misfortune to be completely overrun by a strong force of German tanks. Admiral Cowan was last seen advancing sternly on one of the enemy's tanks, discharging his pistol at it from point-blank range.

Last seen, that is, until, having escaped from his prison camp, he appeared a year or two later in Italy and immediately attached himself to Tom Churchill's Commando Brigade. Those of us who had known him in the desert were delighted to see him reappear on Vis, as frail-looking, as dashing and as friendly as ever. There he was to end the war, adding, at the age of seventy-three, by his gallantry on a raid, a bar to the D.S.O. which he had won half a century before.

With the arrival on Vis of Tito and his staff a German attempt to capture the island once again became a probability, and we lived in a state of constant preparedness. In the event no such attempt was made, largely, I think, because of the disrupting effect of the successful harassing operations carried out by the British forces based on Vis, acting in co-operation with the Partisans. These showed great aptitude for small-scale raiding and were able to give valuable support to the Commandos, whom they furnished with much useful local information. They also used their rather ramshackle old schooners to extremely good effect, employing them not only as improvised landing-craft, but actually engaging and sometimes capturing enemy vessels with them.

In these operations a not unimportant part was beginning to be played by Partisan artillerymen. These were the product of an institution known, somewhat grandiloquently, as the Balkan School of Artillery which had been set up on Vis as part of my Mission under the command of Lieut.-Col. Geoffrey Kup, R.A., a regular soldier of great patience and unflagging good humour, whose life-work it became to instruct the Partisans in the use of the American 75-mm. Pack Howitzer. This was a light mountain gun, transportable on mule-back, if there happened to be any mules, and in general ideally suited to the type of warfare in which we were engaged. After a certain amount of preliminary argument – an unavoidable accompaniment of any enterprise of this kind – the Partisans took to the new weapon like ducks to water, operating the relatively complicated sighting and range-finding devices as if they had done nothing else all their lives. Eventually several whole batteries were trained and, after being successfully tried out on a number of raids, was landed by air, complete with guns and some extremely lively mules, in the heart of Montenegro, a ticklish operation, which, however, was abundantly justified by results.

At about the same time the Royal Air Force carried out in the same area what must have been one of the most remarkable air operations of its kind. I received from my Mission with the Montenegrin Partisans a signal to say that they were hard pressed by the enemy and that their movements were severely hampered by the large numbers of wounded which they had with them. At once the R.A.F. agreed to help. The wounded, numbering close on a thousand, were concentrated near an improvised landing-strip, and one summer's afternoon some thirty sorties were flown by troop-carrying Dakotas and every one of them evacuated under the nose of the enemy.

This was only one instance of the constant help of all kinds which we were now receiving from the R.A.F. The proposal to set up a special R.A.F. formation in support of the Partisans had now been put into execution with the creation of the Balkan Air Force under Air Vice-Marshal Elliot. H.Q., B.A.F. was responsible for the planning and co-ordination of all supply dropping as well as for all bomber and fighter operations in support of the Partisans. This gave me a single authority with whom I could deal direct and was of incalculable advantage in obtaining quick results.

I was lucky, too, in having Bill Elliot to work with. His quick intelligence and ready imagination were essential qualities in dealing with so volatile and uncertain an element as guerrilla warfare. He, in turn, was responsible to Air Marshal Slessor, another outstanding airman, who, despite the innumerable other calls on his attention, was always ready to interest himself in our affairs and come to our help in time of need.

This represented a marked change from the situation which I had found when I had first approached the problem of helping the Partisans a year earlier. Then, such supplies as were available had been dropped and air support had been given as and when opportunity offered. Now help came in a steady flow in accordance with a carefully worked-out system of priorities, while tactical and strategical air support was promptly given wherever it was most needed and a signal to B.A.F. could be counted on to produce immediate results.[1]

Help on such a scale played a decisive part in enabling the Partisans to withstand the fierce onslaught with which the Germans had followed up their attack on Drvar. Like the preceding six offensives, this Seventh Offensive, as it came to be called, gradually petered out. Once more, the Partisans had succeeded in denying the enemy a target at which he could strike a decisive blow. Now, after waiting for their adversaries' assault to spend its force, they themselves were ready to assume the initiative once more. Just as we had helped, by well-timed air support and supply drops, to relieve the pressure when the Partisans were on the defensive, so, now that they had passed to the attack, we prepared once again to back them up.

Meanwhile on other fronts things were moving fast. In Italy, Rome had fallen and the Eighth Army stood before Florence. In the west, the Allies had landed in France and had fared better than anyone had dared hope. In the east, the Russians were advancing rapidly in great bounds, rolling back the Germans towards their own frontiers in the north and in the south pushing down towards the Balkans. By the summer of 1944, the end of the war in Europe at last seemed within reach, or at any rate within sight.

Nor was this without its effect on our relations with the Partisans. The increased speed of our advance northwards up Italy made it more necessary than ever that our operations should be closely co-ordinated with theirs. It seemed possible that, as things went increasingly badly for them, the Germans would decide to withdraw from the Balkans altogether. If so, it was most important that steps should be taken to cut off their retreat. We had also to consider what would happen when the Allies and the Partisans joined hands in northern Italy. Tito had already told me that it was his intention to lay claim to Istria, Trieste,

[1] The following figures for supplies during 1944 give some idea of the scale on which the Western Allies were now helping the Partisans:— over 100,000 rifles; over 50,000 light machine guns and sub-machine guns; 1380 mortars; 324,000 mortar bombs; 636,000 grenades; over 97,500,000 rounds of small-arms ammunition; 700 wireless sets; 175,000 suits of battle-dress; 260,000 pairs of boots.

Venezia Giulia, and part of Carinthia, and the Allies, so far as I knew, had as yet no definite policy with regard to these areas.

Finally there was, once again, the political problem. The probability that Jugoslavia would before long, by one agency or another, be freed from the Germans made it desirable to reach without delay some kind of compromise which would enable us to reconcile our *de jure* obligations with the *de facto* situation which existed inside the country. Tito's presence on Vis, a couple of hours' flight from Caserta, the new seat of A.F.H.Q., seemed to offer an excellent opportunity of reaching a direct settlement with him, and I had not been on Vis long when I was instructed to extend to him an invitation to visit Italy as the guest of the Supreme Allied Commander.

Tito accepted and, after much discussion, an agreed programme was drawn up and a date fixed for the visit. The night before, General Wilson sent over his private aeroplane to Vis to fetch us, and in this we made the flight to Naples. Tito was accompanied by his Chief of Staff and various other leading members of his entourage, by Olga, by his medical adviser and by his bodyguard. It seemed hard, in the circumstances, that the dog Tigger should be left behind and, at my suggestion, he was brought too.

It was thus a considerable party that came tumbling out of the plane on to the sun-baked expanse of Capodicchino aerodrome. The cameras clicked and whirred; General Gammell, representing the Supreme Allied Commander, saluted, smiling affably; the guard of honour presented arms; Tigger barked; and Tito, returning the salutes, stepped with admirable composure into General Wilson's magnificent car, with its blonde Women's Army Corps driver at the wheel and, preceded by outriders on motor bicycles, was whisked off up the hill to Caserta, where he was to lunch with the Supreme Commander. It was his first public appearance outside his own country.

There were not more than half a dozen of us at luncheon in the little dining-room of General Wilson's hunting lodge up behind Caserta, and even so there was very little elbow room. But this did not deter Boško and Prlja, Tito's two bodyguards. Pushing their way past the Italian mess waiter, one took up his position immediately behind the Marshal's chair, while the other kept General Wilson covered with his sub-machine gun. Tigger went to ground under the table.

There was a slight atmosphere of constraint. It was unbearably hot. One could feel the sweat trickling down one's spine. Nobody said anything; everyone, you could tell, was trying to think of a suitable opening gambit.

We were spared the trouble. The strain of passing the vegetables, under the baleful eye of a heavily armed and extremely grim-looking guerrilla warrior, who clearly did not like Italians, was too much for the Italian mess waiter. With an exclamation of despair he let a large dish of French beans drop with a crash on the table, and, at once, pandemonium reigned. The trigger-fingers of the bodyguard twitched menacingly; Tigger, roused from his uneasy slumbers beneath the table, let out a long wolf-like howl and started to snap at everyone's ankles; the Italians chattered and gesticulated. For a moment the situation showed signs of getting out of control.

It was then that General Wilson started to laugh. Gently, almost silently, at first, and then more and more heartily, until his whole massive frame quaked and rocked. Mirth bubbled in his eyes. I have never known anyone with a more infectious laugh. In a flash Tito was guffawing too and soon the whole table was convulsed with merriment. Even the Italians sniggered nervously in the background, while a grim smile spread over the stern features of the bodyguard. All tension disappeared. From then onwards I could tell that, socially at any rate, the visit was going to be a success. I realized too that his gift for putting all around him at their ease was one of the Supreme Commander's most valuable assets.

On the whole the staff talks, which we started next day, went smoothly. In addition to making a careful joint study of the existing strategical position in the areas with which we were concerned and of the way in which it was likely to develop, a good deal of time was devoted to reviewing the supply position. Tito, with an eye, I think, to the future, took this opportunity to ask for the immediate delivery of some tanks, to be landed at some point which the Partisans were temporarily holding on the coast of Montenegro, and it was only by taking him to see the colossal Eighth Army tank-maintenance workshops at Naples, employing some 12,000 workmen, that we were able to persuade him that the maintenance of an armoured force would be rather beyond the Army of National Liberation under existing circumstances. On the other hand we were able to give a good report of the progress of the Partisan tank squadron which was then being trained in North Africa.

Our conversations had been in progress for several days when the Supreme Allied Commander sent for me and showed me a most secret telegram which he had just received. It was from Mr. Churchill, announcing his own arrival in Italy in a week's time, and asking that Tito should, if possible, be induced to prolong his stay at Naples for a few days so that they might meet.

Things would have been much simpler if we could immediately have informed Tito of the contents of the message. But this, on security grounds, we were not allowed to do. We had to invent one pretext after another for spinning out the staff talks, though we had already exhausted almost every subject that we could usefully discuss and Tito was beginning to show signs of wanting to go home. There was, we hinted darkly, 'someone else' who wanted to see him. Time hung heavy on our hands.

I took Tito to see General Alexander at his camp beside the lake at Bolseno, where, for the first time, the question of Trieste was raised. I took him to Rome, the first big town he had been in for three years, where his new Marshal's uniform and the tommy-guns of the body-guard, stacked neatly on the steps of St. Peter's, caused a mild sensation. I took him to see what was left of Anzio and Cassino. I took him to tea with Hermione Ranfurly at her ridiculous little house on the side of the hill overlooking the Bay of Naples. I took him, as the guest of General Bill Donovan, to Mrs. Harrison Williams's villa at Capri.

It was there, as we were sitting under the trees in the garden eating lunch and admiring the incomparable view, that we became aware of a roaring in the sky. Looking up, we saw, high above us, the clumsy form of a York with a dozen fighters weaving and diving round it, like porpoises round a whale. Tito took it all in at a glance. 'Here,' he said, 'comes Mr. Churchill.' He was not an easy man to keep anything from.

The Naples Conference, as it was afterwards called, was, so far as it went, a success. The two main protagonists, Mr. Churchill and Tito, got on well enough with each other.

The Prime Minister was staying at a villa which had once been occupied by Queen Victoria, and there, surrounded by fusty enormities of Italian nineteenth-century taste, we sat closeted for hours in the sweltering heat of the Neapolitan summer, Mr. Churchill and I on one side of the table; Tito, Olga and Velebit on the other. When we knocked off, it was to take part in official and semi-official banquets, freely interspersed with speeches, all requiring translation.

The Prime Minister had no intention of allowing himself to be kept to any fixed programme and the range of questions we covered was wide. Jugoslav Resistance had long been a subject for which he had a special predilection. Now he was allowing himself the luxury of handling it personally, across the table with the guerrilla leader himself, specially brought there for the purpose.

He did it extremely well, with a touch that was generally light and friendly but sometimes heavy with the accumulated dignity and wisdom gained by forty years' experience in the affairs of State. He was generous in his praise of Tito's leadership and in his recognition of the Partisans' contribution to the Allied cause; generous, too, in his estimate of the help they would need to achieve the liberation of their country and to rebuild it once the war was over. Over military matters he took Tito into his confidence, calling for maps and showing him, with appropriate gestures, how in his view the war would develop. Even now, from where we sat by the open windows, we could see the ships gathering in the Bay of Naples for the forthcoming invasion of southern France.

On the subject of our obligations to King Peter Mr. Churchill was quite frank: he made it clear that we could not accord the Partisan regime any kind of political recognition unless they came to some kind of arrangement with the King. Finally, while saying or doing nothing that might be interpreted as undue interference in the internal affairs of another country, he managed to include in his remarks certain counsels of moderation. One, I remember, concerned the collectivization of agriculture. 'My friend Marshal Stalin,' he began (and I could see Tito sit up a little straighter at the mere mention of the name), 'my friend Marshal Stalin told me the other day that his battle with the peasants had been a more perilous and formidable undertaking than the battle for Stalingrad. I hope that you, Marshal,' he added, 'will think twice before you join such a battle with your sturdy Serbian peasantry.'

I watched Tito to see how he was taking it all. He was, I think, impressed. It would indeed have been surprising if he had not been. For him it was a big moment. Here he was, the revolutionary, the outlaw, against whom every hand was turned, honourably received by the highest in the land and dealing on equal terms with one of the Big Three. But he had the strength of character not to allow any feeling of triumph or elation to show or to affect his conduct, which remained moderate and unobtrusive.

Was he perhaps for a moment tempted to consider the possibility of coming to terms with the Democracies, of opening a window on the Occident, of trying to keep in with the West as well as the East? It seemed unlikely but just conceivable.

Sometimes, when questions of detail arose, others would be called in to take part in the discussions. Once or twice matters were referred to a committee of experts, while Mr. Churchill and Tito rested from their labours. On one such occasion a question of supply was being discussed by the Chiefs of Staff, when it was found that no further progress could be made without first referring the matter to the Prime Minister. But no one knew where the Prime Minister was. In the end someone remembered having heard him making plans to go bathing in the Bay of Naples. The matter was of some urgency, as a decision was needed at once, and I was accordingly instructed by General Wilson to go and find him and bring back his answer. The Americans furnished me, in case of need, with a stenographer, a blonde young lady of considerable personal attractions wearing a closely fitting tropical uniform; the Royal Navy gave me a motor torpedo boat; and, thus provided, I set out.

The first thing that we saw as we emerged from the harbour into the wider waters of the bay was a great fleet composed of innumerable ships of every size and shape steaming majestically towards the open sea — evidently the first phase of the invasion of the south of France.

This complicated my task. Trying to find Mr. Churchill in the midst of this mighty armada was like looking for a needle in a haystack, and, to make matters worse, the Captain of the M.T.B., a very young and somewhat diffident officer of the R.N.V.R., showed, quite properly no doubt, the greatest reluctance to risk his craft anywhere near these great convoys as they went sailing past. Disconsolately we chugged along in the general direction of Capri.

It was then that we noticed that something unusual was happening. As we watched, one of the troop-ships slightly slackened her speed as if to avoid something. Simultaneously there was a burst of excited cheering from the troops on deck, and a small bright blue object shot across her bows. On inspecting this through a pair of glasses, I recognized it as the Admiral's barge, and there, standing by the coxswain, wearing a boiler suit and a broad-brimmed Panama hat, smoking a cigar and giving the V-sign, was the object of my search. As we still watched, he swerved out and round and disappeared behind the next ship in the convoy.

Clearly there was nothing for it but to give chase. I put this to the Captain. He did not like the idea at all. It was all very well, he said, for the Prime Minister to go swerving in and out of convoys. But if he did it, he would get into trouble. I said that I would take full responsibility. At this he brightened and, having once taken the plunge, acquitted himself nobly. With the sea foaming and frothing in our wake, we set out boldly on our erratic course down the line. As we passed them, the troops on the transports gave an extra cheer for luck, followed by a salvo of whistles as they spotted my female companion. I have seldom felt more conspicuous.

Eventually we overtook and headed off the blue barge. There followed an intricate boarding operation in a choppy sea and I landed precipitously at the Prime Minister's feet, while the stenographer, anxious to miss nothing, hung over the rail of the M.T.B. Mr. Churchill seemed keenly interested. 'Do you,' he asked, 'often spend your afternoons careering round the Bay of Naples in His Majesty's ships with this charming young lady?' In vain I explained the object of the exercise. I was not to hear the last of this episode for some time.

They were an exhausting ten days and I was relieved when they came to an end. But our excursion into high politics was not over. Already, before his talks with Mr. Churchill, Tito had had a number of preliminary conversations on Vis with Dr. Ivan Šubašić, who, since I had seen him in London some weeks earlier, had emerged as Prime Minister of a new Royal Jugoslav Government, to be formed for the specific purpose of coming to terms with the Partisans. As a result of these, a preliminary understanding had been reached, providing for a measure of co-operation between the Royal Government and Tito's National Committee. Now Dr. Šubašić flew back to Vis in the same plane as Tito and myself, and the conversations were resumed. Vis became a hive of political activity.

In all these conversations, neither I nor Ralph Stevenson, who, as British Ambassador to the Royal Jugoslav Government had accompanied Šubašić, took any part. It was a purely Jugoslav occasion. Ralph, who was an old friend from Foreign Office days, and I spent our days bathing in the warm sunlit sea and speculating as to the outcome of the negotiations.

Would agreement be reached? Would Tito consider it worth compromising with the Royal Jugoslavs in order to gain Allied recognition? Would any terms that he was prepared to offer be acceptable to Šubašić? Would he consider himself as bound by any agreement that he might reach now, when once the country was liberated and he held all the cards in his hands? Might not the Russians suddenly take the wind out of our sails, in any case, by recognizing Tito independently of the Americans and ourselves?

It was hard to say. Rather belatedly, the British Government had done what they could to bring the two parties together. Now they must wait and see what came of it. One thing was certain, namely that, at this late stage, Tito, with so many cards in his hand, was unlikely to give much away.

From time to time the two parties would inform us of the progress they were making. It sounded (and was) too good to be true. The solution towards which they were moving was, it appeared, on the following lines: Tito's Government and Šubašić's Government would be merged into a single provisional Royal Jugoslav Government, which would continue in existence until Jugoslavia had been liberated, and free, popular, democratic elections could be held. Thereafter, it was presumed, the people of Jugoslavia would be governed by whatever type of Government they chose for themselves and would live happily ever after.

On the strength of it, Tito took the whole party out in a motor boat on a picnic to a local beauty spot, a great subterranean or rather submarine cave, which the sunlight, striking through the water which filled it, suffused with a blue phosphorescent radiance. Entering the cave in a small boat, we all stripped and bathed, our bodies glistening bluish and ghastly. Almost everyone there was a Cabinet Minister in one or other of the two Jugoslav Governments, and there was much shouting and laughter as one blue and phosphorescent Excellency cannoned into another, bobbing about in that caerulean twilight.

Then we emerged once more into the sunlight and sea breezes and lunched off lobsters and white wine. It was choppy going home and several of the party were sick. Not long after Dr. Šubašić returned to London to lay before King Peter the results of his talks with Tito.

CHAPTER XIV

RATWEEK

I. PLAN

WITH the departure of Dr. Šubašić there was nothing more to keep me on Vis, and I was glad of it. I had had enough of high politics to last me for some time. I had had enough, too, during the weeks I had spent there, of garrison life and of the eternal sunshine, blue sea and warm winds of the Adriatic in summer. It was time to get inland again — where the stage was set for the last phase of the fast-moving drama, in which for a year now we had all been so closely involved.

On Vis we had kept in constant touch by wireless and by messenger with our officers in the interior. From time to time one or other of them would come out and we would get a first-hand account of what was happening in this area or that. Moore and Jones had arrived from Slovenia; John Clarke from Montenegro, where he had been with Peko Dapčević; Andrew Maxwell from First Corps, burnt black with the sun and wind, and so thin as to be hardly recognizable, for he had stayed behind after the evacuation of Tito's Headquarters and taken part in the long forced marches in the mountains which had followed. Randolph Churchill came over to see me before leaving for Croatia. With him came Evelyn Waugh, a new recruit, whose Commando training and adventurous disposition made him a useful addition to the Mission.

Everywhere the news was the same: the German offensive was slackening and, gradually, the initiative was passing to the Partisans. And now, from various sources, more and more insistently, came a fresh rumour — a rumour that the Germans were thinking of withdrawing from the Balkans, of cutting their losses and falling back on a more easily tenable defence line in the north.

If the war in Europe was not to be unnecessarily prolonged, it was important that they should not be allowed to carry out their intention unhindered. Taking advantage of the presence of General Wilson and Tito within easy reach, I accordingly proposed to both a plan designed to ensure that, in the event of a withdrawal, as few Germans as possible would get away safely.

The scheme was called 'Operation RATWEEK'. My proposal was that, for the space of one week, timed to coincide as closely as possible with the estimated beginning of the German withdrawal, the Partisans on land and the Allies on the sea and in the air, should make a series of carefully planned, carefully co-ordinated attacks on enemy lines of communication throughout Jugoslavia. This would throw the retiring forces into confusion and gravely hamper further withdrawal.

I first put this plan to Bill Elliot. He and the other airmen liked it. With the help of the Americans, they could, they said, find the necessary planes. The Navy, always glad of an excuse for some sea-raiding, agreed too, and General Wilson, after an hour or two spent going over the plan on the large-scale maps, gave it his final blessing.

The next thing was to make sure that Tito would play. It would, after all, have been understandable, if, now that there was a chance of the Germans withdrawing of their own accord, the Jugoslavs, who had suffered so much under the German occupation, had refused to put any obstacles in their way. But it was clear to me at once that this was not a consideration that weighed with Tito. He was all for going on fighting the Germans to the very end. Having listened to what I had to say and to my assurances that the Allied naval and air forces were prepared to co-operate to the utmost, he undertook to instruct his own staff to start planning at once jointly with my officers and representatives of B.A.F. As soon as a detailed plan had been drawn up, he said, he would send instructions to his Commanders in the field to take the necessary steps to put it into execution, in consultation with my officers on the spot, whose task it would be to co-ordinate the operations carried out by the Partisans with those of the Allied air forces.

The detailed planning was done for the most part at B.A.F. Headquarters and my own Rear Headquarters at Bari, where Peter Moore, recently returned from Slovenia, and John Clarke who had just come back from Montenegro, were now in charge. The whole of Jugoslavia was divided up into sectors; a Partisan Commander and the British officer attached to him were made responsible for each, and targets allotted accordingly. Any target, such as a bridge, a viaduct or a railway junction, which was too strongly held by the enemy for the Partisans to be able to attack it with any hope of success, was made the responsibility of the R.A.F. or of the heavy bombers of the U.S. Army Air Force. Where additional quantities of high-explosive or ammunition were needed, special drops were arranged. Plans were made, too, for tactical and strategical air support to be given at the appropriate moment to the Partisan forces engaged. Meanwhile our destroyers and M.T.B.s would scour the sea-routes.

In drawing up these plans, we had recourse to all available sources of information concerning the enemy's order of battle and the disposition of his troops, while at every stage we consulted by signal the British officers and the Partisan Commanders on the spot. Thus, the whole of the German line of withdrawal would be covered and every possible target accounted for. In the light of what we guessed the enemy's plans to be the attack was fixed for the first week of September.

If the Germans withdrew, their main line of withdrawal northwards was bound to be along the Vardar Valley and the Belgrade-Salonika railway. For us, this now became the most important target of all. If their communications could be cut here, their situation would indeed be desperate.

The Partisans in Serbia were still to some extent an unknown quantity, though John Henniker-Major's signals showed that they were gaining ground rapidly. Much depended on what they could achieve. Accordingly, before Mr. Churchill left Italy, I obtained from him and from General Wilson permission to leave Tito and my Headquarters on Vis for an indefinite period in order to go to Serbia, for the purpose of co-ordinating the operations there myself. At last I was to fulfil my intention of visiting Serbia and at a vital moment.

My plan was to join John Henniker-Major in southern Serbia, where Koča Popović had his Headquarters. There I should be within easy reach of the Belgrade-Salonika railway and in a good central position from which I could cover wide areas of country. Tito sent a signal to Koča, informing him of my impending arrival and instructing him to make his plans for RATWEEK in consultation with me, co-ordinating his operations through me with those of the Allied air forces. He furthermore undertook to send with me, as his personal envoy, General Sreten Žujović, or Crni, the Black, as he was usually known.

Crni whom I knew from Bosnian days, was one of the outstanding figures of the Partisan Movement. Indeed, at this time, he was in effect Tito's Deputy Commander-in-Chief. A Serb by race, he had made himself a name as a guerrilla leader in the original rising in Serbia in the summer of 1941. In addition to his military talents, which were considerable, he was also extremely shrewd politically and possessed remarkable breadth of outlook. He was, too, a first-class organizer, and a good man in a tight spot. Tito used him as a kind of reserve, sending him to take charge in any part of the country where things were going badly for the Partisans or where a military or political crisis had arisen. In appearance he was tall and cadaverous, with lank black hair and pale hollow cheeks, which after midday were covered with a blue-black stubble, for, like most Serbs, he had a strong growth of beard. A continual dry cough showed that on him as on so many of the Partisans the sufferings and privations of the war had left a lasting mark. The sadness of his expression was relieved by a pleasant smile and by the vivid intelligence of his eyes. Like Koča Popović he spoke almost perfect French, having lived for many years in France. An older man than most of the Partisan Generals, he had fought in the French Foreign Legion in the first war. His wide interests and pleasant manners made him an interesting companion, and he was sufficiently sure of his position in the Communist hierarchy to be willing to discuss any topic, however controversial. I was glad he was coming with me. His presence showed, too, the importance which Tito attached to the forthcoming operations in Serbia.[1]

The next thing was to get ourselves in. The enemy's general offensive, which in the rest of Jugoslavia had petered out by the end of June, had lasted in Serbia all through July, keeping the Partisans con-

---

[1] General Žujović was disgraced in 1948 in somewhat obscure circumstances. According to the Russians the reason for his disgrace was his loyalty to them.

stantly on the move and making it hard for them to receive parachute drops. In August, however, there came a lull in the fighting, and with it the opportunity I required. John Henniker-Major signalled that Koča Popović's Headquarters were for the time being established on the thickly wooded slopes of the Radan, overlooking the German garrison town of Leskovac on the Nis-Skoplje railway, and that the Partisans were also holding a flat piece of ground near the neighbouring village of Bojnik, where an aircraft could land. There was no time to be lost, for it was impossible to say when the Germans, now thoroughly alarmed at the increased scale of Partisan activities in Serbia, would resume their attacks. I sent a most immediate signal to Henniker-Major to say I was coming and warned Sergeant Duncan and my own wireless operator, Sergeant Campbell, to stand by to accompany me. In a few hours all arrangements had been made for us to go in on the first possible night.

Before leaving Vis, I climbed up to Tito's cave on Hum to discuss with him the final plans for RATWEEK and to say goodbye. The broad outline of the plan was now complete and it only remained to arrange the details with the local commanders. Already additional supply drops were being made and air support laid on for the forthcoming operations. I found Tito cheerful enough, though, like me, tired of life on Vis and making plans to leave it. After we had finished with our maps, food and drink were brought, a plateful of fried eggs and a bottle of sweet Dalmatian wine, and we talked of Serbia, which Tito had not visited since the heroic days of 1941. Then he wished me good luck and goodbye. We parted with jocular assurances that we would meet again in Belgrade.

At first sight, landing by plane had seemed an infinitely more normal and agreeable method of entering a country than what Mr. Churchill called 'jumping out of a parachute'. But, when we reached our destination and, in the pitch blackness of a moonless, overcast night, began to circle lower and lower through the clouds, over hilly country, towards what might or might not be a suitable landing-strip for a Dakota, I found myself wondering whether a parachute jump would not after all have been preferable. Then, through the mist, the signal-fires flared up on the ground below; we circled once or twice more; the flaps went down, the revolutions of the propellers became slower, and soon we were bumping and jolting to a standstill over the uneven soil of Serbia.

There was no waiting about. As soon as we were out of the plane, some Partisan wounded, who had been waiting, were bundled into it, the doors were shut, and the pilot, who had kept his engines running, started getting it back into position for the take off. A minute or two later it was airborne again and on its way back to Italy.

A Partisan came out of the shadows leading some horses. We had kept our personal kit to a bare minimum, and, once the wireless set had been strapped to a pack-pony, we were ready to start. Then the Partisan officer who had come to meet us took the lead and we galloped off. As we left the flat open ground of the landing-strip and, crossing a little bridge, entered a clump of trees, some shots were fired from nearby and the bullets whistled past us in the darkness. It was too dark to see anything, but clearly there were people in the immediate neighbourhood who were not on the same side as we were.

The ride that followed was long and dreary, through thick bush and scrub, mostly uphill, but with occasional abrupt descents, slithering and sliding down the sides of stony ravines. There was still no moon and the horses were anything but sure-footed, needing constant helping and coaxing over the rougher patches. Their German Army saddles, too, were far too big for them and threatened ceaselessly to slide under their bellies or even over their heads. It was with frayed tempers that we eventually reached our destination in the early hours of the morning.

After a good deal of rather irritable groping about in the dark, I found John Henniker-Major asleep under the trees in a kind of wigwam made of part of a parachute stretched over some branches. In a few minutes I had fixed up a similar shelter against the steady drizzle that was now falling, and, spreading out my sleeping-bag beneath it, lay down for a few hours' sleep.

When I woke, the sun was shining through the trees and Campbell and Duncan were busy frying a tin of bacon we had brought with us. It smelt delicious. We were on the edge of a little clearing in the wood. Somewhere nearby I could hear the sound of running water. Behind us, a great forest of oaks and beeches stretched up towards the summit of the Radan. Immediately in front of us, sloping downhill, lay a brief expanse of green turf, like an English lawn. Beyond, the woods began again, covering the lower slopes and the foothills with a blanket of foliage. Then, beyond that again, for mile upon mile, stretching away to the hazy blue of the horizon, the rich rolling countryside of Serbia was spread out before us in the sunshine, a patchwork of green orchards and yellow maize fields, with, dotted here and there the white-washed walls of a village and the onion spire of a church. There could have been no greater contrast with the austere uplands of Bosnia or the stony barrenness of Dalmatia than this peaceful, smiling landscape.

Crawling out of my sleeping-bag and pulling on my boots, I spent the next few minutes rousing John Henniker-Major, always a heavy sleeper. In the course of the night he had rolled out of his improvised tent and half way down the hill. There his progress had been checked by the stump of a tree, round which he was now curled, snoring peacefully. This was to repeat itself night after night during the weeks that followed. The distance which he covered in the course of his slumbers varied according to the steepness of the hill on which we happened to be camping, but he scarcely ever woke on the same spot where he had gone to sleep. He had had a bad time of late and I suppose that the effect on his nerves showed itself in this way. Certainly, there was no other indication that his composure was in any way ruffled.

After breakfasting lavishly off black bread, crisply fried bacon and some freshly brewed tea, we sat down on the grass in the sun, and John settled down to give me some account of his experiences and impressions since first being dropped into Serbia four months earlier.

They had been eventful months. When he had first arrived in April, he had found the Partisans neither numerous nor well equipped. Since the withdrawal of Tito's main forces from Serbia after the disasters of 1941 the Partisan detachments who had remained behind had not had an easy time. Conditions had not favoured them. Geographically the green, fertile, rolling country was for the most part less suited to guerrilla warfare than the wilder and more mountainous regions of

Bosnia and Montenegro. They had been obliged to operate in quite small bands without the same central organization as elsewhere, and lacking proper communications. The civil population, too, had been inclined to prefer the relatively passive attitude of the Četnik forces or the open collaboration of General Nedić to the more strenuous conduct of the Partisans, whose intentions they had in any case been led to suspect. As a result the enemy had long enjoyed greater security in Serbia than elsewhere, being able to count on the help of the inhabitants and of local troops to guard their main lines of communication against Partisan attacks; indeed in many areas these duties were carried out almost entirely by Nedić troops and Četniks. Finally, the Partisans had lacked supplies. The necessarily limited scope of their operations had made it impossible for them to equip themselves at the expense of the enemy on the same scale as their more fortunate brothers elsewhere, while all Allied help, and the prestige derived from it, had gone, not to them, but to the Četniks. Harried by the Germans, by Nedić, by the Četniks, by the Bulgarians and by the Albanians, out of sympathy with the population, out of touch with their comrades in the rest of Jugoslavia, lacking arms and equipment, the Serb Partisans were the Cinderellas of the Movement of National Liberation. It was largely owing to the skill and determination of their leader, Stambolić, that they nevertheless survived and continued to operate.

Then, at about the time of John's arrival in April, there had been a change. The increased interest which Tito was now showing in Serbia had started to make itself felt. Popović, who, after Tito himself, was perhaps the most successful and popular of the Partisan military leaders and who himself came of a well-known Serb family, had arrived to take command in Serbia itself. At the same time a strong Partisan force, largely composed of Serbs and commanded by Peko Dapčević, another of Tito's best Commanders, was dispatched from Montenegro, through western Serbia, to reinforce the Partisans already there.

Finally — and this was perhaps the most important factor of all — there had come the change in Allied policy. The decision, which had hitherto held good, that no supplies should go to the Partisans in Serbia, had been reversed. Supplies to the Četniks had ceased, and arms and ammunition were now being dropped to the Partisans in very considerable quantities. This had enabled local commanders not only to equip the troops under their command on an improved scale, but to arm large numbers of volunteers whom they had up to then been obliged to turn away for lack of equipment.

The change in our attitude had also had an important psychological effect. All the prestige which the Četniks had hitherto enjoyed as a result of Allied support was now transferred to the Partisans. The effect was increased by the news that Tito had come to terms with King Peter and by the King's proclamation calling on his subjects to support the Partisans, which undermined General Mihajlović's claim to be fighting for the monarchy.

As often happens, all these developments, coming one after the other, had a snowball effect. Allied support and supplies had brought more volunteers; better equipped and more numerous, the Partisans had been able to increase the scale of their operations; their successes in the field had, in turn, brought in larger stocks of captured weapons and, incidentally further increased their prestige; so that in the space of a few months the Movement had gone on from strength to strength.

The civil population, too, had at length come to the realization that the more active policy of the Partisans was not as foolhardy as it had once seemed. It dawned on them that it had been this very policy which had won for Tito the Allied support which Mihajlović, however well-meaning, had in the end forfeited by his caution and inactivity. It dawned on them, too, that the Germans, who for so long had seemed invincible, were beginning to weaken, that the early liberation of Serbia was not only possible but probable. The feeling of hopelessness, which had so long weighed upon them, began to lift, and was replaced by a spirit similar to that which had inspired the original national rising of 1941.

With this change of heart, the mood of the people swung over, away from the Četniks' policy of compromise and inactivity and into sympathy with the total war of the Partisans. In response to these feelings, in response, perhaps, also to a conscious or unconscious desire to get on to the winning side before it was too late, daily more and more of their former supporters deserted the Četniks and more and more volunteers flocked to the standards of the Partisans. Again and again, during the weeks that followed, we were to see long columns of men and boys straggling in to Partisan Headquarters to draw their rifles and ammunition, part deserters, part prisoners, part conscripts, part volunteers, some still wearing their old uniforms and the traditional beards of the Četniks, others in their ordinary working clothes.

Nor were these desertions limited to the rank and file. While I was in Serbia I was to meet Radoslav Djurić, until recently one of Mihajlovic's best known Commanders and now Chief of Staff to a Partisan Division. This amusing, somewhat cynical, character seemed to have been received by the Partisans with open arms, although in the past he had always been known, even amongst the Četniks, for the ruthless brutality with which he had waged war against them.

The Partisans made the best of their opportunity. A free pardon was offered to Četniks and Nedić troops coming over before a certain date. Much play was made with the Tito-Šubašić understanding and with a proclamation made by King Peter calling on the people to support Tito, both of which carried a great deal of weight in Serbia, where Royalist feeling was strong. Finally, Communist aims and policy were kept in the background, and very little was seen of the red stars, hammers and sickles, which were so prominently displayed by the Partisans in other parts of the country, but which would have had little appeal in this land of prosperous small-holders.

For the whole of this period during which the fortunes of the Serb Partisans had undergone such a complete and rapid change, Headquarters, Serbia, and John Henniker-Major with them, had been almost continuously on the move. At first their weakness had told against them; then, as they increased in strength, the Germans had put in one heavy attack after the other in the hope of dealing them a decisive blow before it was too late. Many of the Četnik leaders had joined in these attacks with all the forces which remained at their disposal, only too glad to profit by German assistance if it would help them to get rid of the Partisans. The Partisans, for their part, while welcoming Četnik deserters who came over to them, did their best to eliminate all remaining formed bodies of Četnik troops, whether they were collaborating with the enemy or not. Never for a moment did either side lose sight of their ultimate political objective, namely the elimination of all rival factions and their own accession to power.

By now, however, the strategical initiative had begun to pass to the Partisans. Tactically the Germans and Bulgarians by the use of armour and artillery might still be able to keep them on the move; but this was only to be expected. It did not prevent the Partisans from carrying out constant raids on enemy communications and garrisons, or even from liberating considerable areas of territory. There could be no doubt that throughout Serbia the enemy position had of late greatly deteriorated. In other words, everything lent itself admirably to a concerted attack of the kind we had planned.

Next I discussed with Koča Popović the detailed plans for RATWEEK. He was living nearby, and after breakfast we strolled across to where he was encamped under the trees. On the way John pointed out to me a wooded hill-top standing out from the rest a couple of miles away, across the valley, which, he said, was held by White Russians who were fighting for the Germans. To the west and the east, respectively, the Germans were installed in the Ibar and the Morava Valleys. To the north the Bulgars held Niš, Prokuplje and the valley of the Toplica. To the south were the Albanians, and the local Albanian minority, the Arnauts.

I found Koča sitting with Crni under the trees, a brisk, business-like figure in his neat grey uniform with his large black moustache. When he talked the words came rattling out like bullets from a machine gun, and his deep-set brown eyes sparkled with energy and intelligence. Very able and, for all his talk of only wanting to retire to study philosophy, extremely ambitious, he was clearly delighted with his new command and with the prospect which it brought him of being first into Belgrade.

Maps were brought and we got down to work without further delay. He showed me the latest dispositions of the enemy and of his own forces and told me which targets the Partisans could attack by themselves and where the support of the R.A.F. would be needed. I told him what help we could give him from the air and what additional supplies were available. Together we worked out a joint scheme

covering all the most important road and railway targets in Serbia,
with special emphasis, of course, on the Belgrade-Salonika railway,
and this I wirelessed back to Bill Elliot for his views.

During the days that followed we put the finishing touches to our
plan. Signals passed backwards and forwards between Allied Force
Headquarters in the great palace of Caserta and our little camp under
the trees. Almost daily fresh information came in concerning enemy
troop movements, necessitating minor alterations. Supply drops were
made to the points we had indicated. Confirmation was received from
B.A.F. that air support would be given where it was needed.

Almost every day I spent an hour or two with Koča.

One day while I was sitting with him a patrol came in with a
prisoner. He was a German Colonel who had been on a liaison mission
to the Bulgars. His car had been ambushed by the Partisans on the
road between Niš and Prokuplje and he himself had been shot in the
leg in the ensuing encounter. Now he was carried in by two Partisans
and set down on the grass at our feet.

A sallow, slightly built man with an intelligent, sensitive face, in
appearance, at any rate, he was as unlike the German officer of popular
fiction as anyone could be. It was evident, as he lay there, that his leg
was hurting him, and Koča told the man who had brought him in to
make him more comfortable. Then, giving him a cigarette, he started
to ask him questions.

He was, it seemed, a regular soldier and a member of the General
Staff. Much of what he told us was of considerable interest. He had
served on von Kleist's Staff and, with him, had helped to plan the
proposed invasion of England in 1940. Later he had gone to Italy where
his task had been to reorganize the railway transport system which the
heavy Allied bombing had thrown into a state of chaos. His last
Mission had been to try to rally the Bulgars, about whose intentions
the Germans were, it appeared, beginning to have grave doubts.

The questions we asked him were answered readily enough and
with a frankness which, in the circumstances, one could not but
admire. Everything the man said and the way in which he said it
reflected the intense love and admiration which he felt for Hitler and

the Nazi Party and his equally intense hatred for the Allies and above all for the Partisans. Indeed, he made it clear that he was surprised that even the British should have officers serving with such Bolshevik scum.

Before he was taken away, Koča asked him a final question: 'What chance, would you say, Colonel, that Germany now has of winning the war?' 'No longer', he replied, 'a very good chance, for I am afraid that we cannot now hope to hold out long enough to be able to take advantage of the clash which there must inevitably be between Russia and her Western Allies.' It was, in the circumstances, as telling an exit as anyone could hope to make, and, one that was wasted on neither Koča nor myself.

By the last days of August our preparations for RATWEEK were complete, and we started to watch with redoubled keenness for any signs of an impending enemy withdrawal. But still there was no indication that the Germans had made up their minds to move, and we reflected, a little sadly that it would, after all, have been too good to be true if we had really guessed the enemy's intentions to within a few days. At any rate it was something that, when they did start to go, they would find their road and railway communications well and truly wrecked.

As the appointed day approached, I decided to make my way down to join the Partisan force which was to attack the railway in the Leskovac area. Having taken leave of Koča Popović, who was also moving off to supervise operations elsewhere, John and I set out, accompanied by Sergeant Duncan and by Sergeant Campbell, with his wireless set on a pack-pony. The sun was shining as we started downhill towards the valley. It was hot and we marched in our shirt sleeves. Soon we came out from under the trees to find the maize turning golden in the fields and the trees in the orchards weighed down with fruit. From the clover came the hum of bees and a lark was singing somewhere high above us. The track under our feet was white and dusty. The scene had all the serenity of a late summer's day at home.

Then, suddenly, from the other side of the valley, came the crack and roar of an explosion, and, looking to where the sound had come from, we saw, against the blue of the sky, a great cloud of white smoke billowing up from the hill where the White Russians had been encamped. Other detonations followed the first and, as the smoke cleared away, we could see that something was burning fiercely. If these were the results of a Partisan attack, it had clearly been a most successful one. We were only surprised to have heard nothing of the preparations for it.

After we had gone some way, we met a Partisan riding hard in the direction from which we had come. We asked him if he knew what was happening. He said that he had come from a nearby outpost and was on his way to report. The White Russians had blown up their ammunition dump and set fire to their huts and were now evacuating the position.

It was only gradually that the full significance of what we had seen dawned on us. At the places where we stopped to rest, scraps of information reached us, all pointing to one conclusion, and, later, when we set up our aerial and made contact with Bari and with other parts of Jugoslavia, we received still more definite information to the same effect. There could no longer be any doubt about it. The German withdrawal had begun. By a piece of immense good fortune our timing for RATWEEK had, it seemed, been perfect. The knowledge filled us with a sense of agreeable anticipation.

CHAPTER XV

RATWEEK

II. FULFILMENT

OUR first day's march brought us to Bojnik, where I had been landed a week earlier, and the following evening we reached the village where the Commander of the 24th Partisan Division, the formation responsible for the attack on the railway in the Leskovac area, had set up his Headquarters. The Partisan Divisional Staff and Johnny Tregida, my liaison officer with the 24th Division, were living in a rambling white farmhouse opposite the little Orthodox church.

The place was in an uproar. A batch of Bulgar prisoners had just been brought in and were being herded into the courtyard. Dour, swarthy, stocky little men, in dark grey uniforms and German-type steel helmets, they sat or lay about on the ground glumly while the Partisans sorted out the officers from the other ranks. The Bulgar rank and file, the Divisional Commander explained, could sometimes be prevailed upon to join the Partisans, but the officers were for the most part hardened 'fascists'. Until recently they had taken but few Bulgar prisoners; the Bulgars had fought with a determination and a brutality equal to that of the Germans. Now they no longer showed quite the same reluctance to surrender. I recalled what the German colonel had told us about the Bulgars at Koča's Headquarters and, remembering that in the First World War Bulgaria had been the first of Germany's allies to crack, wondered whether something of the kind might not be happening now.

We had our evening meal that night in the Partisan commander's mess, a merry gathering which included two Orthodox priests with long hair and beards who seemed to have attached themselves to the Division as chaplains. The life and soul of the party was Brko (or 'Whiskers') the Chief of Staff, a cheerful character with sandy hair and a flowing moustache in the best Serbian style. With him we discussed our future movements. He would, he said, take us himself to the Headquarters of the Brigade who were carrying out the main attack on the line north of Leskovac. If we started next morning we should just arrive in time.

It was hot down in the plain, and, not relishing the idea of a night indoors in a crowded room, I unrolled my sleeping-bag outside in the yard. But there I was little better off: people stumbled over me; mosquitoes attacked me, while the Bulgars, anxious no doubt as to their prospects of survival, kept up a constant monotonous mumbling.

Next morning we made an early start, though, like most Partisan starts, not quite as early as it was intended to be. Horses had been provided and we set out in fine style. The Chief of Staff's horse, a rather showy chestnut, was called Draža; he said that he had captured it from the Četniks and that it was called after General Mihajlović. The whole subject of Četniks did not seem to be taken quite so seriously here as in Bosnia. John's horse and mine had been captured from the Germans.

The route we followed was a roundabout one, designed to avoid enemy concentrations and to make the best use of the plentiful cover provided by the undulating, partly wooded country which lay between us and the railway. At midday we rested under the trees on what might have been an English village green, a source of interest and amusement to a group of tow-haired village children. We did not take very seriously the startling stories of German armoured columns in the immediate neighbourhood with which their parents regaled us.

A little before nightfall, after riding all the afternoon through rolling, park-like country, we came to the tiny hamlet where the Brigade Commander had established himself in preparation for his attack on the line. From the rising ground on which it was situated, the town of Leskovac could be seen, spread out in the valley below, at a distance of not more than a mile or two from where we were. A mile away to the south, fighting was in progress for the possession of a ridge, overlooking our present position, which the Partisans had captured and which the enemy were now seeking to win back. The issue was still in doubt and, as we entered the village, the noise of machine guns and mortars could be heard, first nearer and then further away. Spasmodically, the sounds of firing continued to reach us during the night.

Next day, the first day of RATWEEK, dawned bright and fine. The battle of the night before was over. The enemy had withdrawn, leaving the Partisans in possession of the ridge, and everything was now quiet. The attack on the railway was scheduled for that night. The Partisans were to attack two points to the north and south of Leskovac, blowing up bridges and demolishing as much of the permanent way as possible. Leskovac itself, the seat of a strong German garrison, including, it was rumoured, a good deal of armour, was to be left to the Allied air forces. Apart from the actual damage which an air attack would do to transport and installations, it would, it was hoped, shake the morale of the mixed German and quisling garrison and help to soften them up in preparation for the Partisan operations against the railway that night.

As we sat at breakfast, Sergeant Campbell came running down from the hillside where he had set up his wireless, with a most immediate signal. It was from Bill Elliot. Air reconnaissance, he said, confirmed the presence of a strong concentration of armour and motor transport of all kinds in Leskovac, and it had accordingly been decided to turn the heavy bombers on to it. A force of fifty Fortresses would attack it at eleven-thirty.

We had not expected anything on this scale. It seemed rather like taking a sledge-hammer to crack a walnut. Up to now the 'Heavies' had not been so easy to come by, being needed for the really big targets in Austria and northern Italy. But evidently RATWEEK was going to be done in style as far as the Allied air forces were concerned.

As the appointed hour approached, we gathered in a little group on the hillside and stood waiting. Seeing that we were watching for something to happen, some peasant women and an old man or two from the village came and joined us, looking out across the valley. A mile or two away we could see the white houses of Leskovac spread out in the warm autumn sunshine. In the trees the birds twittered. From a pond nearby came the occasional croak of a bull-frog. The cornfield buzzed with the hum of innumerable insects. It would have been hard to conceive of a more tranquil scene. Standing there waiting, I tried to think of the German garrison and tank-crews, and not of the population of small farmers, shopkeepers and railway workers, of the old people, the women and children, who at this moment would be going about their everyday business in the streets.

Eleven-twenty came, and eleven-twenty-five. Still there was nothing. The peasants grew tired of waiting and started to drift away. At eleven-thirty the Chief of Staff consulted the immense turnip of a watch which he wore strapped to his wrist and looked at me inquiringly. I began to wonder whether there had not perhaps been a technical hitch.

Then, almost before we could take it in, it had happened. There was a noise of engines, at first barely audible, then rapidly growing to a roar, and looking up, we saw at a great height row upon row of bombers steadfastly following their appointed course, their polished wings gleaming in the sunlight. The peasants started counting them: six, ten, twenty, thirty, they had never seen so many. Already the Fortresses were over their target — were past it — when, as we watched, the whole of Leskovac seemed to rise bodily into the air in a tornado of dust and smoke and debris, and a great rending noise fell on our ears. When we looked at the sky again, the Forts, still relentlessly following their course, were mere silvery dots in the distance. In a few seconds the noise of their engines had faded and everything round us was quiet again, the silence only broken by the wailing of one of the women; she had, they said, relations in the town. What was left of Leskovac lay enveloped in a pall of smoke; several buildings seemed to be burning fiercely. Even the Partisans seemed subdued.

The rest of that day passed in making a general reconnaissance in preparation for the night's activities. Nothing was stirring in the plain, and John and I walked down into the valley to a village just outside the town. We found it in an uproar, full of people who had just come out of Leskovac. The civilian casualties had been heavy; but the raid, it seemed, had achieved its object, for there had been direct hits on several buildings occupied by Germans, they had lost much of their transport and armour, and the morale of the garrison had reached a low ebb, particularly as far as the non-German portion of it was concerned. Many of the Četniks, employed on guard duties, were already on their way out to join the Partisans.

This augured well for the operations that evening and we now set out, while it was still light, to visit the Partisan positions nearest the railway, from which the main attack north of Leskovac would be launched.

We approached the line by a circuitous route, which brought us to the back of a little ridge immediately overlooking the railway. There we left our horses and climbed upwards through a field of Indian corn, which reached well above our heads and provided excellent cover. On top of the ridge we found Partisan outposts established. Crouching beside them, we looked down on the railway a few hundred yards away. An officer gave us some idea of the enemy defences. These consisted of concrete pill-boxes and occasional patrols up and down the line. Suddenly, a machine gun from one of the pill-boxes opened up at an unseen target, and soon there was an answering chatter of automatic weapons all along the line. It looked as though the enemy were expecting trouble. As we mounted our horses and rode off, first one sniper's bullet and then another went pinging and whining past our heads.

It was to a nearby point low down on the face of the ridge and quite close to the railway that we returned that night after dark. A mile or two away to the south, the sky was lit up by the fires that were still burning in Leskovac. Every now and then a great tongue of flame would go leaping up into the night sky as the blaze got a firmer hold on the little town.

Round us, it was dark and quiet. We took up our position at the foot of the ridge and waited. The flat ground below the ridge was marshy and a mist was rising from it. It was cold waiting. I watched the flames leaping and flickering over the burning town and the thin white swirls of mist drifting up from the marshy ground. As I stood there, it occurred to me that all over Jugoslavia other little parties were at this time attacking or waiting to attack.

Then, suddenly, firing broke out at several places along the line, and soon on both sides of us bright fountains of tracer bullets were spurting from a dozen different points, while answering fire flew back to meet them. Here and there, the flash and thud of a mortar, breaking in on the chatter of the machine guns, showed where the Partisans were bestowing special attention on a pill-box. The attack had begun.

Under cover of it, the Partisans carrying the loads of explosive now made their way down to the line and laid their charges. Presently they touched them off, and, for a moment, the roar of one explosion after another drowned the lesser sounds of battle. The charges had been laid under a number of small bridges and culverts at intervals along the line. Now, to round off their task, the Partisans set to work tearing up long stretches of the permanent way. Stacked in heaps, the sleepers were set alight and blazed merrily. Someone had found a goods-wagon in a siding, and this too was set on fire and sent flaming down the track towards Leskovac. It would be some time before that particular stretch of the Belgrade-Salonika railway was again open to traffic. The enemy forces in Greece, if they were to get out at all, would have to get out by road or by sea, a hazardous proceeding in either event. If everywhere else the Partisans had done their job as thoroughly as here, RATWEEK would have got off to a good start.

From some of the pill-boxes there still came an intermittent trickle of tracer, but several had already been silenced and it was clear that the defence was losing heart. Looking over my shoulder as we made our way back up the ridge before dawn, the last thing I saw was a ring of triumphant Partisans who, with linked hands, were dancing a Serbian *kolo* round one of the fires that was blazing near the line, their black figures outlined against the flames like demons in hell.

For the next day or two we remained in the region of Leskovac, collecting information and passing it back to Balkan Air Force. The Partisan attack on the line south of Leskovac had also been successful and so had our air attacks on a couple of bridges. From Bari and from my officers all over Jugoslavia reports kept coming in of operations successfully carried out both by the Allied air forces and by the Partisans. From Slovenia came news of another important viaduct demolished: the Litija bridge on the Ljubljana-Zagreb railway, a key point on the enemy's line of retreat. Here the Americans had given invaluable help. United States Army Air Force Mustangs had 'softened up' the target while Jimmy Goodwin, a hefty young American engineer officer who had been attached to us, had played a leading part in the Partisans' final assault on the ancient castle guarding the bridge — a part for which he was later awarded the Military Cross.

At first the enemy seemed stunned by the suddenness and violence of the onslaught. Then came the inevitable reaction. There was a counter-attack and for some days we were kept more or less constantly on the move.

In the skirmishing which ensued the neighbouring town of Lebane fell into the hands of the Partisans and we attended an impromptu political meeting held on the occasion of its liberation. The principal speaker was a gaunt, rather sad-looking man, suffering from ringworm and wearing steel-rimmed spectacles. This was Stambolić, who up to the time of Koča's arrival had been Commander of all the Partisans in Serbia.

In his speech he referred in flattering terms to Kara Djordje, the swineherd who had founded the reigning dynasty and who had been born in a village a few miles away. This was cheered to the echo by everyone, including the numerous leading Communists present. As in Russia, even royal, or semi-royal personages could be allowed to enjoy a certain amount of popularity, provided they had lived long enough ago and had been violent enough in their methods.

Of young King Peter no mention was made. In the trim little villa where we were taken to rest after luncheon and which had belonged to the bank manager or some other leading citizen, I noticed an elaborate portrait of him in oils hanging in the front parlour; but in most of the peasants' houses that I visited while I was in Serbia the pictures were of his father King Alexander and even of his grandfather. Most of the Serbs with whom I talked were monarchists (even the Communists admitted that in Serbia over fifty per cent of the population were in favour of the monarchy), but their loyalty, as far as I could see, was to the dynasty rather than to the young King himself, who did not seem to mean much to them one way or the other.

We did not stay long in Lebane. Soon we were on the move again, travelling northwards in the direction of the Toplica Valley where I hoped to join up again with Koča. The reports of RATWEEK which I had received hitherto were so encouraging that I was thinking of suggesting that operations should be continued for a second week, and I wanted to discuss with him future plans for Serbia.

Under cover of their counter-attack the Germans were already making frantic efforts to repair the railway, but they had reckoned without Balkan Air Force. Every time that we received reports of a breakdown gang at work, we signalled its location to Bari, and within a few hours our fighters were on to it.

Each evening towards sunset, would come the cry of 'Avioni!' and, looking up, we would see the familiar shapes of two or three Junkers 52 transport planes winging their way ponderously northwards, like geese against the evening sky. The evacuation of Greece and Macedonia had already begun and these, no doubt, were senior staff officers and others, who preferred not to attempt the journey by train and were getting out by air while the going was good. Here was a loophole which needed blocking up. A signal to Bill Elliot, giving the time and approximate route of these flights, did the trick. Somewhere or other our fighters must have swooped down on them for after that we did not see them again.

Brko, by now an old friend, accompanied us on our journey north, still mounted on the faithful Draža. I have agreeable memories of that ride. For several days we were on the move from dawn to dusk through the same green, rolling, fertile country. Sometimes we slept in houses, sometimes in the open; sometimes our rest was disturbed by the familiar shout of 'Pokret!' and reports of approaching German columns. The villages through which we passed bore a family resemblance one to another; a church and a single street of white-washed, red-roofed houses, now clinging to the side of a hill, now nestling in the valley, now peeping from between trees, now sprawled across the dusty plain. Everywhere the villagers were loud in their protestations of friendship for Great Britain. For the Partisans they did not always show quite the same enthusiasm; they had heard, they said, from the Germans and Četniks that the Titovci would steal their property and cut their throats. But in most places Brko's benign appearance and the studied moderation of the views which he expressed soon reassured them. Everywhere we found the same prosperity, so surprising after Bosnia and Dalmatia, and the same overpowering hospitality, the same rich, plentiful food.

I remember arriving at nightfall on the outskirts of a little village which I think was called Dobrovo. We had been travelling since early morning. Part of the time John and I had ridden our two horses and some of the time we had walked and given Duncan and Campbell a spell — a proceeding which struck the good Communist Brko, with his strictly hierarchical ideas, as highly improper. In the end, to salve his conscience, he had got off and walked too, leading Draža after him. It had been a blazing hot day and by evening we were all five tired and hungry.

We did not go right into the village, but camped in a little clearing just outside, amongst the trees. Immediately the news got round that we were there and soon we saw the welcome sight of a procession of peasant women arriving with an array of bowls, baskets, jars and bottles. From these they produced eggs and sour milk and fresh bread and a couple of chickens and a roast sucking-pig and cream cheese and pastry and wine and peaches and grapes, which they laid out on the ground. Then they squatted round to watch us eat, plying us mean-while with innumerable questions: Were the Allies winning the war? Had we come for good, or would the Germans come back again?

Most of them were rosy-cheeked, stolid-looking creatures, broad in the beam, with thick arms and legs, but amongst them, I noticed, was one exceptionally pretty girl, slim and dark, with classical features and a clear, pale skin, holding a little curly-haired child by the hand. I asked her where she came from. She told me Belgrade, and then, pleased at being paid attention, launched into her life history, a typical Balkan story: a husband who had disappeared, who might have been killed or might just be hiding (from whom was not clear); friends who had advised her to leave Belgrade to escape from the bombing; Četniks, Partisans, Germans; collaboration which was not really collaboration; spies, traitors, assassins; financial difficulties; political difficulties; religious difficulties; matrimonial and sentimental difficulties. And what did I advise? And was I really a General? All this with much fluttering of long black eyelashes.

As I went to sleep under the stars, with the horses crunching their oats nearby, I reflected that I had not enjoyed an evening so much for a long time. Feminine wiles and good food and drink were luxuries of which we had almost forgotten the existence.

I recall, too, without being able to place them in the general plan of our journey, numerous isolated scenes and incidents which have somehow stuck in my memory; cold clear water spurting from a pump on the hillside under the trees in a village where we stopped in the blazing heat of midday, one working the pump while the others put their heads under it; a vast meal of milk and scrambled eggs eaten ravenously by the open window of a low, cool, upper room overlooking a valley; sleeping on the grass in an orchard by a little stream and waking suddenly in the dark to find Sergeant Duncan's hand on my shoulder: 'They're moving off, sir; they say the Germans are coming'; and then shouts of '*Pokret!*' 'Get going!' and confusion and plunging horses and 'What's happened to the wireless set?'; long dismal tramps in pitch darkness through pouring rain; discussions whether to push on or to stop in a village with a population reputed to be pro-German or riddled with typhus; speculating as to the meaning of black flags hung outside peasants' houses; knocking and being told that they mean that one of the family has just died of typhus; hoping this is bluff and sleeping there all the same, all crowded into one room; waking next morning to find the rain stopped and the house, where we had arrived in the middle of the night, surrounded by orchards laden with ripe plums; arriving in a village to find a wedding in progress and being swept, before we know where we are, into a *kolo*, twisting and whirling in the sunshine on the green with the village maidens; lying at night out on the hillside in our sleeping-bags and listening to the wireless: the B.B.C., the nine o'clock news, Tommy Handley.

Then, at ten o'clock, loud and clear, Radio Belgrade; Lili Marlene, sweet, insidious, melancholy,

Unter der Laterne,
Vor dem grossen Tor . . .

'Not much longer now,' we would say, as we switched it off. It was a stock joke but one that at last began to look like coming true.

Sometimes, in villages, when we asked where all the men were, we were told: with Nedić or, with Draža; and there was a faint air of embarrassment. In one house I was asked whether I knew Colonel Bailey, the former Head of our Mission to Mihajlović ('Ah, he was a merry fellow!').

Then there was the house where John had lived some weeks before and which in the interval had, it seemed, been occupied by the Bulgars. Knowing the Bulgars' reputation, we looked shocked. 'Did they know,' we asked anxiously of the owner, 'that you had had a British officer living here?' 'Of course they did,' came the reply, 'the neighbours betrayed me. But it was all right,' he went on. 'I told them that you had terrorized me into letting you live here; that you had behaved with unimaginable ferocity. They were most sympathetic.' And we all laughed at the simplicity of the Bulgars. Thinking it over afterwards, I wondered whether a good many Balkan stories did not perhaps originate in this way.

Finally one evening we clattered into a village a few miles south of Prokuplje to find that Koča and his staff were there. We had caught up at last.

But we still get no rest. Almost immediately the whole party starts off again. The Partisans, it appears, are advancing in the wake of the retreating Germans. What is more, the Bulgars have capitulated. This means that the Partisans may be able to gain possession of the towns of Niš and Prokuplje. Then comes confirmation over the wireless that Bulgar representatives are in Cairo, negotiating armistice terms with the British and Americans. Then the news that the Soviet Government, in order not to be left out of the peace negotiations, have somewhat belatedly declared war on the Bulgars with whom they had up to then maintained normal diplomatic relations. Our jokes about this somewhat transparent manœuvre on the part of our Soviet allies are not very well received. Then almost immediately we hear that the Bulgars have entered the war on our side. There is a tendency to refer to them as Slav Brothers. But this goes against the grain with

494

a good many people, for the atrocities committed by the Bulgars are still fresh in their minds. The Bulgars, for their part, do not seem to care very much which side they are on. Having hitherto fought for the Germans with efficiency and brutality, they now fight against them in exactly the same fashion, still wearing their German-type helmets and uniforms.

Prokuplje is liberated, and we enter it in triumph, a typical Serbian market town, at the end of a branch line of the railway, consisting of a single wide straggling sun-baked street of low houses, which at one point widens out into a market square. A group of statuary in the centre celebrates a previous liberation from some earlier oppressor. Outside the municipal building a notice has been posted proclaiming an amnesty for certain categories of collaborators provided that they join the Partisans before a certain date. A little crowd of citizens are looking at it dubiously.

A Liberation dinner follows a Liberation luncheon. Photographs are taken, speeches made, songs sung and healths drunk. I am presented with a bouquet by a schoolgirl. In the intervals we go shopping. It is the first time we have been in a town of this size since we arrived in Jugoslavia and it rather goes to our head. The shops are full of German-made goods and local produce and we buy all kinds of things we do not really want. Just as we are leaving I catch sight of a full-sized enamel bath outside a junk-shop and buy it for a pound.

There is talk of establishing our Headquarters in Prokuplje itself, but for the moment we continue to camp outside. I sleep in a barn which I share with an owl and some largish animal which I hear but never quite see — a stoat, possibly, or a polecat. My bath arrives on an ox-cart and we decide to have a hot bath — the first for weeks. The bath is erected in an orchard and a cauldron of water put on to boil. The Partisans and the local peasants watch the whole proceeding from a distance, now convinced that we must be quite mad.

But at this moment a messenger gallops up on a horse, shouting 'Pokret!' The Germans, it appears, have counter-attacked, not unsuccessfully, and we are on the move once more. Reluctantly abandoning our bath, we stuff our few belongings into our rucksacks, or as we have come to call them, pokret-bags, and set out.

From Prokuplje we headed for the Radan, always a relatively safe refuge in case of trouble. On the way Koča and I, keeping in touch with Balkan Air Force, planned further operations in continuation of RATWEEK. The enemy's counter-attack might temporarily relieve their situation, but, once it had spent itself, they would still be faced with the problem of getting the bulk of their troops out by one or two main routes which were open to attack for the whole of their length. The RATWEEK operations undertaken up to now had already sufficiently demonstrated what could be done in this way.

For the next two or three days we kept on the move. It was the same agreeable existence which I had led ever since my arrival in Serbia. The long early morning marches through the green, sunlit countryside; the halt at midday on the grass under the fruit-laden trees of some wayside orchard; the search, as night approached, for a good place to camp and the arrival of extravagantly hospitable villagers with grapes and peaches, bottles of wine and sucking-pigs, fresh eggs and butter; the evening meal and the brief period of tranquillity in the half-light before it grew quite dark. Then either a night of alarms and excursions, of attacks and counter-attacks, of marches and counter-marches, of rumours and counter-rumours; or else, all the more peaceful by contrast, a long sleep under the stars with the wind on one's face and the trees rustling overhead, until the sun rose and it was time to start. And, bubbling again up within one all the time, a feeling of elation which came from the knowledge that victory, complete and overwhelming, was at last at hand.

Living this life, I looked back with heightened distaste on my existence on Vis; reflected that the political negotiations were, through force of circumstances, likely to remain for some time in a state of suspended animation, that there were no other outstanding questions of any importance, and wondered whether it might not after all be possible for me to stay in Serbia until such time as Koča Popović, having cleared the enemy from the south and centre, swept on into the north for the final encounter before Belgrade. For, as far as one could tell, it seemed likely that it was to him that the distinction of driving the Germans from the capital would now fall; and that was a battle at which I was determined to be present.

Then, one evening, in the second half of September, I received a personal signal from General Wilson. I could tell from Sergeant Campbell's face, as he handed me the crumpled half sheet of paper, that it contained something out of the ordinary, something, that is to say, that would probably mean a change of plan, and I took it without enthusiasm.

It was quite short. It told me, in a dozen words, that Tito had mysteriously disappeared from Vis and that I was to come out at once and find him. It added that B.A.F. would land an aircraft at Bojnik to pick me up at the first opportunity. Mentally consigning B.A.F., Tito, General Wilson and everyone else concerned to perdition, I stuffed such kit as I had into my pack and, after saying goodbye to John Henniker-Major and sending a farewell message to Koča Popović, set out on a dreary all-night march to the landing-strip.

CHAPTER XVI

GRAND FINALE

THERE could be no doubt about it. Tito had gone. As an indignant telegram from Mr. Churchill put it, he had 'levanted'. One morning Vivian Street, who, in my absence, was in charge on Vis, had gone to visit him with a message from General Wilson, only to find that he had disappeared from the island without leaving a trace. Inquiries as to his whereabouts only elicited evasive replies. It was the old story, so familiar from Moscow days: he is sick, he is busy, he has gone for a walk. The more responsible members of the Marshal's entourage seemed to have gone too; the others, if they knew anything, were too nervous to reveal it. On further investigation, it was discovered that an unidentified Russian aircraft had landed on Vis and taken off again, presumably with Tito on board.

This sudden, unexplained departure did considerable harm to our relations with the Partisans. In London and at Caserta it was felt, not unnaturally, that such secretiveness was highly offensive, especially when it was considered that without our support Tito would never have been able to remain on Vis, and that the present phase of the war called for the closest co-operation between allies. Moreover, in Tito's absence, there was no one from whom decisions could be obtained or with whom the day to day business of liaison could be conducted in a normal friendly way. As a result, the causes of friction multiplied and relations deteriorated.

Clearly the first thing was to find him again. There was no point in my going to Vis, let alone staying there. From what Tito had told me before I had left Vis, it seemed to me that the most probable explanation of his departure was that he had gone inland to co-ordinate the final phases of the struggle for Belgrade. The best place to look for him seemed to be Serbia, and I accordingly decided to go back there. Once again my hopes of being in at the fall of Belgrade revived.

Before leaving Bari, I made, with the help of our Intelligence Staff, a careful review of the military situation in Serbia, and, as a result of this arrived at the conclusion that Peko Dapčević, now thrusting north-eastwards through western Serbia, was on the whole likely to reach Belgrade before Koča Popović. The big marked map at my Rear Headquarters, brought up to date in accordance with the latest situation reports, showed that his forward troops had just reached the town of Valjevo, in central Serbia and it was here that, a couple of nights later, I was landed by Balkan Air Force complete with a jeep and a wireless set.

I was met by Freddie Cole of the Durham Light Infantry, my liaison officer with Peko Dapčević, who had been dropped in some considerable time before and had accompanied First Corps on their epic march eastwards, taking an active part in the heavy fighting which had marked those eventful months. With Dapčević, never an easy man, and with his officers, he had established cordial relations and now his popularity had been further increased by the very timely air support which he had been able to call to the aid of the Partisans.

First Corps found Valjevo a tough nut to crack. The retreating Germans, for whom it was a key point, had decided to hold it at all costs and the garrison had settled down to a last man, last round stand, centred on the fortress-like barracks, round which they had built up a well-planned system of defence. In the ensuing battle the Partisans suffered heavy casualties and did not succeed in dislodging the enemy until a pair of rocket-carrying Beaufighters, summoned from Italy, administered the *coup de grâce* to the beleaguered garrison by swooping down and discharging their rockets at point-blank range into the barrack buildings.

For the crew of one of the Beaufighters this was their last operation, for, as they started to pull out of their dive, they ran into a final burst of anti-aircraft fire from the Germans, which sent them spinning to destruction a few hundred yards away. Their bodies were recovered from the wreck of their aircraft and we buried them with full military honours in the graveyard of a little Orthodox church near the spot where they had met their death.

The sudden fall of Valjevo took by surprise many of the local inhabitants who had come to terms with the enemy and now had not time in which to make good their escape. They included followers of Nedić, the quisling Prime Minister, and Ljotić, the leader of the Serbian Fascist Party, as well as some Četniks. The façade of one man's house was still decorated with the inscription in yard-high letters: 'Long live Ljotić. Death to the Bolshevik Rabble', which, despite frenzied last-minute efforts, he had not succeeded in erasing. The house in which we ourselves were quartered belonged to a leading Četnik, who, while expressing the warmest attachment for the Allied cause, clearly found the departure of the Germans and the arrival of the Partisans somewhat disconcerting. After we had been there a day or two, he disappeared and we concluded that we should not see him again. A few days later, however, he reappeared, still nervous, but considerably relieved, having been tried as a collaborator, condemned to pay a fine to Partisan funds, and then set free.

At this time in Valjevo there were numerous other arrests and trials on charges of collaboration with the enemy, but, as far as we could ascertain, the sentences passed were on the whole light and there were relatively few death sentences. To the population, after all they had heard, such moderation on the part of the Partisans seemed too good to be true, and, there was, not unnaturally, much speculation as to how long it would last.

Valjevo was a sizable market town, far larger than any of the villages we had seen so far. The shops were well stocked with local produce and German-made goods, and there was a restaurant where we could get our meals. Our Četnik landlord, whatever his political record, was a man of good taste and education, and his house, with its wide windows opening on to a sun-drenched courtyard trellised with vines, was filled with readable books and pleasant pictures and furniture. Clumping about in our hob-nailed boots on his well-polished floors, and gaping into the well-stocked shop-windows, we hardly recognized ourselves in our new role of town dwellers.

We had not been in Valjevo long when it started to fill up. Daily more members of Tito's military and political entourage kept arriving, presumably ready to move into Belgrade at the first opportunity. Familiar faces began to make their appearance in the little inn where we had our meals, and one day I found myself face to face with Crni.

Hitherto I had not thought it worth while to raise with any of the

Partisans with whom I had come into contact the question of Tito's whereabouts, but this encounter gave me the opportunity I needed. Crni, I knew, had sufficient grasp of the situation to appreciate, if it were explained to him, the resentment which was being caused in London and Caserta by Tito's disappearance and, if he chose, sufficiently sure of himself to help me clear the matter up.

Making no attempt to hide my feelings I told him plainly how Tito's conduct was viewed by the Allies and added that I would be grateful if he would at once convey to him a personal message from me. This he agreed to do, explaining that he was in wireless touch with the Marshal, who was at present in the Vojvodina. I accordingly sat down and drafted a stiff signal to Tito, emphasizing the effect which his absence was having on our mutual relations and asking for an early interview. To this there came back within a few hours a friendly answer from Tito, saying that he hoped we should meet in a few days. The deadlock it seemed, had been broken, though the resentment was to linger for some time.

Not long after reaching Valjevo, I received signals announcing the arrival of Vivian Street and Charlie Thayer. Vivian, whom I had at last reluctantly agreed to release in deference to repeated representations from his regiment, was due to join a battalion of the Rifle Brigade in Italy in a few days' time, and this was in the nature of a farewell visit. Charlie, an old friend from Moscow days, who after numerous vicissitudes, had been seconded from the U.S. Foreign Service, now reappeared, with crossed sabres on his collar and an eagle on his shoulder, in the guise of a Colonel of Cavalry, thus harking back to a remote past when he had played polo for West Point and served, very briefly, under the command of the distinguished but irascible officer later to become famous as General Patton. His official designation was second in command to Colonel Ellery C. Huntington, who had succeeded poor Slim Farish, killed a few weeks before in Greece, as Commander of the U.S. Military Mission to the Partisans. I had hardly seen Charlie since the war. I looked forward to having with me someone who had shared my experience of Russia and who, like me, would be able to detect the reflections of Moscow so readily discernible in the Jugoslav scene.

The military situation was now rapidly approaching a climax. The Red Army, having crossed the Danube, was advancing on Belgrade from the north and the east, and Crni confirmed that Peko Dapčević's troops were to furnish the Partisan contingent for the great battle which was now imminent. A large-scale daylight supply drop by Halifaxes of the R.A.F. brought the Partisans arms and ammunition for the coming offensive. Watching the great white nylon parachutes billow out and come floating down, I reflected that in Serbia, at any rate, this method of supply would soon be outdated. The fall of Belgrade could no longer be far removed.

At Valjevo, as in so many other places, in the desert, in Bosnia, in Italy, Dalmatia and Serbia, we would turn our wireless set in the evenings to Radio Belgrade, and night after night, always at the same time, would come, throbbing lingeringly over the ether, the cheap, sugary and yet almost painfully nostalgic melody, the sex-laden, intimate, heart-rending accents of Lili Marlene. 'Not gone yet,' we would say to each other. 'I wonder if we'll find her when we get there.' Then one evening at the accustomed time there was silence. 'Gone away,' we said.

Vivian and Charlie had scarcely arrived at Valjevo when we moved eastwards to Arandjelovac, some forty miles due south of Belgrade. Now that we had jeeps and that many of the roads were in Partisan hands, travelling was easy, and we reached Arandjelovac in an hour or two. Once a well-known watering place, frequented by fashionable invalids from Belgrade, it was now in a sorry state, with its smart hotels blasted and scarred by shell-fire and the neatly laid out public gardens trampled under foot during the recent heavy fighting. From a broken pipe near the Kurhaus, mineral water was bubbling on to the grass, and we were able to fill our water-bottles with what was reputed to be a sovereign remedy for digestive disorders.

This was just as well. We had been given a rousing reception by the people of Arandjelovac, who, after filling the jeep with bouquets of flowers, forced upon us food and drink of every kind and description. On top of all this, I was warmly greeted by a bibulous-looking individual who announced that he had once been chef to the British Legation in Belgrade and was most anxious to resume his connection with the representative of His Britannic Majesty.

We needed a cook and so I took him on; after which we enjoyed, for the rest of our brief stay in Arandjelovac, almost the best food I have ever tasted, perfect alike in its admirable materials and skilful preparation. Pork, for which Serbia is rightly famous, dominated our diet, the juiciest, tenderest, most succulent pork imaginable. There was roast pork, and grilled pork chops, and pig's trotters and sucking-pig and bacon and ham and innumerable kinds of pork sausages, all swimming in the very best butter and lard. It may sound monotonous; it may even sound slightly disgusting. But at that time and in that place, after years during which such things had existed only in one's dreams, it was highly enjoyable. We felt that we were at last enjoying the fruits of victory.

Nor was the preparation of pork by any means the only branch of his art at which this admirable man excelled. The richest soups; the most delicious omelettes; the most luscious preserves; layer upon layer of the lightest pastry mingled with the freshest cream cheese; all these delicacies, washed down by a variety of excellent wines, were lavished on us daily. Although we did not spend more than two or three days in Arandjelovac it was only by generous use of the local mineral water that any of us managed to avoid the effects of this constant overeating.

Our cook had but one failing and that, as I had suspected from the first, was a taste for drink. When, after each meal, he appeared to receive our felicitations, there would be a marked unsteadiness about his legs, a tendency to sit or even lie down suddenly, coupled with a no less disconcerting tendency to burst loudly and abruptly into song. It was this weakness that brought our happy association to a premature end. When the time came for us to leave Arandjelovac, he was in no state to travel and had to be left behind.

As it turned out, our departure from Arandjelovac was a sudden one. On the night of October 19th, as we sat at dinner, we received the news that the final phase of the battle for Belgrade had begun. On learning this, we made arrangements to leave for the front at first light.

October 20th dawned fine and fairly clear. It had rained during the night and the lanes were muddy. With the Americans, we had three jeeps between us. Charlie Thayer, Ellery Huntington and an American Sergeant set out in one, Vivian Street and I in another, and Freddie Cole and his two wireless operators in a third.

At first we followed country lanes and cart-tracks, between high green hedgerows glistening with raindrops. The fresh, moist landscape, a mixture of greys and browns and greens, had the softness of a water-colour.

Entering a village, we found it full of the Red Army. Even in this Slav country the Soviet troops looked strangely outlandish, with their high cheekbones, deeply sunburnt faces and unfamiliar uniforms. But they seemed to be getting on well enough with the local population, laughing and joking with the village boys and girls in a kind of composite Slav language, midway between Serb and Russian. Red flags hung from some of the windows, and at the entrance to the village a triumphal arch of cardboard had been erected in honour of the liberators.

Thereafter we came upon Russians at every turn, in large bodies and in small, on foot, on horseback, in carts, trucks, armoured cars and tanks, all moving up to the front. They were certainly not smart. Their loosely fitting drab-coloured uniforms were torn and stained and bleached by the sun and rain. The clothing of many had been supplemented or replaced by articles of equipment captured from the enemy. Their boots, as often as not, were completely worn out. The individual soldiers were an extraordinary medley of racial types, from the flaxen hair and blue eyes of the Norseman to the high cheekbones, slit eyes and yellow complexion of the Mongol.

But they looked as though they meant business. Ragged and unkempt though they might be, their powers of endurance and their physical toughness were self-evident. Their weapons, too, were clean and bright. They gave an indefinable impression of being immensely experienced, self-reliant, seasoned troops, accustomed to being left to fend for themselves and well able to do it.

And all this, no doubt, they were, and more, for they had fought their way here from Stalingrad and the frontiers of Asia, and that fighting, we knew, had been no light matter. Most of them wore two or three campaign medals or decorations, not just ribbons or miniatures, but the full-sized bronze, silver or enamelled medals and stars themselves, clinking and jangling on their tunics. Somewhere in my kit I had the large silver and platinum star of the Soviet Order of Kutusov, which had been awarded me some months before, and, seeing that this was an occasion on which decorations were being worn, I dug it out and screwed it on to my battle-dress tunic. This, and the fact that both Charlie and I could talk to them in their own language, had an immediate effect on the Russians, who came crowding round the jeep whenever we stopped, fingering our weapons and equipment admiringly and proudly exhibiting their own.

Scattered over the fields through which we were passing, large numbers of derelict tanks and guns, some blasted by direct hits, others seemingly intact, testified to the violence of the battle which had been raging for the last twenty-four hours and was still in progress. Soviet heavy tanks predominated. In the space of a mile we counted a dozen along the side of the track, their shattered hulks still smoking. Evidently there was still some fight left in the German anti-tank gunners.

Twenty miles or so south of Belgrade we emerged on to the main road and joined a continuous stream of Red Army trucks, tanks and guns flowing northwards into battle. One thing in particular struck us now, as it had struck us from the first, namely, that every Soviet truck we saw contained one of two things: petrol or ammunition. Of rations, blankets, spare boots or clothing there was no trace. The presumption was that such articles, if they were required at all, were provided at the expense of the enemy or of the local population. Almost every man we saw was a fighting soldier. What they carried with them were materials of war in the narrowest sense. We were witnessing a return to the administrative methods of Attila and Genghis Khan, and the results seemed to deserve careful attention. For there could be no doubt that here lay one reason for the amazing speed of the Red Army's advance across Europe. Thinking it over, and recalling the numbers of dentists' chairs and filing cabinets which were said to have been landed in Normandy at an early stage of the

Allied invasion, I wondered whether we ourselves could not perhaps profit to some extent by the Russian example.

Every now and then the stream of traffic was checked. Further on, the enemy were shelling the road and progress was slowed up. Looking at the long defenceless crocodile of tanks and guns and vehicles stretching away into the distance, one felt thankful that the Luftwaffe was no longer in a position to take advantage of the tempting target which it offered.

In one of the frequent traffic blocks we found ourselves jammed against a Russian ammunition truck, liberally decorated with Soviet emblems. Its occupants, cheerful, fair-haired lads scarcely out of their teens, were inordinately proud of it. 'You can't produce this sort of thing in capitalist countries,' they said smugly. From his jeep, meanwhile, Charlie's Top-Sergeant, oblivious of what was being said, had been examining the Russians' truck closely, and discovered what he had suspected all along, namely that, despite the red stars, hammers and sickles, which now adorned it, it was a Chevrolet, produced by General Motors at Detroit, Michigan. 'It makes you sick,' he observed, 'to think of these God-damned Russian bastards having all this good American equipment.' In the interests of inter-Allied friendship, it seemed wiser to leave both remarks untranslated.

For some time past we had heard the noise of gun-fire in the distance. Now, as we moved forward, the sounds of battle came closer. There was a whirring and wailing in the air, and from the muddy fields and tangled thickets on either side of the road came the rattle of machine-gun fire and the thud of mortars.

Before us the sugar-loaf hill of Avala, crowned by Mestrović's monument to the fallen of the first war, loomed above the road. On its steep slopes fighting seemed to be in progress. We could not now be more than ten miles from Belgrade. We decided that, before going any further, we had better secure a more exact estimate of the military position than we had been able to obtain hitherto. The Russians had established an artillery command-post in a tumble-down cottage near the road and here we turned aside to seek information.

We found the post occupied by a Lieutenant and a couple of Sergeants, friendly souls, who, finding that we spoke their language, at once made us welcome. Soon all of us, including the family of peasants who owned the cottage, were sitting on the only bed, drinking hot milk and some kind of raw alcohol and eating black bread and listening to a detailed account, not only of the immediate military situation, but of the Lieutenant's own war experiences and of his early life and childhood in far-away Vologda. In a flash I was back in the Soviet Union: the taste of the food and drink; the stuffiness of the little wooden shack; the cold outside; the heat inside; the droning voices; the soft inflexions of spoken Russian; the stereotyped Soviet jargon; and, above all, the smell: that indefinable composite aroma of petrol, sheepskin and vodka, black bread and cabbage soup, Soviet scent and unwashed human bodies, which permeates every square inch of the Soviet Union and which Russians somehow manage to take with them wherever they go.

From our new-found friend we learned that in the night a large force of the enemy, which in the confusion of the retreat had become isolated from the main body, had sought to cross the road at about this point in a desperate attempt to fight their way through to join the German garrison in Belgrade before they were finally cut off. The result had been a battle of exceptional ferocity which had raged over this part of the road all night long in the rain and the darkness. Now, the issue was no longer in doubt. Practically the entire enemy force, numbering many thousands had been annihilated. The road was again more or less clear. It only remained to liquidate isolated pockets of resistance.

The thought of this victory and of the accompanying slaughter of the enemy had clearly put the Lieutenant in the best of humours. As he drank his hot milk, a broad grin spread over his broad, faintly Mongoloid countenance. He had, he confided, come to hate the Germans more than anything else on earth. He himself had fought against them for three years and found them brutal, inhuman enemies. They had overrun and destroyed his village and massacred his mother and sisters. His only brother had been killed fighting against them. He was glad now to see them finally routed and crushed. In this last battle, he said, they had not taken many Germans alive. I asked him what they did with their prisoners. 'If they surrender in large groups,' he said, 'we send them back to base; but if,' he added, 'there are only a few of them, we don't bother,' and he winked. I wondered how many prisoners it took to constitute a large group.

In the knowledge that the road before us was more or less clear, we now continued our journey. Hitherto we had only come upon an occasional dead body, sprawled in the mud beside the wreckage of the tanks and guns. Now corpses littered the sides of the road, piled one on another, some in the field-grey of the Wehrmacht, others stripped of their boots and uniform and left lying half-naked; hundreds and hundreds of them, their pale faces disfigured with mud stains, greenish grey upon the greenish-grey skin. As we passed, the sickly stench of death struck our nostrils, hanging heavy on the air.

The troops who had tried to fight their way out were a composite force, hurriedly thrown together from elements of half a dozen different divisions, and, looking at the dead, we recognized many familiar badges: the Edelweiss of the First Alpine and the double thunderbolt of the Prinz Eugen. The tables had indeed been turned since we stood opposite these same formations in those early, precarious days in the mountains of Bosnia.

Further along, we passed a great throng of prisoners going in the opposite direction. Many had been left with only their shirts and underpants, and they shivered as they hobbled along in the chilly autumn air, their faces as grey from cold and fear as those of their dead comrades. As we watched, one of the guards appropriated a pair of boots which had somehow passed unnoticed and put them on, leaving their former owner to continue on his way barefoot.

Soon after, Vivian pointed to the side of the road. Looking in the direction in which he was pointing, I saw a hundred or more corpses, lying in rows, one upon the other, like ninepins knocked over by the same ball. They had clearly not died in battle. 'A small batch,' said Vivian. The smell, sweet and all-pervading, was stronger than ever.

Already we were approaching the outskirts of Belgrade. The road, which until now had twisted in and out round the contours of the hills, became straight and broad, with an impeccable surface in the best autobahn style. It was the first tarmac road I had seen in Jugoslavia. Our little convoy of three jeeps bowled merrily along. The thunder of the heavy guns grew louder and more distinct. Over the city a dive-bomber, black against the watery blue of the sky, got into position and, as we watched, went hurtling down towards its target.

Meeting a Partisan, we asked where General Peko had his Head-quarters, and were directed to a villa in a residential suburb outside the town. But when we got there it was only to find that Peko had moved elsewhere. A rear party were busy packing themselves and their belongings into a truck. The position 'proved somewhat incon-venient', one of them explained, a series of deafening explosions from nearby gardens lending force to his remark, as the enemy, wherever they were, settled down to shell the neighbourhood in earnest. Taking advantage of his offer to pilot us to the General's new Headquarters, we climbed back into our jeeps with as much nonchalance as we could muster and followed him gratefully back to the comparative quiet of the outer boulevards.

We found Peko installed in a house on the outskirts of the town. He was about to have lunch and invited us to join him. The house in which he had set up his Headquarters had belonged to a millionaire and was furnished with extreme richness, and the meal which we now ate was of excellent quality and luxuriously served. Having washed it down with plenty of good local red wine, we felt much refreshed and ready for anything. Taking Peko's Chief of Staff with us, we set out in our jeeps to see for ourselves how things were going.

The Chief of Staff, we soon found, had only a rather sketchy idea of the geography of Belgrade. But as none of the rest of us had ever been there before, we left the task of navigation to him, and, under his direction, plunged gaily into the centre of the town. Our first objective was the Kalemegdan. This, it appeared, was some kind of fort, which had just been taken and from which we should be able to follow the progress of the fighting.

The streets through which we approached it were under heavy shell-fire. They were also crowded with civilians, some enthusiastic, some just standing and gaping. From time to time a shell would land full amongst them, killing several. This left the Chief of Staff unmoved. Sitting beside me in the front of my jeep, he was busy showing us the sights of Belgrade, which he had not visited since he was a child. 'That,' he would say, 'is the Parliament Building. And there is the Opera. And now I am afraid we have lost the way again. Ah, that must be the Ministry of Agriculture.'

From the back of the jeep, Vivian, who as a seasoned infantryman had had considerable experience of long-range shelling and its results, was beginning to show signs of impatience. 'Mightn't it be better,' he would suggest politely, as we swerved down yet another side-street, littered with the same little heaps of fresh corpses, 'mightn't it be better to go straight there?'

But the Chief of Staff was not to be put off. Accustomed to the hand-to-hand fighting of guerrilla warfare, long-range shelling meant little to him. Whatever happened, and even though he might not be quite sure of the way, he was determined to do the honours of the capital in proper style.

Next we tried to guess where the shells were coming from and what they were aimed at. But even that was not easy. Nor did the Chief of Staff himself seem to have a very clear idea of the situation. One thing only was evident: that heavy fighting was going on all round us. The thunder of artillery and the rattle of small-arms fire resounded from all sides. It was not until we finally reached our destination that we got a clear picture of what was happening.

The Kalemegdan is an ancient fort, built of stone and red brick, from which, in Turkish times, the Ottoman conquerors held sway over Belgrade and the surrounding country. We approached it on foot through what seemed to be some public gardens, having first left the jeeps under the cover of a clump of bushes. As far as we knew, the Kalemegdan itself was in Soviet or Partisan hands, but in the immediate neighbourhood skirmishing was still in progress and through the trees came the occasional crack of a rifle or a burst of fire from a machine gun. It was not without caution that we wended our way amongst the ornamental flower-beds and clumps of shrubs. 'Keep off the grass', said the notices unavailingly.

Suddenly we emerged from the trees on to a kind of terrace and found ourselves looking out over an immense panorama, in which, as in certain medieval paintings, all sorts of things were happening simultaneously. At our feet, a few hundred yards away, flowed the Danube. Here, at the point where it joined the Sava, it was a considerable stream, its rushing waters swollen by the autumn rains. Of the bridges spanning it, only one remained standing, about half a mile from where we stood.

Across this troops were pouring headlong — guns, vehicles, horses and infantry. Looking through our glasses, we saw that they were Germans, retreating in confusion to the suburb of Zemun across the river, where, it seemed, the main body of the enemy was now established and whence their guns were laying down a barrage to cover the retreat of their rearguard. Suddenly, as we watched, the stream of fugitives was broken, and for a few moments the bridge remained unoccupied. Then more troops came pouring across. As we focused our glasses on them, we saw to our amazement that they were Russians. We could hardly believe our eyes. It seemed incredible that the German sappers should have failed to blow up the bridge as soon as their last troops were across.

And yet there could be no doubt about it. They had. Already the first Russians had reached the other side and were deploying on the flat ground between Zemun and the river. Calmly, methodically, the guns, horse-drawn for the most part, were brought into position and opened up. Little puffs of smoke among the buildings of Zemun showing that they were finding their targets.

Then, as we watched, the Red infantry went into action, wave upon wave, advancing unhurriedly but relentlessly across the shell-scarred fields, firing as they went. Some were armed with tommy-guns or rifles, others dragged behind them heavy machine guns mounted on little wheels. Every now and then one of the sturdy, buff-clad figures would spin round and fall while the advance swept on past him. On the fringes of Zemun the harassed Germans were standing fast and returning the Russians' fire as they tried frantically to dig themselves in.

It was not until later that we heard the story of the bridge. The Germans, it appeared, had duly mined it before they began their withdrawal and a detachment of engineers had been detailed to blow it up as soon as the last troops were over. The rest of the story reads like a fairy tale.

In one of the apartment houses near the bridge there lived an old man, a retired school teacher. He was warlike neither by nature nor by training, but in the course of a long life he had had one outstanding military experience. This was during the Balkan War of 1912, when, in the course of a battle with the Turks, he had, as a private soldier, distinguished himself by removing the demolition charges from beneath a bridge across which the enemy were retreating, thus preventing them from destroying it and enabling the Serbs to follow up their advantage. For this deed he was awarded a gold medal by King Peter I. After which he took to schoolmastering and relapsed into obscurity.

Thirty-two years later, on the night of October 19th, 1944, the old man, armed with this solitary but valuable experience of modern warfare and with a stout heart, was looking out of his window as the Germans made preparations for their withdrawal. With growing interest he watched them laying and connecting up the charges under the supports of the bridge. This was something familiar, something in his line. He knew exactly what to do.

Biding his time, he chose a moment when the attention of the guards on the bridge had been distracted. Then, of his own initiative he went downstairs, crossed the road and devoted a well-spent half-hour to disconnecting the charges under the bridge. When, some hours later, the enemy's demolition party tried to detonate the charges, nothing happened, and, before they could put things right, the Russians were upon them. Some weeks later a second gold medal was awarded to the old man.

As we watched, more and more Soviet troops poured across the bridge and the fighting on the Zemun side became fiercer than ever. In a desperate attempt to make up for their fatal failure to destroy the bridge, the Germans now turned the full force of their remaining artillery against it. From where we were, we could see the shells bursting in the water all round it. Every now and then one would find its target and for a moment the smooth flow of troops across the bridge would be interrupted by plunging horses and lurching, swaying vehicles. But somehow the seemingly flimsy structure of the bridge itself stood firm; and still the Russians came on.

Up to now we had watched these remarkable scenes spellbound, as though from a grandstand. Suddenly, the sound of a gun going off in our immediate neighbourhood reminded us that we ourselves were not so far removed from the battle area. Looking round, we saw that a Soviet gun crew had established themselves with their 75-mm. field gun in the bushes twenty yards away from us, and were now firing over open sights at the enemy on the other side of the river. This, we realized at once, could only lead to one thing. And, indeed, retribution followed swiftly. The comparative peace and quiet of our ring-side seats were rudely disturbed as the German gunners across the river, resenting this challenge to their professional pride, retaliated with some painfully accurate counter-battery fire. A first shell fell to the right of where we were standing; then one to the left; then one over us; then one short of us. It was without displeasure that we received the Chief of Staff's announcement that it was time for us to get back to Headquarters.

In the streets through which we drove on our way back we found the same bewildered crowds as before. At the sight of the Union Jack on my jeep and of the Stars and Stripes on Charlie's some of the on-lookers raised a cheer. The Germans were concentrating their fire on the streets leading down to the bridge. Along these Red Army and Partisan reinforcements were now pouring, and again and again we had to drive our jeeps up on to the pavement to make way for the Russian gun-teams, as, at full gallop, with a clatter of hooves and a rattle of wheels on the cobbles, they went swaying and jerking into battle.

The Chief of Staff had one last bit of sight-seeing in store for us. We must, he said, have a look at the British Legation. In the end we found it, with the Swiss flag flying over it, an unmistakable product of the Office of Works. Georgian or Queen Anne in intention, it nevertheless somehow managed, with its high-pitched roof and artfully toned brickwork, to give the intangible impression of Tudor homeliness which for some reason is thought to be called for in the buildings which today are designed to house His Majesty's Representatives abroad. The body of a German soldier lay spreadeagled near the front door.

By the time we reached Peko's Headquarters, it was nearly dark. We had seen enough from the Kalemegdan to know that the issue of the battle could no longer be in doubt, and what Peko now told us confirmed this. In the battle before Belgrade and in the fighting within the city itself the greater part of the German garrison had been annihilated. The survivors were trying to made a stand in Zemun, across the river, in the hope of thus gaining a little time before continuing their retreat northwards and westwards. Shells from Zemun were still falling freely in Belgrade, but, with the exception of a few isolated pockets of resistance, now being mopped up, there were no Germans left in the city.

As I walked back down the street to the little suburban villa in which we were quartered, the evening sky over Belgrade was bright with innumerable phosphorescent streams of tracer bullets soaring upwards from all sides and at all angles and the rattle of firearms was continuous. The Russians and the Partisans were celebrating their victory in their own way. Coming down the street towards me was a group of Red Army soldiers who from time to time discharged their tommy-guns in the air or, as a variation, straight in front of them down the street. As they went past they shouted merrily to me. Above the pandemonium came the occasional crash of a German shell, and now, from quite near, an entirely new noise as a Soviet 'Katiushka', or multiple rocket-projector, went into action. With a rushing, whirring, hissing sound, like a giant locomotive letting off steam, five or six rockets soared up from behind our house and, trailing after them a wake of fire, went speeding off in the direction of Zemun to land there a few seconds later with a flash and a muffled explosion. Soon the Germans opened up with the inevitable counter-battery fire and once again the shells began to fall all round us in earnest.

Against this background of noise I sat down to draft my signal to the Supreme Allied Commander, announcing the fall of Belgrade. It was a signal that I had looked forward to sending for a long time.

CHAPTER XVII

WHO GOES HOME?

A FEW days after the fall of the city, Tito arrived in Belgrade and held a parade of the troops that had liberated it. Standing beside him at the saluting base, it was impossible not to be moved by the sight of the ragged, battle-stained throng of Partisans of all sizes and ages who marched past us.

Veterans of Salonika and the Balkan Wars marched next to boys of sixteen and seventeen; here and there a girl strode along with rifle and pack beside the men; some were tall; some were undersized. They carried an odd assortment of arms and equipment, with only this in common: that it had been captured from the enemy in battle. Their uniforms, also stripped, for the most part, from dead Germans or Italians, were torn and stained. They were slung about with water-bottles and hand-grenades and strange odds and ends of equipment, for they had come straight out of battle and were going straight back into battle. Their boots were worn and patched. They looked underfed and weary.

And yet they marched well and held themselves proudly and smiled as they marched. Most of them were from First Corps. They had spent the whole of the last three years fighting. Since the spring they had fought their way half across Jugoslavia. Now, after all the hazards and hardships they had endured, after the cold and hunger, the attacks and counter-attacks, the ambushes and the long night marches, after the weeks and months and years of ever-present suspense and uncertainty, they were at last entering the capital as conquerors.

With the fall of Belgrade the guerrilla phase of the Movement of National Liberation had come to an end. There was still much bitter fighting to be done, but the days of true guerrilla warfare were past.

Within a few weeks Serbia, Macedonia, Montenegro, Herzegovina and Dalmatia and large areas of Bosnia and Croatia were free. The

Germans were by now in full retreat and their strategy was solely directed to securing the communications along which their withdrawal was taking place. With this object in view they concentrated the bulk of their resources on holding the main Sarajevo-Brod-Zagreb communication together with the bare minimum of territory necessary for its defence. At the same time they held the lateral communications connecting it with Bihać, Banjaluka and Mostar, thus protecting the south-western flank of the main line of withdrawal against the attacks of the Partisans and against the possibility of an Allied landing in Dalmatia. North-east of Brod, protecting the other flank of their withdrawal, now threatened by the whole weight of the Red Army, the Germans held in force the Srem, the wedge of territory bounded on three sides by the Sava, the Drava and the Danube. Here a fixed front was formed, the Germans desperately resisting the attempts of a combined force of Russians, Partisans and Bulgars to break through towards Brod. Meanwhile, in the north of Jugoslavia, in Croatia and Slovenia, the Germans were preparing the lines of defence on which they ultimately proposed to fall back. In the space of two or three months, the war, from being a guerrilla war, a war of movement, had become a war of position, a type of war which was completely new to the Partisans.

Politically, too, the capture of Belgrade marked the beginning of an entirely new phase. The days were past when Partisan statesmen and administrators needed to creep through the enemy lines at night to transact their affairs. Tito and the members of his National Council were now safely installed in the capital, and it was their business to govern and administer the country instead of stirring up trouble, to quell resistance instead of organizing it. This, also, was a big change.

One thing was abundantly clear. The Partisans had come to stay. Already they were in complete control of practically the whole of Jugoslavia. As I had always expected would happen, the German withdrawal was leaving them in sole possession. There were no serious competitors. The various quisling administrations collapsed as soon as German support was withdrawn. Nedić had left Belgrade with the Germans. Pavelić was preparing to flee from Zagreb. The military and paramilitary forces which they had raised had either surrendered or else were withdrawing northwards with the retreating enemy forces.

As to the Četniks, many had profited by the amnesty and joined the Partisans. Others had thrown in their lot with the followers of Nedić and Ljotić and, like them, were withdrawing northwards with the Germans. Mihajlović himself with a small force of trusted followers had withdrawn to the highlands of Bosnia, to those very parts where the Partisans themselves had held out so long against the Germans. In the drawing-rooms of Belgrade there were rumours that with the spring, when the leaves were on the trees and the weather was better, there would be a Četnik rising throughout Serbia. But for the present there was no sign of any such thing, and the Partisans were busy consolidating their already overwhelmingly strong position by all the means in their power.

These were considerable. In the first place, their political, military and administrative organization was efficient and far-reaching — (it was not for nothing that their leaders were experienced Communists) — and they thus were able without further ado to assume control of all the key positions in the country. War-time conditions favoured centralization. A policy of State control and widespread requisitioning was easy to justify, and soon the greater part of industry and commerce was more or less directly controlled by the National Committee. The Press and wireless had from the first naturally followed the Party line. Finally, the introduction of conscription gave the central authority a convenient hold over every able-bodied individual in the country. while the possession of a very considerable body of armed men meant that its decisions were backed by force. By these familiar processes much power was rapidly concentrated in the hands of the National Committee.

Nor should it be supposed that the Partisans at the end of the war did not enjoy a very considerable measure of genuine popular support. By their gallant struggle against the invaders during the war they had won widespread admiration and approval, which had increased when they had finally emerged victorious. To many people Tito and the Movement of National Liberation seemed to represent the best if not the only prospect of stable government, and that was an important consideration in a country which for four years had been racked by every kind of external and internal strife and dissension. They were known to enjoy the support and approval of the great Allies and, above all, of the Soviet Union, whose Red Army, even after its withdrawal, continued to dominate the situation militarily from beyond the frontier. Thus, the balance was overwhelmingly weighted in their favour.

Such was the background of the negotiations which were now opened between Tito and Šubašić for the formation of a united Jugoslav Government. From the first Tito had all the cards in his hand. All the cards, that is, save one, for he attached considerable importance to obtaining Allied recognition for his regime.

On October 27th I had my first interview with Tito in Belgrade. It took place in a villa on the outskirts of the city which up to a few days before had been the residence of some high German functionary. Originally, I suppose, it had belonged to some merchant prince. The furniture and decorations were dark, heavy and shiny; they had clearly cost a great deal. On Tito's desk, I noticed, stood a small bronze bust of Napoleon.

I had not seen him since his disappearance from Vis. He began by telling me that he and Dr. Šubašić, who had arrived in Jugoslavia shortly before and joined him in the Vojvodina, had agreed in principle to a solution on the following lines. The Anti-Fascist Council would remain the supreme legislative body, but a united Government would be formed, which would include the leading members of both Tito's National Committee and the Royal Jugoslav Government. It would in due course fall to this united Government to hold elections by which the future form of government of the country would be decided. Meanwhile, the form of government would in theory remain a monarchy, but the King would remain abroad and be represented in Jugoslavia by a Council of Regency. In telling me this, Tito made it quite clear that his only object in accepting a compromise of this kind at all was to secure immediate recognition by the Allies.

This was important news. At the same time I was determined not to leave Tito in ignorance of the annoyance which had been caused by his clandestine departure from Vis.

Earlier in October, Mr. Churchill had visited Moscow and, being curious as to Tito's movements after he had levanted from Vis, he had asked Stalin point blank whether he knew what had happened to him. To this straightforward question he had received the equally straightforward reply that Tito had been to Moscow. The mystery of Tito's clandestine departure had thus at last been solved. Armed with this knowledge I could not resist the temptation of asking Tito how he had enjoyed his visit to the Soviet Union. At first he seemed slightly put out and asked me how I knew he had been there. Then, on learning the source of our information, he laughed and launched into a long account of his visit. It had been, he said, the first time that he had met Stalin. I asked him what he thought of him. 'A great man,' he said, 'a very great man.' There could be no doubt of the genuineness of his admiration, but was it not, I wondered, tinged with something very like emulation?

The chief purpose of his visit, it seemed, had been to discuss with the Soviet High Command the part which the Red Army was to play in the liberation of Belgrade and the surrounding areas. As he put it, he had given the Red Army his permission to enter Jugoslav territory. On his return he had gone to the Vojvodina, thence to co-ordinate operations.

I told Tito that Mr. Churchill had been greatly offended by the way in which he had gone off. I told him, too, of the unreasonable behaviour of his subordinates, of the friction and endless minor difficulties which had arisen in his absence.

At this he seemed genuinely distressed. He said that he was sorry to hear that his subordinates had been unreasonable. Matters would be put right at once. He was also sorry to hear of the friction and would do his best to eliminate its causes.

I replied that I was glad to hear this. 'But,' I added, 'you don't seem to understand that what did the most harm of all was the way in which you yourself slid away without letting us know you were going.' But Tito could not or would not see this. 'Only recently,' he replied innocently, 'Mr. Churchill went to Quebec to see President Roosevelt, and I only heard of this visit after he had returned. And I was not angry.' I decided that it would be better not to report this particular remark to Mr. Churchill.

Meanwhile Dr. Šubašić had also arrived in Belgrade. He was accommodated in the Hotel Majestic, and there I went to visit him. I thought he looked a little worn. Sitting amongst the shiny yellow furniture in his bedroom, we discussed the prospects of reaching agreement. He seemed pleased with the way things were going, though he said he found the Partisans tiring to negotiate with. I knew what he meant.

By November 2nd a draft agreement on the lines indicated to me by Tito had been drawn up and accepted by both parties. It remained to see what the Allies and King Peter would think of it. Dr. Šubašić and Tito suggested that I should take it to London and show it to Mr. Churchill. An aeroplane was provided and I flew home at once with the draft agreement in my pocket, while Šubašić and Kardelj flew to Moscow to consult Marshal Stalin.

When, a week or two later, I returned to Belgrade, I brought with me a message to Tito from Mr. Churchill, which, while showing no particular enthusiasm for it, accepted the draft agreement as a possible basis for an understanding.

Dr. Šubašić had by now also come back from Moscow, having seen Marshal Stalin and obtained his approval of the agreement. Stalin, he said, had been particularly insistent on the need for genuine democratic institutions. 'None of your rigged elections!' he had shouted merrily to Kardelj, and they had all laughed heartily. Thus encouraged, Dr. Šubašić, after some further talks with Tito, now flew on to London to lay the draft agreement before King Peter.

Meanwhile, not particularly relishing this new life, I settled down in Belgrade to conduct what was in effect the business of a full-sized Embassy on top of our work as a Military, Naval and Air Mission, which had also increased enormously. That I was able to get through it at all was due in the first place to the keenness and adaptability of a staff, who, coming straight from a relatively active and exciting life in the woods and hills, now converted themselves in the space of a few weeks to a chair-borne force of exemplary efficiency. Vivian Street was now back with his regiment in Italy and Andrew Maxwell acting as my second in command in Belgrade, while John Clarke commanded my Rear Headquarters in Italy. John Selby, who had returned to me after helping to train the nascent Jugoslav Air Force in North Africa, was again in charge of all air matters, and a number of my other officers from different parts of Jugoslavia had been absorbed into the Headquarters Staff: Richard Keane from the Vojvodina, Stephen Clissold from Croatia, Toby Milbanke from Bosnia. Freddie Cole took over our administration. Sergeant Campbell and his wireless operators were in charge of the wireless communications with London and Italy, and now handled the signal traffic of a large Diplomatic Mission. Sergeant-Major Charlie Button and Sergeant Duncan, resplendent in new suits of battle-dress, had transformed themselves into Major-Domo and Head Chancery Servant respectively.

Belgrade, like all newly 'liberated' towns, was a strange place to live in.

There was no lack of reminders of the recent past. Torn notices, signed by the German Commandant, still flapped from the walls, proclaiming mass executions of civilians as a reprisal for Partisan activities. Outside the town lay the grim hutments of a vast German concentration camp. Burnt-out tanks, destroyed in the battle for the city, still littered the streets and here and there little wooden crosses in the squares and public gardens, or by the side of the street, marked the scattered graves of Partisans and Russians who had been killed in the fighting. Every fourth or fifth house, too, in the tree-lined stucco fronted avenues, bore signs of damage, for Belgrade had suffered badly from air-bombardment, both at the hands of the Luftwaffe in 1941 and in subsequent Allied raids during the German occupation, and there had been further destruction during the recent fighting. The royal palace, from the windows of which the bodies of King Alexander Obrenović and Queen Draga had been thrown by supporters of the rival dynasty forty years before, had received a direct hit from a German bomb and lay in ruins.

Nor was the ruined palace our only reminder of dynastic difficulties. Soon after we reached Belgrade, an elderly gentleman, wearing a beret, called at my Headquarters. He introduced himself as Prince George Karadjordjević, King Alexander's elder brother and the uncle of the present King. Then he plunged straight into his life history. It was, he said, an exaggeration to say that he had murdered his valet. His enemies had made unfair use of the incident. If he had his rights, he would be King of Jugoslavia today.

Someone asked him if, apart from this, he had everything he needed. Yes, he said, everything. The Partisans had been very kind. They had given him back his car which had been requisitioned during the fighting, and now Tito had sent him a present of food. It was nice to find someone who appreciated him. And he stumped off, a mildly disgruntled royalty, his beret set at a jaunty angle over one eye.

For several weeks after our arrival the streets were enlivened at night by periodic rifle shots and bursts of machine-gun fire, as stray Germans, who had been left behind in the retreat and had gone to ground in attics and cellars, emerged and sought to fight their way out. The Russians, too, were apt to let off their weapons from sheer *joie de vivre*, and, one day, as some of my officers were sitting in the mess, listening to the wireless, a drunken Red Army soldier lurched in, unannounced, and laughingly discharged his tommy-gun into the loudspeaker.

Then there was the incident of the jeeps. The American Mission kept their jeeps outside their door. Having, like so many of their countrymen, a generous faith in human nature, or perhaps because they were just rather careless, they did not bother to padlock the steering wheels. We of the British Mission, belonging to an older civilization, took a more cynical view of humanity; our jeeps were heavily padlocked and hidden away in a garage. The very first night all the American jeeps disappeared, while ours remained intact. We condoled with our American colleagues, and congratulated ourselves rather smugly on our foresight. We also took the additional precaution of asking the Partisans to post sentries outside the garage. This precaution turned out to be fully justified. Next day, when we went to fetch our jeeps, we found our Partisan sentry contemplating, not without pride, the body of a soldier in Russian uniform, whom he had apparently shot in defence of our jeeps. We hoped that this drastic remedy would at any rate put a stop to this epidemic of jeep-stealing. But our hopes were not justified. Next morning early when we went to the garage, our jeeps were gone. Lying on the floor were the padlocks, neatly filed through, and the body of the Partisan sentry. It was, we were assured, the work of 'Fascist *provocateurs*'.

Bit by bit conditions became more normal. Gradually the debris in the streets was cleared away by enthusiastic gangs from the various Communist Youth Organizations and considerably less enthusiastic townspeople detailed for compulsory labour service. The last Germans were winkled out and disposed of. The bulk of the Red Army moved on to fight fresh battles further north. The exuberance of the remainder was curbed by savage disciplinary action. Food supplies, which in the early days had threatened to fail owing to lack of transport, were re-organized. Shops, schools, churches, theatres and a solitary night club called the 'Tsar of Russia' and much patronized by Red Army officers, reopened. Slowly, very slowly, all kinds of citizens who had thought it wiser to lie low at first began to emerge.

It would be a mistake to suppose that the liberation of Belgrade from the Germans had been a welcome event to the whole of the population. Many, it is true, had cheered the Partisans and the Red Army when they entered the city. But some, convinced by constant German propaganda or by what they had heard from other, less suspect, sources, went in terror of the 'Bolshevik hordes', fearing for their lives, their religious beliefs and their property. Others had consciences that were far from clear. It had not, it must be remembered, been easy to survive in Belgrade under the Germans, unless you were prepared to collaborate with them to some extent, and those citizens who for the past three and a half years had worked for the enemy were not unnaturally inclined to view with apprehension the victorious return of their compatriots who had spent the same three and a half years fighting them in the mountains and forests.

Tito, meanwhile, had moved into the White Palace, Prince Paul's former residence on the outskirts of the city, and there, almost daily, I repaired to confer with him.

Whatever may be said of Prince Paul's political judgment, his taste in matters of this kind was excellent. The White Palace had been built by him a few years before the war in the style of an English Georgian country house at home. It was charmingly furnished and contained a remarkable collection of books and pictures. These had not suffered at all at the hands of the Germans, and Tito had had the good sense to leave them as he found them. He explained meticulously that Prince Paul's property had been confiscated because of his treasonable behaviour. King Peter's on the other hand had as yet not been touched.

The first time that I visited him in his new surroundings, he had only just moved in and together we explored the palace, literally from attic to basement. Upstairs we found Olga, temporarily combining the functions of housekeeper with those of private secretary, busily engaged in having the royal cipher unpicked from the bed-linen. As she pointed out, it would hardly have done for a man of the Marshal's political views to sleep between sheets embroidered with a crown. After admiring the furniture and books and pictures, we went down into the cellar which we found stacked with great black boxes. These, on inspection, proved to be full of gold plate. 'What can this be?' said Tito, pulling out a great gilt pot with a heavily embossed lid. After I had diagnosed it provisionally as a soup tureen, we pushed on still further.

The cellar, we discovered, masked the entrance to a labyrinth of underground passages elaborately fitted up with bathrooms and air-conditioning apparatus, and designed apparently both as an air-raid shelter and as a means of escape from an angry mob, for one of the passages had a secret outlet a mile or two away in the woods. Not perhaps an altogether superfluous precaution, when it is considered how many of the Regent's predecessors had met violent ends. On my way up, I had already noticed the great square blocks of barracks which surround the hill on which the royal palace stands — a piece of town-planning which also possessed a certain political significance. In the Balkans the tradition of violence is old-established and deep-rooted.

Tito, with his natural liking for the good things of life, soon settled into his new surroundings as if he had lived in palaces all his life. His suits and uniforms were made by the best tailor in Belgrade; his shirts came from the most fashionable shirt-maker; he ate the best food and drank the best wine; the horses he rode were the finest in the country. But amidst all this magnificence, it is only fair to say that, to those of us who had known him before, he remained as friendly and as simple in his approach as ever.

But, now that Belgrade had fallen, most of my Mission felt that the original purpose for which we had been sent to Jugoslavia had been fulfilled, and were already on the look out for some new guerrillas to attach ourselves to in some other part of the world. I myself had asked to be allowed to leave Jugoslavia as soon as a united Government had been formed and regular diplomatic relations established, and this had been agreed to.

Meanwhile, it remained to form a united Government and establish regular diplomatic relations — which was easier said than done. In London, Dr. Šubašić, supported by Ralph Stevenson and Vlatko Velebit, was trying to find a formula which would reassure King Peter, satisfy Tito and provide the Allied Governments with a convenient way out of the dilemma in which they found themselves. It was a difficult and thankless task. King Peter, quite naturally, was not easy to reassure, and Tito, sitting in Belgrade with all the cards in his hand, was not easy to satisfy. The Allied Governments, for their part, confined themselves to emphasizing the need for haste and the importance of truly democratic institutions. From Moscow, from time to time, came a casual hint from Marshal Stalin that he was getting sick of the whole thing. I was kept informed by telegram of what was happening and, in turn, passed the information on to Tito.

In the meantime there was plenty to keep us busy in Belgrade. With the advance of the Allied armies into northern Italy, we needed naval and air bases on the eastern side of the Adriatic. Of late, local Partisan commanders had shown themselves highly suspicious of our intentions in such matters, and extremely non-co-operative, and in Tito's absence this had given rise locally to considerable friction. Clearly what was needed was a comprehensive understanding regulating this side of Anglo-Jugoslav relations, and I now opened negotiations with Tito which, after a great deal of hard bargaining, eventually ended in the conclusion of an agreement giving us a temporary air base at Zara, another opening the Dalmatian ports to the Royal Navy and a third regulating the distribution of U.N.R.R.A. supplies in Jugoslavia.

With the enormous increase in administrative and other work which had resulted from the sudden liberation of enormous areas of country, he had been obliged to delegate more and more responsibility to subordinates often lacking in experience and judgment, and this had had unfortunate repercussions at any rate as far as Anglo-Jugoslav relations were concerned and no doubt in other respects as well.

But, fortunately, for the whole of the time that I was in Jugoslavia I enjoyed complete freedom of access to Tito and I did not hesitate to use this to take up and eliminate as far as possible the innumerable minor grievances and sources of irritation which already threatened to embitter our relations with the Partisans, however trifling they might seem. We would hammer these problems out in the White Palace as we had in less civilized surroundings elsewhere, and our discussions, though often stormy, generally led to some kind of an understanding being reached in the end.

In London, meanwhile, Dr. Šubašić had still not succeeded in persuading King Peter to accept the terms of the proposed agreement for the formation of a united Jugoslav Government. Indeed it began to look as if he never would.

And so, in Belgrade, Tito began to turn on the heat. The Press, which had up to now scarcely mentioned the negotiations, came out with violent attacks on the King, and, as though by magic, crowds of demonstrators suddenly appeared in the streets, shouting: 'Hoćemo Tito; nećemo Kralja' — 'We want Tito; we don't want the King.' Tito asked me if I had heard them. I said I could not help hearing them as they spent most of their time shouting their heads off immediately outside my window.

Then, on January 18th, Mr. Churchill defined the British Government's attitude in a speech in the House of Commons. 'It is,' he said, 'a matter of days within which an agreement must be reached upon this matter and, if we are so unfortunate as not to obtain the consent of King Peter, the matter will have to go ahead, his assent being presumed.' At the same time he once again made it clear that we were not concerned to see one kind of regime rather than another set up in Jugoslavia. 'We have,' he said, 'no special interest in the political regime which prevails in Jugoslavia. Few people in Britain, I imagine, are going to be more cheerful or more downcast because of the future constitution of Jugoslavia.'

This reassured Tito, who until then had suspected that we might be going to try to restore the King by force and now knew that he had little more to worry about. At our interviews his manner became increasingly jocular.

But there was a surprise in store. On January 22nd, with no warning to anyone, the King informed the Press that he had lost confidence in Dr. Šubašić and had decided to dismiss him and his Government. He was, he hinted, thinking of getting into touch with Tito direct.

'Do what you can to keep Tito calm,' telegraphed the Foreign Office, now thoroughly alarmed. But there was no need. Tito had never been calmer. The whole thing he said, was 'as good as a play'.

For over a month the affair remained in this indeterminate state. Relations between the King and Dr. Šubašić were resumed and gradually the points at issue were narrowed down to the choice of the three Regents, whose function it was discreetly to keep alive the monarchic principle in Jugoslavia until elections could be held.

On this purely academic question — for it had been clear from the first that the Regents would be no more than figureheads — endless telegrams passed between London and Belgrade; it was clearly essential that all three Regents should be real, eighteen-carat, brass-bottomed democrats. But, as usual, it all depended on what you meant by demo-crat. The rival claims of a number of elderly and experienced Serb, Croat and Slovene politicians were advanced and discussed, and accusations and counter-accusations bandied backwards and forwards in true Balkan style. In the ensuing confusion at least one candidate was rejected by the party which had originally proposed him, on its being discovered that he had already been proposed by the other, while another old gentleman, described to me as being 'universally respected' was found, after his name had gone forward and seemed likely for once to meet with general approval, to have been dead for some time. It looked as if this bargaining might go on for ever.

Then, early in February, while the snow still lay in the streets of Belgrade, we learned that the Big Three, Churchill, Stalin and

Roosevelt, were meeting in the sunshine at Yalta, by the shores of the Black Sea. Jugoslavia, we knew, would be on the agenda, and, in some suspense, we waited for the thunder to issue from the Crimean Olympus. In due course the combined oracles spoke. There was the traditional reference to democratic principles. Shorn of these adornments, the utterance amounted to an exhortation to Tito and Šubašić to get on with it. There was no mention of King Peter.

This clinched it. King Peter gave in. The proceedings in London were brought to an abrupt end. Within a week Dr. Šubašić and his Government had arrived in Belgrade, with a mandate to come to terms with Tito as quickly as possible.

The end was now in sight. It had been decided that Ralph Stevenson, who for nearly two years had been our Ambassador to successive Royal Jugoslav Governments in exile, should, as soon as a united Government (also technically Royal) was formed, simply transfer himself to Belgrade, thus tacitly emphasizing the continuity of the monarchic principle. Preparations were made to fly him in as soon as the new Government was in being, and I got ready to leave.

Shortly before I left Belgrade, Field-Marshal Alexander, who had recently succeeded Field-Marshal Wilson as Supreme Allied Commander, came over on a visit. It was a great success. Tito, who knew something of Alexander's record in both wars, had taken a liking to him when they first met at 15th Army Group Headquarters, while the Field-Marshal, for his part, genuinely admired Tito as a guerrilla leader and recognized his undoubted services to the Allied cause. The visit was made the occasion of a series of entertainments of unparalleled magnificence culminating in a ball given by Tito at the White Palace, which incidentally also served as a farewell party for myself.

From Belgrade the Field-Marshal, taking me with him, went on to visit his Soviet opposite number, Marshal Tolbukhin, commanding the Third Ukrainian Front, which was then thrusting a victorious spearhead far into eastern Europe. For three days we lived in a haze of vodka in a nameless village in Hungary from which all the inhabitants appeared to have been removed and their place taken by high-ranking officers of the Red Army. But, although a great deal of very intensive banqueting and toast drinking was done, very little military information was exchanged, the Russians remaining cordial but evasive.

One small incident sticks in my memory, a reminder of earlier years. Sweet Crimean champagne had succeeded the vodka and had in turn been replaced by sticky brandy from the Caucasus. Enormous sturgeon, roast turkeys and whole stuffed sucking-pigs, gaping hideously, followed closely on a great bowl of iced caviar and a formidable array of hot and cold *zakuski*. Now an elaborate iced cake, surmounted by allegorical statuettes and patriotic symbols worked in pink sugar, had made its appearance and yet more bottles and glasses. Practically no one in the room except the clumsy white-coated waiters was under the rank of General. Everyone was feeling happy and relaxed and expansive. Toasts were being bandied back and forth, and the high-ranking officers present, fresh from their victories, were beginning to laugh out loud and shout merrily to each other across the long, heavily laden table. How different, I reflected, from Moscow before the war.

My neighbour, a solid-looking man of indeterminate age, with a sallow complexion and square, grey, closely cropped head, wearing on his stiff gold epaulettes the four stars of a full General of the Red Army, turned affably towards me. As he turned, the glittering rows of medals and decorations on his tunic clinked impressively. I noticed that he was wearing the insignia of the Order of the Bath, negligently clamped to his stomach.

'And where, Comrade General,' he asked amiably, 'did you acquire your present grasp of the Russian language?' I told him: in the Soviet Union, before the war. This surprised him. He repeated his question; I repeated my answer. There was no getting away from it. He paused to consider the strange phenomenon of a foreigner who had actually lived in the Soviet Union. Then he asked, for how long? In which years? I told him 1937, 1938, 1939.

Suddenly a constrained look clouded his large, friendly face, a look that I remembered seeing on faces in Moscow in the old days. Even now, in the midst of all this jollity, the memory of the great purge was very much of a reality.

'They must,' he said, 'have been difficult years for a foreigner to understand,' and turned hastily to his neighbour on the other side.

On my return to Belgrade, everything was in the air again. Tito, King Peter and Šubašić were back at their old game of arguing about the Regents. Unhappily I resigned myself to further delays. Again I spent long hours closeted alternately with Tito in the White Palace and with Šubašić in the Hotel Majestic. Again I exchanged frantic telegrams with London. Then, suddenly, at the beginning of March, something happened in London; the King's latest objections to Tito's latest candidate were withdrawn; it was announced that agreement had been reached. Everything was over bar the shouting. It only remained to swear in the Regents and to form and swear in the new united Government.

It took less than a week to complete these formalities. The swearing in of the Regents was done in style, the Orthodox Metropolitan administering the oath to the Serb Regent and the Roman Catholic Archbishop to the Croat and the Slovene. The dignitaries of the two rival Churches vied with each other in the splendour of their vestments. Their respective acolytes bobbed and crossed themselves, and intoned the responses. Fragrant clouds of incense billowed up to the elaborate plasterwork of the ceiling. All three Regents, I noticed, swore loyalty to King Peter without batting an eyelid. Afterwards Šubašić and Kardelj asked me what I had thought of the ceremony. I replied that, as a ceremony, it left nothing to be desired.

Two days later, on March 7th, Tito, having resigned his post as Chairman of the National Committee, announced that he had been successful in forming a new united Government, with Dr. Šubašić as his Minister for Foreign Affairs, and six other members of the former Royal Government holding office in it.

As soon as the news was out, I dispatched a telegram to the Foreign Office, and Ralph Stevenson, who had been standing by to leave for weeks, started for Belgrade, where he arrived on March 12th. It had been decided that my military functions should be taken over by an airman, Air Vice-Marshal Lee, who arrived in Belgrade at about the same time.

On the day after the Ambassador's arrival, a couple of days after my thirty-fourth birthday, I left Jugoslavia.

On my way to the aerodrome, I drove to the White Palace to say goodbye to Tito. It was a friendly meeting, as nearly all our meetings had been since the evening a year and a half before, when we had first met under the trees in the ruined castle in Bosnia. He thanked me for what I had done to help the Partisans during the war and said that he was sorry I was going. I thanked him for the high decoration which he had awarded me a few days before. Then we said goodbye.

I was glad to be going. Glad to be going while relations were still cordial, while the comradeship at arms built up during the war had not yet been swept away in the jealousies and misunderstandings of the peace, in the clash of conflicting ideologies.

At the aerodrome the Ambassador and the Air Vice-Marshal, various Jugoslav notabilities and what remained of my own staff had come to see me off. It was a fine sunny day. A strong wind drove big white clouds across the blue sky. By my aeroplane a guard of honour of the new Jugoslav Army was drawn up for me to inspect, resplendent in Soviet-type uniforms, with Soviet badges and carrying Soviet sub-machine guns.

The face of the right-hand man seemed familiar. I looked at him again. He grinned, still holding himself very upright. It was the Economist. I had not seen him since Bosnia. I noticed that he was now a warrant officer. 'You see, Comrade General,' he said as I greeted him,' I have become a real soldier at last.'

There was no doubt about it. He had.

But a Jugoslav soldier, or a Russian soldier? Externally, the transformation was complete. In appearance he was practically indistinguishable from the N.C.O.s of the Red Army who were still to be seen in the streets of Belgrade. But did that mean that he had lost that natural Balkan turbulence and independence, that insurgent spirit which for centuries had made his countrymen such a thorn in the flesh for any foreign invader? I wondered.

Then, followed by Sergeant Duncan, I climbed up into the aeroplane. The friends who had come to see us off waved. The guard of honour presented arms. I saluted. Sergeant Duncan grinned. The doors were shut. The engine roared, and we jolted away towards the take off.

Soon we were circling high above Belgrade. Looking out, I could see the road stretching away southwards to Avala and to the green, rolling country round Valjevo and Arandjelovac. Then we turned in the direction of the coast. Below, the snow was still lying on the mountains of Bosnia. The little paths wound in and out along the ridges. Dense forests reached down into the valleys. Here and there smoke went up from a cluster of huts. Then came the barren crags of Dalmatia, and the islands, bathed in sunshine; and before long we were flying far out over the Adriatic. Westwards.

INDEX

INDEX

INDEX

INDEX

INDEX

INDEX

FOR THE BEST IN PAPERBACKS, LOOK FOR THE 🐧

In every corner of the world, on every subject under the sun, Penguin represents quality and variety – the very best in publishing today.

For complete information about books available from Penguin – including Puffins, Penguin Classics and Arkana – and how to order them, write to us at the appropriate address below. Please note that for copyright reasons the selection of books varies from country to country.

In the United Kingdom: Please write to *Dept JC, Penguin Books Ltd, FREEPOST, West Drayton, Middlesex, UB7 0BR.*

If you have any difficulty in obtaining a title, please send your order with the correct money, plus ten per cent for postage and packaging, to *PO Box No 11, West Drayton, Middlesex*

In the United States: Please write to *Dept BA, Penguin, 299 Murray Hill Parkway, East Rutherford, New Jersey 07073*

In Canada: Please write to *Penguin Books Canada Ltd, 2801 John Street, Markham, Ontario L3R 1B4*

In Australia: Please write to the *Marketing Department, Penguin Books Australia Ltd, P.O. Box 257, Ringwood, Victoria 3134*

In New Zealand: Please write to the *Marketing Department, Penguin Books (NZ) Ltd, Private Bag, Takapuna, Auckland 9*

In India: Please write to *Penguin Overseas Ltd, 706 Eros Apartments, 56 Nehru Place, New Delhi, 110019*

In the Netherlands: Please write to *Penguin Books Netherlands B.V., Postbus 3507, NL–1001 AH, Amsterdam*

In West Germany: Please write to *Penguin Books Ltd, Friedrichstrasse 10–12, D–6000 Frankfurt/Main 1*

In Spain: Please write to *Alhambra Longman S.A., Fernandez de la Hoz 9, E–28010 Madrid*

In Italy: Please write to *Penguin Italia s.r.l., Via Como 4, I-20096 Pioltello (Milano)*

In France: Please write to *Penguin France S.A., 17 rue Lejeune, F-31000 Toulouse*

In Japan: Please write to *Longman Penguin Japan Co Ltd, Yamaguchi Building, 2–12–9 Kanda Jimbocho, Chiyoda-Ku, Tokyo 101*

A CHOICE OF PENGUINS

The Assassination of Federico García Lorca   Ian Gibson

Lorca's 'crime' was his antipathy to pomposity, conformity and intolerance. His punishment was murder. Ian Gibson – author of the acclaimed new biography of Lorca – reveals the truth about his death and the atmosphere in Spain that allowed it to happen.

Between the Woods and the Water   Patrick Leigh Fermor

Patrick Leigh Fermor continues his celebrated account – begun in *A Time of Gifts* – of his journey on foot from the Hook of Holland to Constantinople. 'Even better than everyone says it is' – Peter Levi. 'Indescribably rich and beautiful' – *Guardian*

The Time Out Film Guide   Edited by Tom Milne

The definitive, up-to-the-minute directory of 9,000 films – world cinema from classics and silent epics to reissues and the latest releases – assessed by two decades of *Time Out* reviewers. 'In my opinion the best and most comprehensive' – Barry Norman

Metamagical Themas   Douglas R. Hofstadter

This astonishing sequel to the bestselling, Pulitzer Prize-winning *Gödel, Escher, Bach* swarms with 'extraordinary ideas, brilliant fables, deep philosophical questions and Carrollian word play' – Martin Gardner

Into the Heart of Borneo   Redmond O'Hanlon

'Perceptive, hilarious and at the same time a serious natural-history journey into one of the last remaining unspoilt paradises' – *New Statesman*. 'Consistently exciting, often funny and erudite without ever being overwhelming' – *Punch*

When the Wind Blows   Raymond Briggs

'A visual parable against nuclear war: all the more chilling for being in the form of a strip cartoon' – *Sunday Times*. 'The most eloquent anti-Bomb statement you are likely to read' – *Daily Mail*

A CHOICE OF PENGUINS

Brian Epstein: The Man Who Made the Beatles   Ray Coleman

'An excellent biography of Brian Epstein, the lonely, gifted man whose artistic faith and bond with the Beatles never wavered – and whose recognition of genius created a cultural era, even though it destroyed him' – *Mail on Sunday*

A Thief in the Night   John Cornwell

A veil of suspicion and secrecy surrounds the last hours of Pope John Paul I, whose thirty-three day reign ended in a reported heart attack on the night of 28 September 1978. Award-winning crime writer John Cornwell was invited by the Vatican to investigate. 'The best detective story you will ever read' – *Daily Mail*

Among the Russians   Colin Thubron

One man's solitary journey by car across Russia provides an enthralling and revealing account of the habits and idiosyncrasies of a fascinating people. 'He sees things with the freshness of an innocent and the erudition of a scholar' – *Daily Telegraph*

Higher than Hope   Fatima Meer

The authorized biography of Nelson Mandela. 'An astonishing read … the most complete, authoritative and moving tribute thus far' – *Time Out*

Stones of Aran: Pilgrimage   Tim Robinson

Arainn is the largest of the three Aran Islands, and one of the world's oldest landscapes. This 'wholly irresistible' (*Observer*) and uncategorizable book charts a sunwise journey around its coast – and explores an open secret, teasing out the paradoxes of a terrain at once bare and densely inscribed.

Bernard Shaw   Michael Holroyd
Volume I 1856–1898: The Search for Love

'In every sense, a spectacular piece of work … A feat of style as much as of research, which will surely make it a flamboyant new landmark in modern English life-writing' – Richard Holmes in *The Times*

The Russian Album   Michael Ignatieff

Michael Ignatieff movingly comes to terms with the meaning of his own family's memories and histories, in a book that is both an extraordinary account of the search for roots and a dramatic and poignant chronicle of four generations of a Russian family.

Beyond the Blue Horizon   Alexander Frater

The romance and excitement of the legendary Imperial Airways East-bound Empire service – the world's longest and most adventurous scheduled air route – relived fifty years later in one of the most original travel books of the decade. 'The find of the year' – *Today*

Getting to Know the General   Graham Greene

'In August 1981 my bag was packed for my fifth visit to Panama when the news came to me over the telephone of the death of General Omar Torrijos Herrera, my friend and host...' 'Vigorous, deeply felt, at times funny, and for Greene surprisingly frank' – *Sunday Times*

The Time of My Life   Denis Healey

'Denis Healey's memoirs have been rightly hailed for their intelligence, wit and charm ... *The Time of My Life* should be read, certainly for pleasure, but also for profit ... he bestrides the post-war world, a Colossus of a kind' – *Independent*

Arabian Sands   Wilfred Thesiger

'In the tradition of Burton, Doughty, Lawrence, Philby and Thomas, it is, very likely, the book about Arabia to end all books about Arabia' – *Daily Telegraph*

Adieux: A Farewell to Sartre   Simone de Beauvoir

A devastatingly frank account of the last years of Sartre's life, and his death, by the woman who for more than half a century shared that life. 'A true labour of love, there is about it a touching sadness, a mingling of the personal with the impersonal and timeless which Sartre himself would surely have liked and understood' – *Listener*

FOR THE BEST IN PAPERBACKS, LOOK FOR THE 🐧

A CHOICE OF PENGUINS

Riding the Iron Rooster   Paul Theroux

An eye-opening and entertaining account of travels in old and new China, from the author of *The Great Railway Bazaar*. 'Mr Theroux cannot write badly ... in the course of a year there was almost no train in the vast Chinese rail network on which he did not travel' – Ludovic Kennedy

The Life of Graham Greene   Norman Sherry
Volume One 1904–1939

'Probably the best biography ever of a living author' – Philip French in the *Listener*. Graham Greene has always maintained a discreet distance from his reading public. This volume reconstructs his first thirty-five years to create one of the most revealing literary biographies of the decade.

The Chinese   David Bonavia

'I can think of no other work which so urbanely and entertainingly succeeds in introducing the general Western reader to China' – *Sunday Telegraph*

All the Wrong Places   James Fenton

Who else but James Fenton could have played a Bach prelude on the presidential piano – and stolen one of Imelda's towels – on the very day Marcos left his palace in Manila? 'He is the most professional of amateur war correspondents, a true though unusual journo, top of the trade. When he arrives in town, prudent dictators pack their bags and quit' – *The Times*

Voices of the Old Sea   Norman Lewis

'Limpidly and lovingly, Norman Lewis has caught the helpless, unwitting, often foolish, but always hopeful village in its dying summers, and saved the tragedy with sublime comedy' – *Observer*

Ninety-Two Days   Evelyn Waugh

With characteristic honesty, Evelyn Waugh here debunks the romantic notions attached to rough travelling. His journey in Guiana and Brazil is difficult, dangerous and extremely uncomfortable, and his account of it is witty and unquestionably compelling.

Return to the Marshes Gavin Young

His remarkable portrait of the remote and beautiful world of the Marsh Arabs, whose centuries-old existence is now threatened with extinction by twentieth-century warfare.

The Big Red Train Ride Eric Newby

From Moscow to the Pacific on the Trans-Siberian Railway is an eight-day journey of nearly six thousand miles through seven time zones. In 1977 Eric Newby set out with his wife, an official guide and a photographer on this journey.

Warhol Victor Bockris

'This is the kind of book I like: it tells me the things I want to know about the artist, what he ate, what he wore, who he knew (in his case ... everybody), at what time he went to bed and with whom, and, most important of all, his work habits' – *Independent*

1001 Ways to Save the Planet Bernadette Vallely

There are 1001 changes that *everyone* can make in their lives *today* to bring about a greener environment – whether at home or at work, on holiday or away on business. Action that you can take *now*, and that you won't find too difficult to take. This practical guide shows you how.

Bitter Fame Anne Stevenson
A Life of Sylvia Plath

'A sobering and salutary attempt to estimate what Plath was, what she achieved and what it cost her ... This is the only portrait which answers Ted Hughes's image of the poet as Ariel, not the ethereal bright pure roving sprite, but Ariel trapped in Prospero's pine and raging to be free' – *Sunday Telegraph*

The Venetian Empire Jan Morris

For six centuries the Republic of Venice was a maritime empire of coasts, islands and fortresses. Jan Morris reconstructs this glittering dominion in the form of a sea voyage along the historic Venetian trade routes from Venice itself to Greece, Crete and Cyprus.

A CHOICE OF PENGUINS

Ginsberg: A Biography   Barry Miles

The definitive life of one of this century's most colourful poets. 'A life so dramatic, so dangerous, so committed to hard-volume truth, that his survival is a miracle, his kindness, wisdom and modesty a blessing' – *The Times*. 'Read it to the end' – Michael Horovitz

The End of Nature   Bill McKibben

'An environmental blockbuster ... an extraordinary book, combining an impressive body of scientific detail with the lightest of literary and philosophical touches' – *Daily Telegraph*. 'Even for those who have been living and breathing green issues for the last twenty years this will be a powerful and very disturbing book' – Jonathon Porritt

Coleridge: Early Visions   Richard Holmes

'Dazzling ... Holmes has not merely reinterpreted Coleridge; he has recreated him, and his biography has the aura of fiction, the shimmer of an authentic portrait ... a biography like few I have ever read' – *Guardian*.

The Speeches of Winston Churchill   David Cannadine (ed.)

The most eloquent statesman of his time, Winston Churchill used language as his most powerful weapon. These orations, spanning fifty years, show him gradually honing his rhetoric until, with spectacular effect, 'he mobilized the English language, and sent it into battle'.

A Green Manifesto for the 1990s   Penny Kemp and Derek Wall

Written by two leading members of the Green Party, this manifesto sets out a new political agenda not only for the 1990s but for the twenty-first century.

Heat Treatment   Justin Wintle

On unorthodox tour in the melting-pot of the Far East, Justin Wintle discovered that the women's intentions left little to the imagination and that the food destroyed his digestive system. As fears of massive cock-roaches and of catching AIDS reduced him to a state of persistent hysteria, he learned the full extent of the Orient's extremes.

A CHOICE OF PENGUINS

Trail of Havoc   Patrick Marnham

The murder of the 7th Earl of Lucan's nanny at the family's Belgravia mansion in 1974 remains one of the most celebrated mysteries in British criminal history. In this brilliant piece of detective work Patrick Marnham investigates the Lucan case and its implications and arrives at some surprising conclusions: what was not disclosed at the murder inquest and what probably *did* happen on that fateful night.

Daddy, We Hardly Knew You   Germaine Greer

'It's part biography, part travelogue, its author obsessively scouring three continents for clues to her dead father's identity ... ruthlessly stripping away the ornate masks with which [he] hid his own flawed humanity' – *Time Out*. 'Remarkable, beautifully written' – Anthony Storr

Reports from the holocaust   Larry Kramer

'Larry Kramer is one of America's most valuable troublemakers. I hope he never lowers his voice' – Susan Sontag. It was Larry Kramer who first fought to make America aware – notably in his play *The Normal Heart* – of the scope of the AIDS epidemic. 'More than a political autobiography, *Reports* is an indictment of a world that allows AIDS to continue' – *Newsday*

A Far Cry   Mary Benson

'A remarkable life, bravely lived ... A lovely book and a piece of history' – Nadine Gordimer. 'One of those rare autobiographies which can tell a moving personal story and illuminate a public political drama. It recounts the South African battles against apartheid with a new freshness and intimacy' – *Observer*

The Fate of the Forest   Susanna Hecht and Alexander Cockburn

In a panorama that encompasses history, ecology, botany and economics, *The Fate of the Forest* tells the story of the delusions and greed that have shaped the Amazon's history – and shows how it can be saved. 'This discriminating and constructive book is a must' – *Sunday Times*